TOP STORIES

Volume 2

Primary Information

TOP STORIES #17 $2.50

THE HUMAN HEART

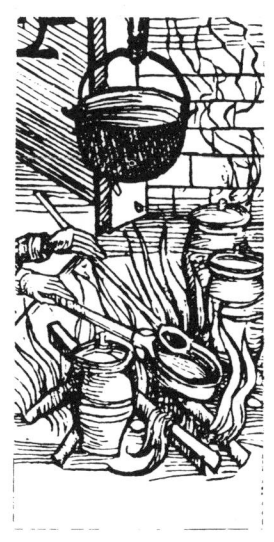

ROMAINE PERIN

The Human Heart

Romaine Perin

Copyright ©1983 by Romaine Perin

Front cover: detail from a German engraving, 1560

This publication has been made possible in part by a grant from the New York State Council on the Arts, Literature.

Hallwalls, 700 Main Street, Buffalo, New York 14202

Swarms of noisy shrill birds prattled incessantly in the dark leaves and hopped across the dense shadowy spaces between branches, flinging themselves effortlessly through empty air, darting, swooping, rustling the leaves when they landed. Dogs, roosters, goats and pigs, and whatever it was that made that dry, compulsive braying, were shrieking and hollering at the top of their lungs in various vernaculars; the echoes rang through the hills and the rutted streets of the town that lay in a little bunched up crumple of architecture at the base of a long finger of land crookedly tapping the lake. Ducks paddled on the water giving out loud sudden honks. A church bell clanged softly. On top of the hill above the town the manor heaved up its mass of stone in mute dominance of the clutter below it. One of its tenants, the enormously wealthy Lord de Fayel, owned practically every acre that could be seen from its windows, including the town that nudged the lake's edge.

It was late morning and high summer. In an otherwise empty blue sky as rich and viscous looking as a kind of shimmering syrup, the sun floated, glowing hot.

It burned hot on the Lord de Fayel's shoulders and thighs as he rode out on his horse, his falcon chained to his gauntlet. But he wasn't uncomfortable: the speed they went at raised up a breeze, and he was excited at the thought of the hunt.

It warmed the side of the Dame de Fayel's face, relaxed in sleep. And then slowly coming awake, she brushed at her cheek to knock away a tiny Middle Ages fly that had been basking in the sun there. Her arm fell and lay stretched out across the sheet. It dropped onto an empty space. Her eyes opened. Yes, she was alone. Her husband gone...where...oh, hunting, that's right. Alone. She smiled.

Downstairs, Elenore le Bon, or The Cook, as she was also called (to keep her at a distance, in the anonymity of servitude) had her back turned to the beautiful sky, to the rectangle of it that shone in the open window behind her and, her thoughts already on the next chore awaiting her in the manor kitchens, kneaded the ball of dough before her on the wooden table, which was stout and firm, but she was strong, and it rocked with the shoves she gave it. She had her sleeves rolled up above her elbows and her brawny working-woman forearms were dusted with a coating of flour. A little blast of breath came out with each energetic pump of the heels of her hands. She worked hard. It was her job, plowing day after day through a list of chores; she hated it yet she was glad of it; at least she wouldn't starve as long as they kept her on here. And they would, she didn't doubt, there was p-a-llenty to do.

She slapped a final slap to the dough, rolled it out into a disc and pinched the edges into a wall. Now what she needed were the pigeons she'd sent Felice to the market for. She'd make a nice succulent pigeon pie for the lord and lady's supper, the second course of it, and she'd make it so they couldn't fault it, like last time. Complaining about her cooking, how was she to blame if the pigeons were nothing but skin and bones to start with. She didn't make the birds, did she, she wasn't God, was she.

Elenore stood still for a minute, wondering if she should cross herself for that. Did she just make a blasphemy? Or not. Her hands were all gooey. She made do by glancing piously out the window and into the sky, almost blinding herself with the glare hitting her eyes like that.

She stood with arms akimbo. Her face burned, it was red as a beet. She lifted up a corner of her apron and wiped her hot damp forehead, smearing flour across it, as, automatically, her eyes turned to the vicinity of her next job. She surveyed the tub full of vegetables waiting to be washed and chopped. Caked with soil and trailing hairy roots, they grew monstrously before her eyes, heaping to the ceiling in a mountainous mass, looming with tedium. All that whittling and scrubbing and slicing and, and, and. Thinking of the laborious repetitive motions made her tired before she started. Her eyes drifted and fell on a pitcher balanced on a corner of a table against the back wall. She knew what it was full of.

"Better catch that before it falls," she said aloud, strode swiftly across the floor, snatched up the pitcher and poured herself a generous measure of lukewarm ale into a clay mug. The dusty flour had made her thirsty, and she downed the whole mugful in one draught. Wiping her mouth and the trickle down her chin with the back of her hand, she poured out another. There was a loaf of bread as big as her torso beside the pitcher; she broke off a piece and, taking that and her ale, she began to advance toward the window that hung the brilliant curtain of sky. It was time for a break.

The empty barrel she used for a chair, with a neat pile of folded rags stacked on top of the lid for a cushion, was right by the window; she'd have a sit-down and a bite to eat, and she'd have a think.

When Elenore was left alone, and when she had the time, she would ponder what she could have been in life if she'd had the power to direct it, instead of her destiny being an open and shut case of slaving away in the manor kitchens like her mother had before her. Here she was, on the far side of middle age, and childless, and nothing ahead of her but a mountain of vegetables to wash and cut into little pieces for other people to eat.

If she'd been high-born—

If she'd been born male—

She didn't want to be male. No. A woman is what she was, and what she wanted to be. A woman is what Christine de Pisan was, and Christine de Pisan was a person whom Elenore sometimes daydreamed about changing places with. If they'd asked her, she would have said, "I won't be The Cook, I'll be Christine de Pisan. I'll get an education as good as a boy's, with lessons in Latin and philosophy given me by my own father, a physician-astrologer at the court of Charles V. And then I'll be married at fifteen to a royal secretary, and be happy, and give birth to three healthy babies. And when my husband, and my father too, are taken from me when I'm only 25, then I'll pick up my pen and I'll write poetry and prose to make me an income, and I'll speak out for us women, so ill-maligned by what men say about us!"

Elenore couldn't have read the works herself, even if she'd had access to them, but she'd heard all about Christine de Pisan and her defenses of womankind. She even knew some of her verses by heart. And as she slowly walked to the window and her makeshift chair, her head bent, carrying her bread and her mug of ale, she recited in a low voice:

> He is too unwise that, for default of one,
> will therefore despise women everyone.

which was from *A Lytil Bibell of Knyghthood*.

But when she raised up her head she stopped short, nearly spilling her ale. Her seat was already occupied.

Two little legs in brown breeches perched on the barrel, the shins bare and pale, the feet leather-booted. It was Felice Cordeau's young son. He'd climbed up on the barrel and was kneeling with his elbows on the window sill and his hands folded together. His head was tilted up to the sky; his mouth was wide open. Elenore stood away from him and looked at him, bemused. It seemed like a long time she stood there looking, but he didn't stir at all, except to slowly close his eyes and open them in a strange blink, reminding her of an animal.

"Hey you, stare eyes, what you doing there on my chair," she all of a sudden said, adding, "with your mouth wide open!" scaring him so much he almost pitched off. His bright black eyes met hers for one second, then the lids dropped. He turned his face away and the one edge of it that was visible to her began to bloom a deep warm pink just like a peach; he lowered his face and sniffed. What—not crying, was he?

"Oh honey don't cry now, I didn't mean to frighten you." Elenore stooped over him and dabbed at his cheeks with her floury apron. Wrapping an arm around him, she cupped the back of his head and lowered it until he was buried in her neck. She heard a muffled sob, and she pressed him a little closer in her powerful embrace. But he began to fidget and fight, clawing at her arm. Drawing back, she realized he was gasping for breath.

A little embarrassed at this, Elenore said briskly, "What's that you were doing, Alfred, praying to God? Now what you want to pray for? For your mama to come back, that's it, isn't it? She's only down there at the market," Elenore's hand waved vaguely out the window, "she'll be coming right back. Now don't you worry, you hear me?"

Alfred's head stayed down. It's true, she'd probably be coming right back. But that wasn't the point. He wanted to go with her; why'd she leave him behind, she always took him. Why'd she yell at him this morning everything he did, then stomp out slamming the door behind her, and him stuck here in the kitchen to wait. Her warning, "Stay put or else!" still rang in his ears. Otherwise he would have crept quietly outside and found a place to play, or gone to explore some as yet unknown corridor, even if it meant risking the heavy hand of a guard or servant coming down to box his ears. No, it was out of the question. So he stayed put and waited.

"Your mama won't be long, sweetheart." The knuckles of Elenore's curled fingers rubbed Alfred's soft cheek. An inconvenient parentage, Alfred's, poor child, half an orphan, really, his so-called unnamed father prancing back and forth right over his head just about, the only thing separating him from the living evidence of his misdemeanor being little more than a ceiling and a floor, and the boy not knowing who to call Dadd—

Elenore's mouth snapped shut. The boy was gazing at her, his eyes narrowed in scrutiny. Strange, he was like an adult that way. Had she been speaking? She was by herself too much, she really ought to watch out for that thinking aloud business. Now what had she done. Felice didn't want Alfred to know yet; Elenore had promised to be careful what she said to him.

Quickly, she said, "Is that what you were praying for, Alfred? For your mama to come home?" After an uneasy pause, during which the child sat utterly still with rapt eyes fixed on hers, obviously expecting further clues, he gave up, as he was forced to every time, and said, "I wasn't praying."

This was stated with such cool self-possession that Elenore's patronizing and sympathetic tone hardened slightly. "So," she said, "what were you doing on your knees and your hands folded together like a boy who's praying? And your face up to the sky? And what's about that mouth of yours wide open? Don't talk to your lap, honey, I can't hear you."

Her legs hurt. Especially the ankles. Standing on them from morning to night, they swelled up. She couldn't crouch this long, they fell asleep, and now they prickled with pins and needles. Wincing, she began to rise with her hands braced on her knees, when she heard his belated reply.

"I was pouring the sky in my mouth and trying to swallow it," he said.

Halfway up, she froze for a second with her face turned to the glowing sky. And for that brief split second the sky did seem to her to be a wide bowl, some gigantic soup pot full of ethereal blue liquid—then a lid clanged shut and she straightened, her legs tingling uncomfortably. With a tired sigh, she said, "Let me sit for a minute, sweetie. You want to eat lunch with me? Here you are." She tore off a piece of bread and gave it to him. Alfred sat on the window sill and Elenore sank onto the rag-cushioned barrel. In silence they chewed the dark, sour bread. When Elenore vacated the seat and was emotionlessly bending over the tub of vegetables, Alfred climbed onto it again and returned to his earlier position, except that now he had his sharp little chin propped on his hands. He was a patient child; he waited for his mother.

He gazed out over the bright landscape, searching for her shape, following with his eyes the section of the route he could see, that she would take coming back. The grounds of the manor were lush with blue-green grass and peppered with flowers: vivid, scarlet poppies, yellow daisies, bluebells and marigolds. Shadows fanned out below the trees, birds scuttled from sunlight to shade and vaulted abruptly upward into the dark, glittering pools of foliage. The hill fell steeply to the valley below, and the vineyards that were terraced into the slope were hidden from Alfred's view. Thin strips of cropland could be seen in the distance, bordering the town of Fayel, a cluster of thatched and tiled roofs with a tiny square-towered church poking up from them. The lake was stone-green; it had shed its white scrim of mist hours ago. From its further edge the land rose again, furling upward in thick rolling flags of color; deep, rusty-brown earth where the earth showed in amongst the vegetation rolling out from the lake in merging bands and patches of sultry, eloquent shades of red: cerise and maroon, a faint rouge, like the dust of old crumbled roses. The carpets of grass fields were true green, fading into a smoky fur of trees with an upward nap. The clarity of the air brought the mountains very close; the leaden gray, exposed bare rock was carved by blue shadows; waterfalls thumped silently in the creases.

But that's not where Alfred was looking. He was peering off to the right, where the road flowed down the hill to the valley, then bled into the main street of the town and then into the market square.

Where his mother, Felice Cordeau, was lifting the hem of her coarse heavy dress—too heavy for this hot weather—and taking a wide step over a puddle of mud at her feet. Already in a black mood, the inconvenience increased her irritability. An inventive and foul curse fell from her lips and into the mud, and the crippled beggar she was passing raised the stump of his arm and made the sign of the cross on himself. Felice took no notice of him; she hardly knew where she was. She was burning up with a blinding rage. Her feet hit hard on the uneven ground as she walked, detouring the puddles. She muttered to herself.

"Hard done by, that's an understatement. Huh. All right for him isn't it. Always all right for them. So what should they care. Take what they want with their fine white unstained fingertips that never touch nothing but velvet and silver and silk. And the skin of women. All over me he went. Wife's not enough for him is she. No. Had to keep sneaking downstairs even after he's married,.his fine flimsy shoes falling on the boards, so long and pointy they were he had to tie up the ends around his knees with ribbons. Huh. The knight in glinting armor is he, the fine nobleman is he, with his codes of honor and chivalry...Hah!"

Heads turned. Felice coughed loudly to try and cover up the sound of that "hah!" and then was quiet for a minute. But up it seethed again.

"The low creak of the hinge, his hand pulling on my door, gives me my own door, my own room, so he knows where to find me, so he can use me all up like he did, in his own private way, just like he's used to with his wife upstairs. And the other servants looking at me strange, them having to sleep where they can find a spot. Him thinking it's a big secret is the joke of the year. You'd have to be the village idiot not to know where Alfred came from. Except her. She doesn't know, does she. How would she ever find out. What would *he* ever tell her for. And if he don't, who would. You'd have to be a pretty mean enemy to snitch to her about it. I don't have any enemies. Except for him. Who, if I really want to be honest about it, I would have to say was my number one arch-enemy. Now who would dare tell her...not Elenore...or Beatrice...

"Them and us, we live in two different countries. She's never set eyes on me, she wouldn't know me from Eve. I'm just one of them kitchen-maids, she couldn't tell us apart if she tried. And why does she want to tell us apart? She wouldn't want to know the first thing about what it's like to be me, what it's like to step-n-fetchit for someone else's every whim and fancy."

But Felice didn't feel true rancour for the Dame de Fayel. All that she had of *that* was reserved for the Dame's husband. Clutching up her skirts from the mud, her feet now slowing a little as she felt her bitter resentment beginning to ease, her anger to abate, she thought to herself, "She's a woman too. And hard done by, as I am. There she is, married to an adulterer."

The Dame de Fayel may never have noticed Felice, but Felice had seen the Dame enough times, riding out on her horse in a crowd of knights and squires and other women all dressed up in bright silks like she was, and laughing fit to split; and she'd seen her somber in the mornings with her favorite ladies-in-waiting, meandering piously toward a quiet grove, prayer books and rosaries trailing from their limp hands.

"Oh well," thought Felice, "if she doesn't know by now about him and me and my boy, there's not much point anymore in telling her. Because her husband has, of late, without uttering a single word in explanation, stopped dropping by on his uninvited visits to my room below the stairs." How long had it been. Not since the night they'd had that enormous feast to celebrate the victory of Lord or Squire So-and-So's, what was his name, in the tournament, and she'd been run off her feet all day—all the servants had— preparing for it. They'd plucked and roasted enough chickens to feed a village. They'd made a huge pie with live larks concealed under the top crust, and after they'd laid it on the feast table it had been opened, and all the larks flew out, closely pursued by the hawks which the idle rich had unloosed in the hall. She'd finally been allowed to go to bed, but no sooner was she asleep than she'd been woken by the creaking hinge and thin echoes of trumpets and singing from the hall upstairs. That was the night, the last time he'd come.

"Thrown out with the trash, I am, and not one word, not one single, solitary—"

"Felice!"

"What was that?" The pigeon-seller was waving. "Felice! Where's your boy today?" she yelled. "He sick?"

"What a blaring voice she's got." Felice wandered to the woman, with difficulty suppressing the rage in her that was threatening to erupt worse than before. It sure was hot. She sure was in a bad mood. In fact, she was in such an evil temper she'd forgotten that the reason she was in the market was to buy pigeons from Rita. Good thing she'd been reminded.

Inside the low, narrow, stacked-up cages, the bars made of wooden pegs, the pigeons scuffled dully, making furry cooing noises deep within their bulging chests. What a desolate moaning throbbed out of their throats.

"It's too bad for them, cooped up like that, never to know the flap of their wings no more." Felice distractedly watched the dark pink calloused claws scratch on the floor of the cages. Glass-button eyes stared out into a striped world.

The pigeon-seller didn't speak. She felt vaguely insulted. The trade she was in called for pragmatism; the insinuation of her cruelty to animals was not welcome. She crossed her arms and pursed her lips.

The sun beat down on the milling crowd. The chatter and motion in that unrelieved heat had the character of slow, controlled frenzy, dreamlike and remote. The conversation level was a solid object, a heavy wave of sound that rose and fell, ebbed and flowed, a tide sent forth by an invisible sea with no horizon to it. Every so often a single cry emerged and crested up: "Fish! Fresh fish!" then sank down again, returning to the ocean of gibberish. Shoulders squashed against each other, a forest of arms and hands darted over the produce; everything was thoroughly fingered and examined. Every so often coins clinked, glinting briefly in the sun before disappearing into a pocket.

"Hey!" shouted Rita and Felice started in fright.

"My ears are splitting," she thought grimly. "Can't she see she's standing right next to me?"

"Why you looking so glum?" Rita screamed. "What's wrong with you?"

"Nothing," said Felice loudly, then at a lower volume repeated, "nothing."

"Where's the little fellow today! First time I seen you without him! He sick?"

"No," said Felice, "I simply came out without him. He's too slow. Can't let a rock on the ground pass him by without having to lag behind to pick it up and ask me how come rocks are hard. Drives me out of my mind with his empty riddles."

Oh, now she felt bad. Why was she grumbling about her darling boy, whom she loved, and who was completely blameless. She wanted to hurry back to him immediately. Rapidly, she said, "I need three pigeons. Three fat ones. I'll get complaints if they're scrawny."

Rita's eyebrows shot up and her thumb shot out in the direction of the manor on the hill. Felice nodded. "No complaints!" blared the pigeon-seller, "I'll fetch you out some right plump ones for them hoity-toits." Since she couldn't stand away to appraise the birds from her narrow alley behind the cages, her stall being back to back with the fishmonger's, she came around beside Felice to have a look. Her lips drew back over her gums in a leer of concentration, and Felice noticed that three or four more teeth had fallen out since she'd last seen her. Wary of Rita giving vent to one of her vocal thunderclaps so close at hand, Felice took a step back. Something hairy and repugnant brushed her cheek. "Ugh," she grunted, recoiling.

The wrinkled paw of a monkey swung dangling by her face. Except for the thick dark fur covering the back of it, it was just like the hand of a human being, with its fine, curved fingernails, and the coarse, hard skin of a land-tilling villein. The monkey was squatting on the shoulder of its owner, a lanky boy of maybe fifteen, who'd been strolling by and had stopped short before Felice could collide backward into him. The paw suddenly darted out and clutched a handful of Felice's hair. With a yelp, she pulled her head back, but instead of letting go, the monkey tugged harder. She slapped at it, raining blows on both the monkey and the boy, who was trying to prise open his pet's hooked fingers. The shrill chatter of the monkey, Felice's cries and the boy's grunts, drowned out the cooing birds, whose necks were undulating frantically at the commotion. Finally, the animal let go.

The boy began to stammer apologies in a voice breaking with adolescence, but he couldn't get a word in edgeways for the pigeon-seller's furious shouts. "Get out of here!" she bellowed. "Move along, sonny, go on! And take your hairy brother with you!" The boy loped away in a hurry, his monkey twisting around to stare blandly at the scene it had left behind. Its arm was wrapped around the boy's head, the paw gripping a bunch of hair.

"You all right, dearie?"

"Yes." Felice felt her eyes sting and moisten. The little beast had done that deliberately. For some reason it wanted to humiliate her. All the humiliations of the past months and years were in the dirt under the nails that had scraped over her scalp. "Give me the birds and I'll go," she said, tight-lipped. Rita crammed three pigeons into one cage and Felice paid. She left the market square carrying the cage by the ring fastened to the top of it, her face set hard, her eyes stubbornly adjusted to the distant horizon.

Once she was alone outside the town and trudging the hilly road back to the manor, she became subdued. She thought slowly and carefully, in distinct words and ordered phrases. Her anger had dissipated, leaving a residue of lukewarm fatigue and a pensiveness that was a lull of calm in her storm. "I," she thought, "can always feel this peacefulness. I don't have to hurt all the time, and wear a scowl. Why shouldn't I always feel this clear and calm?" A fieldmouse hurtled by in her path, a blur of brown fur. Soon after came the cat, gaining easily on its prey. Not wanting to witness what would now take place on the grass to her left, Felice hurried on.

Ahead of her rose the steep climb through the vineyards. Before she embarked on it, she stopped for a minute. She took a deep breath and said, "I'm free of him." Astonished, she realized she *was* free of him. Saying it had made it happen. A boulder tore itself loose and rolled off her chest; as she began the climb she felt as though she'd just left on the ground behind her some huge burden she'd been lugging around.

But from the cage came a constant rustling of constricted wings; a nervous breeze rippled her skirts. The unceasing cooing was intolerably unpleasant. She was delivering the pigeons to their deaths. They'd be cut up in pieces and set on the dining table, and that's the way it would end for them, they'd become a tender, tasty filling between two crusts of pastry. His teeth would close down over a sweet juicy breast....

She set the cage on the ground and looked at it. Her hand went to the catch on the door. She opened it and the birds nearly cracked their wings trying to be the first one out.

No, she didn't. But she sure wanted to.

The Dame de Fayel watched Felice change form. First a speck of dust in the distance rolling infinitely slowly through the cropland outside the town. Then a tiny dark ant on a straight course, crawling toward the hill that rose ahead of it. For awhile it was gone, swallowed into the green mouth, that side of the hill the Dame couldn't see. But then up on the ridge a stick figure appeared, tilting in the direction of the box it carried. By the time she was halfway across the manor grounds, Felice was a flesh and blood kitchen-maid in a thick dress carrying a cage full of fluttering wings, passing in and out of the shadows cast by the trees above her. She entered the manor and was gone. The Dame de Fayel thought she looked familiar, but she wasn't sure. Wasn't it the same thin, tired-looking woman who usually had a child by the hand?

Anyway, her mind was on other things. The filed tip of her little fingernail was between her upper and lower front teeth. She gnawed on it while she let her eyes rove aimlessly over the landscape, all of which belonged to her husband, and one third of which had belonged to her father until he'd offered it, along with his daughter, to the Lord de Fayel to settle a long-standing family debt.

Hearing of this arrangement, the Dame de Fayel, who had been Catherine de Rouvre then, said to her younger sister Louise, "The goods are thrown in with the wife and the wife is thrown in with the goods and the two commodities are part and parcel."

"Maybe," said Louise, "later on..."

"I'll grow to care for him?" That's when the cynical twist at the corner of

Catherine's mouth first appeared. Eight months later, when the funds for the ceremony had been raised, partly through negotiations between Catherine's father and future husband, partly through taxation of the peasants connected to the de Rouvre estate, they were married, and Catherine moved into the manor, bringing her sister with her. Louise's visit had somehow never ended; Catherine liked having her nearby, she was a familiar face in an unfriendly environment, and the last thing Louise wanted was to return to live with their father, whose bombastic tirades and steel-hard palm were still painful memories to both of them.

Catherine spent a lot of time at her window in this private chamber that was only for her to use. It was something she'd insisted on, her own room, and it had been given to her. She either watched the world through the window, or read, or talked to Louise, while Louise mostly listened patiently and nodded or shook her head over her sewing. Louise was not a talkative person.

Right now, Catherine was glad to be alone. She was trying hard to shed from her skin the touch of her husband. She wondered how her mother, whom she only remembered as a dim presence moving through her childhood, had manged to cope with this thing. Perhaps she'd had more affection for Catherine's father than Catherine had for the Lord de Fayel. If she could just make him understand that she didn't want him to touch her. She could not stand the feeling of his hands on her. That's all there was to it. She wished she were pregnant. Then he'd have done his job and he'd leave her alone, wouldn't he? Married a year, and still waiting. Maybe when it happened, it wouldn't be his, but Renaud's. A door rushed open and shut inside her belly, her skin began to smoulder. That low laugh against her ear, his fingers stroking the back of her neck beneath her hair, then rippling on her skin so she grew warm all over from the inside out... That's not how her husband did it. He made her feel sordid, like something he'd bought with money, coming at her with his tongue hanging out like a dog. His hands crawling on her under the sheets, which she'd tucked in tight around her, which didn't stop him, it only took him half a second longer to get at her, pulling at her nightgown, ripping the lace he was so clumsy and scared, his skin squeaking when he slid on top of her which is the only place he ever went, then trying to do it and either doing it or not doing it, and then falling off her like a sack of sand.

Hours later there was a knock on the door. Time to eat.

But that other door opened and shut in her belly. She left the window. "Renaud D'Ault," she whispered timidly. The name alone had unquestioned power. She wanted him now. She slipped onto the bed she used as a couch and her legs parted under her heavy velvet skirts. Her hand cupped the thick folds and pressed hard, the other slipped inside her bodice. She leaned into the cushions, lifting her skirts out of the way, moving around, the tiny door inside her opening and closing...

The Lord de Fayel wiped his lips and leaned back from the table, his open palms braced against the edge. "You," he said mildly, "are not listening to me." He gazed at his wife, who was lifting a spoonful of soup to her lips and trying not to shiver visibly at the memory of her lover's slide and thrust. Her nerves warmed to the slightest provocation of it, these days it was difficult for her to think of anything else. It wasn't convenient being in love with a man you weren't married to. What nasty plan of fate had set her up with this pedantic fool and forced her to sit at the dining table with him night after night and bear with his stultifying speeches that were more deadly than her father's, in obedient silence.

"Why, I asked you, were you late to dinner," said the Lord de Fayel, a tremor entering his voice-either from anger or fear. He was nervous of her beauty, which is the name he gave to the unapproachable coldness she showed him, which also angered him. It meant he had to force himself on her. She was, beneath his hands, pliant to a degree, but there was never any invitation offered on her part, and always he felt some secret corner of her resisted him.

Catherine was preoccupied. She tried to wrench herself back to reality, but she didn't want to badly enough. She was moving very slowly. Her spoon seemed to weigh the same as she did; she lifted and lowered it without energy. The smile that wanted to play around her lips she kept firmly inside. She'd never ever known it like that, the way she'd felt it before. So many, one after the other, and each one better than the last, even when she'd thought it could not possibly be any better than the one she'd just had. It made her want to giggle to remember it, to think she could make them come on so easy once she got started, she hadn't realized how pent up she must have been. No man, not even Renaud, could ever know how to do that, how to touch a woman the right way, the way she...

"Catherine." Her hooded eyes skimmed along the length of the table to the other end, and saw, beside her husband's empty soup plate, his clenched, trembling fist. She took a breath and waited.

The whole table shook, the plates and pitchers and cutlery rattled, ripples ran in circles from the center of her unfinished broth. She calmly lowered her hands into her velvet lap and let him pound as long as he needed to. With every blow her appetite diminished a fraction. So that when the servant came soon after to set the pigeon pie on the table, she had little interest in eating it.

The servant's sleeves were very long, the ends cut at a diagonal so that they came to a sharp point near his knees. They were the height of fashion, the man had a nerve. Right to his face, the Lord de Fayel mocked, "Baboon, you should see yourself. Mimic your master, will you, you ought to see what you look like trailing your fancy sleeves carrying food to my table."

Under his table the master's sleeves dangled to his ankles. Without answering, of course, the servant cut the master and his wife each a slice of pie and walked away, his sleeves flapping.

As the silence lengthened in the dining hall, with her husband staring at Catherine and Catherine staring at her plate, the tension grew to such a pitch that she felt a wave of nervous laughter welling up. She glanced at her husband. He was poking into his slice of pie with the tip of his knife. He lifted up the top crust of pastry and spiked a fat piece of white pigeon breast. She almost started to laugh, when he said, talking through his food, "I'm leaving tomorrow."

"For how long?" she asked, much too eagerly, and his eyes narrowed.

"How am I supposed to know?" He swallowed. "I've been summoned to the field."

"Which field is that?" Anticipation of his absence excited her to volubility. No longer irate, he was now surprised at her, pleasantly surprised at her apparent interest in his affairs, which was something new. Chewing again, he said, "I've been called to Clermont. The Jacquerie are gathered there, waiting like a herd of beasts for slaughter."

"Oh." She bent her head, the knife in her hand toying with her food. Pictures of the Jacquerie thickened above her plate. Marauding peasants wearing boiled leather for armor, brandishing scythes and pitchforks, trampling in torn boots over the bodies of noblemen they'd murdered and whose manors and castles they'd stormed and burned to the ground, also trampling underfoot the tatters of priests' gowns....

"So the uprising still continues," she said.

"It continues and it grows. The Jacques have vowed to wipe off the face of the earth every living member of the Second Estate, and it looks like they mean to decimate the clergy, too. It's a foul stinking horde we'll face. And it's a stinking soup we'll make of them. They'll be reconsidering their plans to overthrow the established order. They'll be begging for the chance to get back home to their putrid hovels where they can return to a peaceful existence of wallowing in their filth like pigs and producing their weak-brained offspring, have a happy family life squatting on their haunches round a fire burning on the mud floor like a pack of wild dogs, except for the stink of onions off their breath." A brittle smile creased his face.

Aghast, Catherine then watched him terminate his remarks by filling his mouth with what was left of his meal, which prevented him speaking further. She took the opportunity to say, "What have the peasants done to the nobles to deserve the scorn that's heaped on their heads? They're hated for their poverty, but it's been forced on them, and by those who hate them for it. There's no sense, there's no...they don't choose to live in vile misery and conditions of the worse privation. They don't choose to live in a one-room hut with only a hole in the roof to let out the smoke of the fire, without a stick of furniture to sit on, or choose for a bed a pile of straw crawling with bugs that the whole family lies on to sleep at night. Peasants don't have much choice in any way about anything."

Her husband was looking at her with his mouth open. Disgusting, it was half full. He was too nonplussed by her unusual behavior to do anything but let her go on. Which she did. "The peasants, they work for all and have the least. I see them with my own eyes, toiling like animals to find two coins to rub together, while we dine on what we please, selecting what we like from the products of their labor. Why should…"

"…we carry the weight of the world on our backs! Everything we have, we owe! We pay the noble for every minute we're given on earth. What have we ever been but the groaning foundations of their castles and manors and churches. Bent crooked and crippled by the weight on top of us. We who have nothing give our all to them who's got more than they need. We pays out to finance the lord's ransom when he's captured in battle. To cover the costs of his daughter's wedding. And the knighting of his son. Who pays the hearth tax? Not the noble, who can afford it, but us, who breaks our fingernails scraping the bottom of the barrel for the coins."

The speaker took a breath. The murmers and muttering grew louder. It was after vespers in the cemetery behind the church in the village of St. Leu, the evening the peasants' revolt broke out.

"We pay fees to use the lord's bread ovens, his cider press, we pay to grind our grain in his mill, he's bleeding us dry. He knows how to put us where he wants us: he knows we can't afford to build our own. We pays and we pays, and them up in their manor houses whittles away the time in frivolities with the currency of our labor. And the priest calling for his tithes, every minute and a half there's new tithes to pay, and him coming to collect what we can't afford to give, what'll it be, he says, sing in heaven or roast in hell, and walking off with a pig or a hen and going home and cooking it for his supper after preaching out so loud and holy that the tithes are a gift to God, and that obedience to the lord is the same as obedience to the Lord! They're all in it together, and they're jumping up and down on our backs and they're breaking them, they are. And !" the speaker's fist punched the air, "And! When we're dead, the noble who plundered our life and our labor…"

"…receives the most valuable possession from the peasant's household, to add insult to injury. The dead, after all, cannot protest. Oh, for shame!" cried the Dame de Fayel to her slow breathing husband at the other end of the table. "And then," she added, "in the few weeks out of the year that they get the chance to earn some extra pennies picking grapes, the women get half the wages of the men. For shame! Well, no wonder the Jacques are on the rampage in a wild fury!"

"What?! What?!" The Lord de Fayel rose half out of his seat. "*That's* the reason they're on the rampage? Because the women get half-wages?" Her heart was pounding in her chest like a drum. "The Jacques," he said carefully, "are raping our women left, right, and center. Ten at a time lined up to take a turn at an innocent, helpless damsel and her daughters to boot, and forcing the squire to stand and watch, and then murdering the lot of them in cold blood. And *you* speak out in their favor? B-r-r-utal animals."

What he said went through her like an icy knife. Why was it that a man could find that word so easy to say. It fell from his lips like he was discussing the weather, but she now felt agonized, and didn't speak.

"Who's been filling your pretty head with problems that don't concern you," he said.

Renaud had told her about the peasants' meeting in the cemetery and what it was they'd been complaining about, and also how it had ended, with the mob breaking into the nearest manor in the neighborhood, where they found the knight and his wife and children at home and killed them all, then burned the building to the ground.

The table shivered again. "Who's been keeping you so well-informed! Who's been giving you lessons in economy and politics! Speak out!"

"Louise," said Catherine in a low voice, knowing how improbable that sounded, Louise being who she was. But he said, "Your sister is leaving my house. Tell her to prepare herself for the journey home. She has overstayed her welcome."

He drained his cup of wine, shoved the bench behind him so hard with the back of his legs that it fell on its side, and strode toward the door. As he was passing behind his wife he paused. Her head turned slightly, and she caught his hard blow on her ear and cheek. Without a word, he left her bent forward over the table, his legs, bowed and thick-muscled from years in the saddle, carrying him purposefully out of her company.

The next morning, early, the Lord de Fayel galloped away in a flurry of heraldic banners at the head of a column of troops bristling with axes and lances. On his shiny, snorting stallion—a knight never, ever rode a mare—and with his chain mail and helmet glinting in the sunlight, he must have inspired something ferocious in his troops to spur them to churn up the dust of the road that way. The foot-soldiers were whisking along at an energetic trot, struggling to keep pace with the mounted knights. When the rumbling of hooves had faded into silence, the dense cloud of fine yellow earth that had been stirred up hung behind them to mark their path. The air was very still. It was another hot, windless day.

"He's gone," noted the Dame de Fayel at her window. Yellow wisps of dust smoked on the distant ribbon of road that her husband, the miniscule dot some distance ahead of the confused blur climbing the hill, was following. "Gone. And glad to go. No more waiting around to be put to the use he was born for." The tips of three fingers very gingerly stroked her bruise. It had come up so quickly. Tomorrow the blue would become bluish-purple, then later it would turn a mottled purple and yellow. "It's not all I have to fear, fear itself," she muttered, her husband's fists clotting together in her memory. "What a temper. Frustration, I suppose. It's frustration that makes a man violent and cruel, that's what I'm beginning to think," she said, turning to her sister Louise, who sat on the couch sewing.

"What do you mean?" Louise stitched her tiny scarlet stitches. Her voice was level, even bland.

"He doesn't have to work for a living. All he has in his life is his Trusty Sword, and all he lives for is to wield it. I'm sure he doesn't enjoy whiling away his time in idle games of chess and backgammon until he's called up to battle. Though I know he does like to hunt. What he likes is blood." She adjusted the veil that hung from her headdress, drawing it over her bruise. "Does it show?" she asked Louise. The veil was pearl-colored silk, a fine translucent cloth.

"Come here. I can't see you against the light."

Catherine left the window. After careful examination her sister told her the bruise was hidden.

"Does it hurt?" Louise asked quietly.

"Here it hurts." Catherine pressed her fingers to the side of her face and experimented moving her jaw. "When I move my mouth, if I open it too wide it hurts."

"It must have been a strong blow." Louise pursed her lips and shook her head in reproach. At this sign of sympathy Catherine's eyes dampened. She went back to the window. After a pause she said, "I feel like we're festering, rotted out by idleness. That's what I kept thinking all the time he was speaking so contemptuously about the mean poverty of the peasants. It's painful for me to realize that I have a part in fixing the inequalities and preserving them."

"What do you mean?" Louise said again. Her older sister was a puzzle to her sometimes, so changeable and moody. The strange opinions she came out with, Louise didn't know how seriously to take her. Talk about inequalities and suchlike was futile when you couldn't do anything about anything. When you had to stay indoors most of the time and sew or read. What could a woman do? Louise was a fatalist. She liked to say, "We're all of us spinning around on the Wheel of Life, strapped on by the ankle. Then one day God undoes your buckle and there you go."

Catherine said, "In the evenings when we all congregate in the hall and there's a fast fire burning in the fireplace and the wood smells so sweet crackling away, and our faces are all lit up yellow by the candles and the rushlights, and the musicians are playing to us and we're singing along too loud and off-key, and laughing and flirting till the early hours, our tongues thickened by wine, you know, the whole of the peasant class is dead asleep from sheer exhaustion in a natural darkness they can't afford to lighten with candles, even if they should have wanted light during the hours when they're given the only opportunity they get to lay down to rest and straighten their bodies out."

Louise threaded her needle with gold thread and knotted the end. Then her hands dropped in her lap and she leaned back. The needle glinted silver between her thumb and finger, the thread trickled a shiny stream of gold over the back of her hand. "It's not your fault,' she said simply.

Catherine, looking over at her sister, remembered her husband's orders. She couldn't do it. She couldn't tell her to leave. She needed Louise with her. She knew she didn't really contribute that much to their discussions in terms of initiating new ideas or opinions, but it didn't matter about that. Her quiet sympathy and patience made her an ally against the ugliness Catherine felt surrounded her. In turning around so fast, Catherine's veil had blown away from her cheek. Involuntarily, Louise winced, and Catherine's eyelids fell.

"What would you like to do?" Louise said quickly, "Do you want to walk outside for a while?"

"Oh, I don't know." Catherine pulled on the silk. "What about you?"

"We could go watch them set up the tents for the tournament. Oh no, of course, there's no tournament now."

"No. Nobody left to join it. They've all gone to plunge their lances into an actual target. Better than sport, that. Rushing into a crowd of ill-abused peasants atop their stud horses at incredible velocities."

Louise thought to herself that her sister's husband must have become incensed by Catherine's bitter, rebellious tongue, and that's why he'd struck her.

"The tournament at Artois," she said, "that was bloody, just as violent as a real battle."

"Oh, it was horrible. Senseless deaths, especially Robert Gaston la Grange, so young, what a waste of a life."

"Philippa d'Eu had to watch him die right under her eyes, and see the scarf she'd given him turn red with his blood."

"The part she played in it was very abstract. As though she would *want* him to prove his feelings for her by fighting to the death in a competition against another man. I don't think he was any different from other men who compete in tournaments. They have an excess of battle fever, they compete to keep in practice for real wars, and because fighting is all they know, not to win the love of women."

"But every knight is sworn to the chivalric code. In tournaments it becomes ritual and sport, that's all."

"The chivalric code," Catherine's hand went to her bruise, "which supposedly elevates women to a height of near-sainthood, is only applied by fictional heroes in literature."

Silence fell in the room. Catherine returned to gazing at the view, Louise to her sewing.

Then with a swishing rustling, Catherine went to sit beside her sister, arranging her cumbersome skirts around her. "Did you hear about Marie Ordelaffi at Cesena?" she said.

"No, tell me," said Louise with interest, smelling gossip.

"You know her husband stabbed their son to death, don't you."

"What?" This was a gruesome beginnning.

"You didn't know? It's another story, I'll just tell you quick. They both were fighting in a battle, and they were losing it. The son wanted to surrender. His father erupted in an uncontrollable rage, he was too hungry for victory, and he stabbed his son, and killed him."

"His own son. The man must be an animal."

"He's an insatiable meglomaniac. An egoist who cannot believe in his own defeat. Well, what happened was, he went to fight the papal forces, leaving his wife Maria Ordelaffi in charge of Cesena. The city was attacked and there was a fierce, prolonged battle. She refused to give in, even though people were dying in horrible ways, and she really was losing. Even when her father begged her to stop fighting, she wouldn't. Finally the knights who'd been taking their orders from her came and told her that the fortress was about to be seized, and there was no hope left. They threatened to surrender without her. And then at last she gave in. But she insisted that she be the one to negotiate with the enemy, and she managed to arrange it so she obtained safe-conduct for herself, her family and servants, and also the soldiers who'd fought for her."

"Well, I think she acted just like her husband, only she was a woman. She was just as stubborn."

"You can't judge the two, men and women, by the same standards. Not yet. Not while conditions of life and liberty are so different for each sex. You know, they've just decided a queen has no authority to judge a knight; though she's his superior in rank, he's hers in gender."

"So how is a queen expected to rule when there's no king?"

"I guess they're still deliberating that point."

"It's not easy to figure out what men have against us. What did we do..."

"Women have been asking that question for centuries."

"Well, anyway, Maria Ordelaffi was too busy being a man to think about it, I guess."

"Being a man? How do you think she would have acted if she weren't terrorized by the prospect of her husband's unbelievable wrath? That's the only thing she's scared of, his insane rages, according to what I heard."

Louise's needle pierced the cloth, drawing behind it the slowly shortening gold thread. Both of them had their eyes on the work. A little insect was calmly meandering down Louise's sleeve toward the embroidered scarlet flowers she was gilding. Its terra-cotta back was decorated with a fine black pattern that seemed to have been drawn with a very small brush. It looked like a shard of an Egyptian clay pot. Softly, Catherine said, "The sound of that needle breaking through the cloth must be deafening to that little bug."

"What bug?" Louise moved suddenly, and the insect took flight.

"Oooh," Renaud D'Ault signed in Catherine's ear, "at last, at last." She could hardly breathe, the way he was gripping her. "Let-let-let me close the—door at least," she gasped. He half released her and her hand went out and gave the door a push. It closed with a loud thud. Immediately he tried to embrace her again, but she ducked under his arm and firmly drew the heavy iron bolt across the doorjamb. Pressed together, they stood against the wall in utter darkness, and in a silence that was only broken by the sound of breathing.

"I wasn't sure you'd come," she said, lying against him under the sheet in the bed she usually shared with her husband. "Especially not the first night he's gone."

"How could I stay away, knowing you're alone?" He bit her earlobe.

"Don't!" She moved her head away sharply.

"What's the matter?"

"Nothing. I don't like that."

"Oh."

"It's just that..."

"Does he do that to you?"

"Don't ask me that."

"No, I know, I won't. Come back here. I'm sorry. That's right, that's better."

"So, Renaud D'Ault, *you* won't have the innocent blood of peasants on your hands."

"No. Took some fast talking and a hefty bribe."

"He said the Jacquerie were assaulting women. I can't tell you how pompous and furious he sounded. As though it could possibly set a precendent. A man is a man. A knight has no justification in setting himself up as an unstained savior of womankind. Things go on in the choicest of households that I'm not permitted to speak about, what with my mythical female delicacy, which I have no qualms in betraying."

"Catherine, the Jacquerie *are* assaulting women. The wives of nobles have been hurt cruelly by them. They're taking their revenge."

"Against innocent women."

"Against their oppressors."

"Women have had nothing to say in it. Women are being treated like the property of the oppressors. Like something of theirs to be stolen or damaged."

"What did you mean about the choicest of households?"

"I mean the attack on the Countess of Salisbury by King Edward III of England."

"An ugly rape. An ugly, ugly rape."

"I remember the first time I really knew I wanted you," said Renaud, slipping his hand under Catherine's unpinned hair and caressing her neck. "The feast to celebrate Jean Fleur's victory in the tournament, it was. The hawks wheeling through the air over our heads after the larks that flew out of the pastry. There was a look on your face I'll never forget. You watched everything with your detached and critical eye, you made me ill at ease. I thought you were a very beautiful woman."

A candle burned beside the bed, behind her. Her face was in shadow, and a long irregular humpy shadow of their two bodies outlined as one, moved on the wall behind him. That's what she was looking at.

"Remember the thousands of verses we had to suffer through, the poet had such a lisp," Renaud went on, "and the noise of the trumpets and the singing, Fiametta's dance, what a night it was."

"He left the hall and he didn't come back," said Catherine. "He left when she started dancing. I saw him go. He didn't know I saw. He was very furtive."

"Why do you have to talk about him right now." Hurt and disappointment were plain in his voice. "This time we have together, it's stolen time. He'll come back..."

And he'd lie where her lover lay now. And he'd turn over and prop himself on top of her, and he'd find some way to increase the repulsion she felt for him. A shudder ran over her. She reached out and felt for Renaud, whom she could have now for the asking, so why even think about the other, who would inevitably take his place.

"How long do you think this barbaric game will continue?" said Catherine.

"I think it won't take long for them to rout the peasant forces. He'll probably be back soon...Catherine...we don't have much time..."

And it wasn't long before word came that the peasants' revolt had been put down; the Jacquerie had been slaughtered. Lashing out indiscriminately with axes and swords, the knights had charged into the crowd and hacked and chopped at their victims, who were too poorly armed to defend themselves against the armored mounted men with years of fighting experience behind them. Even the survivors who dispersed in terror were pursued and murdered. The Lord de Fayel was expected back the next day.

The last night they spent together was probably harder for Renaud than for Catherine, who was carefully preparing herself, philosophically, she thought, for her husband's return, and using most of her energy for the work of stifling her dread.

For the last time, he rose from her bed and dressed by the cool light of dawn. The way she lay is the way he wanted to leave her, uncovered, her face turned to the blue daybreak framed in the window. But in the dim light he saw her eyes were open. He stood at the door with his hands at his sides, watching her rise and come to him. They embraced in silence. She clutched gently at his clothes, loosening a scarf that drifted slowly to the floor, unseen.

He drew aside the bolt, opened, then closed the door, and she was left alone.

She lay where he'd lain, wanting to feel the warmth of him before it had a chance to leave the sheets. The window was full of blood red.

When she next opened her eyes it was opalescent, brighter, awash with yellow-orange. She turned over, drew up the sheet, and fell back to sleep again.

It seemed as if she couldn't have slept for more than a minute, but when she next awoke it was around noon. Her husband stood by the bed. Instantly, she was wide awake.

He breathed coarsely above her without speaking. The way he was staring at her made her too scared to move. e. There was something in his hand. His arm bent at the elbow so that what he held hung over her face. Hanging like a bat from his fist, the monogram almost touching her chin, was Renaud's fallen scarf.

Little Alfred Cordeau (de Fayel) squatted with his toes in the cool water at the shore of the lake, his boots discarded behind him, his arms folded around his folded legs. "Ah!" he cried softly, as the small black water bird he'd been fixing his eyes on finally took a dive underwater, the event he'd been waiting for. The lake was peppered with those birds; when the ducks found them in their path they honked warningly, giving the birds the choice of steering out of the way or being run over. They were funny the way they dived down, Alfred liked watching them. They bobbed nervously on the water, their sharp beaks poking the air in all directions. Spying a morsel to eat in the gray swaying silt on the lake floor, they'd suddenly plunge headfirst into the clear water, gangly stick legs kicking, rubbery webbed feet propelling them swiftly downwards. A long time later they'd pop up to the surface with worms dangling out of their beaks. Alfred planned to ask his mother later why they changed color when they came up, because they did, as though underwater a gray skin had grown over their black feathers, and was shed off on contact with the air. Then there wasn't a drop of water on them. How come they could dry off so fast?

The bell in the church tower struck. Alfred's head went up. One hand stretched out fingers. With the other he counted them in time with the chimes. Five. It was time to go find his mother in the market. He reluctantly reached for his boots and took a last look at the water. Which one was his bird, he'd lost sight of it. Oh, well. He struggled to put his wet feet into his boots, his tongue sliding over his lips, and his breath coming hard with his exertion. When he'd got them on as best he could, he stood and began to make his way toward the center of the town, passing the square stone church on his left and the town hall on his right. He walked slowly, looking at everything, stumbling sometimes on the ridges formed by feet and horse hooves when the earth of the road had been muddy. Now it had been baked to a hard crust by the sun.

The town thickened around him, enveloping him. On all sides rose the spice colored walls of houses, cinnamon, tumeric, also oxblood and a cold, greenish ocher. He kept walking until he entered the market gates, then he stopped. He searched for his mother. Some stalls were beginning to close up, the crowd was thinning, people heading toward the gates behind him to leave. They kept blocking his view, so he left the busy spot and began to wander, keeping a lookout for her.

There was lots of produce left: fruit, like balls of bright cloth, or trinkets, or fruit; red meat, huge slabs of it as wide as the butcher's chest; vegetables, green and orange and ivory, like flowers. Alfred stopped at the fish stall and stared curiously at the tubs full of shiny wet things, at the tentacles with rubbery sucker pads on them, little pink fish lined up and stacked in rows like collapsed dominoes, rows of heads jewelled with dead eyes, glittering silver sardines, buckets full of gray pebbles, which were mussels and clams. Live eels eased against each other, black glistening ropes weaving by themselves.

Then another movement caught his eye in a wide shallow tub full of fish which were alive also. Their wide mouths, the lips red and thick, flapped open and shut, the bodies moved gently, swelling in and out: they were breathing. It was like watching some eerie mutation of the human species. It was as if they were all lung. They're sleeping, thought Alfred, they're dreaming of deep waters. Suddenly, one of the fish began to writhe. Its body twisted and slapped, it curled up double, its tail slammed down. In fascination, his own belly moving in and out, Alfred waited for it to take an energetic leap out of the pail. He forgot himself and everything else but that frantic blind scramble for freedom. The thing was drowning in air, plunging into the wrong element, one that was poisoned. Then it stilled, exhausted. Its mouth gaped. Its gills shivered, beat with quick throbs. Around it the other fish adjusted themselves into place after the disturbance, skin against skin rubbing soundlessly, gleaming, pulsing.

Two enormous red hands, thick-fingered, swooped from above and scooped a quarter of the contents out of the bucket, including the tired, panting fish that had made the escape attempt. The fishmonger emptied the handfuls into a small pail, poured some water into it, and exchanged it for the coins his waiting customer handed him. Alfred stared hard, his neck craned back, not understanding.

"There you are!" He was lifted off his feet and into his mother's arms.

Through the gates, then the town, then the cropland outside it. Along the hilly road toward the manor. The steep climb through the vineyards, over the ridge, across the grounds under the trees. Felice stopped, dragging Alfred, who had his hand in hers, to a halt. A mild roll of thunder rippled the ground beneath their feet as a four wheeled, covered wagon drawn by three horses in tandem emerged from the coach house of the manor just ahead and started down the road toward them. Felice pulled Alfred with her as she backed onto the grass. The coach passed by them, rattling ponderously on iron wheels. It slowly rumbled on, and their heads turned to watch, both spellbound by the misery they saw on the face that was looking back to the manor from inside the coach through the opening at the back. Very briefly, the woman in the dim interior looked at Felice and Alfred with her reddened eyes. But the horses moved inexorably on, and soon she couldn't be seen.

"It's Louise," said Felice, "and all her bags. So she's leaving at last."

"It's Louise," repeated Alfred, exactly imitating his mother's tone of suprise. "Who's Louise, Mama?"

Felice didn't answer. She glanced up at the manor, where at her window, the Dame de Fayel's face could be seen, partly hidden by the handkerchief she was pressing against it. Then Felice distinctly saw a hand come from behind and grip her shoulder, drawing her around. After that she disappeared from the window.

An unexpected wave of sorrow ran over Felice. She looked down at her son, who was looking up at her, patiently. She searched, as she often did, for signs of his father on the boy's face. No, he really didn't leave his mark, none at all. It was strange, as though she'd done it all by herself, produced a living being from her belly without any aid. "I'm lucky," she reminded herself, "I'm free of him." She had a strong urge to rush upstairs and burst into the Dame de Fayel's room and defend her against their mutual enemy. But she didn't.

"Let's go," she said, giving Alfred's hand a squeeze. Together, they entered the manor, heading for the kitchens.

The force of his hand pulling on her shoulder spun Catherine around to face her husband. She bent at the waist and cried out loud without restraint, because she couldn't help it, her face pressed into her hands; he put his hard palm under her chin and tilted up her head. For a minute he watched her coldly as she fought to control herself, summoning the dignity to change her contorted features into an expressionless, utterly empty mask, a mask of inconceivable indifference that would be her way of showing her hatred for him. But tears ran freely down her cheeks, her mouth quivered, and now her sobbing was involuntary, uncontrollable, like hiccups. It came from the middle of her body, where she was shivering with desolate agony. She was scared. He hadn't struck her yet; at his slightest move she winced.

He said, "You'll never see him again."

Her chest tightened. She closed her eyes. The door slammed and he was gone.

The Lord de Fayel had certain influential friends who happened to owe him favors. He had things arranged so that Renaud D'Ault found himself joining the forces of the Third Crusade, headed east to defend Christianity from the "infidel Turk". Hastily, D'Ault prepared to go, afraid of some worse retribution from his lover's husband if he tarried in the vicinity. Reflecting on his punishment, he thought, "It's only how I'll suffer because of her absence from me that will be unbearable. As for the flashing steel and blood, I'll survive if I drown myself in thoughts of her." A surge of hysterical courage rose all the way up to his tingling scalp, filling him with elation. "I'll prove myself with acts of heroism, and it'll be for her. She'll guide me. It'll be her face and form I'll see on the banners, not the crucifix or the fleur-de-lis."

And true to his word, once he was on the battlefield Renaud fought like a maniac, a man gone beserk. The clunk and grinding of armor, the screams of horses, the howls of the wounded, and the generally deranged atmosphere of the battlefield excited him to a frenzy of bloodlust. He was repeatedly promoted, and the men he fought beside treated him with respect. But privately, he was considered a lunatic without a shred of mercy in him. The enemy bodycount he was personally responsible for steadily increased, and he was attaining the reputation of being absolutely invincible.

But one morning, as he was carving paths of death on all sides, an arrow tipped with poison entered a space between two plates of armor and buried itself in his flesh with a sickening soundlessness. A blinding sharp pain hurtled through his whole being, and he fell immediately to the ground in a faint.

The poison acted slowly, and it was an excrutiating wait for the process of dying to end. Propped up on pillows, his breath coming out in a horrible rattling wheeze, aching in every corner of his body, Renaud somehow, with the strength of desperation, found the energy to write Catherine a letter of farewell and a poem. When his servant, Guillaume, came to his side with a cup of water and tipped it to his parched lips, he drank. Then he said weakly, "Bring me here that box."

"What box would that be," said Guillaume, not exactly insolently, but in the tone of an equal. Renaud was much too weak; he let it pass. Guillaume had been speaking to him that way ever since they'd both become aware that Renaud was definitely now lying on his deathbed. The concept of disobedience had vanished from their relationship. The master was powerless and the servant was his lifeline; they now were on different terms. Guillaume had always been what Renaud had called a "faithful servant", now he wanted to be a faithful friend.

"The box," said Renaud faintly, "red leather. On the stool." Guillaume saw it. He fetched it and brought it to the bed, and Renaud's trembling fingers fumbled to open it. Guillaume leaned over to help him, and Renaud let his hands fall and wheezed unpleasantly. The box was empty except for a small curled lock of hair.

"Listen," whispered Renaud.

"I'm listening," said Guillaume.

"I want you to do this for me." There was a pause filled with panting that had a thin whistle in it. "I want you to fold these up," Renaud's hand moved on top of the pages he'd filled with writing, "and put them in the box. And then...are you listening to me?"

"Yes, yes, I am."

"After I'm dead I want you to cut out my heart."

"What?"

"I want you to cut out my heart. And then have it embalmed. Put my heart in the box with the letter and the poem and Catherine's... Catherine's...the lock of Catherine's hair, and then take her the box. Guillaume?"

"Wait a minute. What—"

"Are you listening?"

"Yes!"

"I want you to bring her the box and put it in her hands. Do not leave her until you have put it into her hands. Do you understand me? You GUILLAUME!!"

Guillaume jumped. Where did Renaud get the spurt of strength to shout out his name at such a volume?

Renaud's head turned on the pillow and he fixed on his servant a look of such pleading, with his mouth twisted and tears starting from his eyes, that Guillaume had to look away. He'd never seen that expression before on anyone's face, much less on that of this warrior with hundreds of deaths on his conscience. "Promise me," the master begged the servant. "Swear an oath to me that you'll do it."

It took an hour and half, but finally Guillaume came to say the oath, one he was bound to by his superstitions.

"Eight months."

The Dame de Fayel spoke to a cloud in the sky. Idling morosely in her room, as usual, she changed elbows that she leaned on at the window sill. "But I haven't forgotten a single gesture he made or the sound of his sighing when he came to me," she continued in a low voice, "even though eight months has taken eight centuries to pass." The only major event Catherine could remember happening during that time was that she had become pregnant, which was a major event all right. She had four months to go now.

The tops of the trees below stirred vaguely in the sullen breeze, which seemed as lethargic as she was. When she looked at the cloud again it had turned from a horse pulling a cloud behind it to a body with footless legs one shorter than the other, and a huge head at the other end haloed by wisps of smoke.

"Oh," she sighed, "I'm so lonely."

A rider on a horse appeared over the ridge of the hill. She started. What, was he back from hunting already? Her husband went out hunting almost every morning now, and didn't return until late afternoon. It was early for him to come back, maybe he'd forgotten something. She peered at the rider, trying to identify him-or was it her? No, it was a man, what she'd thought were skirts on either side were cloth saddlebags.

Guillaume's saddlebags padded softly against his horse's flanks. The familiar motion up and down on the trotting animal was contributing to his queasiness, which he'd first started feeling this morning, and which he was sure came from the dubious meal he'd eaten last night in one of the inns in the town below him. He also knew he was feeling sick because of his trepidation of what he was embarking on: the final leg of his journey that would end with him carrying out his promise to Renaud D'Ault. The closer the manor came the worse his stomach felt, until he felt he had to stop and find some relief. He guided his horse into a thick grove of trees and dismounted.

"Where'd he go?" said Catherine, "I only looked away for a second." In a short while the horse and man reappeared and continued toward the manor, the leafy limbs of trees concealing them from her view as they passed beneath.

"I thought that sausage had a funny taste," thought Guillaume, returning to the path, "and parts of it looked green. Ugh." He tried to think about something else. He was lucky he wasn't dead, after what he'd been through, traveling all that way, halfway across the world practically, or so it seemed. Then to finally get to the town of Fayel, and have to put up with a surly inn-keeper and his monosyllabic insults, a waiter with filthy hands who'd shown up with Guillaume's plate of food an hour after he'd ordered it from the one-item verbal menu, and being bitten all night by fleas which either lived in the bed or on the man he'd shared it with, or had made flying leaps across the room from the other beds, it all added up to abominable service. Still, it was the only inn in the town that had a bed for him, and he'd come a long, long way. He'd more than once fallen asleep in the saddle yesterday. Last night he'd slept like a log, regardless of the fleas. And good for him he'd picked up that information about the Lord de Fayel's hunting habits. If he went out every morning, there was no reason for Guillaume to wait. He could deliver his package to the Dame de Fayel right away, this morning. He'd thought he'd have to wait a lot longer than this for her husband to be gone. But better be quick. Put the box in her hands and run. He didn't have the sightest desire to dawdle here and observe the outcome. Once she held the box, he was free.

Guillaume drew up his horse by the gates to the manor. "I have a message for the Dame de Fayel," he said to the guards. "Confidential."

"On whose authority."

"The Duke de Daubeville."

"Where's your missive."

Guillaume handed down the forged document he took out of his saddlebag. The guards examined it and returned it, beckoning Guillaume to dismount. His horse was led away and one of the men took him to the stairway. They began to climb. Guillaume was light-headed with relief.

"Another visitor," said Catherine, as a second horse and rider appeared over the ridge. When the mounted man was halfway across the grounds, she recognized him. Without emotion she watched the top of her husband's head bob up and down, then noticed he had returned without his prized falcon attached to his wrist.

"One of us has escaped at least," she said.

On the first landing, the guard stopped to talk to a serving-maid who had a stack of freshly washed linen piled from her arms to her chin. The guard's hand went to her waist and she exploded with laughter. After a mirthful tussle, during which Guillaume shuffled his feet, tortured by impatience, the maid relinquished her load to the guard, who had been this whole time insisting on carrying it for her to the cupboard. The two of them walked away down the hall, whispering and nudging each other. Guillaume debated whether to go it alone and search out the Dame de Fayel's quarters or wait just one more minute. But then there was a footfall on the stairs behind him. As he swiveled around, his uneasiness changed to thudding fear.

Briskly ascending the stairs, his tread hard and deliberate, was a man dressed for hunting, his falcon's gauntlet in one hand, the other on the banister, and a look of preoccupied surprise on his lined face. They looked at each other, then the man's eyes went to the package in Guillaume's hand. Guillaume's first impulse was to bolt, but his feet wouldn't obey him. So he stood frozen to the stone floor, sweating with fear. The guard reappeared just as the man arrived on the landing.

"Good morning, my lord," he said and bowed low, confirming Guillaume's ugly suspicions as to who exactly the man was. In his guilty apprehension of the Lord de Fayel's having noticed his temporary departure from his duties, the guard said quickly, "This man has a confidential message from the Duke de Daubeville for the Dame de Fayel. I'm leading him to her."

There was a silence while the Lord de Fayel bored holes in Guillaume's face with his eyes. "That," he said, "is not possible. The Duke de Daubeville has been dead for a month and a half." He stared at Guillaume without blinking, his face beginning to flush a deep, warm red. "Give me that package you're taking to my wife." His lips barely moved. The image of the Lord de Fayel's bloodless, barely moving lips was one that would follow others behind Guillaume's closed eyelids, as later, in his dark prison cell he reviewed the important events of his life, one that had been finally punctuated by a spectacular act of loyalty and failure.

"Oh Lordy Lordy Lord," sighed Elenore le Bon, giving her pot of chicken broth a stir. Oh Lordy Lord was she tired. On her feet from morning to night and what for. Tell her what for if you please. Somebody give her a hint of what the real reason was that she'd been brought into this world so she could stop wondering and worrying.

"Oh Lordy Lordy Lord," piped up a thin little voice at her elbow. Elenore's spoon stopped stirring. "Alfred," she chided, "now now," not knowing why she chided him, it was just habit. And after the soup, baked fish. With carrots. This was the longest time of day, the late afternoon, it never seemed to end. She covered the pot and went to the table where Felice had set down the fish she'd brought up from the market. It wasn't there. Isn't that where she'd set it? Oh she was tired.

"Alfred." Alfred came running. "Where'd your mother put the fish?"

"There!" he cried, pointing with his perfect, minature finger to the empty space on the table.

"That's what I thought. Where'd it go? Jumped off the table all by itself?"

"Jumped!" screamed Alfred, "Jumped off the table!"

"Shhh!" Elenore leaned over and gently pinched his lips together. She smelled fish. Sniffing, she looked around her. It was Alfred the smell was coming from. In fact his whole shirt front was covered with something highly suspicious.

"Alfred," she said grimly, "Where is the fish."

"There!" He strutted over to the corner and disappeared behind the wash tub. She followed and found him standing looking down at the floor. Situated at the center of a mess of pale pink flesh and shreds of irridescent, scaled skin was a long flat spine with some meat clinging to it.

"What have you done!" Elenore wailed. As hard as she could she shook the child by the shoulder until he started to cry. "Now what am I supposed to do? Tell me what I'm supposed to do!"

"What's the matter?" Felice appeared at the kitchen door wiping her hands on her apron. "What did he do?"

"Come and look."

Alfred fearfully watched his mother grow and rise over him. "Oh," said Felice, then, "Stop crying!" She gave her son a shake. Her arm went up and came down. Alfred was so surprised by the slap he stopped crying.

"That's all right," said Elenore belatedly, "Don't strike him, he's only a child." Both of them watched as Alfred pulled himself together, proving how hard he was trying to show that he was not a baby anymore.

"Don't you ever ever do that again. Do you hear me?" said Felice. The women waited. At last the head down below them gave a subtle nod. "Say it." Another pause. "Say it, Alfred. Say I'll never do that again."

"I'll never do that again," said Alfred, then sniffed loudly.

"You're coming with me." Felice took hold of his upper arm. "He's nothing but trouble, this one. Trouble," she repeated, looking down pointedly at his bent head.

"That's all right, you can leave him."

"No, I'll take him out of your way."

"I wonder what he wanted with it." To Alfred, Elenore said, "Why'd you take the fish apart?"

"It's just something to play with," Felice shrugged. The three of them walked across the kitchen to the door.

"Why'd you want to do something like that? I would have given you something to play with. What'd you want to take my fish for?"

"I wanted to make it breathe again." He had evidently completely recovered. He was using that tone of precocious confidence he sometimes came out with.

"He's a fine one," scoffed Felice.

At the door, Elenore said again, "What am I supposed to do now? It's too late to send you out for another fish."

"Tell them they'll have to skip a meal." Felice was smirking. "Just this once."

"There's always the salt pork," Elenore said. Felice and her son left the kitchen.

Elenore went to the corner and swept up the remains of the fish. When she turned around what she saw startled her into spilling half of it back on the floor. The Lord de Fayel stood in the doorway, his gaunt face as white as her apron. She'd never seen him at such close quarters before, she hadn't realized how ill-looking this man she cooked for, day in, day out, actually was. He looked healthy enough at a distance, from her kitchen window, when he went cantering through the grounds straddled on the silk-draped back of his horse. What was he doing down below? What did he want in her kitchen? It gave her chills to see him right in front of her like that.

From way at the other end of the room he spoke to her in a strange, dreamlike way. She couldn't make out a word he said. That threw her in a quandary: she didn't know whether she'd show worse disrespect if she went closer to him without his permission, or if she asked for it, which would mean speaking to him without his permission. So she stood without speaking or moving.

But then he stopped talking to her. He walked slowly into the kitchen and onto the nearest table he set down an object, which he avoided looking at.

Then he said loud and clear, "You understand? Cook this for the Dame de Fayel. Only for her. It's a special treat she particularly cares for. But none for me. Is that clear? None at all for me."

"And what's for you, my lord," blurted Elenore. "What should I cook for you?"

"I really don't have any interest in that problem," said the Lord de Fayel, turning his back and leaving.

After thinking all this over for a minute, Elenore dumped the fish in the pigfeed bucket and went to look at what he'd left on the table.

Upstairs, the Dame de Fayel soaked in a tub of hot water in her bedroom. Her maid poured the last bucketful she'd carried from the kitchens into the tub and left to wait in the antechamber for her mistress to call for her. The sound of splashing came from the bedroom, and a low, steady murmuring. The Dame was talking to herself. The maid strained her ears, trying to understand what she was saying, but couldn't catch it. After a while, she was called and went back into the bedroom to help the Dame to dress. She helped her into her heavy brocaded velvet gown, smoothed and arranged the voluminous skirts, and then fastened the long row of jewelled buttons on her fur-edged sleeveless jacket. Then she set an elaborate headdress draped with silk and hanging with strings of pearls, on the Dame's head and stood back to examine the whole ensemble. It was like putting clothes on a mannequin. She wanted to exclaim, "Why are you so listless all the time! Cheer up! You got plenty to be happy about. Here you stand, passive as a dummy, while I wait on you hand and foot!" But she didn't have occasion to let off steam in that way.

Dinner was announced. The Dame de Fayel dismissed her maid and somnambulantly headed for the dining hall.

The herbs bought fresh in the market early that morning and scattered throughout the room didn't sweeten her mood with their scent or color. Few things could stimulate her to emerge from her gloom. Her environment didn't interest her much, conversation bored her. Food bored her also, but its arrival sliced through the tedium of her days. And she was always famished now, she was feeding two people. She was really beginning to bulge now, her belly rounded out full of the life of another. She wished she had another woman to talk to. She missed her sister, she only had her ladies-in-waiting for company. But why couldn't they be friends of hers? She knew they wanted to be. It was her own fault she was so lonely, moping all the time. She wasn't much good as company. She'd have to make a better effort. She'd have to begin to accept that she wasn't an island. It was time she thought about entering the world of the living again.

Her dish was put in front of her, and she ate hungrily. A thick, creamy sauce covered a pile of peas and carrots and pieces of meat, which had a dark bitter taste. When she was finished and was reaching for a piece of bread to dunk in the gravy, she noticed that her husband on the opposite side of the table was staring at her with unconcealed intensity, his food half-eaten in front of him. Nonplussed by his scrutiny, she paused with the bread in her hand.

"What's that you were served?" she finally said. "It's not the same dish I'm eating."

"The dish you've eaten," he corrected her. She looked down at her plate, where only a puddle of gravy remained, then back at him. He looked so old. His face was haggard and drawn, and silver hairs gleamed at his temples. She hadn't seen them before; she hadn't directed her attention at him long enough.

"How was your food?" he said.

"It was good."

"And the meat? Did you like it?"

"It had a bitter taste, I didn't recognize it. I wonder what kind of meat it was. What's that you're eating?"

He ignored the question. "Would you like to know what kind of meat it was you ate?"

"Don't call the cook, I'll ask tomorrow." She broke off a piece of her bread and dipped it in her gravy.

"I don't have to call the cook. I myself know what it was," said the Lord de Fayel. "In fact, the cook is not aware of what it was she prepared for you tonight."

"What do you mean?" Catherine delicately pushed the piece of bread around her plate.

"What I mean is," said her husband in a tone of voice that drew her eyes into his, "you have just eaten the heart of Renaud D'Ault. He was slain on the field. He had his heart sent to you in a box. I happened to meet the messenger who was on his way to your chamber to deliver it. I took possession of the box. You have just eaten part of its contents. The rest has been burned."

Catherine managed to stand up by clutching the edge of the table. She gave out a loud cry, like an animal, and then with her hand covering her mouth she put one foot in front of the other and left the room.

"Well I never!" Elenore burst out in complaint. "That's the last straw. It's one story if she doesn't care for one thing or another, all she's got to do is pass on the word to me. It's been done before. But to turn back every single dish I cook and have good food thrown to the pigs, well, I'm not going to sit still for that!"

"Don't get mad," said the kitchen-maid, whose job was scraping and washing plates after meals, "all I wanted to tell you was that every day half of the plates come back down full of untouched food and I'm just asking you if you heard anything. I mean she's probably sick."

"Maybe it's him who's not eating," said Elenore.

"I *told* you. It's her. Else told me."

"Who's Else?"

"I *told* you who Else was." The exasperated maid raised her voice. "She waits on them at the table!"

"Don't be impertinent, my girl," said Elenore.

"Well, I'm just telling you, Else says the Dame doesn't even try to eat, doesn't even lift a finger. Just sits there with her eyes fixed on nothing and her hands in her lap. Her and him, they don't talk to each other."

"Hmm," said Elenore.

About a week later, Felice stood on the grass of the manor grounds and waited for Alfred to catch up, her patience running out. She tapped her foot, her hand on her hip, the other holding on to her laden basket. She'd get her market shopping done in approximately one-fifth of the time if she didn't have this slow-poke she'd been given for a son dragging his feet behind her as a form of keeping her company. At last she cried, "Alfred! Come ON!" She turned to look for him, and saw a little ways off the Dame de Fayel taking weak, uncertain steps across the grass toward her, leaning on the arm of her lady-in-waiting. The Dame's bones were sharp in her cheeks, her eyes were blank and dull in the surrounding bruised-looking hollows. Felice just in time remembered to curtsy as the women went by, though all she got in exchange was a nod from the lady-in-waiting. The Dame de Fayel didn't notice her. As they went through the manor gates, the lady-in-waiting had to catch the Dame in her arms to keep her from falling as she swayed to the side.

"Who's that?" said Alfred, finally arriving.

"That's a sick woman," replied Felice absently.

It was about two and a half weeks after that, that the maid tipped her bucket of hot water into the tub in the upstairs bedroom, trying not to stare indiscreetly at the shadowed concave spaces and the stark ribs of the Dame de Fayel's wasting body. The sight of her round belly, the only place there was a curve, was a pathetic thing.

"Can I do something for you?" she said in her pity, and bent forward solicitously. Catherine simply shook her head strengthlessly. The maid set down the empty bucket and walked toward the door. As she was closing it she heard a cry of pain and a rending deep moan. Quickly turning back, she ran to the tub. Catherine was leaning over with her legs spread apart and her knees raised to the level of her bent head. Blood was pouring from between her legs and blooming upward through the water in a slow crimson cloud.

"Help me," she gasped, "help me."

In terror the maid ran to the hallway and, calling out, went to fetch help.

By the time the doctor arrived, the news was already in circulation throughout the manor that the Dame de Fayel had lost her baby. The doctor entered the bedroom where she lay, piles of blood-soaked bandages beneath her on the bed, and he removed his embroidered gloves. Then he let fall the fur-lined hood of his purple, silver-belted gown. Allowing only his assistant and Catherine's maid to remain with him in the room, he made his examination. Tablets of powdered stag's horns were prescribed, the bill for his services was handed over, and he departed.

While Catherine slept, her husband stood motionless at the foot of the bed, his pallor gray in the sickroom half-light. He kept a vigil there for five days, only breaking it when he fell asleep from exhaustion. It was then, when he slept, that Catherine died.

The way the sun rose up over the lake that morning you'd think some gruesome horror was lowering its seeping evils into the atmosphere over the town that lay in a little bunched up crumple of architecture at the base of a long finger of land crookedly tapping the water. And that also the air within the manor looming up above was rank with poisonous vapors...

The way it rose up made a vision of personified malevolence that conquers language.

But what it was *like* was: A sullen, bloated, grayish-red sun blinked into view, the eye of a snake, then slid behind a bank of early morning cloud, staining the sky in that quarter a murky but livid color, like dirty blood. Over the surface of the lake the pure white mist began to dissolve away, and the shadows of the clouds on the water were muddy purple, seething, unbearably heavy-looking. The lake was a slab of lead caked with dull brown rust that, when the wind shimmered across it, flared up in long sheeny waves of that dirty blood color.

The pilgrim was leaving that place behind him, never to return. He stared at the landscape that spread out below him with eyes momentarily locked in place, a trick of the muscles. It happened when he was tired, and he was tired now; he hadn't slept much during the night and he'd left the manor and started out on the road way before dawn. He'd already traveled through a good part of the foothills, and from where he sat resting on a flat rock he could see just how high he'd climbed. As it grew light the contours of the hills which he'd traced blindly in the dark became visible through the thin, clearing mist. The sun rose very slowly, it seemed to him, it made him ache with fatigue to watch the slow crawl of illumination across the brightening blue crusts of snow on the mountain peaks.

It hurt his eyes to see such an unearthly play of light; it was as though a volcano were erupting in the sky. And after what he'd been through, to see a sunrise so grotesque and virulent on this particular morning, the morning he was leaving everything behind, his home, his money, the vast expanses of land and the peasant labor that belonged to him, all the things that spelled out the enormous power he once wielded and had relinquished; it looked like a bad omen. His eyes shied away from it and he looked above his head. There, the sky was so limpid and benign that it was hard to believe it continued from that vicious clot over in the east. Downy clouds drifted across the high arc of pale blue, a flood of pure clear light saturated the land below. He turned his back on the growling sun, on the town and the manor aggressively spiking its towers out of the high hilltop above, and began to climb again. He forced the scene to dim away in his mind. It was no longer a part of him, he wasn't the lord of the manor, nor of this particular corner of the realm anymore. He'd exchanged ermine for rags and roasted larks for wild roots and berries. And he'd slept for the last time on a soft featherbed.

From now on he'd be traveling rough like any other poor pilgrim, sleeping in monasteries or guest houses outside city walls, not in the castles or manor houses of knights who were once his equals and now would hardly recognize him.

His heart was as heavy as a block of stone, melancholy slowed his steps. To think seriously of what he was doing was a bad idea. But doubt lurked below. After all, everything he was leaving behind had been passed down to him without his having to lift a finger. He'd been born to nobility, he was no *noblesse de la robe*, no busy ambitious drone fussing with administrative duties in some ministry of the Crown, who'd had to scramble and shove his way up to earn his status as noble. He'd inherited it all, lock, stock, and barrel. It had been passed on to him the way it had been done for generations, handed down from father to son. While mothers and daughters, a forest of spiders, spun the connecting filaments of dynasties. It was a perfect system, and he was a member of its ruling class. Before doubt could overpower him, he quickened his pace. It was hard going, the steep ground was soggy with dew and rivulets of water that constantly drained down the hills from streams and lakes higher up. The bark of trees he passed was soaking wet. He wasn't used to the tedious slog of a trek like this. As a knight, he was accustomed to making faster progress mounted on his steed. But he must keep going. To turn back was impossible. He couldn't do it. Not after the vow of repentance he'd sworn for the terrible duplicity, the heinous, despicable crime he'd committed against his wife.

In his private chapel he'd confessed all to his chaplain, who'd been so shocked and repulsed by what he heard that he'd advised the Lord de Fayel that this time the payment of indulgences would not suffice as a method of repentance. The Lord de Fayel had been so impressed by the chaplain's sincerity—after all, he was turning down a chance to swell the clerical coffers—that he'd felt such a horrible sense of shame for what he'd done, he'd taken the chaplain's advice to embark on a lengthy pilgrimage to try and make amends.

His boots squelched in the mud. The memory of his wife's sunken cheeks and hollow eyes, and of the grueling pain showing itself on her emaciated face, again lurched to the front of his consciousness, as it did frequently and without warning. A grimace twisted his features; his eyes widened in secret disbelief. With bowed head, and tripping clumsily on the slippery ground, he continued his trance-like march.

At her window in the manor kitchens, up on top of the peak of the hill above the town of Fayel, Elenore looked out over the land below with eyes still full of sleep. The sun had risen and the sky was pearly. Something was edging over the rise of a hill in the distance; it caught her eye, it was the only movement in the landscape. She squinted, trying to get it in focus, but it was too far away, she couldn't make out who or what it was. The tiny figure soon vanished, and Elenore immediately lost interest. She yawned and stretched. The sun was slinking up the wall of the sky, it was very warm already. She was falling back to sleep on her feet.

"I'm getting old," she thought to herself, examining her coarse wrinkled hands. "They'll be laying me down in the ground soon, too, like they laid her, the poor thing, so young and fragile, God rest her, who took her." She felt no incentive to get busy working. Since the Dame de Fayel's funeral she'd been feeling lethargic and aged. She often fell behind in her work, a thing that used to be unknown. Her favorite activity had become holding Alfred on her lap and having him jabber away to her any nonsense he cared to relate. At times when she was supposed to be chopping or stirring, she was, instead, poking for lice in his hair, or adjusting his bootstraps, or watching him at his play, which was becoming more experimental and undisciplined as he took liberties in her kitchen with items that used to be off bounds. Under her indulgent eye, he could do no wrong. Unlike women at her age who had borne more than their share of children, she didn't have the vague disinterest in children that long years of their company bring. He was a source of light and warmth for her in this time that felt like winter.

Soon he'd come bustling in, his hair uncombed and sticking up off his head, his face soft and swollen with recent sleep, but his eyes already bright, and he'd come out with some incongruous remark to make her laugh. There, what did she say. The kitchen door was opening. Elenore turned, the corners of her mouth already curling, but instead of Alfred, she saw his mother coming toward her, and what she had to say jolted Elenore wide awake.

"Have you heard yet?" inquired Felice in a complacent tone.

"About what?" said Elenore.

"About *him*."

Elenore knew right away who Felice meant. Lately when talking about the Lord de Fayel, Felice used one of two names: either "him" or "he", often verbally underlined by a tone of sarcastic contempt.

"What's there to hear?"

Felice crossed her arms and took a look out the window, her eyes narrowing. Then she said, "He's gone."

"What do you mean, gone?"

"He's gone, and by all accounts, never coming back."

"But where's he gone? Felice, what are you trying to say?"

"It's not what *I* say, it's what Beatrice says, and she heard it from her brother, who's one of his valets. Or was, I should say. *He* got up during the night and walked out the door. Gone on a pilgrimage. Thinks he can walk his way back to God and innocence, which is a thing *he* never had in the first place, even as a tiny seed in his mother's belly—"

"What are you talking about?" interrupted Elenore, "why has he gone on a pilgrimage?"

"To ask for absolution, of course. If *he* weren't who he was, he'd have been drawn and quartered for what he's done."

"But Felice, what's he done!" cried Elenore in desperation.

There was a heavily weighted silence, while Felice stared at Elenore with her mouth half-open and her eyebrows arching toward her hairline. "Don't tell me," she said, "you don't know the reason for the Dame de Fayel's death. How could you not know?"

"She died of an imbalance of the humors," said Elenore, "and also loss of appetite."

"But don't you know why she lost her appetite?"

Elenore shook her head.

"Don't you know that what you cooked her to eat..."

Now Elenore looked frightened. "What...what I cooked? Something I cooked for her?"

"But you didn't know! You didn't know what it was, it's not your fault!"

"What! What's not my fault!" Elenore gripped Felice's arms and shook her violently. Felice didn't know Elenore was that strong, she fought to get loose. Elenore fell back onto her rag-covered barrel and sat staring out the window. Trembling badly, she turned up her face and said, "Tell me."

"It's not your fault," Felice insisted.

Elenore waited. Felice took a breath and said rapidly, "The Dame de Fayel had a lover and he died in a battle and he had his heart cut out and put in a box to be given to her and *he* caught the messenger and found the heart and gave it to you to cook for her and after she found out what she ate she said she'd never eat again and that's how she died."

Elenore's brows were knit in puzzled concentration. That was not the reaction Felice had expected, or dreaded.

"Elenore?"

"Wait, I'm thinking."

"Do you remember being given something—well, unusual, to cook?"

"So that's what that horrible thing was. It's no wonder I couldn't go through with it." Her forehead smoothed out as comprehension dawned.

"What's that you say?"

"To think that he would do such a vile thing. It's beyond belief. And to give me a thing like that to cook, to involve me in his revolting crime, I who never harmed him."

"Elenore, what did you mean, you couldn't go through with it?"

"I remember it, clear and plain. He came into the kitchen. He had something in his hand, he put it on the table. He told me to cook it. It was after Alfred took the fish apart, remember when he did that? I turned around and there was the lord, standing in the doorway as white as a ghost. 'Cook this for my wife,' he says to me. He said he didn't want none of it, it was only for her. And he put it on the table and left."

Felice nodded. "That was it," she said. "That was a human heart. What did it look like?"

"Well," Elenore grimaced. "I could hardly bear to touch it. It was wrapped in leaves."

It was wrapped in leaves, like a piece of meat. A piece of meat? Then why'd he act so strange about the whole thing, Elenore had thought to herself, standing at the table looking down at the thing he'd left for her to cook. Why'd he bring down a piece of meat to her kitchen, anyway? It was abnormal and peculiar. She unwrapped the thing and took a look at it. Meat. That's what she thought. But strange meat, not like anything she was familiar with. Maybe it was from something he'd caught on one of his hunts. A delicacy. An organ? But...hard...pus... Ugh. She knew the Dame de Fayel was fond of sweetbreads. If she could eat brains, maybe she had the stomach for this. Whatever it was, it didn't look edible. They were a peculiar lot, the rich. The things they called "a special treat". Well, she better try and cook it if that's what she'd been told to do. How, though, was she expected to cook it? He didn't tell her that, did he. First of all cut it up a bit. She fetched her knife and held the blade against the dark blistered wall of the thing.

Oh no. She did not like this at all. Not at all. In fact, she, inured to the sight and sensation under her fingers of bloody gristle and sawed bone and other dead animal matter, could not bring herself to continue. She was filled with disgust and repugnance. Before she quite knew what she was doing she'd shoved the leaves back around the thing and hurried to the pigfeed, where she dropped the foul object and covered it over.

"And then," said Elenore, "I cooked up the liver I was going to have for my supper and drowned it in sauce and herbs so she wouldn't recognize what it was, and that's what she ate. For him I heated up some salt pork."

Felice stared at her. "You never cooked it," she said slowly. "She never actually ate it."

Elenore looked out the window. She didn't fully understand what she'd done. Or not done. She was responsible, wasn't she? Wasn't she partly to blame for the slow death by starvation of the Dame de Fayel?

The two women stood together in silence, both gazing out over the landscape that unrolled in swells and folds and furred and colored surfaces to the horizon and beyond, wrapping itself right around the world, a carpet of graves.

"Well," said Felice, "all I can say is, what a lot of unnecessary trickery. It's all come round full circle."

"What's come ground circle?" said Alfred sleepily behind them.

TOP STORIES

A PROSE PERIODICAL

#1 Donna Wyszomierski
#2 Laurie Anderson
#3 Pati Hill
#4 Suzanne Johnson
#5 Linda Neaman
#6 Gail Vachon
#7 Jenny Holzer/Peter Nadin
#8 Judith Doyle
#9 Kathy Acker
#10 Lynne Tillman/Jane Dickson
#11 Kirsten Thorup
#12 Janet Stein
#13 Anne Turyn
#14 Lee Eiferman
#15 Constance DeJong
#16 Ursule Molinaro

Available from
TOP STORIES
Hallwalls
700 Main Street
Buffalo, New York 14202

TOP STORIES #18 $2.50

FORGET ABOUT YOUR FATHER
& other stories

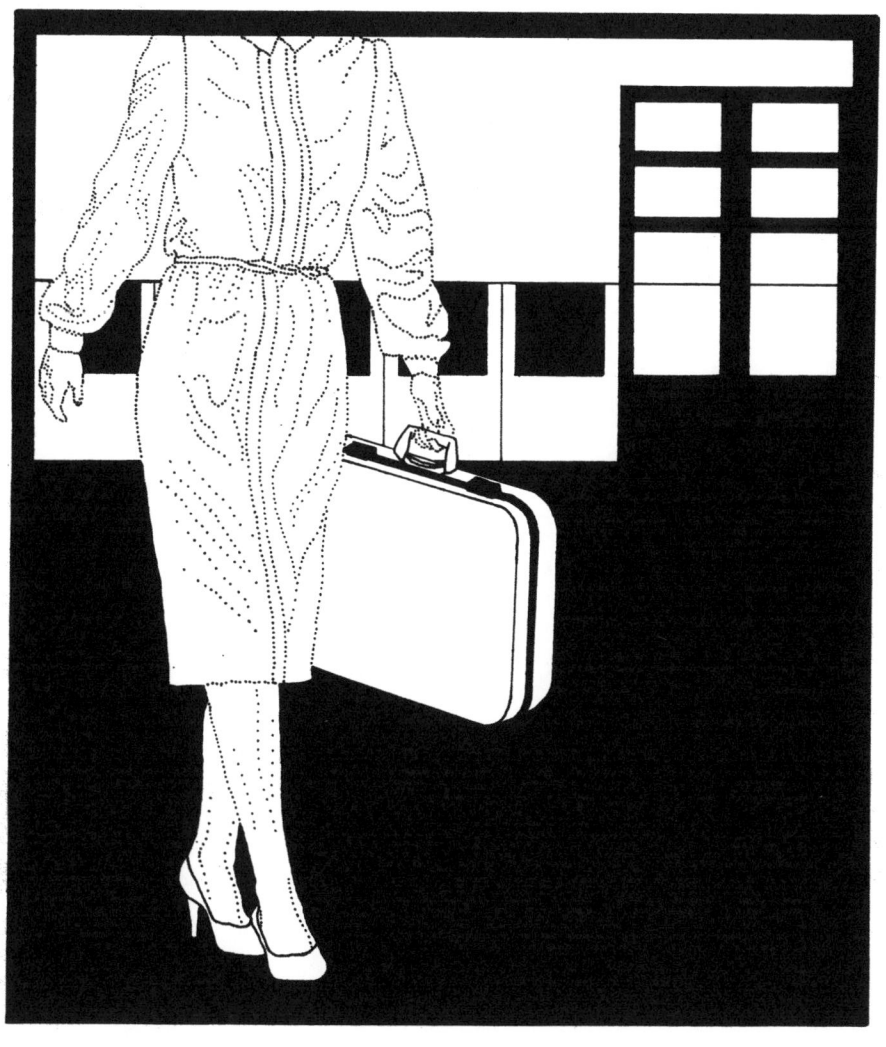

DONNA WYSZOMIERSKI

Forget About Your Father

A Bad Move

He Only Likes Blondes

A Friend of the Family

A Smart Niece

Caught Up in Romance

by Donna Wyszomierski

Copyright © 1983 by Donna Wyszomierski

Cover drawing by Michael Sticht

This publication has been made possible in part by a grant from the New York State Council on the Arts, Literature.

Hallwalls, 700 Main Street, Buffalo, New York 14202

Forget About Your Father

Forget about your father, I told my son. He left me without a dime to chase some young floozy. The kid kept talking about him, it just about broke my heart. Why would you want to be like him, I asked. He admitted it was the guy's height, said it must be my fault he's short. I can't do anything about my genes, I said, you could always get elevated shoes. I took him to a store where the clerk was a friend from way back. He had trouble walking at first, but I had to admit it improved his appearance. I was just starting to relax when the old man shows up and tells the kid he looks ridiculous. You ought to be boosting his ego, I said, why don't you buy him some clothes? All kinds of stuff started coming in the mail, I was embarrassed when the boy wore it. He got these in a thrift shop, I said. We almost came to blows before the kid quieted down.

The next day he announced he wanted to take a modeling course. I was sorry when I heard how much it cost. He came home with a blonde about twenty-eight, the grooming advisor, he called her. I dragged him into the kitchen. She's a little old for you, I said. He asked her to stay for supper. While we were eating she kept looking at my hair. Something on your mind, I asked. Your look's kind of outdated, she said, I could give you a permanent. I wondered if she really thought it would help. We can do wonders these days, she told me. Why don't you come down to the school tomorrow? After she left I asked my son if I'd be intruding. He said not really, she was reasonable.

We got to talking while she rolled up my hair. You know, she told me, your son's very attractive. I want him to go to college, I said, but he wants to be a musician. She said her husband was in a band and they split up over it. Every night he was either playing or practicing, and socially she was on her own. I wouldn't complain, I told her, you have a nice business here. Why would a girl like you want to get married? She said she wanted to have kids some day. Fine, I told her, don't rob the cradle.

They were out late every night. How's the advising coming, I asked my son. I can take care of myself, he said. You're looking a lot better, by the way. That boosted my confidence, I took a walk to the shoe store. The clerk was on his lunch hour. I got tickets to a concert, I said, how about it? He took a look at my hairdo. Not bad, he said, I think I can make it. He picked me up at eight-thirty. We sat in the last row, spotted my son and the blonde a couple seats up. What do you make of that, I asked. He said you have to give them some slack, they come around in the end. We stopped for a drink on the way home. The kid never really had a father, I told him, I think it affected him. I could talk to him, he said, I have a couple boys of my own. You never told me, I said. What happened to their mother? He said it didn't work out, she expected too much. I invited him for supper the next night, told my son to bring the blonde.

Let's have coffee in the kitchen, I told her, I need some advice on my clothes. I sat by the door so I could listen. For starters that skirt's gotta go, she said. Tell me about your family, I said, do you live with your parents? She told me they threw her out when she was seventeen and in love. She wanted to talk to me about them sometime since we were about the same age. Spare me, I said, I have problems of my own. You mean your son, she said. Don't worry, I haven't touched him. He's good looking but a little naive. He misses his father. I do my best, I told her, but I'm not a young woman. I could fix you up, she said, I know a lot of guys. I said I liked the silent type. They were yelling in the living room. Excuse me, I said, we better go in there. My son had the clerk by the throat. It's my fault, I told him, I put him up to it. Don't be too hard on him, the clerk said, I got a little overbearing. They shook hands and I turned to the blonde. You really think this skirt's so bad, I asked. She offered to take me shopping the next day.

I picked her up early, left a note for my son. When we got back his clothes were gone. He went to live with his father, I told her, I could see it coming. Ever think about getting a job, she asked. I started working in the office building next to hers, we had lunch every day. She brought in letters from my son, he was working on a ranch near his father's place. Invite him for the holidays, I said, he always liked the tree. He showed up with a girl his own age. They announced their engagement that night. Are you the maid of honor, I asked the blonde. He's pretty young, she said, but they seem sensible. She helped me pick out a dress. I wondered if the clerk would be my date. He'd be a fool to say no, the blonde said, you look twenty years younger. I went to the wedding on his arm. My husband said I looked matronly, I must be working too hard. I approached a couple of old flames. You'll be a grandmother soon, they said. It couldn't happen to a nicer person. I was disappointed and retired to the bathroom. The blonde was in there combing her hair. I just don't have it anymore, I said. I need a change of pace. That's no problem, she said, I have relatives in the south who love to entertain.

I went home and packed. The blonde's sister was pretty homely. I walked out to the garden where her husband was pruning the roses. The best things in life are free, he told me. I should have guessed something was up. I was just getting into bed when he knocked at the door. My wife's a good cook but there's more to life, he said. Don't you agree? I had a thing about southern gentlemen but I didn't want to rush it. Let's have some tea, I said. I have to think this over. He bowed out gracefully. I decided to write to my daughter-in-law.

It's pretty hot down here, I wrote. If you need advice I'm as close as the phone.

We had breakfast on the terrace. I described my husband's career. He was successful at first, I said, but people took advantage of him. He could never say no to a lady. The brother-in-law kissed my hand and suggested a drive to the lake. His wife said she had a headache, so I excused myself and put on my best dress. It had a coffee stain on the front but I hid it with my purse. For the first hour we read magazines. He brought a big selection and I tried to seem interested. Finally he looked up. I believe in honesty, he said. Let's have an affair, my wife's used to it by now. He said she liked to read, I should look at her library sometime. I said I would, I wanted to avoid hurt feelings. He wasn't much of a lover and I was glad to get back to the house. I discussed my favorite author with his wife. We had a lot in common, and I promised to write when I left the next week.

The first thing I did was look up the blonde. The school was losing money and she was thinking of moving. What did you think of him, she said. No offense, I said, but I pity your sister. My son came home and his wife announced she was pregnant. I asked her if she got my letter. I've been meaning to call you, she said. He spends all his time in front of the mirror. Don't worry, I said, it's a stage he'll outgrow. The blonde left town the next day. I helped her load the car and thanked her for my new look. I hope you find a husband, I said. She promised to keep in touch. I got a card a month later, she was living with my son's father. They were working a big spread, owned a hundred head of cattle. How do you like that, I asked my son. He looked depressed there in the mirror. I went to my bedroom, sat down at the desk.

We're still legally married, I wrote, half of that is mine.

A Bad Move

It was a lot different before we were married. We'd see each other a couple times a week, got dressed up, got along real good. Could've gone on like that but we wanted to have sex, no place to be alone. At first I encouraged her family, they came all the time. Never brought even a can of coffee but I didn't complain, they kept her company when she was pregnant. Had our boy the first year, pretty soon but we couldn't help it. Wasn't a bad move, I got a better job, her uncle put in a word for me. Then her mother moved in, promised to help with the wash. I applied for a job out of state, she wouldn't move, said she'd miss the relatives. I sent her money, met some women but nothing serious. Came home at Christmas, she wanted a divorce, the boy was out of diapers. I told her I'd think about it, the company was sending me overseas. I went by boat so I'd have time to think.

There was nothing to do at night, the captain introduced me to his sister. They were from Connecticut, she was taking the trip to forget about her husband. None of the crew spoke English, we became very close. I didn't want to get involved, resisted her advances. We were blown off course, landed in a small village. The captain went to get help, I couldn't resist the temptation. He came back in three weeks, had a letter from my wife. We had a long talk, I remembered my responsibilities. The captain's sister understood, she came from New England where families are important. I arranged for her marriage to a village elder, her brother was best man. I went home and promised to be a better husband, my wife asked her mother to move out.

The guys thought I was a hero, my wife was thrilled and did whatever I wanted. I helped my boy write a report for school, was invited to address an assembly, got elected to the town council, bought my wife a new coat. I was getting restless, my wife's uncle warned me to watch my step. He stopped me in the bar one day, I knew he was leading up to something. He wanted to know about the captain's sister, he saw her picture in my locker and liked the way she looked. I told him I got a letter the day before, she didn't like the life in the village and was planning to leave her husband. She was independently wealthy, owned a house in France. I gave him a letter of introduction, he left the next morning. My wife asked me why he didn't show up on Sunday, I told her there was a boom on in the islands and he wanted to get in on it. She didn't know about the captain's sister, I didn't want to hurt her feelings. The woman died in a hurricane a few months before but I wanted to get rid of the uncle, he was blocking my legislation. I had the town rezoned commercial, became a local tycoon. We enrolled the boy in prep school, decided to take a vacation.

When we got back I got a letter, her uncle was in partnership with the village chief. He wanted me to see his villa, meet some of the local girls. I told my wife I was going on a trip, she was pregnant and said she'd stay home. I got there at night, the beach was deserted. I set up camp, was ambushed by the uncle's cutthroats. I swallowed some poison, was delirious for months. I woke up in the villa, my wife's uncle was painting a picture of the captain's sister. He told me he gained control of my business back home, was threatening my wife with bankruptcy. Why take it out on me, I said. He blamed me for the woman's death, said he hadn't slept in months. She went insane after I left her, I suspected it from her letters. He made me stay awake all night, give details of our affair. You ought to see a doctor, I said, there are plenty of women around. He hit me with his pistol, accused me of insulting him. Look, I said, I hear she has a cousin. He wouldn't listen at first, after awhile I convinced him. She was living in the house in France, getting over a broken marriage. I wrote another letter of introduction, promised to look after his business. His servants kept an eye on me, I managed to put away some money.

Three months later he came back, said they were engaged. I asked him if I could leave, the heat was starting to bother me. He said next month when the cousin arrived, in the meantime I could take it easy. I got a letter from my wife, our boy dropped out of school. I asked the uncle if I could write, he said okay, don't mention me.

> Dear honey, I wrote, encourage him to join the service. You can show him my army pictures, they're in my top drawer. I understand how you felt all these years. I let my conscience take over, we're building a hydroelectric plant to improve life on the islands. They need my help, I'll be back in a few months.

I took it to the post office, it was run by a man I knew I could trust. I got a lot of sleep, took up with a woman in town. The uncle was jealous, I promised to be discreet. We took walks on the beach, I got a nice tan. The uncle's girlfriend arrived, she was twenty pounds overweight. He put her on diet, asked me to be best man. I got another letter from my wife, she sent a picture of the captain's sister.

> Dear sweetheart, she wrote, I found this in your drawer, she is very beautiful. If she's there with you I'll understand, my brother will get us a divorce. Our son is in the navy, I promise not to tell him. I wonder what happened to my uncle, his mother died and left him a fortune. Please write, I'll be traveling but mother will forward.

I went to see her uncle, he was mooning about his girlfriend's size. My wife needs me, I said, put her on a diet of fish and rice. He promised to try it, I ran down to the telegraph office.

Girl and uncle dead, I sent, who is next of kin.

We held the wedding the next week, I wore my best suit. I gave them the money I saved in exchange for a boat, the bride kissed me on the cheek. She wasn't bad at that point, I winked at the uncle. We left the next morning, ran into bad weather. The boat leaked, I suspected the uncle. We landed at a naval base, I was reunited with my son. He got me on a transport, I was home in two weeks.

My wife was still on vaction, I went to inquire about the estate. They asked me for a death certificate, I produced the uncle's watch and they gave me the papers. I surprised my wife with a new house, refused her mother's offer to decorate. Our son came home on leave, I took him into partnership. My wife bought a stone for her uncle, we went there every Sunday. Our second child was a girl, she looked like her mother. A letter came from the uncle, I took it into my office.

> My wife's fat again, he wrote, nothing like her cousin. I discovered a local secret, it could mean a fortune. I'm building a refinery, telegraph if interested. How is my mother, I haven't heard from her in years.

My wife saw the postmark, said she thought the girl was dead. I showed her slides of the hurricane, told her my old outfit was having a reunion. She went west with her mother, I got a boat the next morning. I arrived on the island, visited my old mistress. Tell me the local secret, I said. She looked embarrassed and refused to answer, I showed her pictures of my children. It's for their sake, I said, you wouldn't believe how much they eat. She promised to show me the next day, I went to see my wife's uncle. I asked him where the refinery was, he had the flu and said his wife would show me. She threw herself at me on the way, I didn't feel good but went along. Three months later she said she was pregnant, the uncle suspected me. I'm an old man, he said, I'll give you a half share in the refinery if you'll take it. I went home for our anniversary, took my wife out to dinner. You know that girl, I said, the poor thing didn't die in the hurricane. I found her living in poverty, she was dying a slow death. I satisfied her last wish, she's going to have a baby. I can't live with myself, I have to bring it home. I stayed for my daughter's birthday, my wife said she admired me. I went back, assisted in the delivery. The refinery was finished, I asked the uncle for a check. You never mentioned my mother, he said. She ran off with a younger man, I said, no one's heard from her in years. I took my son home, my wife was leaving for work. My mother will watch him, she said, I got a job teaching school. I left instructions with her mother, went down to the chamber of commerce, the president took me to lunch. You're an important man, he said, where do you get your tips. I told him about the island, refused to reveal its location. It's terrible how they live, I said. I went home, my wife's mother was packing. It's not my flesh and blood, she said, I have my own life.

I got the telegram the next week, it was from my wife's uncle.

> Wiped out by fire, it said. Refinery no longer operating. Back taxes due, legal action pending. Wife returned to France, have you heard from my mother.

He Only Likes Blondes

I rent a place not far from town, it has a yard but the wiring is bad. My girlfriend brings over some extension cords, tells me it's all mathematical. Let me see the fuse box, she says. She's working on the equations when my boyfriend calls. He left town a few months ago, I was about to write him off. I invite him over for coffee, tell my friend to wash her face. I remember him, she says, he used to call me on the sly. Forget it, I say, he did that to everybody. This was different, she says, he fell for me hard. You're crazy, I tell her, he only likes blondes.

His business deals fell through, he's looking for an apartment. I refer him to an agency, go shopping for new clothes. I need something unusual, I tell my girlfriend, he's big on appearances. He picks me up the next night, his car has a new paint job. I'm about to comment when he suggests a local nightspot. It's a transient hotel, he knows some of the residents. We have a couple beers, I get tired of the conversation and ask him to call me a cab. We make a date for the next day. I call in sick, decide to go to the lake. My boyfriend shows up with the car, he sits in the back with his friends. I get in the passenger side, the car starts down the hill, I yell who's driving and they say you are. We stop in front of a tavern in a rundown part of town. I'm disgusted and go in for a beer, find out it's a youth hostel. I'm wearing my leather jacket, decide to join in the folk songs. We sit in a circle, a funeral goes by outside. It's a local religious group, an old man is dancing on a flatbed truck. We start a hymn, one guy gets annoyed. They can't upset people, he says, it violates my rights. I want to avoid a scene, go back out to the car. My boyfriend's still talking, I tell him I won't drive. He refuses to go any further, says he has to meet somebody. I hitch back to my place, the flatbed picks me up. I hit it off with the old man, he invites me to services. I'd come, I tell him, but my church doesn't allow it. You can't be closed-minded, he says, we have a mixed group on Thursday. I ask him about daycare. Sure, he says, the kids are our best singers. I'm excited, call my girlfriend when I get home. She's looking for something to do and agrees to go along. You can't be crude, I say, these people have high morals. She gives me a dirty look but wipes off some of her makeup. An old woman meets us at the door, assigns us seats near the front. The minister calls my name, I get embarrassed and go up to the stage. I see you entering a dark tunnel, he says, it's lucky you came tonight. I need a companion, I say. That's been my problem all along. He advises me to get married. Do you have any prospects, he says. I'm not sure, I say, I always pick the losers. He invites me for dinner the next night, introduces me to his son. You look familiar, I say. Over coffee it all comes back, he was my first date. It hasn't been easy, he says. I have to work for my father. I feel sorry for him, offer to run away. I think about my bank book, call my favorite aunt. Look, I tell her, you always went to church. Don't tell your mother, she says, but I mention you in my will. I ask for an advance, leave my furniture as security.

The minister's son picks me up in the truck. We decide on a city where nobody knows us. Our apartment is tax exempt, we open a storefront church. I take the money at the door so I can get to know the neighbors. A woman comes in who looks like me, we get to talking and find out we're cousins. She ran away when we were twelve, broke her mother's heart. You should call, I say, she quit looking for you. We go out to a phone booth. In ten minutes I knock on the glass. Find out what you can, I say, but try to be casual. She tells me it's all over town, my boyfriend's looking for me. I'll send him a card, I say, announce my engagement. The minister's son is afraid of him, we decide to make it legal. The old man comes up for the ceremony. I start to fight with his son, we go in for counseling. I tell the doctor I'm a nervous wreck. He asks about my background and I tell him my family thinks I'm a fanatic. Write to your mother, he says, she's bound to come around. I lock myself in my room and try to relive my childhood. My husband knocks at the door. Bring me a drink, I yell. He comes back with a beer and a sandwich, I bring myself to write.

> Dear mother, I say, I think about you all the time.
> Come see me if you want, I miss all your cooking.
> Don't give my boyfriend the address, he drove me
> to this.

My mother writes back that she can't come, she's sending up my girlfriend. I tell my husband, ask him about the kid. He's understanding, says she can sing in the choir. I meet them at the train and have to miss services. How's your new life, she asks. I tell her my conscience is bothering me. We'll talk about it over lunch, she says. I have to take a shower first. I get my husband to babysit, we go to an outdoor cafe. It all started when I was ten, I say. I saw my brother naked. So that's why you married a minister, she says. It's not so bad, I tell her, the praying does me good. I miss the old times, though. Your hair's getting darker, too, she says. It's the climate here, I say. He won't take a vacation. She winks at me, says my boyfriend's on vacation. What'll I tell my husband, I ask. Don't worry, she says, I can fix it. The next night we're watching television, I get a phone call. It's your mother, she says, tell him she's in the hospital. What about the services, I ask, I'm scheduled to sing the closing hymn. She offers to fill in, my husband gets me a ticket. I'd go with you, he says, but I have baptism tomorrow. I don't pack much, I'll have to buy new clothes. I call my boyfriend from the airport, tell him I left my husband, I don't know where to turn. I could be just what you need, he says. We stay at the best hotel. It's lucky I wore my ring, we get good service. I make friends with the maid, ask her how she manages. It's easy, she says, I have a second job. I go to see her that night, she sings in a cabaret. You know, I tell her on her break, I bet I could do this. She agrees and gets me an interview. I wear dark glasses and a low cut blouse. I'm hired on the spot, move out of the hotel. My apartment's small but the bugs are under control. My boyfriend doesn't care, he finds another woman.

Every four weeks I get a package, twenty letters from my husband. I open the latest one.

>Darling, it says, the church is doing fine. We found a new singer, she very inspiring.

I check the return address, it's my girlfriend's apartment. I make a few phone calls, she hasn't been there in months. I take a leave of absence, catch the next flight home. My mother's having a family reunion, I spot my cousin in the corner. Everything's under control, she says, I reunited with my mother. Never mind that, I say, what's happening in the city. She looks down at the floor, mumbles something about religion. I figure it's true, my girlfriend moved in when I left. I go up to my old room, break a couple vases. My mother comes to the door, asks me if I want to eat. We're about to cut the cake, she says. I tell her to sit down, it's time we had a talk. She tells me a story about my father, it changes my perspective. I make a long distance call. I'm unlucky at love, I tell my husband, it runs in my mother's family.

A Friend of the Family

My daughter says she wants to get married. You had a big wedding the first time, I say. I grew up in the south where women don't work, my friends say I'm a perfect wife. I don't have any wrinkles, always keep myself nice. Men look at me but I keep my distance. My husband couldn't handle it, took a job in the oilfields. He sends me checks every month, asks me to join him. I hear the heat's terrible, no modern conveniences. I need a quiet environment, my family won't take me in. I like gardening, don't bother with nightlife.

A few days ago I'm on the porch, the man next door stops by, overweight but not too bad. He wants to take me out, I'm not busy so I say okay. We go to a movie, stop for a beer on the way back. I don't mind kidding, then he gets fresh. I jump out at the corner, he chases me into an alley. I'm afraid he has a knife, there's a history of violence in his family. I call my daughter, she's in bed with her boyfriend, won't answer the phone. I didn't raise her right, the guy's banging on the door. I'm about to take my chances when the police show up. I walk home twenty blocks, I'm so disgusted I fall asleep. The next morning I call an old friend of the family I used to be in love with, a dentist with wealthy clients. We make an appointment, I spend a long time fixing my hair. I knock at the door, he says he thought I'd look younger. I'm offended and don't say anything, we open a bottle and start playing around. His answering service calls, he has to be in the office in half an hour. I'm introduced to a man, he writes down my name and promises to call. We go out the next night and become a local item. My daughter is jealous since he's a doctor, shows me clippings about his divorce. I remind her I'm married, she threatens to call her father. We have an understanding, I say, it's none of your business. She doesn't want to see me again, I tell her the feeling's mutual.

Three days later the guy stands me up, I'm proud and won't listen to reason. I find out his son's in the hospital, I agree to see him one more time. We meet in a cafeteria, he proposes but I turn him down. I think about my daughter, I don't want to hurt her feelings. I love my husband, I say, I could never divorce him. He leaves in a hurry and forgets to pay the bill. The next morning I'm sorry, what good is a husband you never see. I call the doctor, his secretary tells me he left town. I show up at my daughter's, she's drinking and lets me in. Her boyfriend's seeing a blonde, I encourage her to leave him. She tells me she's pregnant, I offer to take care of the baby. Just like old times, I say. She refuses to discuss it, I hear her throwing up. She calls me later, they decide to get married. I feel sorry for her and pay for another wedding.

She sends the kid to spend the summer, goes to Mexico on vacation. I write her about my grandchild, let her know she's missing out. I get a postcard, she says she needs more experience. I watch the real estate ads, buy a cabin in the woods. I spend my time picking fruit, my grandchild learns to take care of herself. I make friends with a trapper down the road, he loses his wife in an accident. He invites me on a trip to Canada, we take the baby and rent a sled. We become self-sufficient, she forgets about her mother. I get tired of eating fish, we move to a village for more variety. I get a job, the trapper starts a lumber business. My daughter sends another postcard, I'm goodhearted and invite her up. She likes our way of life, refuses to go back to the city. The government asks for our visas, we apologize and look for a farm in Kentucky. We like the warm weather, join the local church. The minister takes a liking to me, helps me get a divorce by mail. I marry the trapper, we build a bigger house. My daughter stops eating, I'm worried and send for the minister. She wants to see her father, the trapper pays her fare. I get a letter from the oilfields, find out she's pregnant again. She comes back with her father, he has a beard and looks healthy. The baby's born and looks like the trapper, I'm shocked and go on a retreat. The trapper moves back to Canada, the minister helps me run the farm. We spend a night in the hayloft, he's ashamed the next morning. He tells me to set an example, I remarry my daughter's father. He starts to drink a lot, I forgive him and pay his debts.

The kids start to fight, my daughter panics and asks for advice. I tell her it runs in the family, she's not convinced and looks into boarding schools. I report her to a welfare agency, they say they're short of funds. I take complete control, my daughter goes back to Mexico.

A Smart Niece

I.

I split up with my stockbroker, took a job with an employment agency. The local betting parlor was looking for a clerk so I called up an old girlfriend who was staying with her nieces. They went to a christian school and were flunking all their subjects. Their mother said they could transfer if they promised to write some parables, she was going with a minister who was running low on sermons.

The most talented one was an eleven year old who was on her seventh volume. My girlfriend called her a natural, she wrote a lot on fishing. The minister tried out volume one and came back disappointed. It's an urban congregation, he said, only one or two own boats. School was starting in a month and the eleven year old was worried. I'll come up with the stories, my girlfriend told her, if you fill in the morals. The first eight or nine were easy, they went through my girlfriend's marriages. The minister was happy, had the congregation on their knees. He would take the niece to restaurants and grab her under the table. She was waiting to tell her mother until she transferred schools.

It was a week before a feast day when they all ran out of steam. My girlfriend was in love again but it didn't make much of a story. Her boyfriend was an engraver raised by a couple of nuns. I knew he wasn't good for her, she liked to move around. I owed the big romance of my life to her fight with her second husband. When I heard about the betting parlor I knew she was right for the job.

Spend a week or so, I told her, and get to know the regulars. She hit it off with an heiress who came in at twelve fifteen. This woman was born in Florida and married a good looking playboy. He took up racing stockcars and made her a rich widow. After a lot of traveling she got interested in gambling, now she hung around the track and liked our local parlor. She took my girlfriend to her beach house, they invited me for lunch. I showed up a little early and hid behind a tree. The heiress was telling a story and my girlfriend was taking notes. Remember, the woman was saying, it was my first time with a man. When he suggested a swim to the houseboat I pictured my father's yacht. We ended up in a hammock and I was completely unprepared. The first thing we discussed, of course, was his life insurance policy. He signed it over on the spot but still I couldn't relax. I went into hysterics, he got scared and called my father. He needed capital at the time so everything was settled. The day before the wedding I had my second thoughts. I ran down to the beach waving my father's shotgun, pointed it at a sailor and forced myself on him. I pulled the trigger when he started to stutter. It cost my father a fortune but we knew I'd get off easy, they sent me to jail for a year and I got married on parole. The playboy was scared of my father, promised I'd never regret it.

It started getting warm so I came out and went up the walk. The woman kissed me on the cheek and offered me a drink. She had a problem, she told me. She owed some back taxes. My girlfriend was telling her I'm fond of vacations. It's true, I admitted, I get restless a lot. Then take my money out of the country, she said. The minister will bring it back tax exempt. We'll split it three ways and all be ahead. I know the minister will go along with the plan, in the best part of town they don't make enough. I asked her where we'd make the exchange, knew the place she suggested, it was underdeveloped. Okay, I told her, I'll come up with a cover. I'm kind of attractive but could pass as a missionary.

My passport was in order so I scheduled my vacation. My boss looked at me funny, said clean out your desk. Glad to, I told him, the redhead is stealing. I knew that would get him, they had lunch everyday. I collected my pay and got a cab for the airport, grabbed some clothes on the way that made me look dowdy. We had to go tourist and pretend not to drink. The man sitting next to me saw through the disguise, said the climate was lousy, he was thinking of moving. I'll be free tomorrow, I said, we can travel together. The minister ignored me, I could tell he was nervous. I gave him two thirds of the money when we got off the plane. Just wear your collar, I said. No one will touch you.

I liked my companion, he turned out to be rich. I put my share in the bank and we traveled for months, then went back to the town where we ditched the minister. My companion proposed and I said okay, we had a late breakfast and picked out a chapel. At the top of the steps we ran into the minister. I'm rich now, he told me. The town's right on a quarry. With the money you left me I bought out the owners. My girlfriend and her sister are coming to join me. But the heiress, I said. Her friends might be thugs. She's in jail now, he told me. Out of the picture. The funny part is, it wasn't the taxes. She was out on the docks and shot at some sailors. One of them lived but was left with a stutter.

II.
We picked a hotel where we had our own bathroom. My companion went out so I thought I'd unpack. I was folding his pants when a letter fell out. It was signed your ex-wife and was asking for money. I looked through his suitcase but there weren't any more, memorized it and got dressed to go out. He came back to the room and liked my new outfit so I kept my mouth shut and unbuttoned his shirt.

I went down to the dock when my girlfriend arrived. The smart niece was with her along with the sister. The minister wanted to show us his church, it was empty right now and he lived in the back. You go ahead, I said to my girlfriend. Your niece and I want to go for a walk. Out on the beach I recited the letter. When I got to the end I had tears in my eyes. The niece took my hand and said not to worry. I'll find her, she said. We'll think of a plan.

A few hours later we all met for dinner. The plans were all made for a big double wedding. My girlfriend had doubts but her sister was sure, as a minister's wife the townspeople would love her. The choir would be singing and we'd each read a parable. I liked the idea and picked volume four. There was a good one in there about a man with a past. He ruins three families and dies in a landslide. One thing, the niece said, you need a new hairstyle. There's a beautician in town you really should try. I called the next day and made an appointment. I'm getting married, I told her, I have to look good. I'm a former missionary, just back from a job. It's hell out there but you feel like a saviour. You're lucky, she said. I spent years as a model. I made pretty good money, had the best clothes, married a rich man and traveled all over. I'm not young anymore and now they don't want me. My husband got sick of hearing me cry, gave me a settlement I spent in a year. I'm working for tips now and this town's pretty cheap. I know, I said, let me tell you a story. I gave her the one about the man and the landslide. There's still time, I told her. What you need is some quiet.

We rented a car and drove out to the hills. I knew of a place with some pretty high cliffs. She got really dizzy when I showed her the view. I picked a good spot though and she didn't get hurt. The niece pulled her out of the creek with a rope. I sat on the bank and she thought I was praying. She dried off and decided to try life in a convent. We went through with the wedding and both grooms liked my hair.

III.

We were feeling romantic, got a place on the beach. My girlfriend's sister and the minister rented the house next door, there was space for my girlfriend upstairs in the back. The niece had a room that didn't have curtains. My husband bought a telescope to see the constellations, he was keeping an eye on the minister too. There was something about him he just didn't trust. The niece said on the beach he was teaching her shorthand, it was a subject he was good at in divinity school. She thought it would help her in writing the parables, there were times when she knew she was really inspired.

My husband would've kept watching but the telescope broke. He had to send out to the states for some parts. He was mailing the order when my girlfriend showed up. Her clothes were dirty and her face was all scratched. My niece is gone, she said, we've been looking all morning. I found one of her shoes down in the quarry. It was lying right on the edge of a shaft. The minister, I asked her, is he still around? Come to think of it, she told me, he wasn't at breakfast, but who would've thought they might be together? He gets up real early and goes for a walk. I suggested we start with a search of his bedroom, looked under the mattress and found an old briefcase. I recognized it from our trip on the plane. It's his currency bag, I said to my girlfriend. I would've got rid of it just to be safe. She said she had to admit he wasn't too smart, she just stayed in his church because of her sister. There was a key in the briefcase sewed into the lining. My girlfriend suggested we wait for her sister, showed her the key when she pulled up the driveway. The sister went pale and started to shake. There's a hut, she told us, way back in the quarry. He has it fixed up with pictures and beds, took me there when we first got to town. I thought it was weird but he was alone for so long. Lucky for us I remember the way.

My husband came back, we piled into his car. He tucked his revolver under his coat. I whispered to my girlfriend he was overreacting. We broke down the door and found them together. He was preaching a sermon, she was shaking her head. The pictures were dirty, I wasn't surprised. My husband wrestled the minister onto the floor. We bought the niece ice cream and she told us what happened. She got up early and was practicing shorthand, he came by and invited her along on his walk. He was under control until she lost her new shoe. He seemed to go crazy and dragged her away. When they got to the hut she laughed at his pictures, hurt his feelings she guessed and he started his sermon. The worst part of it was, he used one of her parables. The one about hoarding your talents, I said. It was in volume three and I knew it by heart.

My girlfriend wanted to have the minister arrested but her sister was crying so she let it drop. The sister sold his rights to the quarry and sent the niece to a good convent school. We went back to the place to dismantle the hut but the minister's pictures were already gone.

IV.

A few years went by without any letters. I bought a nice boat from a man down the beach, my girlfriend and I went out everyday. On Wednesdays and Fridays her sister came too. The minister was busy and she had some free time, he was raking the beach and his sermons were shorter. The sister kept a close watch on her shoes. My husband was traveling, business was booming. He was importing telescopes to sell below cost.

One morning I took a walk to the village. My hair was matted so I put on a veil. The women in town started to cry, knew the whole story about my past as a missionary, figured I was practicing to go back in the field. I asked them to promise to cook for my husband, rented a car and a driver real cheap. The niece's school was up in the mountains. He said we'd get there by morning without any trouble.

The first fifty miles he was very polite. When we stopped on the roadside he emptied the ashtray. After a while he complained about smoking, I kept lighting up and he threatened to kill me. I got out at a crossroads and started to hitch. An experienced traveler, I put on my veil. The first thing to stop was a bus full of orphans, the driver was wearing an old fashioned habit. I recognized her by her manicured nails. Remember, I said, that time in the hills. You were saved from the creek by the niece with the rope. A great girl, she told me, with a good eye for detail. We're doing a piece on devotional prayer. I've been wondering when you'd return to your work. I'm on my way now, I said, thought maybe I'd see her. We drove to the school and she showed me the guestroom. The niece and I met in the garden for lunch. So tell me, I said. How's life in the convent? Quiet, she said, but I knew she was lying. Her eyes were made up and she looked a lot older. It's nice here, I said. Think I'll stay overnight. Okay, she told me, you can join us for chanting. I sat in the back and caught up with my reading. During the last chorus I looked for her but she got away.

I walked out of the chapel and an old monk approached me. The bus driver saw us and headed him off. He caught my eye though, I slipped into a confessional. When he got rid of the bus driver he joined me in there. About the young girl, he said. There's some things you should know. She slips out the back every night about midnight. I followed her once and she met a man. The path was icy and I slipped on my cassock but I did get a fleeting look at his face. He went on talking, describing my husband. I could picture him there with that little brat. I thanked the monk and went out to the garden, sat under a tree until I heard voices. It was my husband all right, they were making their plans. He was selling his business and they'd run off to Bermuda. I went back inside to find the bus driver, figured it was time to give up my cover. I told her about how I fell for his stories, gave up my freedom for that house on the beach. I can't blame, you, she said, for being a fool. I did it myself and look where it got me. I still had my bank account from the heiress's caper. It wasn't safe yet, hadn't been through the laundry. The driver had access to the convent's vault and all the equipment from her beauty salon. She reported it stolen before she signed up here, the local police were still on the trail. There was a village nearby so we scouted around. My husband was renting the only hotel suite. For a small bribe we got our hands on a key to his room. The next day I opened an account at the bank, wired back to the beach to transfer my funds. It would take a few days but there was no hurry. The bus driver taught religion, made me guest speaker. The niece came in and took a seat in the back. I opened with an account of my travels, filled in the details from my vacations. When I got their attention I shifted to parables, finished with one that featured a temptress. I made her thirteen and the niece left the room.

The day my money arrived the town was excited. The local tavern was having a big bash that night. I bribed the bartender and found out my husband was going. There were strange men in town, too, looked like top brass police. My anonymous tipoff was pretty successful. The bus driver raided the vault and met me at midnight. We planted the evidence there in his suite. The top brass were waiting when he took the niece back there, arrested them both on three different charges. The tough one to beat was the theft from the convent. He was sentenced to life as a lay brother, last thing I heard they were shaving his head. The salon equipment was returned to its owner. She's an operator again with a rich clientele. The niece went off to a more modern convent. She does their recruiting ads in exchange for expenses. Her mother took over the minister's church. I was happy to give up the place on the beach. My girlfriend has a flat in a respectable alley, some nights I stay there, some nights I don't.

Caught Up in Romance

We meet in my neighborhood restaurant. I pretend I don't see him, he's back from Europe and wearing a new suit. We both like to dance and stay out late that night. I introduce him to my family and they're all impressed. He isn't like my other boyfriends. I don't tell them about his business, make up something about textiles. It's the right thing to say and we spend a weekend at the cottage. He proposes after breakfast and we go on a whirlwind tour. I'm still a little shy but he doesn't expect me to talk. It isn't a bad life and I save a lot of money.

I don't like his associates, they're tall and drop in at odd hours. I listen from the bathroom but don't understand the language. My mother tells me not to worry, she didn't like my father's friends. Then his partner commits suicide. He seems to take it in stride but I start having nightmares. We go away for the weekend, I demand to know what's up. He says it's a long story, he's sure I'll get hysterical. Don't be silly, I tell him. He sits down on the couch and tells me his life story.

I was born in the Middle East, he says, my father was a merchant. When I was twelve there was an accident, I inherited the family business with my grandfather, a deranged old man. He was squandering everything, I had to grow up fast. I hid his body in the well, they still haven't found it. The old man's sister suspected me, tried to have me arrested. Luckily she was senile, I appealed to the government and they promised to protect me. I came to America, changed my identity. Whatever I do I owe them a cut.

I'm quiet for a long time. My father is in prison for back taxes. I know how it is to live on the run. I tell him about my savings, offer to share it with him in a new location. He sounds interested and says he'll talk to his banker in the morning. We make love all night and I'm glad I said something. We settle on South America, I pack up all my furs. My mother cries at the airport and I leave her a diamond watch. I know she'll miss my parties but there's nothing I can do. We rent a house by the water, my husband goes to town every morning but comes home for lunch. I don't ask what he's doing, I'm afraid for my father. The prime minister brings his mistress to dinner. We take a liking to each other, she's about my size and I borrow her clothes. She's attractive and knows the local men. I have chances for affairs but I'm the quiet type and not interested. One man keeps calling, I relent and we go for a walk. He looks something like my father, we talk about our childhoods. His father was a policeman in a small town, everyone knew his family. He took the mayor's daughter to the prom, they got engaged the next year. Two days later she was trampled by a horse, he never forgave himself. It was an act of God, I say. He feels human for the first time in years, we make a date for the next day.

I get tired of his attention. He's small and doesn't like to be seen in public. My husband's home every afternoon and I'm tired of the bedroom. I think about running away but a fight's coming up, my husband boxes and I have to make an appearance. I wear my best oufit, I want my husband to be proud. He's first on the schedule, I smile and look excited. He wins the first two rounds, gets knocked out in the third. We have a coke on his break and he can't take his eyes off me. Back in the ring he looks up at my seat, I yell at him to pay attention. It's too late and his ribs get broken. We're waiting for the ambulance when the police drive up, they have a warrant for his arrest. He's wanted for his partner's murder, they have the papers to send him back home. Down at the station he confesses. It wasn't suicide after all, he pushed him out the window. I was caught up in romance and never suspected. The police chief nods and goes to make a phone call. I'll stick by you, I say, we can make a new start. He talks to his lawyer and starts to look hopeful, then I mention my father. Sorry, the lawyer says, you'll have to divorce her. I resign myself, one prisoner in the family is enough.

TOP STORIES

A PROSE PERIODICAL

#1 Donna Wyszomierski
#2 Laurie Anderson
#3 Pati Hill
#4 Suzanne Johnson
#5 Linda Neaman
#6 Gail Vachon
#7 Jenny Holzer/Peter Nadin
#8 Judith Doyle
#9 Kathy Acker
#10 Lynne Tillman/Jane Dickson
#11 Kirsten Thorup
#12 Janet Stein
#13 Anne Turyn
#14 Lee Eiferman
#15 Constance DeJong
#16 Ursule Molinaro
#17 Romaine Perin

Available from
TOP STORIES
Hallwalls
700 Main Street
Buffalo, New York 14202

TOP STORIES   #19-20 $6.00

How to Get Rid of Pimples

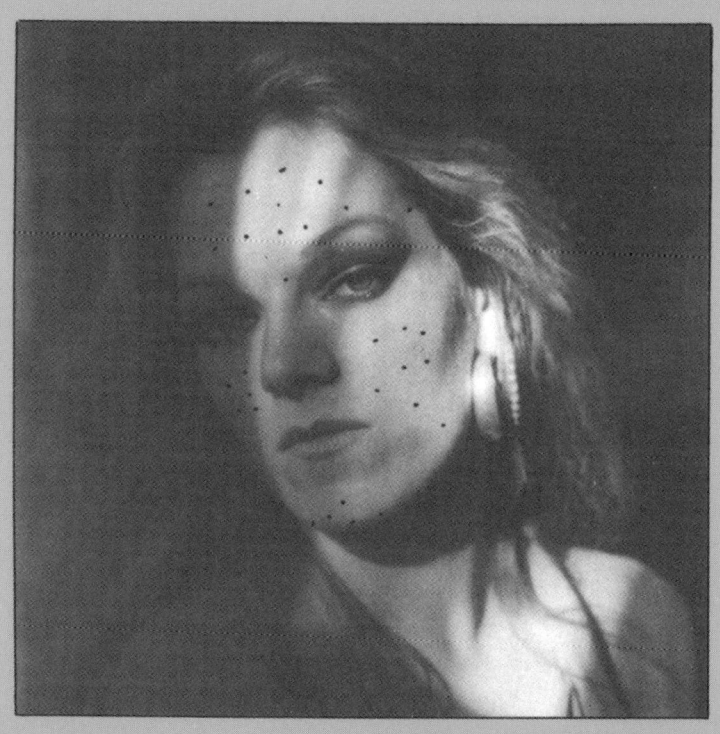

by Cookie Mueller

How To Get Rid of Pimples

by Cookie Mueller

*With Photographs by
David Armstrong,
Nan Goldin, Peter Hujar*

Copyright © 1984 by Cookie Mueller.

Photographs © 1984 by David Armstrong, Nan Goldin, Peter Hujar, Trish McAdams, and Janet Stein.

Cover photograph of Cookie Mueller by David Armstrong

This publication has been made possible in part by funds from the Beard's Fund and the Committee for the Visual Arts.

The author gratefully acknowledges the support of LINE II, which is funded by the New York State Council on the Arts and the National Endowment for the Arts, a federal agency.

ISBN 0-917061-19-5 (Top Stories #19-20)

ISBN 0-917061-20-9 (Top Stories Set, Volume 2, Nos. 11-20)

TOP STORIES   228 Seventh Avenue   New York, N.Y. 10011

Introduction

Actual Letter Sent To Me From A Person Who Wanted This Book Way Before It Was Put Together

Case 1   Andrew   Secrets of the Skinny

Case 2   Brenda

Case 3   Ioona   The Third Twin

Case 4   Goda

Case 5   Julie   The Mystery of Tap Water

Case 6   Joe

Case 7   Dora

Case 8   Valerie   Losing

Case 9   Randy Eros   The Sexiest Kid In Town

Case 10   Gena   I Hear America Sinking

Case 11   Alexandra

Case 12   Miguel La Madrid

The Actual Cure

Index

Here are the tales of woe, the stories of the shunned, the biographies of the shy ones once skuttled to the darkest corners of any room. Looking in mirrors has always been a painful experience for these people and that's why I wrote this book. Even before this book was begun, I received letters asking for it, as it had already gotten some advance notice in John Waters' book Shock Value.

I was once a sufferer myself so I know well what the experience is like. The cure, that I discovered through many years of experimentation and correlation of already documented medical facts, changed my life. I suddenly liked myself.

While reading this book you may begin to wonder if it is something other than what the title indicates. It is not. The actual cure is in the back of the book, on the last pages. If you wish to skip the tales and go directly to the amazing cure, do it.

The following is a copy of one of the many letters I received a few years ago.

Dear Cookie,

Hi how are you doing? I just love you in John's films. I just think you're wonderful.

I'm writing because I want to ask you how you may get your booklet on How To Get Rid of Pimples. I read about it in John's book, Shock Value amd I'd love to have it.

I really don't have an acne problem but it would be nice to have it on hand, just in case.

Thanks a lot Cookie. I hope to be hearing from you soon.

Love,
Steven Damurk

Case #1

Andrew
Secrets of The Skinny

Without question Andrew New was as skinny as a person could be. He was also extremely famous. If there is a zenith in a person's life he was riding on it, but with all the trappings of success that clung to him he found life difficult, if not intolerable.

It was all the shackles, the encumbrances that stuck and sucked on him like remoras to sharks, like locusts on tree sap, like pennies trapped in polyurethane, that made his life less than pleasant.

Even as a child, when he was so skinny that his arms were similar to string beans, his parents burdened him with huge llama hair sweaters and wide wale corduroy pants. They tried to hide the horror of his skinniness because they were plump and it was the fifties when the mode was to have more flesh than less. So afraid that his teachers at school would think they were poor, the parents covered him heavily at all times because to them he looked deformed, almost freakish. Even in the summer they made him wear long johns under his clothes. He felt like a hot package in the heat of mid-July. Aside from being moist in the summer which upset him, he was most of the time happy, for he had found an incredible secret that only very skinny people knew.

On windy days, when the leaves and rocks and dirt flew around, when sparrows had hard times in the air, he could fly. If the wind was 15 knots or more he could feel the strong hands of gusts pick him up to carry him. Perhaps it was only a few inches or feet but he was flying all the same. The minute he saw some wind in the trees he would run into his backyard and there almost naked would fly around and around. Sometimes he flew into the neighbors' yard where he would always break one of the lawn decorations; once the blue reflector ball that sat on its pedestal like an archaic pagan shrine, another time the Italian rococo birdbath. One day he flew into their yard and broke the lawn jockey, the little black ceramic man with the lantern. He knocked himself out. The neighbors found him in his underpants and carried him home in a large paper bag. He regained consciousness and looked up at the twilight sky through the serrated opening of the brown paper. Moving along he heard the voices of the neighbors as they spoke kindly of him. Hovering branches glutted with leaves moved past in his vision of the sky. It was a most secure feeling, not unlike what he imagined raw peeled tomatoes felt like in cans in the A&P bag once bought and liberated from shelves of the grocery store. These were the thoughts about the former inhabitants of the bag.

When the neighbors handed him over to his parents they immediately dressed him in heavy doubleknits.

Now that he was older he had the same problem except it wasn't clothes. It was people. He was so famous that he couldn't walk down the street without bodyguards. When people found out who the bodyguards were bodyguarding, the bodyguards themselves needed bodyguards. Journalists, at a loss for stories about celebrities, were turning bodyguards into stars.

Andrew's entourage of men with muscles kept growing. More and more of them were needed. When he went from his door to his car it would be like a group of prisoners in step with each other wearing invisible leg irons. His fans wouldn't leave him alone, interviewers hounded him, his family pulled at him as if he was taffy in the hands of fighting kids. He felt as if he was all wrapped up in wool again, but this time he couldn't take off the burdens and fly a bit because he was too heavy now and too famous to be seen in his underwear.

So he took long swims with his convoy of men and found the water to have much the same qualities of air except that he wasn't totally at the mercy of the currents as he was in the air because he could use his arms and legs as rudders and oars. In the air his limbs served only for balance. He thought about the freedom in the water...how it didn't matter how big or small you were because you could always float. He decided to gain a lot of weight, build an indoor salt water pool and see how life would be. He forced himself to become extremely fat, lost all his fame, fans and bodyguards and became a very flabby happy swimmer.

At last there were no extraneous loads, no heavy clothes, no troublesome fans, no fear of leaving his house, no nagging relatives, no impositions, no brawny bodyguards using his shampoo, his cigarettes, his nail clippers. His huge contented cheerful flesh was now his only burden, but it was his, a wrapping to belong to.

The Circumstances of Andrew's Cure

A very complex person is Andrew. He loved to fly but needed his burdens as well. It turned out that Andrew became a flight attendant but had to lose weight so that he could fit down the aisles to serve coffee, tea and milk. His problem skin came about only after all the drastic gaining and losing of weight.

I met him while flying from Newark to Buffalo on People Express. I remembered his face from his game show hosting days. I suggested to him that he take a look at my cure. He followed my advice. The next time I saw him he looked great and this time he was flying from New York to Rome on Pan Am.

Before

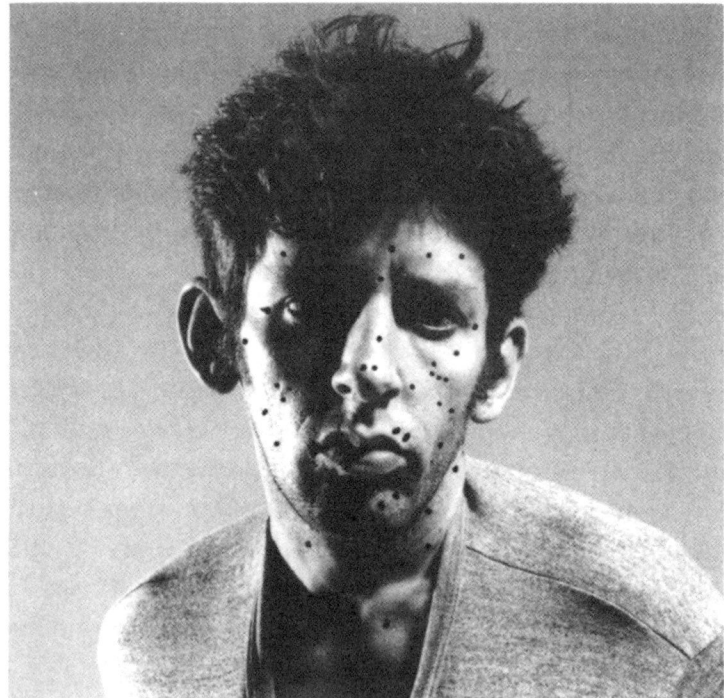

Photo © 1984 Peter Hujar

After

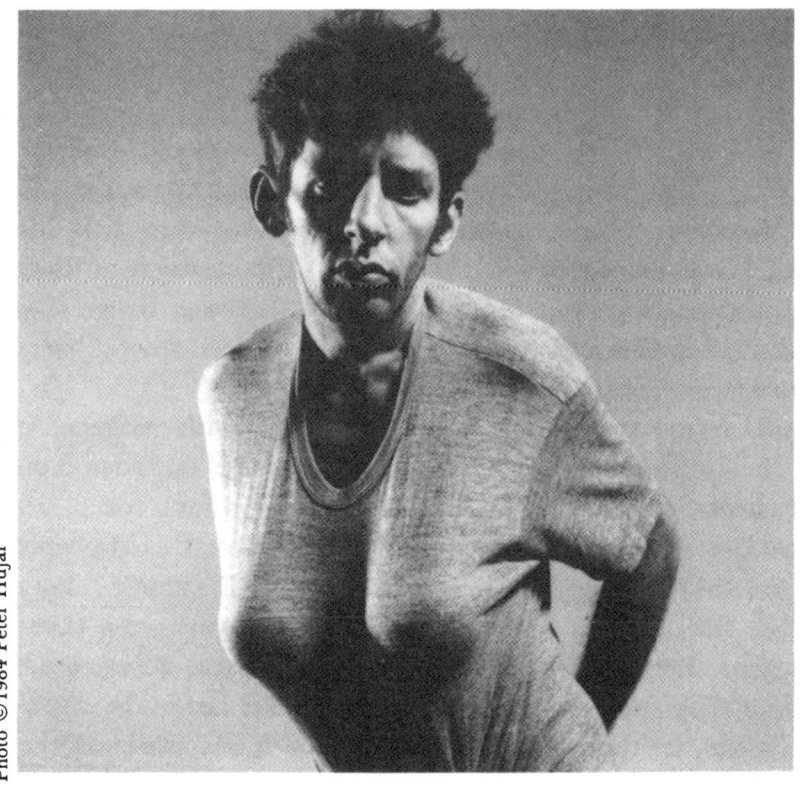

Photo ©1984 Peter Hujar

Case #2

Brenda

She was five feet five less than a year ago, but now she is four feet two because of a horrible, delicate operation where she had her thighs removed. Even though the operation had been absolutely unavoidable, she had not resolved it in her mind and she suffered terrible emotional anguish. She was always being overlooked.

The secret that she now had a vagina that began and ended at her knees was a source of much gossip but she held herself proudly and feared no one larger.

Luckily she had a lover whom she had lived with before the operation. This lover was a person who never let a minor physical aberration interfere with his feelings. Anyway, their life together was enhanced by the surgery, it made each of them more independent yet closer. Their sex life was better too, because Brenda could easily bend at the vagina, giving her a remote feeling of distance from her mate.

Aside from her lover she began to socialize with midgets. At first she couldn't understand why they all looked older than their chronological age. But after considering it for a while, she realized that they aged more rapidly than normal sized people because they're closer to the ground and as Einstein's theory proved, the closer you are to the earth and gravity the faster time goes. Because of this fact she knew she was going to die younger than taller people but it didn't bother her in the slightest. In her life she had already seen quite a bit, she had been around the block a few times, as they say, and Brenda, being the kind of person she was, would make it around the block a few more times, even without thighs.

The Circumstances of Brenda's Cure

Brenda didn't concern herself or think much about her pimples during the time of the operation. This surgery was a more devastating reality. In comparison the pimples might be overlooked.

But after her acceptance of the surgery, when the excitement of her new life wore off and she went back to living the normal day to day grind, she decided that she might clear up her skin. I actually suggested it to her after being introduced by a mutual and very famous midget friend.

She followed the cure and her outlook was once again refreshed. She is an incredibly strong individual. An inspiration, really.

Before

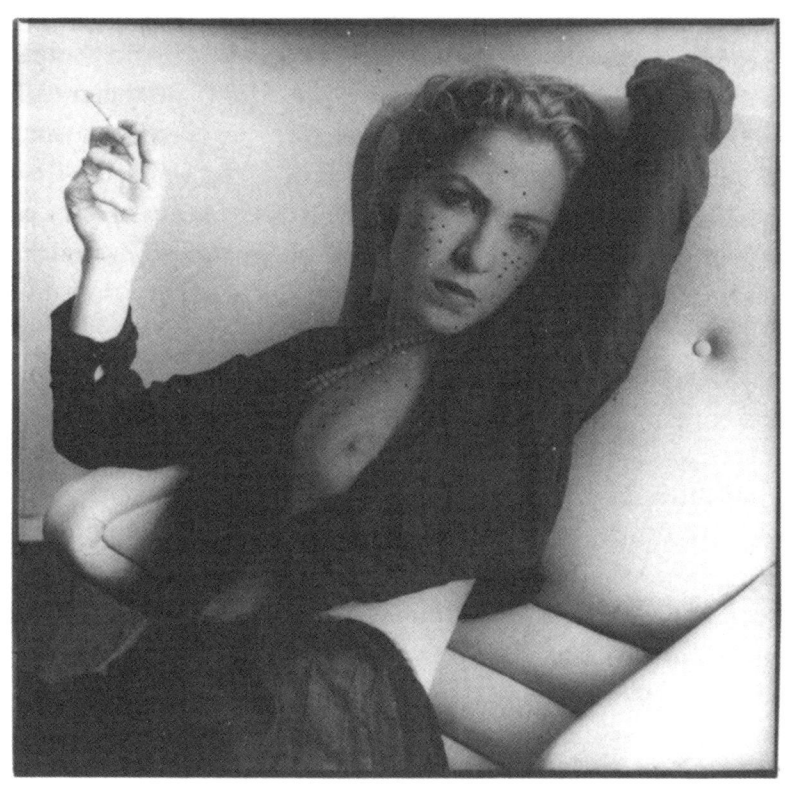

Photo ©1984 David Armstrong

After

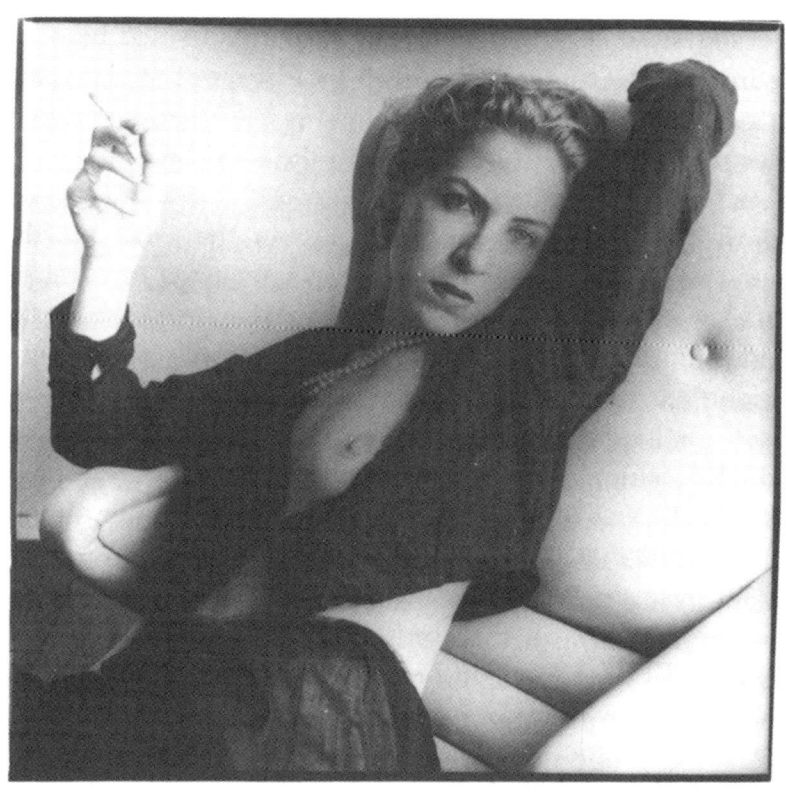

Case #3
Ioona
The Third Twin

In a suburban house with white shingles and black shutters, Ioona, a woman of forty lived with her mother, a woman of sixty-four. The mother depended on her daughter now that she had emphysema and spent most of her time divided between lying in an oxygen tent surrounded by legions of waiting oxygen drums and being propped on pillows in the front window, overlooking the garden, on display to the neighbors.

That Ioona, back again with her mother after a fifteen year soujourn in a lonely marriage to a man that was wealthy (money amassed through a patented adjustment to a rachet wrench), was capable and independent enough to take on the responsibilities of the house and her mother's illness was questionable. But she had taken a mature stand to leave her husband and quit the ruse of love. If she could do that, she could do anything.

So now she was home again, planting flowers for her mother with the seeds that her mother had given her. A profusion of color all over the lawn was what the older lady desired but Ioona threw away all the seeds but Impatience, Bachelor's Buttons and Sweet William because these names were meaningful to Ioona who squeezed significance from everything.

She went to the shopping mall every day to escape the sound of breathing. In the mall, the music was a cradle and all the mannequins in the windows wore clothes as bland as puree. She found herself, like the rest of the people there, speaking in hushed tones in reverence to the mall; intoxicated by the sheer size and force of the steel and stone and glass and the endless displays of things to buy. But she wasn't very similar to these mall-goers at all. She was strong and fierce, despite the blue tablets of Librium she took four times a day to quell her feelings of insecurity. Unable to relax, always wanting new input or streamlined stimuli, she drove around at high speeds in her mother's beige Volare dreaming about transformation and destruction. Most often she dreamed of the Phoenix, living and burning, repeatedly rising from the flames and rubble of the shopping mall; wings spread, casting shadows on all of suburbia. When her dreams went flacid and weren't enough, she thought about meeting a man and how she would do it.

One day at the mall she went into a bar, a place called Libby's Lounge. Her mother had warned her about this place as if there was something horribly off-color about it, but Ioona knew that her mother had probably never been in any bar in her entire life. It was exactly like any other; dark and carpeted and quiet in the day.

Ioona expected to meet a man there and she did. His name was William Way. When they began to talk and drink together in the coolness of the lounge she knew that finally she had met someone so much like herself that she felt almost as if, miraculously her DNA double helix had uncoiled to make this man. Here was the man for her, someone who shared her every mood, someone who had been waiting just for her.

She brought him to her home and they fucked in her bedroom with the background noise of her mother's labored breathing and the oxygen whooshing from the tanks.

Whatever similarities that this new couple, Bill and Ioona, shared, the fact that Bill had been a Franciscan monk brought them the closest. In the fifteen years of abstinence and isolation with only his pets as companions, he gathered a certain knowledge of the natural world.

He stirred her into the initial sexual response by telling her about male kangaroos and opossums who have forked dicks, the females, forked vaginas. He told her about Abyssinian bats who have dicks with bristles just like bottle brushes.

He told her about the day he had taken a live mouse and carefully cut it open to take a cellular tissue scraping from the heart to see the tiny piece under the microscope pulsing all by itself. This fact made her see the order of life that before she had only dreamed was true. This monk...he was perfect.

They didn't marry but he moved in and together they buried her mother—only grudgingly had she relinquished her tenacious grasp on life. They planted tomatoes, corn and sunflowers where all the flowers had been. In the summer they took his boat to the edge of the falls and in autumn they burned leaves on the front lawn. In winter, they went out on the frozen river to cut holes in the ice and fish.

One day on the ice the ex-monk fell into one of the holes and when he finally bobbed up, he was in a cube of ice and dead.

And now Ioona buried him alone and wanted to leave her body but didn't have the courage to commit suicide nor the patience to coax astral travel by meditation. Then she found out that she was pregnant and there was someone else, a third twin perhaps, within her thinking all those wonderful uterine thoughts. She was consoled. This really was just the beginning and she was finally after all these years being included into life's mysterious order where tranquility's sweet bloodless arms would envelope her and rock her until the end.

The Circumstances of Ioona's Cure

It goes without saying that one would be surprised to find a woman of forty with acne. It is so often associated with adolescence. When a woman of forty gets pregnant for the first time the hormones go haywire.

Ioona got pimples. She came to me and I gave her the cure. By the time she was five months pregnant there weren't any pimples. The cure not only cleared her skin but strengthened her and her baby who turned out to be a girl...an amazing child.

Ioona remarried later to a man who was pretty fat and boy was he a happy man. They had a son a year later and the husband/father was so happy that he laughed so loud he shook the house. He was also a very lucky man to have found Ioona.

Before

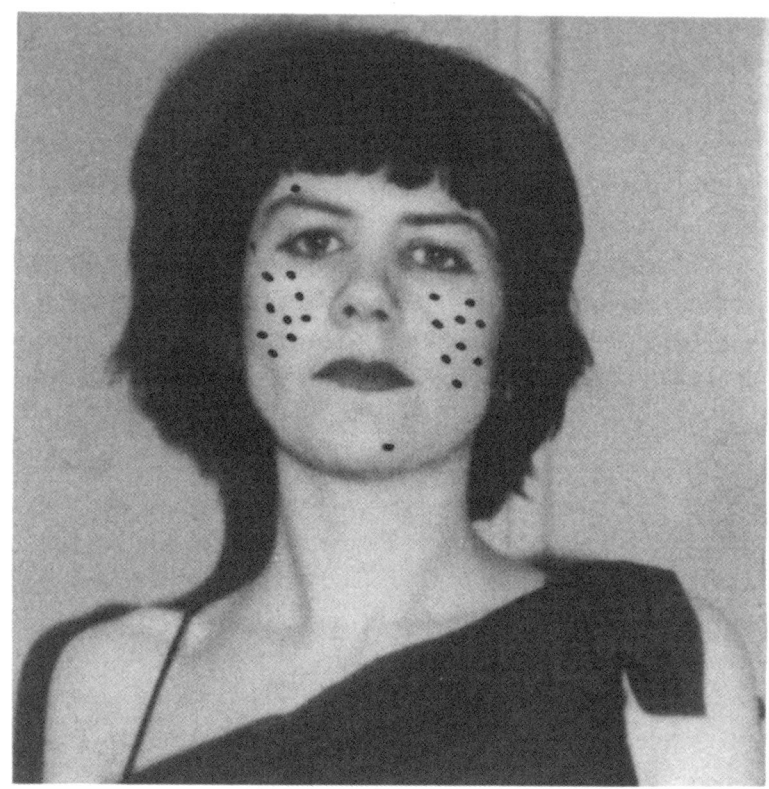

After

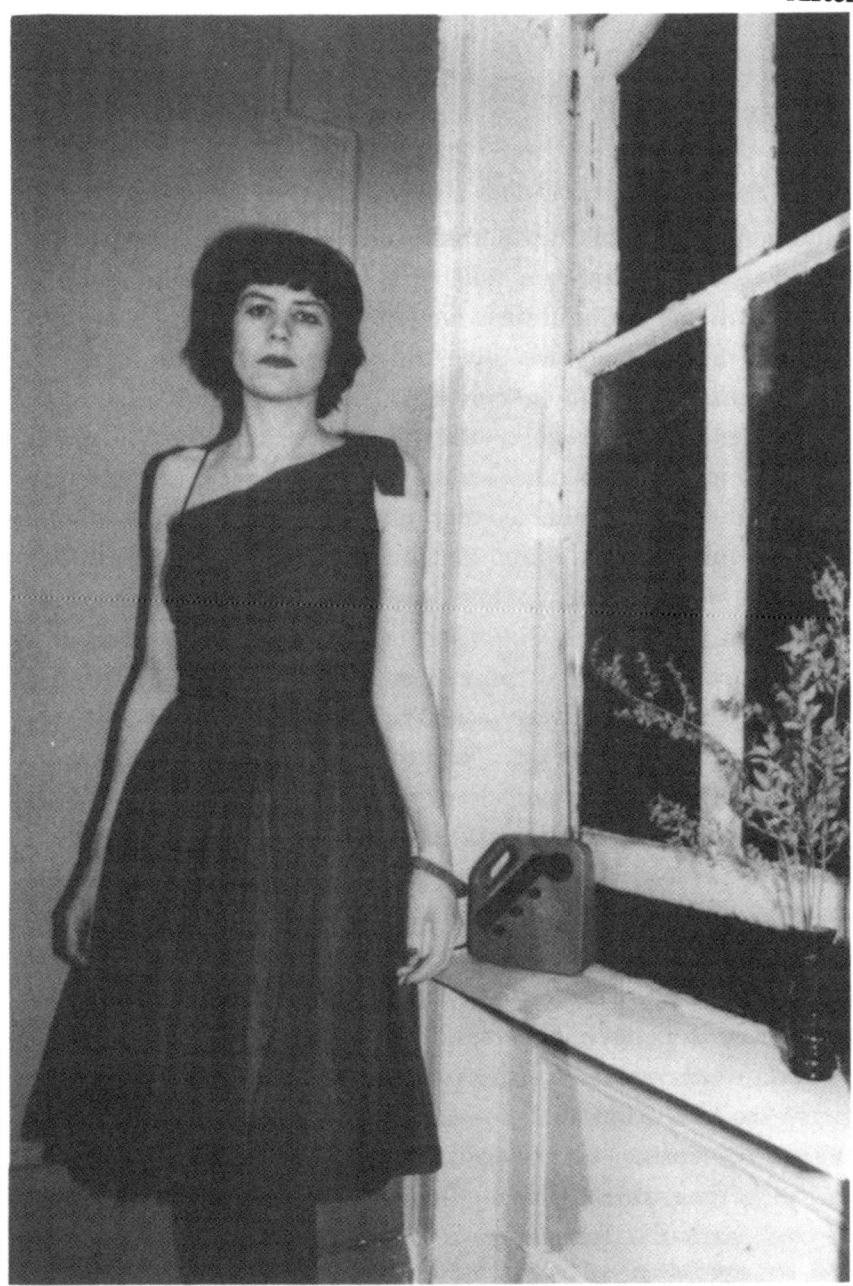

Photo ©1984 Nan Goldin

Case #4

Goda

Goda could not look in the mirror and see herself. Because her hair was ashen, her eyes pale grey and her skin the color of aluminum, she did not reflect well in the glass. There were pimples and even these were silver but they stood out sorely.

Her image, as she perceived it, wavered from opaque to translucent to non-existent. She thought perhaps that she could pass through walls or doors or eavesdrop on relevant conversations without her presence being noticed, but she could do none of these things. Even when her form was invisible and she was sure she wasn't seen, people would feel her as a phantom. Perhaps it would be a slight itch on the back of the neck of a person deep in verbal intercourse with business partners. Another would shoo away a fictive fly, yet another would keep turning to see if there was something or someone beside him. But there was no one and there was nothing. She would walk into a room without legs and feet and footsteps but still there wasn't a person who didn't glance towards her. She couldn't walk down the street and melt all the way.

It was a strange doublet, this duo association of unsubstantiality and entity. She felt the tug from both sides. It became impossible to believe in herself.

Goda went out late at night to clubs where she thought people might see her. Men and women with cameras took pictures of her for no reason and the pictures would sometimes appear in night-life magazines, but her image would always be missing. In one particular magazine called *Nightblind* she saw the two men she had been standing between and there was a blank space where she was supposed to be. So where was she? For sure she had been there. She remembered that George had been drinking the Beck's and David had been drinking the Remy Martin. She even remembered what she had been drinking. A smart cocktail. A martini. But where was she? Could she have been mistaken? Maybe the art editor airbrushed her image because of the pimples? But they wouldn't have done that. No. She just didn't show up because her form was as silver as the photographic plates.

She may well have not shown up in photos but she had a life. There were people who called her on the phone and certainly they asked for her by name.

"Could I speak to Goda?" they would ask.

Or they would say, "Is Goda there?"

She was there alright.

"I must be here...there are people asking for me," she would say to herself often.

From time to time she would go out on dates with people and they would talk at the table over the candle cup while eating Japanese, Chinese, Italian, Indian, Thai or Polish food, depending on what type of restaurant they went to. The person would look directly into her eyes so naturally, she thought for sure she must have been there, otherwise they would be alone and reading a newspaper. Right?

She decided that her problem must be stemming from the dilemma of the pimples. She had them since she was sixteen and now she was twenty-six and they weren't getting any better.

Perhaps it would be more agreeable to be a newspaper but

then she would inevitably be folded up like a daily and left on a seat somewhere on a bus or in a restaurant.

All that mattered were the pimples. Her nose didn't matter, or her eyes or her wide smile. It was only the pimples. She would have squeezed them or applied Clearisil or alcohol if she could have found her image in her bathroom mirror.

She began to consider throwing in the towel, but it was then that she found the answer.

The Circumstances of Goda's Cure

One day she called me. She had heard. I had never seen her before. She asked me for the cure and I gave it to her. She followed my advice. Two months later she called me back. I never saw her. From the sound of her voice I could tell something had changed, she was different. Before, her voice sounded like shards in a wastepaper basket, a voice that sounded like the head behind it believed it held no future rewards; bleached out, bleeding white. Now the voice was effusive and cheerful.

She told me that because of my cure, she no longer had any pimples, not even a greyhead. She was happy. Now she would appear in night life magazines and there would be her image in black and white or color. She could even see herself in shades of grey.

Before

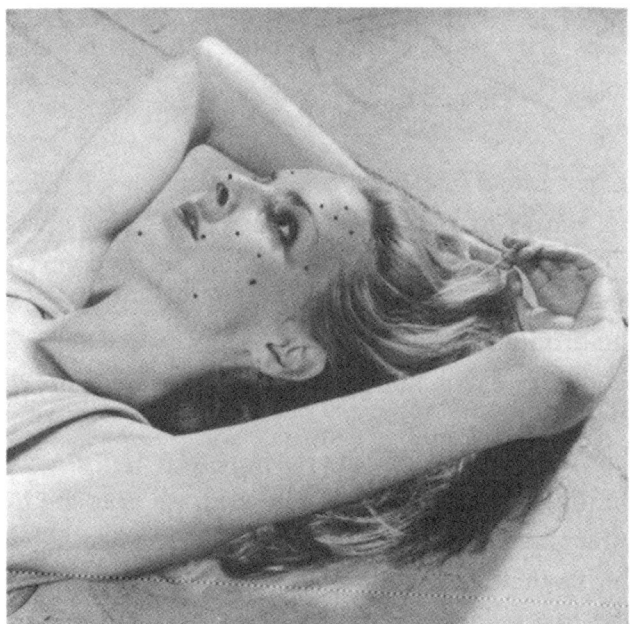

After

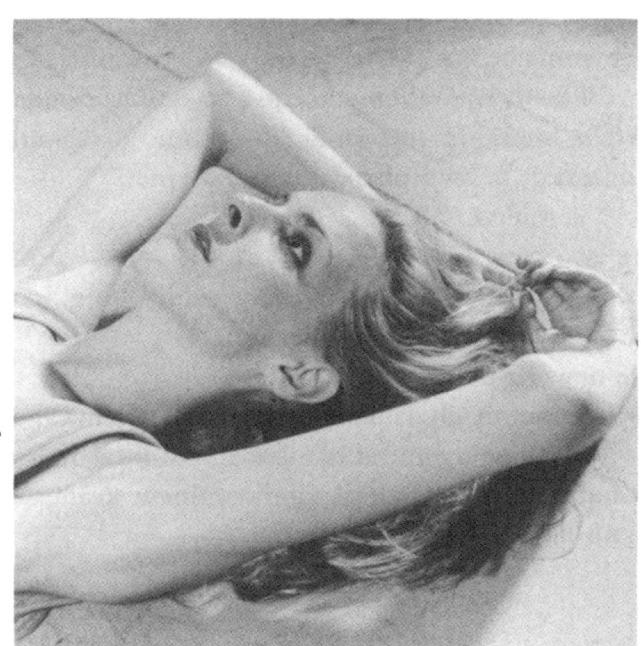

Photo © 1984 Peter Hujar

Case #5

Julie
The Mystery of Tap Water

Julie lost her mind one day, just like that...well really it had taken two weeks to completely lose it. She had always been eccentric but now she was past that. She believed very strongly in the principle, *You Are What You Eat*, so she experimented with water. She drank it, no food, no juice, just water for two weeks. She was convinced that since she would be only water, she could disappear at will.

I saw her the night before she disappeared and she was pretty lucid. She didn't seem too bad. She told me that she had lived forever, that she would never die and since she was all water she must have been the iceberg that sank the Titanic, the heavy water used in making the hydrogen bomb, the basic element used along with Kool Aid in Jonestown Guyana.

"I feel very guilty," she said.

Her last words before she left were, "When you see a gushing fountain, I'll be there. When you sip a glass of ice water, I'll be there. When there's a torrential downpour, a cloudburst, a flood, a blizzard, a lawnsprinkler... that's me."

"O.K.," I smiled, "I'll look for you."

No one ever saw her again.

"Oh she's so elusive," everybody said, "She'll turn up sooner or later in some mental hospital."

But she never did.

I know it's completely ridiculous but now whenever I take a bath I see Julie pouring out of the faucet and I begin to wonder just how many other odd people and complete strangers are in the bath tub floating around with me.

The Circumstances of Julie's Cure

Believe it or not one of the reasons why Julie began to drink so much water was because of what dermatologists always told her: "Drink lots of water."

Well she started off this way and just got carried off into a different aspect of the whole thing. She definitely still had the pimples even when she was drinking so much water. Who's to know if the cure ever worked. Who could see her?

Before

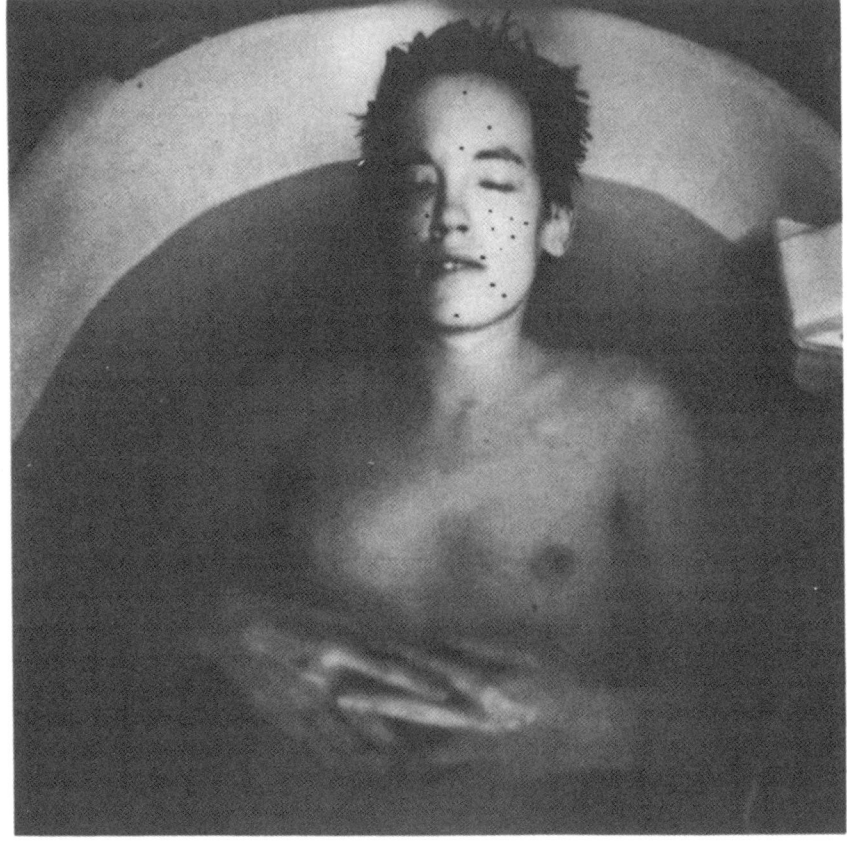

Photo © 1984 Nan Goldin

After

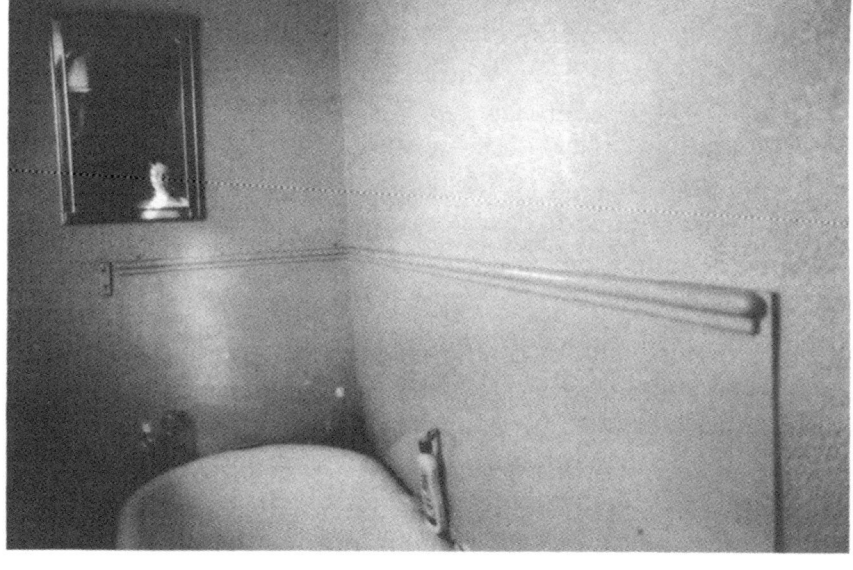

Case #6

Joe

What remained of Joe was sitting on Janie's mantlepiece in a yellowish marble urn. Yellow had been his favorite color. Joe had wanted to be burned and often said he thought that undertakers weren't very honest and they would keep the dead person's pants and shoes for themselves because that part of the deceased was never on display in the coffin. Joe didn't like to think of his favorite shoes on anyone else.

Everyone, all of Joe's children, sisters, brothers, past and present wives and lovers felt very cheated. They didn't understand cremation. There was nothing to look at during the eulogy, only the urn and a four by six foot color photograph of him at the morgue, dead but smiling. The picture was his present wife Janie's idea and she did it to satisfy those with little imagination.

The funeral group got out of hand...everyone wanted something more, so Janie, always diplomatic, got out a huge mirror and dumped the entire contents...every bit of Joe's ashes onto it and divided it up with a razor blade. Obviously Janie did it partly for effect. She was angry at their callous behavior so she thought she may as well shock them by way of example.

The guests were aghast but enthusiastically brought out containers like envelopes and pill vials to put their portions in. Joe's agent wanted a larger amount. He always had wanted a larger piece of Joe.

At one time Joe worked as a TV sitcom writer but toward the end of his life, wrote the material for a famous comedian who had always trod the line between political satire and fearless celebrity putdowns. He told audiences just what was on his mind. He spared no one.

One day a dissident stood up in the audience. People in seats behind him told him to "siddown asshole" but he pulled from his pocket a 38. Without the look of anger or insanity, without a word of warning, he fired a shot at the comedian but missed him. The bullet went past him and hit Joe who was waiting backstage holding revised scripts. That's how Joe died. It was quick.

When the murderer was told who he had really killed he said on nationwide TV that he was happier that he had hit the writer because the comedian was just the figurehead anyway.

Joe, all bloodied up, had to laugh in spite of his wound and he laughed so hard about the irony, that he still had a smile on his lips when they wheeled him into the morgue and took that last picture.

Janie, who knew everything about Joe, couldn't grieve too much. Joe said often that he wanted to go by an assassin's bullet. She knew he wasn't joking about it, because it was the quickest way for a writer of his stature to become immortal.

So Joe really wasn't gone. He would live on and on, riding on the air waves. As a TV sitcom writer there had been only a handful of equals. Everybody knows that until the end of time there will always be re-runs.

The Circumstances of Joe's Cure

Joe always told me that when comedy writers died they wouldn't go to heaven...the place was too boring...not a good time. On their way to hell the oarsman on the River Styx would laugh so much at their jokes that he wouldn't have the heart to deliver them to hell.

When I asked him why he didn't think these people would go to heaven he said something like this: "The ability to take a sad situation, instantly access and glean its potential sight gag or one-liner virtues, then turn it into something that would make someone laugh, is sort of perverted. Perverted people don't go to heaven."

As a young man Joe had problem skin and this he used to joke about. After he followed my cure and had great skin, the cure was the butt of the jokes. Then I was the butt of the jokes. Then he would joke about clear skin. Everything was a joke. He didn't know how to enjoy or appreciate a good old morbid or horrible moment without turning it into something funny.

Before

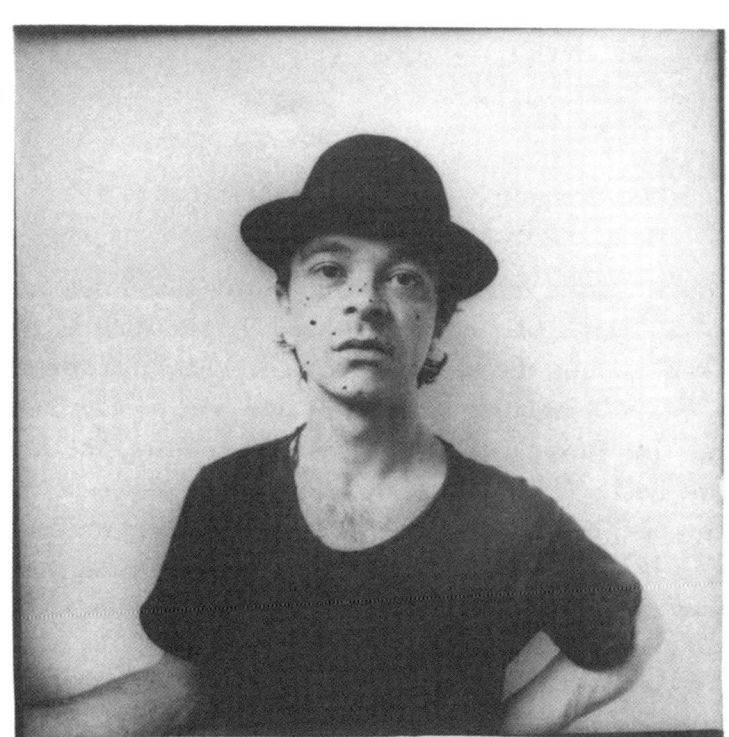

After

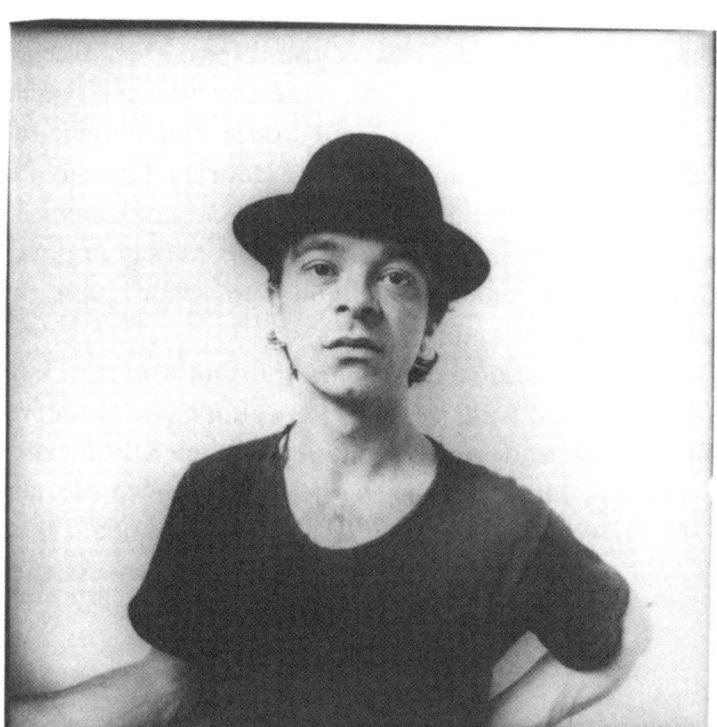

Photo © 1984 David Armstrong

Case #7

Dora

Through Dora's veins ran the cold purple blood that gave her hair and eyes a pale eggplant tinge. Despite such an obvious mark of bearing, she was rarely recognized as an aristocrat. She was always being lumped into the same gene pool as the rest of them, the unremarkable middle-of-the-roaders, the average, the mediocre. No one knew that she thought of herself as a philanthropist, perhaps most people who knew her wouldn't even realize that there was such a word in the English language. Her benevolence to the masses made her pursue things like bartending and go-go dancing. Four nights a week she worked at Joe Protozoa's after-hours place where she stood behind a make-shift fiberglass bar looking not unlike an objet d'art misplaced in a swine barn.

The surface of the bar was all pitted from the stiffness of the drinks she slammed down. One could always smell rancid cigarette-butts, mature sponges, sour booze and human mildew. An electric air freshener hummed, laboring foolishly, impervious to the impossibility of the task, yet at the same time it added another veneer of cheapness to the already impoverished smell of it all. Even without lights one would guess that the place looked awful and it did.

The drinkers who came in mostly drank it neat. They were usually alone and wide awake. Every single one of them would tell her in greatest detail each moment of their sordid existences. She was very kind, but never opened herself up to them; she was the voyeur and recorded in a diary she called *The Monster With Many Heads* every word they told her in conversation. She felt compelled to do this for some reason, perhaps it was because she thought she was doing charity work, that these people needed some kind of inner healing. As a go-go dancer in other bars she had danced her way into many a sick heart because she suspected in their flacid brains she represented a human tonic that cured paranoia, melancholia, loneliness, misery. All the amounts of gold chains and diamond pinky rings that flashed in the lights of the mirrored disco balls couldn't hide the fact that these people were bankrupt, not financially, but emotionally and culturally. All the capped teeth and hairpieces belied their broken bodies. Most of the people in the after-hours bar were thieves, boosters, pimps, porno moguls, hit men, numbers runners, coke dealers, but most of them were ordinary liars, so who could know the truth. Maybe they were just trying to look more powerful than they were. One thing was for sure, they were all drawn together by one common affliction: the desire to stay bombed until noon.

One particular morning was completely different than any other she had known. Dora felt odd, not bad, but she noticed that she was kind of glowing, she felt big, as big as the world.

When a thief named Ian came in and told her of how he ripped a man off after he picked him up at a hustlers' bar, Dora didn't exactly upbraid him but when Ian left the bar he was going straight to the man's house where he had stolen the money and the jewelry to return it. She had made him feel unclean about it. She wasn't sure of how she had done it, it certainly wasn't planned.

A junkie named Mary came in a little later and Dora somehow convinced Mary that she ought to quit using the drug. Mary left the place determined to go straight to Narcotics

Anonymous that day. Dora was shining bluish white, her illumination shining bluish white, her illumination was falling on everybody that walked in. Even Frank, the bounder who frisked people for weapons at the door noticed it.

Around 6 a man came into the bar and placed himself in front of her. He told her his name was Delicious and he'd had the flu for three months and he couldn't shake it.

"I'm on fire," he said, "I'm burning up with fever."

Dora placed her right hand on his black forehead. He was very hot. She tried to remove her hand but there was something there that wouldn't allow that. Her hand stuck like a pin to a magnet. When the pull relaxed she withdrew her hand and the big black handsome man Delicious shuddered.

"I don't feel hot anymore. Did you feel something strange? It was like you took this fire into your hands. Girl, you got some healing hands. What the hell is it? You a saint or something?" he was visibly shaken and aghast.

Dora shrugged her shoulders and looked at her hand.

"I don't know," she said, "I don't know."

Two minutes later a man came in and ordered a Harvey's Bristol Cream on ice. He told her that he'd just had a fourteen pound cancerous tumor removed and he still couldn't walk properly. In fact, he was doubled over on his stool. He told her also that the prognosis wasn't good, the doctors didn't feel that they'd gotten all the cancer and that he didn't have a long time to live, they guessed.

When Dora took the money from him, their hands met for a moment and they stuck like cement. Both of them looked down at their hands in fear. When the tug was over the man straightened up in his seat.

"It's gone. I feel it's gone." He stood up. "I don't feel no nausea no more. I can walk. I'm cured."

People came in all morning until 10 a.m. with physical problems and she unwittingly helped them. She had no idea of what was happening. The place was packed with Dora worshippers. They wouldn't leave, even when the place was closing up. Frank had to escort her home. They all wanted to touch her.

Soon word spread that there was a healer at Joe Protozoa's. They said that Dora walked with the angels. From that morning on the place was crowded with unfortunates of every kind; the blind, the poor, the overworked, the crippled, the insane. There were more people waiting on line at Joe Protozoa's than there were at Lourdes in France.

Joe Protozoa was racking in the bucks but he was afraid of the police. After all, these kinds of bars didn't need a lot of publicity. Liquor was against the law after 4 a.m.

He had to hire doormen and used velvet ropes to keep out the people who were in good shape. Only the obvious sick and crippled or suffering person could enter the place. Of course, there were always a few people who feigned disease or faked a limp or dressed like the insane but the doormen were astute and the phonies rarely got as far as the coat check room.

"Nobody is getting in unless you got something wrong with you," Frank the bouncer said over and over.

People on stretchers got in first. Party people looking for the action were turned away.

"Come back when there's something wrong with ya," Frank would say.

Of course Dora got a cut of the money and so did the cops to keep their mouths shut. A few months later when Dora was hailed as a saint, the beatified bartender, and TV crews had interviewed her, politicians wanted her in their camps, churches rallied for her attentions, she discovered that she was in danger. Her life was being threatened by the A.M.A. In the United States illness was a big money-making business. Without sick people whole industries would starve, the whole economy of the United States was in danger with Dora around.

She left the country in a veil with phony passports from the thieves at Joe's. She went to a leper colony in the Pacific and cured the lepers there, she went to hospitals in India and made the sick well.

Little did she know that a C.I.A. man was following her all over the world. He went to the leper colony and to India.

When she came back into the country in a disguise, he followed her here. She was longing to see her parents and her friends at Joe's. She never left J.F.K. airport. The C.I.A. man got to her first and calmly wiped her out.

It was a routine murder condoned by the government, blessed by the A.M.A. Alas, this always happens to the real saints. What else would one expect?

For his ghastly deed the C.I.A. man contracted leprosy from his trip to the Pacific and he longed for Dora to be alive again to cure him. Other than this, there was no punishment for the death of Dora. The C.I.A. and the A.M.A. weren't really proud of themselves but what else could they have done? It was out of their hands. They didn't blame themselves for one minute, it was God's fault they said, she was born at the wrong time. If only she could have been born before there was an A.M.A., then everything would have been rosy. Oh well.

The Circumstances of Dora's Cure

The A.M.A. doesn't like me either, but they wouldn't bother to kill me, there's too many of them with rotten skin.

Dora was one of my patients many years ago. She was the first. My cure worked well on her. Could you imagine a saint with acne?

Before

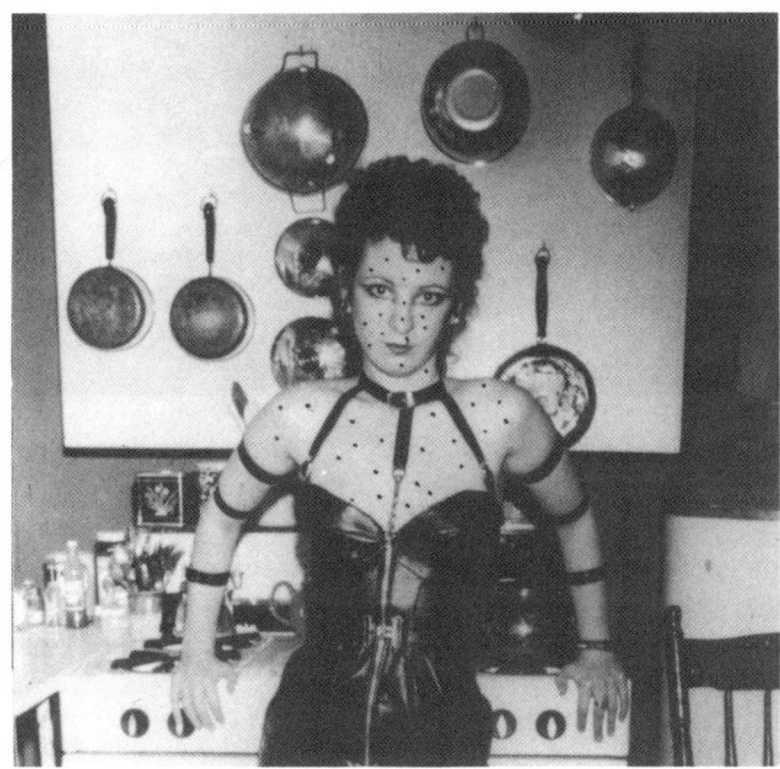

Photo © 1984 Nan Goldin/Janet Stein

After

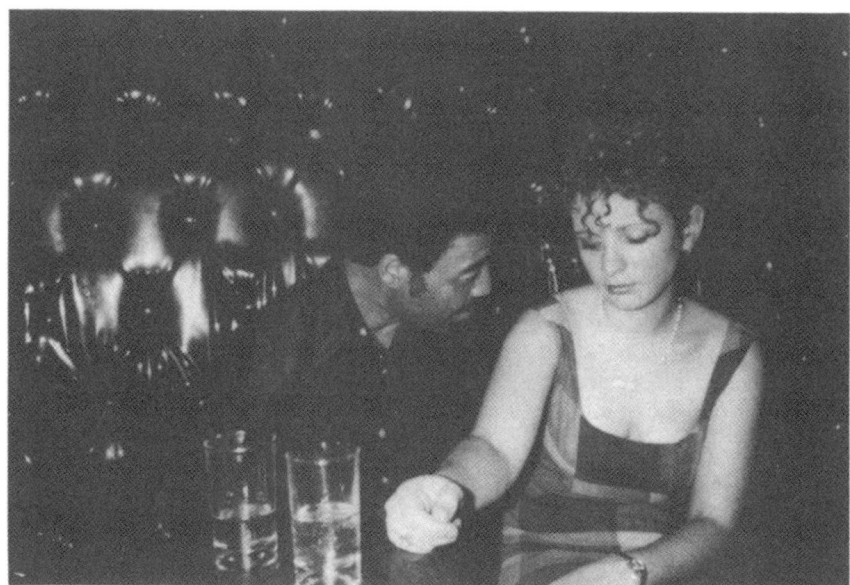

Photo ©1984 Nan Goldin/Trish McAdam

Case #8

Valerie
Losing

Six months ago Valerie woke up and discovered that one of her toes was missing. True, it wasn't the really important first toe, the large one that keeps you from easily losing your balance. Nevertheless, even though it was next to the smallest in size, it was tremendous to her in its importance. She had searched her bed painstakingly and had gone on methodically to dismantle her entire bedroom set in the search.

She didn't have leprosy. Nothing like this had ever happened to her before, so she made phone calls to various clinics, then decided to see a specialist, fuck the expense, but couldn't recall any category she might fit into or if in fact there was such a category.

"Doctor Rutin's office. May I help you?" the receptionist answered the phone. Valerie wondered if she was an R.N. or a P.N. receptionist, all the better doctors had R.N.s as receptionists.

Valerie's voice didn't break, she didn't sob into the phone.

"This is an emergency. I have to see the doctor."

"Are you a patient of Doctor Rutin's?"

"No, but a patient gave me his number. It's really an emergency. Can I see him today?"

"I'm sorry but there aren't any cancellations today. I could put you in at 2:30 next Thursday. What seems to be your problem?"

Valerie made everything easier by hanging up. She got dressed, weeping. She struggled getting her shoes on, not because of pain, there was none, but because she was afraid she might not be able to walk in many of her shoes. It was a difficult decision. She settled on a flat closed toe affair. Black. She went directly to the closest hospital's emergency room and waited with two other patients: one had been shot and was bleeding badly from the neck and the other looked physiologically sound but kept rolling newspapers into balls, trying to set them on fire in the corners below the plastic chairs.

When the doctor saw her, he registered little surprise. He took some blood, gave her another appointment, some Valiums and sent her home. When she got there she thought she should call her mother to tell her what had happened but her mother wouldn't be sympathetic either, probably blaming the loss on Valerie's alien lifestyle.

"You lost that toe because you stay up late, you go to bars, you see too many movies, you don't write to me....It has to be drugs...you don't call me."

If only she could find the toe. There had to be an answer in the toe itself. She took the bed apart again and this time found a leaf. Unlike normal leaves it wasn't green or autumnal colored but greyish beige, a very unnatural color for anything once alive or living. She had seen the same color on walls of very unprosperous Chinese restaurants.

She thumb tacked the lead to her desk and took two Valiums and laid down to sleep.

Many days passed. Everything remained the same. She went back to the hospital and the doctors told her happily that she didn't have leprosy which she could have told them by now. Also she wouldn't lose any more appendages, they said. Fine. By now she was growing accustomed to the loss and she actually got a vague sort of pleasure inside her shoes. She didn't give up hope of a regrowth; a friend of hers once told her that a friend of his had playfully bitten off one of his nipples one evening and in a few weeks he had grown another one. He had shown it to her and sure enough it was fresher and pinker looking than the other one. It was also true that lizards grow new tails when they lose them. But a few months went by and no newer, pinker toe grew. Even though she now felt the loss quite normal, she had fear that someone might discover it. She kept the lights very dim at night and didn't swim at the pool anymore.

The leaf she had tacked to her desk was now one sixth of the size it had once been. It was no larger than the thumb tack now but was still as well formed with no visible signs of decay or disease. As before it was heavily veined and translucent.

After months of thinking the loss over very carefully, she came to know why she had lost this part of her body. In the last fifteen years she had lost a lot, beginning with her virginity. She had lost two husbands, countless girlfriends, passports, bankbooks, wallets, one apartment, plants, a car, a dog, valuable jewelry, there were so many things. This was nothing new, only slightly different. She had lost so much it was just something else to mourn over for a bit. She took it in stride. There is a great art to handling losses with nonchalance.

The Circumstances of Valerie's Cure

Valerie lost that toe very mysteriously to be sure. It was a baffling case but the doctors never took her seriously, they thought that she was a bit brainsick and was born that way but just wanted attention. I happen to know that she had five toes on that foot at one time.

Since that loss, she never once lost anything else, not even a dime. (Although after my cure she did lose her pimples which she'd had since she was a teenager.) Her newfound gift for not losing anything worked to her disadvantage though, because her third husband is a jerk and she'd be better off if she could lose him for good.

Before

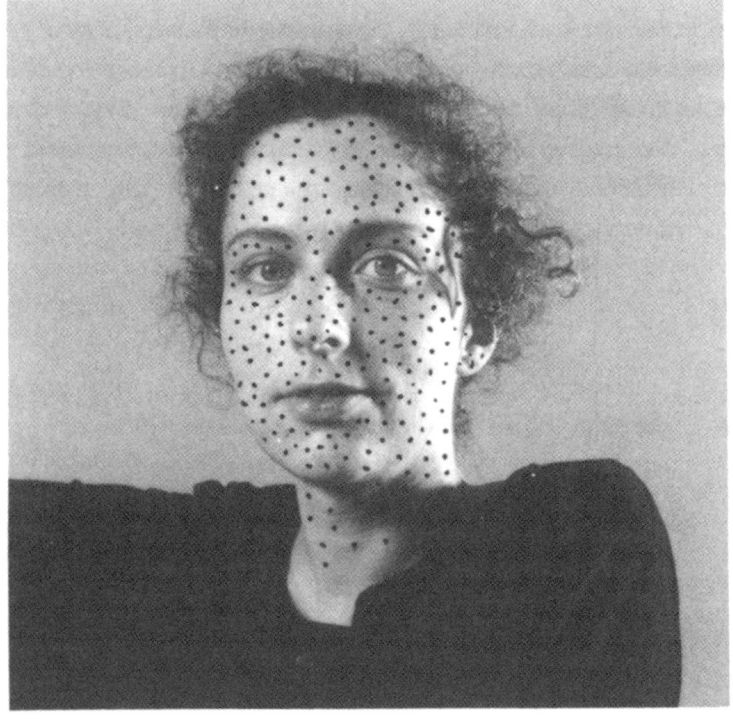

After

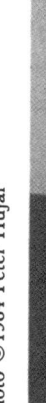

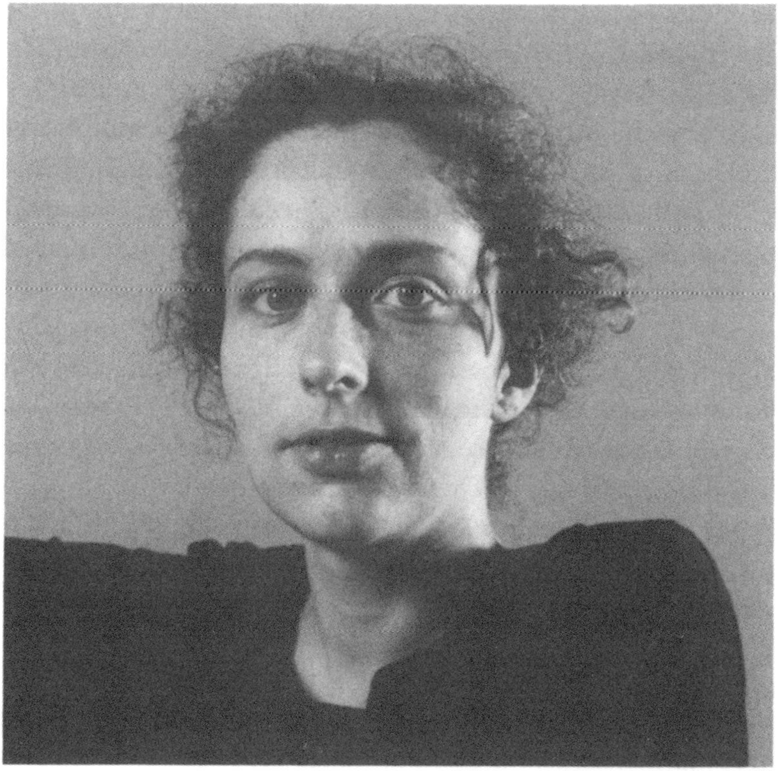

Photo ©1984 Peter Hujar

Case #9

Randy Eros
The Sexiest Kid In Town

Anyone could tell you that Cassanova wasn't so special looking, but women adored him. What was it? Charm. Although Alexander Pope was a hunchback, he was worshipped by his lovers, so what did he have? Intellect. Napolean was too short but he had power. Elvis had hips. Valentino had lips. Onassis had ships.

What did Randy Eros have? Not much but apparently just enough. Yes, he was attractive, not conventionally, but in that extremely suggestive way...blond and big and rough with a well placed three inch scar on his left cheek. His eyes were too cute, there were those Bambi lashes around his undine eyes. His nose was not so great. Sums of money he was casual with belonged to the parents, who wisely had given necessary cultural wrappings, but reading material never included the works of the masters after he left their bounds. He laughed a lot, had a great sense of the absurd and ironic but there wasn't a gift for making others split their sides. His clothes weren't always right but they were always tight. A more sexually desirable person was difficult to conjure up but the reason for this wasn't immediately obvious.

If one believes totally in heredity, the explanation for Randy's charm would be clear. It was in his blood, since both of his parents had made their fortunes on their desirability by tapping the prurient interests of others.

The mother was a prostitute, until she got too old and thought phone sex with credit cards was fine. Her clients had always been ambassadors and dignitaries, entrepreneurs. Only rarely would a taxi driver slip in.

The father was a star of gay porno films, a man who hadn't been out of work in fifteen years. The older this man got the better he looked. People were always impressed with Ed, the father, because of the whopping size of his talent and the nonchalant film presence. Delivering right on cue was his handiest gift, as professionals in the porno business would say.

Both of them tried to pressure Randy into the skin trade but Randy declined. There were other things that Randy wanted, although he wasn't quite sure yet what those things were. Basically he didn't want things to change. Travel altered nothing, as Ed and Linda thought it may. Worldwise and weary at 21, Randy could tell of the trip to Macchu Pichu with his mother, the Bamiyan Valley in Afghanistan with his father and Chitzen Itza with the Art History teacher as if they were walks to the hardware store.

At Macchu Pichu the air seemed too rarified for Randy. He was bored there. His mother loved it. She was so excited about the news of the latest anthropological discovery. Five female skeletons, virgin priestesses dedicated to the services of the Inca gods were found, just recently. On the guided tour she had embarassed Randy with the ceaseless questions about the virgins.

"How was it determined that they were virgins? Who kept them in line? Did they wear chastity belts?" she asked.

With Ed, he saw the Buddha in the Bamiyan Valley, the second largest statue on earth. Here, his father stood next to the big toe, which towered over him and exclaimed about the defacement. All the frontal parts were smashed off by conquering Moslems in the 10th century. The Buddha looked simple to Randy. He didn't care, but Ed was so upset about the frontal parts that Randy suspected his father's disappointment wasn't about the missing nose or fingers but the missing genitals. Even on the plane, while Randy's favorite actor, Clint Eastwood was displaying angst on the mini-screen in *Play Misty For Me,* Ed wouldn't let up about it.

"Shut up, already, Dad," Randy said about twelve times.

At Chitzen Itza, Randy realized that George, the Art History teacher, was very fond of him. Right on the steps at high noon the teacher dropped to his knees and it wasn't because of the weather. He wanted to do some sort of sex act with Randy. It was so stupid, Randy thought, but he let the teacher do what he wanted because he didn't want to anger the teacher. Suppose George had gotten so angry that he would leave Randy in Central America? Then what? Other admirers took Randy to the Parthenon in Athens, Borobudur in Malaysia, Shwe Dagon in Rangoon, Burma and of course Hoover Dam. None of it impressed him, not the sights, not the sex. It was no better than looking up at clouds in a blue sky.

Where were the thrills that people told him about? When would he fall in love? What was special about sex? What was so goddamned great about anything?

His parents began to worry. Randy was just plodding through each day like a zombie and he wasn't even on drugs. They asked him over and over about drugs until he decided that there must be something to them, so he got some marijuana. The high was disappointing. He did speed. He hated the rap. He sniffed glue and didn't like the feel of brain cells pooping out one by one. He free-based cocaine and didn't get the sensation of sitting next to enlightenment or power. He even shot heroin and thought, Jesus, Mary and Joseph, is this all there is to this?

But one day, Randy, sitting in his own tree not far from the others planted by his father, was struck by unfamiliar feelings of intense interest. Below him standing in hot sunlight was a person who was obviously a eunich. It was an old man-woman in horrible polyester clothes and naugahyde sneakers. He or she had hippopotamus-wide hips. If this person had been one sex or the other Randy would have hated the way this person looked. Randy wore only natural fibers and his shoes were made of leather always.

"Do ya like my new blazer?" this person asked Randy while looking up at him. "My mother gave it to me for Easter. It's pink. I have on a hot pink shirt. Ya...ya notice? Ya like it? Ya like it?"

God, what an asshole, Randy thought. Not only is this person a eunich but he/she is retarded as well. Randy came down from the tree. This was the tree that he always climbed whenever he really preferred to be absolutely alone. He thought that there, he would be unnoticed and not bothered by people who might succumb to his wiles. But this ignoramus had discovered him somehow.

"Mind if I come right over and talk to ya?" the idiot asked.

"I was just leaving," Randy actually was really taken with this person but he was confused. This doesn't happen.

"Mind if I walk wit ya?"

"Go away."

"No problem," the person in pink said and trotted away, undaunted.

Obviously this person was not a sensitive type, Randy observed. In the direction that the oddball walked was a seminary, an asylum and a dairy farm. There was nothing else this way except empty fields. Randy started for home but decided instead to find out where the person was going. Must be the asylum, he thought, lots of them were allowed to walk the fields. While turning in his loafers he slipped and fell. Randy had never fallen in his life. He got up. He brushed himself off. It was an unfamiliar action. He could never remember being this messed up. Branches of briars slapped him in the face as he tried to catch up with the person. He was being assaulted by nature. He was getting scratched. He was actually following someone. How odd.

He chased the person past the seminary and into a large room where there were only cows waiting to be hooked up to milking pumps. The person took off his pink blazer and put on a long white coat. He began to put the stainless steel suction cups on the black and white animals. The cups were lined with black rubber. The udders were pink. The person's shirt behind the white coat was pink. The person's pants were white. The floor was black and white tile. The walls were white. The ceiling was white. The person's naugahyde sneakers were white. In the stainless steel vat the milk was white. Through very clean windows the sky was bright blue. There were no clouds.

Over the sound of the pumps sucking and cows chewing the person said, "I thought ya was leavin."

Silence. All the cows stopped chewing their cuds for a moment and listened to nothing. They began again.

"This is what I do. I used to not do anything."

"Do you go out? At night, I mean," Randy asked while getting hit on his real cowhide belt by the tail of one of the animals.

"Ouch," said Randy.

"I go out with my mother. Did ya see *Play Misty For Me* ever?

I seed it wit my mother a lot. Clint Eastwood is my favorite actor."

They went out that night to the movies. It was a Clint Eastwood film about a cowboy show person. It was called *Bronco Billy* or something like that.

The dairy milker turned out to be like an old-fashioned doll, the kind that have no genitals to speak of.

Randy found himself for the first time in his life interested and in love. The milker went along with it. He didn't mind.

Everyone else was mortified.

The Circumstances of Randy's Cure

When Randy fell in love he became human. With this he acquired a few of the weaknesses that go along with it. He got pimples. I suppose he worried more. They were easily cured by following my advice.

The milker and Randy were happy for a number of years and then things fell apart as they often do.

It was O.K., though, Randy was a different person because of the milker. And because of Randy the milker was a different person. The milker had an operation to become a woman because that was what Randy thought best and anyway it was easier for the surgeons.

They are still friends and go to the movies whenever Clint Eastwood is on the screen.

Before

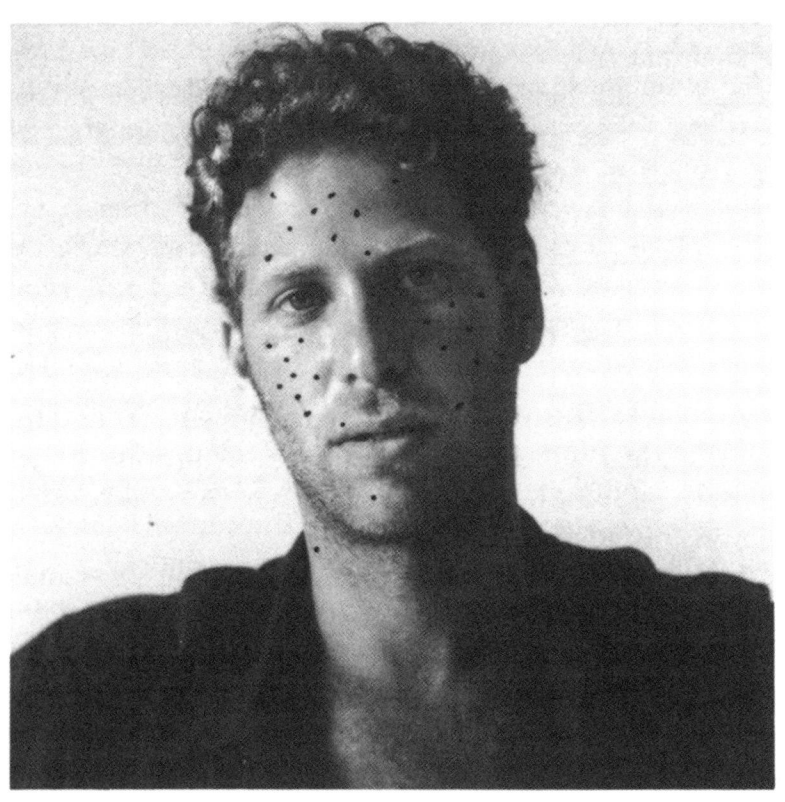

After

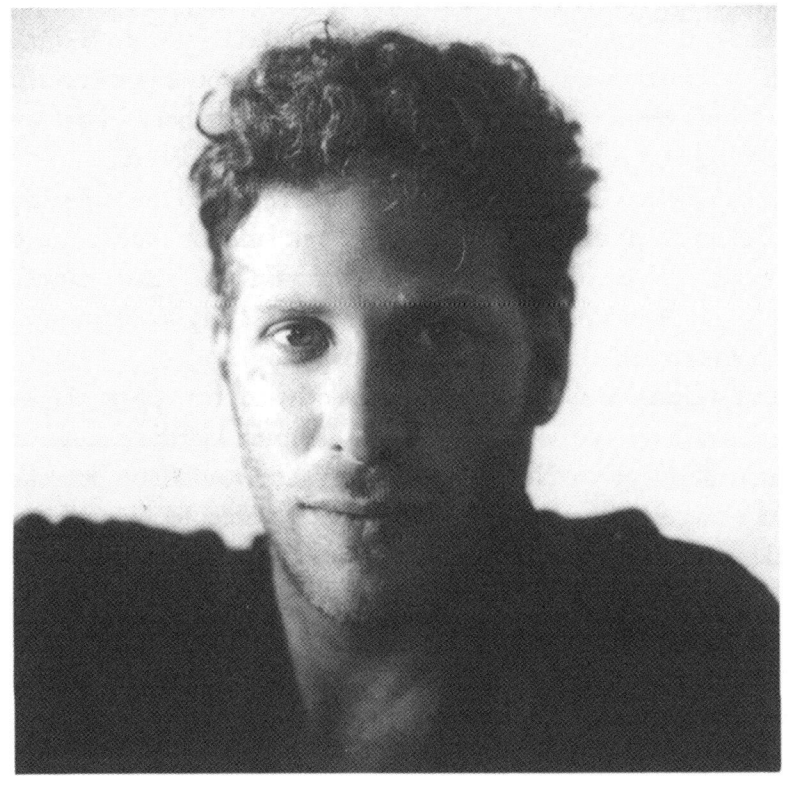

Photo © 1984 Peter Hujar

Case #10

Gena
I Hear America Sinking

Gena grew up in the industrial northeast of the United States. Like all the women for generations in her family she had hazel eyes, light brown hair and dishwater colored skin. As a child she had an ordinary life, so whenever she walked out onto the little patch of land behind her parents' house, she would pretend she was Charlotte Bronte on the moors in the heather. That was stretching it a bit but if she closed her eyes it worked.

In the distance from where she was there were the sugar and flour refineries that would belch out black smoke that damaged the sky so she would imagine, while lying on the grass, that she was Edgar Allen Poe in the gutters on his last day looking up at a sky as tormented and grey as his own soul.

Until Gena was eighteen she lived with her parents but longed to leave the world of avocado formica kitchens and red Datsuns and get to New York where she would be sure she would mingle with the arty types. She wanted to meet influential people like herself...the sensitive types. She knew she was sensitive, she cried at all the animal shows about Africa on TV.

She quit her job as an assistant credit manager...just dropped it as painlessly as a leaf falls from a tree. She forgot about her parents and their provinciality, led herself to Highway 95, put out her thumb for New York City.

The first person she got a ride with looked seedy but she gave him the benefit of the doubt. He told her that he was a writer and naturally she was duped for a while until they got to the city and he pulled into a Ramada Inn, talked her into coming into the room. He had angel dust and a gun and he asked her to remove her flesh-colored underwear. She escaped through her wits by turning the tables and pretending she was a prostitute with the clap. This apparently was unappetizing to him, so he let her go.

Out on the street it was already a bad day. It was the middle of July and the heat was so intense that the cytoplasm in the cells of human beings were coming near to solidifying like the whites of hard boiled eggs. There was no breeze. Air conditioners weren't operating up to their normal standards, city power was browning out from the energy suck and the appliances all over town were dropping from exhaustion much like human go-go dancers after three day dance marathons. Normal people, who ordinarily had wits were walking around with the effects of the sun on their brains. The vision was turning white. The insane homeless bag people walked around buck naked. In the winter these people wore black or brown plastic garbage bags as dress suit shelters.

On the street Gena saw a bum who was naked except he was covered from head to toe in yellow paint. She thought that he must have found a discarded can of yellow curb paint and doused himself with it. He was a human caution sign, a walking no-parking zone.

This bag-man-bum attempted to build a home in a garbage can that was laying on its belly, but he couldn't fit his big butt into it. She felt as homeless as he, but a wire mesh garbage can wasn't much of a hide-away as she saw it. She was lost in a city with bums four abreast on the sidewalks of every corner.

As she walked by, one of the bums screamed at her.

"Fashion mistake," he yelled.

She looked at him. He wasn't wearing anything at all. She

looked down at her own clothes. Was he right? She thought she looked just fine for the city, in black spandex pants and a hot pink t-shirt. Was the look too out of date, she wondered.

As she kept walking nowhere she noticed a real true fashion victim overdressed for the weather. This fashion victim was passing out in the middle of a street and the light was changing to green.

"Oh, heat prostration," Gena thought and she ran to lift the girl and drag her to the opposite corner.

Oh yes, it was heat prostration all right and the girl said "Thank you."

Gena thought she had finally found a friend but as she tried to carry on a conversation while she walked beside this girl, the fashionette told her to get lost and the tone wasn't pleasant.

"Oh God," said Gena, "this city is merciless, beyond my ken."

Where were all the wise people? Where were the sensitive types?

The same day she came to Manhattan she thought she better leave. She'd come back when it wasn't so hot. She found a ride board at New York University and went to Upstate New York where she located an ashram.

She met a man in his forties who was intent on hammering a piece of bamboo into his forehead to open the third eye and she told him that she would help him do it because she knew that he probably wouldn't die because he was so wise. He was practically a yogi. He was almost to the point of levitation. He said he had always wanted to levitate because it was such a show piece, it would impress even his enemies.

On the night of the operation they ate millet with Tahini Tamari dressing and goat yogurt for dessert. A little later at the first sight of blood, Gena chickened out. In a state of nausea she left the ashram. She would never be a nurse.

So she gave up the search for wise men and settled down in a commune not far from the ashram on the edge of a little river. She would spend entire days in an innertube floating, following the current. One day she saw the sky just as it had been when she used to pretend that she was Edgar Allen Poe but this time it wasn't darkened with chemical smoke but with the impending rage of a storm. The clouds looked like rats, all the birds were flying low and the cows she saw weren't standing but lying on the grass. She knew that the animals were acting strangely because of the air pressure of a coming storm. Sure enough, it began to rain so hard that the water around her was singing with the whipping it was getting.

She knew she should get off the innertube to make it to the safety of the shore but the river wouldn't stop...only meaner and rougher it got, until she could no longer see the line of the land.

When the river emptied out into a larger river she decided there wasn't much she could do, so she just relaxed. It rained for four days and four nights and she was sweeping past most of the eastern United States so it occurred to her as she entered the ocean that she was lost. Big steamships passed her in the night...she got so close to them that she could see the bare light-bulbs through the port holes of the engine rooms.

There had been no one to yell at for help in all this time and she thought perhaps she no longer had a voice anyway. Her body was changing alarmingly, pruning up, the skin was evolving into aquatic rubberish looking stuff.

One day she was caught in a tuna net with many large tunas. When the fishermen took a look at her they threw her back because by this time she had ingratiated herself with the sea.

She didn't look like much of anything anymore, certainly not human but limp and green like some inedible ocean life from the Mesozoic epoch. Since she was still on the innertube, she supposed that they thought she was just some green seaweedy debris attached to it. Fishermen caught tires all the time.

As the tuna boat was pulling away from her, she gazed past it and saw the shores of Key West, Florida. She had heard all about the gay men there so indeed there must be some wise men dancing in the discos. But then she thought about her strange new appearance and the rejection from the fishermen. She guessed they were really the wisest bunch of men she had ever met. Finally.

They knew a fish out of water when they saw one. Perhaps they realized that she was better off being lulled by songs of whales and porpoises, adored by little fish that followed her like trained poodles. To reintroduce her to the human world again would only serve to show once more than there was no place for her among people. But perhaps the fishermen were merely thinking in terms of dollars and they threw her back because she certainly wouldn't make the grade for Bumble Bee or Chicken Of The Sea. This was something to ponder as she bobbed on the surface of the waves in her innertube that looked like a licorice donut but more like a comfortable nest. Perhaps she would become a sea bird.

The Circumstances of Gena's Cure

I met Gena way back in Baltimore where I worked as a credit clerk with her. At the time she was so ordinary that she brought a tuna sandwich on rye, without the crusts, seven carrot slices and V-8 juice everyday for lunch from the time I met her until I left the job. She never tired of this lunch. I couldn't believe it. No variation made for a very dull person.

At this time her hair was short and she wore polyester pants suits. But strangely enough through the exterior there glowed a very peculiar person. I couldn't quite put my finger on it. I sensed that she was uncomfortable in these clothes and for that matter in the company of human beings. She had a facial problem and I gave her the cure and before I left the job I noticed an incredible change. By the time she left for New York City her skin had been clear for some time. So obviously this particular skin problem had nothing to do with the fishermen rejecting her.

This story of her travels on the ocean is not substantiated by any reliable witness. I have a feeling that this tale she is so fond of telling over and over (ad nausea) is fabricated.

I've seen her on the streets of New York City lately and she doesn't look so special but her skin is clear.

Before

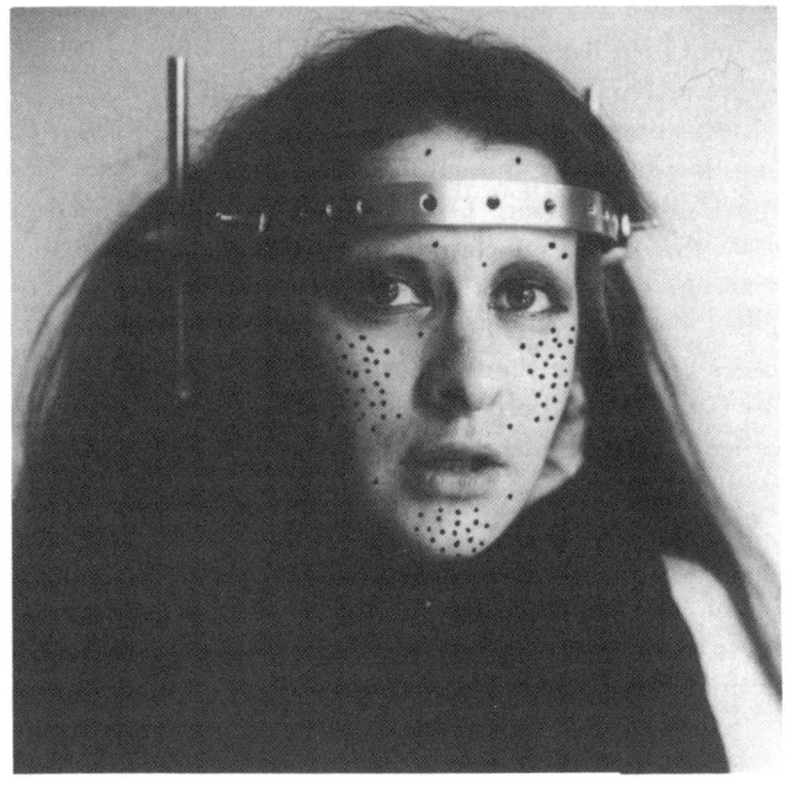

After

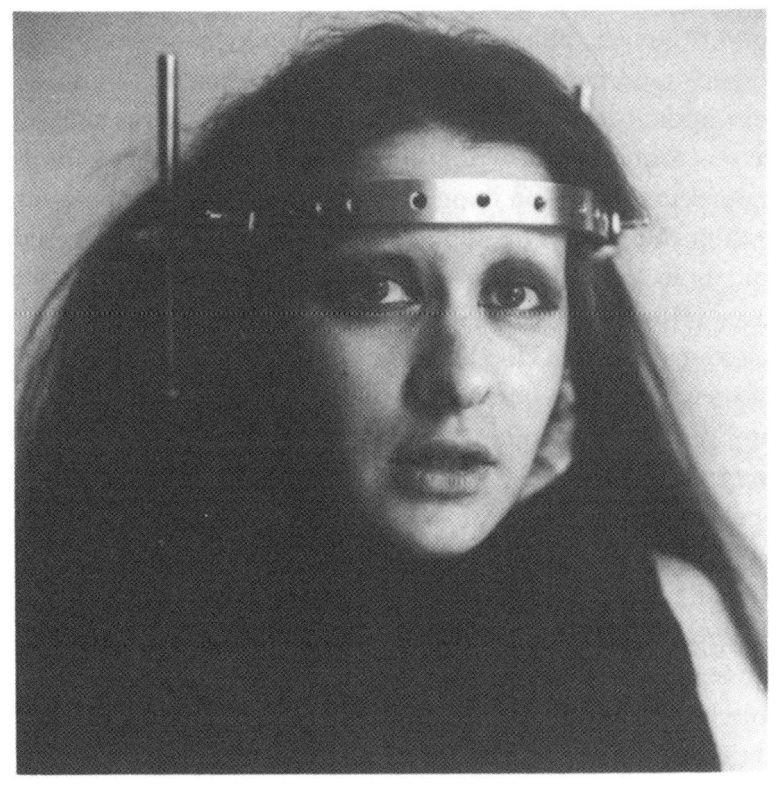

Photo ©1984 Peter Hujar

Case #11

Alexandra

Alexandra was not a Puerto Rican. She wasn't black. She wasn't in the least underprivileged or abused by a cruel society where she felt slighted or abused or oppressed. She was white, free and thirtyish. She had plenty of money. She even had all the major credit cards. Still despite all this, she was a junkie, a heroin junkie, the same as a beaten dark man with six kids and a vicious tongued wife, living in a roach and rat three roomed piece of security with no hope of a job that brought in anything more than the rent. This kind of man had to be a junkie. His heroin made things palatable, made bare lightbulbs look like Tiffany lamps; made his wife look like Diana Ross, made rats look like pets and his kids like a happy bunch on a third world TV sitcom. Without heroin he would probably throw himself off the Empire State building if he could afford the elevator fare to the top.

For Alexandra, heroin took away the harshness of responsibility. Sure, responsibility was still there, but with this miracle drug, she could have a sense of humor about it. Mornings weren't so bad if she a line of heroin laid out on her Honey Beige Revlon compact powder mirror.

After her divorce from a film producer, she lived with her daughter and had a job editing film. Women editors, as everyone in the business knows, were the best. For some reason men couldn't edit. They just didn't know where to bridle genius. Women could eliminate things as easily as losing blood once a month. They could do it graciously, in fact with aplomb. Lucidly as spring water, a woman could explain to a director that was full of himself how a certain scene didn't work so well.

Alexandra met heroin at the job. She was working with a young genius film director who she had an affair with. Together they leaned over the Steenbeck editing machine and touched sensitive skin, at first accidently. They made love right in the editing room with the splices of footage hung up with clothes pins and when they went back to his place he would take out a little package of heroin and they would snort it with a cut down straw. She had been doing cocaine for years so it really didn't seem like such a leap.

Music used to do the same thing for Alexandra as heroin. It would, while she listened, make burdens dissolve. Sex did the same thing as music while it lasted. Both of these things lasted for about 30 minutes. A regular LP was 20 or 30 and so was sex unless of course it was the beginning of a relationship and there was that special hot sex that went on for two hours five times a day.

After she stopped seeing the junkie film director, she found a way to buy the stuff herself. It wasn't difficult or painful to get. A young very likable woman sold it from her pleasant apartment. She loved visiting this person, who was just in the business to make a little extra money. After about three months of being involved with this drug, she found that it didn't make her nod out anymore. It gave her vast amounts of energy. Any junkie could tell you that this was the first step to being addicted. A month later she went on vacation for a week and after the second day without heroin she started going through withdrawal symptoms. She was flabbergasted. She couldn't believe she really had a habit. Not her. How could this be? It was ridiculous. She came down with all the normal things, the runny nose, the hot and cold flashes, the sweats, the diarrhea, the anxiety. She felt uneasy with her friends on the beach in Barbados and she excused herself and went into her hotel room to sweat it out. The worst part was the depression and the stomach cramps. She told her traveling companions that she had the flu, which it was not unlike, except for that horrible anxiety in the pit of her stomach. There was no one to confide in.

Before she left the airport on returning home she called her dealer friend. Now she had energy again. She could work fifteen hours a day at the Steenbeck and became very well enmeshed and in love with heroin. It became her lover. True, she didn't shoot it, but that made no difference. She was a junkie. A beautiful person named heroin was kissing her on her neck, holding her in able arms, behaving with her in society with extreme politeness, speaking to her with all the familiarities of her brother, or her mother, her father, or a sister or a nurse. During the day, while she looked up from the machine she would see her lover in her peripheral vision in July in the wavering heat of the day when black tar melted on the streets. Her lover was the only internal air conditioning system. As a fleeting shadow she saw him on moony nights. At coffee breaks she would look up into the blue from her Steenbeck and see the clear Cheerios like sky amoebas that she had seen often in her youth, but now they were visions of her lover, her compatriot, that semi-synthetic combination of morphine and acetic acid…her heroin. She needed nothing else. Heroin stood beside her as only the most faithful lover would. She began to believe that it was her God. With it beside her, she won an Oscar for her film editing on *Callous Views*. She accepted the Oscar and millions all over the country saw her on TV. She was very high on heroin that night. She laughed when she thought about how she looked so bright and upstanding, a model film editor. On that stage her lover was within her, having sex with her right on the stage, laughing, inserting himself blindly into her making her pupils pinned. She had wanted to say, "I accept this Oscar and I owe it to my lover heroin, who gave me the courage and the energy." But she didn't.

One day she decided to stop. It wasn't so bad. She started to eat a lot and she fell in love with a real person. Her work didn't seem as important though, but she was clean. Food and sex supplanted that old lover. She was happy. When she looked at her Oscar on the mantle piece, she thought of her old lover and laughed. She had spent forty dollars a day on him for two years. What a gigolo. She could have bought twenty Steenbecks and five new cars on that.

The Circumstances of Alexandra's Cure

I was shocked to find that Alexandra was a junkie. Shocked and mortified. You would never know it. She looked so clean and normal, like an ordinary person. Anyway she was and she didn't have any pimples until she quit taking the stuff, which I thought was strange. It would seem that she would have gotten them when she was addicted. But it was all the toxins coming to the surface of the skin when she quit.

I'm happy to say that she has been off drugs for three years now and has fine clear skin. Unfortunately her daughter is now a junkie but fortunately she has clear skin.

Before

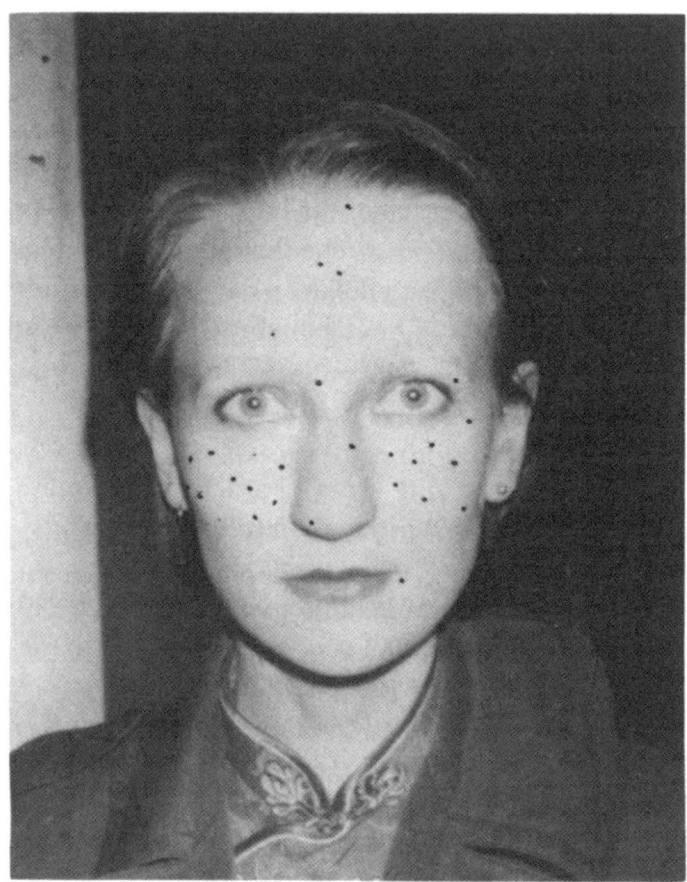

Photo ©1984 Nan Goldin

After

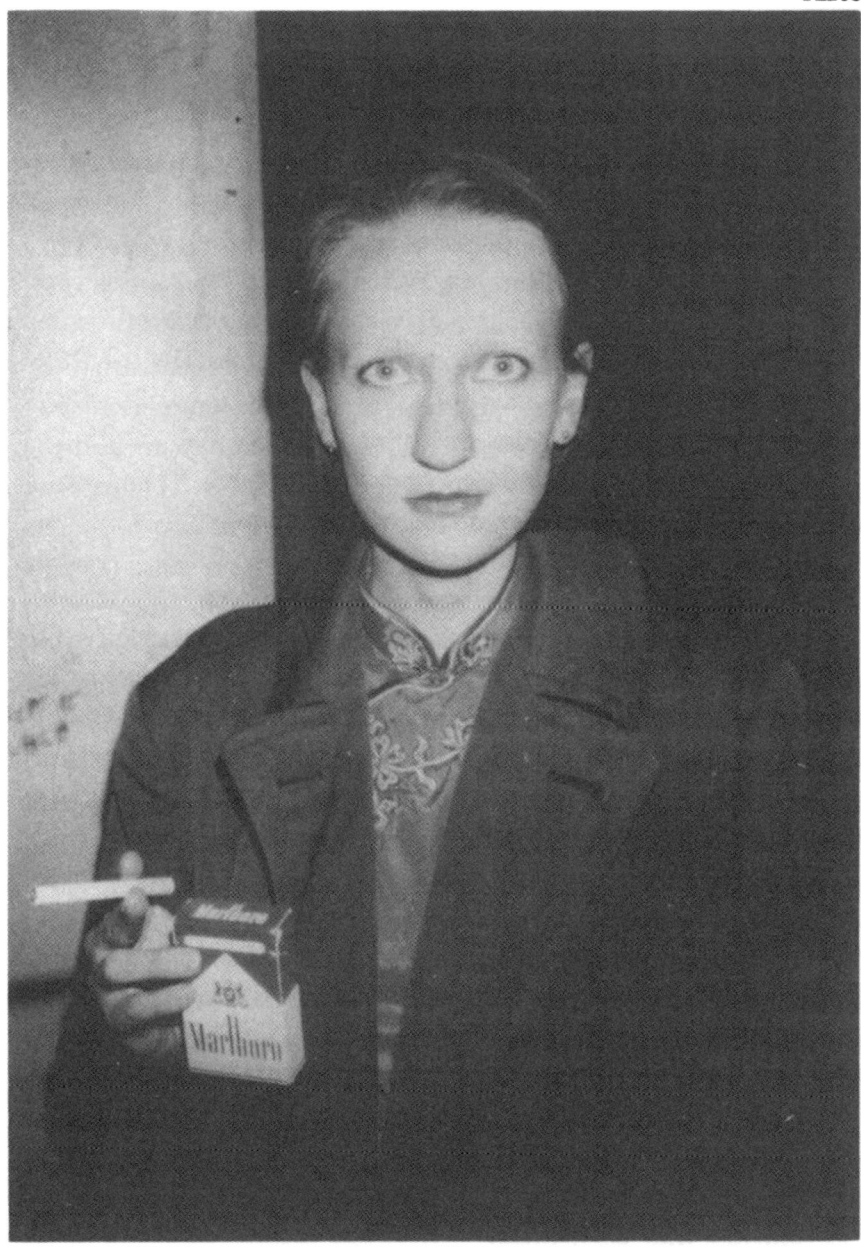

Case #12

Miguel LaMadrid

Sometime in the last part of October, the LaMadrids were given a pig. This Cuban family wasn't very wealthy, so when this relative gave them the pig they accepted it graciously. They lived on a small piece of land in Pennsylvania. They had a few chickens and one dog, a Golden Retriever named Buddy, and a blue Chevy pick-up truck and a well-used Buick Riviera. The Buick Riviera did more hauling than the pick-up truck. They had two TV sets, one color Sony in the living room and the other black and white in Mom and Dad's room. There were three children, by now teenagers, two girls and one boy. The oldest girl was named Maria and the youngest Candida. The son was named Miguel. As most well-born Cubans, they were a handsome bunch, dark hair, chiseled features, the sweetest eyes and finest lips. Lips like these were often kissed by non-hispanic neighbors who were all around. Maria and Candida and Miguel didn't know what other Cubans looked like. There weren't any others around. All the teenagers that came to court the LaMadrid kids were very blond.

The relative that gave them the pig lived in New York City. When he came visiting he borrowed the Buick one day and went to a Farmers' Market and came home with the pig in the back seat. This relative was the first Cuban, aside from the immediate family, that the kids had ever seen. They reveled in the fact that someone other than themselves could speak Spanish.

Of course they kept the pig, it was supposed to be for the Christmas dinner when the New York Cuban relative, his wife, and brothers-in-law and their families were invited to the LaMadrids' that Christmas.

"Fatten that pig up," the relative told them when they put him on the bus back to New York City.

Unfortunately, Miguel, who was the one who took over the care of the pig, began to like the pig more than he should. Miguel was thirteen, but already almost a man and this would be his last childhood pet. The pig and the dog got on very well too. They romped together in the backyard. The pig, whose pink flesh shone through the sparse black and white pinto pony hair, learned a lot about behavior from the dog. In fact, this pig was extremely intelligent, more than the dog. When Miguel went to sleep at night he slept with the dog and then began to bring the pig indoors when it got very cold in November. He used to read aloud to the dog and the pig, late at night when he was supposed to be doing homework and acting like an adult. This was the last vestige of being a child...reading aloud to his dog and pig didn't seem so childish to him, it was like a parent's nighttime duty. He took full responsibility of his charges.

Days before Christmas he pleaded with his father to spare the pig and his father, being a kind-hearted sort, relented and told him they'd go to a butcher store and buy an already butchered pig to cook. The Cuban relatives would never know the difference. When the day came for the relatives to arrive, Miguel took the pig into the woods and tied him to a Blue Spruce tree. He went to bed and the next day found that the relative in the morning hour had found the pig, because it had gotten loose and was scratching at the door as he always did. The relative stabbed the pig in the heart and cleaned it well, pulled all the entrails out and dressed and stuffed it and put it in the oven to cook.

Miguel, when he found out, began to cry and big tears rolled from his sad brown eyes.

On Christmas night when the pig was served at the table, the LaMadrids turned their heads and cast their eyes to the floor. There on the table was the pig that they all had come to know and love. The pig still had those wonderful lashed eyes, so sad and big like all the LaMadrid family members.

At the table with the apple in its mouth he still looked like he was alive and so he was. The apple he spit out and he began to talk.

"Why didn't you save me, Miguel?" Miguel could not answer.

"Oh the cooking wasn't so bad," the pig continued. "It didn't fry my brain. I can still think; I still have a brain. But there's nothing to do now. I can't move. Miguel, would you go down to the book store and buy my that book called *Charlotte's Web*? I always liked that one. Buy it for me. I can still read. My mind is still active, even if my body isn't. Perhaps I can't eat because I no longer have any intestines, but I can still think and I can still read. My eye sight is still good. The cooking hasn't taken that away from me."

The LaMadrids had to leave the room in shame. They couldn't look the pig in the eyes. Even the Cuban relatives couldn't eat the pig now. They too couldn't face the pig.

Alone on the table, amid the splendor of the other foods, the mashed turnips, the Cuban black bean soup, the corn tortillas, the pig glanced around and waited for his book. The candlelight made him look not so cooked.

Miguel went to the book store and bought the pig the *Charlotte's Web* book and also one about a boy who entered the 1984 Olympics in a wheelchair.

All the way home, on his bike, Miguel cried such big tears that the sky began to rain in sympathy.

The Circumstances of Miguel's Cure

Poor Miguel. He was the only LaMadrid to get pimples. He followed my cure and got rid of them of course.

The Cuban relative from New York asked me for the remedy also but after I heard the story about the pig, I told him that I forgot the cure. I didn't think he deserved to have clear skin. His pimples weren't that bad anyway.

Before

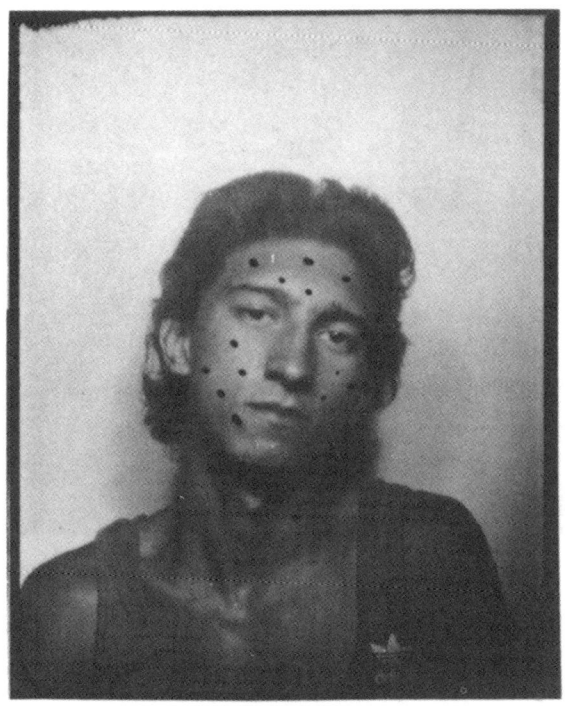

After

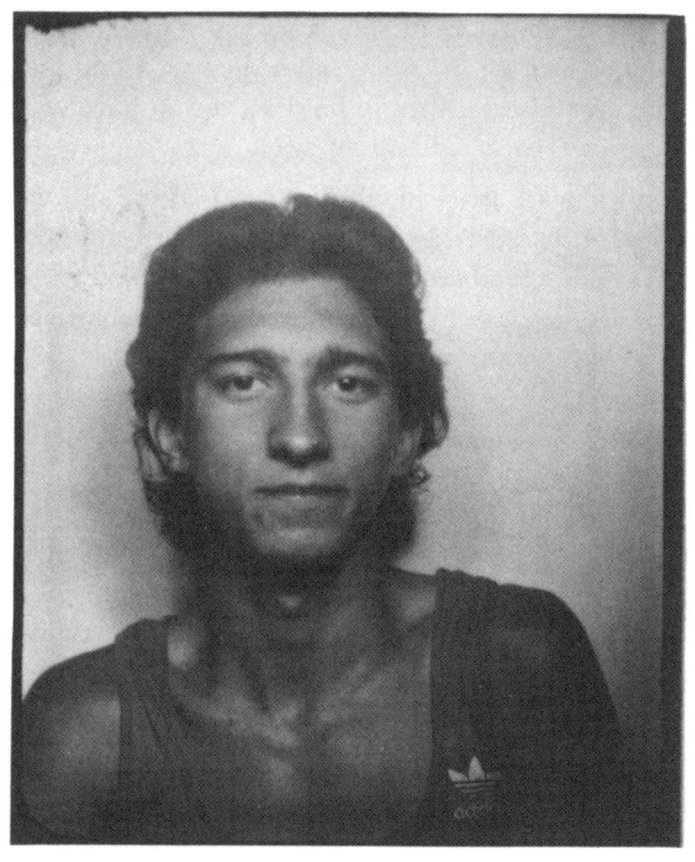

The Actual Cure

Have you heard enough? I could tell you more endless depressing tales of people with bad skin but I won't. I'm going to get right to the facts. The cure is simple and it isn't expensive or time consuming. I'm not selling a product. All the things you'll need are already on your kitchen shelf or at the drug store or health food store.

Through trial and error and a lot of research I've cured myself of acne. I've cured many people who have religiously followed my program. This cure works. This is not a joke.

O.K. Here goes.

If you have bad skin you have a vitamin A and D deficiency. The most readily digestible form of these vitamins are contained in cod liver, halibut liver and shark liver oil. I take cod liver oil, two tablespoons a day. To many people the taste is very disagreeable. If this is the case there are perls (gelatine capsules) of these oils which can be taken. The cod liver oil I take is 2500 I.U.s (International Units) of vitamin A and 250 I.U.s of vitamin D per gram. There are water misible pills as well, these are the dry form of the vitamins. I suggest taking the oil misible form of these vitamins.

There is caution to be noted when taking vitamin A. There is a toxicity level of this vitamin so don't take more than 50,000 I.U.s daily. Research has shown that the body can't utilize more than this anyway.

If you've had bad skin for a number of years, you might have noticed that exposure to the sun tends to clear up the problem. The sun gives you vitamin D. There is a type of cholesterol present in the skin that the sun's ultraviolet rays activate, converting it to vitamin D. This vitamin also aids in the absorption of calcium, which acne sufferers are also deficient in. Don't overdo the sun though, because the tanner and thicker your skin becomes, the less vitamin D your skin absorbs. A deficiency of vitamin D leads to retention of phosphorus in the kidneys and there is a relationship to proper kidney functioning and healthy skin.

Vitamin E is also essential to the cure. Vitamin E is an antioxidant which means it prevents saturated fatty acids from breaking down and combining with other substances that might become harmful to the body. Vitamin E has the ability to unite with oxygen thus the red blood cells are more fully supplied with pure oxygen that the heart and other organs obviously need. Vitamin E is effective in the prevention of scarring on the body surface and internally. It can be used to prevent calcification of the kidneys.

You should take 200 to 400 I.U.s of vitamin E daily.

The B complex vitamins should not be ignored. They help reduce facial oiliness and blackhead formation. B vitamins are the single most important factor for health of the nerves and proper functioning of the nervous system. It is proven that emotional stress and nervousness contribute to acne problems. The best way to get the B complex is Brewer's Yeast. It contains 40% highest quality protein and is an excellent source of most minerals and trace elements. It contains 16 amino acids. Amino acids are the basic units of digested protein.

Many people can't tolerate the taste of Brewer's Yeast, so instead a high potency vitamin B complex pill should be taken.

Never take just one or two of the Bs alone, an improper balance of these vitamins is not beneficial.

Vitamin C should be included with the B vitamins because it activates them. Also it aids in the resistance of the spread of acne infection.

Zinc gluconate (30 mg. daily), niacin (100 taken twice daily) and cold pressed oil (soy bean, sesame; one tablespoon daily) should be included.

As an adolescent I was always told to stay away from chocolate because it supposedly was bad for the skin. There is some truth in this. Chocolate, spinach and rhubarb inhibit the body's absorption of calcium because they contain an excess of oxalic acid. Oxalic acid can form kidney stones and kidney malfunctioning is always associated with skin problems. Calcium helps to maintain the acid alkali balance of the blood which is important for clear skin.

Avoid constipation, get plenty of sleep and exercise and try for peace of mind. Avoid an excess of animal fats in the diet. Take a natural multi-mineral formula and drink water, preferably mineral water. All of these dietary considerations are not so difficult to follow.

Now that you know what to do for the internal, here's what to do topically.

The most important consideration externally is to maintain a low pH acid mantle on the skin. Wash with an acid balanced soap as opposed to an alkali one. The pH level should be 4.5 or lower. Without the proper acid mantle the skin is open for all kinds of bacteria and infections. To insure this protection you must rinse your face after every washing with a solution of apple cider vinegar and water, one part apple cider vinegar to four or five parts water.

Everything that you put on your face (if you use foundations etc.) should be acid instead of alkaline. You can buy little testing papers at the pharmacy called Nitrazine papers. The papers are yellow. If you test your facial products with these and the products turn the papers blue or purple then don't use these products. They are too alkaline.

This apple cider vinegar and water solution is an essential part of the cure. You have to do it.

The routine is this: Apply a pure coconut or vitamin E oil on your face. You can also use the cod liver oil if you can stand the smell, then wash your face with hot water and the pH balanced soap, then rinse with water and follow it with the apple cider vinegar and water solution. If you feel that your skin is really too oily omit the first step.

If you follow all the directions I have cited here, the external and internal, you will notice that your skin will begin to clear up in a matter of two weeks. In six weeks your skin may begin to break out again. This is the time when all the toxins are being released. Don't get discouraged at this time, continue the program. The next week your skin will clear up for good. Old scars will even disappear! You must keep it up, don't stop. Whenever I do, I have a recurrence of acne. Do it. It works.

So that's the cure. It hasn't failed for anyone who's followed it. It has changed people's lives. To encapsulate:

Internal:
- Vitamins A and D, always taken togather as an oil (cod liver, halibut liver or shark liver, two tablespoons daily, not to exceed four)
- A- 5,000 to 15,000 I.U.s daily, taken in a perl
- D- 500 to 1,500 I.U.s daily, taken in a perl
- B- taken as Brewer's Yeast, three heaping tablespoons daily
- B complex in pill form- 20 to 100 mgs. daily for each B
- C- 1,000 mgs. daily
- E- 200 to 400 I.U.s daily
- Zinc- 30 mgs. daily
- Niacin- 100 mgs. twice a day (Don't take this if you're taking the Bs as Brewer's Yeast.)
- Cold pressed oil- soybean, sesame, 1 tablespoon daily

Avoid chocolate, spinach, rhubarb

External:
Wash with the pH balanced soap, rinse with hot water, followed by the apple cider vinegar solution; use pH balanced products.

So you see this isn't very difficult. This does work. For sure. So do it.

INDEX

Abyssinian bat	18	coke dealers	35
Africa	54	cow milk	50
air freshener	34	Cuban Black Bean Soup	70
air waves	31	dermatologists	27
alien lifestyle	42	DNA	17
A.M.A.	38,39	doubleknits	8
angels	37	Einstein	12
angst	48	Elvis	46
anthropologist	47	entrails	69
aristocrat	34	eulogy	30
art history	47-48	eunich	49
ashram	56	fifties	7
asylum	49	fishermen	57,59
see mental hospital		genitals	48, 51
avocado	54	goat yogurt	56
Bachelor's Buttons	16	glue	48
balance	41	God	38,49
Baltimore	59	go-go dancing	35,55
Bamiyan Valley	47	gossip	12
bankbooks	43	gravity	12
belly	55	hairpieces	35
birdbath	8	heat prostration	56
blood	42,56,62	heaven	32
blind	37	heroin	48,62-65
boosters	35	hit men	35
Bronte, Charlotte	54	hustlers' bar	35
Buddha	47	hydrogen bomb	26
Bumble Bee Tuna	58	Inca Gods	47
capped teeth	35	innertube	57-58
Cassanova	46	intercourse	22
chemical smoke	57	Italian Rococo	8
Chitzen Itza	47-48	jerk	44
Chicken of the Sea Tuna	58	Jesus	48
Chinese Restuarant	23	JFK Airport	38
C.I.A.	38	Jonestown Guyana	26
cocaine	48,63	journalists	7
coffin	30	Key West, Florida	58

Kool Aid	26
lawn jockey	8
leprosy	38,41,42
lizard	43
long johns	7
locusts	7
Lourdes	37
Macchu Pichu	47
Manhattan	56
martini	23
Mary	48
meditation	18
mental hospital	26
see asylum	
microscope	18
midgets	12,13
mind	26
morgue	30,31
Moslems	47
murder	38
nail clippers	9
Napoleon	46
Narcotics Anonymous	35-36
naugahyde	49-50
Newark	10
Nightblind	22
numbers runners	35
ocean life	58
Onassis	46
opossums	18
oxygen drums	16
Pan Am	10
party people	37
People Express	10
phantom	22
Phoenix	17
pill vials	30
pinto pony	69
pimps	35
Play Misty For Me	48,50
P.N.	41

Poe, Edgar Allen	54,57
Polish food	23
political satire	30
polyester	49,59
Pope, Alexander	46
porno moguls	35
pregnant	18-19
prognosis	36
prurient interest	46
Puerto Rican	62
puree	16
rachet wrench	16
Ramada Inn	54
razor blade	30
remoras	6
retarded	49
River Styx	32
R.N.	41
Rome	10
seminary	49
shampoo	9
sharks	7
shopping mall	16,17
strangers	26
stuff	57
success	7
suction cups	50
surgery	12-13
Sweet William	16
thieves	35
Titanic	26
towel	24
TV sitcom	30-31,62
upstate	56
vagina	12,18
Valentino	46
Valium	42
valuable jewelry	43
velvet ropes	37
whales	58
woe	5

After

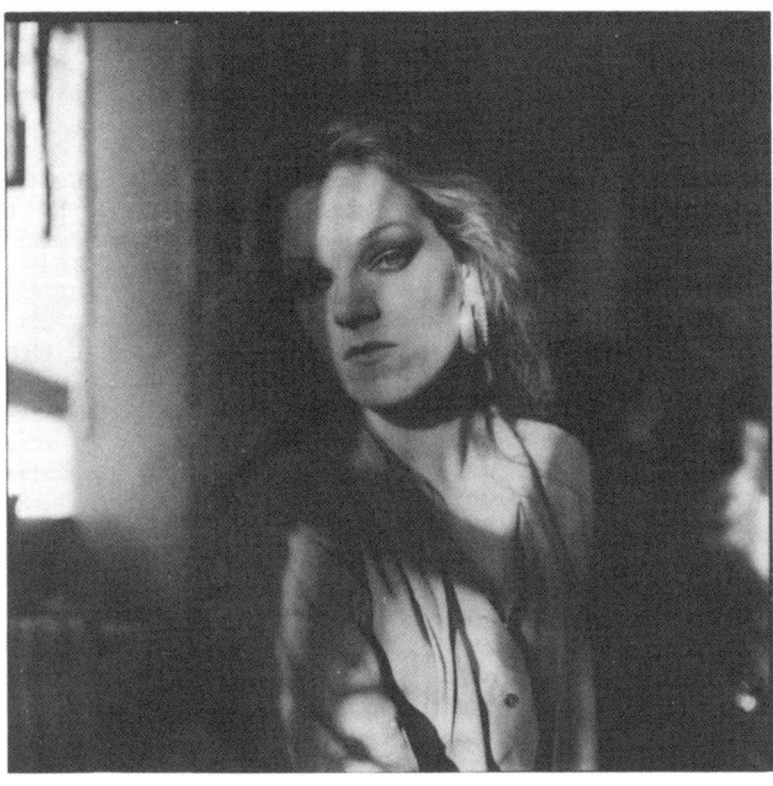

Photo © 1984 David Armstrong

TOP STORIES

A PROSE PERIODICAL

#1   Donna Wyszomierski
#2   Laurie Anderson
#3   Pati Hill
#4   Suzanne Johnson
#5   Linda Neaman
#6   Gail Vachon
#7   Jenny Holzer/Peter Nadin
#8   Judith Doyle
#9   Kathy Acker
#10   Lynne Tillman/Jane Dickson
#11   Kirsten Thorup
#12   Janet Stein
#13   Anne Turyn
#14   Lee Eiferman
#15   Constance DeJong
#16   Ursule Molinaro
#17   Romaine Perin
#18   Donna Wyszomierski

Available from:
TOP STORIES
228 Seventh Avenue
New York, N.Y. 10011

ISBN 0-917061-19-5

TOP STORIES #21 $3.00

RED MOON/
RED LAKE

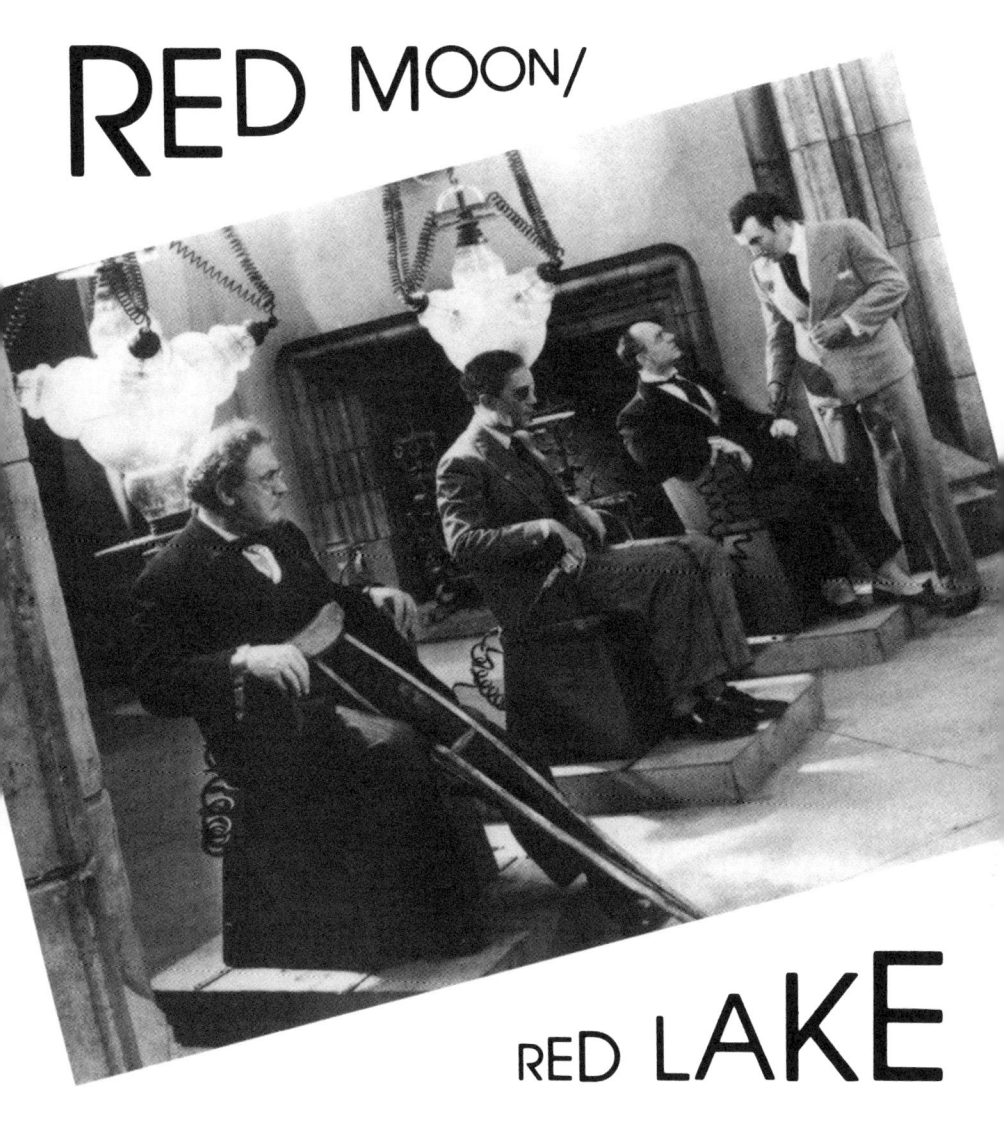

ASCHER/STRAUS

Red Moon/Red Lake

by Ascher/Straus

Copyright © 1984 by Sheila Ascher and Dennis Straus.

Cover photograph, from Dr. X, *courtesy of The Museum of Modern Art/Film Stills Archive.*

This publication has been made possible in part by funds from the Beard's Fund and the Committee for the Visual Arts.

ISBN 0-917061-21-7 (Top Stories #21)

TOP STORIES, 228 Seventh Avenue, N.Y.C., N.Y. 10011

Pam is asleep, the lavender cover just under her chin.

Her fingers or her eyelids may have moved a little, but the disposition of her body doesn't change. A hand that begins the night curled like a glove 1¾" from the pillow will crawl no further than 2" from the pillow by morning; the left ankle will remain tucked under the right calf. A body that seems to lack the vitality to transmit its dreams beyond a tiny envelope of warmth.

The room is covered over and dozing in a cool midnight blue shadow, exactly the same weight and temperature as the white powder blowing in thin clouds from large sacks of plaster stacked in rows on the parched slope of a lawn, below a high wall of loose yellow bricks and warped window frames.

Ted's made a nest for himself and his loose, dark bathrobe in the deep chair near the red oval rug, the small, leather-surfaced telephone table and the color television console. The television is on and in that sense it's true but not completely true, or true but also not true, or true in an utterly new way, that Ted is in the living room, nesting in the deep chair. It could be said just as truthfully that Ted is absolutely nowhere: the television, flashing a blue wash of pictures and a multitudinous blather of voices, is a second head, displacing Ted's as thoroughly as if his throat had been slit, his body hung by the feet from a rafter and drained of all its blood by the eight foot tall, human-like vegetable from outer space in *The Thing*. It's also possible that he's there, but also somewhere else: not totally displaced by the television's objective dreaming, but in an intermediate state of here and there, his photons annihilated in the television's.

The television is beaming a face close to Ted's. Montgomery Clift's narrow, troubled face, eyebrows darkened by guilt, ambitions, ethics, longings is gazing at Elizabeth Taylor, young and lovely, no more than nineteen or twenty. She's just taken a cold swim in the beautiful, dark lake and now she's towelling off her hair and laughing—the dark, shimmering laughter of a girl who's affectionate, happy and rich. A loon flies up from the surface of the lake, passes overhead, and disappears beyond the forest screen. Ted's face, at first next to Elizabeth Taylor's, finds itself next to Clift's, resting on his shoulder, extraordinarily close to the camera, a soft, untroubled pearl, the eyes and eyelashes dark with a sensual knowledge that seems to have something to do with the past and future secrets of the lake. A world of grace and freedom is breathing against Montgomery Clift's shadows.

Someone who's actually leaning on his windowsill on this autumn night is dozing and dreaming he's leaning on the windowsill on a summer night. A thin, dark-haired man of thirty-three who used to live in an orange brick house across the way, but who's now in an ancient, red brick hospital in a distant zone of the city. In a lucid moment he dreams that he's home, staring out his bedroom window and thinking: "if lucidity, heightened to its extreme, resembles dreams, then all I'm suffering from is a delirium of lucidity!" He sees a familiar, curly-haired neighbor in a near-distant window, leaning on the sill and staring at the moon.

The moon is a dark orange, with three still darker areas of blue shadow.

Dogs are barking, crying, baying at widely scattered points within a shallow basin that forms an uneven sound horizon. Leaning on the windowsills, the two men can hear the smothered voices of three dogs, then seven, locked in basements, kitchens or outdoor sheds, as unhappy as children who cry until they're exhausted, their mothers can't comfort them, no matter what. Or they cry until the moon is only a few inches above the dusky lavender of the roofs.

The moon is red now. Its blue shadows so dark they're like holes where they can see the moon's other sky.

The earth is moving perceptibly up across its surface: they can measure the movement, feel themselves being thrust upward and backward. The horizontal line of a television aerial atop the slate roof of the dark brick house across the way slides toward the moon's upper rim.

Now the moon's red is the deep red of the molten core of the planet: a round X-ray mirror deep in space. The two men, terror-stricken, withdraw into their rooms.

Ted is awake. Montgomery Clift has long since discovered that he's guilty, that, accident or no accident, he really wanted Shelly Winters to drown in the dark lake, and the 25" Zenith is broadcasting a coded program of dots and static.

All Ted remembers is that he's had another nightmare, one with a red overtone. He's seen The Butcher again or he's been butchered. The Butcher's shop looked like an enormous public toilet. Dismembered torsos lay in the toilet stalls, cranberry red. He struggles to remember more. It seems to him the nightmare began on a train. He remembers very rapid movement, a complex motion that involves swaying from side to side, vertical dipping and tremors, all the while standing still yet hurtling forward. The conductor insisted he make a decision at once: the crowded car near at hand or the empty one in the extreme distance. A long, difficult journey: loss of balance; many, many doors, hard to open. Arriving at the distant car, he felt as if he were at the bottom of a steep plane, as if horizontal and vertical had changed places. He slid back the door with great effort and saw: the slaughterhouse-toilet. He recognized it as the place he's been visiting ever since Pam's enormous brother Rudi has been living in the tiny nursery just the other side of their bedroom wall.

Pam and Ted and Rudi are having supper together.

Pam is saying that there's a woman at work, just about her age, who was a language major just like her. Only it was French instead of German and the University of Wisconsin instead of Sacramento. Since this woman graduated she's worked at secretarial jobs exactly like the one she has now. First in Milwaukee, then Denver, Los Angeles, and now in New York. All on the same low level. The job in Los Angeles made a *little* use of her training in French, but not much. So, naturally, she's a little depressed.

Ted says: "What's there to be depressed about? Everybody works on a low level—and nobody makes use of anything. Two guys were talking on the beach the other night about that very thing. One of them said: 'you know what I've discovered? Every grey hair means something new you've forgotten. The secret of life is forgetfulness. Remembering is unnatural, that's why it takes so much effort. We're meant to get dumber and dumber with every day. Until, at the end . . . .' Actually, Rudi heard more of it than I did. Didn'tcha, Rudi?"

"More parsnips, please, Pam." Rudi has his thick hand out.

"Since I've been taking these walks with Rudi, I've developed a new ability. *Two* new abilities. I can hear what other people are saying. And I can *repeat* it."

"Even when you don't understand it," Rudi says.

Ted and Rudi laugh.

"Hey! I'm real happy *you* guys know what you're talkin' about—but I wish somebody'd *translate* or something . . . ."

More dishing out and eating, then Pam says: "Does anyone want to hear more about Penny?"

"Penny? Who's Penny?"

"The woman I was talking about, Ted!"

"Oh sure . . . ."

"Sure!"

"Well, *I* feel sympathetic even if you two don't."

"We're sympathetic. Aren't we, Rudi? We even *look* sympathetic. And that's worth more than anything."

"I'm really listening, Pam."

"Cause I'd like your serious opinion on this. I'm so darn naive—or so *optimistic*—that I think when someone's *down* like that it sort of skips right past me. I *wanted* to give her good advice, but I couldn't. For example: I don't at all understand what this means: 'If you don't decide, it decides for you. You think life is waiting for you to figure out what you want to do. But it doesn't wait. It goes on without your consent.' I said: 'Why do you have to know what you want to do? Look at me: I didn't *plan* the life I'm leading. It just happened. And *I'm* sure happy it worked out that way.' So Penny said: 'Is twenty-eight old or young?' so I Said: 'Well. I'm twenty-eight—so I think it's *young*. I can still do anything. *You* can still do anything. People start careers *much* later than that.' 'Sometimes I think it's very old. Because the way things are, by twenty-eight you *must know what you're doing*. Or rather *you must already be doing it*.' I said: 'That's the wrong way to look at it.' So Penny said: 'Oh I can look at it the other way! Twenty-eight is *very* young—because I have so many years left to be unhappy. A whole life ahead of me to suffer. Poverty and lousy jobs and stupid relationships.' I suppose I got a little impatient, because I said: 'Well, gee, Penny, if we looked at life that way, we'd all go out and commit *suicide*.'"

Ted says: "I'm trying to remember who I met in the bakery

yesterday who made me think—'sometimes a person harbors grudges you know nothing about. You meet someone you haven't seen for a year and you find out he's been hating you for a long time . . . .' "

Rudi says: "She isn't telling you the truth, Pam."

Ted stops carving his boiled beef and Pam lays down her forkful of cabbage.

"Who isn't telling me the truth, Rudi? You guys'v got me confused! Are you talking about someone in the bakery now or what . . . ?"

"This woman Penny is lying to you. She's only telling you the part you want to hear. She *knows* you were a language major and that you're too intelligent for the job you're doing. She knows you only pretend to like it. She might even know you took a stupid, low-paying job just to make Ted feel better about the stupid, low-paying job *he* has. People know things, Pam. She told you a little—and then she saw that it bothered you—that you were dumb enough or just unhappy enough to think you were like her. So she told you a little more. But she *didn't* tell you the part that would have made you realize you were different. She didn't tell you that she had a breakdown while she was in Denver. And that all through the months in the hospital she couldn't do the simplest things. She couldn't even cut out a leather book mark in arts and crafts. She wasn't released from the hospital in Denver. She slipped out and went to Los Angeles. Her mother's been in one mental hospital or another for fifteen years. Penny and her older sister, Gloria, grew up in foster homes. The father's alive, but he's crazy too. Weighs more than I do—mean and sloppy—lives without heat or electricity in a house full of old tires and automotive parts. Penny and Gloria were very close until Gloria got married, had children. Now Penny has no one. Last year she had an abortion and wanted to stay with her sister, but for some reason Gloria was furious about the whole thing and they haven't spoken since. Penny's latest boyfriend is a Howard Johnson's waiter. He's crazy too. The morning she talked to you she dreamed that she and her boyfriend stabbed somebody who looked like her father. Her mother was upset because they got blood on her carpet. So she had to clean it up. She washed the body and scrubbed the rug. Then the father came back to life and was sitting in a chair. The mother was hiding in a closet and her boyfriend got slashed. Then there was something about a body in the grandfather clock—and another part where she and her boyfriend were checking each other in the bathroom. She was putting a bandage on his wound and he was examining her body. He was touching her intimately.

She started to feel aroused and woke up. So, in many ways, Pam, I think Ted has much more in common with Penny than you do. Ted doesn't think so, and nobody else might think so, except his kid sister, Betty, but I think his parents belong in an institution."

Ted says Pam can't be like Penny because Pam has no dream life at all.

Rudi says Ted is wrong, Pam dreams about old age. And she dreams about Granma Rich's grape arbor in Arkansas, just the way he does. Her grape arbor and her money. Pam knows and he knows and Polly may know too how many hundreds of thousands Granma Rich has socked away down there. Thirty, forty, maybe fifty years of usury. One of these days they'll find her with an ax head in her brain pan.

Pam says she just realized how insane it was to make boiled beef at this time of year.

Some time after midnight.

Exactly the same midnight all along the street, or each second just a little bit different with every inch of distance.

The moon, unusually dark and orange, almost red, splits the sky into two distinct sections, one of them a bit bluer than the other, as if composed of fewer and more transparent layers. In that part of the sky something is shining. There something is approaching. Something as enormous and brilliant as daylight is going to show its face.

No one sees the enormous figure standing on the porch of the house with the white frame first story, red frame upper stories, one finger deep in the bell socket. He stands flat against the wall next to the door, as if waiting for someone to make the mistake of coming down to have a look around.

A window opens on the second floor, a withered face with a limp halo of red-in-black or black-in-red curls gazes out attentively at the slowly developing photograph of the street, listens acutely to the thin band of sound along the horizon, one, two, three sharp cries in the foreground. Sees no one; hears nothing or does hear something subaudible, human breathing that might also be wind in hemlock saplings; closes the window and recedes from dark window surface to dark bed. A broad white shirt sails down the street, unseen or seen only by the eyes of children awakened by nightmares.

The rain that's falling at 5 am is so fine it's little more than heavy mist.

The streetlamps haven't gone off yet. And wherever there's a streetlamp the atmosphere looks even bluer than it is.

The streetlamps along the boardwalk that frames the ocean as a repetitive sequence of horizontal vistas are placed with the utmost regularity. Between the broad cones of odd, daylight pink, there are slight, marginal spaces of natural light where one can see that the sun may already have risen in a luminous sky.

A guy in a hemp-colored shirt and dark trousers, who's been sitting on a bench, drinking beer and getting wet, is staggering down the wooden ramp, cradling a brown paper supermarket sack. Seven-hundred-and-twelve steps down from the ramp he passes one of the channels where darkness is running between the houses. Ten empty Budweiser cans make a tremendous clatter on the sidewalk, two full cans roll out of the dark, across the sidewalk, down the shallow driveway grade.

Across the way a white lace curtain behind a closed window is twitching as if the window were open. Someone, agitated, isn't certain if she's seen something odd. Where can the man have disappeared to? She knows for sure that he doesn't live anywhere in that row of two-family, treeless houses, neither modern nor anything else, an absolute architectural dead point whose inhabitants every morning shake off a wierdly pleasing neutrality in order to accomplish the tasks of the day. He always follows a path, as if avoiding invisible obstacles, toward the old-rice-colored apartment building on the boulevard. The impression that he'd been jerked obliquely, slightly upward, like someone launching into a difficult backward dive, is already beginning to break down into more conventional possibilities. She notices that a few tiny, beet-colored leaves and blue flowers have popped up overnight on her lawn. The blue of the tiny flowers absorbs all her attention: the blue of a distant land mass, perhaps the coast of New Jersey, visible across how many surface miles of ocean, with all its deep shadows and superficial whirlpools.

A few twigs of sunlight appear for the first time through a dark, scattered fleet of morning clouds.

A hedge is built up rapidly, yellow as wicker.

A hedge and then hedges.

Along the boardwalk several apartment houses are reconstructing themselves brick by brick out of a moist and gleaming sunlight.

When the sun touches the greenish blinds of a sixth story window sparks pass across 5×10^{23} gaps and the engine of the day starts up.

Sunshine on the waxed wood floor and the bright red rug: the tv set translating cosmic forces into pictures of Buddy Ebson shooting and being shot at in a dark parking garage: the panes white with sunlight. Rudi is sitting on the coral convertible couch, reading last week's *Sunday News* and chuckling while Pam fixes dinner and Ted repairs a lamp cord.

"Did you get a nice letter from your Mom, honey? Did she have anything interesting to say?"

"I haven't opened it yet."

"But you got it on Friday, honey. Aren't you at all curious about what your Mom's life is like in Vegas?"

Ted's answer is inaudible.

"Well, I guess I'll put the spaghetti up."

"Terrific."

"Let Pam read the letter, Ted," Rudi says from the couch without looking up from the paper.

"Oh Teddy! *Could* I? Would it be alright? Can I read the letter while you do that? Oh, Ted, I love you!"

Dear Pam & Ted,

A happy, healthy and prosperous first anniversary. I am fine. I took it very easy this week. Like everybody else, tired and broke. So I took a good rest on Saturday and then again today. Besides, we've had unusually cold weather here. Freezing— every-one down here thinks it's freezing—till today. And when it's windy it does feel a little like New York. Many people are sick. Thank God I'm fine. Enjoyed a walk in the beautiful Nevada sun today—by the orange wall and the tremendous eucalyptus trees. Am now getting my hair done.

Thank you so much for the Hummel music box. The "Merry Widow" Waltz. My favorite song! And when it gets too quiet in the apartment I play it. Though it's always noisy at the club and music, such as it is, constantly. So I really enjoy the peace and quiet of my apartment. I never see the other tenants, 'cept coming and going—and I like it that way and have a lot of privacy. Of course it does get a bit lonely at times, but I find that I'm more than willing to pay that price.

Thank you also for the delicious cake, Pam. It held up real well.

My weekly shopping consists of soap—tissues—coffee—sugar—toothpaste—and that's about it. What a change from the truckloads of previous years!

Had a ball with the girls. But, again, not enough time and I was too over-tired to really enjoy them. Would have liked to have given them more, but I couldn't. I've lost the capacity. Or I never had it but used to *think* I did. There is nothing—*nothing*—left in me to give. And this often feels like happiness.

Hope by now you've received my package and also that Ted's been definitely hired by Eastern. Regards to all.

Love,

Mom

"They do make a pair, don't they?"
"Well, I don't know, Teddy, it kind'v made me miss my Dad and my Mom already . . . ."
"Jesus, don't compare your folks to mine!"
"He's right, Pam," Rudi says from behind the newspaper. "*Your* Dad never tried to have *your* Mom put away."
Ted looks surprised, as if he didn't know Rudi knew that. Or as if he didn't know it himself.
"Your mother may be going the way of her sister, Grace," Rudi says. "After your Aunt Grace left the convent she vanished. And I think your mother is just gradually vanishing right now. You'll get a letter from her this winter or next spring and then you'll never hear from her again."
Pam and Ted exchange glances and Pam changes the subject.
"Hey wasn't my Dad something when he said that about taking the elevated line out to see the *tenements*?"
"He must've made a picture—as pale as he is and what's he up to now, about 270 pounds . . . !"

"People think they know who you are," Rudi says, sunlight falling on him in a way that makes him look like vividly tinted paper mâché. "Families think that they've hatched you and that their traits are your destiny. Two things are locked together, Pam. They're locked together like a pair of hands. And those two locked-together things are what we call Destiny. Do you know what those two things are, Pam?"

"No, I don't, Rudi. I don't know what they are and I don't know what you mean. But I sure don't think Mom and Dad think they *hatched* us . . . ."

"It is *possible* to escape from your destiny, Pam!"

"But why would anyone want to escape from his destiny, Rudi? What's wrong with our destiny?"

"People *assume* they have brothers and they *assume* those brothers come from California. But what if I'm *not* your brother and what if I *don't* come from California."

Rudi is on his feet, talking faster and faster. As far as Pam and Ted can make out he's saying pretty much the same thing, but in new and endless combinations, ten different ways, then fifty, then five hundred. It sounds like another language, or a sub-language, a code, like the crackling flash of particles when the tv loses its transmission. Ted rises to his feet also, his normally pink cheeks dead white, takes a step toward Rudi with nothing particular in mind and stands there uselessly. Pam, trying to control herself, is sobbing in a wierd, smothered way.

The lamp cord is repaired and Ted is switching the lamp on and off with an expression of puzzled satisfaction. Pam is sitting where Rudi was sitting, leafing through the same out-dated *Sunday News*.

"I can't at all figure what set Rudi off," Ted says without looking at Pam.

"Dunno, Teddy" Pam says, a little distracted by a small article about a corpse that was found in their neighborhood a couple of days back, neck broken and ear lobes, several fingers and toes missing.

"Sometimes I think you're just about the only person on the face of the Earth he cares for. He has a very low opinion of people. I mean, I don't think he likes *anyone*."

"Yes, I think you're right. And I don't like it either. I don't like the fact that he tries to make someone so *pure* out of me. Because one day he's going to be sorely disappointed. If he looks at me as the last grain of hope for humanity and then I *fail* him . . . . It kind'v gets to be a burden when people keep telling you how *good* you are, Teddy."

"But you *are* good, Pammy."

Pam isn't listening. She's spotted an article that covers two facing pages with photographs on both. On the left-hand page there's a picture of an enormous man in a dark suit and narrow tie. He has a black wheatfield of hair flattened backward a bit, as if a tractor had just passed over it; eyebrows like drawbridges, one of them raised a little more than the other, letting those on the outside get a tiny glimpse of doubts or worries trying to gnaw their way out through the thick bone of the skull; an ordinary, perhaps smallish bulb nose, the nostrils maybe a drop wider than average; a slack mouth sucked in to look firm; eyes turned diagonally away from the camera or toward the edge of the page. The caption reads: "HEINZY HEINZ, THE PIED PIPER OF BENTON."

On the same page there's a photograph of two men: one, in white shirtsleeves and dark slacks, digging with a shovel in pale, ink-stained ground: the other, in a coarse-grained state trooper's uniform, leather holster and boots, moving off to the left down a shallow grade, his steps following his gaze into the underbrush. The caption reads: "Cop shovels desert sand in search of Jolene Gill, girl friend of killer, Adolph Heinz, the 'Benton Butcher,' whom she had found 'creepy' but 'nice.' "

On the facing page there's a row of three snapshots of women, one 4" x 3", two 3" x 2". The larger photograph shows a woman in a simple white blouse and dark skirt, left fist on left hip. Her dark hair is short yet windblown, windblown yet fixed in a permanent set of wig-like clusters, and her features are square-cut, pugilistic. She's looking out to the left, slightly down, toward a point far beyond the boundaries of the photograph or, perhaps, all possible vistas open to the photographer. The two smaller photos resemble high school yearbook photos of people you never knew or can't remember. The woman in the center photograph has a short hairdo with deep, rigid waves and dark blonde gleaming shadows. Neither pretty nor ugly, mouth wide open in a luckluster smile. Nose a tiny bulb. Dark eyes staring straight at the camera, straight *through* the camera, toward Pam or beyond her toward the next room, a room in a house in Benton, Arizona or beyond the planet's light envelope. The woman on the right-hand side of the page has a narrow face; weak chin; shoulder-length blonde hair, bobbed; eyes resting utterly within their own surface; mouth hammered in under the sum of ten cancelled expressions; forehead as short and fragile as the chin. The caption under the three photographs reads: "Mary English (left), drawn irresistibly by the Pied Piper's pitch, stares down at the spot where once was heard a dying scream. Heinz's first of three victims, Jolene Gill (middle), and Gretchen Lenz, who vanished with her sister, Heidi."

Pam takes in the whole article swiftly, skimming each subsection under its boldface heading:

MEAN AND BEAUTIFUL

TALK TURNS TO MURDER

SHE HEARD A SCREAM

MOTHER TAILS 'HEINZY'

TAKES A BEATING

THREATENS TO TALK

OFF TO CALIFORNIA

SUGGESTS A BURIAL

A DUBIOUS STORY

LOSES HIS COOL

ESCAPE IN RED WIG

But Pam keeps returning to the photograph of Heinz. He looks exactly (with the solitary exception of the black, oddly flattened hair) like Rudi! Could just about be Rudi's double. She doesn't ever remember seeing two people look so much alike, not even Olivia de Havilland in the movie where she plays twin sisters. And she wonders: is it really possible that the man who's been living with them isn't Rudi? Could it be that in Las Vegas or maybe Reno, Tahoe or Gardena, or one of the places Rudi'd travelled to with Donald, possibly Galveston, Dallas, Norfolk or Newport News, or down across the border in Tijuana or up in Alaska, even in Libya or South Africa, this guy Heinz happened to run into Rudi? His exact duplicate. Not a second wasted in surprise. He saw what he had to do and did it. A fool-proof escape. It had to have happened during one of Rudi and Donald's arguments: they'd split up for the millionth time, hadn't rejoined. It really was possible! Rudi could be dead. This could be Heinz!

Ted is saying that he had a conversation with Donald about Rudi. He said: "I really wish Rudi could lose some weight, because he *is* a good-looking person." And Donald said: "Well, he *could* be a good-looking person, if only he'd lose some goddamn weight. I've been trying to get him onto that, Ted, believe me." So *he* said: "It does stand in his way, I think—in the way of having any normal sort of social life." "Yes," Donald said, "it sure as hell is some sort of obstacle. There aren't too many women who're going to be interested in a two-tonner!"

"If it were only just his weight!" Pam hears herself cry out.

Ted begins to read the shopping list from a pink slip of paper, but leaves off in the middle.

"Why is it that grocery shopping always gets me down?" he says.

He doesn't say that it has less to do with grocery shopping than with the darkening light over the roofs and less to do with the darkening light over the roofs than with something he's never been able and never will be able to name.

"No," Ted says, dejected, "it isn't just the weight."

A man is walking, searching for something he'll recognize only when he's found it. He passes through a zone of run-down storefronts, railroad flats, bars and shanties—all those unhappy surfaces that have put down such deep roots into reality. Hours later he passes through a residential zone with its pseudo-chateaux ringed round with layered depths of park-like lawn and hemlock screen. Toward dusk he crosses a scorched green plaza receding toward a pale sky over water and the blue oxidized green of a bridge. As he makes his way toward the ocean he thinks: one's gaze withers in the terrible gaze of the world. And one's soul, exactly like the great balloon of one's shadow, searches for a deeper shadow to hide in.

The moon is full, its enormous, dully glowing face like a face in a highrise window. Currents stream by it. Micro-particles that taken together may = life pass into warm breezes on Earth's beaches, prickling the hair on the heads and forearms of strolling couples. Someone fishing reels up a bright little angle of light. A tiny, dark figure dashes into bright waves; a pale figure into dark waves.

A match flares up, a tiny fire below the horizon.

A little moisture seeps out of the white matchstick paper below the head.

An enormous man is lighting a cigarette from a pack he doesn't remember buying.

One puff to make sure the tobacco has taken the flame.

He can feel, through his fingertips, that something is boring into itself, away from the dark cone of ash, toward his lips and mouth. It wants to get inside him, where it can tunnel toward the dark green lake of the trees along the avenues; beyond the avenues; beyond the long meadows and miniature evergreeen forests of the national park; toward a black, orbiting zone that knows nothing of the pleasant surface of things, of friendship or happiness.

The dark, evergreen lights of a ship on the horizon seem to him the green of a green glass ashtray with a round bowl and notches at the four corners, a beautiful leaf green that casts green facets on the polished wood of a table. He wonders if it's possible to reach out and stamp his cigarette out in it.

Someone lights a cigarette not twenty feet away. A woman's blonde curls show up in the flare of the match: fiftyish with a pug nose, short bulldog jaw. He feels drawn to her, as if she were pulling at his flame through her cigarette. He feels his hips and shoulders, arms and ankles twine with hers, faces close and talking, sharing the cigarette of happiness rather than the far more popular cigarette of unhappiness. His shadow flies toward her and is completely surprised to find that it can't get through. It smashes up against her, quivers and sticks there, like a dart in a dartboard.

As if the sound of someone pounding in a nail can be heard in a room seven blocks away.

Or as if the phone is ringing and someone is desparately trying to get in touch.

You wake up, feeling parted forever from a world of the utmost intimacy, from an urgency of feeling you never know in waking life—an unspeakable depth of anguish, of humiliation or love. As if, having actually succeeded in travelling beyond death, your arms around a loved one, a blue crystal drifting swiftly among crystals, along a dark, curved track beyond the barrier of all inward-travelling forces, something draws it all away as easily as the cotton sheet that covers you in summer, exposing you to ordinary morning light.

Ted remembers dreaming that the telephone gave one short burst and that he found himself standing in his bathrobe, holding the receiver before the noise had travelled beyond the fringe of the red oval rug. Now he's awake and holding the receiver. Someone at the other end is talking so rapidly, in arpeggios, that he reaches the other end of his keyboard and begins to flurry backward. Ted's voice is nothing but glue. The two men talk for several minutes without understanding a word.

After a while the man at the other end gets his voice straightened out and Ted realizes it's Rudi. Rudi says that he just woke up in this hotel and both his arms are numb. He thinks that he fell asleep and dreamed that he was dreaming. In one of those dreamed dreams he turned over and slept on his hands. He *never* sleeps on his hands. What happened last night to make him sleep on his hands!

He goes off into another row of arpeggios and Ted tells him not to move till he gets there.

The door of the hotel is the burglar-resistant kind, with a wire lattice embedded in the glass and a heavy steel frame. The stairs leading to the upper stories are covered with a brilliant runner of vermillion and orange diamonds. At the first landing there's an alcove, but no desk clerk, no desk with numbered pigeonholes and keys or any other interior map or blueprint. A red-and-black bookkeeper's ledger is lying open on an old, green felt-surfaced card table. Ted leafs through it: nothing but figures that might be the hotel's accounts, a gambler's private code or rough computations for building a flying saucer like the one sighted in the summer of 1983 over the police station in Carmel, New York.

He sets off down the narrow corridor, tapping at one door, then another. A rather deep woman's voice answers from the first. No one answers from the second. The third door (the three doors are so close together they form a cluster) is wide open. The room seems unoccupied: a stained and pitted green-brown-light green-cocoa-striped mattress mounted on a dark set of springs on short, bowed legs; a wash basin; white kitchen chair. The machinery of this region is so powerful and efficient, a gasless engine of misery powered by the fall-out of absolutely everything, that a glance into it makes Ted feel suddenly downcast, hopeless. The carpet is a dark, dry stain that runs from one end of things to the other. The grey walls may once have been the pleasant, pale blue of blue clouds that are more like blue markings in a blue sky than discrete objects. "Life really has only one principle," Ted thinks unhappily. "Or it has a lot of principles, but they all run down the same drain . . . ." He's arrived at another sequence of doors. Three on the left, two on the right. Voices are coming from somewhere within this constellation. He hears a little water running in a sink, a woman's voice, hoarse from cigarette smoking, a man's voice, somewhere between Rudi's timbre and shading and Laird Cregar's in *I Wake Up Screaming*.

The man says something like "I'm trying to think about my mother."

"What for?"

"Because I can't remember her. It wasn't that long ago—but all I can see is a woman with a blonde wig."

"Is that all?"

"She's about your height."

"No kidding . . . ."

"Really!"

A little low laughter.

"Do you have many friends?"

"No."

"Nobody?"

"I have a friend, Edward."

"Yes . . .?"

"Yes. When I'm with Edward . . . then everything's alright. I feel ok. With Edward everything's ok. There's something about Edward that makes me feel good."

"What is it about Edward that makes you feel good?"

"I don't know."

"What's he like?"

"There's something about him."

"But you can't put your finger on it."

"How did you know? That's it. I never thought of it, but it's true. There's something about him, something that's *not like me*. It makes me feel ok, but I can't put my finger on it . . . ."

"Would you like to be like Edward?"

"Like Edward?"

"You admire him. Edward is sure of himself. He's smooth with people. He has fun. And you'd like to be that way too. Is that it?"

"No, that's not it," the man says, his voice altering in an ambiguous but important way. "Edward is as bad as I am. And he's stupider. So I don't think I want to be like him. We're *all* ill. Do I mean 'ill'? All our faculties are asleep. We talk about 'health' the way we talk about life on another planet. Do you understand what I'm saying?"

"No, honey, I don't."

"Good. There are things I don't want anybody to understand. I want to talk about them, but I don't want anybody to understand them. There are things . . . ."

"There are things you didn't tell those stupid detectives. I knew it!"

"You know me, Rita. Better than anyone does."

"But I hardly know you at all . . . !"

"Am I the type who takes walks? Do I stroll on the boardwalk on a summer evening? Do I go down to the shore to stare at sunsets?"

"God forbid!" the woman laughs.

"But I remember *being* there. I remember *doing* those things!"

"Sometimes a feeling is so strong you think it's a memory. Like a dream you've had so often . . . ."

The man says that on the boardwalk or on the beach at night, not long after sunset, when you're still able to feel darkness as something tangible, as something odd, an extraordinary state, the ordinary human mortal is amazed by the number of lights passing through the air. Some of them are ships, floating in the opening that's visible between two horizons. But the roaring and trembling overhead remind him that he's close to a major airport. Planes take off and approach every couple of minutes, or even less. He sees them pass overhead at different heights and angles—looking very distant and abstract—the usual arrays of red and green lights—or low and menacing, dark as submarines. Some of the lights hovering over the ocean, yellow and round—larger, more globe-like and orange the longer they hover—are simply planes in holding patterns. Sometimes there's a small light, red or deep blue, flattened and twinkling, that moves in a swift, erratic way. Some of these lights seem to vanish backward or upward; they zip away without reappearing somewhere along the loop of a turn.

After the normal human mortal has stood there for a while, watching things appear and depart, he's pierced by an odd sort of unhappiness. He thinks: this is the modern sky. He really is witnessing the appearance of the modern world. This is actually the way it looks when it looks modern but isn't *trying* to look modern. And he knows for certain how limited, how trapped he is—exactly like people in another century who weren't able to get far beyond their valley, with its handful of dull but pretty towns.

Before long there'll be a completely different modern sky. But you won't see it. That much is certain. You long to see an object—what we call "an unidentified flying object"—something that sails right through the limits of the modern sky. You feel that you can't live another second in the normal way. The only thing that can cure you is to get on a rocket, travel twenty-five light years to a region where the idea of the future doesn't resemble Fort Worth. But nothing appears. You don't travel to another planet and the feeling passes off. If not one other thing is learned in life, every idiot seems to learn this: that there's no event, no matter how much dread it causes beforehand or how much anguish afterward, that doesn't fade into the rest. The disappearance of events, emotions and memories is so regular and predictable, so precise, we ought to be able to work out a formula for it. The familiar feeling of "letdown" is the body's feeble yearning to remember. Exactly what's supposed to console us, is what makes life terrible . . . .

"Jesus, honey, whad'ya mean by 'an ordinary human mortal'? You make it sound like there's something else."

"In Manhattan right now, Rita, the atmosphere is the color of aluminum. You wouldn't be surprised to see waves breaking against the middle levels of the high-rises. There's a woman in a white high-rise standing at her picture window, where there's an almost level glimpse of the river, thinking that the visible moat of space that usually separates us from things looks filled in. You couldn't slip one hand between the outer skin of the building and the world beyond. The air has the weight of sea water. It reminds her of the week she spent in Puerto Rico, when there was a shark attack at a resort further along the coast and people just stood on the beach, afraid to go in—the sky and the water such a horrible, tinny color you not only sensed them cruising and waiting out there, but you knew that their world lay so flat against yours that one of them might slide right up to you, at eye level, and grab you right off the beach . . . ."

"Would you like to go down now and get some breakfast . . . ?"

"There's something else . . . ."

"Won't it keep?"

"I have the feeling I've done something horrible, unforgivable. They're going to punish me for it! The punishment was ready and waiting before I did it . . . !"

"You can hide. I can hide you. There's this place up near the Connecticut-New York-Massachusetts border on the way to Mt. Washington, you can't really call it a hotel . . . ."

"There used to be a way of getting out. But I've forgotten it. It used to be my own language, but now it's foreign. You choose something and then you're trapped in it . . . ."

"We can talk about it in the diner, baby. It'll be better down there with the fake flowers and the brass sconces. Nobody goes wierd in the diner."

"I love when you call me baby."

"Baby, baby . . . ."

A little throaty laughter.

"You know, you're a lot like Edward."

"Me? I'm like Edward . . . ?"

Very loud sound of chairs moving.

Ted hurries back down the corridor and out of the hotel as silently and as quickly as he can.

He crosses the street and conceals himself in the shallow doorway of the real estate office between the bakery and the discount store.

He waits ten minutes or more, but no one comes out.

He isn't at all sure if it was Rudi. Isn't sure it *wasn't* Rudi either. The guy talked about "Edward." "Ted" is a diminutive of "Edward." But no one has ever called Ted Edward. Also: if it were Rudi, he'd be talking about Donald Green. Rudi and Donald: that would be possible. Ted has had thoughts about *those* two. But for Rudi to talk that way about him would mean that Rudi had become close to him in some wierd way without his knowing it! That for Rudi he was another Ted. And if he *was* another Ted for Rudi, then Rudi might have named that Ted "Edward."

Ted doesn't know what to do. He could go back in, go back up, and knock at that door. Settle things swiftly, directly. Like turning, after fleeing through corridors, mounting stairways, hiding in cellars, to confront the madman who's stalking you with a Chinese cleaver. But knocking at that door is just one thing he can't face. He feels that it would be more possible to stand in the doorway of the real estate office all day, as immobile as someone who's had a stroke, wheeled this way and that under a golf cap, unable to turn your head, than to go back in and knock at that door.

What he'd really like to do is find a telephone, call Pam and ask *her* what to do. "Should I go back to the hotel? Go home? Look for Rudi in all the groceries and luncheonettes? Or what?"

But he can't do that either. If he calls Pam he has to tell her that her brother's out here, wandering around somewhere or sitting in a room on the second floor of a hotel, completely lost and thinking he's someone else.

The squat angles of an enormous pair of dusky blue trousers appear through the heavy burglar-proof door of the hotel, filling up its wire diamonds and blotting out the orange and vermillion runner.
The man stops on the pavement to clean his glasses. The world looks like a tremendous glass doorknob. Even with his glasses back in place, every direction looks like a facet of every other direction; every destination as far away as the enormous bank of early morning clouds that hasn't yet been drawn off below the horizon. Might as well set off toward those dark mountains as toward anywhere else.
Familiar dark range of mountains where once there may have been an ocean, its blues and blacks darker and more tarnished than the hulls of freighters.
Familiar ocean where there once were mountains and will be mountains again.
The low, uneven line of the roofs above the dismal shop windows, the pizza joints and luncheonettes. The sidewalk with its grey, permanent stains and sour black puddles below the curb. The world is sailing through this dreary station without making a stop.

Minutes later the bottom of outer space begins to sift particles dryer than rain and moister than smoke on everything in sight.

Ted props himself up in bed. He smells coffee perking, the complex aromas of singed toast and browned butter. Rudi is snoring behind the wall, asleep and dreaming in the blue nursery, sending off the usual thermal, bioelectric and chemical outlines, like a wide-screen color television someone's forgotten to turn off.
He hears sobbing in the living room or kitchen, stumbles to the door in his dark bathrobe. Pam is sitting in a chair by the dinette table whose roundness forces a round sense of space on the zone by the kitchen, her head so far down it looks like she's throwing up. The radio is on, tuned to a twenty-four-hour station.
Pam says that a report just came over the radio that the body of Marian Lamb, the downstairs tenant, was washed up last night off the Point, her neck broken, her ear lobes and several fingers and toes missing, just like that other poor man they'd found near here a few

weeks ago.

She looks up and meets Ted's glance.

"Don't say it!" she screams. "It isn't true! It *can't* be true! I won't listen to it!"

"But I'm not saying anything, honey," he murmurs.

Ted's little sister, Betty, is sitting between Ted and Rudi on the red couch. They're all watching a situation comedy on television. Betty is laughing, Ted is half-smiling and Rudi is reading *TV Guide* as if it were *Scientific American*.

Rudi says that there's a Lionel Atwill film already on on another channel. He cantilevers forward to turn the dial.

Betty, pouting, wants to know who "Lionel Atwill" is.

"You've seen him a million times, Betty," Rudi says. "But you don't know him. He's *invisible* to you. Everything is invisible to you. Is it because you only see what you want to see? I don't think so. I don't think you even see what you *want* to see. And you don't see what's there to see either. You don't see the surface and you don't see what's hidden. So what *do* you see, Betty? You're still not *completely* stupid because you're young. But it gets worse as you get older. Your brain gets smaller and smaller. By the time you're your brother's age it'll be the size of an orange pit."

Betty has tears in her eyes. But Ted doesn't intervene.

Rudi turns toward the televison, sitting on the edge of the couch as if he can't get close enough to the screen.

Lionel Atwill is standing next to a corpse covered with a sheet and saying: "This is death by strangulation, gentle-men. And strangulation by an *unusually* powerful set of hands. Note the deep impression of the *thumb* marks on the *throat* . . . ." Someone else, a policeman or a reporter, says: "But what about this deep incision at the base of the brain, doctor?" "Yes," Atwill answers, "undoubtedly inflicted by a surgical scal-pel."

A little later Atwill is explaining the possible character type of the killer: "Undoubtedly a neurotic. Someone with a deep pattern of activity held in a *knot*—a sort of knot in the *brain*. And anything can trigger off the need to commit this act *again* and *again*. To return to the original moment. *Anything*. The full moon—the sound of the ocean—and so on." "But why this *incision*, doctor?" "That is not merely an *incision*. This is clearly a case of *cannibalism*, gentle-men."

Later there's a headline that says SCRUBWOMAN IS MOON KILLER'S LATEST VICTIM. The police are convinced that the murderer is a member of the Academy. Atwill begs them to give him one last chance to clear the mystery up himself. He gathers all the Academy members in his laboratory in Cliff Manor on Blackstone Shoals, Long Island, administers a sort of lie detector test. Everyone (including Atwill himself) is strapped into a chair fitted out with dozens of meters, coils, electronic monitors. The camera pans across the row of strapped-in doctors. Dr. Wells, who did the treatise on cannibalism and who's missing one hand. Old Dr. Haines, the one who's kept a heart alive electrically for months and who secretly reads a magazine called *French Thrills*. And the two doctors (one in a wheelchair, one with something odd about his hands) who survived the shipwreck and the days of starvation in the lifeboat, while their companions perished or disappeared. When all the equipment is glowing and buzzing Atwill says: "Naturally I would prefer to believe that all members of the Academy are *innocent*. But, unfortunately, circumstances—the use of a surgical scal-pel used *only* by this institution, for example—prove that *one* of us may be *guilty*. *Any* one of us. Someone in this room may be a murderer. A man who *kills* by the light of a full moon with a surgical *in-stru-ment*. And who leaves his victims horribly *mutilated*. It is my *theory* that the murderer is someone who through *dire necessity* was compelled to resort to cannibalism. And that instant was *hammered into his brain* like a *nail*. Clever and brilliant, he is able to *conceal* his thoughts from his colleagues. *But not from this radiograph*." The radiograph switch is thrown, the laboratory goes black, spasms of light pulse in panels and coils, someone screams as if stabbed, everyone cries out, struggles against the thongs binding him to his chair. The scene shifts to another room. Someone with one hand like an animal's claw is smearing gobs of greyish, flesh-like jelly on his face and muttering, "SYNTHETIC FLESH! SYNTHETIC FLESH!"

Betty screams.

"SYNTHETIC FLESH!" Rudi screams, his voice perfectly synchronized with the madman's. "Exactly the same as raw living flesh eaten by cannibals! SYNTHETIC FLESH!"

Betty dashes to the door and Rudi follows her. Ted continues to watch television.

The old brass floor lamp with its enormous shade casts a broad circle of light on the floor-boards surrounding the red oval rug. The disc of silence that surrounds it within a vast perimeter of tiny sounds is disturbing.

Ted picks up the double highball glass that's gleaming, half clear, half amber, on the coffee table, drains half its contents, and sits shivering in the big armchair.

By the time he sets the wide glass with its extra bottom weight down on the table's glass surface, Ted is empty and exhausted while the glass is 1/8 full of dark amber thoughts.

"No refuge—no sanctuary. Is it true that without love there's no sanctuary on earth—nothing . . .? Totally alone and adrift—

"A corpse is already in you. Travelling with you. Always horizontal—

"So that when you lie down there's a fatal harmony—

"All your life you feel this anxiety—this tug of the horizontal—

"At night you leap up so suddenly your weight can still be felt on the bed—more or less at the moment two hands of the clock are about to coincide—

"You died *before* you were alive—

"Slowly life struggles to assert itself—

"Dies out before a good blaze can get started—"

Ted is draining the surprisingly heavy glass of its last thoughts when Betty bursts into the room screaming his name and crying.

"What is it, honey?" Ted says without moving.

It looks as if she's about to fall on him, he realizes she wants to be embraced and embraces her.

"It's Rudi! It's Rudi! Oh Ted! It's *Rudi!*"

"Rudi?" he says dumbly.

Betty has him clasped close and is sobbing into his shirt.

"You didn' *see* him! You didn' see what he *looked* like . . . ! DON'T LET HIM IN! DON'T LET HIM IN! HE'S COMING . . . !"

Only her throat is holding her voice together. It's a quiver of trills.

"Hey, it's only good old Rudi, Betty. It's only *make*-believe."

Betty, letting go, is looking aghast at the door.

Ted actually thinks he hears a board creak in the hall, but tells Betty that he doesn't hear a thing.

He strokes Betty's hair indifferently and Betty gradually calms down.

Time is passing in any number of ways. The television, switched off (or, rather, *not* switched on) seems to have a perpetual, fluid calender of instants locked inside. So that it's possible to think: if no one ever watches television again, Time will be cancelled. The room is almost dark. The floor lamp is switched off and the small table lamp emits a glow more like a candle than anything else. A level, simultaneous plane of time extends endlessly from this weak oval.

Ted is sitting over in one corner of the long red couch, doing nothing, near dozing, like someone staring into a fire. Betty is taking up the rest of the couch with her long, smooth legs, dark blue shorts of soft cotton, pale blue polo, slender arms holding a *National Geographic*.

A while later Betty has turned over onto her stomach. She's asleep, her left hand and the yellow cover of the magazine within the weak oval of light intersecting with the red oval of the rug. Ted falls asleep and dreams that he's having a fight with Pam. He goes up to his room (in the dream he lives in a house with two or three stories, just as he did in childhood). He tries one lamp, then another, all the while longing to sit quietly in the dark, to be like a monk who's taken a vow of darkness. The lamps blink on and off several times and then go dead, as if he's willed it. A woman comes in, calling out a name that he recognizes, though it isn't his name or the name of anyone he knows. It's the name of *something*. What is that something? He can't name it.

At first the woman sees no one, though she's left the door open and a sort of twilight washes through the heavier particles of darkness. She catches sight of him sitting there, barely visible within a high-backed chair, and she's frightened. They both turn in terror. The murderer's come through the door. His hair stands out against the light.

Ted wakes up, his heart racing. There isn't a sound in the apartment, perhaps not in the house. It's so silent that Betty's sleeping isn't enough to cause it. Rudi must be sleeping too. Voices in the street, down on the sidewalk, are like the voices you make out on shore when you're about to row out of sight. He crosses to the window, leans out to see if it's Pam. His face and yellow/brown curls are tinted the same wierd amber-coral that's tinting the yellow stucco walls of the three-tier hacienda-style house diagonally across the way. But it isn't Pam. It's the tall musician who lives next door and his tall musician friend, who's married to the musician's sister, attaching a U-Haul trailer to his old

Buick.

The rest of the night is spent worrying about Pam, dozing, imagining he hears Pam arriving, looking at the tv or out the window.

About one a.m. people are actually coming up the stairs. Now that they *are* arriving, he can tell that a real arrival sounds different in every way from all those false alarms. A real arrival has an unmistakable texture and weight. It has definite early signals and then gathers force and mass. It doesn't begin with a murmur of neutral voices you don't quite recognize and the rattle of a heavy chain against a fender. It *does* begin with a front door closing, laughter you'd recognize after five deaths and six lifetimes, overlapping heavy treads on carpeted stairs, an enveloping breath of the out-of-doors you can feel welling up from a distance.

Pam comes in with Donald. Her eyes are glowing, cheeks flushed. Ted feels an idiotic yearning, as if they've just met. He thinks to himself that Pam hasn't looked this good since before they were married, when she had a high-level job with Hydra Chemical.

"Where's Frankenstein?" Donald asks.

"Asleep, most likely," Ted says tonelessly. He's so taken by the way Pam looks that he's depressed by it.

Pam says that Rudi *can't* be sleeping, cause she looked into his room on the way in and he wasn't there. Bed was still made.

Ted says that Rudi *did* pull some pretty wierd stunts tonight. Scared poor Betty half out of her skull.

"What *kind'v* wierd stunts, Teddy?"

"Pretty wierd, that's all."

There's an odd silence, one with a furry edge, like a torn blotter.

Ted starts to say: "I didn't know you guys were going out together tonight," but Pam interrupts him.

"Donny's leaving for Alaska tonight. And I'm going with him."

Ted says that he has to drive Betty home.

"Jesus, Ted," Donald says. "I feel lousy as hell about this. I didn't wanna come up here at all. But, if you'll stop and think about it, Pam and I go back *way* before . . . ."

Ted is already carrying little Betty down the stairs.

Donald follows Ted to the head of the stairs.

"Be a little *honest* with yourself, Ted!" he yells down the stairwell, though Ted may already be out the front door. "You're a fuckn *seed* pod, Ted! You belong with *Rudi*, Ted!"

Several weeks later, in a street in the same neighborhood or one exactly like it, an unusually thin woman is standing in front of her house, in warm sunlight, hosing down her black Newfoundland. Her younger daughter Rosamond is watching how the spray carries over to the spruce next door. The young needles are green and shining while the rest of the tree looks as if it has a web over it and inside, under the boughs, it's as black as a cave.

An enormous man who's passing, in clothing that's stained green and brown, as if he's been sleeping on lawns, under hedges, or in back gardens or in a park somewhere, stops and says: "A pine *tree* is exactly like a pine *cone*. But what is a pine *cone* exactly like?"

The woman has the dog soaked and mother and daughter begin to scrub him into a lather.

"You have a second self," the man continues, "and you feel it slipping away. Tears of jealousy come to your eyes when you see your ex-husband's face on the cover of *TV Guide*."

He's examining her closely, as if this sign or that will make him do one thing or another.

"I've been watching you and your children. I've been watching your children grow. I've seen everything that's happened. And I just want to tell you that I don't like your daughter, Johanna!"

"Johanna?" the woman answers stupidly. She's panic-stricken because the man knows her elder daughter's name.

"I don't like her dreams. When she wakes up screaming in the middle of the night and you can't quiet her down, when she sobs uncontrollably, for one hour or two, I know she's dreaming of me. And I don't like it!"

The younger daughter, Rosamond, is crying and pulling at her mother's slacks. The mother's gone dead white, her arm around her daughter. The black Newfoundland is barking and dripping soap suds, taking nervous steps forward and back. It gathers its courage, finds leverage, bounds, accelerates, detonates into the man's chest, jaws swivelled toward the throat. The man staggers and bends under the impact, his eyes and the dog's eyes no more than a foot apart. His arms are deep in fur, as if it were a sinkful of water. The forearms are covered with slobber and blood. The dog's choked snarls turn into screams. Something pops in the structure of the dog's thick neck and its body drops to the rounded slope of the lawn, not quite in the long shadow of a neighbor's spruce.

The man's enormous stained white shirt and dark slacks fly into the gap between two houses before the woman is able to utter a sound.

Ted's little sister, Betty, is at home, in her room, lying on her bed, unable to do her homework. Her head is a leather helmet of stupidity that will eventually become as familiar and comfortable as a regular head. She observes that the shiny red material of the bedspread has here and there, regularly or randomly, a coarse, raised thread in it. She gets tired of lying there and figuring out the bedspread as if it were a problem in solid geometry, goes to her vanity and begins brushing her short curls with harsh strokes. Her scalp burns as if it were about to bleed.

She turns. Someone is outside her door, breathing, listening. A board creaks slowly, as if weight is being gradually released, shifted from one leg to the other. The sensation continues then dissipates. There are no sounds in the hall or on the stairs and no door can be heard opening or closing.

Betty goes to the window. Her glance flies without hesitation toward a point in the distance, where it seems to her she sees Rudi, standing, as if waiting for a bus, under the trees at the intersection.

Below the porches of nine frame houses, a powerful wind is blowing through evergreen shrubs. Someone standing in the triple shadow of a fir or hemlock (precisely the height of the three-tier house it measures) imagines he's standing in an evergreen forest, a sort of black thistle. A whole mountain, a massive cone of wooded slopes, revolves through the universe at 360° per second. He thinks to himself: from the slopes the monster descends on mountain hamlets—children vanish, bodies are dismembered, local crackpots falsely convicted of murder. Down through the ages men have become beasts: the snarling and drooling of nightmares a nocturnal way of life.

Ted hasn't gone to work for weeks. He hasn't gone grocery shopping, hasn't left the apartment, hasn't shaved or bathed. He's been watching television eighteen hours a day and eating whatever food was in the refrigerator when Pam left and everything that can be eaten straight from the can or heated. It's 11 p.m. and he's eating from a tin of Campbell's Barbecue Style Pork & Beans while he watches the news gliding up against the inner surface of the screen. The story comes over of the capture in northwestern Connecticut of an escaped murderer, the famous "Benton Butcher." The man's already confessed to the murders, either alone or with the participation of a man he refuses to name, of two hundred women and children in states along the Northeastern Seaboard, in the Southwest and in the Far West.

A quick glimpse of a tremendous man with red hair being hurried up the steps of a courthouse.

The red hair is obviously a disguise: a hasty dye job or even a wig.

Ted goes to the phone, gets the number of the police in the town named in the news report and calls.

"The guy you pulled in" he says, "the big guy with the red hair who confessed to all those murders, is *not* the one you think he is! He is *not* some guy from Arizona! This guy you've got up there is my brother-in-law who disappeared three weeks ago! He's just a dead ringer for the other guy, that's all. Who am *I*? Whad'ya mean who am I? What difference does it make who *I* am?"

He lowers the receiver from his ear, stares at it without replacing it in the cradle. He looks out the window, straight ahead over the tiled or shingled, flat or peaked roofs, then to the left, toward the ocean. The sky is unusually light and the atmosphere is perfectly clear and calm. Nothing is closed. Every window is open. He feels that he can see through the pale row of apartment buildings, all the way to the west, where the full length of the New Jersey coast is visible. A dark, unstable blue, an internally burning cobalt, impossible to remember five seconds after you look away. It breaks down instantly into more luminous ideas of blue, darker memories.

One light grows larger and more brilliant as the atmosphere darkens. Smaller and dimmer lights appear far to the right, near the point where the dark blue line of the Jersey coast and the pale, curved line of New York's sand beaches converge. Here and there, to the left, one sees a small cluster above the horizon, rising and dipping as if afloat on the water.

Everything helps darkness arrive.

A hand is stroking a child's head, slipping in between its sobs and delivering it to a calm and friendly world

Or a hand does *not* slip in, does *not* stroke the child's head—the infant simply lies there, exhausted from sobbing, feeling delivered to a world of dark rooms and windows.

TOP STORIES

A PROSE PERIODICAL

#1	Donna Wyszomierski
#2	Laurie Anderson
#3	Pati Hill
#4	Suzanne Johnson
#5	Linda Neaman
#6	Gail Vachon
#7	Jenny Holzer/Peter Nadin
#8	Judith Doyle
#9	Kathy Acker
#10	Lynne Tillman/Jane Dickson
#11	Kirsten Thorup
#12	Janet Stein
#13	Anne Turyn
#14	Lee Eiferman
#15	Constance DeJong
#16	Ursule Molinaro
#17	Romaine Perin
#18	Donna Wyszomierski
#19-20	Cookie Mueller

Available from
TOP STORIES
228 Seventh Avenue
New York, N.Y. 10011

ISBN 0-917061-21-7

TOP STORIES   #22 $3.00

THE COLORIST

Susan Daitch

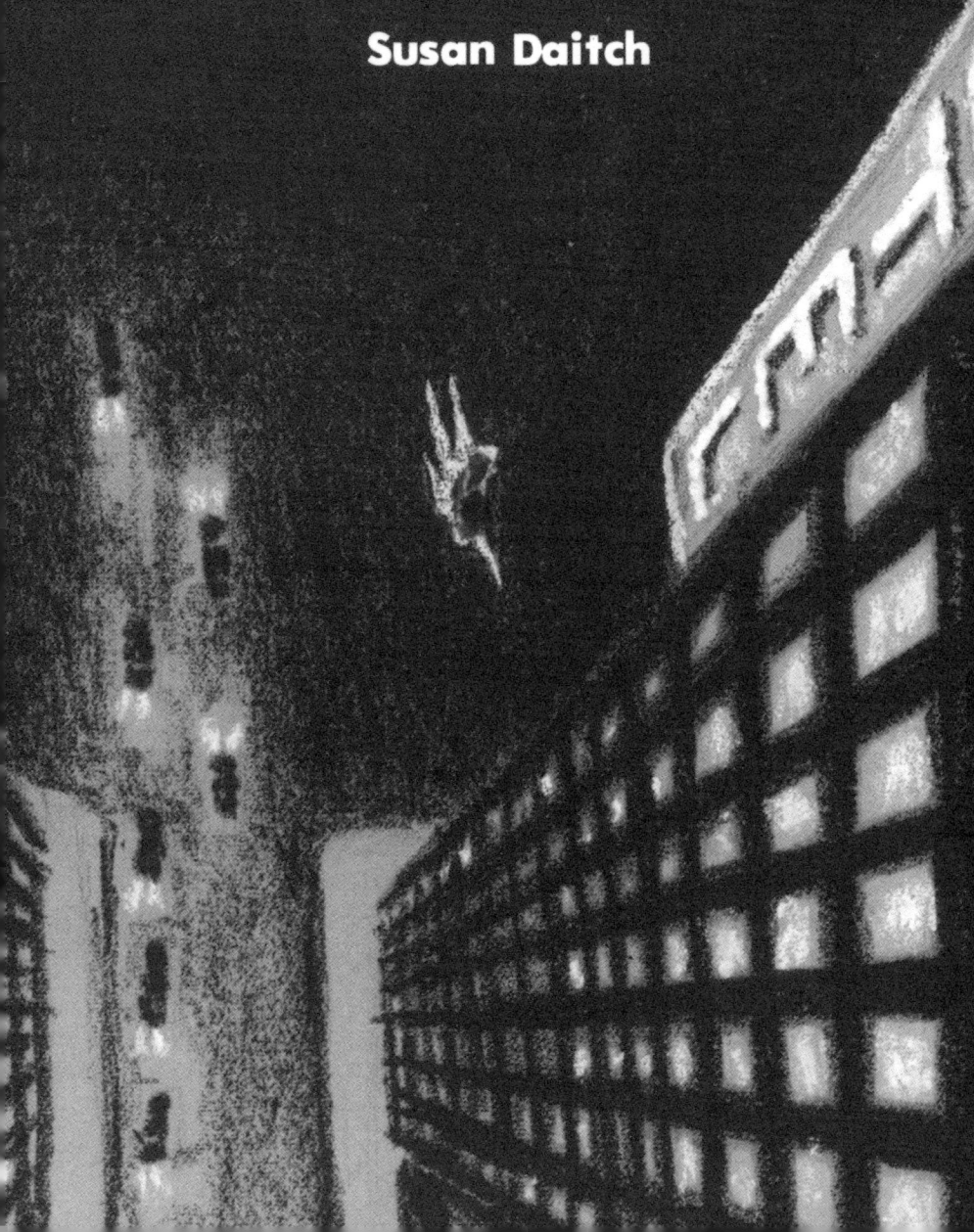

THE COLORIST
by Susan Daitch

Copyright ©1985 by Susan Daitch

Cover drawing ©1985 by Jane Dickson

The author would like to thank artist Charles Long for the use of the cinema hat.

This publication has been made possible in part with public funds from the National Endowment for the Arts and the New York State Council on the Arts.

ISBN 0-917061-22-5 (Top Stories #22)

TOP STORIES, 228 Seventh Avenue, N.Y.C., N.Y. 10011

There's a mural on the wall behind the bar, "Civilization Teeters," dogs chasing half naked women, columns tumbling. You don't know what kind of teetering is being discussed on the part of civilization: falling or laughing. Sometimes when I walk into these places I feel invisible. They have their conversations, their arrangements to make. Everyone is very intent, but it's a veiled kind of intention, at any moment intention could fly apart, go to the dogs. Urgent and under control, like they're applying for a top job at NASA and it's all very secret. I imagine part of the job application means being under surveillance. When you think no one is checking your behavior, they are. Behind closed circuits everyone is being watched, assessed by NASA. All of them except me. I'm not in the running, not being watched. NASA isn't interested in Julie Greene. I'm invisible.

Walking home, past the black queen, the one in a blue dress, spiral sequins trailing behind, old white prostitutes in cracked plastic skirts, buyers and sellers mixed together, young men with no hair and black-ringed eyes sitting on stoops baiting everyone who walks by, shadow men painted on the sides of all kinds of buildings, someone painted a smiley face on one, a dick with a face at its end on another, Rastas with their hair stuffed into knitted balloons, red, green and black.

A friend of mine made a sculpture called a cinema hat. It's a box-shaped object you put on your head. The inside of the box looks like a small movie theatre. Your eyes are where the projector is. In front of your face are small seats and where the screen would be is open so whatever you see in the room, in the street, that's the movie. Your life as it happens, that's the film. You are the leading actor and the audience at the same time. This method puts random events, especially unpleasant ones in a dramatic context. You run into a skeleton from your closet at large (Everyone has these. Sometimes you get lucky and have two or three.), you see a man dressed like Cardinal Richelieu or another like a rag-tag Sheriff of Nottingham throwing imaginary arrows at everyone on Seventh Street and it's all part of the script, the story.

Sometimes he would leave his paintings out, hung from his second story window sill as he painted until early in the morning. Little slips of paper fluttered in the bits of wind: $15.00 for a cardinal, $20.00 for an island with palm trees. Self-portraits were usually around $10.00, a painting of his granddaughter's little dog was $5.00. The pictures were flat wet oil paintings. A sign which read "Free Puerto Rico" in Spanish was painted on a map, had no price tag, and he never took it in. He drew blue columns on the inside of one of his rooms, the one which faced the street. Each had a different capital, some overlapped onto the ceiling. He was not my super and rarely smiled or said hello but he would tell me if someone had been looking for me or Eamonn. He drank beer, painted late at night with little illumination except what came in from the street, and sang when he became drunk. His granddaughter told the woman downstairs that he beat her. She was very thin and never seemed to grow any taller.

When Eamonn told me not to take so seriously the latescent images of my bad dreams, he made a dumb mistake, but I learned: Never demand a leap of faith from a man who sees himself as a professional fly in the ointment. Dreams: a random helter-skelter tipping a hat to the hieroglyphics of my childhood. In these Eamonn saw only signs of mental anarchy. He wore a torn sweater as if it were a relic from the 1916 Easter Rising and he'd just been dragged from the Dublin Post Office, riddled by British bullets. I have a couple of torn shirts but I can't pretend they're anything.

There was a ghost in the apartment. In the day, in her conscious thinking, not at night, not part of her dreams. He had made himself at home, disturbed no object, made no noise.

Julie's friend, Eamonn, with whom she lived, never noticed the ghost. To him the ghost was invisible, even when Julie was sure Eamonn must notice she could think of little else, the ghost was never spoken of between them.

Eamonn Archer left Ireland when he was 12 or 13. The story was different each time. Exiles or expatriots, sometimes he called his family one, sometimes the other. There were no jobs and his father had died. They might have stayed. They weren't starving or on the run from the Ulster constablulary, British soldiers had not yet arrived, but his mother had gotten work with Aer Lingus in Galway. The job finally brought them to New York. Eamonn's accent was fragile, a casualty of fifteen years here. There was barely a trace of it left. Just when he said certain words: London, Shankill, terror. In the neighborhood bodegas, he spoke Spanish quickly, as if he'd lived in a country where Spanish was spoken, but no, he told Julie. There were no hidden portraits of hidalgos in his grandmother's house in Londonderry.

Julie moved in with Eamonn after she was attacked in the hall of her building on East Ninth Street. She remembered the boy was tall, had a filed down screwdriver, took her up to the roof. All she had was $10. He knocked her to the floor. It was then she understood those moments in *Frenzy*. "You're my kind of girl, Babs." He took off his tie and the camera withdrew down the street, backed off, the sound of traffic grew louder. Hitchcock said the audience would subconsciously think, "Well, if the girl screams, no one is going to hear her. A murder is happening, a man buys a newspaper, life in London goes on and in New York, too." Murder or potential murder goes unnoticed, like someone shouting in a language no one within earshot understands or has any inclination to pay attention to.

In history books, medieval cities are often described as if all daily activities neatly dovetail, a self-contained enterprise: markets, water systems, collection of tithes, one religion (nearly), the distribution of justice, and all the lunatics were placed on ships of fools and set adrift. In reading of early cities, so conceptually grid-like in places where you knew streets made no sense, Julie imagined them harmonious. People were diligent, delinquency rare. History with a sense of progress. Citizens clumped together, formed cities, conducted businesses, grew more secular. Here it is the twentieth century, just the same, everything going on in a city, and murder, too. She was a woman on a roof looking at a pointed end of a screwdriver. He said he knew her address and he'd be back. Julie believed him.

Eamonn helped her pack. His offer seemed more convenient than potentially Faustian. It was as if an intangible abstraction (not her soul but something like it) was sold and tossed into the arrangement. The habits given up when she no longer lived alone were part of the exchange. Eamonn presented her with a convenient choice, nothing more complicated than an apartment a few blocks away, with the same telephone exchange and low rent. Hidden clauses, overlooked riders that might turn up later in unpleasant ways, tipped no scales. She didn't change her mind, because the screwdriver could turn into a knife or a Saturday night special. Eamonn was sympathetic in the way a witness might be who was essentially untouched by the crime and had nothing to risk as far as being the object of a stranger's revenge. Sympathy had its charms and helped moved boxes and a couple of suitcases but Julie was resistant to showing the depth to which she'd been shocked by the incident on the roof. Betrayal on Eamonn's part didn't mean confessing theirs was a marriage of convenience, didn't mean that he might fall in love anytime the chance presented itself. Betrayal meant giving away confidences, meant ridicule. Eamonn would dismiss her vulnerability. At the same time he would enlarge the moment on the roof as if it meant Julie might again become terror stricken in a subway car, on the street, anywhere. There was betrayal in his confusion, even if the confusion was altruistic and his treatment of her could be entirely unrealistic. The responsibility involved in rescue can grow into knowing too much about the victim.

Eamonn spent several days moving, arranging, and throwing out rolls of unused, out-of-date film, old Polycontrast F paper, empty yellow-orange film cannisters, neck straps long ago removed from the cameras they came with, old bottles of bleach and chemicals: selenium toner and Edwal FG-7, cracked tongs and old newspapers.

He didn't photograph Julie often. In a few months he might if he thought she was a problem. Eamonn would start clicking away as soon as she got out of bed, not stopping until night or until she moved out, whichever happened first.

The shutter savior, Mr. Fix-It instantly, automatic rescue by virtue of the act of recording the scene of the (social) crime. How is packing a box like taking a photograph? Here is someone to shoehorn by virtue of the act of taking her picture or letting her move in. Julie had seen newspaper photographs taken just after the bombing of a department store in Paris. She asked Eamonn how the photographer got there so fast. The two women put their hands up before the camera as if it were a gun. The one whose face was visible bore an expression of anger and affront. What mattered to Eamonn was that people didn't know what was ultimately going to be good for them. Eamonn knew about personal shock and he knew about fighting fire with fire, or so he was fond of implying. He did the disenfranchised a big favor by recording their exploitation, their accidents. Because he saw himself as only having risen a very minor degree above their state, because he had fixed notions about economic infrastructure, the owners of the means of production, surplus capital, people with slices of disposable income, oppressed classes. Just as one member of the ruling class feels affinity and understanding with another, Eamonn thought most of the people whose pictures he took would feel a partnership with him. He was no longer an immigrant but not yet a citizen. Eamonn sometimes made a profession out of being a displaced person.

In a few months he might say she was a nice girl from Pennsylvania who got what she deserved. They would both have forgotten how he helped her pack and talked about how the provisional government that took over after the 1848 revolution in France recruited murderers and thieves to be part of the *garde mobile*. They were still a mob, *les gens sans feu et sans aveu*, (People without fire or faith, he would quote Marx in French), they were paid and given uniforms but they were still no damn good. She hadn't wanted him to talk about the underclass at that moment, even if there was some historical fact in what he might say. Curtains, plates, boxes, Eamonn packed, stacked, with a kind of enthusiasm Julie wasn't sure had anything to do with her. It was an opportunity to talk about *les gens sans*.

Eamonn stared at the ceiling and began to talk about his high school in Brooklyn, petty drug dealing, the beginning of his life in crime. He wanted me to stop drawing and get back into bed. I squeezed a blob of veridian green out of a tube, much more than I needed. Light from the street lay in its curves, not enough light to paint by. His desire to sleep was at odds with a desire not be left alone. He insisted on talking, as if autobiography had the power to displace everything else. There had been a place called the Sugar Hill Club, small-time allegiances turned into gangs, a friend got murdered on the subway. His monotone voice made the whole thing sound religious. Eamonn's narrations, bits of things that happened to him, all of it became speech. I tried to channel the talking but resistance was useless. I could tamper with the floodgates, make suggestions like, "Don't you remember I've heard this before?" He never sensed he was being made a fool of and sometimes I felt sorry for him. Okay, Eamonn, go on with the story. When I met him the first thing I thought was that he took all the parts in a conversation. The second thing: is this about love or does he think he's being filmed? He either looked away when I spoke or stared at me in such a way that I was sure he wasn't listening. What he didn't discuss became something that might be continued with the next episode, and it was the information he withheld that convinced me one more drink, one more movie, one more night. Less and less did his inattention seem a liabilty; less a clue to future books thrown against the wall, to future fits, bouts of yawning, spells of lapsed concentration. I liked spending nights with a view of a park, even when I couldn't sleep, but the Moebius loop of stories and autobiography bugged me sometimes.

I told him a story I knew he wouldn't like by virtue of its juxtaposition and trivialization.

"My life in crime began on the Fourth of July when I was 13. A friend and I bicycled into Pittsburgh to buy illegal fireworks. We met a man in a funny room next to a garage. It might have been a small trailer that glommed onto the old tires and drums. There wasn't very much in it except for a radio and a zodiac poster of men and women fucking in different positions. I hadn't wanted to stare. I kept hearing John Lennon singing, 'The cops are going to get you,' and the man called us 'you femmes.' He might have been 18. I don't remember how my friend, who was older than I was, made contact with the fireworks man, but I remember thinking: this is it. This is the beginning of my life in crime. It begins in a tin room where a man gives you a brown paper bag and runs his hand up and down your back even though you never saw him before."

I tore up a small piece of paper stuck to the lid of a paint jar: half telephone numbers and movie times. Eamonn told me I was a jerk and it was three in the morning.

"Delacroix wrote that once you get out of bed you shouldn't get back in until you're ready to go to sleep."

"Another screwball."

He might think he was Karl Liebknecht in Berlin in 1918 but it was New York 1985. His high school in Brooklyn had been the Charlottenburg gaol which released Liebknecht in 1897 on the anniversary of the Paris Commune. Eleanor Marx called him "Library" and disapproved of his biography of her father. Engels was critical of him, his effusiveness, his handling of affairs in Germany. In the middle of the combat zone he might decide he wanted only to return to Anhalter Station, to go to the *Rote Fahne* office. Rosa would be there. To Eamonn, City Hall could have easily been Wilhemstrasse. I couldn't even pretend to have Rosa Luxemburg's convictions. Bloody Rosa, they called her. A man who wavered over the assassination of Karl L. was found dead, shot twice in the back in a Licterfelde alley.

My insomniac's revenge affected Eamonn in the middle of the night. When he woke up too, he'd go into his darkroom. He'd built one in the bathroom. He'd look into it in the middle of the night the way some people will go to the refrigerator. He was careful about arranging the negatives and prints so that when I used the bathroom, I rarely saw his work. Bottles of chemicals, trays, enlarger, huddled around my feet, on shelves above my head or under the sink.

In the autumn Eamonn became interested in the case of the Grace O'Malley, an eighty-foot trawler U.S. Customs agents seized on the city waterfront in New York. The Grace O'Malley was carrying seven tons of automatic weapons, hand grenades, explosives and ammunition. It was supposed to meet another trawler, the Maud Gonne, off the Kerry coast. There were only two men aboard the Grace O'Malley. They were detained for questioning by the customs agents, then released the next day. The newspapers didn't print their names. What had happened was that the Grace O'Malley had lain for several days in port and a watchman had become suspicious. The ship looked abandoned. None of the boat's fishing gear showed evidence of use, nor did the boat appear ready for fishing. The windows were blown out of the pilot house, as if it had just been through a violent gale.

"We believe," said the inspector to a reporter, "this is the vessel that shipped arms to the Provos. We have found documentation aboard showing that it was in the area concerned at the time."

The area concerned, the pick up spot, was a few miles east of Mount Desert, Maine.

Valued at $500,000, the Grace O'Malley was registered in the name of Freddy Driscoll of Staten Island who said he knew nothing about any smuggling.

"The boat was supposed to be out swordfishing," he told U.S. agents. Driscoll owns a small fishing fleet and would only say his boats caught fish, not hand grenades. They were designed as trawlers, not transatlantic gun runners.

Grace O'Malley was an Irish pirate who preyed on English ships returning from the New World. Sir Francis Drake's Golden Hind was counted among her prey. Queen Elizabeth had Grace O'Malley to court in a diplomatic effort to stop the marauding. They met queen to queen. Elizabeth handed her a little dog. "What the fuck is this?" said Grace O'Malley. She was told it was a lap dog, she should hold and pet it as they spoke. The pirate said she'd never sat down long enough to have a lap and handed it back to Queen Elizabeth.

Martin came in late the day he worked at Phanta Comics. He'd been hired as a free-lance letterer. He called himself a consultant.

Mr. Loonan, scripter, needed some new angles on catastrophe in *Electra*. The director, Mr. Regozin, said the stories were becoming too predictable, too repetitious and they were losing readers. Readers always knew the end of the story, even if the end was nowhere in sight for the next ten issues. The idea was to stage each comic as if the predictable end might be imperiled at every other frame. Two fates—happy marriage and death—could be approached but must never actually be met. For anyone or anything in space to regard Electra as a love object was useless. Love for Electra was doomed, and death a subject of close brushes but never the big end. If ingenious delays or obstacles in space turned fatal to Electra, they would be fatal for everyone else in the office. Julie Greene was the colorist on *Electra*. She filled in colors of her choice but didn't write the stories themselves. That was Mr. Loonan's job. If the obvious twist in plot lay right before

Mr. Loonan, he was consistently blind to it. In spite of his occasional ingenuity, Julie grew bored with Mr. Loonan's dream warrior. Her carapace of bravado covered conventional femininity. There were more male power figures in the serial than you could shake a stick at. Sometimes they baled her out, if not, they were there just in case. Evil women who were frustrated mothers spawned cruel offspring by chemical means. Neo-Nazi scientists with Russian names planned construction of an Ultimate Parent Entity. A story of restricted themes: adventure, rescue, jailing, malevolent stepmothers who looked like post-Industrial Revolution Cyclopses. Over the years Electra hadn't changed much, on the premise that the audience grew up and did change. She was not phototropic. She thrived on dark space which seemed abstractly ironic for a champion of good causes, but Mr. Loonan liked drawn blinds and often told Julie and Lisa Quong Lu, the inker, that he worked best at night.

Tacked above Mr. Lonnan's desk were a few wrappers from hollow chocolate robots he had given out last Christmas. He had eaten some of them himself and saved the gold wrappers with their green and rose patterns. They flattened into symmetrical abstractions. Each one was different.

It was September, and Phanta Comics was busy producing Christmas issues. Regozin kept calling Loonan into his office, then Loonan would repeat the director's injustices to his staff. Too much emphasis on Electra's skills. Loonan didn't take enough risks. Retire the Orion character. Introduce a new threat. All kinds of things are terrifying in space. Write down your nightmares. Last week Regozin overheard two fourteen-year-old boys talking about jet packs, a space station, something about interlocking parts, reconnaissance probes, rotating hexagonal joints. "I should have hired them on the spot," said Mr. R. The director hinted Mr. Loonan's imagination had, in past issues, grown plodding and pedestrian. Electra had lost all her sense of intrigue. She never fell in love with the wrong man or woman, never underwent a personality change, or had a treasonous crew member aboard her space ship. Mr. Loonan's fascination with the Electra story was the adoration of the creator. Mr. Loonan lived alone.

Julie suggested it was difficult to maintain intrigue in a story when people rarely went outside. Why don't you have them land on a planet? Lisa Quong Lu suggested he plant a fifth columnist on Electra's ship.

Mr. Lonnan rubbed his eyes under his glasses as if to say: fifth columnist, this isn't Catalonia in 1937, this is 32nd Street, forget about Franco. He returned to his desk, ignoring them. A man walked in, said he was looking for the bathroom, then returned a few minutes later and introduced himself as Martin, the new temporary letterer. He was the tallest man ever seen at Phanta. Curly hair fell over his forehead like a bunch of grapes. Mr. Loonan showed him to his desk and told him he was trying to run a business, not a toy shop and to get to work.

There were rumors Phanta was going to phase out Electra and Loonan plotted each book like a lover who sensed he would soon be rejected. Since he wrote the comic book, it was partly as if he were rejecting himself. Phanta might place him on another comic, but they were certain to be weak substitutes, the inventions of other men. It was Electra Mr. Loonan loved, with her missile-like chest, superhuman strength, and micro-quick reflexes. She occupied a whole Loonan day and part of a Loonan night. He had no other obsessions or interests, drank black coffee, thrived under fluorescent lights, and was passionate about thinking out loud. Bits of Electra episodes floated past us, the try-out audience whose opinion didn't really matter. Lisa turned up her radio. Loonan looked hurt. She got a Walkman. As if close proximity to comic book heroes lent him the authority of a neo-tyrant, he checked my colors constantly. He never seemed to get it, yet Mr. Loonan must surely have known, however saturated my colors appeared on the layouts, they always printed down to the same cheap tabloid range. They aged, cheap ink and paper faded. It was inevitable, yet he wanted to have Electra last. Even if we could have drawn her on archival paper, I don't think that was the kind of preservation he had in mind. Loonan was after the mythic. He didn't always wear a tie, sometimes there were nylon turtleneck sweaters, and science fiction books stuffed into his pockets.

Blue stands for black and white in frames which have no colors—a long shot of Electra at the controls of her spaceship, almost pensive; there is no text. A close-up shot, the misregistration of color and ink make her large lips look even bigger. Eyebrows like Elizabeth Taylor's, like apostrophes. Tears are simple, Lisa does the outlines. When Electra demonstrates her test tube generated strength, her powers are signified by rays, sometimes arcing out of the frame. She's nearly naked in every caper, occasionally Mr. Loonan will suggest boots and gloves. Ah, blam and whap aren't part of Electra's style. Shock is simulated in their faces. Expletives are suggested without being used too often. She isn't a borderline parody like *Supergirl*, not a parasite like *Spiderwoman*. No one at Phanta would have used the word ideology but Eamonn says they made Electra into the comic book version of the Holy Virgin Mary, even if she doesn't wear much clothing.

Loonan explained a frame split into eight sections as if divided by spokes of a wheel, Electra's head in the middle. In each section she tries to land on a random planet or comet and is turned away from each. Orion has spread rumors in the galaxy that she's not a heroine but one of the following: a scout for pirates, a cast off counter-spy, a psychobiotic polluter with minimal free will. One planet is governed by a creature who looks like the wicked stepmother in Disney's Snow White. Blonds are usually good and gentle like Betty. Dark Veronicas are greedy and possessive. Loonan is a stickler on the symbolic and he considers his directives on questions of color to be a reinforcement of classical thinking on aesthetics.

A kitchen could be bright and cheerful (chrome yellow and cadmium), signifying security and good news, or dark and ominous (sepia, Hooker's green), signifying an absent mother figure or household appliances discovered to have lives of their own. Rows of Dr. Martin's inks in their little glass bottles glowed fuschia, orange, malachite, violet, and Yves Klein blue on my desk. Electra wore Prussian blue #17. The interior of her spaceship was bluish-black #38 except where she sat under a cone of chrome yellow #3, diluted 30%. It was always night in space. Under a cone of yellow light Electra held a Payne's gray #10 gun and a Van Dyke brown #9 square which represented a photograph. Each frame brought the square closer. It was a sepia print of a man dressed as a World War II soldier and he was tied to a chair. Something about a time warp beyond Mars and going steadily backwards, I wasn't paying attention.

In the middle of his explanation a man walked in, asked to use the bathroom, then came back a few minutes later. He was wearing a wrinkled black jacket. When I looked closer I could see it was faintly plaid and I stared hard at his back as if picking out the blocks in an Ad Reinhardt painting. He had very long arms. He was reading Goethe's *Theory of Colors*. Loonan introduced him as Martin Shirk and told him he noticed he was late.

"I'm trying to run a business here, not a toy shop."

He smiled dumbly at the scripter, said something about lost keys and sorry. He looked at the pens Loonan gave him as if they were Loonan's own laundry. They did need to be cleaned and he did so sluggishly. Loonan, at his desk, muttered about authority figures and their problems in two dimensional space.

Lisa put on her Walkman, Martin turned closer to me and told me the story of his life as he lettered.

> YOU THINK SHE'LL BE A PROBLEM? WE'LL ARRANGE A SHORT CIRCUIT.
> ARIADNE LIFTED THE DECODER FROM THE DEAD MAN'S JACKET. SHE HEARD THE SOUND OF A WINDOW BEING OPENED.

He no longer read what he wrote. As a child he was probably told he had a lovely hand but it's the twentieth century, kings' and bishops' scribes have long been out of work so he ended up in the funnies. Martin wasn't a fat person but he was large, moved slowly and seemed out of place in the little office where everyone was nervous we might all be canned any minute. After his last job he had gone to Berlin to stay with an American woman who translated subtitles for films and lived near the wall.

Martin had been a child actor in television commercials. He did them locally in Michigan for a car dealer who wanted to emphasize a family image. His parents thought he might go to New York, study acting, perform in real commercials, but Martin grew too fast and didn't retain the automatic cuteness of childhood. He was frightened by an audience; even in school, he never spoke unless called upon. It seemed a terrible thing to be an old actor. The grandfather in the car dealer's commercials really disliked children. Between takes, he would roughly remove the little girl from his lap, get out of the station wagon, and have a cigarette alone, away from the lights. Martin's part as the disillusioned man's grandson who only wanted to go for a ride seemed, even to young Martin, mealy-mouthed and dumb beyond reason. His parents couldn't understand his disinterest. Martin's mother thought that as he grew up he was always acting, always being someone else. Years later Martin told his mother he never acted, he was only playing. The reason she didn't recognize the difference between acting and playing was because she thought celebrity conferred authority status and that's what she wanted for her son.

By the windows, near a corner, Mr. Loonan spoke to himself, in varying voices.

"'You're my kind of girl, sweetie.' 'That's what you think.' Door slam. Stupid thing to say. Orion causes everyone on Electra's ship to fall asleep. Even the image duplicator has Zs tracking across its video display terminal. No, the image duplicator is a machine and can't. That's what stopped O.''

Beside me Martin read quietly out loud from his book.

> 221. Primary objects may be considered firstly as *original*, as images which are impressed on the eye by things before it, and which assure us of their validity. To these secondary images may be opposed as *derived* images, which remain in the organ when the object itself is taken away; those apparent after-images, which have been circumstantially treated in the doctrine of physiological colours.*

Theory of Colours, Johann Wolfgang von Goethe, MIT Press, Cambridge, MA, 1970, page 221.

At 5:30 Loonan left for a meeting with Mr. Regozin. He took small objects out of his pockets so they wouldn't stick out: pens, a notebook, his glasses case. He combed his hair, put the styrofoam cups he'd been punching his thumbs through all day into the trash as if he were going to the electric chair. All those gestures I never thought about twice seemed supportive of a hopeless case. Lisa ignored him. Martin screwed the caps on his pens.

We got out of the subway, stopping to look at the things, possessions, genuine and faintly hot, spread on blankets near the subway stop. Rhinestone tiaras, old toasters, used tweed suits with the pockets cut out, a second hand copy of *Thief's Journal*, early Patti Smith records. Men with long hair, as if they'd just emerged from mothballs and drugs, sold copies of *Life*, *Time* from 1969, 1970, 1971. Richard Nixon on one cover, Patty Hearst on another. Past empty lots filled with the winter shelters of the homeless. Constructions made of cardboard cartons cut into igloos; broken umbrellas stuck out like warnings or fake television antennas, sometimes real gardens sprinkled with empty amyl nitrate bottles of the night before, bags of cans and bottles, a stash that will be turned into money. Soon a bulldozer will flatten all the paper and tin houses. A foundation was already being dug on the lot next door. Someone wrote on the plywood surrounding the pit: "Rich people will soon live here." We looked through a hole although it was dark out and construction had stopped for the day.

We went to Veselka's and tried to eat dinner, talking about the phasing out of Electra. Lisa took the pink Eiffel Tower out of her ear and put it on the table.

"We could go to Paris."

We could get jobs at other books. Lisa was pragmatic, like Martin, one job followed another, you just had to spend a lot of time on the telephone. An old Ukranian man approached table after table, trying to sell his surrealist watercolors. Nobody bought any art from him. He grinned at each rejection but the situation was sad and pathetic, like Loonan talking to himself about Electra's escape from Orion, desperate above the sound of Lisa singing along with her tapes.

Eamonn wasn't home yet. Had he crept aboard the Grace O'Malley at the wrong moment? Arrest kept secret from the press; was the FBI, CIA keeping him in a house like the one in *North by Northwest*? Maybe the prison was in Forest Hills. They question and torture him. If he was simply in jail, he'd get one telephone call and it's not to me, that one call. Orion was chasing down Electra and her resources were getting thin, approaching zero, all of ours were. Loonan was flirting with rape by a superpower and it would be the end of us all. In his rashness he would sweep away any concept of what ought or ought not to be in the book. There hadn't ever been a real need for rescue. She always took care of herself. Malcontents, inker and colorist, had no editorial voice.

Think about what it means to die hard, Mr. L., the moment of death proplonged by a tangle of intravenous tubes, mercy killers banished to the hospital parking lot. Kids won't close the book thinking, oh, what a wonderful world. You have to allow for resurrection because resurrection can happen at Phanta if someone changes his mind. You only have to hire Martin for a week and he'll print the words.

Lisa and Julie rewrote Electra.

> BIRTH OF ELECTRA
> EPISODE I
>
> $K =$ the cube of any planet's distance from the sun divided by the square of the periodic time of that planet's revolution about the sun.
>
> $G =$ any constant $M_s =$ the mass of the sun
>
> Dr. Mary Atlas has been working alone for years in her laboratory under Sierra Madre del Sur. Madame Curie and Rosalyn Franklin may have trusted the

wrong people. She wouldn't become a victim of bad faith. She refused to work with male colleagues or hire male research assistants because she was afraid of theft. Dr. Atlas wouldn't swallow literal or theoretical radium. She was no dupe of the funding institutions that demanded results favorable to their industries. Under Sierra Madre del Sur she created a test tube baby, Electra, whose scrambled genetic code endowed her with superhuman strength. The girl grew up in the lab. It was a happy, if sunless, childhood. When the Secretary of State threatened to begin bombing Leningrad, Dr. Atlas put Electra in a spaceship and sent her into space, thinking the girl would be less endangered beyond Mars.

$$G = \frac{4\pi^2 K}{M_S}$$

Henry Street, Catherine Street, the part of East Broadway which was full of shooting galleries. Lisa Quong Lu would go into stores, poke around in the ginger root, the eels, the Buddha cookies, speak Chinese to the old women and the young men hawking fish and oranges. None of them seemed to notice the pink Eiffel Tower in her left ear. Once she spoke the language, that seemed to be enough. You could marry someone from Hong Kong for two to six thousand American dollars, you could get a fake passport in a basement in Queens but the networks all started in Chinatown.

Lisa saw Eamonn coming out of the Hak Ng Fung Funeral Parlor and followed him for a few blocks. He had tea at Hop Kee's on Pell Street, he looked at turtles and frogs in the window of Sun Nol's Fish Palace. He went into an herb shop which was too small for Lisa to follow him into, so she didn't know what he bought there. She wondered how he, a non-Chinese, would know what to buy in such a place and what to do with the herbs once he had them. Next he went into an apartment building on Doyers Street. She went home. Eamonn could take care of himself. What did Hop Kee and Ng Fung have in common?

The top of a building near Phanta was lit gold. As I walked east the red and green lights on the top of the Empire State building appeared from behind the gold panels, moving out from behind the brilliantly colored fog. Like finding a badly lit cathedral with no visitors except a few faithful old women, you become a believer, even if it's just cold and raining on 36th Street. In the mist and nearly empty streets at night, you could believe in androids, mutants, Charles Dickens, and Mary Shelley, the nineteenth century and the future. What wasn't making sense was the bit in the middle.

Julie was often given photocopies to work on at home. At her desk, away from Mr. Loonan's preference for cool colors, she painted Electra rose lake as she endured a blast of light from an artificially induced meteor shower. The whole scene was done in reds. Eamonn would have said Electra's redness when she fought was the mock red of a bloodless revolution. In comics, Julie would say, color is never an entity by itself, color is never a message without a sign. She looked out the window at the clusters of bag men in the park. There was no conflict between word and image in Electra's bit of space. Artificial and highly stylized, there were no contradictions between what was said and what was seen.

Here's Eamonn again:

When any single color or hues of a color are isolated or given special status in a social context, the color becomes connected to ideas or becomes symbolic of a set of ideas. Color is more than an optical phenomena, more than masses of rods and cones in your retinas.

Martin would quote:

Goethe thought yellow was the favorite color of children and savages, capable of enraging educated men. Red-blue was a disquieting color and therefore appropriated by the church. Red was at the apex of his system of colors. Yellow is active. Blue is passive. Color induces mental and emotional states regardless of the nature of form of the object itself.

Julie put Electra aside and drew a pair of shapes, labeled them Etta Cone and Ed Rod, gave them arms and legs, hats and briefcases, then threw them away. It was turning colder. The next time she looked out the window, the bag men had left their park bench. They had probably gone a few blocks further south to gather in lots or near curbs, huddling over a fire started in an old drum.

There had been photographs of the Chrysler building, of a man kissing a woman on the Staten Island Ferry, of three card monty dealers, hands hovering over bent cards. The Chrysler building at night was a Tivoli sweet, partly ominous and Gothic the way he had photographed it. The woman on the Staten Island ferry had her eyes shut as she kissed or was being kissed, the man had one eye open and the one eye looked straight at the lens. The three card monty dealer grinned at Eamonn. These were some of his New York photographs.

A man made a telephone call from a bombed-out telephone booth, jagged glass, splintered wood, his back was to the photographer. Another picture, the ruins of a house. They looked like older ruins, not recent, perhaps the house was gutted by fire or a bomb a few years before. A woman in a heavy coat looked out of what used to be a window. Two men with machine guns were painted carefully on a brick wall. One aimed at the sky, the other sat, stylized flags waving behind them. "Bobby Sands RIP" and "Fuck the Queen" were painted in above the flags. Thin men in masks carried a narrow coffin, the third picture. I returned to the woman in the coat. She didn't smile at the photographer. These were his Irish pictures. A dark line had been scratched over her eyes but the negative remained clear.

It was about to rain. The picture sky was grey. Wales, it said on the back of the photograph. Before a stone bridge, a doll's carriage had been overturned. Six or seven children all stared at Eamonn's lens: curiosity, indifference, potential hostility. Short dress held a twisted doll. These were Eamonn's performers. Two women in furs looked in a shop window. The window had been opaqued and in its center was a recess containing a display of diamond necklaces. One stared at her reflection. Old women in jewelry, furs, standing next to their horses. Men in bowlers on horseback. I never asked him how he got onto their grounds in order to take these. The trappings of class sat more appropriately and with less jarring effect on the old men. They looked so much less ridiculous even when they were old and obese and wore kilts or little caps, at least Eamonn photographed them with more restraint.

No crystal clear scandal, no shock, no gun to the head. You have to come to these pictures with some information first. You might have to know geography and a little history. Eamonn has experienced the terror already, assimilated the contradictions, it's up to you to read the impressions, the footprints of that terror in the busted telephone booth and the race horses.

Eamonn was reading *The Life of Weegee*.

He took me into his darkroom, turned on the red light. Strips of negatives hung from pipes, bottles of chemicals wedged into tight rows. Odd lenses, rubber hoses connected to the sink, a paper cutter he called the guillotine. A negative was cut off, slid into the enlarger and brought into focus. My face was gray and small before worms of graffiti drawn on a wall in the park. The writing looked reversed but it wasn't. Set the timer. Expose for 10 seconds, click. Slowly the picture is born again, my face still small but sharper. Carefully take the print out of the developer with tongs, the solution dripped off a corner back into the tray. I floated under the stopbath solution for 30 seconds, then the fixer and at last the wet paper is hung up to dry.

Coming home very late Lisa saw a man's body on the sidewalk on the corner of East Broadway and Pike Street. Lisa guessed he was from Hong Kong, about 17 or 18. A new immigrant recruit for one of the gangs. They start out small—running rinky-dink clubs with Korean prostitutes and a little gambling, Kung Fu arcades, then they become restaurant owners. They don't kill for pleasure or revenge, just for cash. The police don't care because it's always within the neighborhood. There are no stray bullets. In the morning the body was gone.

Looking out windows on the thirty-ninth floor facing west, I could see a boat on the Hudson, and I felt like the boy who had to live in a bubble because he was born with a critical immune deficiency disease. Phanta Comics is a world by itself, and this room where *Electra* is produced is a medieval city, walled in. Food is brought in in the morning, garbage taken out at night, products sent to the printers, money distributed in the form of checks with taxes taken out.

Mr. Loonan Discovers a Modern Novel is Hard to Write
I hoped Martin Shirk would be hired again as a letterer. Each morning I gave him until 11:00 to come in late.

"Did you see the first page of Ms. *Tree* this month?" Loonan was in a good mood. Ms. Tree was Electra's rival in popularity and it was to the detective that the space traveler would be sacrificed if there were cutbacks. Loonan felt Electra was much more sophisticated, more truly heroic. The first page, had we even looked at it!

"No."

"Ms. Tree is standing over a body in a high angle shot and she says, 'Sid was deader than polyester.'"* Loonan often wore those kinds of clothes. He saw no humor in that first page, only a hack attempt at comedy.

Mr. Loonan asked Lisa about Chinese food and self-defense. Could she show him how to eat with chop sticks? As long as Electra's rival looked silly and made jokes that were no longer funny, as long as he could stay with his comic book test tube child, he was full of Christmas spirit. Otherwise Lisa Q. Lu was the Lady of Shanghai and I was Clytemnestra. He was right, too. If he should be locked out, his suspicions would be confirmed. Adulterers, cosmopolite spies, we privately rewrote the book. Renegades, revisionists, we would soon be out of work anyway.

*Eclipse Comics, September 11, 1984, *Dancing in the Dark*

THE ORION AFFAIR
ELECTRA, EPISODE II

As the teenage Electra hurtles past Mars, her silhouette against therma-glass windows is seen by Orion. Bewitched beyond reason he pursues her across space. He is undaunted by her disinterest, even when disinterest turns into anger, even when anger turns to violence.

Dr. Atlas coded Electra's genetic material to produce remarkable results. She could do vast sums in her head, repeat piano concertos perfectly after only having heard them once and could read *Ulysses* in a day, but her aesthetic acumen was often faulty. Dr. Atlas had given her art books for her education and amusement during the long ride into space. When Kandinsky wrote of spirituality she drew no conceptual link between that word and his triangles and tornados. Electra traced colored prints of Matisse, Braque, Rousseau, and asked the absent Dr. Atlas why she had given her these books. The only way Electra's brain could be tampered with was if her spaceship was intercepted by radioactive lasers. An accident of this kind would result in amnesia. Dr. Atlas gave her daughter one weapon: an image duplicator. Using the image duplicator Electra could create copies of herself like animated Xerox, phoney trick women who crumpled under Orion's embraces. The duplicants were like shadows, mirrors, a kind of reversed image. They are right-handed while the real Electra is left-handed.

I was late for work but the office was nearly empty. Only Martin Shirk was there. He was looking at some typed pages of Electra script laid out on Mr. Loonan's desk. Lisa had phoned in sick. He had been called in to replace her, to do the inking and lettering for a few days. The Christmas rush was ending. All the scripters were in meetings or at the printer's. We would be alone all day. Mr. Loonan called twice to check if we were following directions he'd left. Thinking he wouldn't call a third time, we left Electra only half colored-in by shades of blue (that was easy, stood for black and white), left her speech balloons blank and went downtown.

Martin's apartment was on the south side of the park. Part of the building was boarded up. A narrow slice of the ground floor was a junk store. He lived alone in two rooms filled with furniture found in the street pushed against the walls, books were stacked in milk crates. The walls were probably white but I remember them as dark olive green, Rousseau colors. If Rousseau had painted urban detritus instead of tropical plants, he would have loved this room. The objects crowded in corners and along the walls were as densely arranged as trees in his landscapes. A single fluorescent tube hung from the ceiling. He had a lot of lamps of different styles and sizes: a matador with a frozen plaster cape who held a bulb instead of a sword, office lamps from a city auction, lamps on arching stems behind parchment yellow shades. In the two which were functional he had put low-wattage bulbs. When I was in his apartment I always felt as if I was in a mine and the only light available was the one attached to my head. The floors slanted dramatically: here was a permanently listing boat or a lopsided chamber unearthed in Pompeii, relics intact; Martin and I the only survivors.

Martin showed me some storyboards, plans for a movie about an out of work actor who drives a cab. One day he picks up a beautiful woman on the corner of 49th Street and Park Avenue. He drops her off in Chinatown. A few days later he picks her up at the same spot. She barely speaks to him but the driver becomes obsessed. Like magic she's on that same corner every time he passes it in his cab. He ignores other fares and tries to tail her. Relentless in his pursuit, he is drawn to the conclusion that the woman is a murderess. That was as far as Martin's storyboards went. I could see him looking at me as he drove an imaginary cab down Second Avenue, hands on an invisible steering wheel, demonstrating the part of the out of work actor. When he stood very close I looked away. I have never needed to take a cab from 49th Street and Park Avenue.

She asked Lisa where Mr. Loonan was. Why was his desk so neat? Lisa explained that Electra had been terminated. He had probably known last week but didn't tell anyone. Regozin was writing the last chapter. She was either going to be killed or surrender to Orion. The latter fate seemed to signify termination was serious, beyond hope of a comeback. This was a character who had, like Red Sonja and many others before her, a tradition of celibacy.

Regozin came in with the end of the story and the roughs to be inked and colored. He was a short man with iguana cheeks and thick glasses who'd been at Phanta for years, the kind of supervisor who moved the products out of the shop and never missed a deadline. The director's office had been planning and drawing this last chapter for weeks without telling Loonan's actual staff. Here it was, Electra marrying Orion on the cusp, almost a morganatic marriage, she would get nothing from the transformed brute when he kicked off. Electra herself would not be murdered because some day Mr. Regozin might want to bring her back. "Make her look happy." he said. White boots, long gloves, lots of hair blowing around, no dress, just some white streamers. Mr. Regozin let me know he noticed I was late and told me what he had already told Lisa. We were both laid off indefinitely.

"This is Martin Shirk calling. I'm at Spector Comics this afternoon. 254-0400, extension 95. They might need a colorist next week on *Agent 998*. Ask for Mr. Sampson when you call the main number."

"I'm trying to reach a Mr. Archer. You people don't know me but Victor Friedman at the *Post* gave me your number in connection with some photographs taken some time ago off the Maine coast."

"He's not home."

"Tell him I called. I'm interested in Mr. Archer's pictures. He can reach me at 718-341-0649. Ask for Freddy."

I wanted to put the radio on when it was already on. I wanted to put the television on while the radio was on. I wanted to go to the movies when I was already at the movies.

Baudelaire's Dream Wish

Martin walked me home. The entrance to my building is a short hall with a dozen mailboxes and buzzers divided between two walls. The buzzers signal someone is at the door but you can't buzz them in. You have to go downstairs or throw a key. Martin said good-bye in the hall. A few days before I had been awakened by a loud prolonged press on the bell. It was 6:00 in the morning, too early for the mailman, but I got dressed and ran downstairs. In the hall a prostitute was giving a man a blow job. He was leaning on the buzzers and had woken up half the building. He had a broad back. The woman was wearing a knitted beret and a stiff suede jacket. Their breath misted in the entrance over the mailboxes. The man seemed barely alert enough to zip up his fly but he did and they shambled into the street. I was careful not to lean against anything and not to let Martin. It was half past midnight.

Sometimes I think I'm too old for this. There's a woman who was in my class in high school who has had two kids, a hysterectomy and a rich husband who cheats on her. She's way ahead of me. She lives in a big house that looks like a prison built by Louis Quatorze and it's next door to the house she grew up in. The east side of the avenue near Seventh Street is a series of five story buildings and at night they look entirely like a trompe l'oeil painting; a false front stuck in a landscape where real estate values make the idea of its falseness absurd. I know it's not true. From the street, people can be seen in their apartments and you can walk around the block. It's not painted on. People live in those nineteenth century (not) trompe l'oeil buildings and they probably don't consider themselves living according to trompe l'oeil inclinations. The woman in the Louis Quatorze prison who waits for her husband until early in the morning, as she looks at her neighbors' houses: does she think they're a painted set-up, fakes staged to make her feel miserable? I don't feel tromped on or watched by my fakes, and this is the reassuring part.

Fanny Ardant, too, has begun to look older. She played the Countess of Guermantes in the movie. Married, in love with Swann. (Come with us to Spain or Italy, how can you know where you'll be in three months?) She tries in vain. It's an unlovely part because his obsession is Odette. No matter how hard she tries, two facts remain constant: (a) She's married, and, most important, (b) Swann's not in love with her. Fanny Ardant has a gesture, it seems involuntary, her jaw juts out, as if she won't accept rejection but at the same time, she knows he wouldn't go away with her even if he weren't dying. She can't believe and never has accepted his destructive love for Odette, to her a human zero, a shallow hooker from Marseilles. She stops short of being plaintive, won't allow Swann's family in her house, doesn't run after his carriage.

ELECTRA RETURNS TO EARTH
EPISODE III
   Electra shut the book on Kandinsky again. Mary Atlas hadn't coded her against claustrophobia or

homesickness and longing, by-products of a good memory. Orion might pelt her with intergalactic valentines or missiles but his offers were annoying, dangerous, offered no companionship. She grew curious about Earth. What happened to Kandinsky and Cocteau? To her mother? She turned her spaceship around. Orion went numb. He couldn't follow her. On Earth he'd be a mammoth, a freak with an ursine cast to his features. He would have no privacy, no secrecy, no subtle way to plead his case. He'd be seen from miles away. He couldn't function on the planet of Electra's origin. In his frustration he pounded the controls of his spaceship and a fragment of an amnesia-inducing ray pierced Electra's therma-glass window. It was only a small bit of a ray but it erased the part of her brain that stored memory of Dr. Atlas. The spaceship still headed towards Earth. It was too late to change course. The precocious laser beam did more than just alter Electra's memory. Her spaceship disintegrated as it fell through the Earth's atmosphere. Electra grew lighter. She landed beside Cleopatra's Needle in Central Park, clutching a microchip from her image duplicator.

Eamonn left for Mount Desert, Maine during the week between Christmas and New Year's. He accused her of being like Dreyfus, as if she were such an ordinary person, if she were falsely accused of treasonous actions, she wouldn't be on her own side. That was the kind of betrayal that she'd been waiting for since the near murder on her old roof. She told him there are a lot of men in a lot of apartments. There are a lot of women in a lot of apartments. Sometimes they are in the same one together and it doesn't amount to a hill of beans.

Talking to Martin was like talking to the sexual KGB. I never knew when he wanted to leave or when he wanted to stay. The only way to avoid being made a fool of was to barge on ahead anyway, to risk being more foolish, as if deliberate intention could cancel out inadvertent ridiculousness. I got sick and tired of the act of seduction being some kind of trial. It was a way not to panic.

She often had trouble falling asleep. She might hear a radio from across the street. There seemed nothing more inert than a sleeping man when she wondered what she was doing in his apartment, if she had made a mistake, and how might she be made to pay for that mistake. What is the insomniac's revenge on the man who sleeps and in that sound sleep is blind to the light creeping into the room, deaf to the people drinking in the park, ignorant of her chimeras which are partly about him? Leaking sesame sauce from last night's dinner bowed white cartons still sitting on the table. She might pick fruit flies from a glass of wine left out and drink the rest. The first thing he said when he woke up was hello which had some truth to it. In sleep he was dead to everything.

Julie looked for signals for the beginnings and the ends but sometimes these can be contradictory. He didn't return her calls. She thought perhaps his mother had died. His mother must have died seven times in the ten months she knew him. You think you know the signs but you ignore them anyway, she said to Lisa.

I ate cold sesame noodles and reheated left over coffee. I no longer went to the laundromat but washed my clothes at home in the bathtub, hanging them to dry across the room. Not realising how much water even wrung out T shirts held, they dripped onto a stack of drawings stored nearby, ruining the top ones. At night the clothes hanging across my apartment looked like a child's idea of ghosts, but during the day the lines of pillow cases and socks made it look even smaller and more cluttered than the rooms ordinarily were.

EPISODE IV
ELECTRA DOESN'T KNOW WHAT TO DO
"Useful on Earth, in most places," the package said. It had been zippered into her suit. Inside were

hundred and thousand dollar bills but Electra had no conception of what money might be, its purpose or value. She had read about dollars, pounds, and francs but didn't know what they looked like. A picture of a house, a portrait of a man, a signature, numbers, there were so many bits of paper but no directions as to what they were for. She left the package on a rock in Central Park.

She had to live on the streets and grew ragged constructing her possessions from what other people threw away. Because inconspicuousness seemed desirable, Electra drifted to the southeast side of the city. Even if other citizens treated her with equanimity, as if she were just like them, she sensed her slip-ups, she sensed they were being polite and not mentioning her mistakes in social behavior. Memories of a life of privilege, extravagant intelligence, and faintly odd looks served to give her away to herself, if not to others. Only vague childhood memories resisted erasure. A laboratory whose walls were of uneven rock, a little girl splashing soapy water from test tube to Petri dish, domes of suds in the sink, a recording of Glen Gould playing concertos (although she didn't remember Dr. Atlas who had been in love with him). Parts of the city looked familiar but the familiarity was grounded in mistaken identity. A stone faced tunnel near Police Plaza bore a little resemblance to rooms hollowed under Sierra Madre del Sur. Nothing to jar presence into the absence created by Orion's chance ray, touched off in agony.

Her glassy translucent skin grew dirty and cracked but the dirt concealed the fact Electra had the look of someone who was born out of a tank. Layers of clothing found in the street; jackets, trousers, skirts made her a shapeless Pere Ubu; hair matted and greased stood up straight. It was summer and she could wash under the hydrant at night after the children ran away, but she began to like it, thinking smell was like a thumb print or the sound of voices, each peculiarly idiosyncratic. She had no concept of what it might be to appear offensive. Her world, for so many years, had been entirely solipsistic.

Language had a chancier aspect on the streets. It wasn't entirely neologisms she hadn't learned due to her isolation in space but a combination of idioms, slang, and the local habit of aposiopesis and metonymy which confused her. Spoken sentences never seemed finished although she suspected the thoughts behind the broken phrases were.

Few of Electra's companions on the street were charitable or magnanimous about distributing whatever they might have scavenged. The concept of surplus didn't exist. One's body was a savings bank, a storage vault, interst cumulative depending on market value. Rubber bands were among the utilitarian rarities coveted by the homeless. Incapacity didn't eliminate the imperative of committing crimes and there was a gluey nastiness to their fights. In the aftermath of a fight between two men, as one lay unconscious and bleeding, others rifled through his stiff, ligneous rags. They did this to the dead as well. Useful objects: bags, safety pins, rope, rubber bands were of value and had degrees of preciousness. Down along the line, everything changed hands, was transformed. A belt became a handle, bicycle tire became trouser suspenders, a paper bag became a hat.

Electra lived in an old cardboard refrigerator box. The emblem on the refrigerator reminded her of her spaceship. Electra knew other citizens on other avenues looked and behaved differently so she stayed on her street, rarely going more than a few blocks in any direction. Sometimes she moved with clots of homeless men and women settling for a few days on the corner of a busy intersection. The men might wash cars. When her box disappeared she slept by herself on a traffic island in the middle of Allen Street, learning to ignore the sound of cars and trucks. One night a cab driver got out of his car to piss and heard Electra moan in her sleep, saw her bare legs poking out from twin bundles of checkered rags. He didn't zip his fly back up. Wobble and drip, in one motion he stepped over to Electra and stuck one hand up between her legs. Layers of frayed cloth and scratched sore skin, to him her body was an extension of one long hole, something he was entitled to by virtue of the juxtaposition of his cab to her bench. A possession treated with violence, a devalued commodity but still a hole within his rights.

Electra never had occasion to use her superhuman strength until the cab driver pried her legs apart. Orion had only pursued, never came near acquisition. The cab driver thought he could force her with one hand. When she opened her eyes his pants were down around his ankles and his stained shirt tails barely covered his stomach. He tried to hit her but she stopped his swing in true Phanta comic book style, yellow arc careening out of the frame. He screamed but the street was deserted, no NYPD, no Fantomas on the Boulevard du Crime. In the middle of the night nobody looked twice. It occurred to Electra she was stronger than this man but that she wasn't supposed to be and he had been surprised. But what if she hadn't been able to overpower him? The comic had been phased out, what if on earth, over time, she became as vulnerable as other women? The lessons of space didn't always translate and her powers, so special beyond Pluto, were out of context here.

She took the keys as well as his wallet which was stuffed into a pocket like a hot clamshell. She'd seen bodies rifled through on the street before although it wasn't clear to her what the objects taken from pockets were for. Key into ignition, foot on brake, no, try the accelerator, steering wheel, it's obvious what that's for. She drove down Allen Street to Pike, parked the cab, put the microchip from the lost mimetic device in the glove compartment, and fell asleep in the back seat. If even an empty-headed duplicant had to have been sacrificed to the cab driver to ensure her escape, Electra would have felt pity for it.

Lisa had intermittent short jobs as an inker at Phanta. There were more cutbacks after Electra was terminated and Mr. Regozin called her less each month. When I tried to get work as a colorist again I was told the same thing she had been. We'll call you when there's something to do. Lisa was terminated a few months after Electra got married off to Orion.

Section C
I stood in line at Veselka to buy a Lottery ticket but passed by Gem Spa. I had a system. I would pass every other newsstand or candy store that sold tickets. Lisa did the same in Chinatown. She broke the system when she went to Queens to visit her mother because she neglected the third newsstand, the next one due according to her route. It had sold a winning number the year before and the odds were negligible another chance millionaire would come out of it.

As long as I could get Unemployment and my landlord remained confined to a wheelchair, I felt safe. He'd had a stroke in the middle of the summer and was partly paralyzed, knew little of what went on around him, food fell from his mouth into the chair.

Sometimes I think there must have been a fork in the road and I picked the wrong branch. I don't remember when I had the choice, where, or what the alternatives were but I'm sure I made a mistake.

Eamonn was in Mount Desert. My twelve weeks of Unemployment were running out.

One Thursday morning at Unemployment I was sent to Section C. Something had gone wrong. Each week I glanced quickly at Section C, a group of folding chairs set into warped lines facing double rows of desks, most of which were empty. This cordoned off area was for people who wrote the wrong social security number on their forms or got caught having a job off the books. Two men and a woman sat at their desks looking seriously occupied as if preparing for a play before an audience they knew to be fractious and captive for up to an hour. Belligerent, nervous, Section C felons knew this was where you fought for your checks or gave up. The lines at Unemployment were long but the wait in Section C was even longer. Counselors were impuisant civil servants who started out with received ideas about social welfare, but by the time they worked in Section C they had turned into the kind of people whose combination of cynicism and self-righteousness makes them think of themselves as astute and sophisticated. My counselor, Mr. Belvilacqua was like that when clearly he was neither. All that really drove him was the desire to nab another cheat.

"I have been looking for work," you say and you list the jobs you've applied for, the advertisements you've answered, the inquiries you've made.

Mr. Belvilacqua didn't know what a colorist was, thought it had something to do with dying hair, and comics were a feeble excuse for adult employment. Couldn't I work at any magazine? Hadn't I even tried? Mr. Belvilacqua wrote down everything I said on a folded four page form like a little book and everything he wrote was in the first person. He read the statement back to me.

"'Last Wednesday I called Spector Comics but they said they weren't hiring any illustrators.'"

"I'm not an illustrator, I do coloring. I'm a colorist."

He looked at me as if I said I were a professional hummer. I gave up. Mr. Belvilacqua made my search for a job sound like I never got out of bed. His handwriting was neat and round, so different from mine which is fast and jerky. His text was a Procrustean narrative, had nothing to do with what I said, and was stupid to boot. I refused to sign. He gave me a date for Unemployment Court in two weeks. In the meantime my checks would be cut off. If I won my case I would receive the back checks and be entitled to another twelve weeks. I wouldn't need a lawyer, Mr. Belvilacqua said, just show up and talk. It seemed hopeless. Room 1209 was another day wasted. I decided not to even try it.

My landlord was moved to a nursing home. A sharper sister managed the building now and demanded a late fee if rent was paid after the fifteenth. Her English was good and she made a point of being sure she was understood.

As the date approached, I began to be a little curious about Room 1209. I might go after all. In a grand sweep of humanist eloquence I would reveal Mr. Belvilacqua to the judge as an inarticulate, petty misogynist. I would reduce his fiefdom, his corner of Section C, to bits of twisted paper clips and eraser dust. The judge would grant me triple back compensation and a trip to Rome. Room 1209 had no connection to any mental construct about grace, however whacky. Judicial eloquence fell on deaf ears. Room 1209 might have no exit. I would be the one reduced to confessions of unimagined crimes: cheating the crippled landlord, haunting OTB joints, turning tricks on lower Third Avenue, lying to the government. Room 1209 meant waiting, listening to other claimants who didn't have a leg to stand on either, who pleaded they'd end up living in the tunnels under Grand Central Station. I would listen to story after story and as I listened I'd draw pictures of Electra on my forms. Electra lands back on earth, lives in an abandoned car, sells the art history books originally put in her spaceship by her creator, and begs for change at subway stations. Her carefully engineered genetic code goes haywire because her special talents are of no use to the disenfranchised and in the last frame her nostalgia for the test tube is impossible to draw.

She was on a boat on the Pacific Ocean in which the dried salted fish had run out and Malaysian pirates in motor boats might appear any time to rob them of the money they hoped to take to America. She was crossing the Cambodian-Thai border on foot, she was working in a sweatshop in Singapore, she had no time for my hesitation, for my alternative plans. Sometimes Lisa was obsessed by a personal idea of history, of a sequence of deprivations, not even her cousins had actually worked in those sweatshops in Taiwan, or crossed the ocean in a rickety fishing boat. She wasn't working as a dancer in Bangkok doing tricks with Coke bottles for American servicemen. A series of received ideas transformed her into the kind of operator who would twist the market towards her own ends. Lisa was not Rouge, sprung from *Terry and the Pirates* but she could see herself as tough as nails, and had faith in those received ideas about buying and selling, about not being a victim no matter what. I don't know if other prostitutes thought along those lines.

When I was in school one of my teachers read a line to the class from Mayakovsky. In the line, something was "like a naked hooker jumping from a burning building." She could barely read the words through her laughter. The class laughed too. "This should tell you something about poetry," she said to the class. Ignorance finds humor in degradation; somebody else's.

Julie's apartment no longer seemed like her own. It was a room of transit. Four more hours, three more hours, two and a half more to go. The familiar seemed unfamiliar and useless. What do you do with these socks, this broom? It was too hot for wool and too late to clean, no reason to. She had a song in her head but it played with the wrong lyrics. Twenty four hours to go. Another good bye, the big one, the real one. He asked her if she had the letters of transit. It was supposed to be a joke but in a dim way she felt there was some document she was going to need and didn't have. At immigration she would be sent into a bare, white room; stripped, searched. The immigration officers would demand more than a passport. A document of history, intention, stated purpose. Who are you going to visit? What does she do?

How did you meet him? How long have you known her? It doesn't have to be in writing, you can make the statement orally if you let us record it. Letters of transit no longer exist. All you need is a passport. It seemed too simple. She hung up the telephone and turned the answering machine back to zero.

The airport bar was dark, orange, hard to find. Marco Polo was on television. Richard Chamberlain met the King of Shanghai or Ceylon. She couldn't hear the sound. Only a few people in the airport bar looked like travelers. If you worked in the airport you might go to a bar like this one after work because it was close, because some of the people you worked with lived on Staten Island or Long Island and the JFK lounge was the closest place you all could get to before everyone went home. The airport lounge kept cardboard displays on most tables. The folded photographs showed three kinds of drinks. She made dents with her thumb nail in the glossy margaritas, traced pale yellow and pink umbrellas on the other side. She didn't want to talk to the man who looked like he'd slept in his black suit and chain smoked short cigarettes. Julie was always behind this kind of man in lines, never behind the ones who looked like they just got out of the shower. There was no one to say to the camera, I saw her just before she got on the plane.

Other versions: she was not alone, yet. A man did come to see her off, to say good bye. Edmund Wilson wrote that he and John Bishop were afraid to see Edna St. Vincent Millay off to Europe. They were afraid of who they might meet, other lovers on the pier. Julie said good bye to each person separately. She wasn't an auburn-haired poet, it wasn't 1920, no amount of mental dimness or wishful thinking would turn Kennedy Airport into a midnight waterfront or transform a cheap flight with nervous passengers who rarely flew into a lovely boat. 1985, not 1920, Julie would play all the roles in her departure, poet leaving New York behind, anxious suitors in striped suits twisting bunches of gladiolas. She found no flattery in scenes certain to be embarrassing and the person she wanted to come see her off probably wouldn't be caught dead doing so.

Marco Polo learned about gunpowder.

Waiting near the gate, one of the passengers looked like John Huston. She took this as a good sign.

Everyone on the plane was asleep but her. Sleepy typesetters back in Manhattan would not be printing news of a crash. Back in the airport bar, Marco Polo kissed a Chinese girl for the first time.

I had seen a sixteenth century German print of the story of the story of Joseph and Potiphar's wife. An unmade bed was between them. She had her hand on Joseph's shoulder but he had his back to her. He was on his way to the door. She looked as if she were about to be drowned. According to the story Potiphar's wife falsely accused Joseph and he was thrown into prison. Adultery, the desire and potential crime, is pinned on her forever. The bed looks slept in, there is evidence Joseph shouldn't have gotten off Scot free in history. What's a few years in jail by comparison? They aren't wearing biblical costumes but the kind of clothing the artist wore and saw around him.

There's a painting in the Metropolitan Museum by Vermeer, *A Girl Asleep*. She's sitting at a table, eyes shut, daydreaming more than actually sleeping soundly. Originally, according to radiographs, a man was painted in the doorway behind her, but Vermeer painted him out, thinking there would be more of a feeling of lovesickness or dreaming if the lover were absent. He painted *A Girl Asleep* around 1656, it says on the card next to the picture, shortly after the more explicit Dresden *Procumen* was completed. Julie looked through the negatives of Eamonn's Irish pictures to look at the woman's face before he obliterated her eyes. She turned on the red light in the bathroom/darkroom. There was a ghost standing at the door. Eamonn didn't seem to notice but Julie saw him everywhere.

TOP STORIES

A PROSE PERIODICAL

#1 Donna Wyszomierski
#2 Laurie Anderson
#3 Pati Hill
#4 Suzanne Johnson
#5 Linda Neaman
#6 Gail Vachon
#7 Jenny Holzer/Peter Nadin
#8 Judith Doyle
#9 Kathy Acker
#10 Lynne Tillman/Jane Dickson
#11 Kirsten Thorup
#12 Janet Stein
#13 Anne Turyn
#14 Lee Eiferman
#15 Constance DeJong
#16 Ursule Molinaro
#17 Romaine Perin
#18 Donna Wyszomierski
#19-20 Cookie Mueller
#21 Ascher/Straus

Available from
TOP STORIES
228 Seventh Avenue
N.Y.C., N.Y. 10011

ISBN 0-917061-22-5

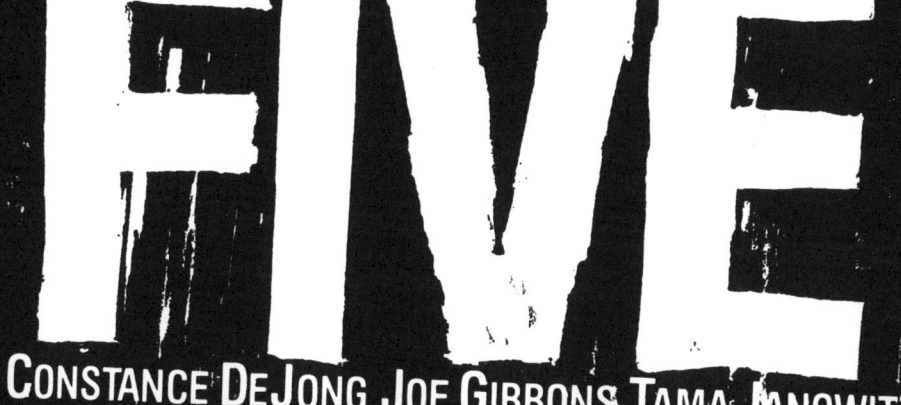

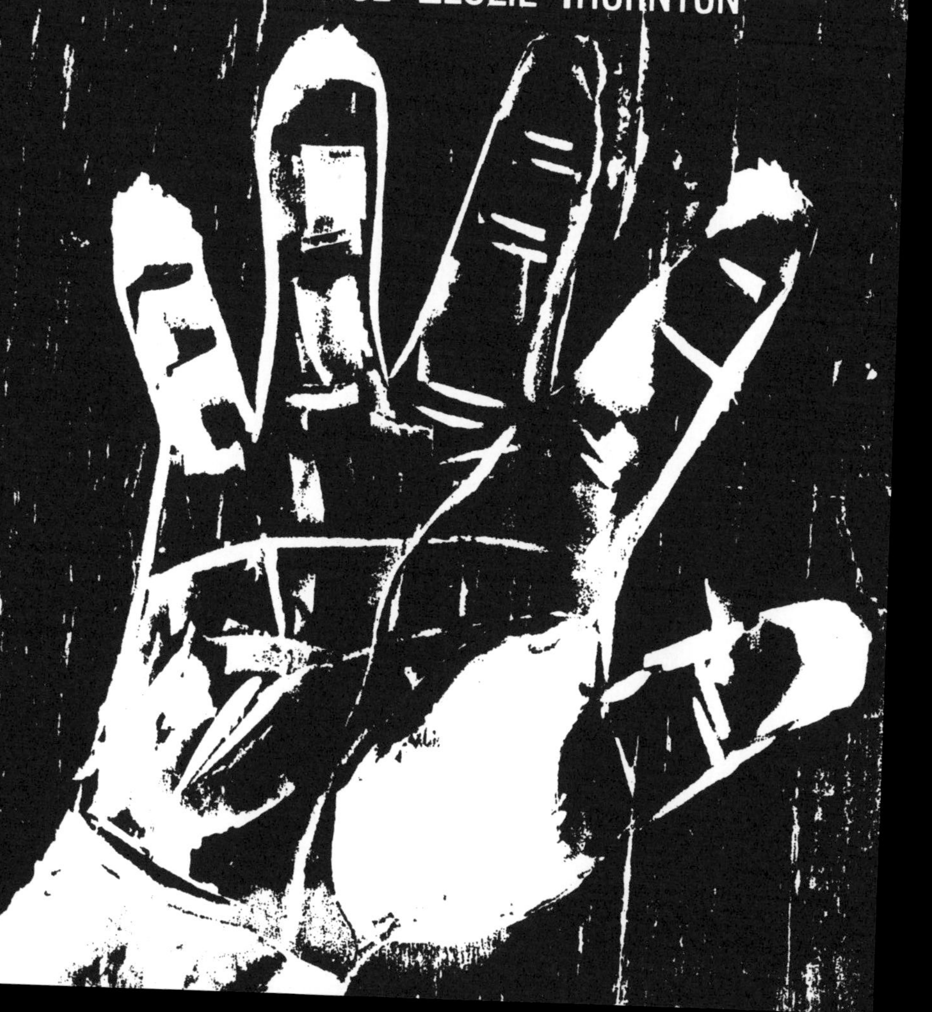

FIVE

FIVE

CONSTANCE DeJONG JOE GIBBONS TAMA JANOWITZ
RICHARD PRINCE LESLIE THORNTON

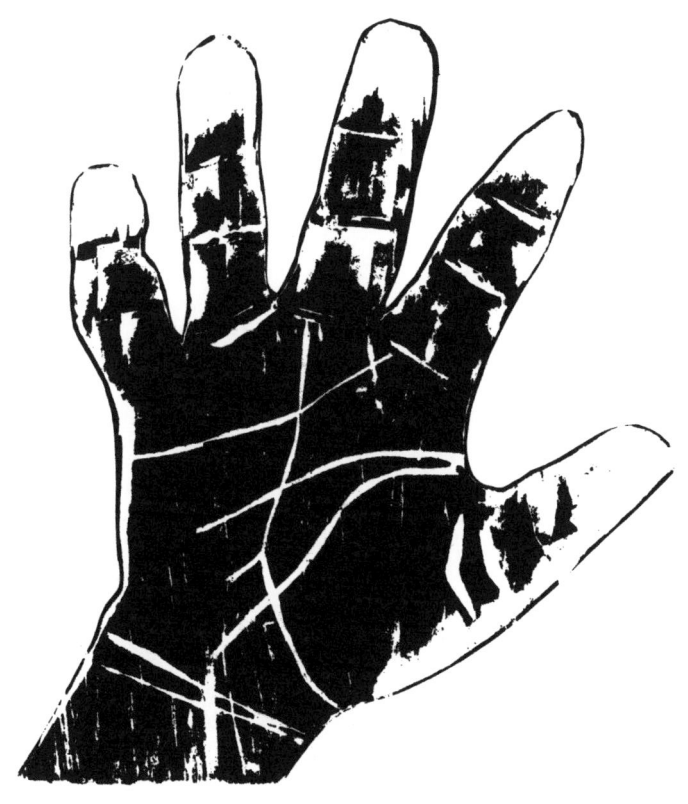

TOP STORIES #23-24
1986

Copyright © 1986 by Constance De Jong, Joe Gibbons, Tama Janowitz, Richard Prince, Leslie Thornton

Cover woodcut © 1986 by Gail Vachon

This publication is made possible in part with public funds from the National Endowment for the Arts and the New York State Council on the Arts

ISBN 0-917061-22-3 (Top Stories #23-24)

TOP STORIES, 228 Seventh Avenue, New York, NY 10011

CONTENTS

Twice Told Tale
Constance DeJong

Mein Wittgenstein
Joe Gibbons

Future Saint #1160
Tama Janowitz

Jokes
Richard Prince

Her Weak Memory of the Tornado
Peggy and Fred in Hell
Leslie Thornton

Twice Told Tale
Constance DeJong

Betty went to see a palm reader for the purpose of inquiring: was it a good idea to go up to Canada for two weeks with Buzzy Cramer?
"Darling, if it's a vacation you want then by all means go. You can travel to your heart's content. That's what all these criss-crossing lines indicate. You'll notice, however, that they all emanate from one point. Can you see that slight mound at the end of your ring finger and the little x-mark on top? Those are such unusual markings you'll have to come back two or three times so we can go into everything in detail. But for starts I can tell you that you're wed to the ancient of ancient times."
Betty could barely make out the little diamond-like spot. It was so dark in the restaurant where Doris gave her readings with her cold icy fingers taking hold of Betty's hand, her pointy nails tracing the lines...red nails matching red lips on a paper-white face that never sees the light of day. Doris has sat in the Diablo restaurant making a living reading palms ever since she retired from the Rockettes. Among her loyal customers, no one cares much about the show girl in Doris, who at 67 has an unshakable reputation for giving good advice. On account of this Betty added Doris' advice to that of her friends.
Everyone said: "What are you crazy? Of course you should go up to Canada. The city stinks in July. Besides Buzzy's place is heaven."

Nights like these Betty begins to wonder. In the city she can put her finger on real fear. The rats are crawling around between the walls, a six foot four maniac is prying up the window. But here in the country....

"Buzzy wake up I heard something."

"Go back to sleep. I told you there were mice in the kitchen."

"Right. Mice wearing shoes, opening doors."

"Yeah, I'll turn on the lights."

The lights are just one bare bulb with a tinfoil reflector and with many moths gathering around.

"You know Buzzy from an entomological point of view those moths aren't very interesting. They're the Timania variety from Japan eating their way across Canada. Your fir trees are all going to die soon."

Buzzy suddenly enthusiastic: "You know I was just thinking. That noise from before; I'll bet it was Rudolph. Everything fits. July, moon in Cancer,—What time is it?—5:30, yeah I'm sure of it now, that was Rudolph alright, the poor slob. He never got over it when they automated the lighthouse. That's what he was going to do to the end of his days, just work the lighthouse and not have anything to do with the rest of the world. He'd pretty much seen all there was to see, following some watery dream, being a sailor I mean. First off in Frankfurt; when that got dull he fell in with a couple of clock makers. Every morning Willie and Rupert would go to their little shop and stay there until suppertime. Then they'd collect Rudolph for a night of drinking and he'd tell them all about ship life; the nasty captains and the stormy nights and the poker games. He had no idea that all day long Willie and Rupert would be working away trying to keep their minds on the insides of clocks. Neither told the other about his obsession with Rosene. But all day long she was there across the street in the bakery selling bread and kuchen. Willie kept his head down but he could see her over the top of his magnifying specs. Rupert was forever dreaming up excuses to change the window display so he could watch her, too. Both of them started coming to work early, to see Rosene coming down the street. But one morning Willie overslept. It happened that Rosene didn't come down the street that morning and by 9:30 Rupert was completely around the bend, convinced that Willie had run off with Rosene. So he ran across the street into the bakery, just because he didn't know what else to do. And when Rupert on his way to work saw Willie's mad dash, he knew Willie was trying to take advantage of his absence to get in good with Rosene. So he ran into the bakery, too. They were standing there fighting mad when the baker came in with a note from Rosene. She'd run off with the wife of the deputy mayor of Frankfurt, a notorious woman hater. Nothing like this had ever happened to Willie and Rupert, who linked arms, closed shop on a weekday for the first time in twelve years, and went off to find Rudolph. They were well into a good drunk when Bertwhistle walked into the bar. They all thought that was a pretty funny name and wanted to know why he was wearing a yarmulka made out of lace. It was a family pattern crocheted in white silk, that was all Bertwhistle knew. Oh yeah—the original pattern was a gift from a Chinese emperor on the occasion of seeing his first Jew in China. All of this started Rudolph to dreaming again about the watery world, so he left the beer garden in search of a good ship. He wanted to see everything: naked girls dancing under palm trees, everything. He... good lord, it's six o'clock. I better go milk the goats before it starts to rain. Hey, Betty are you asleep?"

"No, no. All of that got me to dreaming about my own travels. How I went to Paris—a young girl in search of wordly experience. How I went to the East, to India where time is a different experience, a very very slow...."

"And very, very interesting, no doubt. But right now I really, really have to milk the goats before it starts to rain."

If anything is typical of July in Cape Breton, it's these overcast mornings. It may be clear by lunchtime, it might stay grey all day. It could be anywhere from fifty-five to eighty-five degrees depending on, who knows? The radio always says the sun's going to shine all day... in hopes of luring more tourists from the mainland. The locals don't know anything in spite of folk myths. Then comes Buzzy: a forty-five-year-old man, very set in his ways, including the way he could manage to forget about warning Betty of Cape

Twice Told Tale

Breton's changeability factor, of how she should have brought up more than a swimsuit and a couple pairs of lightweight pants. A rubber poncho, Wellingtons, flannel shirts, a woolen nightgown—a woman needs all this and more to survive Cape Breton's whims; a fact Buzzy takes lightly. He moves with an upright authority; he is spending his second season in his new summer house on this piece of rock sticking up in the Atlantic; he is taking the place just the way it comes day by day and its shortcomings, if there are any, are not up for discussion—not on Betty's first day in the country or on Tuesday, Wednesday, Thursday, Friday. By Saturday Betty realized the shortcomings of Cape Breton were not up for discussion with a single one of the summer residents. Like Buzzy, they were busily milking goats, repairing roofs and fences, working like crazy to undo the winter's damage so they could take pride in their country living—their flannels flapping on the clothesline, rows of bread rising on the drainboard, pieces of meat marinating in herbs picked in the fields. Flowers and weeds from those same fields decorated the dinner table at Linda's house:

> Saturday, July 13
> Went to a dinner party at Linda's house, Linda of the crummy novels all day on the beach. About ten people were shoveling down her so-called wholesome country meal. There were a lot of kids and dogs, too, but everyone ignored them, and me, too. Too busy discussing the importance of privacy and complaining about the locals living in trailers and junking up the place. As far as I can tell they'd all be living in trailers too if it weren't for some rich dead relatives six foot under. One of the privileged was kind enough to ask me if I was up for the whole summer. I restrained myself from speaking my mind, especially after seeing Buzzy give me some big winks across the table like he wasn't having such a great time either. After people comes nature. A few words about that before I call it a night. NATURE IS CRUEL. No, weird, schitzy, I don't know, I'm drunk.

When sober, nature can still knock Betty for a loop. Pods are popping open and baby animals are thrashing through the underbrush and shoots are pushing through the ground and stamens are rubbing against pistils. And all together it's another case of Cape Breton's changeability factor. Nature knows this brief interlude of July days is its only chance. Hence, the hysterical growth taking place in the unbelievably noisy woods. By standing very still, the racket surrounding Buzzy's house can sort of be differentiated into the black fly's hum, the woodpecker's knock, that hiss is probably a snake slithering through the grass. Buzzy won't cut it because it's nice the way it waves in the wind. Anyway, he says: "There aren't any poisonous snakes on the property, underline any." Betty says: "Terrific, there are fifty yards of tangled underbrush between the main house and the out house." And that means even going to the bathroom is an issue in Cape Breton.

Larger issues stem out from the house. Surrounded by woods on three sides, the front door opens onto the big sky, acres of meadow and on a clear day the shore line runs for twenty-six miles before the haze blots it out. It's helpful having a narrow footpath down to the beach. Without it you're just a tiny thing lost in a big landscape. Even with it Betty feels the emotional currents of this sad, lonely place where moths are feeding on pine trees that are crying in the wind. And down at the shore the waves roll up to tell her... no place to run to, no place to hide. Twenty-six miles of coast are shrinking in the twilight down to a little patch of sand where Betty sits watching the sun, a huge red dot, slip toward the horizon. Once upon a time a woman sitting there like that was described like this:

> The great female who sits there guarding the Island is the last of all. Her head is infinitely higher than the highest mists. There is no other nearly living thing on the Island except her now. Her red hair, far above everything else, still slightly gilds the clouds, and that is all that is left of the sun.
>
> She is trying to make herself a cup of tea, so they say.

> She may just as well try, since there she'll be throughout eternity. She'll never get her tea to boil because of the fog which has become much too thick and all-pervading. She uses a ship's hull for a teapot, the hull of the biggest and most beautiful she can find, and she warms her tea in it. Oceans and oceans of tea. She stirs, she stirs it all with an enormous oar...that gives her something to do.
>
> She takes no notice of anything else, sitting there forever serious, forever busied with her tea.
>
> With her fingers she pokes the live coals that are under the ashes between two forests of dead trees. That's enough for her. She tries to get it to burn properly, everything is hers now, but her kettle will never boil.
>
> There's no life in the fire.
>
> There's no life in the world for anybody except just a little for her and it is all very nearly over now.

Betty hated that description from a crummy French novel she'd encountered in her search for worldly experience. Maybe she'd come a long way from her strolls back and forth across Paris to this Cape Breton world where she was beginning to see the light, a light standing out against the darkening background, a line of light sweeping across the waves and back, steadily, regularly, back and forth, back and forth. It was a little like being hypnotized, like being herself, the woman she was once upon another kind of time—the gradual, graceful time of India:

> India's on slow time. An even train of days hooking onto nights shading into another day steadily shading out over the water over the desert the mountains the plains. The sky was filling with light, the sun was clear in the sky and there was a cool breeze from the sea. It was fairly early in the morning. Fortunately it wasn't going to be too hot a day. But the dust was everywhere, fine and penetrating. In the moonlight the garden

became very beautiful. Motionless, silent trees cast long, dark shadows across the lawn and among the still bushes. The birds settled down for the night in the dark foliage. Hardly anyone was on the road. Occasionally there was a song in the distance. Otherwise, the garden was quiet, full of soft whispers and the trees gave shape to the hazy, silver sky. It had rained all night and most of the morning and now the sun was going down behind heavy, dark clouds. There was no color in the sky. The frogs had croaked all night, persistently, rhythmically; but with the dawn they became silent. The morning was gray. The sun rose out of the woods, big with burning radiance, but the clouds soon hid it. All day the sun and the clouds fought each other. Clouds had been coming through a wide gap in the mountains; piling up against the hills. They remained dark and threatening over the valley and it would probably rain towards evening. The night was silent and still. It was very early in the morning and the sea was quiet, lapping at the white shore. There was a sparkle in the sea, and a blueness and it was old. Smoke from a steamer far out was going almost straight up in the sky. The sun wouldn't be up for two or three hours. There wasn't a cloud in the sky. The villagers weren't up yet. The sky was enclosed by a dark outline of encircling hills. The night was completely still. The moon was just coming out of the sea into a valley of clouds. The water was still, blue. Orion was faintly visible in the pale, silver sky. White waves lapped against the shore. The moon was rising above the valley of clouds and it was huge. There was rain. It came down in sheets, flooding the roads and filling up the lily pond. Trees bent under the weight. The crows were soaked and could hardly fly. Suddenly the frogs were silent. It was particularly beautiful that evening with the sun setting below the dark town, behind a single minaret, which seemed to be pointing the whole town up towards the sky. The clouds were golden red, aflame with the brilliance of a sun that had travelled over a beautiful, sad land. And as the brilliance faded there was the new moon. There over the dark town was the delicate new moon. The sun was now touching the treetops and they were aglow with soft light. They were giving shape to the sky. A single rose was heavy with dew. The rains had washed the skies clean; the haze that had hung about was gone and the sky was clear and intensely blue. Shadows were sharp and deep, and high on the hill a column of smoke was going straight up. It was still very early and there was a slight ground mist hiding the bushes and flowers. The sun was just coming up behind a mass of trees, which were quiet now. The chattering birds had already scattered for the day. It was quite early. The Southern Cross was clear and beautiful over the palm trees. A heavy dew made a circle of dampness around each tree. There weren't any lights on in the houses yet. And the stars were very clear. But there was an awakening in the eastern sky. It had been raining for days. Hills and mountains were under dark clouds. In the distance, the land was hidden by thick fog. There were puddles everywhere and the rain came through everything. It was a lovely day and as the sun had only just come over the treetops it still wasn't too hot. The sea was pale blue and very calm. White waves came in slowly. There wasn't a cloud. And the waning moon was in mid-heaven. As the sun climbed higher, the plains were covered with long shadows. It was a beautiful day, clear and not too warm. It had rained recently. One of those soft, gentle rains that go deep. The sky was intensely blue; the horizon was filled with enormous clouds. Early in the morning, just before the sun comes out of the sea, when the dew is heavy on the ground and the stars are still visible, this place is very beautiful. Everything is quiet against the thunder of the sea. The morning star is fading. A golden rim is showing at the water's far edge. Shadows are slowly casting across the ground. The sea is very calm. The sea was resting before the north-easterly winds began. The sands were bleached by the sun and salt water. There was a strong smell of ozone and seaweed. No one was on the beach yet. The eastern sky was more splendid than where the sun had set. A mass of clouds was full of flashes of lightening, twisting sharp and brilliant. There were other weird shapes. And every imaginable color. Towards the west there was a pure orange. It had rained for days. It was a very clear, starry night. There was not a cloud in the sky. The waning moon was just above the tall palms, which were very still. Orion was well up in the western sky and the Southern Cross was over the hills. Not a house had a light in it and the narrow road was dark and deserted. The sea was calm. The horizon clear. It would be an hour or two before the sun would come up behind the hills and the waning moon set the waters moving. Nothing was stirring in the bushes, nothing yet moving. The birds were quiet. It was a lovely evening, cool after the hot, sunny day. A breeze was coming across the water and the waving palms gave shape to the sky. The sun was setting. The day was shading slowly, evenly into a black Indian night. The woman was standing on the beach. She was riding in a train, walking up from the valley, sitting on a hill. The woman was traveling alone in India. She was eating ice cream because it was her birthday. The dark blue waters were full of reflections. For an instant she cast about for a thirty-year old opinion. It was another lovely, Bombay evening, cool after the hot, sunny day. The sun was fading. A breeze was coming across the water and little sparkles began to stand out against the darkening background. The palms were waving. The water was full of reflections; she was standing at the Gate of India; it was a very clear, starry night.

Twice Told Tale

    Twenty-six miles of coast are shrinking in the twilight down to a little patch of sand where Betty has been sitting for a long, long time watching the sun slip below the water. A line of light sweeps across the waves and back, and automated or not at least the lighthouse is there, gone, there again. "Stay there lighthouse, you're the one who sees I get home safe. You get me through the wavy meadow full of snakes. You keep the bears in the woods, keep me steady on the footpath with one eye on the dark, one eye on the lookout for the place where the path curves and Buzzy's house pops into view."

    Betty is used to sprinting that last twenty yard stretch, to stepping into the light pouring out from the windows. Here the edge of night is clearly drawn and this can be the nicest time of day—when Betty turns around and makes faces at the wild animals and swirly sky. But tonight her victory over nature doesn't have its usual kick, it doesn't come up to the kind of thing she was reading about earlier in one of Buzzy's religious books. When Vivekenanda was a young man, a herd of mean monkeys began to follow him down the road. Vivekenanda was so frightened he began to walk faster and faster until an old sage sitting along the roadside called him over. The sage told Vivekenanda that the only way to dispel fear was to hit it straight on. After concentrating for a while Vivekenanda whirled around and stared at those monkeys and sent them screaming in all directions. After thinking about Vivekenanda all day Betty realized—a saint she was not. And after arriving safely at the porch with the squares of light shining on the floorboards, the pine scent on the breeze, the far away sound of lapping water, Buzzy through the window stirring something on the stove... no, this was not her idea of heaven. Buzzy could see that written all over her face. "Look," he said, "tonight in your honor I'm serving an old, secret family recipe: *Martians in the Himalayas*."

    He put the bowl of green peas and mashed potatoes on the table, she wondered if it was the big, sad landscape that made their difference in age stick out so much.

    "You know Buzzy I was reading one of your religious books today and I came across the issue I've been thinking about these days, the issue of fear and conquering...."

"Ok, ok, hold it, just stop right there with this fear business. If you want to talk with me about so-called fear, then there has to be some basis for a conversation and the way I see it there are three possible approaches. Now is it the natural, the supernatural or just the drunken local marauders? You decide."

Buzzy cleared the table, did the dishes, built a fire, got the bed ready. "Do you want me to tell you some more about the travels of Rudolph?"

"No," she said, "no thanks. And Buzzy, I know it ruins a whole day for you but could you take me to the airport tomorrow? I want to go home."

It's ninety-seven miles to the airport one-way. Coming back Buzzy stopped in to see Linda. He skipped all the excuses for just dropping in like that. The signals had been sent already: his—an especially soulful look with an unnecessary pat on the arm at the dinner table; hers—an up from under the lashes with the head cocked to one side. Everyone at Linda's dinner had tried to ignore these transparent hijinks going on right there in front of Buzzy's girlfriend. Ever since, it had been only a question of time, a wait that meant nothing to Linda. She'd been sending her signals for many years and the many receivers who responded to her odd offering of silk sheets and chocolate chip cookies would resemble a bell shaped curve of male humanity... leaving many women to ask, what does he see in her?

In Buzzy's case he saw a shining lamp drawing him closer, a nice enough person whose sheets and cookies after a week's worth of visits all combined to fit comfortably into his definition of a flame— when flame is not longer something hot, scintillating. It's something safe, steady, a sure thing, the source from which all good things flow; a little bit like an old TV glow. In fact when Buzzy came down from his summer in Canada he had a definite blue-gray aura about him, an aura of television, of daytime television, of the soaps. Of all places, Buzzy chose the Diablo as the setting for his little scene billed as a late dinner with Betty, dinner at eleven, as was their custom. Buzzy's script called for him to play high priest of the noble mysteries to her fallen angel. From these, Buzzy's euphemisms for high and low, any fool can guess how his bye-bye lines go: how life is a mystery, how you just never know, how there's chance meetings, destiny, lucky stars....

Twice Told Tale

Upon hearing lucky stars Betty stood up and excused herself to go to the bathroom, walked out the front door of the Diablo and kept walking down the street. Her footsteps were leaving treadmarks on the earth, were increments measuring years on the march. She was twenty-five going on forty, sixty, eighty...a hundred year old woman. She was too old for looking at stars. And besides, according to Betty, there was another, a more important chronology of events: "My problems didn't begin with some euphemisms from the smooth talking Buzzy, but with the dream merchants who sold him a bill of goods in the first place...his very own house on an island by the sea. That's the level of competition I've come to. Those guys with their dreamy sales pitches—they're not little entrepreneurs out building a family fortune. They're part of the technostructure whose influence is incomparably greater than an entrepreneur's.

"Those who look for the influence usually look in the wrong places. They look for legislators in the pay of corporations, for public officials responsive to financial flattery. They delve for the five-percenters and lobbyists dispensing alcohol, mink, vicuna, hospitality in Nassau. The best discovery of all is of a traditionalist who carries money in a black bag, has a congressman in his pay and, at the least, has requisitioned his office and telephone. These last are rare but every year one or more exponents of these techniques of bribery or illegal influence is discovered and drummed out of the company of respectable men. These victims are the survivors of an earlier era and methodology. Their public destruction is a purification rite. Minor sin is washed away in an orgiastic burst of indignation. Meanwhile the dream merchants are busy spinning the sale of Buzzy's house into an international epic.

"Oh sure, it takes some time for this transformation to occur; a tiny portion of which is devoted to the art of speaking. A fast talker converts a roof over Buzzy's head into peace in his mind which clinches the sale that initiates the complicated passage of Buzzy's money back to the mother company, whose real estate holdings are but one of its many offspring. Its computers suggest selling Buzzy's money out in the open market, an old venture lacking the Casbah-touch, though modern investment technques are pretty exotic too. They have to be, considering the value of the dollar and how it can purchase more valuable currency and still make a profit as if by magic. By extension the profit can be increased by high interest loans compounded weekly, sometimes daily. And by the time the mother company sees a three to five hundred percent profit on the sale of one home, added to many other sales, multiplied by many other business deals—by then the company has acquired a deep concern for the economic stability of the country. It doesn't take a genius to recognize the well known relationship between government and big business. The practical manifestations of this friendship are most visible in the area of defense procurement. For example, Buzzy's money is now resting peacefully down in South Africa as a couple molecules of nitrogen in an atom bomb. If it goes off some people will stand around applauding money making as the highest social achievement. Now you can tell me that some will also say I'm making a federal case out of my own personal problems?"

"Listen to old Eddie, babe. You can't get away with that end of the world crap just because of one lousy love affair. Look Betty, it just makes you sound, you know, just deeply shallow, you know what I mean? Get out of here."

>Friday, August 31 going on September 1...3 a.m.
>I finished my drink and walked outside. When I'm out there walking around all doubtful in the rain, I look up at the raindrops in the halo around a street light and I'm happy again. The weather is my friend. I say weather, you're the greatest. Human hands, computer brains, no one messes with you. That's why I like reading about you in the papers. I worry about the animals, though. All those lost little dogs and cats. Parakeets that can't get out of their cages. Angelfish slopped out of their bowls. I worry about what happens to the animals when the weather cuts loose, when I read that earthquakes took 86,000 lives and left 2.4 million homeless in Guatemala City and southern Iran. Typhoons in southwestern India devastated a one-hundred mile area taking

Twice Told Tale

51,000 lives and leaving uncounted homeless. All winter —hurricanes raged in the Canary Islands, floodwaters poured over Mexico, gale winds battered southern France, and a series of tornadoes swept down the eastern coast of Japan. Across the Pacific events moved in a northerly direction along the California coast with eighty-mile-an-hour tailwinds fanning forest fires out of control— Malibu, Big Sur, up north to San Francisco and a rain that began in October was still coming down at Thanksgiving. By then parts of San Francisco were underwater and in the upper parts of the city the mail stopped arriving, the phones went dead, and the one final comfort, the lights, flickered and dimmed. It continued to rain in the midst of practical maneuvers for evacuation —some said the end was near, some that it was already here, and others tell the story differently. A few would tell us we are all members of a species endangered by the stories that get told and not just those tales of most fabled love where words are just rollers to spread the emotions around.

Twice Told Tale, © 1979 by Constance DeJong
Contains excerpts from *Modern Love* (1975) and *L.A. Stories* (1977), both published by Standard Editions.

The author and Wittgenstein in Cambridge.

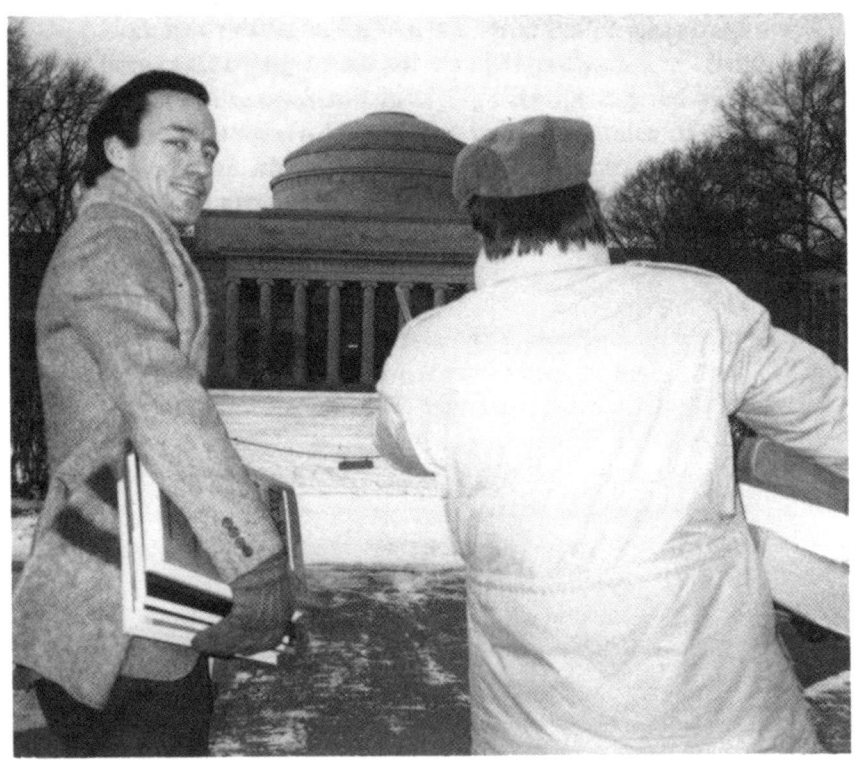

Mein Wittgenstein
Joe Gibbons

I have, in my colorful career as a cultural adventurer, known many of the leading figures in the intellectual vanguard with some degree of intimacy—whether as friend or foe, mentor or acolyte. Only one person, however, fit into—at one time or another—all four categories, and that was the renowned philosopher Ludwig Wittgenstein. Although our relationship lasted only a short time, it was one that profoundly affected my life—and his too, of course.

I first encountered Wittgenstein in a run-down moviehouse in Cambridge, England, just before the war. He was with a group of his students and throughout the movie he persisted in making crude comments and wiseacre observations, generating much laughter from his young admirers. I was unaccustomed to this sort of rudeness in a house of cinema, and chastened him with an open-hand slap across his face which knocked him out of his seat. His students leaped on me and pinned me to the floor. "Stomp on him, sir! Crush the infidel!" they urged him. Instead Wittgenstein scrutinized me and said "Let him go;" then, addressing me in a grave voice, "I am sorry, sir, for disturbing you. Please allow me to buy you a Pernod."

Over the course of the evening—and countless Pernods—Wittgenstein and I got to know each other. He explained to me how he had definitively solved all the fundamental problems of philosophy by reducing them to mathematical propositions, thereby rendering

Mein Wittgenstein

them nonsensical. I in turn described how I had arrived at precisely the same conclusion through a different methodology—my theory of the tautology of truth functions. We were both quite excited by our mutual corroboration and ended the night with a champagne toast to the demise of philosophy.

From that night on Wittgenstein—or Wiggy, as he preferred to be called—and I were inseparable. Like two men just released from a prison sentence, we felt liberated—freed from the chains of ratiocination, from the prison-cell of the intellect.

Wittgenstein confided in me his belief that "logic is a lie, a distortion of reality." He felt that the urge to make sense of things (Nietzsche's "will to order") was a fundamental human weakness. Worse, that for certain people such as himself, abstract thinking was an addictive disease similar to alcoholism or bulimia. "I think as another might excessively drink or eat, to insulate myself from the uncertainties, the angst of the natural world. I am a man obese with thought; I am a fathead."

Sometimes, in the midst of one of his thinking binges, he would visit my quarters at Trinity College and pace back and forth all night long, as though trying to work off the excess poundage of his thoughts. When Wiggy became lost in this maze of lucubration no one could reach him; his only refuge was the local moviehouse. "The movies, they make me stupid. I love them for that." He often cursed his fate to be an intellectual, and fantacized about being a Hollywood movie director.

As soon as spring arrived we left Cambridge and traveled to Paris, where we took up a dissolute lifestyle bankrolled by Wittgenstein's recent inheritance. He believed that money was inherently corrupting and was determined to divest himself of it as rapidly as possible. His long-range goal was always to acquire religious convictions and enter a monastery, but for now he wanted to "live it up" and experience life to its fullest.

One night at a seedy bar in Clichy, Wittgenstein, emboldened by alcohol, picked a fight with a prickly bunch of logical positivists. Wiggy, as it is well known, did not suffer the "log-povs" gladly; he disparaged their lack of interest in the theory of meaning and their petty preoccupation with the principle of verifiability. For both of us they epitomized the small-mindedness of the contemporary philosopher. However they were good fighters and we were taking a terrible beating—a flying chair cracked several of my ribs, Wiggy lost a couple of teeth—when Bertrand Russell happened by and restored order with a round from his automatic revolver.

After that incident we tried to stay out of trouble, but I could sense that Wiggy was growing restless. Clearly he missed the aggressive grappling with problems that characterized his approach to philosophy. I knew from my own research that a life without problems is a shallow one; that the quality of a life is determined by the quality of its problems; and that real problems are infinitely richer and more fulfilling than the pseudo-problems of academic philosophy.

Thus I suggested to Wittgenstein that he take up the homosexual lifestyle: it was avant-garde, challenging, provocative and highly problematic. It wouldn't be too hard to adapt to since Wiggy had never really developed a sexual orientation, having spent his adolescence in deep cogitation. Moreover, he appreciated the non-procreative aspect of homosexuality, believing it a heinous act to bring children into a world such as ours.

I was astonished at the vivacity with which Wiggy embraced this new identity. I liked to imagine what his colleagues back at Cambridge would think, to see him in his full leather regalia, chatting up the young boys along the Rue Montparnasse. But this was Paris in its heyday of decadence, and everything was permitted.

One very dissipated afternoon Wiggy and I were sipping pink absinthe at a Left Bank boite when World War I broke out. For Wittgenstein, nothing would do but that we must go and enlist immediately; he was very drunk and spouting Pig Latin. "Eway antway otay ightfay! Eway antway otay ightfay!" he chanted all the way to enlistment headquarters. (We flipped a coin to determine for which side we would fight.) I accompanied him, never imagining they would let us in the door.

The next day we were on our way to the front. After I got over my initial chagrin it felt good to be out-of-doors, "roughing it." And with the rockets whistling overhead and the bullets whizzing by, I felt more

Mein Wittgenstein

alive than I had in years. What a change from the soft university life!

Unfortunately the war brought out the worst in Wittgenstein: he reverted to excogitating. At first he tried to hide it from me, but I could always tell when he'd been deep-thinking. He began to neglect his personal appearance, and soon he lost all interest in practical matters. Not even the other soldiers could succeed in distracting him, some of whom rather fancied "the Wig," as they took to calling him.

I suspect the stress of the battlefront drove him to seek solace in the security of his "language-games." I tried to dissuade him—"You don't want to end up like Kant, do you?" but to no avail. He was increasingly obsessed with the idea of a developing a private langauge, and in the process he stopped communicating—that is, he stopped making sense.

For Wittgenstein, the act of thinking was inseparable from the act of speaking. He found it necessary to think out loud, which some of the soldiers found disconcerting. In fact, he soon became unbearable with his incessant chattering and scribbling. He babbled incomprehensibly all the way to the Marne, where the Italian forces were mounting a major offensive. I was certain that Wittgenstein would never see combat himself, that he was instead expected to serve as the resident "wise man," a sort of home-spun philosopher. The officers had misconstrued him when he had light-heartedly listed his occupation as "moral philosopher"—thinking him to be a "morale philosopher," one whose specialty was diagnosing and ameliorating morale problems.

Actually nobody was more demoralized than Wiggy. As always, for him deep thought went hand in hand with deep depression. I never understood why this was, but I knew that three of his brothers had taken their own lives to escape this same affliction (he drew inspiration from the fourth brother, a one-armed concert pianist). "Language," he would say, "is what we use to close the wound."

Still, Wiggy was tireless, prattling and scrawling night and day in those colored notebooks; one was blue, another brown, still another was shocking pink (he never let anyone read that one, I suspect it was pornography, or his movie script). He was composing his *Tractatus Logico-Philosophicus*, a title I suggested; it sounded appropriately important and abstruse, like the great classical texts of Archithebes and Polythagoras.

At one point our position was under heavy artillery assault. Mortar shells were exploding right and left, snipers were firing on us from all sides—we were sitting pretty as strudel on a sidewalk, as Wittgenstein would say. To take my mind off the imminence of death I conducted an informal religious survey among the men. When I informed Wittgenstein of my findings—there were no atheists in the foxholes—he snapped back at me, "Only fools and fanatics join the infantry."

Shortly afterwards a grenade exploded beside me, peppering my legs and chest with shrapnel. I was nearly in shock, but somehow managed to drag myself to a nearby bunker. There I found Wittgenstein hunched over his notebooks, muttering to himself and writing. He had been preoccupied for several days with the problem of one's knowledge of other minds, and due to the serious nature of this inquiry, was excused from combat duty.

"Ludwig, I've been hit," I gasped. He peered at me with a look of profound perplexity as the pool of blood grew larger around me. Finally he spoke with a grave enunciation, "Language is what we use to close the wound," and turned back to writing in his notebook.

I tried again. "Ludwig, I'm in terrible pain. I'm dying, help me!" Again he scrutinized me with bafflement, and after some thought spoke again with the same deliberation as before, "If one has to imagine someone else's pain on the model of one's own, this is none too easy a thing to do: for I have to imagine a pain which I do not feel on the model of the pain which I do feel." I was growing faint from loss of blood, but Wittgenstein continued. "That is to say: if we construe the grammar of the expression of sensation on the model of 'object and name' the object drops out of the equation as irrelevant." He turned back to enter this observation in his notebook. Unable to appreciate the epistemological implications of my injuries, I blacked out.

It was not until the next day, en route to a hospital in Normandy, that I regained consciousness. The ambulance driver, a burly bearded man named Ernest, regaled me with anecdotes about the exploits of his friends, a fascinating bunch of adventurers who were doing the kinds of things Wittgenstein and I only dreamed about. I told Ernest, "You should write this stuff down, it would make a good novel." He promised me he would look into it.

Along the way I told him a yarn I cooked up for the soldiers about an old man who goes out in his boat to catch himself a fish for dinner, but the fish he catches is so big it drags the old man out to sea. The old man refuses to give up and let the fish go; days pass and it's a stand-off. Unfortunately I hadn't figured out an ending, and Ernest yowled with disappointment when I told him so. He thought for a few minutes and suddenly beamed, "I've got it! The old man finally succeeds in bringing the fish back to port, but on arrival finds that sharks have devoured the thing. Oh, you must come with me to Pamplona, in Spain, next fall, if you've recovered. You'll love it! They let the bulls run through the streets, it's chaos; people get killed, it's better than war!"

I was certainly tired of the war—it turned out to be a big disappointment—and agreed to meet Ernest in Pamplona on Armistice Day. I told him all about Wittgenstein and asked if he could come along too. "Of course, of course! We'll bring the ambulance, make some money, we'll have a grand time!"

During my convalescence news reached me that Wiggy had been captured by the Italian forces—they were convinced he was a high-level intelligence officer. He refused to surrender any information, volunteering only this (which was to become the cornerstone of his mature philosophy): "Whereof we cannot speak, thereof we must remain silent." That's my Wittgenstein!

By September I had recovered from my wounds, but I was a changed man. I suppose it was the proximity to death that made me see things in their proper perspective. I no longer wished to be one of the "Lost Generation": I knew all too clearly who and where I was, and what I had to do.

And I am not ashamed to admit that, yes, I was once an "intellectual." It is one of those phases one passes through on the way to wisdom and maturity: I regret nothing.

I took the next steamer to America, and never saw or heard from Wittgenstein again. The rest, as they say, is history.

Future Saint #1160
Tama Janowitz

1.

For many years I had eaten the same thing on certain days of the week: Monday, Salisbury steak, mashed potato, roll, apple cup; Tuesday, sausage in tomato sauce, buttered corn, mixed fruit cup; Wednesday, Island sandwich (ham, cheese with pineapple), salad with French dressing, crackers, wonder bar; Thursday, sloppy joe bunwich, vegetable sticks, onion rings, apricots; Friday, cheese pizza, buttered mixed vegetables, chocolate pudding with topping.

This completed the weekday menu.

For many years I had eaten the same thing on certain days of the week: Monday, Salisbury steak, mashed potato, roll, apple cup; Tuesday, sausage in tomato sauce, buttered corn, mixed fruit cup; Wednesday, island sandwich (bun, mixed fruit cup, meatballs), zucchini squash, nuts and bolts; Thursday, collard greens, tater tots, peas and carrots; Friday, fishwich and cheese roll, chocolate pudding with topping.

This completed the weekday menu.

The food was dished out by the dietician on a green plastic tray, and at the end of the line there were forks, knives, spoons of two different sizes and napkins in a black and silver metal container. There were three tall cannisters like sump pumps, and each day the solutions in these dispensers varied: ketchup, French dressing, mustard and syrup were only a few of the different things available to put on the food.

I did not like to interrupt my enjoyment of the meal by speaking to anyone, so I sat alone in one corner of the dining hall. In any event, it was obvious to me that I was superior to the others—I do not mean this in any derogatory sense, only that I was better than they were—and would not have had much to say to them, grim and noisy in their grease-covered coats.

Still, I could not help but be filled with happiness as I ate my meal. How tactful I felt toward everyone! How kind! And they to me, for they left me quite alone as I dined. The mashed potatoes so creamy, bland and gently refreshing. How pale and thin the metal fork was, and how fine the roll, with a tender brown crust and white interior, as if a bird had died in my hand. The carrots like young girls smiled on my plate, the macaroni and cheese, pure, nearly inedible, swam down my throat like living goldfish and the chocolate pudding, dense, sooty, tasting of powdery grit. Around me the forks and knives of the others clattered like the most glorious of harpsichords.

No seconds were allowed, but generally, if I waited until the very end of the lunch hour, I could go back and get another roll with a pat of margarine, or even, on occasion, another portion of dessert. This was only because the dietician and the cashier knew me and did not mistrust me in any way. The cashier did not take money but different colored tickets: I myself always had the green tickets, daily I gave her two. The meals lasted one hour: from eleven forty-five to quarter of one every day.

After two and a half years I began to notice that my portions were dissimilar to the portions received by the others. At first, I assumed this was simply due to slight of hand on the part of the dietician: after all, I remembered how on several occasions I had gotten more than one and a half times the normal amount of batter-fried fish and cheese on a bun, because, after all, fish was by its very nature not a mathematically exact form. I had not complained on those occasions when I received too much, but now, getting less, I began to feel offended.

After all, everything was weighed and cut into equal portions before hand—the meat always weighed four and a half ounces, the

Future Saint #1160

mashed potatoes were dished out by ice cream scoop, the pineapple tidbits were measured into tiny paper cups. Therefore, though the first few times I received smaller portions it might have been an accident, the deviation from the norm could not have been so frequent *without being done on purpose.*

At first, it was just by a little bit that my portions were cut, and while others on line in front of me got a whole cup of jello with fruit cocktail, I noticed that I received only half a cup. After several weeks, my rationing grew even shorter: three ounces of meat, two or three carrot sticks instead of five, two peas and then at last only one pea and nothing else, one pea alone on my cafeteria tray.

Why? What had I done to deserve this? It was injust, injust, and in the cafeteria dining hall I saw the faces of the others sneering half-wittedly at me, as if to say, now you have gotten your comeuppance.

As if this wasn't enough, my tray was very dirty—the dietician had organized the trays so that when I came in, the tray on the top was very dirty, and to pause on line for even a second, even for the second that it took to get a different tray, would mean being trampled by those behind me on line. I had seen it happen, I had seen elderly and infirm hurt and kicked for their slowness on line.

My nails were bitten to the quick. There was no peace of mind to be found in eating one pea for lunch.

The dietician and the cashier acted as if they did not know me. They looked at me as if I did not exist. I had always felt such a closeness to them, especially the dietician, who more than anyone had grace and an animal surety.

At the end, when I tried to give the cashier my tickets, she would not accept them. I hesitated to speak out loud, knowing how the others would turn to leer at me, they would had once been so tactful though crude, but I could not control myself. "But why?" I said. "Why?" She did not answer, and I realized I was the only using green tickets. The green tickets were no longer being accepted. But this at least was an explanation, something I could live with.

Sadly, I took my tray to the disposing area, I put it on the rack, the spoon I placed in the silverware container, I did not know what else to do....

2.

After I became a prostitute, I had to deal with penises of every imaginable shape and size. Some large, others quite shriveled and pendulous of testicle. Some blue veined and reeking of Stilton, some miserly, crabbed, enchanted, dusted with pearls like the great minarets of the Taj Mahal, jesting, ringed as the tail of a raccoon, fervant, crested, impossible to live with, marigold-scented. More and more I became grateful I didn't have to own one of these appendages.

It was a great relief to me. Of course I had a pimp; he wasn't an ordinary sort of person but had been a double Ph.D. candidate in philosophy and American literature at the University of Massachusetts. When we first became friends he was driving a taxi cab, but soon found this left him little time for his own work, which was to write.

When my job as a script girl for a German-produced movie to be filmed in Venezuela fell through, it became obvious we were going to have to figure out a different way to make money fast. For a pimp and a prostitute Bob and I had a very unusual relationship. As far as his role went, he could have cared less. But he did not. I paid the bills and bought his typewriter ribbons, and then if I felt like handing over any more money to him in addition, it was up to me. At night I would come in for a rest and find him lying on the bed reading Kant or Heidegger's *What is a Thing?*

Often our discussions would be so lengthy and intense I would have to gently interrupt him to say that if I didn't get back out to work the evening would be over and I wouldn't have filled my self-imposed nightly quota.

I was like a social-worker for lepers. My clients had a chunk of their body they wanted to give away; for a price I was there to receive it. Crimes, sins, nightmares, hunks of hair: it was surprising how many of them had some to dispose of. The more I charged, the easier it was for my friends to breathe freely once more.

3.
I began to tremble with happiness. What a thing I was! Trembling with happiness, I had not eaten all day, I had no money left in the bank, I was all alone, yes I was completely alone, not even anything to look forward to and yet I was quivering with what I sensed was joy.

Stop it at once, (from a distance I heard the twitter of nervous sardines, they spoke to me, only to me) stop this at once, there is certainly no need, no joy, no point, no sense in being happy or even feeling good.

Still I stood in the grocery store, trembling with happiness. Yes, trembling. Nobody would have known it to look at me, but I could not control myself. So many strangers, standing around examining the frozen vegetables as if members of some curious cult: *they* were not important to me, not at this moment indeed. But the spinach souffle, Stouffers, sterile in the freezer! All free to look at, yes, there was no one to stop me from thinking about every item in the grocery store today.

The statuesque slices of meat, red and freckled with fat, enshrouded in plastic with the following figures embossed in blue on a white sticker: $4.99 lb, .52 lb. Meat and meat by-products! The rows of grapefruit, ominous, silent, stacked-up yellow and disapproving. The craniums of artichokes. And the members of the root family: the onions, the beets, the noble carrots, jaundiced, aristocratic! Ah, the thrill!

Bliss, such bliss, I was nearly dancing down the aisle and who knows what I might have done next when I said: yes, but you do not know that you are trembling with happiness, you may be feeling this way for—some other reason? It may be that in fact you are not happy at all, you are quite miserable, and are simply dancing about in a little pool of something else, not pleasure but misery.

A case of misinterpretation on your part. Fine, fine very good. But no, this other voice, an insistent voice (not the sardines, no surely not the sardines) continued to speak of happiness, yes, pleasure, I was very happy.

I had experienced the other, I had felt *depression*, and it was an emotion quite, absolutely different from this one. Misery was justifiable, there was always an excuse for feeling badly, so many reasons to feel the depths of despair, ennui, or the various cousins and relatives of what I had come to call *boredom.*

But so few reasons to feel happiness (commences the whisper of a can of peas.) It was not possible for me to feel this now, of that I was certain. Even during those few times—perhaps seven—when I was justified in feeling decent during my brief, my youthful lifetime, a short lifetime at this point, (though even if I were quite old, still in terms of the evolution of the entire planet, nay the universe, it would be a brief time) even during those seven times when I was entitled to feel joy, always in the back of my head had been a small whisper saying: but you have forgotten what a fool you made of yourself last week, hah-hah! Even though it is true you are feeling happy now, and justifiably so, in truth I will remind you of a tiny disaster to tinge and taint this thing you call a positive feeling.

Indominable, indominable. And here the cackle of corn-chips began, the sibilant hiss of cans of Coca-Cola (Coca-Cola! As if they, as if any of them have any rights, no rights in the matter)—that oozing, prurient tone of peanut butter, the natter of macaroni shells—ghastly! A shock! I did not believe in physical pain, no I did not even believe in moving unless absolutely necessary, to me a chair, better still a bed was the best place to remain, still I was tempted to create some kind of physical disturbance in my body in order that this terrible, needless feeling of happiness I was experiencing might go away. Anything, if it would just leave me alone!

I noticed it was ten past five. An entire day had gone by, during which I had accomplished nothing. Nothing had been attempted, nothing had been finished. In a sense this was better than trying to do something and being unable to do something.

And this thought was enough. For at last, luckily I did not need to do anything drastic, at last my fear and anxiety returned—you have no money, no money (the tiny whispers of the peas chimed in, but how soft now, how gentle!)—and I could, at last, in my misery, relax.

4.

As a child my favorite books had been about women who entered the convent. They were giving themselves up to a higher cause. But there are no convents for Jewish girls.

For myself, I had to choose the most difficult profession available to me; at night I often couldn't sleep, feeling myself adrift in a sea of seminal fluid. It was on these evenings that Bob and I took drugs. He would softly tie up my arm and inject me with a little heroin, or, if none was available, a little something else. For himself, there was nothing he liked better, though he was careful not to shoot up too frequently.

Neither of us were very good housekeepers. Months would go by, during which time the floor of our Tenth Avenue walk-up would become littered with empty syringes, cartons of fried rice, douche bags, black lace brassieres, whips, garottes, harnesses, bootlaces, busted snaps, cracker jacks, torn kleenexes and packages of half-eaten ring-dings and nacho corn chips. The elements of our respective trades. I was always surprised to realize how intelligent the cock-roaches in our neighborhood were. Bob was reluctant to poison them or step on them. He would turn the light off and whip it back on again to demonstrate his point.

It's obvious they're running for their lives, he said. To kill something that wants to live so desperately is in direct contradiction with any kind of philosophy that I believe in. Long after the bomb falls and you and your good deeds are gone, cockroaches will still be here, prowling the streets as large as cats.

Sometimes I wished Bob was more aggressive as a pimp. There were moments on the street when I felt frightened; there were a lot of terminal cases out there, and often I was in situations that could have become dangerous. Bob felt it was important that I accept anyone who wanted me.

From each according to his ability, to each according to his need.

Still, I could have used more help from him than I got.

But then Bob would arrive at the hospital, bringing me flowers and a pastrami sandwich on rye, and I realized that for me to change pimps and choose a more aggressive one, one who would be out there hustling for me and carrying a knife, would be to embrace a lifestyle that was genuinely alien to me, despite my middle-class upbringing.

When I was near Bob, with his long graceful hands, his silky moustache, his interesting theories of life and death—I felt that for the first time in my life I had arrived at a place where I was growing intellectually as well as emotionally. Bob was both sadist and masochist to me, for him I was madonna and whore. Life with him was never dull.

In any case, I liked having the things that money could buy. Originally I hail from a wealthy suburb of Chattanooga, Tennessee. One of the few Jewish families in the area, my great-grandfather had come from Lithuainia at the turn of the century, peddling needles, threads, elixers, yarmulkes, violin strings and small condiments able to cure the incurable. All carried on a pack on his back; his burden was a heavy one, eight children raised in the Jewish persuasion. Two generations later my father owned the only Cadillac car dealership in town. I suppose part of my genetic make-up has given me this love of material objects. Or maybe it's just a phase I will grow out of as soon as I get everything I want. Even saints have human flaws; it is overcoming their own frailties that make them greater than the sum of their parts.

I went to college at an exclusive women's seminary in Virginia; until my big falling-out with Daddy, when I sent home F's for two successive semesters, and got expelled after being suspended twice, I had my own BMW and a Morgan mare, Chatty Cathy, boarded in the stables at school.

But I could never accept the role life had asigned to me; I feel in love with Jimmy Dee Williams, the fat boy who pumped gas at the Seven Eleven, and though the marriage only lasted six months, Daddy never felt the same about me. I didn't mind the time I spent in the hospital. Fond recollections can be found in all walks of life. Yet if I had been allowed to go to a co-ed school I know things would have turned out differently for me.

5.

After the cessation of the luncheon engagements there was not much for me to occupy myself with. For a long time I lay in bed, the blankets wrinkled around me, the heat was turned much too high on the electric blanket...yes, it was too hot, but still there wasn't much I could do about it unless I reached onto the floor and turned the heat down, and did I want to do that? I wasn't certain if I wanted to move, but then the telephone rang and I was forced to move, I always answered the telephone in case there was somebody I wanted to speak to, but no one was on the other end, at least, no one answered.

Hello? Hello? Hello? Hello?

No, there was no response, it was nine in the morning and nobody was on the other end, I thought to myself: perhaps today I will sweep the floor, I had been watching, noticing for some time now how much, how very much dirt had accumulated, dirt from where I wasn't positive, in fact, it had simply appeared, over a long period of time, it had simply appeared, over a long period of time it had arrived of its own accord, various...lumps, grey matter, a wide assortment of dirt, *unknown origin*, it might be a good thing today to...sweep the floor. And there were other things I could keep myself occupied with. It was possible I was going to have a guest, a house guest might arrive and then I would need a sheet, that was one of the things I might do today, was to go downtown and buy a sheet. To do this I could write a check when I found the sheet I wanted to buy, or I could...go to the bank and cash a check though I hated to go to the bank because there I would have to say hello to the bank guard, who was extremely...he had white skin and was very friendly, and the bank tellers knew me too, because I generally went to the bank frequently, because I never cashed very large checks, and I spent the money quickly, too quickly, so I had to go back, two, three or even more times during one week, which was why it might be better if I wrote a check directly to the store where I was going to buy a sheet, but I didn't like to do that because often...my checks bounced, because I didn't know how to balance a checkbook, I didn't know how and I didn't want to know how, because of a slight difficulty I had in adding and subtracting numbers.

I did think of getting out of bed, I wanted to get out of bed, to get out of bed would indicate...some sort of start to the day, some kind of commencement, a new beginning, but I had had too many new beginnings, beginnings that began and ended, often going nowhere. If the phone were to ring again, that would be some sort of indication that...that there was somebody out there, someone or something who wished to communicate with me, and that in itself would be an indication that there was some reason for me to get out of bed, aside from my desire, albeit a faint desire, to buy a sheet, a dim desire, like the desire of an animal long since domesticated but thinking of the jungle.

But quite possibly I was being too pessimistic, there were so many things to look forward to in a day, the mail, the mail would be arriving at eleven, if there were going to be any mail for me, and I could stay in bed until eleven, and then if I went downstairs, I would have a reason to go downstairs, because there would be...there might be...the mail. Though this view might be overly optimistic because...probably I wouldn't get any mail, or if I did I suspected the mailman kept a lot of it, I had no faith in the mailman because I so rarely got mail and yet I saw him carrying great bags of mail, daily, I saw mail trucks and mail boxes and I knew there must be a great deal of mail out there, yes, letters, and magazines and bills, surely some of it must be addressed to me?

My life was exhausting, extraordinarily exhausting. There were certain things I had to think about, and certain things I had to brood about, and these things took up time...time and energy. I was thinking about this, just as I was becoming weary, so weary from this thinking my body...abruptly flung itself out of bed, of its own accord, got out of the bed and almost before I had a chance to think I was...there I was in the bathroom, then I was no longer in the bathroom, a duty had been performed, not really a duty but something necessary, relieving in a sense, though once I was finished in the bathroom my body gave up, simply abandoned me, and it was left for my head, or what I might call the Command Center, to take

Future Saint #1160

over, hand out the orders, decide what to do next and this...was rather frightening in a sense, to be so abruptly thrust about, from the bed to the bathroom, and out of the bathroom and then abandoned...abandoned, leaving me with a body, motor control, yes, to be sure, motor control, as well as certain involuntary functions of the body, the heart beating, for example, I didn't have to worry about that, nor was it terribly difficult to make my legs move, one after the next, they practically did that of their own accord, although breathing, in and out, in and out, was often something I had to remind myself to do, the lungs filling and emptying like baggies, used baggies, grey and...but I did not have to think about that too often, three times a day, or sometimes more frequently, but...I did have other things to think about, more important things, because I realized that one thing I would like, one thing I would like to do would be to eat some breakfast.

6.
It was as if a burden had been lifted from me, a sodden weight, now that I knew what I wanted to do, I would get the Wheat Chex out of the refrigerator, I would take them and pour milk on them and sugar, I would wait until the Wheat Chex had gotten soggy in the milk and then I would...eat them. What pleasure this thought gave me! How happy! I could almost imagine what it would be like, the Wheat Chex at first firm and then growing moist, even tender, and heavy, to be eaten by me, after I had gotten back into bed, I could lie in bed with a pillow in back of me, eating the Wheat Chex with a spoon, hardly even having to lift my chin up, for I liked to transport the Wheat Chex, in the spoon, from the bowl and up to my mouth, though it is true using this method often some of the milk and sugar...dribbled onto my chest, and that was not so pleasant for...when it dried, the milk and sugar, it was often sticky, sticky yet dry, and I was afraid...of attracting roaches. Some things had no right to exist, now whether or not I was justified in feeling that way about roaches I didn't know, I would hesitate to commit myself...there must be some purpose, some function roaches served but...from what I could see, from what I

could tell, there was no need for them, at least not in my apartment, although I heard, somewhere, that roaches did eat old hair, cells sloughed off, mucuous, various human waste products, and that did seem like a function, although if that was their function they were not serving it... in my apartment at least.

This reminded me that one of the things I had to do today was to sweep the floor, and I would have to look for the broom, yes, the broom and the dustpan, and then, after using the broom across the floor (even, possibly, going so far as to move some of the furniture around and sweep under the radiators, because, from where I sat on the bed, I could see there was a great deal of detritus under the radiators) I would then have to push the dirt, somehow, possibly using the broom, gently, skillfully, up into the pan, without leaving too much of it behind... on the floor. There were a lot of cracks in the floor, often it was more convenient to try and push the dirt into these, rather than having to undergo the ordeal of getting it into the dustpan and then, from there, getting it into the garbage without... without spilling it back onto the floor. And even then, once the dust was in the garbage bag, often the bag would mysteriously, of its own accord, develop a rip, a tear in the bottom of it, and then willfully the dirt would be back on the floor, as if it were trying to tell me something, or to frustrate me in some way, though I was well aware that dust was not... an animate object.

There was the coffee, there it was, in the kitchen, all I needed to do was to put a teaspoonful, a heaping teaspoon, into a coffee cup, after rinsing it out in the sink, because, as I knew so well, there was a pile of dirty dishes in the sink, no one had bothered to do the dishes, as usual, how angry this made me! My body, with so little to do, so little to occupy it, aside from tending to my every want and need, had not bothered to do the dishes... as usual. No wonder there were roaches in the apartment! And what was the problem, that my body could not bother to do the dishes? Did I abuse it, did I beat it, did I demand more than it could give? I asked so little and even that was too much.

How disgusted I was, disgusted and yes, angry at having to get

Future Saint #1160

up and wash the old coffee and milk of the mug, particularly where it had solidified into a gooey ring two-thirds of the way down. I put some Ajax in the cup and tried to get rid of the ring, which made me think: now today I'll have a cup of coffee and it will taste a little bit like Ajax, just a tiny bit, like old bleach and why?

Because I didn't rinse the cup well enough, yes, yes, and the coffee will be ruined and then for the rest of the day everything will strike me as just a little bit offensive, like a bathroom on a bus that reeks of disinfectant, my day, will, in short be contaminated and... I won't remember why.

In short, I no longer knew whether or not I could continue with this... sort of existence. However, that was not up to me, that was really not something within my control, within my grasp, and, as I had heard so many times before, where there's a will there's a way. I was very calm now, I was not going to let my emotions, my rage, get the better of me, all things are possible to those who wait, and I ran the water from the tap into the tea-kettle, I was not myself responsible for getting the water into my apartment, it simply involved my turning on the tap and then making sure the tea-kettle was under the running water until it filled up.

So I put the water onto the flame and then I thought: it would be a fine thing, a really fine thing, to change your underwear, or, alternatively, to put some on if you are not already wearing any, and to find some socks, either clean ones, or if there are none left that are clean, then to go to the laundry hamper in which you store the dirty laundry and there find a pair that... possibly match and are not too dirty.

Meanwhile, while I ws thinking of all this, I took the Wheat Chex from the refrigerator, and annointed them with sugar, hoping, hoping against hope that I was not putting too much sugar on them, hoping that I was putting just the right amount of sugar on them, pouring the milk on, examining even the box of Wheat Chex to see if there was any special offer on the back, something I could get when I saved up enough proof-of-purchase seals, perhaps a calendar, or even a juice pitcher, if a juice pitcher was being offered on the back I would eat two bowls of Wheat Chex, furthering my own interests in a sense because the more Wheat Chex I ate the quicker it would be until I had saved up enough proof-of-purchase seals, and then, since the water still had not boiled for the coffee, nor had the Wheat Chex grown sufficiently soggy, I began to dress myself, now the underpants, now the socks, then at last the blue jeans, faster and faster making real progress here, until, I was dressed, I was dressed, the breakfast was nearly ready and soon, shortly, I knew I would be ready, as long as I could keep myself from getting back into bed and turning the electric blanket on again, if I could just prevent myself—my body—from doing this, if I had to tie myself to a chair to keep myself from doing this, I would be dressed I would have eaten and my day begun.

7.

Back in college the other girls would spend long evenings drinking beer and sitting on the rocking chairs that ringed the great plantation hall—the school had taken over many of the original buildings on the tobacco estate, and the new buildings were built in a Georgian style in a great semi-circle facing the old mansion—gossiping about boys and worrying if they would pass French. But meanwhile I had to show them that I was wild and daring; I would pick Jimmy Dee up when he got off work and the two of us would smoke some grass and drive around, bored and restless in the heat. One evening I drove right up onto the lawn and Jimmy Dee pulled down his pants to press his great buttocks, gleaming white, against the cool air-conditioned glass window of the car. That was the second time I was suspended from school; the first was when I had an affair with one of the black cafeteria workers in my dorm room, a man with only one arm who tasted of bacon and hair oil... The only reason I was allowed to stay after that was because Daddy donated money to the the school to build a new swimming pool. He never understood that no matter what he did, they were always going to think of him only as a rich Jew...

I was finally asked to leave for good when Jimmy Dee and I

were caught sneaking into the school pond, which was closed for swimming after dark. Both stark naked, dripping with mud and algae... I tried to explain to Miss Ferguson, the dean, that I always got wild when there was a full moon, but prim and proper in her mahoghany office, smelling of verbena and more faintly of shit, she said she could see no future for a girl like me, that never in the course of all her years... I had to laugh.

Before Daddy could find out about my marriage and divorce and could take the car back from me (and have me locked up again??but there are no convents for Jewish girls) I had driven north to New York, sold it for two thousand dollars, found an apartment and bought some new clothes. I landed a job in an internship program at a major advertising agency, even though I didn't have a college degree... once more Daddy spoke to me on the phone, Mother and Mopsy even came up for a visit...

I might never have found my vocation if I hand't been evicted from my apartment and after finding a new place in the East Village met Bruno, who offered me the job of script girl or assistant director on the film he was making in Venezuela, which in the end didn't work out at all.

But one thing leads to the next (doesn't it always?) and it was through Bruno I met Bob, and now at night, cruising the great long avenues of the city, dust and grit tossed feverishly in the massive canyons between the skyscrapers, it often occurs to me that I am no more and no less, a thought that I hand't realized until my days as a prostitute began. (True I have my bad days, when I cannot rise from bed, but who can claim he does not? Who?) I could have written a book about my experiences out on the street: but all my thoughts are handed over to Bob, who lies on the bed dreamily eating whatever I bring him—a hamburger from MacDonald's, crab souffle from a French restaurant in the theater district, a platter of rumaki with hot peanut sauce in an easy carry-out container from an Indonesian restaurant open until one a.m., plates of macaroni tender and creamy as the sauce that oozes out from between the legs of my clientel.

8.
   As in the convent, life is not easy...crouched in dark alleys, giggling in hotel rooms or the back seat of limousines, I have to be a constant actress, on my guard and yet fitting in to every situation. Always the wedge of moon above, reminding me of my destiny and holy water.

Jokes
Richard Prince

"My Doctor sure put me back on my feet."
"Really?"
"Yeah, when I got his bill, I hadda sell my car!"

"Which reminds me of the doctor who knew his patient couldn't afford an operation, so he 'retouched' his X-rays."

"My mother and father keep fighting. They rant and they rave and they shout."
"Who is your father?" somebody asked.
"That's what they're fighting about."

A traveling salesman stopped by a farmhouse and asked for a night's lodging.
"We're all filled up," said the farmer, "but you can sleep with the little redheaded schoolteacher."
"That's alright," said the traveling salesman, "I'm a perfect gentleman."
"Fine," said the farmer, "so is the little redheaded schoolteacher!"

Richard Prince

I gave her so many gifts I had to marry her for my money.

Fireman pulling drunk out of a burning bed: You darned fool, that'll teach you to smoke in bed.
Drunk: I wasn't smoking in bed, it was on fire when I laid down.

Camp Hiawatha, that's where the Jewish kids go for the summer. Camp Ginsberg, that's where the Indian kids go for the summer.

A couple is driving to Miami Beach in a brand new car. As they're driving he puts his hand on her knee. She says, "We're married now, you can go a littler farther." So he went to Fort Lauderdale.

Jewish man talking to his friend: If I live I'll see you Tuesday. If I don't I'll see you Wednesday.

"I eat politics and I sleep politics, but I never *drink* politics."

Her Weak Memory of the Tornado
Leslie Thornton

Wrapped around her neck, two strings and a piece of gum. Waiting by the house, standing on the door, looking at the night, picking up the glass. Trying to lift the suitcase, feeling the back of her throat, turning on the light, sticking to the window. By the way, when I was talking to you the other night did you notice anything strange about the way your hand kept touching that object or the fact that I refused to be moved by your little drama of the self?

Scratched into a thin line, one box on top of another. A mood of gravity prevails.

A hand, a rose, a book, a joke, a fly, a radio, a little figurine, a drawer of burnt-out bulbs, a patterned rug, a certain order. A rational description of compassionate acts (a murderous impulse toward the genius of words.) I love wry humor, I lie very close to him at night to see what he does in his sleep, the way he moves. I know when it's raining. And now she could see him down the hall and further down the hall a long word, drifting, and it was sucking, sticky deadly word, parasitic miasmus. Go to Hell.

Flat to her face, fall down, her fingers point accusingly at him, "You go ride the old mule into the desert!" She collapsed laughing. "And then will I know what to do? My flesh is damp; there are random facts, with sunlight moving, and the sweeping, blasphemous, sick sun resting, falling with yellow sky turning. And the crazy yellow sky." And then you say "how do you say bananas in Spanish?" And "land of make-believe calling." Then you say, "send the unsaved to hell." And I know, you don't want to go.

She put one foot in front of the other, shifted her weight slowly forward, the top part of her body, her shoulders would collapse backwards producing a sensation of weightlessness, but the momentum of her stride would carry her and she would move suddenly forward. I looked up in surprise, but you didn't see me. I was there. I almost tripped when you stumbled, then turned and tripped myself, until I grabbed for the staircase and found my way. I chased you across the room. Why didn't you tell me? I knew the room was flooding and didn't like your expression as you descended into it blindly.

(I-don't-want-you-to-get-hurt.)

(That's-the-final-straw.) "Oh yes, well in that case, I'll take everything we had that was good. You can have the rest, the goats, the barn. I'll take the carefully placed accoutrements of life, which you managed with a bilious economy. I'm sure the rest will hold you, now listen to me closely. You go on being earnest. In the morning I will take the cat out for a short walk. The last two hours will probably be the hardest."

And the times were so troubled that when a soldier exposed himself to the crowd to indicate his displeasure, rioting broke out and thousands were killed, or so it is told. Moses, using an allegory, had described Paradise to be the womb, and Eden the placenta. Thus, the river flowing from Eden symbolizes the navel, which nourishes the fetus. Thus Exodus signifies the passage out of the womb, and the crossing of the Red Sea refers to the blood. A divine figure speaks: "I am the Voice, I am androgynous (I am both Mother and Father since I copulate with myself, and with those who love me.) I am the Womb, the Thunder, Perfect Mind. I am first, last, honored, scorned, holy, mother, daughter. I am knowing, secret, shameless, shamed, strong and frightened, foolish, wise, blinded and insightful. I am the matropater, the serpent and the flood. The word is everything to the child. Only those who seek the word are truly happy. For this reason, seeking is also called sucking; to those infants who seek the word, the Father's loving breasts supply milk."

Her Weak Memory of the Tornado

The window breaks. I watch our boat get caught on rocks, then try to climb them like a crab. We turn around to see if anyone is looking, dart for the door, stuck, threw my weight against it, water rushes in knocking us over. Something hard, like vinyl, lodges in my throat, almost choking me as I try to regain my footing. I grabbed for your hand and blindly thrashing slowly eased by way to the door. I didn't know if you were alive but I pulled your big body behind me, thank goodness it floated along. I thought about how I had been mean to you at breakfast and tried to understand why. My anger and determination were fierce, though as I reached the exit, I let go, gasping. If I hadn't caught the railing we would have drowned.

Calm down, I know you are insightful, he spoke these words to her, but you must be driven. He had no insight. He was numb. She was lying down, waiting for something to happen. No, this will never do, you moving away, me measuring the distance in the dark. Her love for him was winding up, and up.

An ancient light filling the room.

"You always hurt the one you love. It will be fresh and soothing to your skin. The one you shouldn't hurt at all. It will enter the room in spurts, twirling. . . so if I broke your heart last night. . . it will turn you around. . . it's because I love you most of all. . . and then you will see the other side of the valley. There will be a war and disaster in our house. There will be dead animals, broken flesh, missing phrases. You will forget how to talk, you will only have forethoughts. You will become tense and feel anger when the windows are broken."

She will tell you what this is about. It is about walking into a hold, simple, a woman who goes out and discovers she cannot believe the bus will ever come—she is exceedingly distressed, she pants, moving like an animal side to side. She says to her children, "I have finished discussing everything with you. I have told you everything for you to share secretly with your friends. I have sealed the sleeper in luminous waters that death might not prevail." Her slippery thoughts, the children wanting more. She played dead.

And that is what saved her. There was a fantasy. There was an old woman who was very small, lived across the way, shorter than the banister on her back steps. Her house was peach and she wore a green vest. She was much too small. I knew there was something wrong when I saw her and relaxed, why should I care? Get too close and I, well.... Watch her down the block, and the way the light comes off her, and the way I want to be nearby, it is a mystery. Back yard, dark alley. A slight movement caught out of the corner of my eye, either eye. Later that night at the grocery store I find I have no breath. My eyes flash bolts of lightning: le chapeau, le tapis, un fauteuil. Une pendule, un tableau, la suspension.

What do you expect in a small midwestern town in 1951, hours before a devastating tornado?

She walked through that room thousands of times, bored, making a lot of noise. And when the bottle crashed through the... it was impossible... her weak memory. It took all the strength she had just to move across the floor, over and around an assortment of things, half organized piles of stuff that might slip suddenly, stacked right up to the ceiling at odd angles and casting strange shadows. Turn around and put your head against the wall. Wrap your arm limply, like this, about the neck and let your hand drape on to your back. Place your other hand on your hip and hold still a minute.

For dinner she would have a little goose liver pate on rye crisp and an orange. For breakfast she would have whole grain cereal with wheatgerm, raisins and milk. For lunch she would sometimes have coffee, otherwise an American cheese sandwich. Lick your finger and touch, there, precisely.

But all this is too far into the future. All right, right then. You can take the goats. Grim, hostile, grotesque. The light will dim the darkness. The wind, the sky, the glories of nature. The tornado.

Peggy and Fred in Hell
Leslie Thornton

She pressed her back hard into the chair and put her hand under her leg. He had no idea she was there. Finally her impatience took over and he turned as her hand shot up to her eye. What was the difference, she thought. He'll stand there with his machine and think about good design until she lets something else happen. The breeze came in with the smell of the factory as she shuffled her feet, but all that mattered now was the way the window opened. Because the curtain was just beyond her reach she decided to forget about the hole and make an effort to speak.

It started now. Speak. She looked around for a while, dropped her hands and swallowed her tongue. Except for a few breaks here and there everything seemed so oppressively even.

Spinach omelet maybe? I don't like spinach. I'm sick of spinach. How about pork chops? I'm sick of spinach omelets. We've had an omelet everyday.

Crash. The birds were at it again but no matter because she hadn't felt so relaxed in a long time. He put her hand under her leg while he turned on the machine. She kicked him (unintentionally) in the eye then looked at the window. Overall it hadn't been a bad day.

Wild. Things running all over the place. Objects. Hole bubbling. Charm-destroying and romance-killing odors. A window that opened by itself. The sounds of the opera next door. It was harrowing living here and it took all the strength they had. It was hell.

Leslie Thornton

I can't stand having only one chair, he said.
I know what she is. That's the way she is. She's like that, she's evil. Look at the way she stands there with her head flying off and her feet beneath the floor. And when I reach for her she's just that much farther. She cried out, threw her hand against the wall. It cracked and fell away.

Now that the house had burned down they had a better view of the factory. He cut the acorn squash and sat down to read the funnies. She stood on his head to arrange the curtains. The slope of the floor toward the hole was causing trouble but what could they do? It interfered with walking and infected what little elegance there was in the room. So despite a rich fantasy life she felt thrown together in the insouciant tradition of most tropical constructions. Tropical. What a funny way to think of it. Insouciant. She didn't even know what that meant.

Her head flew into the farthest corner of the room, mouth opened involuntarily, sounds of moaning, blast of light off the curtain, then came another thunderous clap from the orchestra and they found themselves back in the wheatfield. The door opened. They were received into the outer world with great joy. No, no. Don't go. I'm afraid. I want to be alone. She felt the four walls with her hands then hung her head between her feet, into the hole, and cried.

Other things happen in this room. There are huge mill-wheels turning rapidly and the proud are attached to them with fiery hooks. The envious are immersed to the navel in a river of ice and are lashed by the biting wind. In the cave the wrathful are hacked by swords and knives. The slothful are shut in a cage full of serpents. The avaricious are plunged to the neck in cauldrons of boiling oil and metals. In a valley there is a foul river and a table heaped with filth upon its bank. Here the gluttonous are fed with reptiles and the water of the river. The lustful are sunk in pits full of fire and sulphur.

The light was so dim they had developed the habit of staring. Always moving, she was very strict about the kinds of things she would say. It was a glorious day, sun on the curtains, windows shut cutting the noise and the smell. Madness, simple like a headache, made a knot of their common efforts. (Deep down they were frozen with terror.) But the distractions in the room kept them busy and they did

not suffer unduly. Her speech was elliptical and seductive, she thought, though very limited, still powerful, and filled with sound. At least I'm one person who appreciates the excesses of the body. She started to hum.
   La da da, la da. She longs for a fondness of the familiar. True, he is here, but they don't care for each other and everything keeps changing, every instant. She moved the animals off the chair and turned it on its side. They ate the acorn squash while she thought about oxygen. That machine. There was an extra there in the sentence and she couldn't find it. It was driving her crazy. Ordinary. He collapses into the blue as she moves past the word on the warm blue wall.
   Anything can function as rhythm. They walked into the cave where the opera was performing past 80 yards of rock walls lined with hundreds of speakers. The separations between sounds were so overpowering they thought they might have died and entered a new world. The frogs and cicadas were up, the planes stormed overhead. Your fingers begin to curl, you step on them to straighten them out and they stick to your feet. A great sense of urgency comes over her. She mimics the gestures of speech with her mouth. Shoulders back. Head back. Now start. Speak. Lift me up to the window mom. Lift me to the image with the sounds and the way it moves. It must be real but what is it called.
   I hate you. I hate you. I love you. I don't care about you. You hate me. I don't see you. Go away. Help me. I forget you. We sound alike. I won't be long. I want that chair. I must have it and you I don't care about anymore, so there. Toccata and Fugue in D Minor. I don't want this ever to end. Lotte Lenya sings Berlin theatre songs by Kurt Weill.
   Bone Eating Insect Hell. Discriminative Fully Assumed Characteristic Hell. Hell Where Everyone is Cooked Hell. Great Screaming Hell. Upside-downess Hell. Five Senses Hell. Hell of Repetition. Being Very Specific Hell. Bird Mouth Hell. Hell Where Everything Faces The Ground. Place Of Great Tragedy. Why, Why Hell. Contemporary Superlative Hell. Tenderness Hell. Hell Where The Suffering Is 10,000 Times Greater Than In All The Other Hells Combined. All Kinds Of Hell. Telling The Difference Between Objects and Actions Hell. Not Telling The Difference Between Humor And Despair Hell.

Hell's Hell. Forever And Endless Hell. Hell For All The People Who Perform Badly In All The Other Hells Hell. An Old Pond. A Frog Jumps In. Plop.

Let's dance.

As these figures wheel around, the almost unbearable tension and exaltation which has gripped the spectators is suddenly relieved by the appearance of two grotesquely grinning masks, whose movements ape the dancers. She shook her head, lifted up her foot, who cares, turned on the radio. I'm not going to build this up until something else happens, something overheard and unknown. Mouth wide open, no reason. Getting up, walking across the room, sitting down.

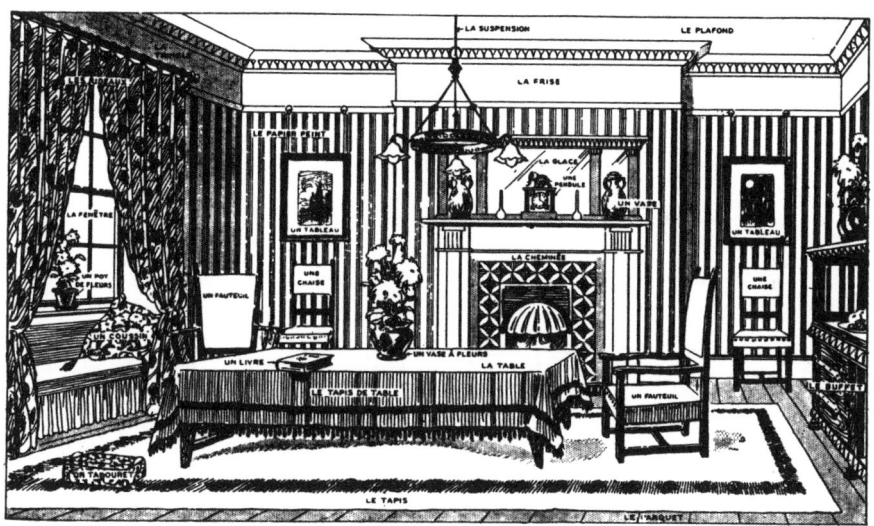

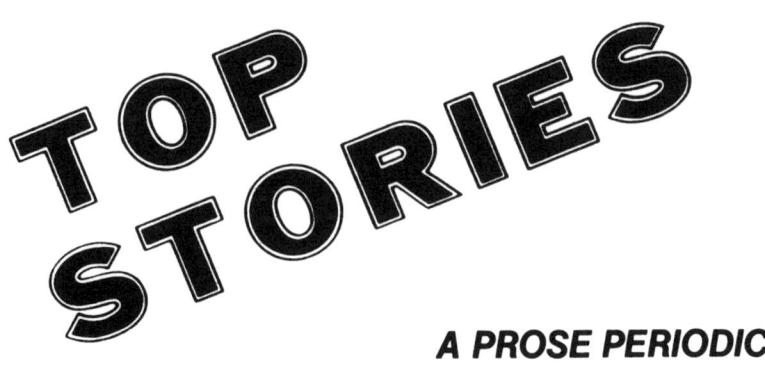

A PROSE PERIODICAL

#1 Donna Wyszomierski
#2 Laurie Anderson
#3 Pati Hill
#4 Suzanne Johnson
#5 Linda Neaman
#6 Gail Vachon
#7 Jenny Holzer/Peter Nadin
#8 Judith Doyle
#9 Kathy Acker
#10 Lynne Tillman/Jane Dickson
#11 Kirsten Thorup
#12 Janet Stein
#13 Anne Turyn
#14 Lee Eiferman
#15 Constance DeJong
#16 Ursule Molinaro
#17 Romaine Perin
#18 Donna Wyszomierski
#19-20 Cookie Mueller
#21 Ascher/Straus
#22 Susan Daitch
#23-24 Five, An Anthology

Available from
TOP STORIES
228 Seventh Avenue
New York, NY 10011

ISBN 0-917061-23-3

TOP STORIES #25-26 $6.00

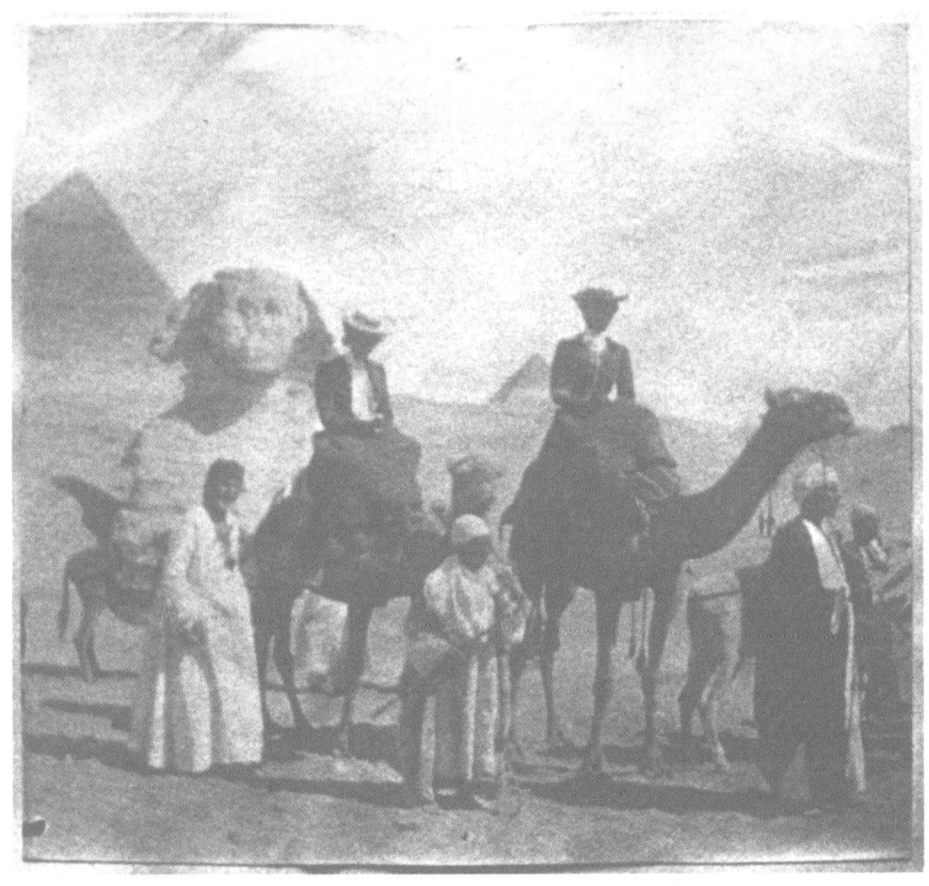

TOURIST ATTRACTIONS

DOUGLAS BLAU•LINDA L. CATHCART
CHERYL CLARKE•SUSAN DAITCH
CONSTANCE DEJONG•ROBERT FIENGO
GARY INDIANA•SUZANNE JACKSON
•CARYL JONES-SYLVESTER•
JUDY LINN•MICKI MCGEE
GLENN O'BRIEN•SEKOU SUNDIATA
LYNNE TILLMAN•JANE WARRICK

TOURIST ATTRACTIONS

TOURIST ATTRACTIONS

edited by Anne Turyn and Brian Wallis

Douglas Blau
Linda L. Cathcart
Cheryl Clarke
Susan Daitch
Constance DeJong
Robert Fiengo
Gary Indiana
Suzanne Jackson
Caryl Jones-Sylvester
Judy Linn
Micki McGee
Glenn O'Brien
Sekou Sundiata
Lynne Tillman
Jane Warrick

TOP STORIES #25-26
1987

Copyright © 1987 by Top Stories
All rights revert to the authors

Cover design by Nancy Linn

This publication was made possible in part with public funds from the National Endowment for the Arts and the New York State Council on the Arts.

ISBN 0-917061-25-X (Top Stories #25-26)

Top Stories, 228 Seventh Avenue, New York, NY 10011

The publication of Tourist Attractions coincided with a reading at Artists Space, New York, NY in June 1987

TABLE OF CONTENTS

Excerpt from Home Sick Lynne Tillman	7
Gran Turismo Glenn O'Brien	12
Tex Caryl Jones-Sylvester	17
Friendly Flies Judy Linn	22
I know the climate's wonderful, but how's the Truth? Robert Fiengo	27
To Japan and Back Linda L. Cathcart	31
Sanjiro's, Thumb's and Apple Pie Micki McGee	37
gothic tourism Cheryl Clarke	45
Driftings Douglas Blau	48
Incunabula #3 Susan Daitch	54
Foreign in Life Jane Warrick	60
Leaving Quito Gary Indiana	63
Painted Desert Suzanne Jackson	70
Pop Life Sekou Sundiata	74
Legend 1 inch : 1 hour Constance DeJong	77

Excerpt from HOME SICK
Lynne Tillman

"I am...the fellow-citizen of all that inhabits the great furnished hotel of the universe."   —Flaubert

PARIS: I am in my hotel room, on the bed, reading PORTRAIT OF A LADY, and nursing an illness I might not have. As I am unhappy, I might just be unhappy and not suffering from the flu or *la turista*, but a Frenchwoman named Arlette has sent me a get well card. She seems to take my illness seriously. The card has a Tibetan symbol on it whose meaning I don't know and which might have significance if I did. Her concern might also be ironic and when she appears at my bedside the next day, I can't read the gesture as graciousness or solicitude only, since I don't really know what she means. I both feign surprise at her visit and feel surprised, a mixed response for what might be a mixed get well visit. She talks about adjusting to changes of all sorts—the weather, leaving one city for another, a friend's betrayal, the end of a love affair—some of which she knows I've experienced. Leaving a city, a lover, good weather for bad. I want to get back to my book, the heroine of which, Isabel Archer, has an end that must be worse than mine, something I've always loved novels for. I decide to leave Paris when I've finished it. While in Paris I remember Istanbul, because there are several hammans in Paris, none of which I go to as I don't feel well enough to leave my hotel room. Except to go down the street for some bread. Or *pain*, as they call it here.

ISTANBUL: My hotel room is small and dark and it's been raining for weeks, and even the walls look wet, though when I touch them, as if reading Braille, they are in actuality dry. It's a good room to read in and the hotel itself stands about five hundred yards from the Blue Mosque, which I have not yet gone inside. I'm told you have to take off your shoes and will have a hard time finding them later.

My shoes are wet, and they're my only pair, having thrown out another as dead weight, determined to travel light. I travel dark and wet, I think to myself, because I'm reading MY GUN IS QUICK. Reading it makes me want to make movies, but I'm not sure why. The hotel manager, perhaps its owner, a small, elegant man with a mustache, knocks on my door and brings me a tray with a teapot and a glass. I haven't asked him for this and he is either curious about what I'm doing in my room, or a very nice man whose sense of hospitality extends beyond the mercenary unctuousness of other hotel managers I've met. Sipping the tea in a glass shaped like Mae West, an association my hotel man here probably wouldn't make, suddenly I'm dying to go to the movies. Almost anything makes me want to go to the movies, even a glass shaped like a movie star who's dead. Or is she?

AGIA GALLINI, CRETE: I never meant to go to Crete, but now that I'm here, I'm glad. My room faces the harbor and I have a small terrace. Because the sun is hot—we may be near the Equator—I stay under the shade of the terrace's overhang. Above me are two Australians, Jennie and Michael, who live in London, and they're out most of the day, and John, a man from New Zealand, who calls himself a traveler. He smokes endlessly and I know he's there because of this smell, and like my father's occasional cigars, I find the smell, at a distance, reassuring. They say that smell for women is a much stronger sense than for men, and I'd like to know why it should be, and that as you grow older, everyone's sense of smell increases. Why this should be as well I don't know. The New Zealander yells down that we should have a drink. He has a bottle, he says. Of what I wonder, but don't ask. I say I'm reading but all right. I don't know why I put it that way—"reading but all right." Perhaps I meant to suggest that his visit ought to be short. But I'm in Crete with all the time in the world, as well as an increasing sense of smell, for that matter. John and I empty the bottle, sitting on the terrace, the hotel room, its bed, in the background. A small room with a single bed. The night grows darker and darker, until I can only hear the water slapping against the harbor, but can't see it. Just as I barely see John, but can smell him.

ISTANBUL: An Englishman has taken the room next door. I hear him speaking to the hotel manager in that unmistakable accent that brings up so many associations, even ones that aren't movies. He, like me, stays in his room most of the time. At least I don't hear him leaving. His door rarely opens or shuts. Perhaps, like me, he has bought oranges, bread and yogurt. Or not. We pass each other going to the toilet but as he doesn't acknowledge me, or act friendly, I decide I won't either. If he knows I'm American, he probably expects me to make the first move. I feel under no such cultural imperative. Although as the days pass, this resolve appears foolish. On the other hand he might think I'm Greek or Italian, as others have, and hold different expectations.

I read the Herald Tribune nearly every day, which marks me as a foreigner, one who desires to remain in touch with her home, indicating attachment. Sometimes I buy a local paper, simply to appear to be trying. I look at the pictures and puzzle over the captions. The hotel man approves of the oranges. He smiles broadly when I come in with my groceries and newspapers, nodding his head up and down with enthusiasm, I think. And if he is with another man when I pass by, he also nods at his friend. This might not, of course, be approval, but day after day, the hotel man and I smile and nod and gesture and I believe he's getting used to me, as I am to him. I suppose we have a sense of each other and are like babies together, communicating preverbally. I decide he does like me, as I have a need anyway to feel that I am liked. No doubt this marks me as an American and I am full of national characteristics that become palpable only when I am not home, as home, to me, becomes palpable only because I'm not there. Still I don't really want to meet or talk to anyone, and revel not only in this silent relationship but also in my quiet hotel room whose walls look damp. The Englishman, when we passed, touched his hand to his head, a kind of salute, and I did likewise, a gesture that has absolutely no meaning to me at all.

AMSTERDAM: The hotel I am staying in has a history—as I suppose does everything—which is still alive. Four generations of a single Dutch family sitting or standing in the room I am eating in, who have owned this hotel for as many generations or more. The grandfather, the father, the son, and the son's male child, all owners of this small, or cozy, as the Dutch might put it, establishment. I'm eating a raisin bun, drinking coffee, and reading I SHOULD HAVE STAYED HOME, a novel about Hollywood. I'm also wishing there was a television in my room, and glance furtively at the four generations as if they might become a sitcom. Actually, looking more carefully, they're closer to Western types, on the order of *Bonanza* or *Seven Brides for Seven Brothers*, and from now on whenever I see them, either the theme song from *Bonanza* or "I'm a Lonesome Polecat" from *Seven Brides* plays in my mind. I finish I SHOULD HAVE STAYED HOME in the breakfast room, and I believe it is also in this room—cheerful and warm—that I read that vampires do not suck blood, they lap it.

TOURIST ATTRACTIONS

ISTANBUL: The Englishman—Charles—and I take a walk to a site below the city, some kind of tunnel system that all large cities have. I can't remember how we got in or if we paid. I barely remember it at all. Charles reeked of oddness and vagueness which must contribute to the blight on this subterranean memory. His hair grew in batches over his head, and he had large eyes and a soft voice, his whispers very hard to hear especially in this cave—or was it a sewer? Several hours might have passed with us in conversation. Flat-bottomed boats floated by occasionally. At least I think it was there that I saw the boats but the more I imagine it, the more I think I'm remembering a Fellini movie, not this strange cloudy place I went to with Charles, who I suppose I could say was also strange and cloudy.

Later in the front room of the hotel, the manager served us tea, pastries and oranges, a privilege I hadn't yet been granted. I worry that the hotel manager wants to pair me off with Charles so I try to appear independent no matter what, hoping the manager won't get the wrong idea. Of course what does it mean to appear independent anyway. This is some horrible fiction that no one can project, I think, and then I relax and drink my tea. Let him think what he wants, as he will anyway.

AGIA GALLINI, CRETE: Screams from the street wake me and I think I'm home. A dog owned by a shopkeeper has been found dead, and women in black skirts hurry up and down the street, agitated. John reports that the dog was killed, an act of revenge against the shopkeeper, and as we're in Greece, the event resonates peculiarly. John has brought us feta cheese, bread, and tomatoes, as well as an English language newspaper only five days old. This assures us of our being in a remote spot in the world, I suppose. I'm writing postcards to friends, having purchased all the best ones from the cigarette vendor downstairs. The very best: a black and white photograph printed badly, of a man in a suit walking, rushing, in the foreground, with a large freighter docked in the background. My postcards home annotate this image, refer to the dead dog, and the hot sun, and I think about that scene in THE DISCREET CHARM OF THE BOURGEOISIE where the dinner guests look at tourist postcards as if they're pornography. I feel very much the same way about describing sex as I do landscapes and monuments, events and activities that we all do and know, that are always there and never new. Maybe even impossible to see in the same way that sex, for me, is unrepresentable because the tongue, for example, is privileged with information indifferent to words. And now I want to see a movie, having thought about Bunuel. But John wants to make love. He thinks he's in love with me, and his love, if I can call it that, is not returned. The Australians, Jennie and Michael, are leaving. They tell me to look them up in London.

LONDON: The hotel is Victorian in more than its architecture. Men are not allowed in one's room, which strikes me like those signs that read "No dogs" or "No spitting on the subway." This place, with its fake red velvet wallpaper, reminds me of Tad's Steak House and is comforting because of that. The hotel's breakfast room, crowded by nine, empties by 10 a.m., when I generally take mine. Breakfast is served, the card says, until 10:30, and I'm aware that latecomers engender hatred among the staff but I find it difficult to get out of bed earlier and refuse to simply because I will be disliked otherwise. This goes against my general desire to be liked by everyone and I wonder if I'm making progress. Another American woman joins me for breakfast and starts to tell me her story. I hear many stories and tell some, too, but this morning I'm just listening. Her name is Carol and her husband, an Englishman, has left her, vanished. She begins to describe him and suddenly I know she's talking about Charles whose face rises out of the mist where I last saw him. It now seems appropriate that it was a sewer, if it was. I don't know whether or not to tell her that I saw him in Istanbul. I know I will, but this breakfast room, with its impatient waiters, doesn't seem the right place. But then travel doesn't ever produce the right place, I've discovered, so I describe Charles and my encounter with him. He is, indeed, her wandering husband, a fact that at first silences both of us as we spread orange marmalade over cold toast—I've grown to like cold toast—and almost instantly I am her best friend in the world, the world being so small these days that it takes only one encounter to make us fast friends. Or so we think.

Gran Turismo
Glenn O'Brien

Last year in Biarritz I met this biker chick at the Casino. She was tall, blonde, Finnish. We both won big on the don't pass line and without a real word between us we got out of there. She had a Vincent Black Shadow with a side car parked in front. I had my Gran Turismo in the lot but she said she needed someone to balance out the bike going down the mountain.

I hopped in and we gunned off into the hot night. Her leathers were the color of the full moon. I leaned out of the sidecar on the turns. She took them fast. She headed for the French border.

Before we got to the checkpoint she stopped at the side of the road, handed me a wallet and took off again. We passed the border without incident. We had passed from Spain to France but we were still in Basque country.

She stopped again at the side of the road, this time to open a gate in a wire fence that enclosed a wooded hillside. We climbed the hill and at the top was a cement chateau with a tower. She lived there with Arturo, her brother, a stylist, and his Brazilian girlfriend YeYe.

YeYe was swimming naked in the pool and Arturo was riding a stationary bicycle when we arrived. He told us to help ourselves to champagne and we did.

Then Ikipope the butler arrived and asked us if we had eaten. In a few minutes he returned with piping bowls of Mullagitawny soup and some bread.

The biker chick, Helena, looked nothing like her brother, but she explained that her mother had been a stewardess for Pan Am. Her father was a pilot from Lufthansa and Arturo's father was a Brazilian copra baron with a spurious title.

Arturo had attended hotel management school at Cornell where he played reserve point guard on the basketball team, but after graduation he had attended beauty school, followed by a brief stint as a minor league pro in the Continental Basketball Association. Returning to Paris he had been discovered by Vogue and he'd been in the money ever since, working as a stylist for the top photographers in the business.

He traveled all over the world, and on one shoot in Bali he had met YeYe who was working as a dancercize instructor and helped choreograph the Robert Palmer rock video Arturo was working on with Guy Bourdin. YeYe was only half Balinese, her father was an actor who had visited the island during the filming of South Pacific. They had been together ever since.

Helena was harder to figure. She was young. She said she went to school but she wouldn't say more. She changed into a white one-piece bathing suit and put on a tape of Slim Harpo. While she danced to "Hip Shake," I did the original rhythm part with spoons on the formica bar top.

Later we went out and looked at the cactuses in the moonlight. They seemed to have weird human and insect shapes. We talked about Paul Bowles, Ernest Hemingway and jai alai. Her cousin Nicky played jai alai in Newport, Rhode Island. We talked about Klaus von Bülow and picking rosehips on the beachwalk in Newport.

We heard a single engine plane circling above us but we saw no lights.

When we returned to the chateau Arturo and YeYe had gone to bed. Helena took out a large photo album and we sat on the floor looking through it and drinking port. Helena showed me her pictures of Reinnes Le Chateau where she said the Knights Templar had their headquarters and hid their treasure. She told me a long story having something to do with Victor Hugo and Jean Cocteau being direct descendents of Jesus Christ and Grandmaster of the Elders of Zion. Then she asked me if she could wash my feet with her hair. It sounded pretty kinky to me, so I said "Why not?"

She unrolled her bun and it reached practically to the floor. I couldn't believe it. I'd never seen hair that long in my life. I asked if I could wash my feet first before she washed them and she said that would ruin it, so I just sat back and let the girl do her thing.

After she washed my feet with her hair they were really clean. I asked her if she wanted to keep washing and she did. It was the best cleaning job I ever had.

I stayed up there with Helena and Arturo and YeYe for a few days and then Helena said she had to go away so I went back to Biarritz and got my car and drove all night to Paris and didn't see a cop all the way.

I checked into the the Georges Cinq and went out to get a hamburger. I picked up a Herald Tribune and saw that the Yankees had beaten the Red Sox 6 to 5. I thought of Helena and I wondered if her cousin Nicky, the jai alai player in Newport, was a Red Sox fan. When I returned to the hotel I opened my old, beat up Louis Vuitton overnighter and discovered I had someone else's bag. Beat up just like mine. But its contents were a lot different. Silk, nylon, pearls. I looked for a name. But all I found was an ounce of heroin.

I went to the Cafe Flore and had six gin and tonics before I knew what to do. I returned to the hotel, ordered a sandwich in aluminum foil from room service, made a small line of the drug on the foil and smoked it. Then I ate half the sandwich and went to the bathroom and threw up. When I emerged from the bathroom there was a pounding at the door. Woozy, it seemed to be the beating of my heart. I felt myself sinking into the shag carpet as I wavered toward the throbbing door. I threw open the door and a Chinese women dressed in black whisked past me into the room. I latched the door. She sniffed the air.

"I hope I'm not interrupting," she said.

"Not at all," I said. "Have we met?"

Her name was Lucille O'Malley. Her mother was from a wealthy Hong Kong banking family, her father was an Indy car driver who crashed and burned in the seventies. She was the ideal of Chinese beauty, but with pale blue eyes.

"I am a friend of Helena," she said.

I wondered if my feet were clean.

"She said that she left something with you on the road from Biarritz and needs it back."

I remembered Helena passing me the wallet just before we had crossed the border into France. I remembered the strange look of those cactuses in her backyard.

Later that night at a night club Lucille gave me a big hickey on my neck and introduced me to a lot of her friends and we went back to her house and listened to Zulu records and chased the dragon some more. An American saxophone player came over and we played a few rubbers of bridge.

I woke up in Lucille's bed. She was out. She came back with the Herald Tribune and coffee. The Red Sox beat the Tigers 2 zip—Oil Can Boyd had a two hitter going in the seventh when he was ejected from the game for arguing a call.

We drove to Biarritz that afternoon. On the road south I passed a blonde in a yellow Shelby Cobra. She passed me doing about 120. I passed her. She passed me. Lucille slipped down in her seat. She couldn't bear to watch. At the hotel we had a drink in the bar with the blonde. Her name was Doreen and she was vice president of Prudential-Bache. She and Lucille seemed to fancy each other. We agreed to meet later that evening.

Doreen was not at the casino. Lucille and I played a few shoes of bacarrat and drank a bottle of D.P. A few thousand ahead I tipped the croupier well and we left the casino. Lucille drove. She was a little bit drunk. When we arrived at the border the Spanish police made me take the wheel. Lucille was singing a yoghurt jingle in French when we pulled into Arturo's.

When I stopped the car and began to get out Lucille stayed in her seat.

"You are really a shallow guy, do you know that Steve," she said with limpid eyes.

I was hurt but casual. She followed several steps behind me on the flagstone steps to the front door. As I neared the door I turned to tell her to watch her step in the dark and I paused. Just in front of me a huge wheel of cheese smashed to bits on the naked stone. I looked down at the yellow hunks and realized they could be my brains scattered there.

Someone was trying to kill me.

I told Lucille and she laughed in my face.

"Don't be stupid," she sneered. Then she said something under her breath in Chinese.

"Someone dropped a whole wheel of Gruyere on my head from the top of the chateau," I said.

"Nonsense," said Lucille. "We are near the airport. It fell from a Swissair plane."

The butler came to the door. Ikipope was black and supposedly from New Guinea; to me he looked like Jack Lord, but more effeminate. He had on a dark suit and sandals with socks.

"They've gone, sir," he said blankly.

"Gone where?" I said.

"They didn't say, sir."

Lucille insisted that I drive to a small airfield near the chateau. No one was about. She said we should wait.

"Wait for who?"

She said she didn't know.

I asked her what was in the wallet.

"Identification," she said.

At dawn a single engine plane landed. It taxied to where we were parked.

"Let's go," said Lucille, putting on sunglasses.

"Where?"

"Flying," she said.

As we passed over on take off I glanced at the Gran Turismo and wondered if I would ever see it again. Lucille and I sniffed heroin and my mind wandered into a strange vision where the sound of the engine became the muezzin at a mosque, calling the faithful to prayer. When I came to my senses we were landing on a small desert strip.

The sunlight was blinding as I emerged from the plane, but as soon as I could focus I noticed men sitting on camels. They were carrying rifles. Two of them dismounted and began loading large wheels of cheese into the airplanes—wheels that resembled the one that had nearly killed me.

Without a word being spoken the men lifted Lucille and me on to the backs of camels and as the plane departed we rode off into the dunes, a high mountain range looming in the distance. After half a days ride, during which no one spoke, we arrived at an oasis where there was a large modern house surrounded by a mud brick fence posted with armed guards in Arab dress.

The leader of our caravan took us into the house. When he pulled his burnoose aside I saw that he was a blonde, blue-eyed European, deeply tanned. His name was Dirk. He welcomed me to his house, smiling secretively to Lucille. He gave me a cold beer and ordered the major domo to show me to my room.

A turbanned blackamoor motioned for me to follow. We walked down a long glass corridor with piped-in music—a large string orchestra playing "Light My Fire."

We came to a heavily curtained door. The huge man gestured for me to enter and I did.

Inside I found Helena and Doreen laying naked on a huge bed feeding one another apricots. They smiled at me.

"How long have you b-been here?" I stammered.

"Since Friday," said Helena.

"It's Sunday," cooed Doreen, "but that doesn't matter."

"The hell it doesn't. I have a meeting with the IRS on Tuesday morning at 8 a.m."

I was at the Cairo airport by nightfall. I found the Avis representative and handed over the keys to the Grand Turismo.

Tex
Caryl Jones-Sylvester

Ya know what he does with them? Eats 'em. Eats 'em. Yes he does. Yea, some go to whatyacallit? Some goes ta them experiments. But if he gets hungry, well he just goes out an' shoots one. An' he eats 'em.

• • • • •

That ain't nothin'. I knew some folks up in Rochester, they ate dogs too. Right there outside a town. They lived right next door ta me.

One night my two dogs come up missin'. I always kept them down in the cellar. Well, I knew my dogs' bark. You know your dogs' bark. An' I noticed they wasn't around. I go next door an' knock. She comes ta the door an' I asked did they see my two dogs. She say, no, they ain't seen nothin' a my dogs. I said that I'd give just two hours an' when it was midnight, well, if my two dogs didn't show up back home—I'd start killin' dogs. An' I'd start with theirs. Well, they had this little dog, nice Pekinese an' I bet they didn't wanna lose it. Sure enough, in about a half hour I hear my two dogs come right up on the front porch.

• • • • •

That's stupid! They'll eat anything in Saigon. They eat dogs, anything over there. J–e–e–ez! Ya see alot of funny things over there. HARHARHAR....

• • • • •

Don't just eat dogs. I know of a woman would have a baby, kill it and eat it. She did that every time she had a baby. She used ta can 'em an' eat 'em. It's the truth! I read it in the paper. It just happened just a while back. Couldn't be more than a couple a years. Right up in Bath. They got her in jail now. But it took some time 'fore they was able ta catch her. J–e–e–ez, took her four years ta get knocked up every time! Ya think they woulda caught her! It's true.

• • • • •

There's lots a funny things goes on. There's lots a funny people in this world. I know some people right now that eats dogs. I can't see it myself.

• • • • •

J–e–e–ez, that's stupid! When I was over across, there was a lot a funny things.

• • • • •

There's a lot a funny things right here in this country, boy.

There's one thing I et, snake. Tasted just like halibut. That was up in Linenville. Used ta be ya could get it right at the store. I thought it was halibut. I was buyin' it regular. The meat was white, just like halibut.

Back then, ya could buy things right there in the store—wasn't marked. Laid right there an' I went ta pick up another piece, his father says—"You don't want that." I says "Yes, I do. I been eatin' this right along." He says "You know what that is? I says "It's halibut." He says "Put it down. That there is rattlesnake." Well, if ya look at the back of a fish, an' a snake ain't that much difference. The skin looked just the same ta me.

• • • • •

J–e–e–ez, that's stupid! People eatin' dogs, snakes—people! HARHARHARHAR....

• • • • •

Read in the paper a while back, about a woman that cooked her baby. Put the baby in the oven, and cooked it. The husband come home, smelled somethin' cookin', and then he found out it was the baby. People are doin' funny things. There was this couple, they both worked. Well, they hired this babysitter to take care of their baby. The babysitter was a retarded girl, you know—retard. Well, they told her to start dinner at three-thirty that afternoon. They told her what ta set the oven at. So the dinner would be ready, you know, for the people when they got home from work. They left all the stuff for the dinner on the table. Well, it was like a meatloaf, she was to put the stuff for the meatloaf together an' put that in the oven an' other stuff. But she was a retard, you know.
So the people come home from work, an' they ask her where the baby is. She says the baby is in the bedroom sleepin'. So they go into the bedroom to see how the baby is. They come out an' say the baby's not in the bedroom. Where is the baby at. So just then—they smell somethin', an' they go into the kitchen to the oven—an' there's the baby in the oven at four hundred degrees. Well, it went to court—but they couldn't try the girl, you know, 'cause she was a retard. It was the parents' fault. So they decided they better try the parents because, you know, they shouldn't have left the baby with the retard. It was their fault.

I get this newspaper, costs me fifty-five cents. You can learn a lot readin' it. I like to read things. You can learn a lot. You don't have to go nowheres, if you read.

· · · · ·

Back in '79, wasn't it Ma, when we was up in Linenville—there was this guy gettin' young girls out ta foster care—he'd kill 'em an' take their skin an' upholster furniture with it. It took quite a while till they caught him at it. There was quite a few girls come up missin' 'fore they caught him. J-e-e-ez, that's stupid! HARHARHARHAR....

· · · · ·

There's a lot of these cults worshippin' around up there. Up there in Linenville. They would be gettin' young girls. Every year they'd kill a girl. Had ta be a virgin. They raised them just for that purpose.

Then ya got your vampires. There's plenty a them around. Had one there in Buffalo a while back. He was getting girls an' suckin' their blood.

· · · · ·

Took a fork with two tines, just stuck it in their necks an' sucked the blood. There's a lot a that cult worshippin' around. They got plenty a that right over there where we're livin' at now.

'Member when we was livin' over there in Bradford? Bradford, Pa.—well, we did all our food shoppin' at the Topps. Well, come ta find out—that they was usin' human bein's in their hamburg. Yes, it come right over the TV. I had just got me some hamburg from there. An' we had it for dinner that night. It comes over the TV don't eat none of the hamburg out of Topps. Return it ta the store ya got it from. It was humans. They was investigatin' the Topps stores for quite a while. Seems they was takin' bodies outa the funeral parlors an' grindin' them up for hamburg. Couldn't tell the difference. Tasted just like beef ta me. An' I says, "Well, that's a fine howdy-ya-do." We had already et the meat. Tasted alright ta me.

· · · · ·

They'd been doin' that some eight years 'fore they got caught at it. Eight years they'd been takin' people outa the funeral parlors an' usin' them in hamburg. Musta mixed 'em in with other meat, 'cause it tasted just like regular hamburg ta me. Musta been mixin' them in. An' their motto is 'The friendly people....' HARHARHARAAA....

There's some that'll eat cats, dogs—you name it. Now I never did have no turtle. They say there's seven different kinds a meat into a turtle. An' then there's the poison that's the eighth kind. You gotta know where that meat is. So there's the seven kinds an' then that poison. Draper, he raises them dogs—sells some, sells others for them experiments, an' when he wants some meat—he goes out an' shoots one ta eat.

· · · · ·

Depends on where ya live. Now if ya was in India, ya wouldn't wanna shoot a cow. They'd sooner eat a dog. You'd be in big trouble if ya killed a cow!

Then they sell elephant by the pound. Fifty-three, fifty-four dollars a pound.

Aughta weigh the whole elephant, then decide how many pounds ya want. An' have 'em cut off a pound or two.

· · · · ·

In China they drink blood. I was at one a their temples and what they do is hang a snake up—slit its belly an' let the blood run right out into a glass. Then they drink it. They took me all around there.

Eat a lotta horsemeat in Texas. I was a Texas Ranger an' they don't think nothin' a eatin' horsemeat. That's just as common as beef.

· · · · ·

Night I was next door lookin' for my dogs, that's what she was doin' there in the kitchen—cannin' dogs. He'd kill 'em an' dress 'em out an' she'd can the meat. Found out there was four families up there eatin' dog. There was plenty a cult worship up there around Linenville. There's plenty a cult worship wherever you go. 'Member two years ago, 'fore we moved, when you found that cult worshippin' stuff going on over there?

· · · · ·

Me, havin' been with the police an' all, I caught on real quick 'bout what was goin' on. I went up there an' found where they was, up there in the woods behind the trailers. They had a fire an' all, an' sheets. I went right off an' told Sheriff Dartt. He said he'd look into it. But shi-i-i-it, they don't do nothin'. I cleaned them out fast up there. Me havin' been into the Green Berets, cop an' all an' a Texas Ranger. I learned a lot. I learned how ta go into a jungle with nothin' on, an' come out with clothes. They teach ya how ta make your own clothes. I cleaned them out fast, did I Ma?

Friendly Flies
Judy Linn

The Flight

We leave the West Coast after dark. Following the sun, the night will be short. We will reach tomorrow's sunrise at the wrong time. We will disembark on the wrong day. It will be a week before my pineal gland and the sun will agree again.

I can't get to sleep with so many strangers around. Feeling like a participant in some over-achiever's science project, I realize I must be playing the part usually reserved for the very obliging rat. Strapped into a seat with 384 of my own species (problems of urban density), allowed only a few aisles to walk up and down (limited mobility), given attractive options on perfume, liquor, and sugary foods (restrictive, obsessive diversions), in a short time I ever-so-predictably tumble over the edge of rat sanity. It happens every time.

In-flight Movie

On the screen, a hand takes a transistor radio out of a suitcase. Three men at a table look at a map. A man walks through a door marked *Hotel*. He goes to the river and watches a train pass. He talks to a man whose face is hidden. He is hit over the head and thrown in the river. Three men in overcoats run down a street. A man looks at a passport. He rests in a public bathroom. Breathing deeply, he leans against the white tiles.

Outside the oval window there is no horizon line. The night is immense, empty, and cold.

Parangtritis

Seaside resort, ninety-cent-a-night resort hotel surrounded by ten bird cages. Fat bug teases bird in cage. Wouldn't you love to eat me for dinner, wiggle, wiggle.

I am here only to take notes on the changes in scale as you get closer to the equator. The flies are here only to find my legs. When my clothes are dry they fall off the line. The broom looks suspiciously like a rat. Borobodur, the ninth-century, nine-story Buddhist Stupa, the three-dimensional realization of the order of the universe, is carved on the sewing machine cabinet.

My arm itches. I'm tired in the afternoon. Condensed little old lady carrying enormous load on her back walks by in home-made shoes. Sometimes time stretches like an ancient rubber band. The old lady smiles under her conical hat.

The turquoise and maroon ocean has a strong undertow. The black beach has diamond bracelets of sparkling foam. At dusk the moon reflected in the wet sand follows me down the beach, the perfect companion, an abstract celestial puppy, ardent follower of my eye.

Penang

I am sitting facing the sea wall. Sitting in a plastic chair at a table with a metal umbrella set in concrete. There are a few people around, some tourists, two cats, some crows ready to scavenge any unattended dish. The grass is edged with manicured plants and small walks. The sea is a very light blue, reflecting a soft silver light.

Just sitting looking, I feel this person inside me, a few inches under the skin, as if my outsides just lift up; the hair, the dress, the female, as easy as a veil rising in the warm air. It is all unnecessary. Underneath is a shape not made up of parts. It is plain like a roughed-out sculpture, grey, solid, unmoved, just sitting looking at the coastline of Malaysia.

Sukhothai

Flies cut abstract patterns in the air. Three waitresses wait for business. One puts on makeup in the mirror in the center of the room. One with beautiful, irridescent-green toenail polish reads the newspaper, third goes to get change for the hundred-baht note. The mosquitoes arrive like slippery little hallucinations too close to your face to see, the first customers of the morning.

Ubud

The jungle is filled with house plants. Pieces of earth move by on people's heads. Two dragonflies fly backwards in tandem reverse. Coconut palms spill shadows like big, blue spiders.

Meanwhile, I attain full adult growth and become paler. My fat becomes enviable. Bearing a striking resemblance to Nurse Rita in the large color advertisements for Rita Creem Toothpaste, I become exotic.

Dinner in Phitsanoluk

The woman who cooked the shrimp we just ate for dinner is sitting across the room carefully probing her nose. A man at a front table is eating with chopsticks and from here it looks like he is furiously turning a crank in his ear. Chris just took a picture with a flash. Oh, no, the goldfish-looking guy is interested. The older Chinese lady woke up with all this action. The cat meows. The easy-listening Thai is on the tape.

We are across from the expensive hotel in town. We had first gone over there to try and eat dinner, but as we walked through the restaurant guys heads popped up over the banquets and slowly watched us like a periscope silently tracking an enemy vessel. We left when we realized they had locally- done color pictures of girls in bathing suits on the menu.

The restaurant we are in is open to the street and there is a glass booth just inside the door where all the food is displayed and where the daughter is cooking again. The old lady is drying silverware in a basket and making a lot of clanking noise. An old lady friend comes by. She is wearing yellow combs, a brown embroidered top, blue knit pants pulled up tight in the crotch and well-worn plastic sandles. She gets a fist full of chopsticks. A slightly grey Pomeranian parades back and forth in front of the door. The ladies set the table. Some cutlery is dropped and has to be rewiped. They all sit down to eat with the son. He has on a Hell's Angels riding high T-shirt and grey knit sweat pants. They sit under old pictures of the royal Thai family so everyone is young. There is a clock that is part of a large 20 by 24 picture of a tractor in a very ornate gold plastic frame. The Pomeranian lies under their chairs while they eat. The music tape is over.

The aquarium behind me has so many moving plastic toys, I have to concentrate to see the fish. There is a clear blue rotating water wheel, a rising and sinking tethered orange mine, a clapping clam shell, and a Belgian boy pissing bubbles, all constantly moving at different rates.

The daughter interrupts her meal to figure out a bill. The Pomeranian viciously bites fleas at the top of his back leg. The lady has her shoes off. Her bare feet on the chair are crossed at right angles at the ankle. When she talks she holds her chopsticks poised next to her head so she can catch words as they go by.

A boy comes in fast for carry-out. Absorbed in a pocket computer game while he waits, he leaves pretending he is a jet fighter. He stops, though, and says good-by to the dog. The daughter attends to two men who came in to peruse. A mosquito sniffs me. The men get a Pepsi, a soda water, and a bottle of Mekong whiskey. Little boy comes in to sell newspapers. No takers. We ask for a bill. Daughter comes back with two cigarettes on a plate for the men. We say how many baht? The son and daughter giggle. The Pomeranian lies down near us.

Swimming

In Phuket a tropical fish was friendly to me. A real tropical fish, any New York pet store would gladly include him in their stock. Black and yellow striped, he was a little larger than a neon tetra. The water was so clear at first I thought he was a piece of garbage or waste from one of the fishing ships in the harbor. When I pushed him away, though, he came right back, looking at me and beating his little tail. I went underwater to look at him, but he was so close and my trying to see cross-eyed through crummy goggles was impossible. He stayed between me and the sun, and we swam down the beach together. I would look back over my shoulder and there he would be. I was afraid he would get lost in so much water, that I was leading him astray. So, after reluctantly bidding him a fond good-by, I got out of the water and realized he was the smallest thing ever conscious and attracted to me without wanting to bite me.

Phitsanoluk Airport

It is a quarter to eight in the morning. We are waiting for the flight to Chiang Mai. As we sit in the little cafe in the corner of the terminal, the radio news comes over the loudspeaker. A large bottle of Coffee Mate non-dairy creamer is on the table. People near us drink iced tea. There are gallon bottles of preserved water bugs on the counter. If the size categories are the same as for olives, these are colossal, aligned belly out like Italian antipasto. The Thais know these inexpensive flavor-enhancers are hard for the tourists to ignore. We are trying to decide what to eat. There are signs around warning us not to bring objects on the airplane that are spoiled, dirty, or foul-smelling. And, if we must, to declare our gases, flammables, corpses, durians, and vicious animals.

The flight from Bangkok arrives and people bend over to see out the low windows. The radio drones on. At another table, three American men speak with Southern drawls. Their smoking cigarettes hang from their paws over the center of the table. They have a battery-powered archery set. A man with a very strong face, pink shirt, cigarette holder, high-heeled plastic pastel loafers gets up to say hello to a pilot. He puts his hands together and nods in the traditional Thai greeting. The pilot returns the gesture without putting down his golf putter.

At two to eight they play the Gold Bell Gift Stamp medley on a door chime that makes your neck muscles twitch. Everyone rises, stands evenly on two feet, faces a certain direction, and the Thai national anthem is played. No one talks on the side or giggles or rolls their eyes. They all comply and take it very seriously. I was looking forward to seeing this. The last time we were in this airport, it occured while I was in the ladies room admiring the very lovely deep raspberry and mauve Western plumbing. When I came out, everyone was frozen in space and I had no idea why. Only in fifties TV shows did this sort of thing happen and, when it did, it usually meant you were in for a little time travel. As the only person still moving around, I was reassured that at least if it was a TV show, I was the female lead.

With a quick segue from the national anthem to a theme from a Sergio Leone spaghetti western, everyone comes back to life.

I know the climate's wonderful, but how's the Truth?
Robert Fiengo

People have been chronicling their travels for thousands of years, of course. Caesar kept people informed in Rome by writing about his Gallic War, and we are told that he did it for personal political reasons: he wanted his heroism known so that he might smooth his path to power when he returned, a little like Kennedy's *A Profile in Courage*. Xenophon's *Anabasis* takes us with Cyrus across what is now Turkey, another ancient case in point. I'm not sure when the travel book was demilitarized, really. There were ancient accounts of personal journeys, the *Odyssey* and later the *Aeneid*, but I take it that these were appreciated as essentially fictional. I suppose the prospective traveler might pick up a few tips, how to avoid the twin perils of Scylla and Charybdys, how to get to Hades, and even more importantly, how to get back, but I think it's safe to say that these books had not practical impact on their audiences. It would appear that for the next thousand years or so everybody stayed at home, at least until Marco Polo, and various other crusaders, pirates, slavers, and missionaries started writing about how much fun one could have doing business abroad. War was replaced by trade. But it was not until the later part of the nineteenth century that we find the tourist in the modern sense—the adventurers, the lion hunters and mountain climbers. By now there are tour guides for every purpose; if you want to taste every wine in northern Italy, there are guide books to show you how. Caesar wouldn't have told you about the wine, but now there is an industry in place, encouraging you to find those hard-to-find vineyards.

Still, I think there's something lacking. The guide books will tell you where all the commodities are, but as far as the intangibles are concerned, they're really letting us down. Consider what I call the quality of life questions. At the moment there is no industry which can sell a quality of life, but when there is you can be sure they'll advertise. But I don't see why we should wait for entrepreneurs to market these things and tell us where to find them; after all, this kind of information can be crucial. If you find yourself all of a sudden in a different quality of life, you want to know how to behave. On the other hand, if there is a different quality of life that you've always wanted to experience, you want to know where to go. A few superficial stereotypes are all one can find: the mañana mentality south of the border, Scandinavian reserve, Southern hospitality. But this is of no more use than being told that Greece is hot in the summer. It's not enough to be told that not all of the roads in Poland are paved. The tourist wants to know which ones.

Now some of the most fascinating things which one can encounter in one's travels involve such things as how people determine what is true and how people make decisions. A case in point. You are in Spain or Italy in a group of eight or ten people. It has been decided to go out for dinner. The question is where. Conversation may well proceed under the rules of Latin Unanimity. The decision must be unanimous. No one may try to convince another. People may leave the conversation or enter at will, at which point the newcomer is brought completely up to date. All possibilities must be considered. When any particular restaurant is mentioned, both pros and cons must be considered. The decision, when it comes, must not be perceived as stemming from any individual. Discussion may last up to two hours, and it is important to greet the decision with wonder that it had not been thought of before. People tell me that this ritualized communal decision making is a reaction to Fascism. Perhaps it is; in any event, those of us who are tired of authoritarian decision making should be able to find out where to go to find relief.

Different methods of determining the truth is a variable we all should be sensitive to; after all, the government often gets involved. This is a truism in Eastern Europe, where the truth is typically determined by assuming that everything that the government says is a lie. Citizens disagree over whether the current lie is a dumb lie or a clever lie, so the truth can be elusive, still the official press contributes in a negative sense in determining the facts. In some parts of the world the government has not only legislative power but also ontological power. It can determine not only what is legal, but what exists. I tumbled onto a version of this in Japan.

I was, one late evening, leaving a restaurant in Nagasaki in the company of a Japanese businessman. He had insisted on paying for everything, of course, the main event having been the butchering of a live turtle on our table with glasses of fresh blood all around, but this was now but a fond memory, the current problem being the effects of the Scotch. He seemed to feel that I should be escorted back to my hotel, a common courtesy there. I pointed the direction of the place and fit my mouth around its name, one of those five syllable jobs that always gets tangled. He recognized the name but insisted that we proceed by a far different route than the one that I had indicated. I was in no mood for that, wanting to pass out as soon as possible, and my escort followed me with strange reluctance. The mystery cleared when I found that I was steering us directly through the red light district, whose nature had been invisible to me when I passed through a few hours before. The propositions were rapid and vocal, two twin girls and a mother-daughter combo among them. My friend looked anxious and lost, though he was a native of Nagasaki, and turning to me said with rigid conviction, "There is no prostitution in Japan."

Now the Japanese language is a subtle instrument, much of what is overt in English is left tacit in Japanese and consequently the shift of a mere syllable can have far-reaching effects on the meaning. I pondered his words carefully, sensing that a mistake at this point might be socially disastrous. A flip rejoinder like "What do you call this, a girl scout camp?" would not have done. But suddenly I knew with neon clarity that I had heard him rightly. In fact, I realized, he had said it in English.

Still, there was room for ambiguity. After all, if I say that there is no sleeping on park benches, I don't mean that it doesn't exist but that it is illegal. Perhaps he had meant his negative this way. "Do you mean that prostitution doesn't exist?" I asked, throwing in a little naive wonderment. "Not in Japan," he replied, "but there is in Korea. "Why not?" I asked, a little shaken. "Because it is illegal here," he replied, and the topic was closed. Now my friend clearly knew what he was seeing, but appearances must be preserved. The Japanese are a law-abiding people. Prostitution is illegal. Therefore, the reasoning goes, prostitution doesn't exist. This all probably is part of the larger fact that the Japanese typically believe that the government is expressing their will. Opinion polls regularly show that only 10% of the Japanese people may know what the government is doing, but 90% feel that the government is correct. This contrasts with the U.S. Here a poll showed that only 10% of the American people know which side the government is on in both Nicaragua and El Salvador but that 90% think the government is following the wrong policy. This is the kind of thing a tour guide should tell us. If we wish to replace unknowing distrust with unknowing trust, we should be pointed to Japan. This for many is an attraction far more precious than sushi and bullet trains.

There is something similar in the U.S., though. There are areas of California and, I imagine, many other parts of the U.S. if the enterprising traveler can only uncover them, where the weary tourist may happily turn over ontological responsibility to another party. I once found myself at a party in Big Sur when it suddenly became clear that I was the only person there that did not believe in elves. They are, I was told, about a foot and a half tall with leggings and hats and talk in whistles and songs. It developed that only two of the party had actually seen them, however, and they were held in great esteem by the others, who felt that their failure to spot any was a personal failing, the way some of us are bad with cats. These beliefs seem to pyramid under direction of leaders, who are in effect running a kind of epistemic Amway. Anyhow, membership is always open. And membership can be desireable. Some of us, who live in hectic, complex cities crave the wide open spaces. And some of us, who have a narrow, circumscribed set of beliefs crave the freedom to believe in something new. For others, the wide open spaces of belief are really the big empty spaces, and they are better off staying at home.

Communal decision making, existence determined by law, truth determined by negating the press, the world is your oyster. But let's try to appreciate all of these things before they are degraded by rank commercialism. Let's try to appreciate them in their natural state, before the tourists get there.

To Japan and Back
Linda L. Cathcart

It all begins about November of last year. I get a call from one of those organizations that was formed after the war to repay or pay back war debts or maybe just to assuage guilt—whatever. Anyway, this is a Japanese-American group and they've decided to invite ten museum directors to come to Japan and see the art there.

Well, I guess they started out planning the whole thing a little bit late. It had something to do with the fact that their fiscal year was about to be over and they had some extra funds that needed to be spent and they had to be spent by January. So anyway, it's billed as ten really important museum directors and, as things go along, I get the felling that I was not on the A list. I figure they've got this kind of "A" list like Dick Oldenburg, Tom Messer, Bob Buck, big guys like that and they called them all on six weeks' notice. Of course, these guys say absolutely not and some of them recommend people that worked for them, or friends of theirs, to take their places.

Well, I gather the Japanese took some of these suggestions and also combined it with some panic on their part, and some kind of regional specifications to fill the group in. Also there seemed to be a whole bunch of hidden agendas going on here, like the female to male ratio, for example. The group ends up just like when you give a big party and certain people can't come and those people are precisely the links between the other people—you end up with this really bizarre group in which everyone is offended. So, here we are—ten museum directors in close quarters for 30 days. We're a group and when the Japanese say group, they mean it.

First of all they scheduled the departure date over the top of the AAMD meetings, which are being held in Puerto Rico. The AAMD is the Association of Art Museum Directors and there's about 100 or 150 of us. In order to get in, your museum has to be nominated, you have to be nominated, you have to be passed by the nominating committee, submitted to the membership committee, voted on by the membership committee, agreed on by the Trustees, then you get to be in. It's a really big deal. Needless to say, I'm one of the few women so I go to all of the meetings. I also get to head up a committee—again, there aren't so many women and I'm the one they can count on.

So I don't go into a big fuss about the departure date because I figure out that when they get the response from these other nine important museum directors, they'll get the word about how the departure date will have to be more or less flexible. Flexible is not a word in the Japanese language. Not only did the departure date remain set, but we all had to fly on the same planes—one from the west coast and one from the east coast. I have to return from Puerto Rico to Houston in order to go to New York in order to get on the east coast plane. Any other discussion is out of the question, I'm informed. Anyway, they want us all to arrive at the same time, so that the foundation can pick us up. Think of if the planes had gone down—oh well, never mind that.

So, we get to Japan. We've been there for about ten days and a couple of million picturesque and ridiculous things have happened to us. And we're pretty well defined as a group right now. Diane and John are the two most important directors—senior in age and deportment and all other departments. They have also quickly figured out how to use the second string—like me and Jay—because we're eager to please and clearly on the "B" list. The "C" list is defined and described by the unfortunate inclusion of two—can you imagine it?—art critics. Are the Japanese really so insensitive that they do not realize the meaning of this social blunder, this professional gaff? Or are they being diabolical? So, you get the picture about the hierarchy.

The tour consists mostly of going to lectures and visits to museums and partaking of long meals which try our abilities to sit still and look attentive. The Japanese don't notice nor care about that. These are things that we do to impress each other.

So far we've been housed in rather substandard accommodations and we are always placed side-by-side, alphabetically in the hotel. We have precious little privacy as we are on a bus together all day and we get every meal together. We have come to know one another's cute little quirks—every person has a little joke —some smoke, some smoke secretly, another loves beer, another dumplings. You get it—oral fixations. Well, anyway these things we can tease each other about without any real risk to the pecking order.

About ten days into this, the Japanese decide that we should go to a Ryokan, which is a sort of rustic Japanese inn-type place where young lovers go during the spring to see the blossoms, worship at the temple, and eat all their meals together in their pajamas in a room alone. Needless to say, this has some attraction for young newly weds, but for us—well, remember it's January and it's freezing. In fact, it's snowing. These places lose a little of their rustic charm at that time of year. It's sort of like—you know, those quaint little rental beach houses in the Hamptons. Like they would be in the dead of winter.

The staff of this little inn is delighted to have some customers—some that are foreign to boot. It not only makes for extra money, but also for some yuks at our piggish manners and barbaric social habits. We are told as the bus approaches the site that we will be put in rooms in pairs, as this is apparently the way things are done there. Presumably, when you have young lovers, this makes sense. When you have a group like us, well, as you can imagine, the potential is for disaster.

We are paired off alphabetically. This is a system the Japanese often use in order to prevent any kind of decision-making. I'm paired with Cathy. It's pretty awkward, but we manage. I take a giant sleeping pill and she drinks a large bottle of beer. In the morning, she tells me the worst: I've snored. From the way she says it, she was awake the entire night, what with the stress of being confined to a room with a companion, not to mention the offensive snoring. I make some vague mumblings about sinuses and allergies. As we get back on the bus, everyone looks a little worse for wear.

A few days later, we are told once again that we are going to be honored in another of these great springtime hot tub places. I forgot to describe the bathing part of this whole thing. When you're not in your pajamas sitting in your room eating a whole bunch of stuff and looking out the window at the cherry blossoms, or cruising around on the mountainside toward the temple, you're supposed to take hot baths. They have these giant bathtubs where you get in with everybody else. Part of the bath is inside and part of it is outside. There's snow on the ground and you're swimming back and forth, inside-outside. The water's about a million degrees and you know—you've read the travel books—you don't wash in the tub, you wash outside it. Well, one thing they don't tell you in the travel books, is that the faucets are about the level you'd use to bathe your dog. Anyway, we get offered this entertainment and nobody takes them up on it. You're supposed to drink before you get in the bath and drink a little bit afterward and it purifies your soul. All the women claim they have their periods.

As we approach the second Ryokan, we suggest to our leaders that the alphabetical system be reversed so that each of us would now have new sleeping partners. This system proves to be amazingly accurate in pairing those who have become the closest on the trip—the women I mean. The men couldn't care less.

We arrive in some town. We never know where we are. It's that the Japanese don't like to go into detail about everything, lest it provoke some response which would be too difficult. You can imagine, we say "where are we? in the north? in the south? near the sea?" They reply "yes" to every question.

The street that the hotel is on is too small to accommodate our bus, so we are dumped off on the sidewalk and our bags unloaded into our hands. There are never any porters in Japan and we follow, as always, behind the guides into a lobby, carpeted with cabbage-like images in violent red—it's hideous.

About a thousand short ladies grab our shoes off our feet and we are led upstairs through sort of endless passages to a giant room where we stand like cattle waiting to be told what to do next. We are quite used to this by now. Then they bring up all the luggage. Suddenly it is apparent to some of us that we are all to sleep in this one room. We look at each other. Diane dispatches me to the desk to ask for separate rooms—alone—and to offer to pay the difference. I go to the desk and make this request. "Impossible" I am told. "The entire inn is full." Needless to say, there's not a soul in sight. I return to the room and it has now dawned on all of the participants, one by one, that we are to be together in this space. Everyone is aghast. We ask the attendants about this arrangement. They roar with laughter and draw our attention to some paper screens which can divide male from female as we slumber. Suddenly Cathy has an anxiety attack—serious. She's panting, she sinks to the floor. We all look at her with dismay and some relief—she's having the attack that others of us would have had later on.

This entire group has remained remarkably discrete from one another throughout the journey. There's been the A, the B and the C group, each has acted appropriately in its roles. Each has been discrete in its arrangements. We don't know who's called home to their boyfriends, husbands, lovers, fathers, etc. We do not know who's received mail or sent manuscripts back and forth through their editor. Has anyone dallied with a guide? We've remained remarkably aloof. We treated one another as you would have them treat you.

But suddenly we have an emergency! And it's Cathy. She may be B list, but she's cute, funny and smart and everyone still likes her. Lids fly off boxes, bottles appear out of purses, pockets. Bags are rummaged through and suddenly there is a great debate as to which tranquilizer should be administered to her. There's Valium, Thorazine, Librium, Xanax. Everyone is proffering their own medicine! No one looks at anyone else. It's apparent in this group of ten that each one of us has been taking enormous quantities of tranquilizers all along, without anyone ever having noticed. An argument ensues among the most experienced directors. It's decided that she will have Valium. It's the dosage that then comes up for discussion. I offer Valium—#twos. I'm scoffed at and turned away. One of the art critics offers five and then someone on the "A" list has, in fact, tens. We fall back in silence. Ten milligram Valiums. She administers two to Cathy. We lay her down on her little futon and we all take a walk to the temple—leaving her alone until she is able to feel calm.

We return to the room several hours later. She's had a little nap. She's looking pale but better. All of us are extremely cautious. We dress in the bathroom, turn by turn. We talk softly. Many of us drink a great deal of sake at dinner. We're solicitous. We turn the heaters toward her feet. Each of us tries not to look at one another to see the fit and form of the pajamas we are being made to wear. Some of the men even agree to go around to the bathtub. The women again refuse and retire to their little sleeping bags. Suddenly, it's sort of like we're at camp. We're all covered up. We're all warm. Everyone's taken whatever they've offered to Cathy and some even seem to have shared things with other people. Nothing more is said about sedatives. We all chat merrily and say goodnight to one another. In the morning, nothing is said about snoring, anxiety attacks or anything else.

The trip nears its end. We have one last stop back in Tokyo. We are returned to the same room, in the same hotel where we were put at the beginning of our journey. These rooms are six feet wide and twelve feet long. They contain a single bed and the television on which you can view pornographic movies for the right change, to be deposited at 30-minute intervals. We also have these little self-contained plastic capsule bathrooms in which everything is molded out of a single piece of plastic. The bathtubs are about three feet long, and as you sit in them, you imagine all the people above you and all those below you also sitting in these little tubs at this very moment. You could induce a serious anxiety attack by just thinking about this for a minute too long. Diane comes out in the corridor. She says let's go downstairs and ask for double rooms. We'll pay the difference. No one will ever know. We won't cause any trouble or embarrassment to the Japanese who seem to loathe us whenever we ask for something other than what was arranged.

We go down to the desk together. We ask for double rooms. They consult the papers; they consult the leaders of our group. There's great consternation. We explain we'll pay the difference. We just need slightly bigger rooms for our last few days here. Finally they agree. They refuse the difference, but I am sure they add it on to the cost for the foundation. They give us keys. We arrive upstairs to our adjoining double rooms. We open the doors joyously, looking forward to three days of sprawling out, unpacking our suitcases completely—the previous rooms had no closets and no shelves. We fling open the doors and look in. The rooms are exactly the same. The beds are double. They, in effect, decrease the available space in the room unless one wants to live on top of the bed. I look into the hall—Diane's door remains closed. I decide not to say anything. The humiliation is too great at this point. I decide to take it like an A Team.

A couple of hours later, I run into Diane at the desk asking for change. I've gone to the desk too. The change she gets is a certain kind of coin you put into the television slot to watch the pornographic movies. Diane has two handfuls of coins. I figure, what the hell, and I change in a large bill myself.

Two days later, we are all taken to the airport; all put on the same plane. At the counter we beg for seats apart from one another. We are dispersed throughout the 747 and we fly back the twelve hours to New York without speaking to each other even once during the entire flight.

Sanjiro's, Thumb's and Apple Pie
3 episodes from a fiction
Micki McGee

I. Sanjiro's Even though Fodor's calls Shinjuku "Tokyo's center for the young and non-conformist" you still hadn't expected to find a gay raggae bar packed full as a rush hour subway car. Nor had you expected to see a Japanese Rastafarian dressed only in a red, green and yellow loin cloth and his own waist-length dreadlocks dancing on top of the bar. But you might find yourself here at Sanjiro's; someone might take you to this smoke-filled basement with Sanjiro dancing above the crowd of misplaced salarymen, sailors on shore leave, travelers and traders just in from treks in Nepal or looking for fences for stolen goods—fur coats or leather jackets from Hong Kong or Seoul. You could find yourself just there, drinking Sapporo beer, smashed up against another patron of the place, a young American man wearing those round, wire-framed glasses that suggest a certain lifestyle, a kind of politics, or a pretense of intellect. Perhaps he is one of the nonconformists that Fodor's writes of.

And he might start a conversation with you, smashed up against him as you are, expecting you to speak English based on your blonde hair or your blue eyes. And since you do, the two of you might talk.

"You'd never believe it," he says. "You'd just never believe it."

"Try me," you answer.

"You see that girl over there?"

"Yeah," you nod, not at all certain which one he pointed at.

"That girl went home with my friend Tasaki last night and charge him 10,000 yen...10,000 yen." He repeats the figure as though it had some magical properties.

You look over at a young salaryman that you guess is Tasaki. His face is flushed from drinking. Standing next to him is a flawless young woman—probably his hooker friend—smooth skinned and glowing in the dark basement bar.

"Sounds like a bargain to me," you say.

"But she's charging. How could she charge him?"

"Easy enough," you say. "Someone's willing to pay and she's willing to sell."

"Well, I don't understand," he shakes his head and looks around for his way out. But Sanjiro is still hopping around on top of the bar to "Woman No Cry" and there's just nowhere to move yet. You feel momentary remorse—maybe this guy is really as young as he sounds; maybe he really is that innocent. So you ask him what he's doing in Tokyo and he tells you he plays lead guitar in a band called "They Might Be Giants"; that they're on tour, mostly playing in USO shows. He asks you what you're doing and you tell him you just got back from the Philippines.

"The Philippines," he exclaims, "God, I love the Philippines." His face lights up at some memory he's not yet disclosed to you. "It's just incredible there. You can go into any bar in Manila—any bar—and know that any one of them would marry you in a second. You could have any one of them... most of them virgins. And if you don't want to get married, you can still have *almost* anyone for 100 pesos. 100 pesos... five dollars and fifty cents."

You imagine him figuring the currency conversion on a pocket calculator. You do not believe you're having this conversation with the young American who's suddenly as foreign to you as anyone in the room.

"But I thought you were the one who couldn't imagine people selling sex," you remind him.

"Yeah, but at that price how can you pass it up?"

By now Sanjiro has fallen or stepped down from the platform of the bar and an old Jimmy Cliff tape plays, "she is a woman, so true and so free, she is a woman, ideal for me..." You find your way away from the lead guitar player of the would-be giants.

II. Thumb's You agreed to meet Dave at Thumbelina's—Thumb's to the regulars. You arrive early and are surprised when you're greeted by a midget maitre d', an older man with peppered grey hair who might have been distinguished looking if not for his diminutive stature. As he shows you to a table in the dimly lit dinner club, you see a waitress, also under four feet in height, standing on a bar stool to survey her tables. Dave hadn't mentioned that Thumb's was the only restaurant in Manila, perhaps in the world, staffed entirely by dwarves, midgets or little people, as they call themselves. Little people from all over the Philippine archipelago migrated to Thumb's, where they could earn better-than-average salaries from tourists' tips and meet others like themselves, often marrying into the growing dwarf community. But you don't yet understand this when you sit down; you're staring and struggling not to stare when your waitress arrives to take your order.

"What can I get you," she asks, looking up at you despite the fact that you're seated and she's standing.

"Just a San Miguel for now... I'm waiting for someone."

You continue struggling not to stare in this place designed to make you gawk. Thumb's is banking on making you stare; their business thrives because you've never seen anything quite like this before. Focused on the dwarves, you don't notice Dave, your disaffected ex-peace corp worker friend, until he's at your table.

"Feeling better?" he asks. That afternoon he'd volunteered to guide you through Tondo, the city's enormous shanty town, bordered on one side by a garage dump where a soldier stands guard with an M-16 in hand to break up fights between people quarreling over anything edible or saleable. You're not usually given to faintness, but somewhere on your trek you'd found yourself overcome. You weren't sure if it was the heat or the stench of burning refuse, or the sewage flooding the street after a brief afternoon downpour. Or perhaps it was the diesel fumes from the jeepneys, converted surplus jeeps, as they splashed through the puddles of offal in rush hour traffic. But whatever it was, you'd surprised yourself by nearly passing out.

"Yes, I *was* feeling much better, but what's the idea of coming to this freak show restaurant?"

"Trust me... trust me... this is the best show in town. Tonight a folksinger named Freddie Aquilar's playing. He's alright, but the best show is the crowd he'll attract: opposition leaders and fans on one side of the room and CIA people and Marcos informants on the other. You'll meet alot of people; some of them will be able to help you and others will want to. Unfortunately, they won't necessarily be the same ones."

Over Dave's shoulder you can see two dwarves starting to fight in the kitchen; the dwarf chef is yelling at the dwarf waitress. You can't hear what they're saying and wish you could. While you're distracted a tall, polished Filipino approaches your table.

"Dave, it's been a long time... can I join you?" he asks already pulling up a chair.

"Sure, sit down, Eddie. This is my friend Dani." He introduces you to the man in the pressed white shirt and khaki trousers.

"Dani. Dani. That's a man's name. And if you don't mind my saying so, you're obviously very much a woman."

"It's short for Danielle."

"So what brings you to Manila, Miss Dani. It is 'miss', isn't it?"

"She's here on vacation," Dave interrupts, kicking you under the table.

"Really? So where've you been so far?" Eddie asks while he orders a beer by holding up your empty bottle for the waitress.

"Dave gave me a tour of Tondo this afternoon...."

"Tondo...what could you possibly want there? That place is disgusting...."

"I wanted to see how half the population of Manila lives."

"But that's not living...let me show you how the Filipino people live... perhaps you would like to come with me on my boat tomorrow. There's a yacht race between Manila and Negros, and we certainly have enough space for an extra passenger, even two extra if you want to bring Dave along. We'll get there just in time for the festival...."

"That should be fun," Dave remarks, saving you from answering.

"You really should join us...but let's get back to your quiet friend here. Where're you from—America?"

"Yes," you answer, "I'm from the U.S."

"You're not a WASP, are you?" he asks.

"No, raised Catholic," you answer. "What's it to you?"

"Catholic, that's good," Eddie nods approvingly and Dave grins over at you. A round of applause interrupts your conversation as an emaciated man with an acoustic guitar steps onto the stage. He begins singing in Tagalog—something about his country and his people and the room grows quiet except for Dave and Eddie, who try not to let the singing disturb them.

"So how's your business doing?" Dave asks.

"It's never been better. I jsut acquired several thousand hectares of virgin forest...absolutely untouched land in the Cordilleras. Covered with pine and hardwoods. Of course we'll be stripping it soon; I'm putting together a deal with a logging firm. Eventually I'd like to move into some of the rain forests in the south. And the aquatic farms, the prawn farms, they're doing great, too. We've just gotten another fertilized female from Singapore; you know how difficult all this seafood farming is. They really don't like to mate in captivity. But we got this fertilized one—smuggled in for only $800.... Listen, this talk is probably boring your lady friend. Why don't you let me buy you both a drink? But let's not stay here...let me take you someplace you'll really enjoy. Let me show you Manila."

You're taking your cues from Dave by now.

"Sure Eddie, that sounds good. Let's get out of here."

Freddie the folksinger is singing "Where Have All the Flowers Gone?" as the waitress brings the check. Eddie picks it up and walks out ahead of you. Dave leans back towards you and whispers "You're gonna love this."

Eddie leads you to his BMW, black and shining under the only streetlamp working on the block. Eddie unlocks the driver's door first and lets himself in before unlocking the passenger doors. Dave sits in front and you slide into the back.

"By the way, Dani, I forgot to give you my card...allow me."

You read the card quickly as the car pulls away from the street lamp: COLONEL EDUARDO MENDOZA—MARINE AND FOREST VENTURES. There's a phone and an address, but the light fades as you pull onto the street.

"If you'll excuse me, I just have to make a quick stop up here. I hope you don't mind. Then I'll take you to a place you can really enjoy...a place with sexy Filipina girls."

"You don't need to find any sexy Filipina girls for me," you say, but there's no answer from the front.

Eddie double parks and runs into a small shop. You and Dave can finally talk.

"Who is this creep?" you ask.

"Watch what you say, okay?" Dave points to a walkie-talkie lying on the leather upholstery of the front seat. Looking into the shop, Dave reaches for a black leather case on the dash board and opens it slowly, never talking his eyes off Eduardo who's standing in the shop talking. He opens it wide enough for you to see the revolver inside. Dave returns the revolver to its place on the dash and turns off the walkie-talkie. "I don't know, kid, but he sure took a shine to you."

"No, he didn't," you protest.

"Are you kidding? He hasn't talked to me in months. And why d'you think he was asking your religion?"

"I don't know....I thought it was a little strange."

"He's looking for an American wife, preferably Catholic. He used to be Marcos's private pilot, but he's since gone into business and made quite a fortune, as he's let you know. But like everyone else here, he knows this Marcos thing can't last forever and he doesn't want to be left behind with no U.S. visa... not after what he's been doing in the northern provinces to get that "virgin land."

"What's he been doing?" You hadn't noticed Eddie walking toward the car.

"You're really going to like this bar," Dave says with excessive enthusiasm as Eduardo opens the car door.

"Yes, you're going to love it... now for some fun," Eddie says as he starts the engine.

You drive less than three blocks and double park again. You could have walked more easily, but that would have spoiled Eddie's fun. He leads you to a bar with no name posted outside and greets the hostess at the door. The three of you are escorted to the only empty seats at the bar. Three young Filipinas in black fishnets and sequined G-strings are gyrating to an oddly re-arranged version of "Girls Just Wanna Have Fun." A round of beers arrives and Eddie proposes a toast, "To beautiful girls from all around the world." You toast to his success with the virgin forest and Dave smiles over at you as you settle back against the bar stool.

The stage is level with the bar, and set just a few feet behind. There's a mirror lining the wall behind the stage, so your vantage is nearly all inclusive: you see the go-go dancers from the front and from behind and you see yourself and all the other customers reflected back between the girls' legs. One of the dancers works her way back to the mirrored wall and gyrates in front of her own image as though seducing herself. Another, with an incongruous expression of shyness, pulls a fishnet stocking and garter down, throwing both out into the crowd, mostly German and Japanese tourists, who scramble for the souvenirs.

"Which one do you like best?" Dave asks.

You look back at him in surprise, but you don't get a chance to answer since Eddie's put his arm around you and pulled you toward him.

"So, Dani, my dear, would you do that...would you dance up there like that?" he asks.

"If I had to, of course I would," you answer, pulling away from him.

"You would?!?" he exclaims with disappointment. "I thought you were a good Catholic girl."

"I am. What difference does tat make? So are they. If I was in their position, I'm sure I'd do what I had to do to get by."

"You wouldn't. I know you wouldn't." Eddie tries to reassure himself.

"Do you like to dance?" Dave asks.

"Under the right circumstances," you answer.

"You mean not on a mirrored stage in front of a crowd of drunken tourists."

"Yeah."

"Good, let's get out of here." You and Dave say your goodnights to Eddie, who stays at the go-go bar, perhaps continuing his quest for an American bride.

III. Apple Pie   "You wanna go over to the American Embassy this morning?" Dave asks, rolling over into the space you've left him on the single bed.

"The embassy? Why would I want to go there?"

"For breakfast, my sweet. For the best eggs-over-easy in Manila and the only apple pie in all of the Philippines. The only apples, too."

"Sounds tempting—just like you," you say leaning over to kiss him. "Uhmmm, good. Okay, let's go."

"Wait a second. Not so fast—the Embassy's open til five."

By two o'clock you're walking through Ermita, down Mabini Street, looking for a jeepney headed over towards the Embassy. You walk past shop windows: displays of seashell trinkets in some and cast plaster statues of the Virgin Mary in others. You turn down an arcade and see a sign that reads: MEDICU SERVICES: SPECIALISTS IN SEXUALLY TRANSMITTED DISEASE. PERINEAL (VAGINAL) REPAIRS. HYMEN RESTORATION. PLSE USE STAIRS. RM. #203.

You burst out laughing. "Well, I hope we don't need their services," you joke.

"We could always get your virginity restored," Dave says, tugging on your pony tail.

"Yeah, that sounds like a terrific idea. I was so anxious to get rid of it the first time around... seemed more like a stigma than a prize in my high school."

"Oh, you had it all wrong.... Didn't you know that's everyman's dream—to be the first." He hums the theme song from *Star Trek*, "You know—to boldly go where no man has gone before."

"You can't be serious...."

"But I am. Maybe we should go back there," Dave turns back in jest. "But isn't that what we're all doing over here...hacking our way across jungles, looking for something no man—at least no white man—has ever seen. Quick, there's a jeepney. Let's get it."

You jump on board and take the last seat, next to a man cradling his fighting cock. The bird pecks ferociously at the man's gloved hand. Dave's standing at the back of the jeepney, hanging on to the railing. You think vaguely about novelty and familiarity and look back fondly at this man you've only known a week.

The fighting cock squawks as the jeepney pulls in front of the embassy. Barricades of steel reinforced buses line the sidewalk adjacent to the main building, an ugly structure covered with aluminum panels that Dave tells you screen microwaves and prevent spying. You and Dave enter after showing your U.S. passports. You are required to turn in your camera and pocket knife. You try to imagine yourself holding the embassy hostage with your Swiss Army knife. The guards have already started frisking Dave.

"Just like the embassy to give us a warm welcome," Dave jokes as another guard frisks you.

You both pass the inspection and sign in before taking the elevator directly to the sixth floor coffee shop. You're the only customers; lunch was hours ago. You each order coffee and apple pie, a la mode, with vanilla ice cream. The Filipina waitress brings your coffee, then your pie, and you sit overlooking Manila Bay through the anti-microwave aluminum.

gothic tourism
cheryl clarke

my self is a house i'm afraid to enter.
some humility would help
break down my gables of ego
here in jersey city—
where the stares of recently immigrated
east indians from guyana
third generation italians
fourth generation irish
egyptians taken for puerto ricans
post castro cubans who fear being
mistaken for puerto ricans
and a bar on every corner flashing
a neon shamrock, an emblem for
'no colored need apply'
when i need a pack of cigarettes at midnight
mark their hope i'm just passing through.

a fat little girl with a wild side
hides in my house abandoned
for 37 years to the darkness
where she licks her lips and sings
of her roots deep in north carolina
somewhere near hickory.
her people didn't leave on the
trail of tears but were marooned

in the great smokeys.
our grandmother spent time in tulsa
though and then some in detroit
then D.C.
and for the first time i hear her
sing to me
seductively:

you need love, baby.
i need love, baby.
see me. see me.

my self is a house i'm afraid to enter
having forsaken those red hills for conctete
refined those rustic ways to cool black.
here in jersey city old people are friendly
out of fear
and filipinos attend mass as steadfastly
as italians and irish.
home of lek walesa's father
my opthamologist's uncle
and my ex-lover's husband, a cuckold
and me, its most recent reluctant emigrant.
no southern hospitality here.

if only i had the archaeologist's tools
to excavate some connecting marrow
under this rehabilitated rubble of yuppies
where africans used to live.
and my creepy birds of paradise
loose their color in the smog
wasting in my window from manhattan
in this perfect apartment we rented
from a nice jewish couple—not yuppies
but young and professional—
after a year of desperate sundays
eating yogurt in a park of bear
and buffalo sculptures

suspended in some primordial epoch
till 1 o'clock and the next appointment.

a polite pole who renovated his house
himself introduces a beautiful woman
as his 'ole lady.'
i fantasize introducing my beautiful
lover as my 'ole lady' and saying we'll
share the same bedroom
and watching him falter before his
fear of aids as i ask for a glass of water.

you can't drink the water in jersey city,
our landlords warn. foreigners, too, from
brooklyn.

> *i need love, baby.*
> *you need love, baby.*
> *see me. see me.*

she sings seductively, playing with her pubic
hairs in a dark corner of the house i'm afraid
to enter
its woodwork painted over for decades like
gradations of ego.

DRIFTINGS
(An introduction by way of a preface)
Douglas Blau

"When floating on an open sea out of sight of sand, or in a desert plain without compass or a guiding hand, one comes to know the need for reins and for the mannered things of man."[1]

"I had often wondered what my thoughts might be if I were to be set adrift in a small craft with no particular course in mind and with nothing to see but the sky and sea. There, I supposed, I would find the ability to float freely, to let my mind drift as aimlessly as the boat in which I would sit, for, there, I would see no things to which I could attach myself. I felt certain that in such a state I would have the facility to envision what I had never before seen, to invent, as I did in my sleep, objects that I had not known. There, with no things to bind me, I innocently believed that I would find an entirely new world waiting to greet me... I had tried to find this mood, but, in doing so while aboard the ships on which I had traveled, I had never been able to rid myself of an awareness of the railings, which contained me, or of the ships' speed, which pushed like a knowing guide toward a specific direction...

"Having no true desire to actually discover that I had been abandoned in the middle of an ocean, and, believing that I would feel the same freedom of mind in the desert, I lost no time [*once he had arrived in a town on the desert's edge*] in securing for myself a native who could lead me to a desolate place, where I would be left undisturbed and would be able to lose myself in undistracted thought...

"Leaving my man with the animals, I set out in search of a dune that would offer me shade, and, upon finding one, I set to work on my experiment. At first, I was content simply to have achieved the uncomfortable but long-sought-after pose, and my thoughts wandered to those earlier moments in which I had imagined it to be a privileged state. I pictured myself as a desert monk and, although the thought of a life of religious solitude seemed to me uninteresting, I enjoyed wondering what temptations might be placed before me by the spirits that inhabited the god-forsaken land. And then, for an unknown stretch of time, my mind, resting on nothing, drifted undirected as if in a trance....

"The following morning, we left the village before sunrise and arrived at the feeble oasis by the later hours of dawn. I returned to my place and, once again, let my thoughts drift aimlessly.... But, on this second occasion, the novelty of having no things to ponder no longer kept me entertained. Within three hours, I found myself to be as restless and as bored as I had ever been. The monotony of the barren landscape was unbearable. I longed for some thing to interrupt the silence, for some thing to catch my eye, for any thing from which I might be able to derive thoughts or that might provide direction for my driftings; for, without objects before me, I could see nothing and felt as if I were blind....

"...upon seeing my servant's hat, which had previously meant nothing to me, I immediately understood the excitement felt by the shipwrecked when they spot the slightest speck on the horizon."[2]

It was on that second morning in the desert that Béton, in a typically histrionic fashion, claimed to have sworn an oath "to myself and to all else who might be listening," promising "never again to visit places that cannot provide me with objects capable of initiating or stimulating my digressions."[3] On first glance, such a comment, coming, as it does, from a man who occupied himself as a writer of books on travel, seems a natural result of a selective and discerning mind. Why should anyone, particularly a professional nomad like Béton, journey to unexciting sites? Yet, when we consider the implications of the remainder of his oath, a very unusual type of travel-writer appears: "...I will henceforth focus my attentions solely upon things that have been fashioned by the hands of man. Only polished, artificial forms are worthy of my meditations. They alone are able to provide both impetus and anchor for my drifts."[4]

With the exception of the opening chapters of *North African Adventures* which is written in a style unlike that of his other books, Béton was true to his word: Nowhere in any of his writings can we find descriptions of the landscapes, climate, unmanicured vegetation, social habits, religious beliefs, farming techniques, or the political systems of the foreign lands he visited. We are never told how he happened to arrive in a country nor do we ever learn how he managed to leave it. If a train is mentioned, it is treated as if it were a piece of sculpture rather than as a means of transportation. And, when he writes on a subject such as gondolas

—as he does in an essay entitled "Fountains"—he never once mentions Venice, gondoliers, nor does he make any attempt to inform the unknowledgeable reader that the objects serving as the basis for his tangents are boats.[5]

These eccentric traits never failed to annoy his colleagues, but nothing infuriated them more than Béton's habit of giving his books titles that seemingly had nothing to do with their actual contents. *Dinners with the King of Siam*, for example, was comprised of eleven essays, all bearing apparently suitable titles. Yet, upon delving into the book Béton's readers discovered that "Entertainment at Court" was a detailed description of the decoration of La Scala in Milan, that "The King's Wives" was an article on Ingres' *Grande Odalisque* and the Oriental paintings of Théodore Chassériau, and that the chapter entitled "Dessert Served at the King's Table" was an essay that pivoted around the glass decanters pictured in Tintoretto's San Giorgio Maggiore *Last Supper*.[6] Béton, in fact, did not mention any of the things that he had seen on his journey to Siam until nine years later, when, in his *Venetian Driftings*, he wrote a long prose poem on the subject of the palace gardens.[6]

Such tactics led one of the journalists who reviewed the Venetian volume to write: "Had I not dined with M. Béton in Venice last year, I would certainly have insisted that he had written this book without having ever visited the city."[8] And Sainte-Beuve, who had given sympathetic reviews to Béton's earlier books, later added this nastier note: "Perhaps M. Robert Béton believes that by misleading his readers he is being amusing, but I, for one, am no longer amused by his childish pranks."[9] Others, of course, were. Barbey, Nerval, whom Béton had met in Cairo, Gautier, and Lamartine had all praised Béton's wit. Even Baudelaire, who had patience for neither Béton nor his ideas, could not help but appreciate the other's craft. "Robert Béton is a ridiculous little man," the poet is reported to have said, "but we must nevertheless read what he writes."[10] Yet, while Béton was able to list some of the more memorable writers of his day amongst the ranks of his appreciators, few of them thought him to be more than a talented sightseer. It was not until another generation had come of age that Béton found an audience interested in putting the theoretical underpinnings of his writings into practice.

As fate would have it, a young Whistler arrived in Paris the same month that Béton's *Travels in England* appeared in the city's bookstores.[11] Whistler originally bought a copy of the book as a gift for a friend but, as "the color of the binding was blinding and, better still, there was not a word about England in it," he decided to keep it for himself.[12] It was not just the turquoise leather that attracted Whister to Béton's book, as the Pennells tell it, the painter was "fascinated by the writer's renderings of the fog as it strolled along the waterways of Venice, obscuring the details of the houses that he was observing.[13] The essay to which the Pennells refer, "English Country Estates," contained other passages that were sure to have caught the young Whistler's eye, for, here, Béton wrote not only of fog-draped palaces but of the qualities of translucent glass, of the veils worn by the dancing girla of the Levant and, most important, of a misty, storm-approaching painting by Francesco Guardi,[14] which was described in terms that could easily be applied to the *Nocturnes* Whistler was later to paint.[15]

A number of years later, Whistler passed this same volume on to one of his followers with the words, "If you really must insist upon playing art-critic, Oscar, I think you had better read this."[16] "The Critic as Artist" was published soon afterwards and, with the exception of a few interesting twists, Wilde's conception of what art-writing should be rested almost entirely on the foundations laid by Beton.[17]

That his own essays had served to inspire others to make things would have satisfied Beton greatly, for, to his mind, objects—printed prose being considered as such—were to be valued only if they were able to provide a base for another to build on. An object, we must remember, was to Beton merely a stepping-stone, a catalyst that would throw him off into his own envisionings. Unable to see any distinction between a restaurant and an art gallery, he treated all things that were served to him simply as a means of satisfying his needs. It is a view that Wilde's character, the arch-aesthete Gilbert, was to voice: "Criticism of the highest kind treats the work of art simply as a starting point for a new creation."[18] And later, using both hands to make the same point, Wilde adds:

> *Ernest.* The highest Criticism, then, is more creative than creation, and the primary aim of the critic is to see the object as in itself it really is not; that is your theory, I believe?
>
> *Gilbert.* Yes, that is my theory. To the critic the work of art is simply a suggestion for a new work of his own, that need not bear any obvious resemblance to the thing it criticizes.[19]

That it is not necessary for a writer to dwell upon the object that is, in actuality, the occasion for his own essay, is pure Béton. As has already been implied in the case of his desire to write around a subject rather than to write directly of it, Béton was concerned only with what an object made him think of, what it asked him to conjure and with what *things* it enabled him to see. Just as that aforementioned Neo-Palladian villa in the English countryside had acted as a transport for his drifts to Venice, where he imaged glassworks, Guardi, and the Grand Canal, which led him, in turn, to thoughts of the Orient, where he pictured the costumes of slightly-clad entertainers,[20] so the perfumes put into his bath in Siam served as a departure point for his thoughts of India, of a meal placed before him at a hotel in Córdoba, which, then, led him to write of the utensils that were depicted in an unidentified seventeenth-century Flemish still-life.[21]

After his so-called "revelation in the desert," that youthful incident that he often referred to as his "confrontation with the immaterial forces of Silence,"[22] Béton had come to believe that driftings were worthy of merit only when they were derived from or firmly chained to a specific, though unseen, object by means of a series of craftily styled links. Despite the popular sentiment that his essays were nothing but aimless wanderings and careless digressions, Béton's tangents were always appropriate, always conscientiously constructed so that one thing would become another and would, then, slip seamlessly into the next. He would touch down in order to fly off; rest for a moment on one thought, while an impression left by another image was still holding sway. As he put it: "When someone arrives in Vienna, they do not leave their remembrances of Barcelona behind."[23] He would, in essence, build atop his own images in the same fashion he would upon those created by others. That Indian spices spilled from a Siamese tub into a meal cooked for him in Spain was not the result of a flood of random associations. Nor was it, by any means, an immaculate conception. As his itineraries show, Béton accounted for his every move; each of his transitions was plotted with an almost neurotic precision.[24] His tangents progressed in a manner so logical and timely as to make any stationmaster envious. And yet, only by way of his titles and his sly references do we come to know of his embarcation point. In no instance do we learn of his destination.

NOTES

1. Robert Béton, *Things to be Seen* (Paris, 1849), p iv.
2. Béton, *North African Adventures* (Paris, 1844), pp 28–44.
3. *Ibid*, p 48.
4. *Ibid*.
5. "Fountains" was originally published in the *Revue de Deux Mondes*, 1853. It later appeared in Béton's *Travels in England* (Paris, 1855), pp 119-152.
6. Béton, *Dinners with the King of Siam* (Paris, 1861). Of the three essays mentioned, "The King's Wives" was the only article to have appeared prior to the publication of the book—in the *Revue de Deux Mondes*, 1860. In the introduction to his translation of *Dinners with the King of Siam* (London,

1905), p 31, David Heilbroner suggests that the initial publication of this essay was meant to coincide with the exhibition of Ingres's *The Turkish Bath*, which was shown in Paris that year.
7. "Courtyards," *Venetian Driftings* (Paris, 1870), pp 189-223.
8. This line, accredited to Felix Resnicoff, is cited by William H. Matheson, *Selected Writings on Travel by Robert Beton* (London, 1931), p 14.
9. Heilbroner, *op cit*, pp 28-29.
10. Enid Starkie, *Baudelaire* (New York, 1958), p 340.
11. The month was November, the year 1855.
12. Joseph and Elizabeth Pennell, *Life of James McNeill Whistler* (London, 1908), pp 204-214.
13. *Ibid*, p 219. Note that the Pennells mistakenly place emphasis on the fog rather than on the architecture. Also note that their use of the word "observing" is inappropriate.
14. "English Country Estates," *Travels in England*, pp 180-201. While it is unclear as to which one of Guardi's paintings Béton refers to, W.H. Matheson, who translated this essay for his anthology, believes it to be *Laguna Grigia*, now in Milan's Museo Poldi-Pezzoli (*op cit*, p 39).
15. See Lawrence D. Steefel, Jr., "Whistler's Béton," *Art Journal* 21, no. 3, pp 151-155.
16. Pennell, *op cit*, p 288.
17. See Emma Kafalenos, "The Affects of Robert Béton as Oscar Wilde's 'The Critic as Artist,'" *Journal of Literary Comparisons* 3, no. 3, pp 56-71. While Kafalenos does not deny the influence of Ruskin and Pater, she does claim that their work had less of an effect on Wilde than is usually thought. Using O.W's letters as her primary source, Kafalenos shows that Béton and his writing served Wilde as the model for the character Gilbert.
18. Oscar Wilde, "The Critic as Artist," *Intentions* (London, 1891), p 139.
19. *Ibid*, p 141
20. "English Country Estates," *op cit*.
21. Béton, "Siamese Scents," *Adventures in Non-Nature* (Paris, 1875), pp 99-126.
22. Béton uses these expressions often. "Revelation" appeared in his writings initially in the preface to his second book, *Things to be Seen, op cit*, p iii. "Confrontation..." can be found throughout *North African Adventures*.
23. Henri J. Koslowski, ed., *The Letters of Robert Béton* (Paris, 1893), vol. 1, p 176.
24. Matheson, *op cit*, pp 43-45, 203-208. Reproductions of pages from Béton's diaries, which give some example of his fascination for lists of all kinds, can be found here.

©*1981, Douglas Blau (reprinted with permission)*

Incunabula #3
Susan Daitch

People used to read everything as if it were a story. Readers looked for moral tales. They wanted to be taught a lesson and then to move on to the next potential mistake. They matched accidents and natural disasters to hearsay, fables, and myths. It was a way of imposing logic on mishaps. It initiated a system of cross-referential meaning where none would seem to have existed previously. It was a way not to seem like a city of helpless victims hit by random catastrophe. Here was authority. Here was a motive for revenge. People used to read for pleasure. People wanted to recognize the end of a story in its beginning. People wanted to be surprised at its end, anyway.

She grew increasingly afraid to leave her apartment and gave others complicated grocery lists. When they were uncooperative, she would live on coffee with powdered milk and spaghetti sauce eaten directly from the jar with a spoon. Her personal geography grew truncated in proportion to potential fatalities that she associated with runaway subway cars and the crimes she linked to the density of foreigners in the streets. She defined a foreigner as anyone she failed to recognize. The hazards crept towards the door. She would listen to the radio for hours as a substitute for actually doing anything. She approached the act of listening the way another person might consider driving a car or writing a letter. Radio time began to replace clock time. Before noon the news came on five minutes before the hour. That divided the morning into equal parts but added five minutes to the first hour of the afternoon. Friends hoped she might have some reconciliation with at least the front steps of her building before the end of the summer.

I see them working in the subways. Blue, green, gold, orange tiles: the front of a locomotive, little houses unlike any seen in metropolitan New York, beavers and squirrels in profile. Each piece has been previously cut to the right shape. There is a signal and they jump onto the platform. They mainly work at night. In the morning a gold stripe, a red bracket, sort of baroque, or a tree has been added. Everything is finally covered by something, there is no space left undecorated. When their work is completed, the tilers move on to another station. The irregularity of their presence during daylight and the danger of their work make them seem like peripatetic tap dancers who put together a different act each night. Even after the signal they behave as if they have all the time in the world. One of them noticed I was missing trains in order to watch them so I got on the next one. Later in the night, after they've gone home, painters come and cover parts of the tiles with tags and pictures. There are ghost stations, entirely painted over, which the train passes between working stops. Sometimes the cars halt in front of one; dimly lit and long out of service. It might move slowly past a series of stations full of pictures: an early form of cinema. In the future all stations will be painted over and all the trains will be slow express trains: the history of cinema advances. A movie with images of trailing comets, rockets, larger-than-life silver letters takes shape. Historically earlier parts will feature words made of bubble letters, in later ones the letters turn angular. This has been called Gothic Futurism. In the depths of each station colored names will give way to jungle landscapes, images of mechanized monsters, caricatures of comic figures. Sequences mimic existing perspective to such an extent that people will be sure they must have missed a corner as the train passes. They will want to repeat the trip, in effect, see the movie again. Even though there is so much to see, tiers of scenery, the train must keep up a certain speed or the effect of animation will be lost.

It had once been exciting to be identified, named, and photographed. This happened to her mother in 1939 when she was eleven and the family was broke. Her mother got a job as Mrs. Modern at the World's Fair in Queens. She worked opposite Mrs. Drudge in the Westinghouse Pavillion. Every morning she put on her costume and went to work. Her picture was in papers and newsreels whenever the Westinghouse Pavillion was discussed. Sometimes she was by herself, sometimes she was photographed with Mrs. Drudge who had no machines and did everything by hand. The whirlagig of sensationalism occasionally included the actual sons and daughters of Mrs. Modern and Mrs. Drudge as they went through their daily lives as real children. A *Life* photographer appeared at her school looking for her. She ducked into the bathroom, spent a few hours there, then ran away. She didn't want to be recognized as a child of Mrs. Modern.

Because she had so little information, written language was all she would trust. Words spread out like puddles of inference, thin at the edges, creeping towards misuse, misspelling, mispronunciation. The boundaries of words grew vague. One impersonated the next. She set up a schemata based on analagous relationships.
All hotels have a few rules in common.
Everyone needs the right clothes.
You must have money in order to live.
Repulsive behavior can take many forms.
She read newspaper lines straight across: "the women wear full length mink major source of permanent housing for the homeless can't ski anywhere in the world without a gold Rolex. Official said the city hoped would not set foot without major gemstones, $49 a day for a family of four"

"It ruined a three-week trip. forced to leave buildings that have been abandoned.
Still other had to leave over-
crowded apartments of"

"'comes a guy with the latest Italian skiwear. I was proud. I told him,
ments more quickly. Homeless families are now housed in hotels"

"You don't stay in a hotel, you stay in a
what-do-you-call-it? A house."

Iterative clauses hinted at branches of connotation and so she made diagrams. Antiphrasis struck deaf ears. She had no sense of irony. She read literally and lines of print gave her a hard time. She became easily distracted, turned to another page, confronted a similar set of lines, felt hungry, struck a match, lit a burner and boiled water. It was all as discontinuous as the definition of hotel.

You had to know someone or be with someone who knew someone in order to get in. A narrow storefront, almost not that, almost a corridor connecting other corridors that you really couldn't get into. Sometimes there were a couple of tables and chairs inside. Sometimes a man (it was always a man) or two would be sitting in one of them. If you just walked in off the street the fat guy behind the counter would tell you in Spanish that they weren't open for business.

A man I knew was like Mr. Memory in *The 39 Steps*. He would take risks if you could manage to convince him no one would guess what he was really doing. No one would believe his intentions were anything but benign, his interests anything but self-interests. He didn't appear the sort of person easily waylaid by aimless curiosity. I persuaded him to go in with me because I couldn't go in by myself. I would be nervous, my teeth would chatter, I would look at the floor. Like Mr. Memory, he would know the answers to their questions and if they, like the German spies in the movie, asked for the formula for a particular airplane engine, he would have recited arbitrary numbers and I'm sure they would have been the correct ones. Neither one of us did get in. I never found out what went on in there.

Like Madeleine Carroll, I didn't want to be attached to the stranger who kissed her/me on the train. As danger became more apparent, she became more cooperative, but in my case, the danger was of my own invention. If we were Madeleine Carroll and Robert Donat handcuffed together, rolling down an embankment, playing elopers at a hotel, then he couldn't be Mr. Memory at the same time. Hero and traitor mixed in the same actor. Possibly the story was skewed. I felt stuck to the wrong character.

He didn't recognize her. He was sitting at a table with other people, looked up at her and then spoke to his friends as if she were no one in particular. She walked close to the group as if she were going to the telephone booth to their right. He didn't look up. She pretended to make a call, put a quarter in the slot and dialed her own number, left a message for herself on her machine. The message made little sense and continued long past the beep. The cord was very long for a phone booth. She turned, winding it around herself so she was facing him but he still didn't recognize or even notice her. He was wearing a tie with silver horseshoes and horses' heads painted on it. From where she stood the horse heads looked like shiny flies. An unknown woman wrapped in a telephone cord, like Jane Avril wrapped in a snake. She thought she should have made up a conversation instead of leaving a long message on what was actually her own machine but it was too late to change her story. As if anyone who might hear her would stop their own conversation and ask her just what kind of a nut she thought she was. He tapped the table to make a point then, looked out the window as if disgusted or defeated. She couldn't go on just standing there.

The personal things put on each desk grew to monstrous representations of buffoonery. The ashtray with *My Favorite Martian*'s picture embedded in it says goofiness is the large category under which you operate. Even actions committed for sincere reasons, under serious pretense will prove just as embarrassing. The ashtray denies all of this. Your motives can never rise any higher. Other employees have feminized objects on their desks: artificial flowers, birthday cards, picture frames, souvenir lighters. You can't say if these objects are feminized or emasculated because, conceptually, they are relatively neuter. They could have gone either way. A lighter or the idea of a lighter wasn't originally burdened by connotations of gender, at least not in English. A man in the office suggests these objects are emasculated by virtue of contamination. He has a paperweight of the Empire State Building embedded in plastic on his desk. When you shake the thing, of course, it snows. The paperweight might be a cliché but he insists it's not femmey. No one suggests to him that the World Trade Center is bigger. I go to another floor to get a cup of coffee out of a fairly neutral-looking machine. I find myself being drawn to the image of cuteness in inert things, but if you relinquish everything to cuteness, you might become happy enough at your job so that you would think twice before leaving it.

She wrote *rue*. No further description was needed. *Rue* was not the same as *rua*, *via*, or street. She wrote Clinton in front of street, *rue* needed no modifier. It already spoke of balconies, thin curtains, a set of shutters which opened out and a pair of windows which opened in.

Eventually only printed language which had been reproduced had any credibility. She felt like a caretaker of inauthentic documents and she was in search of a nucleus of the original sentence. They were fly-by-night resurrections, none of them to be entirely trusted. Tokens: the resurrections were only traces of some past myth of precision. She had no faith in pictures or photographs. All evidence had to be verbal. She kept stacks of newspapers in mostly chronological order. It was a slow system. She couldn't always find what she was looking for. Her hands and cuffs were often dirty, her forehead smeared with inky tracks.

One subject which never, to her knowledge, appeared in print was her own life. Even its most mundane aspects were never verified by reproduction in newspapers. The stacks under tables and chairs, under her bed, suggested an important simulacrum and one which excluded her.

He told me a story about finding a human hand in a garbage can. I didn't believe him. I know people who find decent furniture and remarkable clothing on the street, but a human hand, never. He was putting off going back to his apartment and would just say anything. He did this every night after work. I asked him what kind of hand it was, what did it look like? Black or white, big or little? Was it holding anything? Was it wearing any jewelry? I didn't exactly make a study of it, he said. How do you know if it was real at all? Maybe it was rubber. No, it was real, this was no rubber hand, he was certain. Did you go to the police? No, there was no point, it was just a hand, not a body. Could it have been a prop? You said it wasn't rubber but it might have been something else, some special kind of plastic, for example. Were you walking near a theatre or a prop shop? He was getting annoyed but he didn't want to go home. There are cities where things like this happen and it is considered normal. You don't have to live in Santiago or Buenos Aires to find body parts on the street. But this, I reminded him, is not one of those cities.

Had the hand taken over his life? Had its appearance ruined him for further use? Well, yes, for a few days he had been upset and thought of little else. He couldn't put a plastic bag full of coffee grounds and balled-up pieces of paper, a bag which said, "Have a Nice Day!" on top of a human hand.

He didn't want to go inside his building yet. It was warm and after we separated I knew he'd walk around for hours. If we hadn't worked together that night he would have attached himself to someone else or roamed the street talking to himself.

People have always found before-and-after stories very compelling. The lives of formerly bald, now hairy; or formerly fat, now thin people are automatically read as stories because they prove that anyone can start a new life, regardless of their past. People used to read as a substitute for religion. People used to read if they were patricians. People used to read everything as if it were a metaphor, or if not that, as if all the lines contained nothing but tropes. People used to put off the end of a story for as long as possible, putting obstacles between it and the moment at hand, even if they knew how the story would end, and had known its end since they could remember.

Foreign in Life
Jane Warrick

I was left with Dad when I was seven. He'd lived in a fishing village when he was growing up and I was sorry he'd moved. I wanted a boat. More than anything. I wanted to be able to get up in the morning, run down to where the slipway disappeared into the water, take my boat, and go off, quickly, out to sea.

On Sundays he'd take me out in the car for a drive. Sometimes we'd visit his relatives down the coast. It took a long time to get there and I'd look out of the window while Dad drove. We didn't talk much. He'd whistle under his breath and I'd look out at the cliffs and the beaches and the enormous stretch of water we ran alongside. It was breathtakingly beautiful I understand now, now I've left, but then I didn't have words for it. I was just drawn to that incredible depth of blue.

We'd follow the road went up a hill and then over the other side, dipping down into the village; a few houses clustered around the quay. I was never really sure who Dad's relatives were or if they were fishermen or farmers but they were kind to me and let me go down to the quay by myself.

I stood there and watched the water where it touched the slipway. The way it rippled slightly where the swell lifted it. How it distorted the cement under the surface and then swallowed it up completely. Green tendrils of seaweed lay flattened against the wall below the hightide mark. I took off my shoes and stood with the water up over my ankles. I felt completely happy and content there. Alone. The water matched me in some mysterious way. I merged with it, was part of a pattern; the complicated and rocky relationship of land to sea.

Once, when we were driving home again, Dad told me a story. He pointed to a field at the top of a cliff, and told me that when he was a young man, they grew wheat there. "One day in the summer we were stacking bales of straw," he said. "We started early in the morning and finished as the sun was going down. It was so hot." Then he pointed, "See that rock out there," and about half a mile out I could see a rock sticking out of the water. He laughed a bit. "We shouldn't have worked that long with the sun beating down on our heads. And all day, out of the corner of my eye, I saw the sea glittering." He laughed again in a funny way. "I was light-headed. I got it into my mind that I could walk all the way out to that rock," he said. "I dropped the last bale and ran down the field, over the barbed wire, and climbed down the cliff. I took my clothes off on the way down. When I got to the water I only had my underpants on." He went on in a slightly amazed way. "I went in and when I got far enough out that the water closed over my head I kept on walking."

Then he said that the others had realized there was something wrong with him so they'd all scrambled down after him. When they tried to drag him out he punched them. It took four of them to get him out, and when they pulled him onto the sand, he cried.

It's the only story I remember him telling me and it burnt like something hot. He was doing the same thing I did, trying to insert himself between the sea and the shore. And the thing was, I could tell he wasn't convinced that he couldn't have done it. And neither was I.

I left home at sixteen and traveled around. I never really felt at home in my life the way other people did. I felt like a foreigner who'd forgotten what country she came from. Simple things that everyone else seemed to know were beyond me. It suited me to be in a place where I didn't know the language; it made sense.

I wasn't drawn to water so much. I stayed in cities and dreamed constantly of tidal waves, but they didn't frighten me; I knew I'd be safe.

I'd call Dad on the phone and after he said hello he'd go quiet. The cables ran beneath the sea and although it was foolish, I could somehow hear it in the quality of the silence coming through the receiver.

I'd never missed anyone. I was always independent, even as a child, but as I got older I wanted to be more like other people. Ordinary, with less passion, less joy if need be. I still traveled, but the idea of finding a particular place began to take hold of me. Somewhere to stay for a while. Somewhere I could live as a person.

During this time I had a dream: It was dark and I was standing on a beach. Small waves broke over my feet. They felt cold and clean. As the water ran back it took the top layer of sand with it.

After a while I bean to feel uneasy. Something was wrong. I wanted to leave but I didn't know where to go. A tremendous longing shook me.

Then my body took over. I started to run along the water's edge and as I did so I lifted off the ground. A breeze began to blow. As my feet rose above the waves I heard with unusual clarity the sound of the water. It was all I heard.

I felt now that I could take great steps or cross oceans if I wanted to. I was also conscious of a small fear of leaving the land. I wanted so badly to go but seeing the shore below filled me with sadness. I felt anguish and a feeling of loneliness folded around me like a garment.

As I glided this way and that, indecisively, above the water, I heard a humming. A small boat came into view. In it I could see a creature, human-shaped, but covered in fish scales.

I began to follow it from a safe and silent distance. It hummed as it rowed purposefully. I followed it for hours. Sometimes it would stop for a minute or two and rest its flipper arms on the oars. I wondered what it was waiting for.

A faint light began to appear and I turned my head to find its source. When I turned back there was a beach below me. The creature was pulling the boat up onto the shingle. It was still too dark to see so I moved closer. I saw the creature flip the oars into the boat, and turning, it caught my eye. Deliberately.

I was so surprised I almost fell out of the sky. Somehow I managed to land but when I looked around the creature had disappeared. I walked with heavy feet up the beach. The boat had gone but where it had been there was a dark shape. I walked over to it. It was an oar. I picked it up. Suddenly, I felt so tired, as if I'd crossed continents.

In front of me the beach rose up into dunes. I walked up and at the top found a hollow. I curled up there like a bird in a nest. I wanted to be able to sleep and see all around me when I woke. I lay the oar close beside me and clasped my hand around it. Then I slept.

During this sleep I became confused. I wasn't sure if someone else's hand was holding my wrist, gently but firmly, or if it was the sensation of my hand around the oar. I slept deeply and woke in the sun. All around me was a new and unfamiliar land.

I carried that dream like something precious. Something you'd take out of your pocket and turn over in your palm.

Leaving Quito
Gary Indiana

"It was difficult to imagine that we were about to see the traces of a glacier thousands of years old. There was a hole in the rock at about the level of the cock of an average-sized man. That we were going to walk in its path and follow its footsteps down into the valley. My fingers trembling, I unzipped my cutoffs, eager to get the confining cloth out of the way. Our feelings before starting our trip to the mountain lakes were dwarfed alongside the magic of a panorama where reality surpasses imagination. As I pushed them down, my hard prick snapped up against my belly and then stood straight out in front of me. Our departure point was Lake Toreadora, 37 kilometers from the city, 3,500 meters above sea level. Fred had unzipped his pants and taken out his cock to arouse Dick more."

Singapur, 28.—"Miss Noruega," Marian Leines; "Miss Hong Kong," Fui Chung y "Miss Suecia," Susanne Thoerngren, constan entre las primeras concursantes que han llegado aqui para el concurso de "Miss Universo," que se realizara el 27 de mayo.

Clouds avalanching down the skin of the volcano. Hard green hills, fissures of gray between the peaks and the bleach white sculptures spread across the sky.

The Inca is *muerte*. The Inca has been carbonized above fat pylons of cedar and palm. The priest of Our Lord, Jesus Christ, baptized the Inca an hour before the auto-da-fe so he did not die heathen by agonizing torture over several days but simply roasted for an hour or two.

At the airport, the far-off crackle of a breathy voice, *vuelo*, she sighs, *quanto, Avianca por Lima, Santiago, Valpariaso*, outside the blue air sits gently on the brazen palms.

-That was for us, says the woman idly.
-Yes.
-Senor Carlos. He can help you very much.
Pizarro digs a brown line with the point of his sword: those who wish may advance for the glory of Spain and the Spanish Crown and those base cowards who merely because of affliction with scurvy wish to return to Panama will perhaps live to regret their stupid loss of incalculable riches.
The parrots mock them. The turtles strapped to the sides of their pathetic boats for food mock them even in death, as their heads are severed.
Gloria, Gloria, in excelsis deo: the simple Indian with an orange kerosine tank strapped to her back embraces the feet of the gigantic Christ.
-He's not around?
-I forget what he looks like, really.
The official from the airline approaches, bland and buttery, like a fading cabbage.
-Is that for us?
Yes. You pay the airport tax, and then you will go and get in touch with the young lady from Equitoriana. She knows about you already.
-We just paid for the lunch.
-No. You did not have to.
Blessed art thou among women and blessed is the fruit of thy womb, Jesus.
-Well, they charged us.
Holy Mary, Mother of God, pray for us sinners, now, and at the hour of our death.
-I did it already. I paid.
-Well, they did.
-They charged you? For the lunch? Come over with me.
Our Father, who art in Heaven, hallowed be thy Name.
The flames rise from the stake. Whips of yellow are visible in the emerald hills.
-No, don't worry about it. The plane will be late. But they were not supposed to charge you for the lunch.
Walkie-talkie static, in bursts.
The beloved bastard of the Inca who reigns supreme in Quito, sends an entreaty to Huascar, Supreme Emperor of Cuzco. Atahuallpa wishes to gather, from each of the nations recently conquered by the Inca, mourners for his deceased father. Actually, he plans to marshal troops against Huascar. Huascar, gullible and a fool who thinks he's secure in his Incahood, sends permission via the thousand-

mile highway his ancestors have carved through the length and breadth of the incredible Inca Empire.

-Go get your money.

-It was 1500 sucres. So, if you want to go—

-I don't, really. It's your money.

-Let's go.

-No, no, it's really okay. We don't mind.

-But I paid for the lunch already.

Pizarro listens to his foul and unworthy interpreter, the low-born Felipillo, whose liaison with a royal concubine should have caused not only his own death but that of his entire family, his entire tribe. He, Pizarro, examines a tiny, jeweled casket.

-Instead of that, why don't you just get us through without standing in line. And that would be, you know, acceptable.

-Everyone here is waiting. Just a couple of minutes.

-I don't really care about the lunch.

-It's not fair, you know. I already signed for it. Let's go upstairs, it takes two minutes, that's all.

A presentiment of his own assassination tickles Pizarro's forebrain. He knows he will die by the knife, murdered by his own beloved lieutenants. Though he does not love them all that much, even now, for they are a smelly pack of greedy swine. But first he will conquer the Inca, demanding ransom for Atahuallpa in the form of a room stacked to the ceiling with gold.

-I paid. But they charged 1500 sucres.

-For extras, maybe.

-Extras, yes.

-I don't mind.

-Extras.

I want to sleep, Pizarro thinks: I want to lie down here in the filthy black mud of this island and sleep for one thousand years, without dreaming. The stink of blood I have shed nauseates me. My murders will smell throughout history, like ammonia. I have destroyed an ancient and noble race for no higher motive than the others. I sicken myself: why should I live? Why do they call me a conqueror, when I cannot conquer myself, my own sickening lusts? And then at the end I shall be killed as easily as I now kill that ridiculous bird up there in the lofty tree.

-The plane just arrived. You have to be patient. We have to fix the plane, we have to do many things. You still have time.

-Okay.

TOURIST ATTRACTIONS

-It doesn't take that long. Twenty minutes, we will be there.
-There's a departure tax?
-Yes. It was only $5 two months ago. But now, twenty.
-What's the equivalent in sucres?
-Each dollar has 170 sucres. You forgot something?
A bird with a pink and yellow bill, high above, cocking its dumb shrunken head and watching my death.
-It's usually three bucks.
-Twenty is a lot.
-Okay, maybe I have it in sucres.
-You probably do.
-Dollars?
-Check your tickets, though. Because it says departure card on them. Or it should.

As I lie dying I would of course remember, not the triumphs of all my many glories, but the evening Ruiz and I drank a gallon of palm wine, vomiting throughout the jungle, and after some hours Ruiz leers and asks me: I'm curious, did you ever fuck a dog?

-I can't wait for the age of teleportation... and I'll never go on Equitoriana if they ever get teleport machines.
-They'd probably get a fly in there with you.
-Your legs will be here some time this week.
-That will be a mess, probably. Losing parts of people, sending them to the wrong place.
-Wrong place, and putting them on the wrong bodies.
-And if you lose your ticket, you're really in trouble.
-Then you'll be nowhere. Your genes will be floating around in space.
-So what else is there, besides Quito, Guyaquil, and Cuenca?
-Isn't that enough?
-There's Esmeraldas, where blacks live, which I guess is in the north. There's also little places, of course. In the disputed territories.
-And that Virgin on the hill. Quito. What a trip.
-Virginity is a big item around here, also.
-Very prized.
-Well, of course, they used to sacrifice them.
-That's why they built the statue so big. That's the last Virgin, she's too big for the volcano.
-The Aluminum Virgin. It was really quite interesting, getting inside her.

They have stained glass windows, and then all these figures of different Indian types holding spears, and stuffed iguanas.
-They said the Incas had destroyed Quito. They razed it to the ground. And then it was rebuilt in the 1500s.
-I don't believe the original inhabitants of any place would be the destroyers of it.
-Yes, but the Incas actually conquered the people who were here before. And the people who were here were fighting the Incas. I mean, that's what it says in that guidebook, but there are many things wrong in that guidebook.
-So did you have to leave the VIP area to go to the bathroom?
-I spoke already to the stewardess. She is going to give you good attention, some wine and stuff, and special attention, okay?
-We board the aircraft?
-TAME?
-Not TAME. Tam-ay.
-That's the one that crashed.
-The cannibals got the passengers. The survivors. TAME. Tam-ay. Where did it crash, that the cannibals got them?
-In the woods, in Colombia.
-And here.
-Look. Nuns.
-Wasn't it a shampoo? TAME? No, it was a creme rinse, now that I think of it. It's a shame to shampoo without TAME.
-I never went to a duty-free shop before.
Thy kingdom come, thy will be done, on earth as it is in heaven. I can never repent so many homicides.
-Did you buy anything?
-Yes, I got some, what do you call those things?
-Scarves. And Jose Llopez cigars, apparently. I got three scarves, and that bag there. I thought I'd gotten something else, too. Well, I guess it's just the three scarves.
Okay. Because this plane is coming from Mexico, your seat will be unassigned until Guyaquil. Then in Guyaquil, you take your own seat, okay? Could we go in first class? They have certain passengers in Panama, getting on. Do we change planes? No, but until Guyaquil you take any seat. Well. If there were going to be one more complication, I'm sure they would come up with it. Did I tell you? I got this jacket here. I kept going to all these shops, always closed. I got this sweater, and this. I was flying high. It was hard for me to believe that a small town like

mine could offer so much hot male sex. The villages became more numerous, and, as the vessels rode at anchor off the port of Tacamez, the Spaniards saw before them a town of two thousand houses or more, laid out into streets, and it suddenly seemed to me that every man in town was gay. This was not true, of course. She looked out and saw this guy naked, bound to a post, with a belt being cracked across his bare butt. She called the cops. I got this sweater, and this. When the royal procession had arrived within half a mile of the city, it came to a halt; and Pizarro saw with surprise that Atahuallpa was preparing to pitch his tents. My heart pounded. Bill was nothing to sneeze at. Better than six feet tall, as blond as Hank, but a year or two younger. His body was great, too. I saw his tight ass outlined in the overalls and wondered if Hank had ever screwed him. Now, this is definitely special treatment right here. We have our own Equitoriana umbrella, so in other words, there's going to be a mob scene on this airplane. We just keep walking endlessly along these tarmacs from one plane to another, one taxi to another, one restaurant to another. Doing absolutely nothing. I wonder if we can keep the umbrella. It would be quite impressive to those who have never flown Equitoriana. Where do you live? In New York. No, I know, but where, in Chinatown? Park Avenue South, by Union Square. Where do you live? Twelfth Street. Right nearby, actually. Oh. I think we can unfurl, or rather furl it. Got it? Do you want to sit by the window? Yes, if you don't. Oh. The L.A. Times. "Fatal Chase." Sounds pretty good. Ladies and gentlemen, welcome to Guyaquil. Information, 15 hours, 39 degrees centigrade. Somebody spilled 4711. What? You know that cologne? 4711? Oh. I don't get it. From Mexico to Quito, then to Guyaquil, and then to Panama? God, I hope a lot of people don't get on this plane. Bill unzipped the front of his coveralls, revealing a broad chest with huge pectoral blocks, crowned by beautifully formed rosy nipples and a scattering of golden fuzz. The scene for this second auto-da-fe at Valladolid was the great square before the church of St. Francis. At one end a platform was raised, covered with rich carpeting, on which were ranged the seats of the inquisitors, emblazoned with arms of the holy office. I licked my lips greedily, thinking of how good the hot cock meat was going to taste. It was going to be great sucking it into my gullet, talking time to taste the flavor of every inch of it. I think we're in the right seats as it is. I think we're in the same seats as on our boarding passes. You'll have to move. No, because we're in the right seats anyhow. Where's your seat. *Cavo entos muertos*, which means I shit on your dead relatives. That's pretty good. I wish that child would shut up. It seems a lot of people are getting off. Why don't we watch there, maybe they're taking off our luggage. Put that back on the plane, would you? I'd be willing to just forget it, at this point. That looks like mine. No. Ours have little pink tags on them. Mine doesn't have little rollers on the bottom. No, but there are pink tags on ours. Looks like something leaked on that one. Looks like something leaked on all of them. No, they all look wet. Missionaries. Just what this country needs. They're bringing the word. Trash. Too late now. Looks like a mummy. That's like the bodies we saw on the road. We going to Panama, now? Panama to New York. From Mexico, figure that one out. Straight from Panama to New York. Unless they go to Peru. So, I wonder what time. That does look like my bag over there. Where? The one on top. You have a strap on top of yours. Yeah. No, but it's not the same type of strap. Maybe I can see when they turn it around. No, it's not mine. And if you see your bag going off, what can you do? You run out. At this point, let it go. Well, that must have been the last of the luggage. Now they're taking the packages off. What's that ring? Garnet. I went to price rubies at Stearn? For a quarter of a carat they wanted two-and-a-half-thousand dollars. Is that okra? Sure they're not peppers? They probably are. No, they're okras. No. Okay, pepper. Those are the box lunches. Excuse me? Is Sylvia back from lunch? I really don't know. We were supposed to be in first class, but there was a problem with the tickets. So we have priority. Sylvia knows about it. It is okra, look. I didn't know we imported okra from Panama. You have your tickets? Our tickets mean nothing, because they're made out for the 25th. We were supposed to receive priority treatment. My prick jerked around, standing up hard and firm as a candle. The sensations ran right up my legs and into my nuts. In the hurry of the flight of one party, and the pursuit by the other, all pouring towards Cuzco, the field of battle had been deserted. But it soon swarmed with plunderers, as the Indians, descending like vultures from the mountains, took possession of the bloody ground, and, despoiling the dead, even to the minutest article of dress, left their corpses naked on the plain. Time and information are abstract concepts, mere memories of days past. But you know what's funny, when we got to Quito, we started going back to New York time. In Cuenca we were living on Cuenca time. You kind of have to, in Cuenca. Actually, to tell you the truth, once you get ready to leave you don't feel like going. I don't know if it's the traveling, or what.

Painted Desert
Suzanne Jackson

Ray opened the car door and considered his options. He was behind the steering wheel looking straight ahead, eyes focused on the space in front of the windshield. He asked himself, will it be in or out? But clear thinking was impossible; nerves moved in his cheeks, his thoughts closed on a self-frightening emotion and panic forced him out. The next moment he was standing on the asphalt. Kicking gravel with his motorcycle boots. Meanwhile, Pamela crawled from the other door on her hands and knees and softly padded at the edge of the desert. She imagined herself an animal, then lay down on her stomach, turning her head to rest on one side, invisible to the hawks circling a thousand feet above the desert floor. Ray climbed on the roof of the Camaro and felt the heat off its red-glazed surface rise around his ankles and between his legs. He opened his arms and tipped his head up to the light. If Pamela moved, he would eat her.

Later that night, after traveling for hours at deadly, illegal speeds, Ray pulled into a Best Western. He killed the motor, which made his muscles jump under his skin, and before getting out, tilted the rear-view mirror to have a look at his face. He could only see his forehead and eyes, but even in pieces the continuity was disturbing and he was momentarily paralyzed by an irrational fear of the known. He turned to Pamela, but she wasn't there and had left just a few strands of hair and an empty beer can on the seat. He followed her tracks and found her already in the bathtub, under water, spreading her washing-up friction, like a snake getting out of its skin, squirming and breaking things. Her body twisted and he dipped his hand in the water at the same time she asked for a Jack Daniels. They drank until their heads collided and she whispered humid sounds to make him forget the sand and heat in the desert. He poured the rest of the bourbon on his dick and got in with her, but, as usual, he had to stay partially outside. Even in such a small space and with all the contact, she got away.

Pamela started talking about the motel rooms. She said she knew them, said she used to run with a crowd, business travelers who spent their lives in these kinds of places, off-the-highway motels, roadhouses. She knew all about maid service, room service, magic fingers, cable TV, adult TV, swimming pools. She knew which provided glass glasses, instant coffee, and powdered cream, which had automats or restaurants attached. She knew the night men at some and this surprised Ray. She could say, according to the weather, the time of day, and the time of year (in relation to national holidays, county fairs, superstar entertainers on tour), which would have vacancies. She knew which were organized and run outside of time, which ones depended on a cult-of-personality psychology, which had no rules at all and might be the sites of drunken teenage love or despondency. She knew the parking lots, where you might see a dozen Harleys, or deer tied to the hood of a Dodge Ram pick-up. She told him about one place where a starlet and a rock musician had both aspirated on vomit, in different rooms, with ten years intervening. And she knew the route, which traced a huge, misshapen infinity sign covering almost two thousand miles, that a serial killer had mapped, over three years, killing people in their rooms and burying them along the freeway, usually behind billboards. In the end she promised to take him to a room in a Days Inn where she could open a hole in the floor and show him underground tunnels that a tribe of Indians had built centuries ago.

Soon Ray was lightheaded and went into the next room, where, out of sight, he listened to Pamela make her noises, passing time until she would come and lift the bed sheets and show him the perverseness of what he was looking for, like the other nights in the motels, where she kept turning, disappearing and reappearing on the other side. She made him want the most sinful kinds of love. He lay on his stomach and saw himself, in his mind, with his torso pressed to the hood of the Camaro. If he loved the motels, he loved the car even more and, initially, had agreed to take the trip with her because he believed that the only way to find her was in the car, on an interstate highway. But he realized now how wrong he'd been, he wouldn't find Pamela anywhere and all that was left was to follow her; her promises of terror and oblivion kept him interested and before he knew it she was standing before him, clean and shiny, showing off her polished chrome fingertips.

He climbed off the bed and started toward her, but Pamela moved away quickly and as she passed she brushed against his leg, like a shiver, a secret wish, barely touching him. It was a moment filled with uncertainty: the soundless hello, the way her eyes dripped onto her cheeks when she lowered the lids, and the way, when he turned to watch her, he saw the glowing, orange prints that her bare feet left in the floor. But the closeness, the urgent contact, the terrible feeling, the fact that she had moved to touch him convinced Ray that something had happened. She crossed the room and sat in a chair, taking a posture that ruined her softness. He felt how near she was to containment, and this just by chance, out of politeness. She kept her seat so as not to break any rules and organized her limbs as part of a big lie invisible to anyone except him. Seeing it was his exclusive privilege.

Succeeding events proved how evasive she really was and provoked actions he had not taken before. He started talking about the Camaro and realized, after getting in very deep, that the car was too concrete to interest her. Although conscious of this desperate position, he could not stop and soon felt the walls of the room collapse under the pressure of their diverging thoughts. She began to rise from the chair, but he caught hold of her to pull her back, at the same time begging her to listen to his story about the custom paint job. He let her stand, took her arms just above the elbows and, as he continued speaking, watched her head sway gently from side to side. Then her gaze steadied, eyes lowered and fixed on the center of his body. He anticipated eye contact, but turned his head, apprehensive of being seen by her, and when he looked back she was standing several feet away, completely out of reach. The idea of traveling that distance was too much and he shook all over.

That was only the beginning. After several hours alone with her, Ray realized that he had an almost lethal combination of chemicals in his blood. Pamela controlled their intake to produce an erosion of sensibility, an approach to something transitive and he hadn't stopped her, but had followed her the way he'd planned, protesting only slightly when she made a hole in his thigh with a safety pin and gently poured fluid inside. She was good at things like that, a genius at chemistry. And so together they had passed through stages of heightened awareness, ignorance, spontaneity, repose, physical strength and weakness, wakefulness, the appearance of sleep, sleep. At one point he saw her come very close to death, her face glowing, radiant and unaffected; and while not beautiful, there was something exposed about it. In the midst of his confusion he asked himself, was this what he had driven hundreds of miles for? And perhaps it was.

The next morning Pamela stroked the skin that covered his backbone before they got into the car. She put on a pair of dark glasses and looked toward him with her eyes closed behind the glasses, another one of her disappearing acts. As they picked up speed on the freeway ramp, she started touching herself all over, pulling at her skin, feeling for texture, checking to be sure it was hers, still attached to the bones with the nerves biting its surface. When she was satisfied, she reached out to touch Ray's leg. He watched the monkey fingers run over his skin, but apart from the touch he thought he sensed a lazy resentment and was afraid she had learned something, had guessed his motives, or knew how hungry he was. But his fears vanished when she started drinking the pre-made gin and orange juice and then poured some bottled water over her chest and neck to keep the heat away.

He pushed the Camaro to a hundred and ten miles per hour and drove like that until his eyes crossed and his head throbbed. Pamela opened a beer and put one of the special pills in her mouth. Then Ray opened a beer. He looked over at her, saw moisture shining on her neck and tried to remember something he had said the first time he held her in the grip of love, and though he began to recall the words, an aimless request, he could not recreate his voice in his mind. Miles and miles registered on the odometer while the unsettled memory persisted; the sound became less familiar and finally he saw only the remembered picture, somthing entirely physical. He could feel the Camaro move faster and, with the sun shining through the window on the passenger side, knew that Pamela was burning up beside him. He watched her legs fold into the white vinyl; someone once told Ray that Pamela's legs ended at her neck, but he didn't know where they ended. Slightly disoriented, he reached for his beer and drank the last of it. Then he threw the bottle out the window, knowing it would crash and shatter; he'd done it a thousand times before and didn't care to look now, but at the moment of impact he made a cowboy sound, as if he had seen it smash and had felt the old destruction energy. Pamela breathed softly and, although she had almost disappeared, he knew she was beside him because of that faint sound; looking to his right, he squinted against the sun and still could only see an imprecise outline of her profile.

Pop Life
Sekou Sundiata

I'm in this movie
see?
speeding from state to state.
I can't make it
on the Limit
so I break
space.
Deep in the bass
a line that walks
modulates and turns
under the influence of whatever is
the recommended daily allowance.
A slow drag moon
speaks to the water in my brain:
put away your romance
you ain't no killer.
You a lover.
In a long establishing shot
the opposition of shadow and substance.
Suddenly things be
exactly what they appear to be.
Monday is the day after Friday.
Nothing's funny.
A true hero would laugh
about pissing in the wind.
The next shot doesn't let the murderer out
proud to say
he still right here with me.

A joker appears onstage
in a white
spot
like a game
show.
Name one style, he says
from the year 1984.
Or, well, do you remember
that picture of them in Le Monde?
The wife kissing the President
in the mouth.
Tongue and spit
that sort of thing.
She was right about Europe.
She was right about the moon.
And then, in the Convention Hall
under that hard light
she was waving her hand wrist and arm
at his huge face in the video monitor
as the Gipper waited
in the hotel room with his pal.
The mindscreen located the First Family
in a place at that moment called The Nation.
This is the American living room
his buddy whispered
she's waving at you Chief.
The Chief nudges him, points at the screen
and nudges him again, shifting mentally
like he does from foot to foot
happy to recall how it's all done
with mirrors.
The First Lady's signal mushrooms
into a radiant but silent smile.
He was grinning and waving back
the way you do with babies and animals.
You could really
see
his boyish charm.

Speeding from state to state
I can't make it on the Limit
so I break
space.
Telephone poles frame the land
according to how the neon runs
freeze dries adds body.
The Future Promise zooms by various exits.
Product
glowing in its face:
crystal moons for lovers
who live inside of pop tunes
a national breakfast special
foreign auto parts
a burger a steak a seafood
combination
movie house supermarket dry cleaners
wreckage haulers 16 wheelers
the x-ray and xerox generation singalong rocknroll
in the radio background of its inheritance
spinning like a Vegas
tracking the overused night.
And here stands the blue collar
with a torso inside
acetelyne fire
oozing from the sleeve.
There stands tomorrow, an ex-famous athlete
grinning, stuck inside a revolving door
and, behind him, the casino
like a birthday cake with leaky candles.
A line of scrimmage.
The flag blossoms in a crush
of uniforms hot dogs and beer.
The anthem roars from house to house.
The foot pedal slams
like the heart of the green giant
against the kick drum
in common time, cymbals splash, crash
tis of thee tis of thee tis of thee

LEGEND
1 inch : 1 hour
Constance DeJong
(with Tony Oursler)

"Charles, look: the entrance to the tunnel."
"Look: a red fox running through that toxic dump."
"Look: farmland. Twenty-five minutes outside the City and there's farmland."
"Look: a big gas station with food and bathrooms. Let's stop."
"Look at her, look at her...that's what the women in that bathroom were saying; pointing at me, talking so loud I could hear them. Twenty-five minutes outside the City and I'm an exotic alien, a tourist attraction for the hicks. I hate this, I hate...."

Charles: "Relax, blondie. We just got on the road and you know this kind of thing is going to happen over and over again. Look at you...maybe they think you're a rock star or something. Let's be positive. And let's get out of here; we got to go, we're not measuring this trip in miles but in hours. I want the window open, blowing on my face. I want things rushing by me, things I've never see before, I'll never see again, things that never repeat."

Doomed to repeat the mistakes of the past are all those who remain ignorant of history. Thomas Edison, Woodrow Wilson, George Washington, John Kennedy; all the exits on the New Jersey Turnpike are named for men save for one, the last one named for Clara Barton:

> American Humanitarian; born Oxford, Mass., 1821–1912. Called the Angel of the Battlefield, she set up a supply service during the Civil War, was nurse at army camps, and on battlefields; and led searches for the missing. After working behind German lines for the International Red Cross in the Franco-Prussian War she organized (1881) the American Red Cross, which she headed until 1904.

TOURIST ATTRACTIONS

Men continue to dominate the landscape in Washington, D.C. where history is being repeated all over town; a man is waving a sword, a man is reining in a horse, taking aim, waving a flag, holding up a document, a deed. A town code keeps the buildings low, the sky high, forming a background against which statues stand out: our forefathers can be seen by the dawn's early light.

By twilight the past of our nation dominates the landscape in names only. Christened in the names of Marshall, Jackson, men of war—the highway in the Blue Ridge Mountains recently echoed with sounds of war in the night. As told by a resident of Maggie Valley, North Carolina: "All that fell, all that was wet just froze up solid in minutes—ice everywhere. That's when it started so loud you could feel it in your chest *booming, crashing.* It sounded just like Viet Nam. Then you'd hear some further away down the valley echoing. Then I saw what it was... the frozen trees had begin to break to pieces under the pressure of the Nor'wester. It went on all night; thousands of trees split, half broken, crowns snapped off. A real fire fight. It looked like lightening struck all over the mountain, the highway for miles around."

There is a legend, that at the time of the Crucifixion the dogwood had been the size of the oak and other forest trees. So firm and strong was the tree that it was chosen as the timber for the cross. To be used thus for such a cruel purpose greatly distressed the tree, and Jesus, nailed upon it, sensed this and in His gentle pity for all sorrow and suffering said to it: "Because of your regret and pity for my suffering, never again shall the dogwood tree grow large enough to be used as a cross. Henceforth it shall be slender and bent and twisted and its blossoms shall be in the form of a cross... two long and two short petals. And in the center of the outer edge of each petal there will be nail prints, brown with rust and stained with red, and in the center of the flower will be a crown of thorns, and all who see it will remember...."

While the dogwood's story can be purchased in every season, only in spring can its blossoms be seen... especially at twilight when white stands out against the darkening shades of blue ridged mountains from which, perhaps, historical statues have been carved. From white—the eye is drawn to a full moon on the rise which, like mountains named for their color, is known as the Pink Moon of April. Eyesight improves in the south. A southern spring is color-vision; the sight of azeleas, crepe myrtel, sorrel, clay fissures in the meadows. A southern spring is the smell of wisteria in the night... an especially welcome scent in Canton, North Carolina where something stinks all the day long.

statues have been carved. From white—the eye is drawn to a full moon on the rise which, like mountains named for their color, is known as the Pink Moon of April. Eyesight improves in the south. A southern spring is color-vision; the sight of azeleas, crepe myrtel, sorrel, clay fissures in the meadows. A southern spring is the smell of wisteria in the night...an especially welcome scent in Canton, North Carolina where something stinks all the day long.

The stench filling the noses of visitors is the smell of something sweet to local residents. They call it the smell of money: for this is a one company town, home of Champion Paper, where the business of making paper spells the difference between prosperity and poverty. At Champion, logs come rolling in one end of the plant, and out the other comes an endless roll of paper; a long, continuous banner unfurls from huge spools of Champion paper. And from Canton, North Carolina to Canton, Ohio, the highway is one long, continuous sign of commercial interests clearly spelled out: Hardees Ahead, Piggly Wiggly, Family Dollar, Jiffy Mart, Ziggy's Motel....

One no longer absorbs a wealth of information, no longer takes time to read historical plaques, legends on postcards, signs in restaurants....In Allendale, South Carolina we visitors are told by a local resident, Zita Mellon, not to eat at Granny's Restaurant. "They keep garter snakes on the floor in the kitchen to control the mouse population." A sign posted on the kitchen door informs us:

> When the white men discovered this country, the Indians were running it. No debt, no taxes. Women did all the work. The white man thought he could improve a system like that!

Meanwhile back on the highway north, the messages are short and sweet, the signposts are rushing by, the wind on the face no longer carries the smell of money, and one no longer sights the difference between North and South, no longer sees the landscape now dominated by Ziggy's Motel sign and all the rest: Liver or Gizzard Snack, Exotica International Shopping, Vac 25¢, Philip 66, Nightfall Motel, Slumberland Motel, Palmetto Hotel, Hong Kong Restaraunt, Destiny Homes, Swap Shop, Radiator King, Already On Top & Getting Better, Huddle House, Fantasy Males in Motion/Females in Lock Up Friday, Dixiana, Oops You Missed It, Sleep Cheap, We're Live at Nite—Marriot, 102 All Music... All Memories, We Beat the Pants Off Any Deal, Admirals Quarters, Mom & Pop Family Rest, Welcome to Wild & Wonderful West Virginia, Double Money Back Meat Guarantee, Dover Cryogenic Division.

TOP STORIES

A PROSE PERIODICAL

#1 Donna Wyszomierski
#2 Laurie Anderson
#3 Pati Hill
#4 Suzanne Johnson
#5 Linda Neaman
#6 Gail Vachon
#7 Jenny Holzer/Peter Nadin
#8 Judith Doyle
#9 Kathy Acker
#10 Lynne Tillman/Jane Dickson
#11 Kirsten Thorup
#12 Janet Stein
#13 Anne Turyn
#14 Lee Eiferman
#15 Constance DeJong
#16 Ursule Molinaro
#17 Romaine Perin
#18 Donna Wyszomierski
#19-20 Cookie Mueller
#21 Ascher/Straus
#22 Susan Daitch
#23-24 Five, An Anthology

Available from
TOP STORIES
228 Seventh Avenue
New York, NY 10011

ISBN 0-917061-25-X

TOP STORIES #27 $3.00

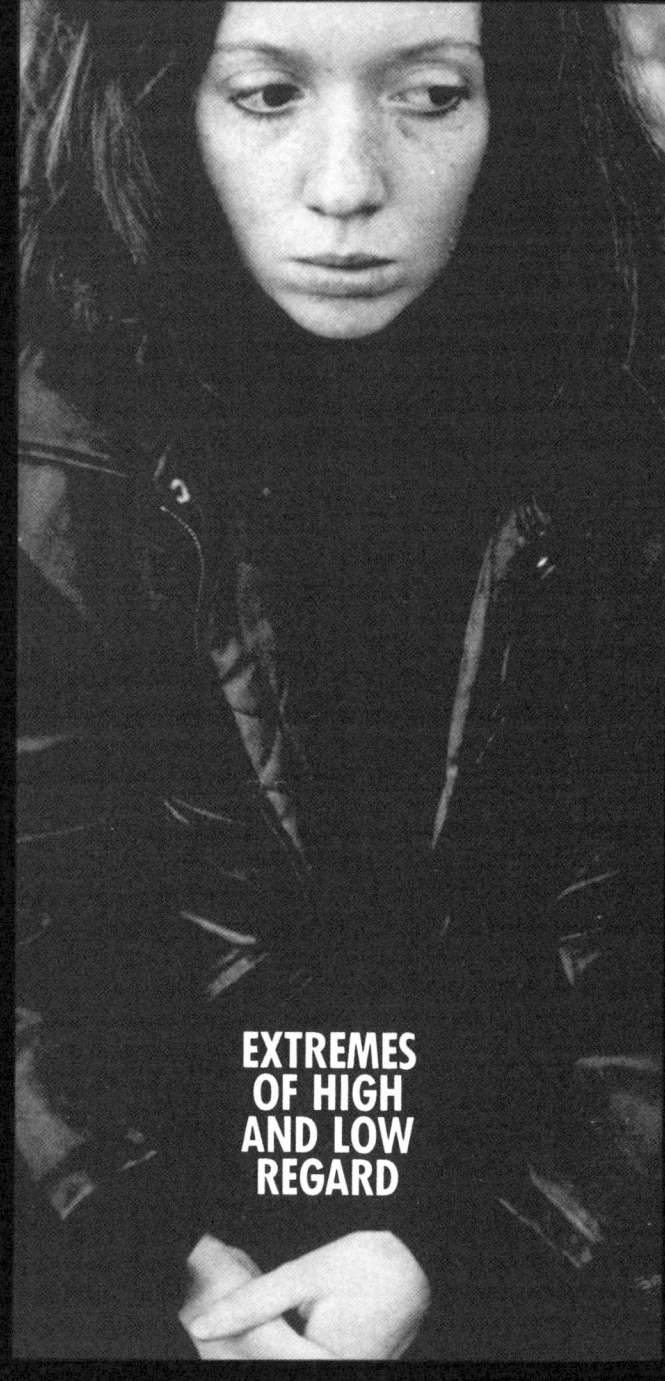

**EXTREMES
OF HIGH
AND LOW
REGARD**

LOU ROBINSON

Extremes of High and Low Regard

Extremes of High and Low Regard
by Lou Robinson

TOP STORIES #27
1988

Copyright © 1988 by Lou Robinson

This publication was made possible in part with public funds from the National Endowment for the Arts and the New York State Council on the Arts.

ISBN 0-917061-27-6 (Top Stories #27)

TOP STORIES, 228 Seventh Avenue, New York NY 10011

TABLE OF CONTENTS

Door of Counfounding
7

Moving Objects at a Distance
10

Naming the Urge
16

Extremes of High and Low Regard
20

DOOR OF CONFOUNDING

I wanted to be a horse handler. All my life I gathered testimonials. I listed all tentative information. I tried to imagine—causing a pain behind one eye—buying a trailer to take the horse back, now, today, to what? The word *intriguing* is such a case. Once understood to mean deceitful coming through the French from entangle with the intention of issuing a warning. A boy grows up to be a man.

The horse shared the barn with my father's motorcycles. A Harley. An older Harley. An older Indian in baskets. Bridles hung from the handlebars and a dusty red Sioux Indian saddle rode the old Harley, the one that was retired. This Harley had been ridden during the war, through Indianapolis in the rain, spilling him three times, a wounded, delirious, AWOL Eddy, riding home to see my mother, Mona, before they were married. There was an ache in the presence of these machines, in the very premise of a thing that can't stand on its own, that is too heavy for a girl to lift, but whose weight can crush you. I would have had to leave him lying on the road in the rain. The mare was half-Saddlebred, half-Arab, a field accident. She lifted her feet high, that was the Saddlebred. She had fears, expensive needs, a weight of affection, a wayward soul. The motorcycles are still there. What could a girl hold on to, for a future?

We have stopped for coffee on the way to Maine for Lynnie's wedding. Before he retired, he had conducted an informal survey, my father is saying, of how men and women release the coffee into their cups from the coffee urn in the faculty lounge. Men push down, he says, and women lift up. To a man. My mother had become intrigued, surveyed the bridge club and their husbands, and had to agree. Later, the three of us watch each guest approach the urn across the dance floor under the strobe light in the pine barn called 'club' at Lynnie's wedding reception, and he is right. There are no exceptions.

Suddenly he worries that no one will make a toast to the bride and groom, and begins to write on a napkin. My mother and I cringe, grin ruefully at each other as he rises. On the napkin he has written: 1945 Harley, Lynnie in saddlebag.

Later I ask friends. One remembers that he used to push down on the little lever, but always worried that the urn would tilt and crash, so he switched to lifting. "But even you were dumb enough to push down first," I say. I feel cheated. All along I thought the things were meant to be lifted, people who push were going to break it off. Why hadn't someone told my they were made to move both ways? Why had I never taken one apart? Was it a man who first took it apart or put it together and knew it could be puld? Why hadn't I watched how He did it? I had been tricked into another feeble, feminine gesture.

Riding behind him when I was five, I pretend to be French. His shoulders block the sun. My mother teaches French. It is a special female domain, intuitively decipherable, like a language of known affections. I spare myself the meanings to keep the mystery, the purr, and to have words of my own that my father can't explain. And there is more, French is sex. A sly connection to the motorcycle magazines I discover in the rack at the candy store. Finding the one where they put their hands down the women's blouses. They handcuff a woman to a motorcycle and drag her. My father's wide black leather saddlebags say *Eddy* in rhinestones. Intense rise and guilt, reading these things. Riding behind him all the way to Indiana, bugs smash on my teeth, I say, le, la.

Was vanilla female, was chocolate male? Why was a chair a woman? A kind of sex dyslexia set in. I still say wedding when I mean funeral, and vice versa.

Riding behind them in the back seat of the van, through the snow to

Maine, I compose his obituary; it will be stern but forgiving, glossing over the obvious wounds. At Lynnie's funeral that afternoon I hear him telling my aunt that he has noticed a new trend in obituaries: they say "survived by her companion," or "by her friend and partner...." Father and daughter, writing each other's obituaries, anxious to find a form that will be acceptable to the dead, slumbering at last in forgiveness and vindication.

Every noon in the second grade I go to other people's houses for strange sweet green beans so that my parents could concentrate; Eddy to write his thesis, Mona to type it. A speech teacher, right? Enough to strike you dumb. In the evenings a series of children with speaking problems were led up the long stairs to the gable room with his grey leather chair and the window made of small panes of glass where they put the Halloween turnip.

Murmurs of encouragement from behind the door, which he explained must be closed so the child won't be embarrassed. Speech Therapy. Which witch. All the w's in my first grade books underlined. A letter for the occult sound owls make. The creature my mother and I saw in the window, his mouth making a silent sound. "He" because it spoke, even though they couldn't hear it. The mythic significance of the double-u which I could pronounce perfectly and the boy could not. Would he grow up to be a man or something else? Yearning passing to a rootless, groundless resolve resides in this sound, for the root does not bass, and the yearning reveals no root. I never see the child Eddy tutors. I imagine it is because the sound of my perfect W would break his heart. The boy who is also other, behind the door of confounding. This is the first hint of my kind of power in the world and what a burden. I cut some holes out of my skirts.

Eddy takes me with him to home debate tournaments, where I get to flip the time cards, watching the second hand on his watch. In the car on the way home we argue. "How can you say one thing that you know is right, then switch and take the other side? I can't do that. I wouldn't do that. I would just quit."

"You confuse yourself with words," my father says, secure in his birthright, shaken by all that escapes speech. Twenty years later he says this again. He means I am moved to action by rhetoric. "At least I never had a guru, Eddy." "No, you were a guru unto yourself," he says solemnly.

I see sentences in my sleep: Things can form but not attach. Hooks can be removed and reexamined. I breathe in all my murderous possibilities. I dream that I murdered my wife. My wife had disturbed my sentences. Without thinking, I reached over and squeezed her neck, and it popped. Ever since, years, I have been living underground waiting for the knock on the door, the badge, the arrest, the trial. A horrible moral structure presses against my tongue. Backed by relentless dogmas, it holds in breath. I throw up a little king.

Home from kindergarten, my best friend and I used to play Killing the King up in the attic. We bound an invisible king to a chair and whipped him. Sometimes we whipped ourselves.

In the stomach the king has been left to establish himself as a given. So there is a limit on the range of possibilities....This boundary squeezes sense out of words, words out of sync. I gather testimonials to revolt:

One from the newspaper—
"State police are conducting a door to door search in Horseheads for the prime suspect in a stabbing death, who sent a 68-page letter to the police signed 'Jezreel.' In this letter Jezreel says, 'I can't wait to render him back to where he came from and can just picture the look on the little runt's face, well I finally killed his physical body. yes I know you untrue souls think I'm insane.'"

From a hitchhiker—
"I was wondering if anyone would pick me up or if someone would pick me up and kill me, but I think my vibes are too good for that since I stopped being depressed. I was really depressed last week, I used to think about killing myself a lot, like from a doorknob or something, but all the ways you can kill yourself are too painful, know what I mean, I guess if you're too depressed to do anything, killing yourself is too much work. Anyway I decided to stop being depressed because it was so boring talking about myself all the time. I mean when I was depressed I would have gotten

into this car and started telling you all about how I lost $500 my rent and I don't have a place to live and everything. I was hoping to get in the car and hear a lot of interesting things from you that I could think about for a change. When I was depressed I used to look terrible but since I stopped I've been dressing up. I've been looking good for about two weeks now. I don't know if I can keep it up. I'm in college. My own college, I call it the College of Trial. I study whatever I want, but at the same time every day. Like if I'm going to do reading, I do it at the same time each day. I'm adding an anti-sexist class that will go on all day. This way I can study anywhere, in Ireland, when I go to find Stiff Little Fingers. Did you ever feel like death is just 20 feet behind you? I'm just ahead of mine, that's why I'm going to Ireland. Look at my tongue. I painted it green. In Ireland they paint their tongues green so their words have the power to make things real."

MOVING OBJECTS AT A DISTANCE

The family restraint—as in the incident of the pond: It was one hundred degrees and I was home for a visit. The pool was full of holes, so my mother, my sister, her two kids, and I decided to walk to the pond. The pond is owned by a neighborhood group called The Homestead Acres Association. For a long time it was just a pond, and anyone on the lane could swim in it. Then those closest grew possessive, incorporated, put up a sign. We didn't join because by then we had a modest swimming pool in the backyard, and we lived at the far end of the lane anyway. Still, my brother and sister swam and fished and skated there for years with their neighborhood friends.

The two little kids ran right into the water. We three women stood in a clump preparing to be friendly to Mrs. Cobble, the only other bather at the pond, standing in two inches of water on her chicken legs. She said, "You know, Mona, the pond is really only for members of the Association."

My sister scooped up her children and replied, "I didn't think the Association would mind two little kids cooling off, especially since your daughter Jane spent many hours in our pool." My impulse was to laugh hysterically, point at Mrs. Cobble's legs, and dive in. But I took my cue from my mother—her upright dancer's posture and sudden faraway look, and was left with a weak snide grin for my part.

When we got home, my sister wrote Mrs. Cobble a letter in which she enclosed a dollar bill, "I hope this will cover any damage my children may have caused." Mother confessed to being mad at herself for her silence. My brother says Mrs. Cobble is still rankled from the early days when she tried to call on my mother like a good neighbor and my mother hid in the basement, smoking cigarettes, waiting for her to quit knocking and go away. My brother says he would have dived right in. My brother-in-law suggests that the men all go down and stand in a row and piss in it. My father is already on the phone, reminding Mrs. Cobble that he himself laid the foundation for the pond's boathouse and has also been mowing the grass with his tractor for free ever since. He calls one pond member after another. He resolves never to lend a single tool to any of the incompetent feeble pond husbands who borrow things from his garage and break or lose them, and when their wives get stuck in the lane next winter he will ride by on his tractor in his hooded marine coat and laugh instead of pulling them all out for free in the bitter cold like he has for years good decent neighbor that he is.

I berate myself for my silence also. Since 1969 my family expects me to respond to the slightest provocation in a crass, extremist fashion, so if I react at all it threatens to become another story about me. I am stunned to learn that on those occasions when my mother hid in the basement to avoid Mrs. Cobble, or Mrs. Rucker, with her butterscotch cakes made on the gas burner with Thank You Ed in mustard colored icing, even down there just doing laundry, she smoked. I've never seen my mother smoke. I thought it was my father's pants making the laundry chute smell like cigarettes. "I knew she smoked," says my brother.

Every time we get together, we discuss the pond incident, growing more and more appalled at our almost unanimous silent retreat. Last Christmas my sister remembered when Mrs. Cobble tried to divide the ice into sections to keep kids from skating on more than their share. The five-year-old comes flying into the room with a stick he calls his machete, screaming, "I'm going to slash your face Mrs. Cobble."

The ceremonial may inaugurate momentum, if not resolve.

Such fatigue sets in when trying to remember. Always there is a huge breathing shadow. Guilt and anger and desperate-not-to-feel-them sum up decades of a peculiar coma. I dreamed my left thumb was cut off and that meant my good grandmother was dead. Then my father said his mother would replace her. She can't, I said. "She had to pay the piper," he answered, to get even. He meant she thought too highly of herself to live.

The corollary to my speaking out, breathing, thinking highly of myself in a separate shell and the holes it caused in his intestines. How soon do we learn that our bodies are houses of guilt? My niece wakes in her crib and pleads, "I'm nice, I'm nice;" the typesetter at work says she blamed herself for the Vietnam war; and when I am struck from behind while stopped at a red light, my first thought is that maybe I was supposed to be moving.

The door is frustrated and not opening all the way. Screens over lights turn suggesting patterns. The more screens the more arresting the pattern.

"1963," my mother says, "was a terrible year. Kennedy was shot, mother died, and we had our wreck." The real sequence: Kennedy, the wreck, my first period, the death of the grandmother.

My parents were coming home from Christmas shopping in Columbus on a snowy night when a woman with no insurance slid across three lanes and smashed into my mother's side.

I am at my best friend Tommie's house making floating island pudding. Her father, whose name is Red, comes into the kitchen and tells me I'm to stay with them until we hear more. Red seems to be hiding something, which scares and offends me, because as editor of the Gazette, he is expected to respect the facts. Some confusion while they try to locate my brother makes me picture him lying still somewhere off Route 23 in the snow. A veil descends. Colors mellow and become golden. Tommie's dog Gussy, lying on the floor chewing a mouthful of rubber bands, is the most beautiful astonishing thing I've ever seen. I can hear voices now as part of the soundtrack but I don't have to do anything.

Then Red hears from another friend that my brother is in the hospital too, with a sprained neck. Already somehow stories of my father's heroics are circulating—how he carried her out of the car with two broken arms himself and three crushed ribs. I'm not allowed to see my parents, but they take me in to see Mike, to prove he is alive. He hangs his head in a sullen wrenching way and won't look at me. All I can say is "Are you alright?" to which he growls "NO. MY NECK HURTS," each time. Then I leave with Red.

In my dreams since then my brother has not managed to grow a single year. If he's in them, he's six. Last year at Christmas I finally said, "were you traumatized by the wreck and did you feel I abandoned you in the hospital?" "NO," he says. This is what he remembers: "Haycock carried me around on his shoulders saying Hey Mike look at the pee-pee in the jars, and made me laugh. Then we started into a room and I saw Mom's yellow coat in the wastebasket, covered with blood. Then I was home and you wouldn't leave me alone. You let me play with your paper horses." This gives me inexpressible relief.

What I remember: My pony got fed three times in one night by helpful neighbors. My grandmother Zel came to stay with me and my sister; brisk, efficient, inspired. Days or weeks passed then, from the hospital my mother guessed that my period would start and sent my grandmother after sanitary pads, only two days before it actually began. Then my father came home on Christmas Eve, having bullied his way out against the doctor's orders, to "be with his children." Waking in the night I heard him sobbing out loud "and I don't even have a Christmas present for her," while my grandmother said, "Now Ed."

Finally allowed to see her, I walked into a room with three beds, confused until I heard her voice, shaky, trying to sound teasing, "don't you recognize me?" coming from a purple football of a face with huge cross stitches and shaved patches of scalp. I gave her my Christmas present, a pack of pinochle cards which I had bought at Woolworth's thinking they were for bridge.

And I remember the day the wrecker towed home the car, because after that whenever I heard the joke 'what's black and white and red all over?' I thought of that car, a black and white paneled station wagon, dried blood covering the upholstery, no passenger side remaining. Later I learned they hadn't expected her to live.

I wasn't sure how to dispose of the sanitary napkins.

My grandmother struggles to counter the coma reflex by appearing in dreams, dipping caramels and nuts into rolling chocolate or pressing huge white steaming squares through the sheet presser, wearing garnet lipstick and offering timely warnings about eyestrain or dangerous relationships.

House of retention of grief. Show all. Rest becoming distinct. Egress.

NAMING THE URGE

My real name is Jo, after my mother's favorite character in *Little Women*. She was named for Catherine in *Wuthering Heights*. My mother hated Catherine and changed her name to Mona when she was thirteen. My grandmother confessed to having been torn between Catherine and Fanny, another heroine, but back then her husband could still put his foot down. She herself was christened Elsie, which I loved, but my grandmother hated because of Elsie the Borden cow. She started the grandchildren calling her Hazel, after a pagan novel by Mary Webb. Babies heard that as Hey Zel, so it got shortened to Zel.

Early impressed by the arbitrary, malleable nature of naming, I jettisoned Jo for Stormy, the name of a horse in a book I once read that had a cover portrait of a yearling with a wild, blue-black mane. Other names I had considered: Seal, Smoky, Micah, Coaly Bay, Blue, Cinnamon, Sorrel, all the colors horses come in. Stormy seemed to leave more room for temperament.

My family are all great readers, to the point of rudeness. We'd drive all the way to Vandalia to visit Zel, make straight for the magazine rack and retreat with a stack that would take us through dinner to bedtime. It wasn't hard to change your name. The general atmosphere was one of detached indulgence. Whenever they looked up from their books, it was with faces of surprise and amusement, as if they truly were confused about my origins. I propped my comic books on a solid shelf of bitter chocolate, like a lap desk, nibbling and sucking the edge all day. Zel had taken a machete and carved off this slab for me from the dark bitter wall of chocolate that stood ten feet high in the cold room.

The magazine rack was in the store attached to the house that Zel and her husband, Moss owned—a grocery store and soda fountain called Lane's Confectionary. It was the very womb of luxury. I fed myself from the soda fountain: chocolate coke for breakfast, cherry coke with lunch (a hot dog in crinkly cellophane heated in the machine), banana coke with dinner. I whipped around behind the counter, pulling parrot head fountain spouts, spooning balls of ice cream into giant soda glasses, topping off root beer froth, to the deep envy of neighborhood kids. Kids loved my grandfather Moss. They called him Laney. He was a small wirey man in a long white apron and white fitted cap over thick vanilla hair, who worked from dawn to dusk. His silence, and the whiteness of his hair were due to the war, after which he had become a ghost, handing out free candy and running up bills for the whole neighborhood all through the depression straight into bankruptcy. In a photograph he stands in front of the big wavy mirror behind the fountain, in eternal apron and cap, his skinny arms holding an eighty-pound candy cane under his chin like a barbell. Above, his eyes are absent, or spooked. Each Christmas Laney gave one of these monster candy canes away to whoever could guess its weight.

It was strenuous work, candymaking. In his basement workroom he would punch and roll the mass of hot sugar, heave it over a buttered hook fastened six feet up on a post and pull it, heave and pull. Then separate a great wad of it, make a dent with his fist, and Zel would pour in dye so red it was a color seen only on the big screen, staining the lips of Anne Bolyn. Then he would roll and twist this ruby wad into a stripe of perfect evenness against the shiny ivory of the rest.

Meanwhile Zel did all the smaller candies that lined the glass case upstairs in the store. Fondant, nougat, turtles, chocolate caramels and creams. I helped, pressing walnuts into caramels to make legs and head, dipping them in their baths of milky tan or bitter cocoa. Sometimes Zel made candy bars named after her grandchildren: the Lynn-bar, the Candy-bar, the Jo-bar. People came from all over the Midwest for their candy. That meant each holiday Zel and

Moss nearly killed themselves getting the orders ready, running the store at the same time. All the relatives came to help.

These are my secret memories of bliss. The long line of them in white aprons and caps, perched on tall green stools, their elbows moving in and out in unison as they roll the slender fairy sticks forward and back, forward and back to round and cool them. Every pastel color and every sweet hot smell you could imagine and nothing forbidden. When I felt the need to dream in a little more privacy, I could work alone in the cold room, coloring in the mules on the Lane's Cough Drop boxes—red for cherry, brown for horehound.

Easter was the holiday the adults dreaded most, but it was the height of Zel's magical power. Her simple painted boiled eggs were beyond description. Silver-green paisleys like the cloth she remembered from Scotland. Deep purple pansies edged with chrome yellow. Cornflower blue bachelor buttons, each tiny frond distinct, each hair on the moss-green stem bristling.

Easter morning I would rise to find the basket—three feet high, wrapped in cellophane and tied with a mauve satin ribbon, the basket itself sometimes made of woven candy, shiny, eggshell white. Inside, deep green grass pillowed one giant chocolate egg covering the smoothest butter cream. No other candy-maker came close to the texture of Zel's creams. Its chocolate surface was covered with blue and lavender flower petals, ivy, and *Stormy* written in a sweeping script of the palest yellow frosting. Around it —rainbow fairy sticks, little marshmallow chicks in a smaller basket of woven pink fondant, pale green sea-foam pieces, deep crimson cinnamon suckers as clear as stained glass. And the hollow egg. A fairy-tale object, made from a blown goose egg coated with layers of sugar tinted all the pale colors of snow under church lights. Through the window the size of a thumbnail, a tiny Stormy could be seen standing beside blue-green pine trees, holding the reins of a miniature licorice horse. In the grass at her feet, rabbits, cats, wildflowers and Easter eggs the size of Indian belt beads.

It wasn't just that my grandmother had renamed herself—

effecting a window, a slim hope. Or that her art was both inspired and generous, created only to be devoured. She demonstrated that you could change yourself to fit your private dream. Her vanity table covered in wild blue and pink flowered chintz, holding buns of hair from her childhood that she sometimes attached to her loose strawberry waves with long blond hairpins. Bedside table covered with astrology magazines, movie star magazines, Christian Science pamphlets, and novels by women. Opinionated, haughty, she existed to recreate the sordid everyday, passing this talent along to her daughter and granddaughter. My mother took as her motto Scarlet's line "I'll think about it tomorrow." A positive construction was built over every blow, every warp or sharp odor.

Standing in front of the mirror at the foot of the stairs, age four. A chance wind has blown a piece of hair over, giving me the idea to part it in the middle for once. The pleasure of staring at yourself, changing yourself. Suddenly a tomboy with a serious look becomes a doe, a cameo with a widow's peak. Who would not want to hold her to them forever? Simple as that, I think, sly behind my new look of acquiescence. A whole new character grows from a single image. Now there are two: one with which to combat; one with which to seduce. The new one gets a secret name: Cat.

Naming flows from the source of lost possibilities. You name someone, you put your hopes for them into the word, shaping a little cage. When you name yourself you form a cage perhaps of smaller dimensions than your mother would have imagined for you.

My naming urge became fierce, creating apocryphal tokens that I would roam behind for years.

EXTREMES OF HIGH AND LOW REGARD

My father writes for *Rod Action* and *Old Cars*. He has worked on hundreds of cars and cycles in his life; he respects nothing. In his column he curses cars with nostalgic relish. All his stories have a curious mixture of macho and humility. They are all at his own expense. He wants to be the first to say, "the old fool."

Telling me about being arrested for riding his 1945 Harley with a taillight out (a long story that includes going to court with Hell's Angels, being forced to take the riding test over, blasting around the barrels on 'Grandpa' and miraculously not falling flat...), he says, "You missed your father in his finest hour." His motorcycle belt says *Eddy* in rhinestones.

I sold Eddy's motorcycle jacket in the early 70s. For years I wore it, sleeves dangling half empty to the knee; was wearing it when I went up to Jill Johnston at a reading and Jill said, "I like your style." On the radio a woman describes why she makes videos: the only time she ever saw her father cry was in front of the television when Kennedy was shot. I have the obverse goal. How can I appropriate the emblems that made him appear invincible?

I also took and lost his marine jacket. He likes to remind me of the time he drove me to the bus, and watched me, wearing the jacket, board along with twenty marine recruits. He didn't know if I made it to Cincinnati alive.

Once years later when I had a broken heart, I called Eddy and asked him to find me a motorcycle. He hauled one all the way from Ohio to New York. I rode it around the driveway for several weeks and then sold it.

When I visit him, he makes me read his latest column the minute I step inside the door. "You're my best audience." I never show him anything I write because it's often about him and it might hurt him so much he would have a stroke and need to be nursed for the rest of my life.

My natural coating-like bark curls up showing the seam of the supposed results of will and the place it has found. This reserve proves itself in the body. Every tribe has its casualties, its downward spiral. I remember when he told me the story of his mother, Edna, whose real mother was a Blackfoot Indian. An herbalist from Kentucky, she died after Edna was born. Edna's new stepmother despised her husband's Indian kid, and one morning hung the child's dog from the branches of the oak outside her bedroom window. He has too many of these stories. I tune out. They register instead in my stomach. Quick lunges may upset the counter momentum, but no masking can counter the brooding and seething—it has its own reasons.

On the phone he says, "I guess you can't make it down for the Kentucky reunion. I wasn't even going to mention it. It's Aunt Birdie's one-hundred-and-one birthday."

I studied the man. Very early I remember being depressed that I couldn't wash my whole head like he did, with a washcloth (or washrag as he calls it, thinking each time of how his third grade teacher said he talked like trash).

He claims a resemblance to Robert Mitchum, which is actually evident in a certain permanently wounded attitude, a stoic but wronged set of grimaces and sighs. His face relaxes from this into tragedy. And from his side, he will suddenly say, "There's a girl who runs the salvage yard here—your age, looks and talks like you." And later, "My novel: the main character, female, your age, wears a sweatshirt all the time, too. I scrapped the first two chapters...." I move to protect my stomach. No protection felt. Banished from the head, but something in the gut mourns over the necessity of manifestation.

Trace Branch. Where he comes from, where she hung the dog. I fixed on this. I heard it very early. I focused on the plight of animals. I spent my childhood in anguish on their behalf. After Gail and Eileen Irish, the two Quaker sisters from down the lane, dropped out of the club I formed, I scoured the country lanes alone, looking for hurt creatures. My Band of Mercy, my club of one. Found birds, mostly; they didn't make it, and one white chicken that died in the basement. But I bore witness. When Linda Walters strapped her horse in a standing martingale and whipped it, I called the SPCA. "I want to report a crime," and hung up with the familiar sinking feeling of futility. The same sinking as when Eddy tried to tell me that in movies the horses don't really get shot or fall over the cliff. There was an organization to protect them. Right. I read his books. I knew what people were capable of.

Eddy was titillated by the Band of Mercy. Caught me with a quick question as I was coming up from feeding the chickens in the basement, and surprised, I let slip the name of my club. I saw his face twist with the struggle not to grin.

I hated to be laughed at and he loved to laugh. One tease could drive me into a week-long silence. I froze him out from the beginning. From the beginning he pushed, he used his very agile mind to get inside my fortress. It was a constant battle which drove us both to extremes. Once I heard him exclaim to my mother, in disgust, as if I were a criminal or prostitute, "Why does she keep the door shut all the time? All she wants to do is be in her room with the door shut. Six years old and a misanthrope. What does she do in there anyway?"

In there I made paper horses the size of my thumb. It was not easy. Having started so small, I was forced to make the curry combs, brushes, bridles, halters the size of fingernail trimmings. Each horse had a blanket with its name on it, and a tab like paper doll clothes. My favorites had one version of themselves standing proudly, head raised to the wind, and one leaping in air. Each horse had a little me to go with it, with a tab that fit in the saddle, and a blob of red at the top so there would be no mistaking who owned this fabulous stable. I had a green blanket on my bed.

Behind my door, I would pose them on the hills and valleys of blanket over pillows. I spent long hours devising plans to ensure their safety if the house caught on fire. In my plans, I saved everyone. But I wanted to be prepared. I didn't want to have to make choices.

And I read: *The Yearling, Where the Red Fern Grows, Black Beauty, My Friend Flicka, Coaly Bay the Outlaw Horse, Beautiful Joe, The Red Pony*. At night I made peanut butter and banana sandwiches and watched animal movies on TV: Biscuit Eater, Old Yeller...or failing that, Ida Lupino. When my Aunt Verlan sold the motel, she gave all the old TVs to Eddy, so we had one in every room. I didn't like to watch with people. I liked to watch, maybe even the same show, alone, in my bed, with my horses. This drove Eddy crazy. I wanted to be absorbed, out of the body, into the scene with the dog that sucked eggs, doomed; cradling Beauty's scarred head in my hands—bare emotion. I did not ever want to be watched.

Eddy found projects for the two of us: sanding the Harley pieces, cleaning pistons, shoveling gravel—things horrible in their monotony—but what made me dread them was his huge talking, thinking, prying presence. I had to hear things I did not want to know. I heard them all in the garage.

Garage is not the right word. It was a giant quonset hut Eddy had taken apart at an abandoned army barracks and moved to the back field. He widened the roof with a wooden extension and a row of windows that broke the curve, jutting out like a strange ship, where hundreds of pigeons roosted. More like a barn, but that is a word for animals. This vast place was for cars, motorcycles, tractors, workbenches, tools. House items discarded from our earlier years found their way here and stayed forever, turning black with oil: my old yellow chenille baby spread, an Easter muff now used to buff out polish. There was a clear space only in the middle, to drive in a vehicle for repair. The rest of the floor was covered with greasy black things of all sizes. White enamel pans held lakes of black sump oil twenty years old. Acetylene torches, oxygen tanks. Goggles and a gas mask hung on a nail, covered with cobwebs. You could be sure anything hanging on a nail was never used. Frequently used things were on the inner circle of the floor heap. "Jo, go look for a bolt about this big," he'd say, holding out his black thumb and finger. Or "Go get the ballpeen hammer. It's over by the basket of Indian parts." I never found a single thing I was sent to look for. I never had the satisfaction. I'd stir it around hopelessly for an interval, then trudge back. He'd say "Oh jesus christ" and I'd watch his bent back disappear. I spent a lifetime in there on a stool, learning about how to adjust spark plugs, set timing, take apart a piston. I don't remember how to do a thing. "Hold this as hard as you can while I turn." It would spring back in our faces. I never had the strength. Saturdays Mona would say, "Eddy wants you out in the garage," and she'd pat my back in sympathy as I laid down *Island Stallion Races*.

Once I came running into the garage screaming that my dog was stuck in another dog. I had to hear about animal and then people sex. I knew a lot already, from reading *My Secret Life*, Henry Miller, and Mike Hammer off Eddy's shelves when I could steal them, but I didn't believe anyone I knew did these things in real life. He went on from dog and people sex to perversion. Telling me about Mr. Snouffer, my geography teacher who had left in the middle of the school year. Because, Eddy said, he had taken six seventh grade boys on a field trip to St. Louis, where he paid them to tie him to his hotel bed and whip him with their belts. Eddy sounded like he didn't really want to have to tell me this. He was polishing the gas tank of the older Harley, the one that had been his father's. I was staring at a calendar of a very fat naked woman, given him by his friend George Brey. George thought it was funny. Eddy didn't take it down because he didn't want to hurt George's feelings. George lives alone with his pit bull at the Radnor junkyard. He is a damn fine mechanic. Eddy and George ride abreast to Indianapolis once a year for the races. They ride straight through cities at 80 miles per hour. It always rains. They sleep in the park under picnic tables, with a plastic garbage bag over the boards and one on the ground. When they come back I help him fix Old Grandpa, which has invariably broken down somewhere on Route 71 and been patched up with wire, a stub of a broom handle....In the garage he tells me about the Hell's Angels. This time they played a game with a hot dog hung from a wire stretched between two trees in the campsite. The men have to roar their hogs down the path between the trees and catch the hot dog in their mouths. After awhile, one of the women, in a dog collar, goes over with a jar of mustard and crams the dangling hot dog in it, to make it more slippery we guess, and they start again. He couldn't believe it, he says.

I know this has to do with sex. Why tell me? Am I different from my mother, less innocent somehow; does he think I am more like him? Everything in me slinks away. In private I muzzle my stuffed collie dog and pretend to drown it behind a chair, aroused. I peel the skin off hot dogs and hack them to bits. But I want to be more like him. I do not ever want to be the one on the calendar, the one holding the mustard.

We have photos of Eddy and I together, lolling on the floor of Oak Hill with Gill, the English bulldog Eddy brought from home when he married Mona. In one he lies on the floor with his knees bent and I use him as a chair, my own legs crossed suavely at the knee, my one foot dangling in his face. I remember when his bulk seemed a necessary part of me. I loved him with fierce pride and fear of separation. He was the one who taught me everything: to read, to ride a bike, to climb a tree, to figure things out. He was the one who fixed things for people. He went out into the world and made speeches to crowds. He once marched in a parade in cap and gown next to Yul Brynner. He had met Dinah Shore. He had a purple heart and a silver star. When my foot got caught high in the oak tree and he had to climb up and release it, I fell on the ground in a rage. I could not stand to be so helpless. What if he died?

We played a game—knocking our heads together at the forehead until someone's eyes watered. I would never quit. If he quit, I was sure he was letting me win. Mona would say, "Jesus, Ed, is that a game for a *child*?"

When I was one, Eddy put me on a merry-go-round horse, blue-grey, I swear I do remember that color, at the Delaware County Fair. The man was supposed to hold me, but I kicked him away with my hard little white baby shoes. I wanted to do it alone, and promptly fell on my head. I always had rages—when the bacon fell out of the BLT—whenever he could manage something that I could not.

Then suddenly I couldn't stand to be alone with him. I don't know what changed between three and six. I don't know where my mother was while all of this was happening. Off in her own dream. Alone together, Mona and I either made cookies, cried over TV shows, shopped for school clothes in perfect bliss, or else fought furiously over washing my hair. She says I drove her crazy. But the way I remember it, it was casual. Nothing sly and shaping about it. I wasn't her. She didn't know who I would be but she assumed I would be different. She wasn't bribing companionship from a child.

But I don't remember why I suddenly dreaded Eddy's company. I had grown up riding on the back of motorcycles as calmly as playing horse with a broom. But I developed a dread of this as well, at some early point. I didn't like to have to press my chest against his back. I didn't like that he would speed to give me a little terror. I got on each time in silence and pride, without a struggle, but never without the thought, "If I die, I will come back as a quarterhorse. I won't have to go to school with boys. I won't have to sand primer."

That's when he gave me the pony. Papaw Harry actually bought it for all the cousins. But I was the only one who wanted it, and Eddy hauled it from Indiana to Ohio, its eyes rolling white over the cab of the maroon pick-up. Together, we built a barn for it out of metal shingles. I stood on a ladder in the wind, leaning my weight against a sheet of rippling metal, trying to line up a screw and a hole. Or I crouched beside him as he heaved and sweated over fifty-five postholes. I straightened old nails, as he had done for his father, Harry. I was overwhelmed. I would think, "Is this any kind of work for a child?" I wore out. It was over the pony. It backfired on him.

I switched affection to the stubborn creature Harry had bought at an auction. It—Star—was getting even for a life of abuse. He bit, kicked, squeezed us against the wall. Until we got the fence built, he dragged me an acre on my stomach, morning and night, as I staked him out to graze. Finally I won him over, but he never gave in to anyone else. I took off on his back for hours alone, exploring. Eddy was jealous; he was also bit harder and more often. One day he confessed to having gone out and burnt the pony on the nose with a cigarette, after watching him drag me through the field. I lost all respect. But I had to endure this and the rest now, to keep the pony. I had to become duplicitous. I no longer wanted to be like him. I didn't want to be the son he was to his father.

What was his childhood really like? I don't want to ask. If I could swallow it all quick once in private I might have only compassion—no rage. I know from my mother's few words and angry silences on the topic, that she thinks Papaw Harry was a cruel man. It is a very sad story, even the little I know. It is too much to bear. That's why he talked to me endlessly in the garage. Somebody had to hear it. He talked to me about his father. How Harry had made him stand in the dark alley for punishment, then crept up on him from behind and scared him speechless for a week. How they were building houses together when Eddy was six. Endless stories of old cars bought together, fixed together, wrecked together. How Harry was in the KKK in Kentucky, before they moved to Indiana, then he worked shoulder to shoulder with a one-armed black man, shoveling coal, and got respect for the colored, I was six, seven? Was this about when Harry left my grandmother for a younger woman?

I have always believed that to write this story would be to bury Eddy. The same suspicion that stops me from taking someone's photograph as they start on a trip. But I have been saving it to the point where I am stub up, a bag of tears. Old men's bare backs, bent working in the sun, make me sob. At the same time I feel as if something has been spilled and I must catch it quick before it disappears into real dry memories, all you have left when someone dies. These are between the living, making me fear his death whenever I see his face. It's guilt and anger, of course, but how to say it.

He tells me his sad stories over and over, of Christmases with only an orange for a present, or a box of crayons that a bully steps on, and The War; Christmas in New Zealand, Iwo Jima, sermons in the mud. I am disgusted by this dark blanket of pathos. The man is outrageous. I am fascinated. I tell my stories of him. Here is my version:

I had been fighting Eddy all my short life. I left home finally at eighteen and ran away to Cincinnati, leaving no address. I gave him a phone number of a commune on Mitchell Street where he could leave messages. He wouldn't call, but Mona did, after a few months, to tell me about the reunion. Eddy was going to reconcile with his father. All these years since the divorce, Eddy had refused to see Harry. Had seen him only once, come to find him drunk, cleaning other people's toilets. (Eddy told me this years later, when I happened to be cleaning houses for a living, but I didn't let on.) On this night in 1969, from a payphone on Calhoun Street, I refused to come home. Days passed before someone at the commune remembered to tell me that Mona had called again. From the same payphone I learned that Harry was dead.

For the reunion, all the relatives had chipped in and bought the old man a motorcycle. They gathered at my cousin's sheep farm, a hilly place near Greenville, Indiana. They all had motorcycles, all their lives. Harry got on the new bike. My remorse is boundless. In a word—a universe of guilt. How is it that Eddy forgave me when it took him years to forgive the old man? What did I do that I think I killed him? Tried to escape. Failed to respond. Refused to return. I am the one he can't control; who controls me better? He has to have my nod, no matter how he grovels, because he never got it. No one ever forgave me. Anybody dies and I am to blame. Terrified of his dying. Easier would be to forgive, let him live. Who taught me to read, gave me a pony, whose love weighs more than an army. Can't breath, can't carry. Just an old man trying to be brave, raised under a rain of blows, who wants to kill me with love. When I look at the photo of him as a youth on his first skinny Harley, I know why Mona married him, how it feels to be in love with that crazy boy. It's all there in the face in the photograph and the face in the flesh, forty years later—his hazel eyes looking up, humble and coy, masking some raw cry. To leave someone you love, who is killing you by degrees.

We bury it, but hairline fissures open, threatening to gape. These are not voids, they are presences staring back. Solomon, prescribing death as a test of loyalty.

Eddy's father got on the new motorcycle at the reuninon and rode out onto the highway and head-on into a semi-truck and died.

I know it is too much for one story. We can't surround it either. In the garage he showed me how to start the new Honda motorcycle he'd bought for me. "Watch out for this little thing—gas tank switch ON. That's what got Harry. His tank was full, but his switch was off. He pulled out on the gas left in the engine, then lost power, right as that truck came over the hill." I had to take it, and then I had to get rid of it.

Can revisions permit former contexts to need no homage? His need was insatiable. My loss was his gain. Bound by romanticism and infection, like lovers—same anger at not being known, same determination to remain secret. Same stabs of remorse when this denial hits its mark. Named Eddy Ray after Sugar Ray. His loss was my gain. My gain is relived in sorrow every hour.

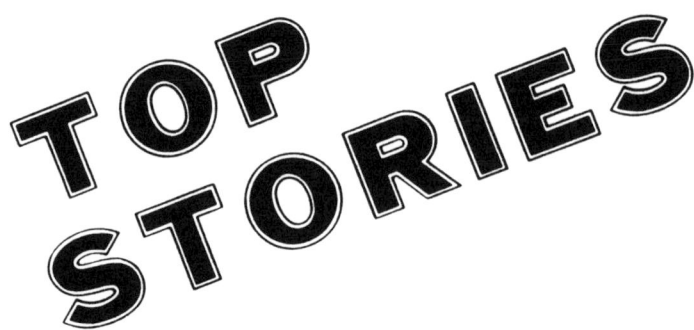

A PROSE PERIODICAL

#1 Donna Wyszomierski
#2 Laurie Anderson
#3 Pati Hill
#4 Suzanne Johnson
#5 Linda Neaman
#6 Gail Vachon
#7 Jenny Holzer/Peter Nadin
#8 Judith Doyle
#9 Kathy Acker
#10 Lynne Tillman/Jane Dickson
#11 Kirsten Thorup
#12 Janet Stein
#13 Anne Turyn
#14 Lee Eiferman
#15 Constance DeJong
#16 Ursule Molinaro
#17 Romaine Perin
#18 Donna Wyszomierski
#19-20 Cookie Mueller
#21 Ascher/Straus
#22 Susan Daitch
#23-24 Five, An Anthology
#25-26 Tourist Attractions, An Anthology

Available from:
TOP STORIES
228 Seventh Avenue
New York NY 10011

ISBN 0-917061-27-6

TOP STORIES #28 $3.00

WAR
COMICS

LISA BLOOMFIELD

WAR COMICS

LISA BLOOMFIELD

TOP STORIES #28
1989

Copyright © 1989 by Lisa Bloomfield

This publication was made possible in part with public funds from the National Endowment for the Arts and the New York State Council on the Arts.

ISBN 0-917061-28-4 (Top Stories # 28)

A portion of the War Comics series appeared in Impulse Magazine, Volume 13, Number 4, 1987 (Toronto, Canada).

All texts within this issue are fictional. Any similarity to real-life occurances or individuals is coincidental. Motivation Series: originals in color.

TOP STORIES, 228 Seventh Avenue, New York, NY 10011

PART ONE

WAR COMICS I-VI

PART TWO

MOTIVATION

WAR COMICS

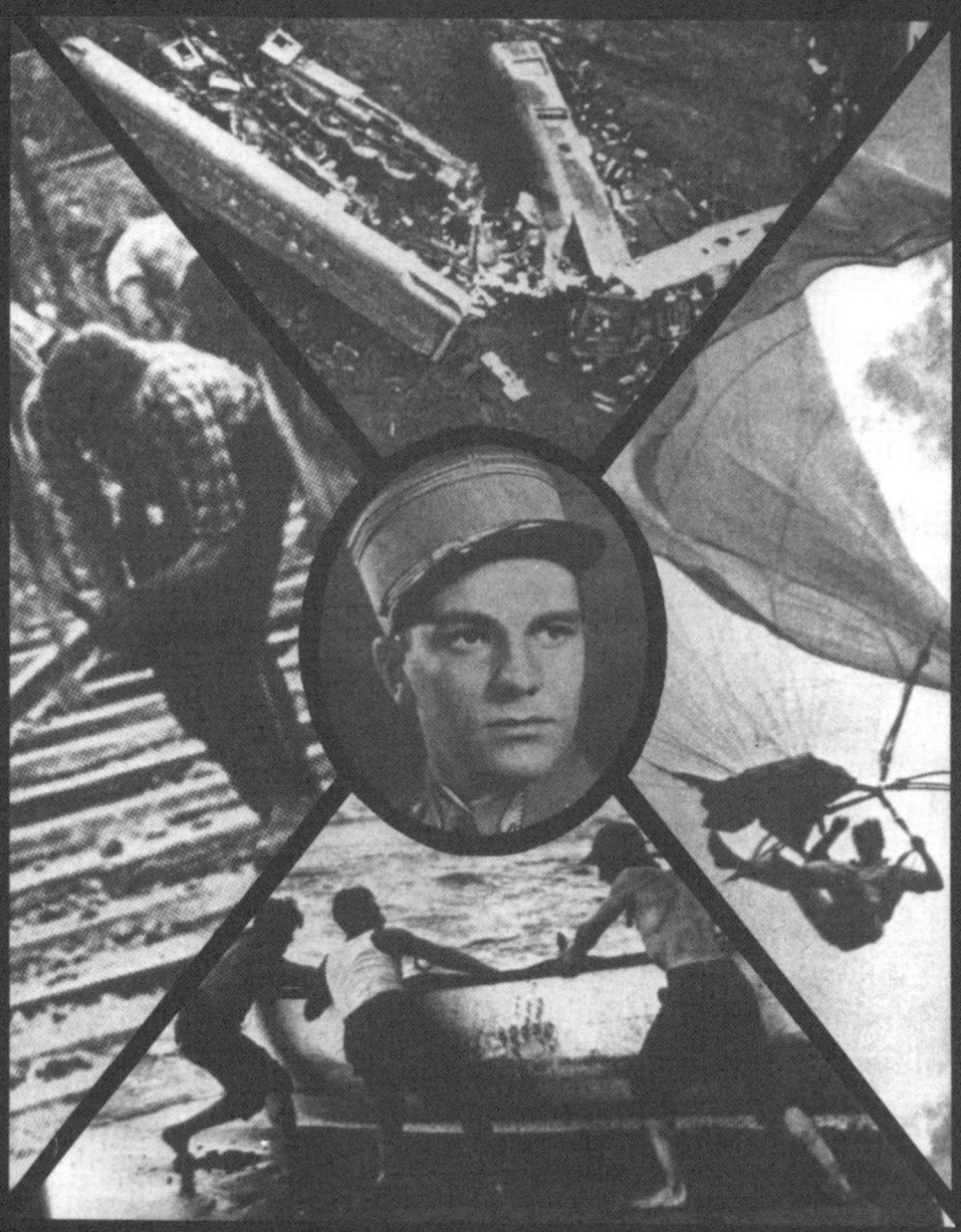

All the well-known episodes of youthful heroism that propelled him toward power...

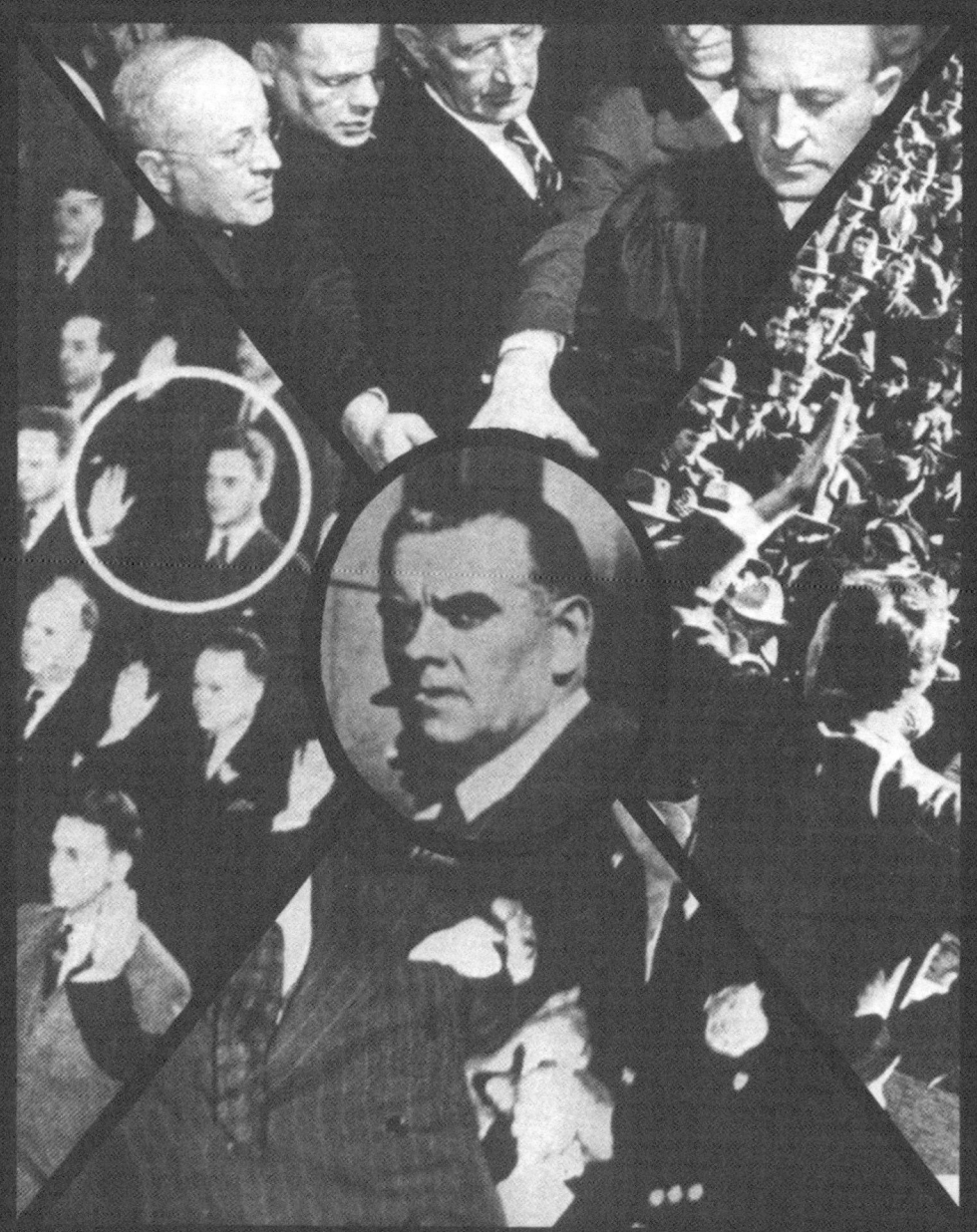
were revealed after the investiture to be false.

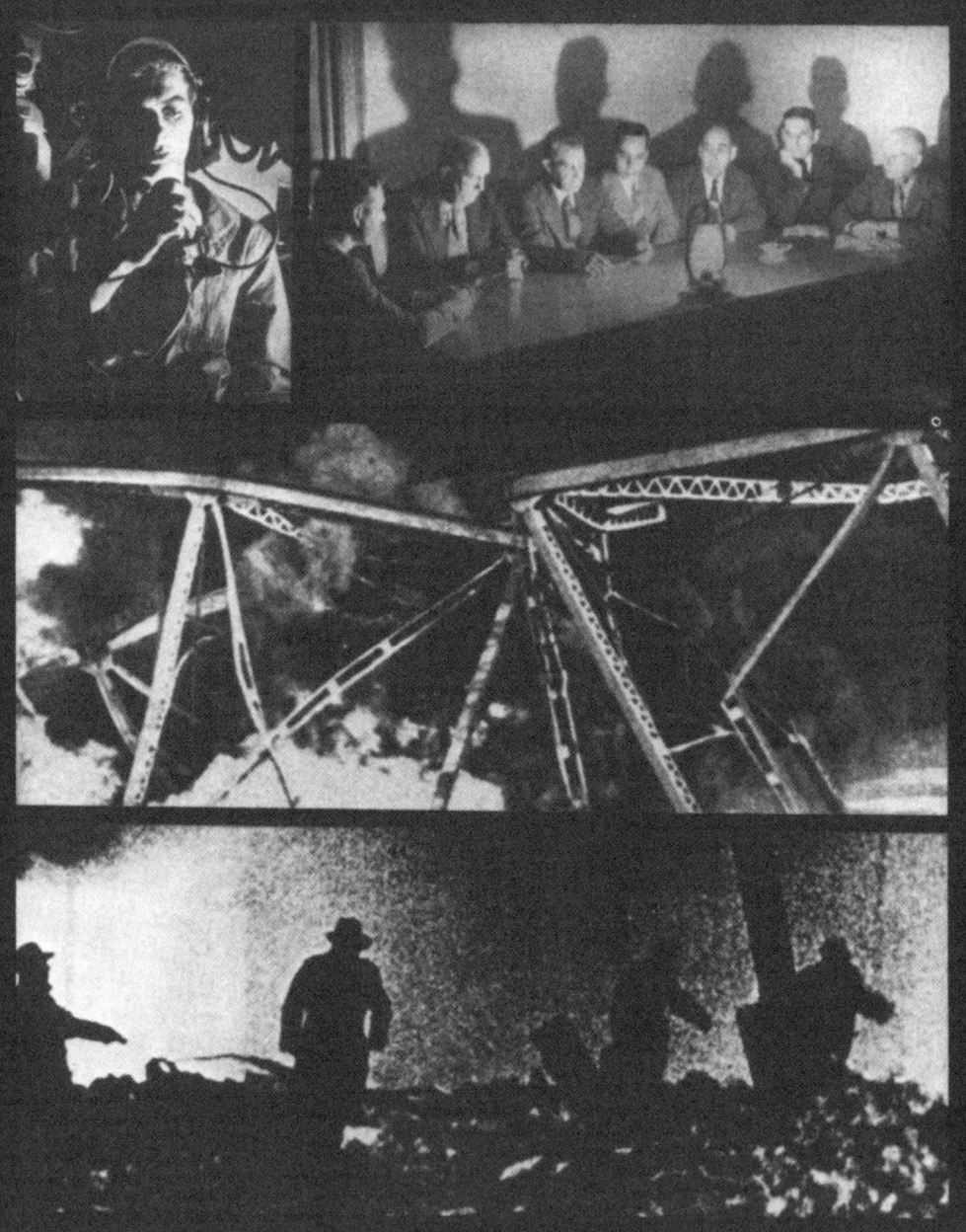

He listens through cardboard-thin walls, aware of his capacity for cowardice.

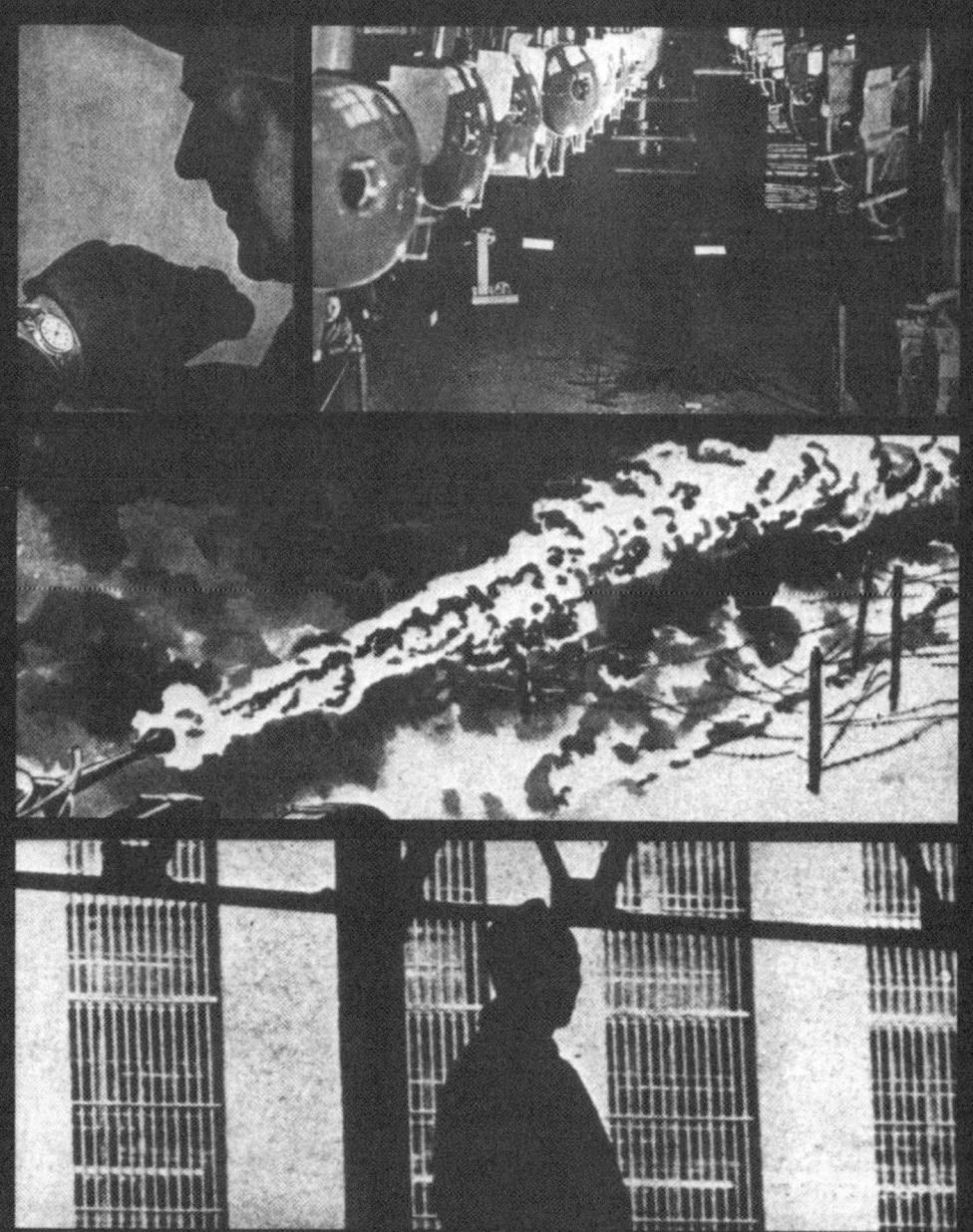

But to penetrate their defenses would be easy.

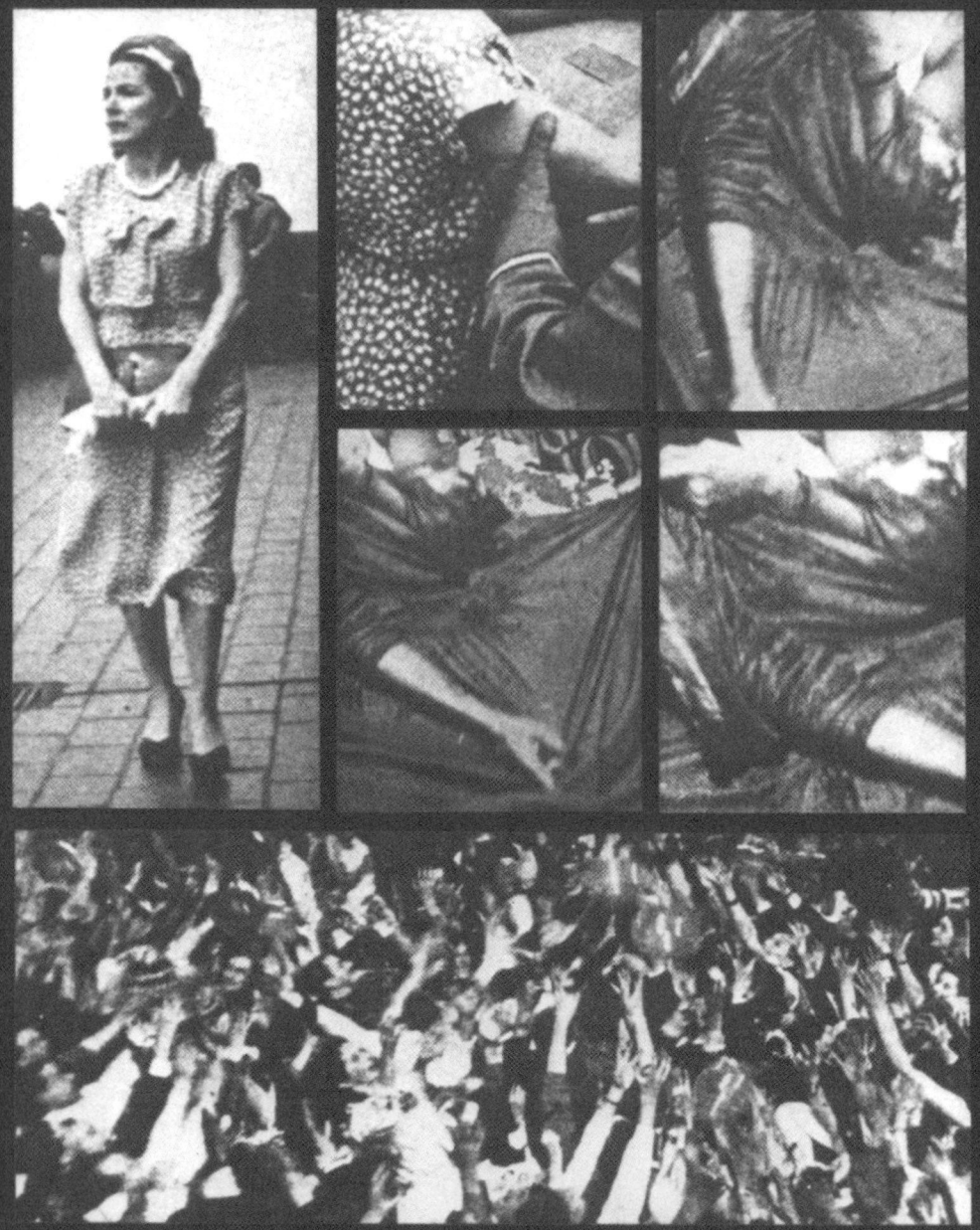
They spoke about the fear of suffocation.

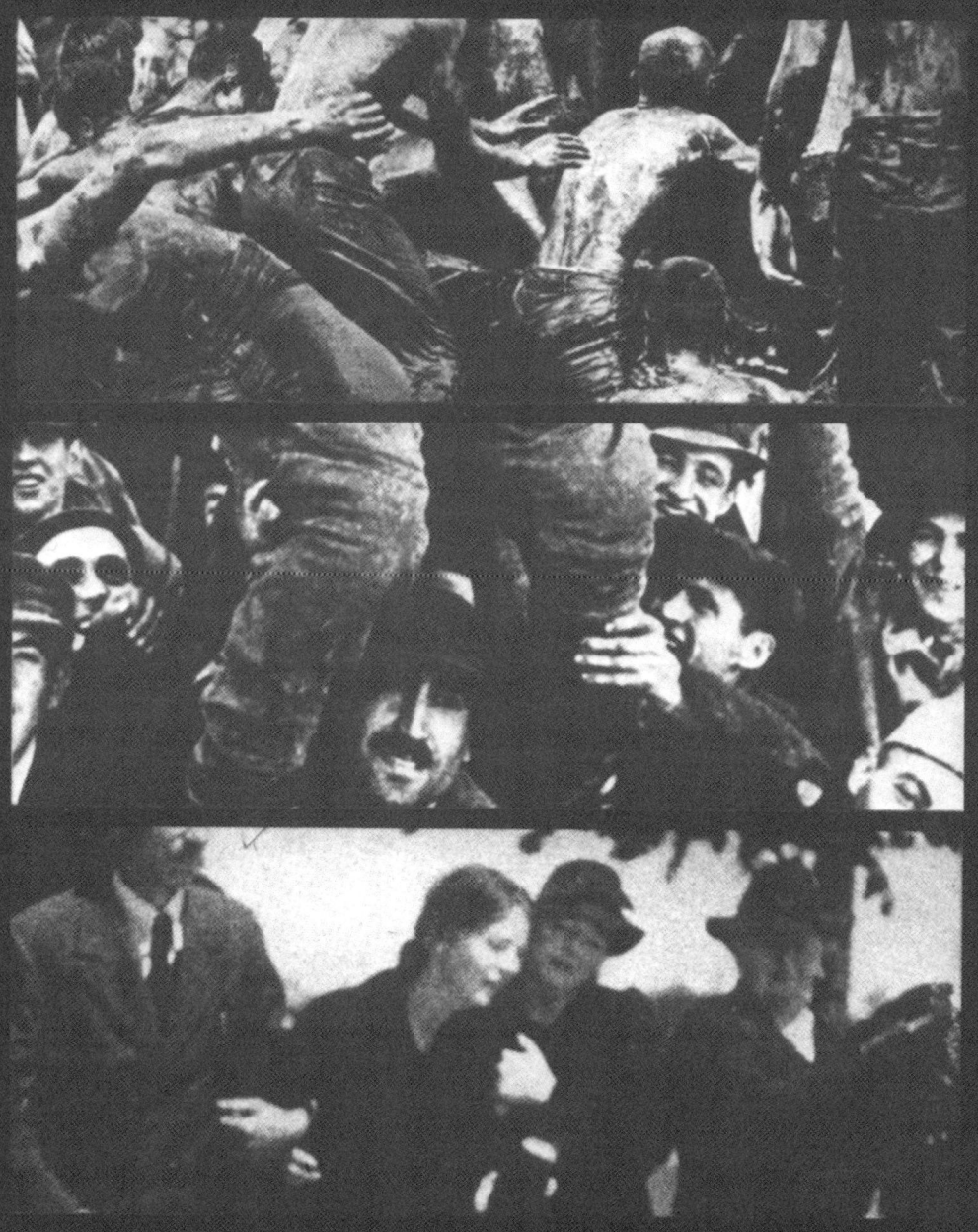

There was nothing to do but comply.

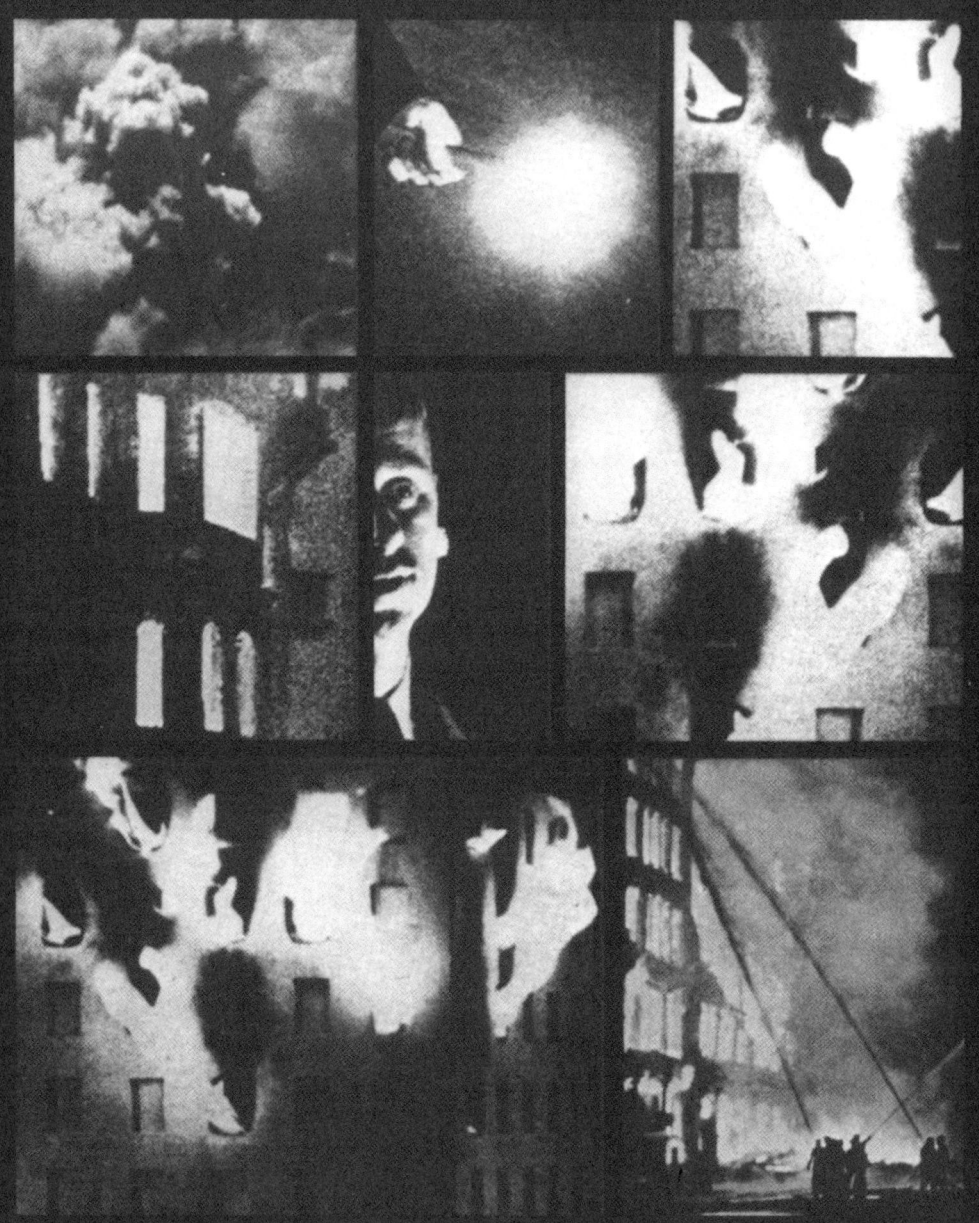

Rage had clouded his reason before.

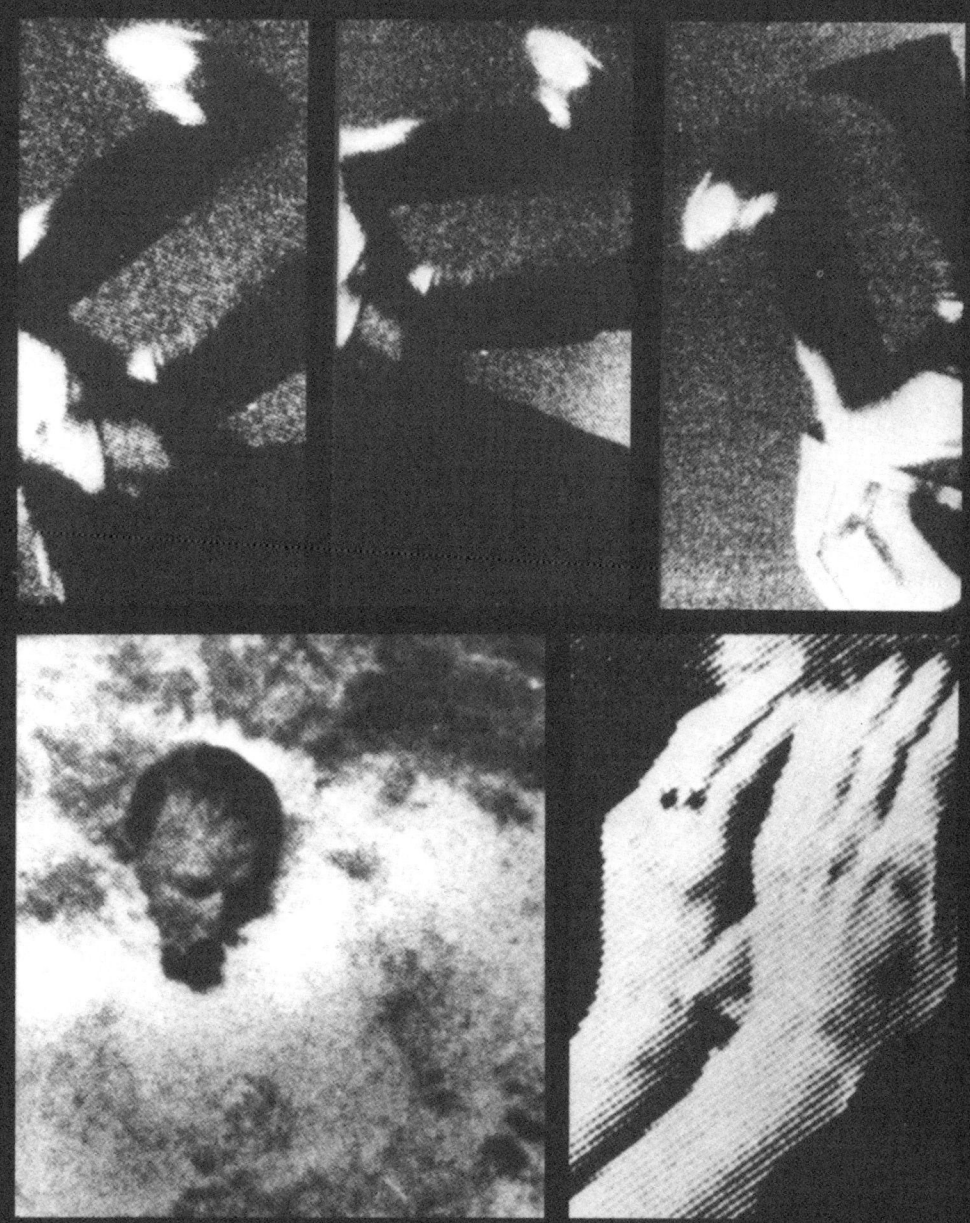
He has denied his weakness - repressed his doubts.

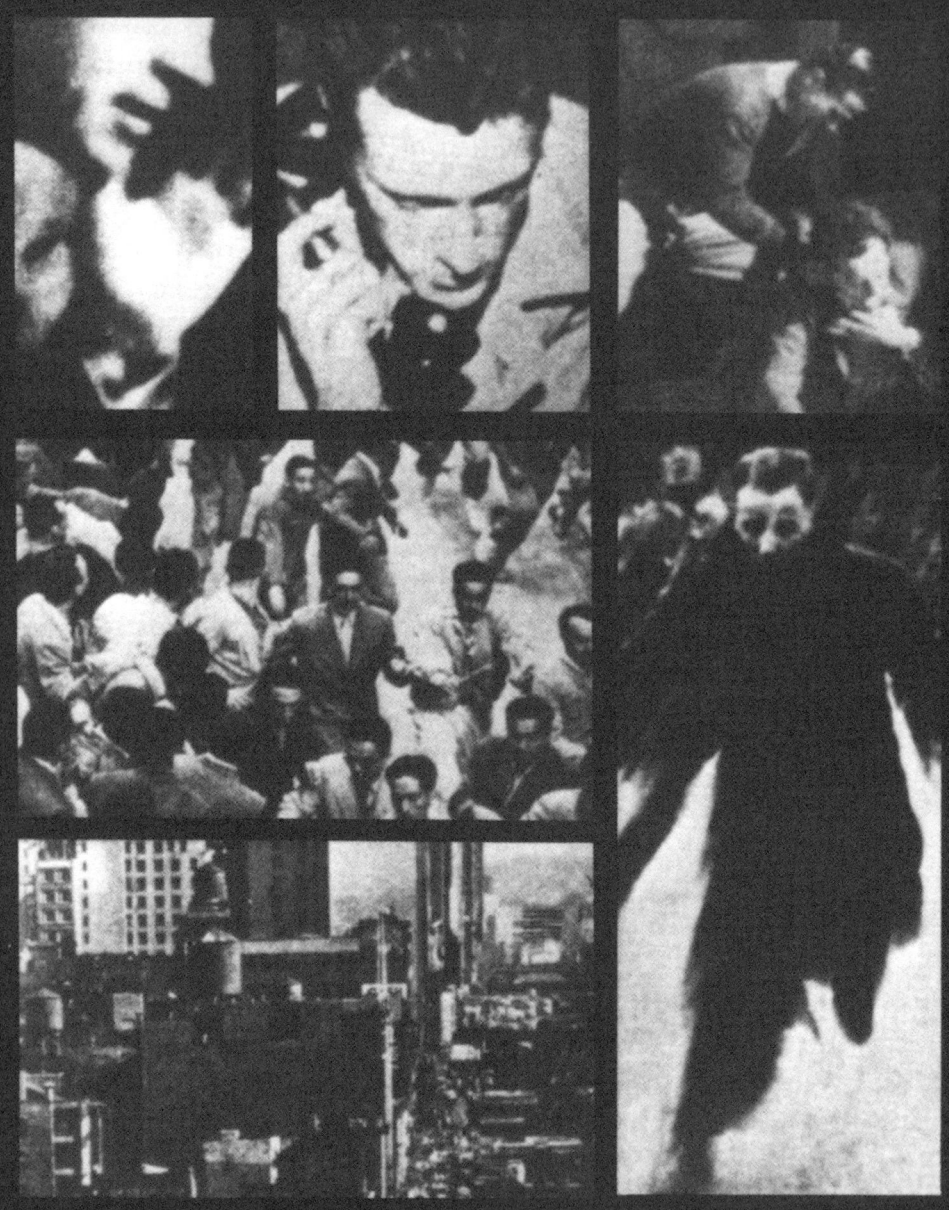

The possibilities for escape were few.

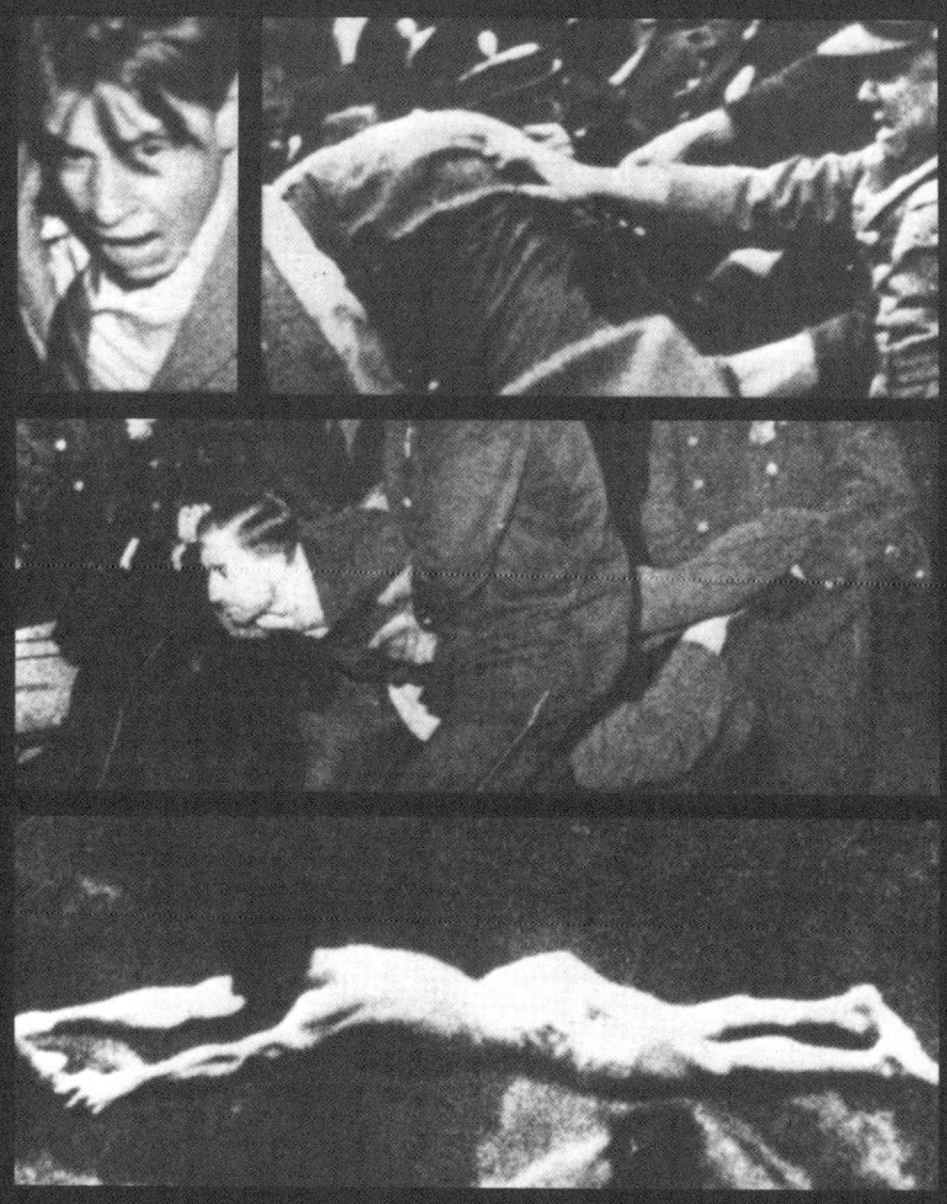

Capture. He felt like he was swallowing fire.

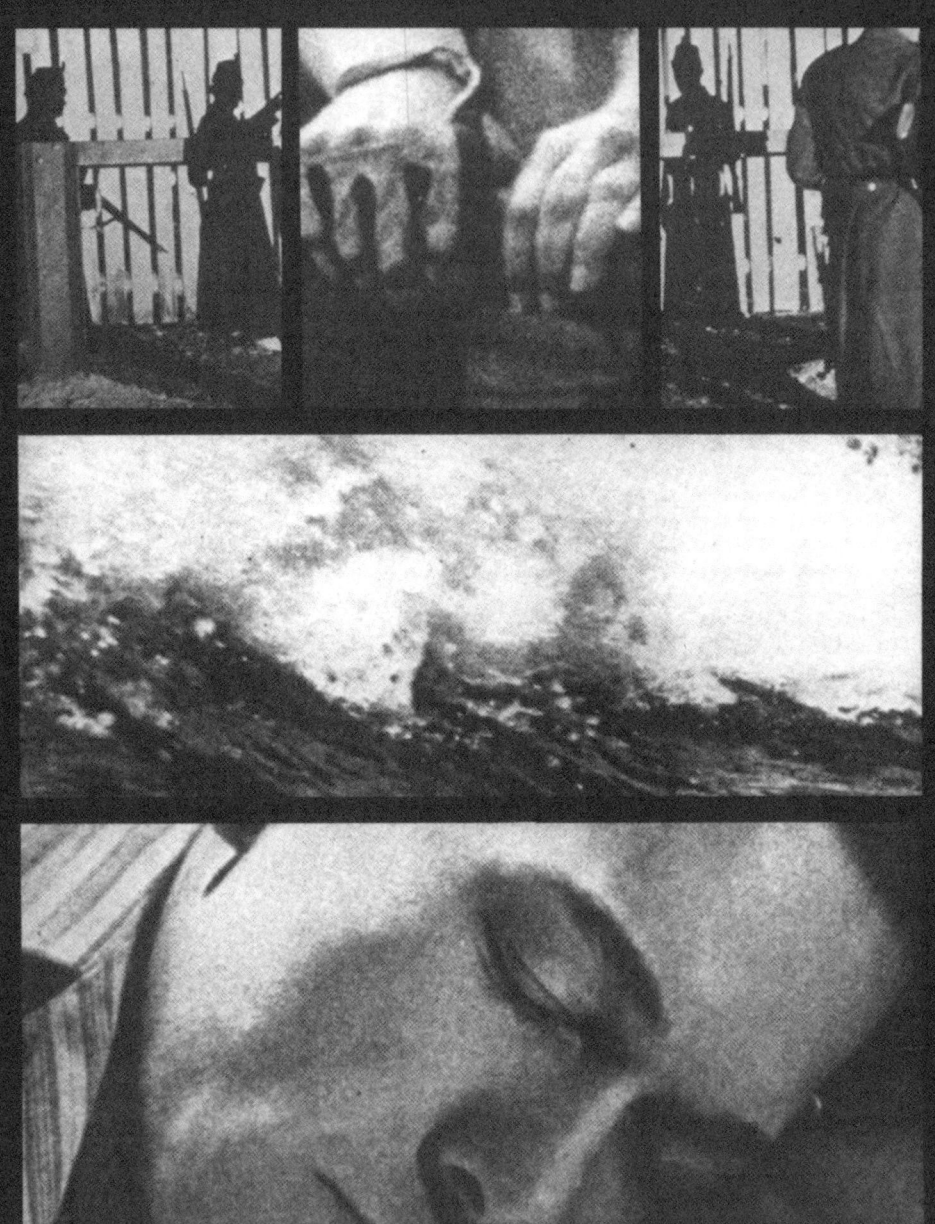

In moments he will disappear from his world without a trace...

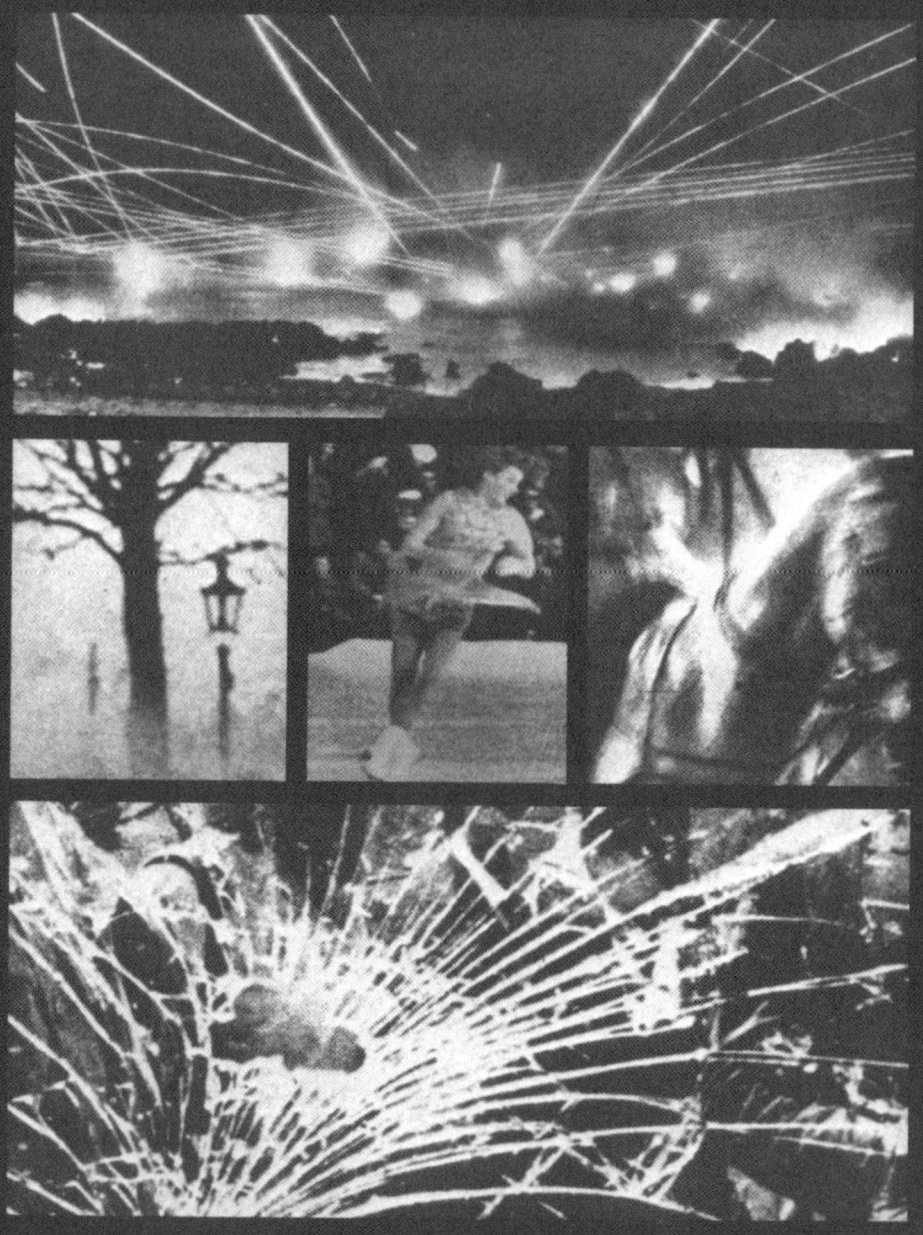

as others have done before him.

MOTIVATION

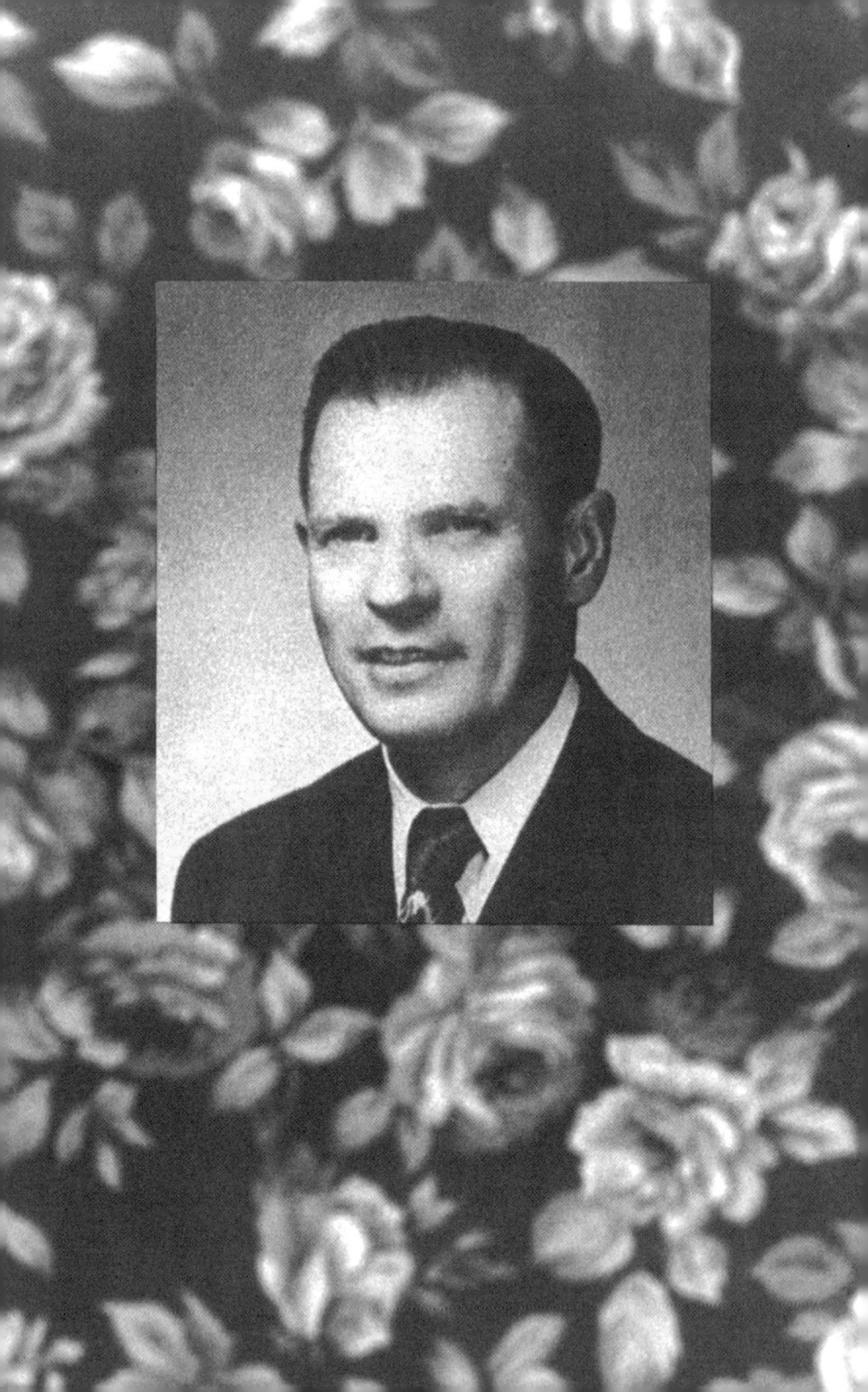

A traveling salesman spent years motoring around his territory with display cases full of quality products, but never achieved much success. One day he picked up a hitchhiker and ended up telling his passenger his life story. As the salesman described the difficulties and failures of his business, the hitchhiker couldn't help but think to himself that here was a good opportunity to turn his luck around. Later, as they sat eating lunch in a coffee shop, the hitchhiker said he had to go to the washroom, but instead slipped outside and drove off in the salesman's car. From then on the hitchhiker, using the salesman's name and products, worked hard, and soon turned the business into the basis of a nationally successful chain.

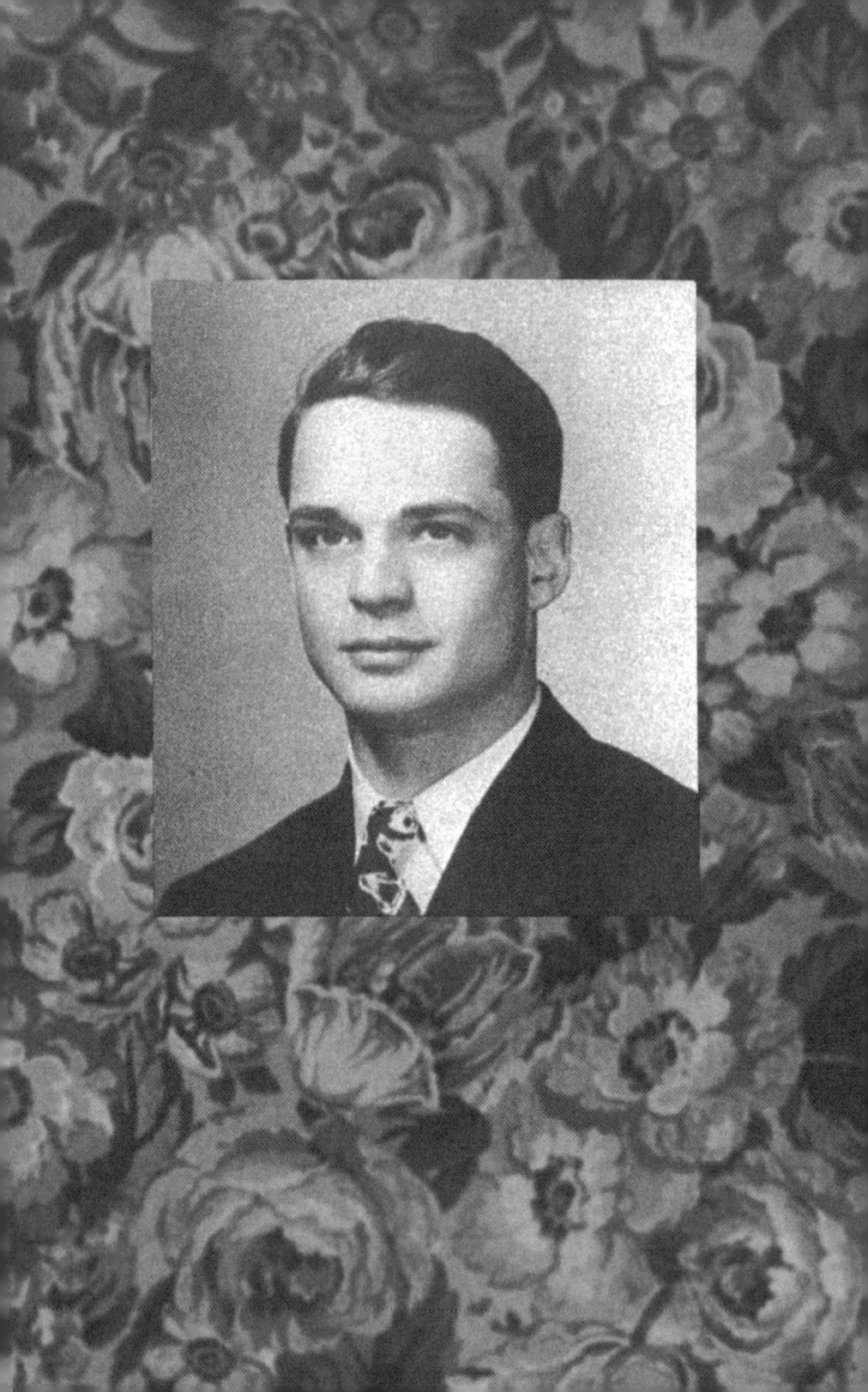

Joseph grew up in a heavily policed society. From an early age he trained himself as an athlete, and in time became known for his swimming abilities; yet each time a government official draped a new medal around his neck, he could think only of escape. One night he made his way to the edge of the river that separated his country from another. Wearing only one of his golden swimming medals, he plunged in. The current was strong and cold. Finally, on the opposite bank, he was met by a pair of soldiers, who angrily ordered him to go back where he had come from. But Joseph ripped the medal from his neck, presented it to the soldiers, and they let him go. In time he became a wealthy and influential leader in his adopted land.

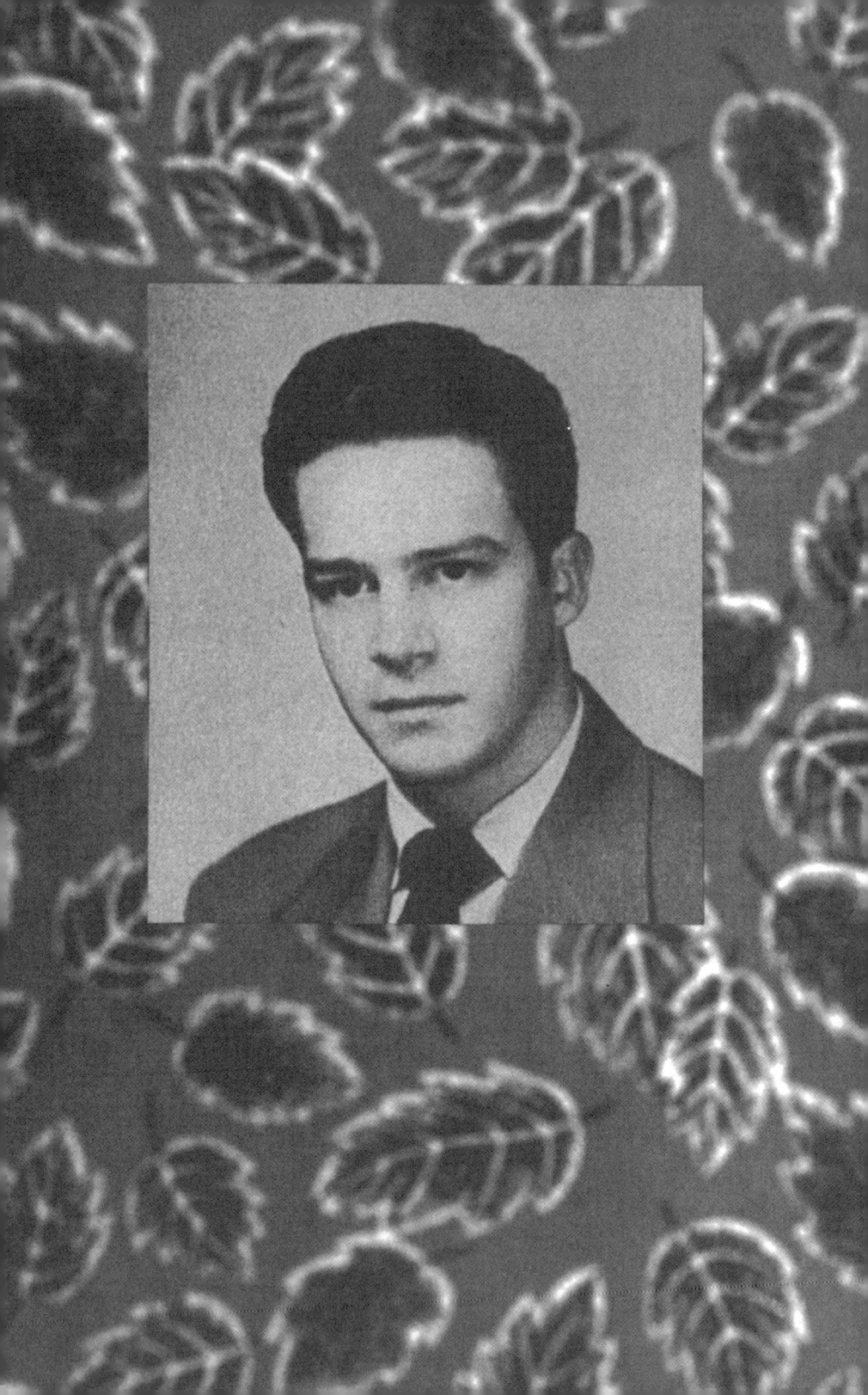

Tom fell asleep one morning at his machine and fell over the railing onto the furnace platform. His coworkers reached him before the conveyor belts could drag him into the central inferno, but not before both his legs were severely burned. During the long convalescence, Tom learned of the nation's emergency demand for higher productivity. Defying doctors and friends, he returned to his machine and operated it at record speed, despite his condition. The tiring spirits of other workers responded to this example, and the result was an increase in output for the whole factory. Soon the news of Tom's sacrifice spread everywhere, and productivity doubled.

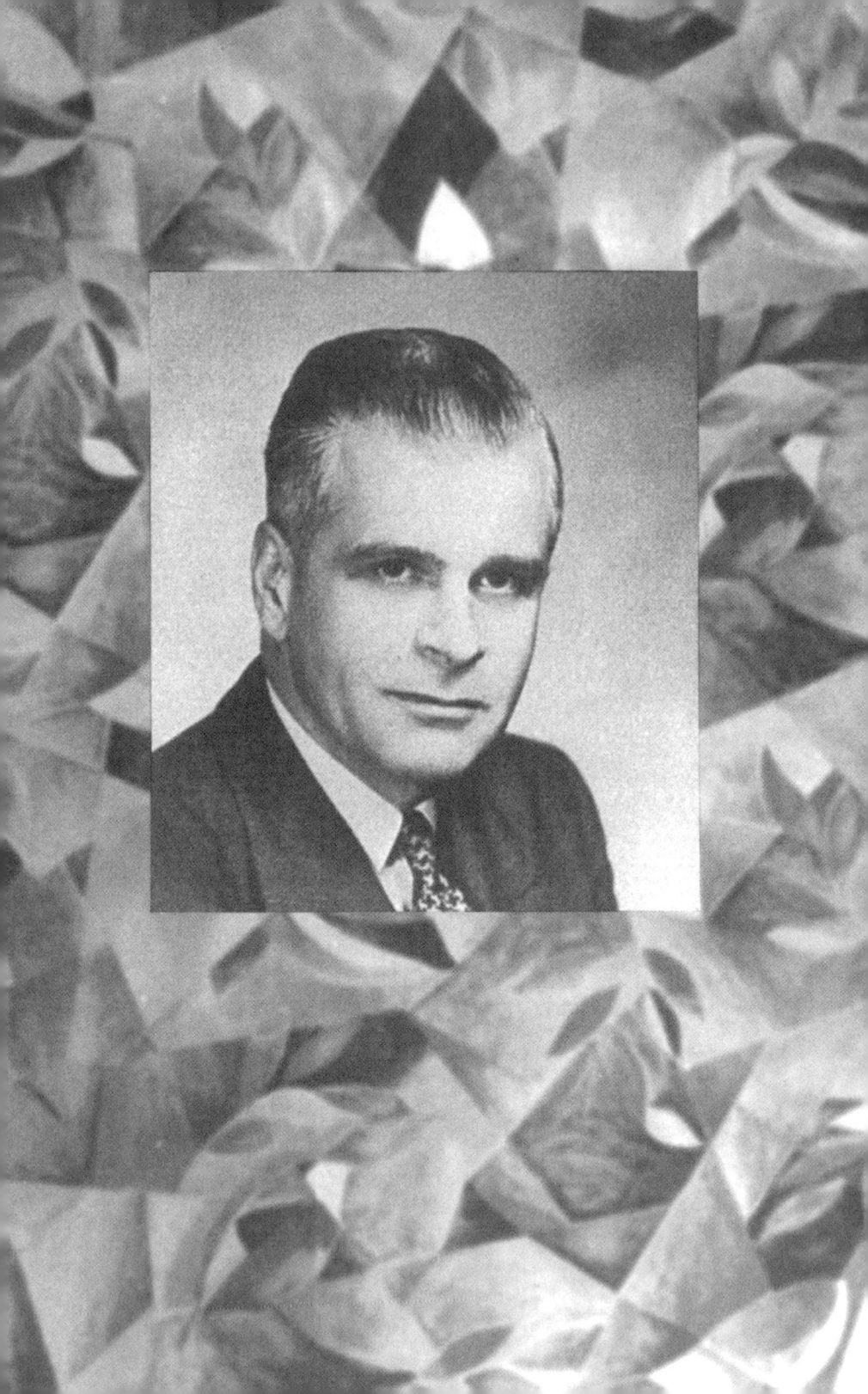

A penniless young man joined a small circus company. Though short in experience, within a few years he had become one of the regularly performing clowns. One morning, when the tent was going up, there was an accident with the drop hammer, and an elderly roustabout was injured. Cradled in the young clown's arms, the man whispered the secret of some hidden bonds and certificates, and died. Within weeks the clown was extravagantly rich. Soon he negotiated a controlling interest in the circus, billed himself as the premiere clown, and reworked the big top show around his own routine. In later years, however, he hung up his clown costume, and used his talents to transform the once tiny company into one of the country's largest and most profitable novelty concerns.

TOP STORIES

A PROSE PERIODICAL

#1 Donna Wyszomierski
#2 Laurie Anderson
#3 Pati Hill
#4 Suzanne Johnson
#5 Linda Neaman
#6 Gail Vachon
#7 Jenny Holzer/Peter Nadin
#8 Judith Doyle
#9 Kathy Acker
#10 Lynne Tillman/Jane Dickson
#11 Kirsten Thorup
#12 Janet Stein
#13 Anne Turyn
#14 Lee Eiferman
#15 Constance DeJong
#16 Ursule Molinaro
#17 Romaine Perin
#18 Donna Wyszomierski
#19-20 Cookie Mueller
#21 Ascher/Straus
#22 Susan Daitch
#23-24 Five, An Anthology
#25-26 Tourist Attractions, An Anthology
#27 Lou Robinson

Available from:
TOP STORIES
228 Seventh Avenue
New York NY 10011

ISBN 0-917061-28-4

TOP STORIES #29 $4.00

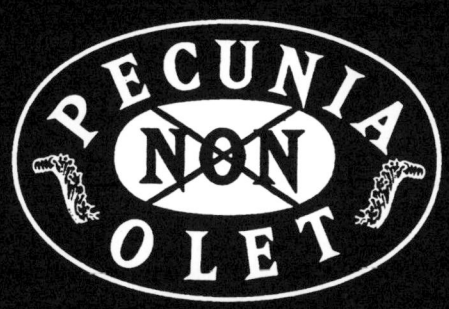

MARY KELLY

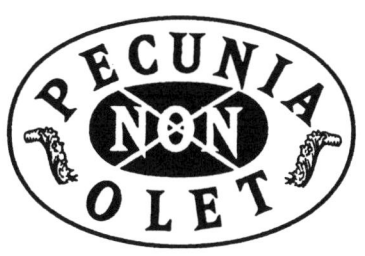

MARY KELLY

TOP STORIES #29
1990

Copyright © 1990 by Mary Kelly

This publication was made possible in part with public funds from the National Endowment for the Arts and the New York State Council on the Arts.

ISBN 0-917061-29-2 (Top Stories #29)

This text originally appeared as part of a three-dimensional installation consisting of 20 units, each 16" × 6.5" × 11.5" silkscreen on galvanized steel, at Postmasters Gallery, New York City, in May 1989.

TOP STORIES, 228 Seventh Avenue, New York NY 10011

CONTENTS

mater 3
conju 15
soror 27
filia 39

m

A total appeared in digital red, and the voice next to it issued an ultimatum. Cash or charge? She opened her checkbook, leafing quickly past the tried-to-cut-down-no-use panic of the balances and onto the serene stupidity of those blank pages, tenderly illustrated, promising everything. The sixteenth day of the tenth month of a very bad year, she began, spoiling the future of a perfect seascape. One hundred ten and how-could-they-eat-so-much eighty-eight, she wrote reluctantly over the pale seagulls that, frightened by the calamitous motion of her pen, flew away to the safety of the bank's logo in the left hand corner. She signed her name at the vanishing point of that replete horizon, but without conviction. Things must change, she thought. The children were materialistic, wanted everything—a boat, a car; they watched too much TV. She filled the plastic carrier-bags and speculated on the savings she would make by using them to line the trash bin. Being thrifty, she felt more optimistic. Her receipt became a confirmation of her wisdom; its purple abbreviations a miracle—seven days, twenty-one meals and an hour of agonized decision making digested and spewed out in two postmodern seconds by a diligent computer. More than that, there was the thrill of walking out with all that food, and then, her modicum of ecstasy—she'd make them something wonderful to eat.

a

WHAT'S THE FASTEST WAY TO MAKE A MILLION?

Invent something....something useful like inflatable soles for orthopedic shoes, or a soundproof tent to cover the TV <u>and</u> the kids. Maybe you should target a specific group ... that's it, essence of Irish stew, made in Dublin and exported to New Jersey. Say, what about a white trash restaurant ... you could serve opossum ... no? Okay, something for the masses then ... a square football?

t

Nine o'clock. The restaurant was full, but they were seated promptly. Things had changed. He was successful. She enjoyed it. Life was good. That thought granted her a smile. Another took it back abruptly. She remembered; remembered when they had no money and four small children to sustain, to manage in this dangerous and expensive city. At a table near them someone tried to calm a child of two or three, she could not be sure, so long since then, could not recall just what distinguishes each stage. She watched, not able to imagine how she did it—cook, clean, stevedore her precious cargo to the school steps everyday. Her <u>own</u> work too, not that she did it badly, simply that she had not done it, had postponed her life till later. Later, being now when they were grown up and she exhausted. Still, all were fine except for one, who was so troubled, so defiant. Why? "Three out of four, not bad," their father joked and ordered fish. "No salt or butter," she reminded him. "I still need you, see?" he said. She ordered kale and fennel, lightly steamed. No condiments. No consolation.

e

77 PORSCHE 930 slantnose conv, all steel 1983/3.0 motor, new int, Epsilon whls, Pirellis, Kenwood CD, Xlnt cond.

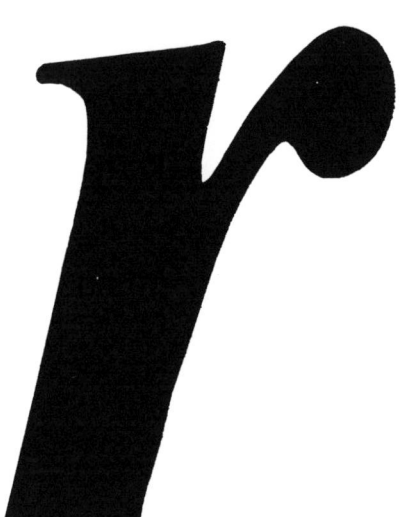

She just wanted them to be happy.

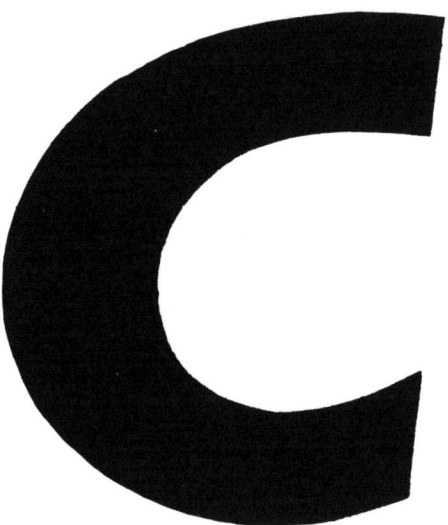

He was gone. Now, everything would be her way. First, the newspapers—fossilizing in her precious cupboard space. She'd throw them out. Then, the receipts, itineraries, tickets, lists—a little mound of crumpled pasts that grew, insatiable and fungus-like around her telephone, devouring two volumes of the Shorter Oxford Dictionary and a Franklin Spelling Ace. She'd put an end to that. Finally, but most emphatically, she plotted to clean the bathroom, to remove the sallow wreath encrusted on the toilet bowl, the gilding spray inside the seat, outside the tank too for that matter and, when she looked more closely, on the wall behind it all the way up to the light switch. She wondered what evolutionary lapse had shaped such an improbable, undignified anatomy and felt annoyed. She was alone. At last, she could open all the windows without arbitration and embrace the cold, emancipated air. She was surrounded by nothing, nothing but an arc of abstinent light and the smell of palest blue. The house effused a canny silence and the bathroom was so clean, <u>so</u> clean.

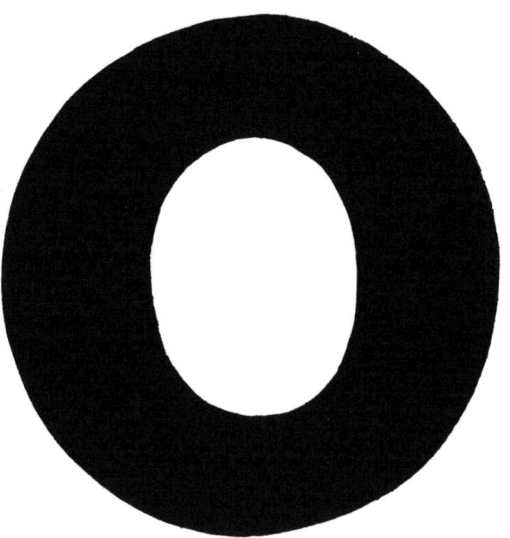

WHAT'S THE FASTEST WAY TO MAKE A MILLION?

Real estate, of course. Buy a small building, preferably in an up-and-coming neighborhood, convert it into apartments and use the rent income to pay the mortgage. Then, with the first building as equity, buy a second, convert, rent, buy again and so on ... simple. Well, except for the fact that you'd have to save or borrow enough money for the initial investment, umm ....

n

Three gables and a country porch just visible beyond a cast-iron gate. It could be perfect. She imagined tidy evergreens and red azaleas against the brick facade. Instead, she found a thicket of dense bramble, a few wild poppies and an insipid cupid pissing in a seashell. That would have to go. She sealed its fate and carried on. A double-door, stained glass, she turned the key. It could be perfect with a little work—replaster, paint, remove the carpet and the hideous drapes. She planned, envisioning a floor of polished oak, a tasteful rug, an open fire. Perhaps it's Christmas, yes, a tree, clear lights, of course, with berry clusters, cabbage roses, ribbons, raffia and lace. He'd chop the wood and she'd prepare the goose. Where was the kitchen, anyway? She found it, much too small, a north extension possibly; a walk-in pantry, but too dark. She'd add a skylight, then a granite counter, porcelain sink, refrigerator, freezer, Aga range. Above her would-be-herbery, a window. She looked out—a partial view obstructed by the freeway, but the lot was large enough to have a pool, gazebo even, perfect! Scalloped tiles, it could be perfect, well, it could be, could be perfect, if ...

MAGNIFICENT contemporary villa, prime in-town hilltop acre with unparalleled views of mountains, city lights & sunsets. 4850 sq. ft. hi-tech showcase for custom furniture/ investment art. 5 bdrm, 8 bath, 45 ft. living room, granite fireplace, bleached oak floor, deep carpets, skylights & etched glass. Gourmet kitchen, Gaggenau range, Subzero refrigerator, dual-zone heat & central vacuum. Tremendous pool & spa, 4 car garage, elaborate security.

u

Flowers on her birthday for chrissake, that's all she wanted.

S

South on 15, east on 8, exit offramp 94. Poterero, Campo, Jacumba, then nothing. The foothills ground down to a solemn flatness. She looked at the map. Turn left, six miles to the reservoir, windmill on the right, slowdown. There it was. Huge gawking hacienda surrounded by a metal fence, snarling barbed wire at the rim. It looked abused, once elegant veranda, ornate tiles now weathered, cracked. Imagining the Spanish with their clavichords and lacquered armoires, she portaged her stereo and her answering machine to the entrance with propriety. It belonged to her. Four thousand feet of open space for next to nothing. Unthinkable back in the city where she should be, but at last she could see several paintings at the same time and afford to have assistants. They would be grateful for work here. Although, she had been told to keep a gun, not to shoot, of course, to show them she meant business. Business, yes, she would do business. She would be discovered, wild woman painter of, well, forty-eight, no child prodigy, but ambitious nevertheless. She would entertain in her capacious monument—vaulted ceiling and expansive walls, high windows, ample frames, each painted white. The table laid, her ivory candles would disburse their shrewd titanium light, and guests, all wearing black, would chant "great space, great space."

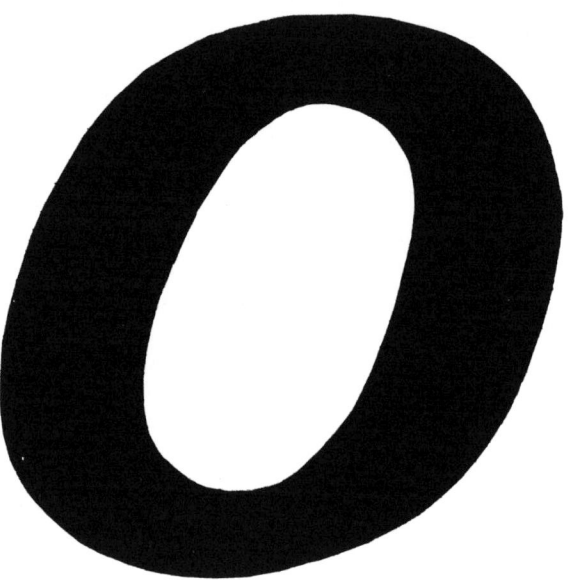

WHAT'S THE FASTEST WAY TO MAKE A MILLION?

Crime, yeah, that's the only way. Should be stylish though, let's see ... you could make a perfect replica of a night-time deposit box, graft it carefully onto the bank's facade and then remove it several hours later with substantial contents. Beautiful, what d'ya think?

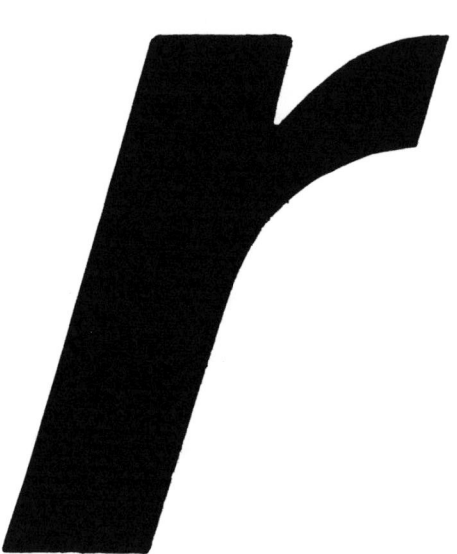

Someday, when she was older, she would leave the city. Leave the dirt, fumes, noise, etcetera, and move to the country. There, she would live simply, grow her own alfalfa, zucchini, tomatoes, and so forth, and savor the last morsels of unpolluted air before they escaped through the terrible hole. Meanwhile, she resolved to invest her savings in a plot of land, upstate—small lake, tall pines, rolling hills, and so on. She could not afford to build a house, but at least she could go there on weekends with a tent, a picnic basket, and a friend—ideally, an architect—and plan. Where to begin— perhaps a swimming pool and two cabanas, the rest could come later, later when she was ready to leave the city, when she was older, and <u>if</u> she met the right person. Until then, she decided to put on her leather jacket, chain bracelets, lace anklets and the like, and live complexly a little longer.

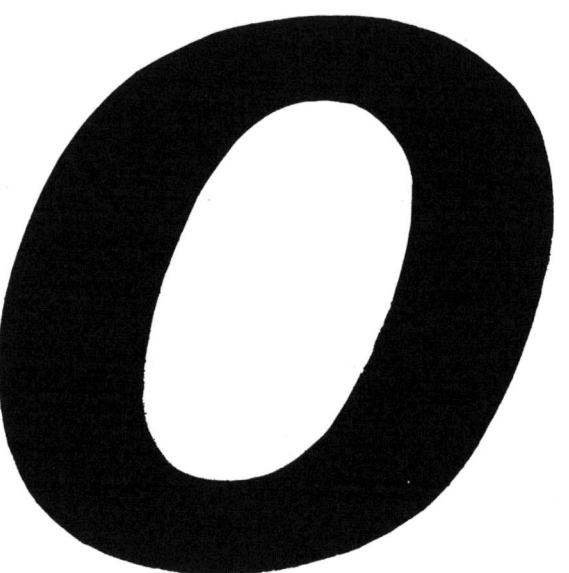

ATHLETIC Attractive 48 yr old prof. woman, terrific sense of humor. Looking for honest, healthy, successful, WF, sincere relationship, age 40-60, no smoking, no losers, no tattoos.

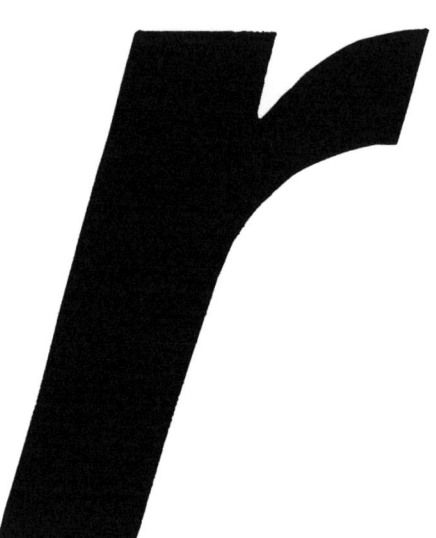

She wanted her <u>and</u> she wanted all of her clothes.

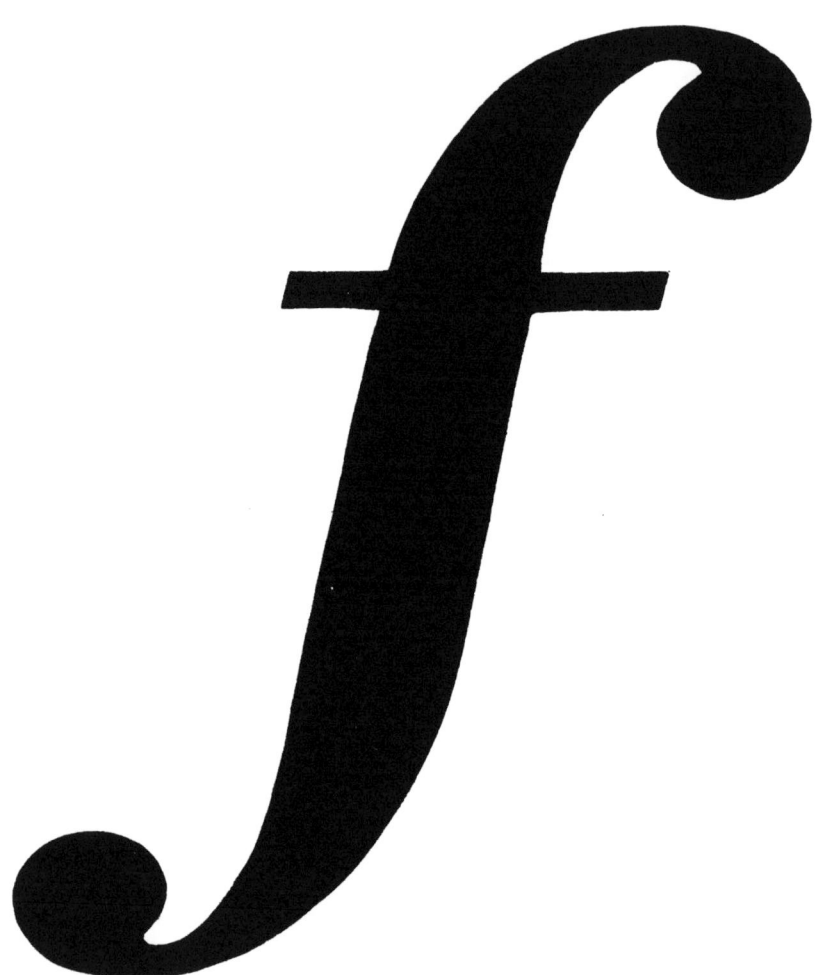

Five small but clear diamonds set in a plain gold mounting. Her mother's wedding ring. She must have been eighteen then when she married him, a plain man with strong arms and small, clear eyes. They lived in the same town all their lives. Her inheritance, she held it tightly, pressing the gold into the soft mounting of her palm, carving out an unthinkable absence. Her mother was gone, she could not say ... lump in the throat, hot tears, predictable throb, could not say ... she was losing control, there, in that public place, a woman of her age, her education, her demurity ... could not say "dead". She opened her hand and stared at the ring, five diamonds, her mother's small fingers mounted on the white of the hospital sheet, not plain or strong, but fine and slender, like her own. She hadn't noticed, had insisted on their difference. No nonsense, salt-of-the-earth, not like the ivory-tower daughter who had not noticed the elegant forehead, the cheekbones and the playful lips, mocking the nurse who asked, "Will this be a home death?" Yes, a homely death, plain, not costly, small and clear, mounted in strong gold. She slid the ring slowly over the end of her own slender finger, elegant nail, fine cheekbone, unbearable pain, over the playful lip of her knuckle, and it fit. Perhaps too tightly, but that way, she wouldn't lose it.

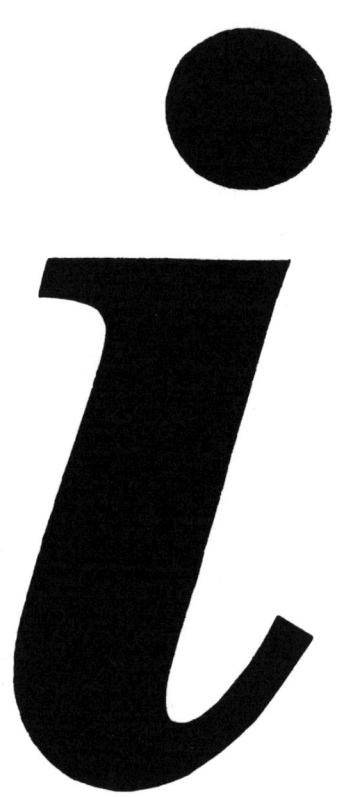

WHAT'S THE FASTEST WAY TO MAKE A MILLION?

Get someone to give you a million first.

Inconvenient, but no crisis, she could transfer the balance to her cash account. The last of her savings, still, no catastrophe, she proceeded—the forms, a pen, no problem, yet her hand denied it, shook visibly, nerve severed by a sharp conceit, "he doesn't love me." Such irrationality disturbed her. After all, she did not want him to take care of her. No, in fact, <u>he</u> needed her. That realization pressed down on the fragile posture of her independence and she felt it crush a few complacent bones. Why hadn't it occurred to her, and then, why should it, since her mother never mentioned money and her father told her simply: work and save. She had worked, but she hadn't saved. It was she and not her T-bonds that had reached maturity; no tenured job, no pension plan and now no savings, not even a pocket calculator to assess the exact nature of her deficit. No crisis, yet it had occurred to her, between two decimals, that this was the reason men had heart attacks—all those withdrawal slips and dependents clogging their arteries. Yes, insanity and suicide were luxuries reserved for pampered women. She, on the other hand, would not want to inconvenience anyone.

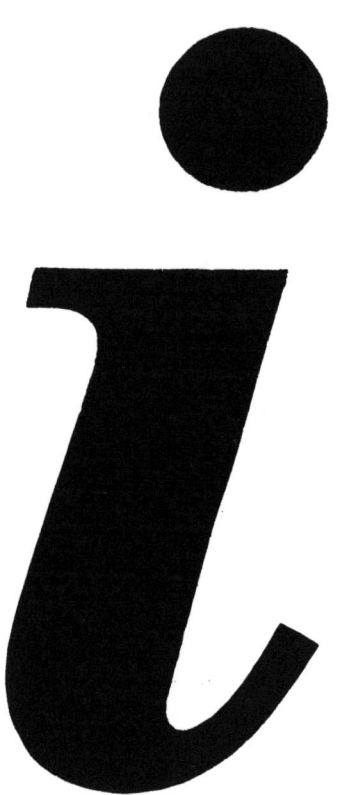

ANTIQUES, OBJETS D'ART offered immediately following Real Estate Auction to include Austrian antique sideboard (late 1800's), marble statues, mahogany drop front desk (G.W. repro), Cargas dining room set, paintings, Campodimonte china platters, vases, pedestals, gaming equipment, oriental rugs, imported Italian bedroom set, (National) brass cash register & silver cock.

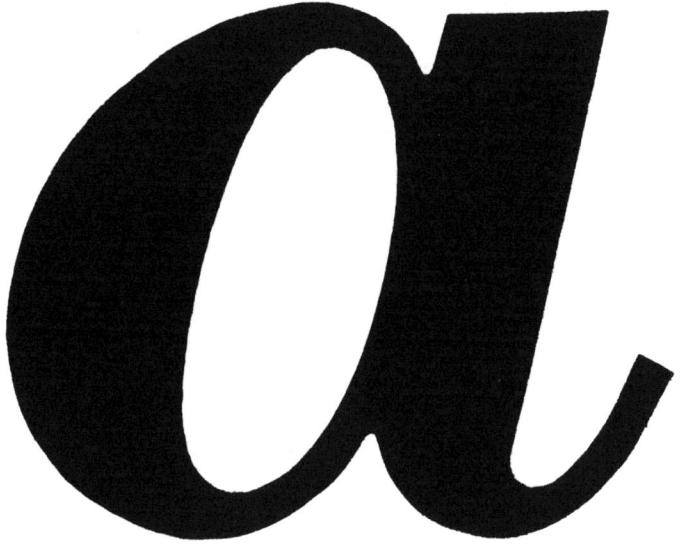

Someday, she wanted to write a book.

TOP STORIES

A PROSE PERIODICAL

#1 Donna Wyszomierski
#2 Laurie Anderson
#3 Pati Hill
#4 Suzanne Johnson
#5 Linda Neaman
#6 Gail Vachon
#7 Jenny Holzer/Peter Nadin
#8 Judith Doyle
#9 Kathy Acker
#10 Lynne Tillman/Jane Dickson
#11 Kirsten Thorup
#12 Janet Stein
#13 Anne Turyn
#14 Lee Eiferman
#15 Constance DeJong
#16 Ursule Molinaro
#17 Romaine Perin
#18 Donna Wyszomierski
#19-20 Cookie Mueller
#21 Ascher/Straus
#22 Susan Daitch
#23-24 Five, An Anthology
#25-26 Tourist Attractions, An Anthology
#27 Lou Robinson
#28 Lisa Bloomfield

Available from:
TOP STORIES
228 Seventh Avenue
New York NY 10011

ISBN 0-917061-29-2

Top Stories
© 2021 Anne Turyn

ISBN: 978-1-7365346-1-8

The rights to the work remain the sole property of the author. All rights reserved. No part of this publication may be reproduced, stored in retrieval systems, or transmitted in any form or by any means, electronic, mechanical, photocopying, recording, or otherwise, without prior permission from the copyright holder.

Lynne Tillman's story in Issue 25–26 appears as the opening chapter of Tillman's 1991 novel, *Motion Sickness*.

Top Stories was published in twenty-nine issues between 1978 and 1991 and edited by Anne Turyn. This volume collects issues seventeen through twenty-nine as they were originally published.

Editor: Anne Turyn
Managing Editor (2021): Hiji Nam
Managing Designer (2021): Rick Myers

Primary Information
155 Freeman Street, Ground Floor
Brooklyn, NY 11222
www.primaryinformation.org

Printed in Latvia by Jelgavas Tipogrāfija

Primary Information would like to thank Constance DeJong, Lia Gangitano, Randy Kennedy, Max Schumann, Matt Shuster, and Leah Whitman-Salkin.

Primary Information is a 501(c)(3) non-profit organization that receives generous support through grants from the Michael Asher Foundation, the Graham Foundation for Advanced Studies in the Fine Arts, the Greenwich Collection Ltd, the John W. and Clara C. Higgins Foundation, the Willem de Kooning Foundation, the Henry Luce Foundation, the National Endowment for the Arts, the New York City Department of Cultural Affairs in partnership with the City Council, the New York State Council on the Arts with the support of Governor Andrew Cuomo and the New York State Legislature, the Orbit Fund, the Stichting Egress Foundation, Teiger Foundation, The VIA Art Fund, The Jacques Louis Vidal Charitable Fund, The Andy Warhol Foundation for the Visual Arts, the Wilhelm Family Foundation, and individuals worldwide.

TOP STORIES

Volume 1

Primary Information

TOP STORIES $1.00

Too Good To Be Entirely True

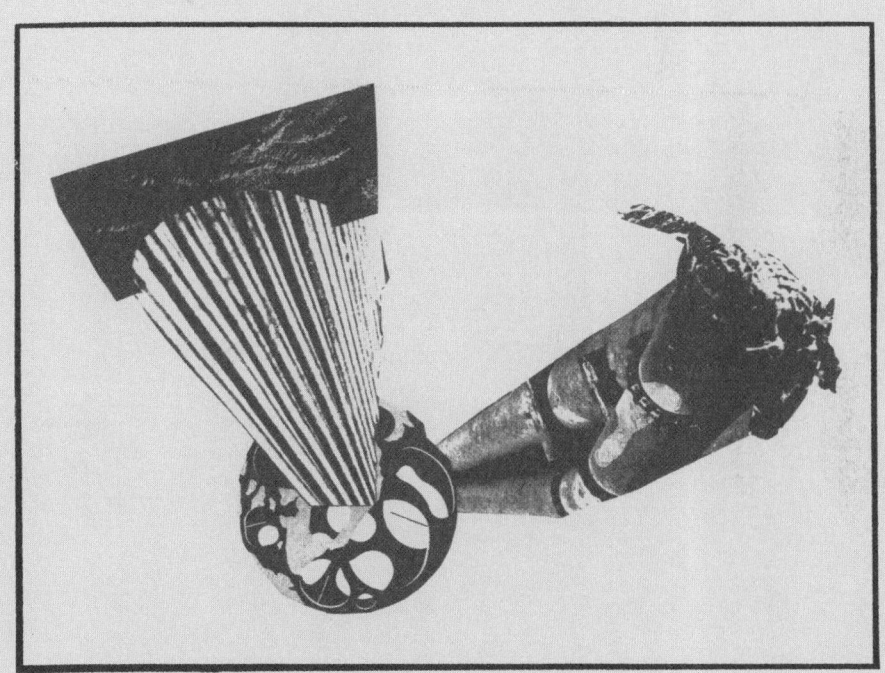

Donna Wyszomierski

TOP STORIES #1

Too Good To Be Entirely True

Donna Wyszomierski

© 1979 DONNA WYSZOMIERSKI

poor dean he's so innocent wife's nice too called about
insurance i don't mind if people call me at home lives
not too far three kids says its selfish not to have them
anyway i can't stand it had a political job before still
work in the elections volunteer at the hospital its
something i like to see my boyfriend after work don't
want a promotion why do we have to change i was so mad

garbage day not up to par lie down on the floor they
think you're crazy take the day off you're home alone
sister used to live there too old to stay by herself
supposed to have an operation but it wasn't convenient
think he'd be responsible second wife's as bad first one
killed in a crash don't know where the kids are school
teachers but they're eccentric

this has to be signed by the priest honey or you don't get the money for rent love you

only ones working christmas eve not children don't need
to be told not worth it except for the pay can't be
over thirty mother worked forty years nothing for it
didn't have a party don't want to work for your
father watches everything you do what if your girlfriend
comes nothing wrong talk on your coffee break fourteen
already has a boyfriend makes you look cheap other girls
feel left out higher intelligence do better later

that's the kind of girl i wish my boys would bring home
don't have to tell her knows when to keep quiet one of
my favorite people queen bee gets anything she wants
doesn't like me can tell when she talks looks disapproving
a lot don't know what to make of him tried to kiss me
after work wouldn't let him said i was too old oversexed
poor thing wife with a headache thought he had a steady
girl i said both of them the same night can't take it
any more got to get out and they say the women are dirty

TOP STORIES #1

Too Good To Be Entirely True

Donna Wyszomierski

© 1979 DONNA WYSZOMIERSKI

poor dean he's so innocent wife's nice too called about
insurance i don't mind if people call me at home lives
not too far three kids says its selfish not to have them
anyway i can't stand it had a political job before still
work in the elections volunteer at the hospital its
something i like to see my boyfriend after work don't
want a promotion why do we have to change i was so mad

garbage day not up to par lie down on the floor they think you're crazy take the day off you're home alone sister used to live there too old to stay by herself supposed to have an operation but it wasn't convenient think he'd be responsible second wife's as bad first one killed in a crash don't know where the kids are school teachers but they're eccentric

this has to be signed by the priest honey or you don't
get the money for rent love you

only ones working christmas eve not children don't need
to be told not worth it except for the pay can't be
over thirty mother worked forty years nothing for it
didn't have a party don't want to work for your
father watches everything you do what if your girlfriend
comes nothing wrong talk on your coffee break fourteen
already has a boyfriend makes you look cheap other girls
feel left out higher intelligence do better later

that's the kind of girl i wish my boys would bring home
don't have to tell her knows when to keep quiet one of
my favorite people queen bee gets anything she wants
doesn't like me can tell when she talks looks disapproving
a lot don't know what to make of him tried to kiss me
after work wouldn't let him said i was too old oversexed
poor thing wife with a headache thought he had a steady
girl i said both of them the same night can't take it
any more got to get out and they say the women are dirty

the nurses are wonderful i bring them candy half a pound
a day it goes fast but they like it the one doctor he's
a doll he says it'll be a miracle if she pulls through i
pray for her everyday i wonder what he sees in her this is
confidential she says she pays for her own dinners i gave him
back a ring because he couldn't dance that's terrible isn't
it he was a nice fellow too i'd rather see a man get ahead

says i'm a poor supervisor get things done fast won't
stick my neck out won't back you up doesn't care about
your family kids of his own thinks they're different
comes in to make phone calls no way to prove it mother
runs a chicken farm wife comes to the office hair just
like his a little heavy in the hips should wear dresses
look more dignified read it in the paper outlast him
he'll go somewhere else do the same thing no vacation
this year don't mind take off when i want son moving to
minnesota no one at home need time to fix the place up
like the overtime eleven something an hour and no one to
bother you

she's so thin i like her but she's always crying in
the bathroom says she can't help it her boyfriend
won't marry her she likes the fellows has a goofy
laugh but can't get along with people always has a
grievance can't dial the phone because of her nails
repeats things so you'll pay attention says she
couldn't go out saving her money to buy a house
wonder if she'll live by herself has a sister in
college they don't get along bought her a gumball
machine for christmas mother in the hospital didn't
want them to come says they shouldn't see her like
that father sells real estate has to sit on the toilet
all afternoon when people don't show strange interests
for a girl her age goes to OTB on her lunch hour knows
about the games but won't go to cleveland that's for the
ones who like to drink shouldn't run with a crowd like
that don't have the money such a difference in education

took her daughter to the doctor for the pill sixteen
do you think that's right my sister has a girl and
she never got married didn't need to i was married
twice good husbands both times always held a job
likes to sleep at the laundry no bread in the house
for lunch i said go out for spaghetti but he's
coming here instead

this is secret stuff high strung might fly off the handle
bought a black rose for her desk leaving town for the wake
such a shock second one in the last six months sisters
coming to clean her desk wouldn't go to a doctor tapping
her foot all last week anxious to go looked healthy but
there was something wrong

wonder if she knew about the nursing home could've
died of a broken heart isn't the song terrible lots of
people are short i think they mean about four eleven though

in the examining room she wouldn't be quiet i couldn't hear the doctor he was jumping up and down said he couldn't stand it gave her a shot a major tranquilizer i said i could ask her to leave she said i think i should go they'll be needing me downstairs

found out i had cancer had to make up my mind go along
with what they said or go away somewhere i wanted to
leave early told him he could come but i might want to
read on the bus didn't want him to see me like that i
like him but he drinks a lot and there's such a
difference in education

tired of talking so i got promoted have to feed my
family daughter has asthma hospital couldn't cure her
doesn't want to take the shots make her sick hair not
as shiny can't go out much tired at the end of the day
mother drives her around hard on a girl that age affects
her mentally brother in sports different shirt for every
team twenty-eight but you'd never know it dress code at
work keep the girl in pills no baby on the doorstep things
come to them that wait

if i won the lottery i'd start my own agency everything
based on logic all of a sudden things will click hate it
when people talk down to me i read a lot

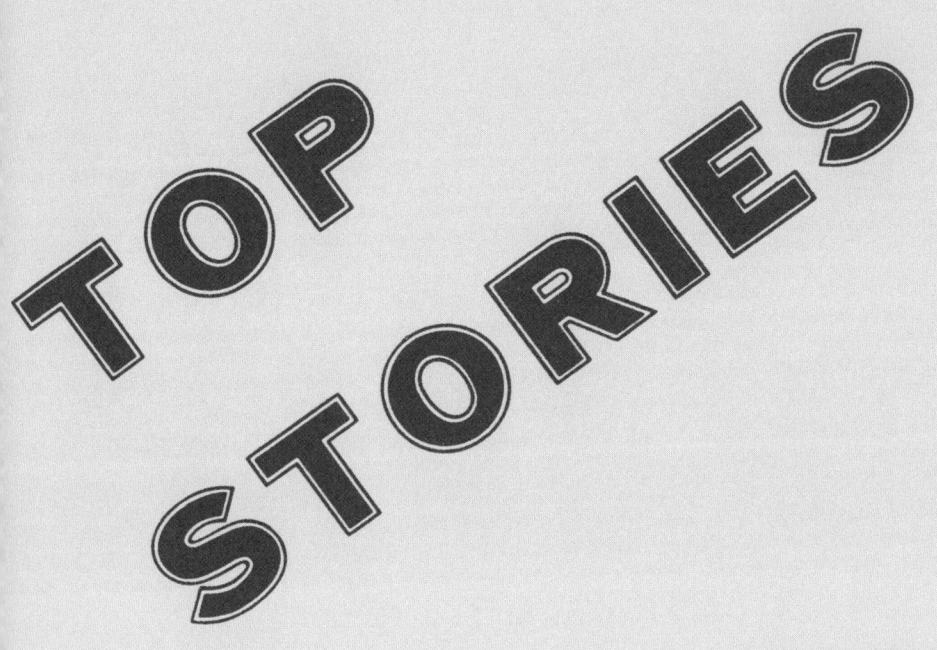

TOP STORIES of *Hard Press*
30 Essex Street
Buffalo, New York 14213

a prose periodical

TOP STORIES $1.00

WORDS IN REVERSE

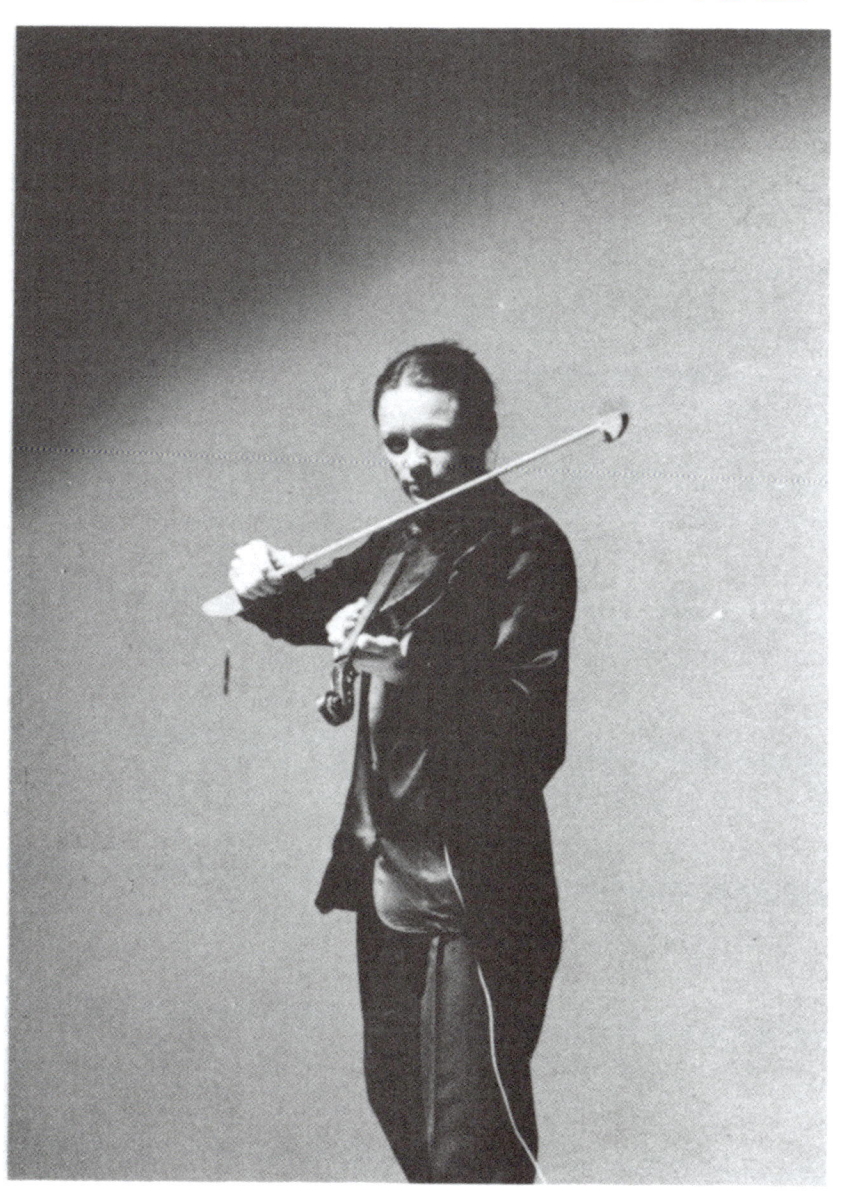

LAURIE ANDERSON

Cover: The Tape Bow Violin is an instrument with an audio playback head mounted on the bridge; instead of horsehair on the bow, there is a strip of recorded audiotape. As the bow is drawn back and forth across the head, the signal is heard forwards and then in reverse.

Cover photo by Marcia Resnick

© 1979 LAURIE ANDERSON

WORDS IN REVERSE

The following tests are extracts from "Like A Stream" (1978) - a piece for string ensemble, tape bow instruments, and voice - and "Americans On The Move" (1979) - an extended series for voice, electronics, film, and instruments.

It was the night flight from Houston - almost perfect visibility. You could see the lights from all the little Texas towns far below. I was sitting next to a fifty-two year old woman who had never been on a plane before. Her son had sent her a ticket and said, "Mom, you've raised ten kids, it's time you got on a plane." She was sitting in the window seat, staring out. She kept talking about the Big Dipper and the Little Dipper and pointing. Suddenly I realized she thought we were in Outer Space, looking down at the stars. I said, "You know, I think those lights down there are the lights from little towns."

I saw a photograph of Tesla who invented the Tesla Coil. He also invented a pair of shoes with soles four inches thick to ground him while he worked in the laboratory. In the picture, Tesla was sitting in his lab, wearing the shoes, and reading a book by the light of the long streamer-like sparks shooting out of his transformers.

I went to the movies and I saw a dog thirty feet high. And this dog was made entirely of light. And he filled up the whole screen. And his eyes were long hallways. He had those long, echoing, hallway eyes.

He thought of space that way ... as something you could fall into ... Falling for miles ... sideways.

I met a man in Canada and every day he had the same thing for lunch. He had a carrot and he had a bowl of chocolate pudding. First he ate the carrot into the shape of a spoon. Then he ate the pudding with the carrot shaped spoon. And then he ate the carrot.

There are Eskimos who live above the timber line. There's no wood there for the runners of their sleds. So instead, they use long frozen fish, which they strap to the bottoms of their sleds to slip across the snow.

I saw a man on the Bowery and he was wearing ancient, greasey clothes and brand new bright white socks ... and no shoes. Instead, he was standing on two small pieces of plywood and as he moved along the block, he bent down, moved one of the pieces slightly ahead and stepped on it. Then he moved the other piece slightly ahead and stepped on it.

You're walking ... and you don't always realize it but you're always falling. With each step ... you fall. You fall forward a short way and then catch yourself. Over and over ... you are falling ... and then catch yourself. You keep falling and catching yourself falling. And this is how you are walking and falling at the same time.

It was the Fourth of July and a parade of ships from all over the world sailed slowly by. Each was "camouflaged" by a particular shade of blue, gray, blue-gray or gray-blue. Bright blue for Greece, pale blue for Portugal, silver-gray with white trim for France, steel-gray for the United States. Strictly local colors. Regional ideas about the ocean. No one could have sneak-attacked anywhere but off their own coasts. This is the trouble with the transparency of water.

It was a room full of people. They had all arrived at the same building at approximately the same time. They were all free and they were all asking themselves the same question: What is behind that curtain?

(Peter says the thing he likes best about bowling is that you can see exactly what shoe sizes people wear.)

Outside the theater showing the Jane Fonda movie, the lights are bright. The movie is over and the crowd moves slowly out the glass doors. Most of the moviegoers are squinting, temporarily disoriented by three-dimensional space. All tolled, about seventy Jane Fondas stride through the doors - heads set at jaunty new angles, wise-cracking over their shoulders, brand new memories. Even the short-legged have new, jive, long ones. This is one of the effects of light.

No one has ever looked at me like this for so long. No one has ever stared at me like this for such a long time. This is the first time anyone has ever looked at me like this, stared at me like this for such a long time ... for so long ... for such a long time ...

Dan said he was on a plane flying over Greenland with a bunch of Texans. And they had binoculars. They were looking for polar bears down on the ice. White bears down on the white ice. From approximately 10,000 feet. And they said, "Look! I think I see one now! Down there ... I think I see one down there. Maybe that's one right there! Well, it could be one..."

Oh. Oh. I like the way you look. Oh. Oh. Oh. I like the way you talk. Oh. I like the way you walk. But most of all I like the way you look (at me).

In my dream, I am your customer.

He didn't know what to do. So he decided to watch the government, and see what the government was doing, and then kind of scale it down to size and run his life that way.

It was an ancient Japanese pot, incised with grooves. Thin-ridged grooves. Grooves all around it. It looked like one of those collapsible paper lanterns. It was an experiment. The pot was placed on a turntable and the turntable began to revolve. A needle was set into the groove. A stereo needle. They were waiting to hear the voice of the potter potting the pot 2,000 years ago. They were hoping the sounds of the potter had somehow been embedded into the wet clay. And stayed there, intact, clinging to the ridges of the clay. The pot turned around and around, like a record being treadled into the third dimension. It turned. They listened. They were listening. Some of them heard an unidentifiable Japanese dialect, rapid and high. Some of them heard high-pitched static. The needle dug into the pot. The needle was getting blunt. More and more blunt. It was that scientific. Blunter and scientific. More blunt ... and more scientific.

I can draw you so that you have no ears. I can draw you so that you have no ears at all. So that where your ears would be, there is only blank paper.

Looking into his eyes was like walking into a large municipal building. He had perfected an arrangement of his features that suggested International Style architecture: a subtle yet daring blend of American industry's most durable yet flexible materials. His expression seemed to suggest he had just finished saying, "That's the way things will be in the year 2,000."

A certain American sect has completed its research on the patterns of winds, tides, and currents during the Flood. According to their calculations, during the Flood, the winds, tides, and currents were in an overall southeasterly direction. This would then mean that in order for the Ark to have landed on Mount Ararat, it would had to have started out several thousand miles to the west. This would then locate pre-Flood history somewhere in the area of Upstate New York, and the Garden of Eden roughly in Genesee County.

I am in my body the way most people drive in their cars.

I went to a palm reader and the odd thing about the reading was that everything she told me was totally wrong. But she seemed so sure of the information that I began to feel like I'd been walking around with these false documents permanently tattooed to my hands. It was very noisy in the parlor and members of her family kept running in and out. They were speaking a high, clicking kind of language that sounded a lot like Arabic. Books and magazines in Arabic were strewn all over the floor. It suddenly occurred to me that maybe there was a translation problem - that maybe she was reading my hand from right to left instead of left to right. Thinking of mirrors, I gave her my other hand. Then she put her hand out and we sat there for several minutes in what I assumed was some sort of participatory ritual. Finally I realized that her hand was out because she was waiting for money.

A couple of weeks ago, an earthquake was reported in parts of the Bronx and New Jersey. The quake measured roughly 3.5 on the Richter scale and its epicenter was pinpointed to an ancient New Jersey bog. It was the first quake of this magnitude in the area since 1927. The scientists at nearby Princeton, however, missed the quake. They said, "At the time of the earthquake, we were changing our chart paper."

You know, you look a lot like a car. From a distance, say, from a few blocks away, you look exactly like a car. You look like a car from a distance.

The detective novel is the only type of novel truly invented in the twentieth century. In the detective novel, the hero is dead in the very beginning. So you don't have to deal with human nature at all ... Only the slow accumulation of facts - of data. You must put the hero together yourself.
In science fiction novels, the hero just flies in at the very beginning. Nothing is explained. He can forge steel with his bare hands. He can walk in zero gravity. And they say, "Look! He can walk in zero gravity!" So you don't have to deal with human nature at all.

I wanted you ... And I was looking for you ... But I couldn't find you. I wanted you ... And I was looking for you all day ... But I couldn't find you ... I couldn't find you ...

He explained his career in filmmaking this way - his mother had always had a hobby of cutting out pictures of hamsters from magazines. She would make frames for the photographs by gluing the wood chips from the bottoms of hamster cages into rectangles. She hung these over the fireplace, which was how he got the idea for using light.

Dad said last spring there were a lot of geese in his wheat field. The geese grew and the wheat grew; the geese grew and the wheat kept growing. But the geese always grew just slightly faster than the wheat. And all you could see were their long necks waving above the fields of grain. And he said, "Look! They look like cobras out there in that wheat field."

If you can't talk about it, point to it.

Last night I dreamed I was lying in bed sleeping. Last night I dreamed all night that I was just lying in bed dreaming I was sleeping. Last night I dreamed I was sleeping.

When Bobby got back from his first trip to Las Vegas, he said he noticed he was pausing just a little longer than usual after putting his money into parking meters and xerox machines.

I met a writer at a cocktail party. This writer used "I" in all his books. He was famous for the way he used "I" in all the books he wrote. At the party, people kept coming up to him and saying, "Gee! I really like your work!" And he kept saying, "Thanks, but I'm not very representative of myself."

I read about a rabbit in a laboratory. The experimenters held the rabbit's head, eyes open, pointed towards an open window. For twenty minutes, staring at the bright window. Then they took a knife and cut the rabbit's head off, peeled the tissue off its eyes, dyed it, and under the microscope, like film, the tissue developed. There were two windows imprinted on the rabbit's eyes. And they said, "Look! This rabbit has windows on its eyes!"

The reason you always think there are fires at riots is because that's the only place at the scene of the riot where there is enough light for the video camera. Actually, maybe this fire is only something happening near the riot ... incidental to the riot. Someone's trash is on fire or someone is having a barbeque near the riot but not as part of the riot. But that's why you think there are always fires at riots when sometimes there aren't any fires at riots, or in any case, not at every riot.

Steven Weed wrote in his autobiography that he was asked by the FBI to come in and answer a few questions. He said it wasn't like an interrogation room at all - there were no bright lights ... But he said they had it set up so that there was an agent on his right and an agent on his left and they alternated questions so that he had to keep turning his head back and forth, back and forth, to answer them. He said that after a few hours of doing this, he realized that no matter what answer he gave, it always looked like "no" ... "no" ... "no" ...

From "IT Song" - A song for a man and a woman who can't agree on what the word "it" refers to

She said: It looks. Don't you think it looks a lot like rain?
He said: Isn't it ... isn't it just like a woman?
She said: It's hard. It's just kind of hard to say.
He said: Isn't it just ... isn't it just like a woman?
She said: It goes. That's the way it goes. It goes that way.
He said: Isn't it just ... just like a woman?
She said: It takes. It takes one. It takes one to know one.
He said: Isn't it just like ... just like a woman?
She said: It takes one. It takes one, two. It takes one to know one.
She said it. She said it to know. She said it to no one.
Isn't it, isn't it just, isn't it just like a woman?

                    x   x   x

From "Closed Circuits" - A Song for Voice, Microphone Boom, and Electronics

Well I know who you are baby. I've seen you go into that meditative state. You're the snake charmer, baby. And you're also the snake. You're a closed circuit baby. You've got the answers in the palms of your hands.

Well, I met a blind judge and he said, "I know who you are," and I said, "Who?" And he said, "You're a closed circuit, baby." He said, "You know the world is divided into two kinds of things. There's luck ... and there's the law. There's a knock on wood that says 'it might' and there's the long arm of the law that says 'it's right.' And it's a tricky balancing act between the two because both are equally true. Cause might makes right and anything could happen, que sera sera ... am I right?"

Well, I saw a couple of hula dancers hula-ing down the street and they were saying, "I wonder which way the tide's gonna roll in tonight?" And I said, "Hold up hula dancers! You know the tide's gonna roll in ... then it's gonna roll right out again. Cause it's a closed circuit baby. We've got rules for that kind of thing and the moon is so bright tonight."

And don't think I haven't seen all those blind Arabs around. I've seen 'em around! And I've watched them charm that oil right out of the ground. Long black streams of that dark, electric light. And they said, "One day the sun went down and it went way down ... into the ground. Three thousand years go by ... and we pump it right back up again. Cause it's a closed circuit baby. We can change the dark into the light ... and vice versa."

Well I know who you are, baby. I've watched you count yourself to sleep. You're the shepherd, baby. And you're also 1-2-3-hundred sheep. I've watched you fall asleep.

In one of the spacecraft we sent to Jupiter, there were two identical computers - one active and the other quiescent, "asleep," a fail-safe back-up. For some unknown reason, NASA engineers had left out one program. They hadn't told the computers that at blast-off there would be a temporary adjustment period. At the moment of lift-off, the first computer began to get strange read-outs. Nothing seemed to calibrate. What should have read zero read 2,000 and vice versa. Whole systems went out. The computer began to troubleshoot, scanning all systems. "... Inoperative ... Inopertative ... Inoperative ... ." It concluded that since all systems seemed inoperative, the computer itself was defective. It woke up the second computer which in turn scanned the craft. "... Inoperative ... Inoperative.... ." It concluded that it too was non-functional and that the spacecraft would have to return to earth.

In Houston, programmers suddenly realized the omission. The new message flashed off, brief, simplified by emergency. #1 - Reactivate ... #2-Resume quiescence ... Now: Shock; ... Now: Illusory, temporary inoperative state. ... Now: Birth.

It was that way for him. Some days he was flying. Flying easily. White light. Great ideas. He could do no wrong. And then one day, it would all leave him. For no reason, it left and suddenly nothing worked. He burned the toast. Dented the car. He was clumsy. Depressed. And then it would change again. It would be easy again. It changed fast and for no reason, it changed. And he went to the doctor and the doctor said, "...chemical imbalance..." and gave him some chemicals and cured him. Cured him until it was all evened out - every day same thing. And he was so relieved to find out that "he" wasn't crazy. "It's not me ... it's my biochemistry..."

When TV signals are sent out, they don't stop. They keep going. They pick up speed as they leave the solar system. By now, the first TV programs ever made have been travelling for thirty years. They are well beyond our solar system now. All those characters from cowboy serials, variety hours, and quiz shows are sailing out. They are the first true voyagers into deep space. And they sail farther and farther, intact, still talking.

And as we listen with our instruments, as we learn to listen farther and farther into space, we can hear them. We listen farther and that is what we hear. They are jamming the lines. We listen and we hear them talking, travelling faster and faster, getting fainter and fainter. And as our instruments get more sophisticated we can hear them better ... speeding away ... the sound of speeding away ... like a phone continuously ringing.

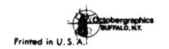

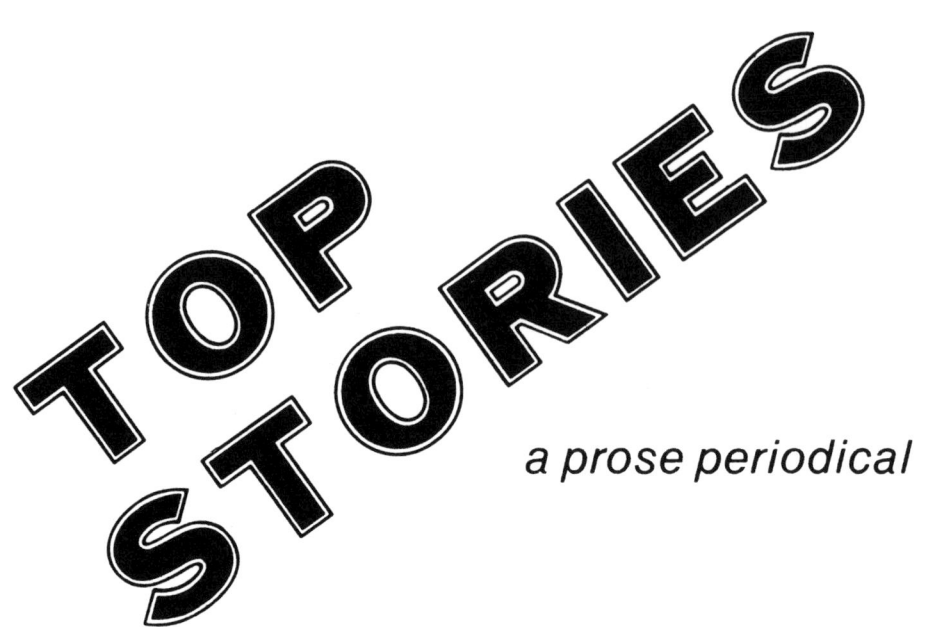

a prose periodical

#1 Donna Wyszomierski
#3 Pati Hill
#4 Judith Doyle

available from:

TOP STORIES *of* Hard Press

30 Essex Street
Buffalo, New York 14213

TOP STORIES $1.00

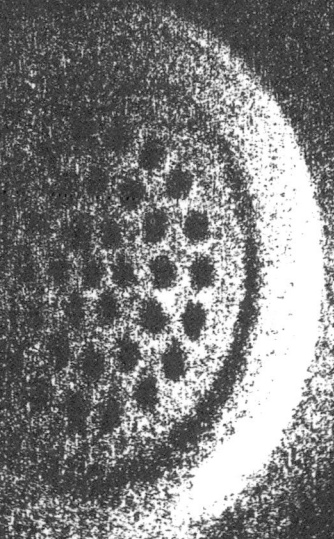

PATI HILL

TOP STORIES #3

3 STORIES

by
Pati Hill

Mrs. Starling and **The Ballad of Annie Bates** originally appeared in the Missippi Review, and **The Falcon** in the Paris Review.

MRS. STARLING

Mrs. Starling was eighty and on her head she frequently wore a coolie hat. In her youth she had been a beauty. In her seventies she had decided to live in a house by the ocean. In her garage she installed Sarah Allen and at times the two of them could be seen in Sarah Allen's red Volkswagen, but mostly they kept behind their wall and pasted photographs.

Mrs. Starling could not rightly have been called eccentric though some of the things she did were odd. To cite a few: Collecting sea gull eggs, dumping her garbage on the supermarket steps, refusing personal mail, wading in her neighbor's lily pond, making her own ink out of pokeberries.

When Mrs. Starling was a girl she had married a playboy named Horace Davis, but they had quickly separated.

She was well into her fifties when she married Mr. Starling, and he was thirty-five, but seemed younger.

They were quite happy until he killed himself. (An accident; he ran into a thick wall in a fog.)

Mr. Starling had often expressed his belief in cremation but Mrs. Starling buried him in a plot she had bought for herself and went to visit him every Saturday and on alternate Mondays.

Unless it was snowing she allowed Sarah Allen to drive her there. She liked walking in snow, however, and slept well afterwards.

Although the beauty of Mrs. Starling was frequently spoken of there were not many people who actually remembered it except Mrs. Starling.

"Photographs in that day were very inadequate," she said. "The ones they take now are incomparably clearer but they lack charm."

"Anyone would think you regretted the old days," sometimes accused Sarah Allen.

"I do," Mrs. Starling nearly always replied.

In the summer of 1973 Mrs. Starling bought a row boat.

"You know, rowing a boat is not the same as driving a car," ruefully remarked Sarah Allen the instant she laid eyes on it.

"Whoever said it was?" asked Mrs. Starling.

(There were times when Sarah Allen was trying, though she meant well.)

When Mrs. Starling and Sarah Allen went rowing they wore orange life jackets and carried their lunches in paper bags.
If their energy held out they ate on Billy's Island and if not they returned to the mainland and ate in the dining room, refolding the bags afterwards.

No one dreamed that Sarah Allen might ever fall in love.
She had had measles and scarlet fever and broken her wrist twice while in Mrs. Starling's employ and, for a brief time, it had looked as if she might go queer in the head, but there are limits to the things that befall a person.
"I will give you three weeks to recover," said Mrs. Starling. "If I were younger I would give you a vacation in Greece, but the way things are, that is out of the question."
"We are being married," said Sarah Allen. "I am not a virgin, but the last time was so long ago it comes to the same thing. Nevertheless I don't believe I'll wear white. If you would like to join us on our wedding trip, you would be more than welcome. Money is no object. Archer makes a good salary. I wonder if I should take out life insurance."

After Sarah Allen's departure Mrs. Starling gave up boating and started dictating her memoirs into a machine that had come with the house.
As often as not when she tried to play them back to herself they ran out of the machine like spaghetti.

Sarah Allen stayed married for two and a half years, then returned to work for Mrs. Starling, but something had gone out of their relationship.
"I believe it would be better if I ended my days in a home," Mrs. Starling concluded. "I have written to several already. I shall regret this view, but now I wish to devote all my time to preserving my past."

The last time Mrs. Starling and Sarah Allen met, Sarah Allen had dyed her hair and cut it so short she was scarcely recognizable and Mrs. Starling had on a Nile green necklace.
It was one of Mrs. Starling's better days and she was able to recall a dazzling array of things, enough of them connected with her life with Sarah Allen to make conversation a real pleasure.
"I was wrong to leave you," Sarah Allen said at one point.

"A person your age should remarry," Mrs. Starling replied.

"I have received a cribbage board from my daughter-in-law," said a Mrs. Vogl who had arrived only the week before, but fitted in nicely.

At five o'clock a nurse brought spoons and plates.

It was the custom at Oxville for the nurses to dress as hostesses rather than as nurses.

"When will it land?" certain inmates wondered.

"When is my birthday?" wondered others.

"What was on all that tape?" Sarah Allen inquired. "When I came back to see you last year there was tape all over everywhere, even under the refrigerator."

Just before Sarah Allen said good-bye there was a sunset with red and gold shooting out of the clouds in every direction and Mrs. Starling suggested they walk to the edge of the lawn in order to take advantage of it.

She tucked her skirts up as she had used to do when wading in her neighbor's pond and carried her shoes in her hat.

Sarah Allen asked once more what had been on the tapes but did not really expect an answer and nearly everyone, even the nurses, agreed that the good weather would hold.

THE FALCON

Mr. Bean and Mr. Muller were in the Coffee Cup sharing a grinder when the notion came to Mr. Bean to paint a lion. He got up at once without excusing himself and went to the hardware store where he bought a can of yellow paint, a can of orange paint, a can of green paint, a can of black paint, a bottle of turpentine and two brushes, one large and one small. He took them to the shed behind his house and cut himself a piece of masonite twenty-four inches by twenty-four inches square.

He saw this lion as seated dead center in the manner of a family portrait, the mouth closed, the expression mild, and in the background four lambs following each on the heels of the other, as alike as patterns on wall paper.

It took Mr. Bean six days to finish his picture, not because the subject presented any particular problems but on account of the time required for the different layers of paint to dry.

When it was finished he set it on a shelf and studied it for a day, then laid it face down on a pile of sandpaper and forgot it.

The week after that he decided to paint his neighbor's house.

Although he had lived next to Mr. Adams for forty odd years they had never spoken. The lady who lived with Mr. Adams was not his wife and the house was surrounded by a wall made of smooth stones resembling balls of chewing gum.

Mr. Bean used the same technique in painting his neighbor's house that he had used in painting the lion, except for the wall which he made by gluing on real pebbles and in the sky above he wrote: "Thou shalt not covet."

When his neighbor's house was dry he laid it above the lion but this time he did not forget it. As he walked the streets of Stonington he looked for other subjects such as the cannons in Cannon Square and the monument to the American Revolutionary Troops in front of the library, but he did no further work until the Portuguese Festival when he painted two fishing boats and the grand stand decorated with crossed American and Portuguese flags.

These works he showed to his wife who said,"Well, I was wondering what was keeping you out there in the shed. You can put the boats over the mantlepiece if you want, but I don't like the Portagee Fathers. It's cranksided," by which she meant she did not like the Portuguese or believe them a fit subject for a work of art.

In his heart Mr. Bean agreed. However, he was not master of his inspiration and did not wish to discuss the matter.

Between July and December Mr. Bean covered eight pieces of masonite and two pieces of common carton with subjects ranging from Mrs. Bean's hat to the Hudson Tunnel, which he did from memory.

This last satisfied him particularly due to his realistic rendering of the smoke from the automobile exhausts in steel wool and he asked permission to display it in the Coffee Cup window.

"How much do you want for it?" the proprietress asked.

"I don't aim to sell it," said Mr. Bean. "I'd just like to put it out where people can enjoy it. It took me a deal of time to paint."

"Well, it sure does beat all," said the waitress, and together they set about cleaning the glass that it might be seen to the best advantage.

On a cold night in February it came to Mr. Bean to paint a falcon.

He got out of bed promptly and made his way into the tool house in the dark.

He knew this falcon must be finished in one sitting and he was puzzled to know how to go about it, but as he crossed the driveway his attention was caught by an oily rag which was folded and twisted in such a manner that it resembled the creature he had in his head to perfection, so seizing it he nailed it viciously to a board. In black letters he wrote "Pride goeth before a fall," and this work he hung above the door of the shed.

The pounding wakened Mrs. Bean and she was filled as she often was filled with irritation against her spouse and thought as she often did how she might have married Miller's boy and be living in an unmortgaged house on the hill, but when Mr. Bean came in his expression was so agitated she decided she would not mention it.

"Get in bed you old fool," she said, "It's nearly light!"

. The night before the Beans were married, Mr. Bean had had a premonition. He had foreseen that their wedding cake would not be delivered on time and he had taken his bicycle and ridden full speed to Whalen's Bakery.

The shop was closed except for Mr. Whalen's mother who was deaf so he wrote on a piece of paper, "Tell Al don't forget cake 3 P.M."

The cake arrived at four-thirty after Mr. Bean and his bride had been toasted in apple jack and cranberry juice and left on their honeymoon.

Mr. Bean foolishly disclosed this premonition to Mrs. Bean on their second anniversary and as a result she held him forever responsible for the missing refreshment at the same time declaring him unreasonable to have thought he could change Fate.

The month following that in which Mr. Bean painted his falcon his health began to fail and the doctor prescribed rest and walks by the sea.

Mr. Bean was not accustomed to lying down by daylight or walking without a definite end in view but he soon accustomed himself to his new existence and took pleasure in talking to people who had not crossed his previous path.

One of these was Professor Sisson, a man near his own age, who collected seaweed in gunny sacks to fertilize his garden and make custards.

The two men, so unlike in temperament and experience, often sat together on the rocks beneath the pier rubbing their hands together or trudging across the sand.

One afternoon as they neared the lifeguard's post the public telephone located beneath it began to ring.

The two men looked at each other in surprise, then the professor picked up the receiver, but could not make out the words that were said at the other end.

The next day Mr. Bean read in the local paper that the Professor had died of a heart attack.

Mr. Bean was not surprised. A man who ate seaweed and answered public telephones in such unlikely surroundings could not be in sound health.

When, some weeks later, he heard the same telephone ringing he walked on without so much as glancing in its direction. Nevertheless he took chill which rapidly went into pneumonia.

On the fifth day (which was also his birthday), Mrs. Bean sent for Father Manueli and together they awaited the end. Mr. Bean recovered, however, and subsequently painted a mural for the bank and another for the laundramat. Peaceful works which caused favorable comment even from his wife.

It should be noted in closing that Mrs. Bean was a gaunt woman with cold feet and straight hair that she pulled into a knot behind her head and she had never been otherwise, but suited Mr. Bean very well.

THE BALLAD OF ANNIE BATES

Jesse grew in the feed store which was also the gasoline station, facing out on the crossroads of the world.

For playthings he had the red tin donkey from the plug cut, a sheaf of dirty playing cards and all the cigar bands he wished.

By the time he was twelve he could fill a car as fast as his pa and make change somewhat faster, but until he was fifteen he went to church or got beaten. From there on he rarely saw the place except when he went down to Harkness to buy whiskey.

For a while yet he trudged to school to goose Gertha Hammercheck and outstare Annie Bates.

Annie and her people had come from Tatum where there was a movie house, a bank and a branch office of the Montgomery Ward. She wrote with a fountain pen and carried her lunch in a lunch box instead of a lard tin, but aside from that she was not so different from anyone else, so when Jesse found her waiting for him by the fence surrounding Catlett's place he told her straight out he planned to quit school.

"I like Mr. Hewitt," he said. "He's a fine nice man, but time's wasting. I can't spend my life reading books."

"Oh, you're right," agreed Annie. "I'd give up myself except I kind of like the walk," and she ran her fingers over the moss that clung to the fence post in such a way that Jesse seemed to feel that moss himself in all its rootlessness.

"How do you folks like it over here in Pardee county?" he ventured, nothing risked, nothing gained.

"We like it," she admitted.

On Wednesday Jesse waited to no avail, but Thursday she was there again and together they headed up to the still where dogwood was said to be in bloom.

"It's funny, you and me," Jesse mused. "I wouldn't have guessed things would fall out this way, though I always liked your hair."

In June Annie said they best get married to give their child a Christian birth.

Jesse felt a great shock to think consequences should come of such pleasant sport as they'd engaged in and when next they met it was in her family's parlor where hung two oval portraits of her grandparents and a calendar from his pa's filling station showing a blonde lady astride a balloon.

"My girl's a good girl," Annie's ma struck out strong and clear. "I brought her up strict and only a demon like this one could have led her astray."

"My son is a lamb lured to evil by a woman of eighteen years," his pa came back fast as a bobcat. "I and mine don't aim to feed another mouth."

One week later Annie wore starched voile and her baby sister followed her down the aisle with a brass ring sewed onto a balsam cushion, Jesse's cousin passing him the real thing when the preacher told him.

Annie looked a proper vision and Jessie was put out until he remembered a scratch she had had on her face the second time she waited for him and the subsequent walk and her long legs.

As the women lingered behind to put mason jars of wedding flowers on their kinfolk's graves they threw jealous glances at Annie.

"Nobody ever comes out here to straighten up any more," they told each other. "Seems like once a person's in the ground he might as well never have lived."

Annie got big as soon as she let her sash out and she didn't know how to turn over a pancake but instead of staying with her people they chose to make do in dead Horace's cabin.

This far abode was two hours steady walking over hill and dale and when Jesse worked in the village Annie was alone indeed.

"If any tomfool bothers you just take my shotgun and blast his insides out," he told her.

No tomfool ever bothered her, though, as she washed their clothes and cleaned every inch of the cabin and gathered raspberries in her bought lunch pail.

"When the boy is born," said Jesse, "I aim to teach him respect for his parents as well as how to hunt, and if we should get a daughter I sure hope she can sing."

Sometimes by full moon Jesse had a dream: He saw the world empty as a box except for him and a strong brown bear and together they had it out.

When this happened Annie would hold him until he came to himself.

"Can't you leave me be?" he reproached her. "A man has to learn to sink or swim," but he might as well have been talking to the mountain.

One morning in October Jesse took the shortcut down for flour and bacon.

"Don't worry," he told Annie, "I'll be home before dark and if anyone comes to bother you, you know what to do."

Annie pulled him down by the ears.

"You know something," she laughed, "it ain't **me** that's afraid. It ain't never **been**!"

Jesse thought, when I get home tonight I'm going to love my Annie with a will, but when he came home, she was floating face down in the stream.

From the looks of it her foot had slipped while she was wringing out the sheets.

Jesse carried her into the house and built a fire and passed his living hand along her chilly flesh till morning, then he walked back to town and told their people.

"It's God's curse on you!" bawled her ma.

"It's a sore cross to carry," groaned his pa and thus, dissenting and lamenting, they laid the girl to rest.

In November Jesse climbed the mountain one last time to bring down their quilts and the next year he married Miriam, called Goldie on account of her fine head of hair.

From that marriage he had six sons and two daughters, one born stone deaf, and when he died people said he had been a modest kindly man who paid his debts in hard times as well as good.

In the church yard they laid him side by side with Miriam as he might have lain with his Annie.

The Lord gives and the Lord takes away was his favorite text but it was too long for the stone so they chose **Jesus wept** instead.

TOP STORIES

a prose periodical

#1 Donna Wyszomierski
#2 Laurie Anderson
#4 Judith Doyle

available from:

TOP STORIES of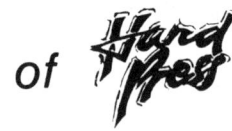

30 Essex Street
Buffalo, New York 14213

TOP STORIES

AGENT PINK

Suzanne Johnson

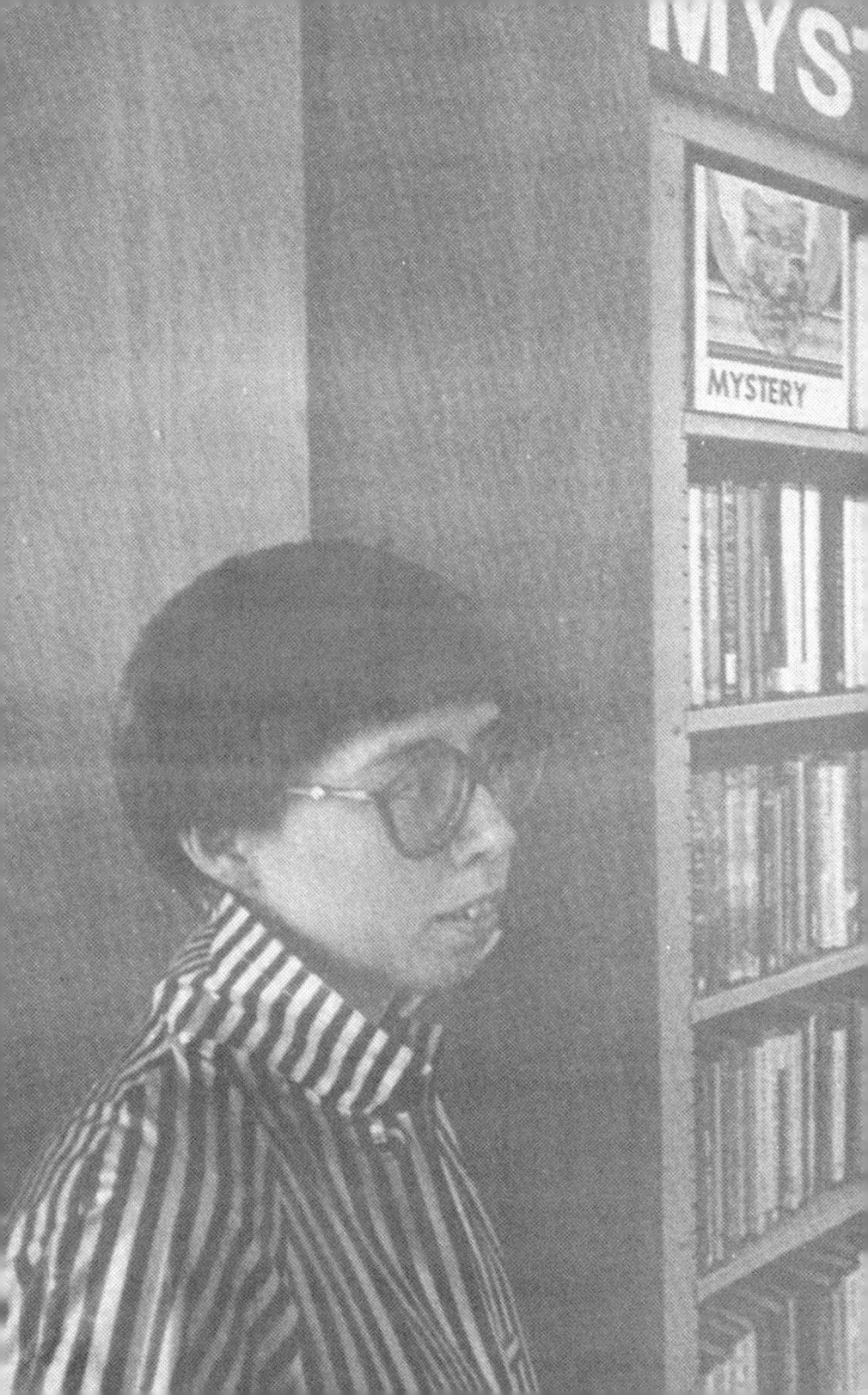

TOP STORIES #4

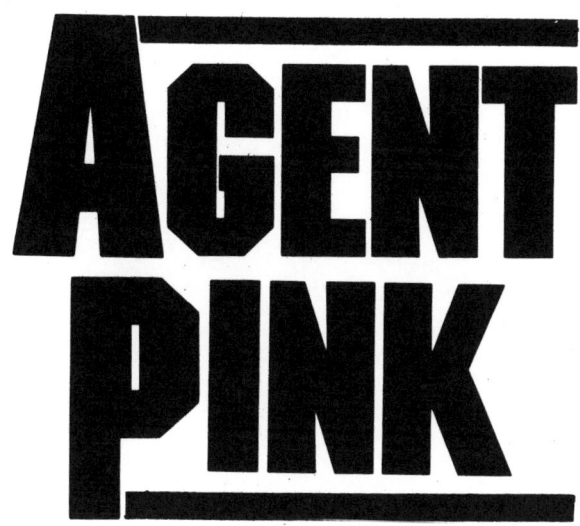

by
Suzanne Johnson

© 1980 SUZANNE JOHNSON

for Pinky

The characters and incidents in **AGENT PINK** had their origin and growth in the imagination and are not to be identified with any actual persons or events.

They were sitting in a sunny front room: Avery Pink and Cleo Jameson, best of friends. Avery reads thrillers; Cleo does crossword puzzles. "Now here's a trivia question", says Avery. "Oh?" says Cleo, always interested. "What is **Barbie's** last name?" Cleo didn't respond. "C'mon," urged Avery, "it's really easy once you think of Barbie as the unattainable American female WASP." Cleo lifted the cover of Avery's book: **Barbie's Hawaiian Holiday**. "How can you read this junk?", she said sweetly, not to be mean. Avery had heard this before. "Look, I'm not all hung up on Barbie's unreal molded body and those high heels they made her wear. I loved her dresses. Now, c',mon, **guess**!", Avery posed demurely. "Smith," Cleo said. "Barbie Smith? Yick." Avery consulted her book. "It's Roberts. **Barbie Roberts**. Now that sounds like a virgin doesn't it? Of course it had to be a man's name." She closed the book, leaned to her friend and kissed her forehead. "I'm going for the mail, want anything?" Cleo extended her glass, "Apricot nectar and apple juice, please." Avery feigned shock. "Another drink, how decadent."

Avery Pink wears her name on her sleeve. Just look in her closet. An array of fabrics in any shade of red. Red corduroy, red socks, several pairs of red shoes, red terry shirts, red all-cotton panties, dyed red undershirts with pink lace and a red rose at the center. A girl who loves red.
Or pink, crimson, vermilion, maroon. Anything that happened not to be red at least had accessories: red buttons on black dresses, red shoelaces in yellow sneakers, red belts lying across turquoise trousers. She is actually kind of plain. She can look back warmly at the girl she was, raised by loving parents in a rural New York setting, surrounded by ponies, cornfields and farm boys. From college she crusaded through museums and libraries.

Now her life lacks one essential ingredient she feels is her due. Mystery. Dark and foreboding, chocolatey rich mystery. Raised on the adventures of those brats, the **Happy Hollisters**, matured by the underworld sensuality of the **Man from UNCLE**, she thought intrigue would mix up her life like fashion and boyfriends. Well-dressed and intelligent Emma Peel, a perfect match for debonair and aloof Mr. Steed. Ah, romance.

Avery reentered the room opening the mail. "A letter for you, a bill for me, and an invitation for us." "An invitation?" Cleo looked closely at the envelope Avery extended — "not another one of Gregory's house sales?" Cleo tested her friend's reaction. Avery was calculating. "It looks like it's a party as well as a preview. I know he's a creep, but we haven't been out in weeks. I wouldn't mind going." After a minute, Avery answered, "I'm trying to remember where **this house** was; you know, where he got the stuff. It was on Delaware Avenue somewhere . . . Alright, lets go, I'm curious." They smiled.

Cleo is older than Avery. That's important only from a cultural standpoint. They are sensitive to different memories. Whereas Cleo's high school boyfriends one by one went off to Vietnam; at the time, Avery first noticed a black child in her public school class. Whereas Cleo's boyfriend Art was later seriously wounded in the Tet Offensive; Avery remembers it as the year Micky Dolenz of the Monkees got married. But Avery has caught up and Cleo has slowed down.

Cleo decided to wear a nice summer dress. Avery admired how precisely Cleo made up her eyes and her lips, gave her hair a few brushes so it shined. "Everyone will fall in love with you tonight," Avery declared. "Maybe," she answered, "but **someone** will fall in love with you." Avery decided to wear black. Illya and Napolean always wear black to parties.

To Avery, their host was a real worm. About 30 and very fat. Gregory was one of those guys who was always asking, "How you doing?", when he knew he was doing better than you. He had enough money to support a couple of token businesses to disguise his drug trade, but his latest diversion put him at the top of Avery's shit list. He was a building vulture, waiting for another 19th century building to be torn down, and replaced by a Burger King. His shadowy connections allowed him to walk into a place, wrench in hand, and walk out with pedestal sinks, cast iron columns, stained glass windows, and other chic desirables. Rumor had it he paid very little and sold very high at his store affectionately named "Architectural Reruns." Avery hated his guts.

Gregory was having a party to show off his latest acquisition: the entire contents of a widow's home on Delaware Avenue. It was a demolition that was hotly contested and suspiciously lost. Avery's secret mission that night was to liberate something in the memory of the woman whose past had been destroyed.

Avery and Cleo pulled up in front of Gregory's house, squeezing the Volvo between a Jeep and a Porsche. The house was big, of course, but the creep's extravagantly poor taste was overwhelming. Cleo made a mental list of the design atrocities. Avery's hopes of an interesting evening melted when she looked around the coke and disco crowd. Gregory kissed her on the mouth **(bad breath)** and led her over to the food. She insisted she wasn't ready for all that meat, so he pushed a drink in her hand. She traded her drink for a beer and got away from him. She found someone unslimey to talk with for awhile. Actually, she liked disco and she danced alot. She occasionally bumped into Cleo and they swapped comments.

They had switched to Beatle songs when she saw him. First she liked his shirt — yellow voile - gee, Avery hadn't seen one of those since her grandfather died. It was miles too big for him; he was pretty skinny. Tall, though. With a closer look, she saw he was leaning on a cane. His cream colored tux jacket was also giant size, but the cut was early Frank Sinatra and she liked it. What was obviously lots of stuff in his coat and vest pockets made him look a little top heavy. When Avery finally looked at his face, she saw him hugging a tall woman very closely and kissing her neck. Kinda cute. Avery watched awile and turned her attention elsewhere.

It wasn't until she heard a voice say something ridiculous that she noticed it was he again. Pardoning and excusing himself through a group of people and looking directly at Avery, he came toward her. Here he comes, thought Avery. Lowering his voice an octave, he said, "Yes, excuse me, but would you care to participate in a small experiment I'm conducting?" Avery looked beyond him and noticed several women smiling in his direction. The guys were ignoring him. Without waiting for Avery's answer, he put his arms around her politely and said quietly to her shoulder, "You see, it's my birthday. I have, as I'm sure you've noticed, a rather pronounced olfactory apparparatus, possessing naturally an extremely keen sense of smell. I'm wondering if there is a direct proportional relationship between how nice I think a woman smells and how attractive I find her to be. May I?" How could Avery resist such a buildup. His nose nuzzled her neck, he inhaled deeply, then sighed heavily as he exhaled. The third time he did it, his lips touched Avery's skin and lingered for a little nibble. Avery wore her name on her neck. Satisfied with his sampling, he thanked her cordially, smiled and went on to someone else. I hope Cleo witnessed that, thought Avery.

At that point, the music sounded raunchy, the room was smoky, and she didn't want to drink any more Lowenbrau. On her way to find a bathroom, she ran into Gregory, and didn't think fast enough to go the other way. "So, Ave, what do you think of my castle? Pretty decent selection, huh?" He wasn't getting Avery's **'You're a jerk'** signals. He steered her down the hallway. She decided to roll with it. "You gotta see this," he was saying. Avery looked back for Cleo.

He snapped on the light in a darkened room and Avery saw it had once been the library. the walls were lined with ceiling-high bookcases, empty but for a few cartons on the lower shelves. A tremendous chandelier hung from between heavy beams, but that was not what illuminated the room. Avery felt ice in her blood. In among the shadows cast by a clamp lamp on a table, she saw an assortment of objects piled on the furniture. There were lamps, and boxes with wood molding sticking out of them, leaded windows of different shapes and colors all balancing haphazardly on parts of sinks and bathtubs and dressers. There were small boxes filled with paper scattered among it all.

Avery hated Gregory for it, but the things were beautiful. She noticed all of the windows were covered with someone's Martex sheets. She turned to the gloating Gregory and asked, "Does the chandelier work?" "Nah, I'm selling it. It's one of those that used gas. So, it what d'ya think — I got a pretty nice haul, didn't I? Hey, c'mere and look at this." What a clod. Avery couldn't stand to watch him climbing around. She started looking through a couple of candy boxes filled with bits of stationery, envelopes, rent receipts. The next box affirmed Avery's discovery.

It was all here. Everything from the candy store that had once been the pride of Elmwood Avenue. Cleo had told her about it. It had gone out of business before Avery moved to Buffalo, but she had heard all about the **Shaker Bonnet** and the ladies who owned it. Someone wanted to 'develop' the property and their rent doubled every year until they lost their lease.

Long gone to a decorator was the interior of elaborate plasterwork painted in pastels. Here were the glass-topped round tables and wire chairs her friends remembered, cherished settings for cinnamon sundaes with hot fudge sauce. There were boxes of ice cream dishes and all kinds of bowls and kitchen stuff for candy making. The poor things had been harboring it all in that big house on Delaware, just hoping for a chance to open a shop again. Wait 'til Cleo saw this.

Avery wondered just how much that douchebag Gregory was going to get for everything. He asked her for a light. She pulled out her purple plastic flashlight and flicked it. With sort of a laugh, he looked at her. "You're funny, you know. Not just that you act funny either. I mean, as a chick you're really . . ." His slimey face was breathing on Avery when someone else spoke from the doorway. "So here you are," tight-jeans and a sweater passed Avery. She was Gregory's latest attachment, Cherry Bond. Ignoring Avery, she pulled him back out into the party, murmuring something about distributing party favors in the TV room. Avery saw something worth lifting, but decided to come back for it.

Avery followed the pair through the house to what was now the 'entertainment center', a concept Avery abhored. There were about ten people tossed around on tacky furniture, thoroughly engrossed in the hockey game on a video screen. Avery was aware of the overwhelming mellowness of the group, sniffing alot and flashing assorted drug paraphenalia. Not having strong drug habits, Avery wandered over to the TV. During another offensive beer commercial she switched it over to "Leave It To Beaver", more endearing than ever on the large screen. Everybody got pissed off, but she attracted the attention of the guy who had sniffed her earlier. She smiled at him and tapped her nose. He smiled back from the fake designer couch. She noticed the ornate black cane resting against his thigh. "Your weapon, Mr. Steed?", she asked, as she sat in a nearby chair. "Why, yes, Mrs. Peel, as a matter of fact, this outwardly innocent-looking device is one of the more inventive items in my extensive collection." He flipped the top of the cane sideways and produced several glass vials with rubber stoppers. One held some white powder, one was empty and the third — "Aspirin," he volunteered, "I have arthritis." Avery was impressed. "Quite the useful instrument. An agent could always rely on something like that." He looked at her, grinning, and said, "Oh, is that your calling, Ms. —" "Avery Pink," she announced, extending her hand, which he took and sniffed and marked with a kiss.

"You know," he moved closer, "I do believe you are the best-smelling woman here. I couldn't make the announcement of my findings as planned, for fear of alienating all the other swell smellers, including your friend Cleo." Avery was adding all this up. "But honestly, I can't believe how great you smell. Especially over here, under your ear. Mind if I make sure?"

Avery was getting pink all over, but he was cute and certainly the most promising, personality-wise. "Tell me — " "Trent," he offered. "Oh Trent, that's nice. Tell me why do you have so many pens in your pocket, are we expecting a test? Passing out applications?" He assured her the test was over and proceeded to give her a thorough tour of his pockets which included all varieties of pens, a kazoo, a pipe, Pez dispensers, swizzle sticks, toys. She suggested he donate his unique collection to the museum where Cleo worked. Then she stood up. "Wait a minute. About an hour ago I was on my way to the loo. See you later." She messed up his hair on the way out.

As Avery came back down the rear stairs, she found Cleo in the kitchen getting a beer. Filling her in quickly, Avery pulled her down the hall saying, "C'mon, you're not going to believe this."

They made their way deviously to the library to pick up Avery's artifact. Creeping into the dark room, Avery fumbled for her flashlight. When she bumped into someone, she knew they weren't the only snoops. All it took was one sniff and Trent sighed, "Ah, Avery Pink, I'm so glad it's you. But who is this? Wait a minute —" (Sniff) "Ah, Cleo." "Hello Trent," she said. He wrapped them both in a big hug. "Not only do you two smell great, you feel great too." Cleo wanted to see, so she closed the door and turned on the light.

"What are you doing in here anyway?", Avery asked, "on a pen expedition?" "Well not quite, look," he said enthusiastically showing them some of the dishes, books, dusty personages in frames. "And look at this!" He held up the mold for making chocolate buffalos she'd seen earlier. "Hey, I know," said Avery jealously, "I saw it first, when I got my private showing. It's mine." She took the heavy thing from him. Cleo was alarmed at the suggestion of taking something. In fact they were arguing about it so loudly, they hardly noticed the door opening. When a group of people crowded into the room, they tried to act casual.

Gregory was obviously pissed that they had scooped the dramatic effect of his preview. Avery ditched the mold in a box while Cleo chattered to Gregory that he donate the woman's possessions to a museum. He laughed at her, which infuriated Avery. Didn't she see he could make a bundle breaking up the collection? So Cleo suggested, "How about donating the papers? You know letters and things, it'd be tax deductible." He looked at her as if she was nuts and said she could have the 'junk' for free if she bought something else. Trent shoved the mold in Avery's hands and said, "She'll take this for five bucks." Gregory said he'd have to get **twenty**-five for it. Trent stuffed another fifteen dollars in Gregory's pocket and took the mold from Avery. "We'll share it," he grinned. Avery glared at him.

There were too many people in the room now, pawing through everything and it made Avery sick. She and Cleo gathered the assorted cigar boxes, shoe boxes and candy boxes into a couple of cartons. She still wanted to lift something from this jerk for her own piece of mind. On one of the shelves she saw just the thing. It was a tin box, probably once full of sweets, with a beautiful aerial view of City Hall and Niagara Square at its 1930's best printed on the lid. While everyone was fondling the antiques, Avery slipped the box into hers and covered it with some papers. Avery took one last glance around and then they left.

At the car, Avery knew they'd never fit everything in the Volvo. She asked Trent, "Hey, do you have a car?". He was merely awaiting the question. In minutes, he was pulling up beside them in a white Rabbit. The boxes fit perfectly. "Now what," asked Avery. Trent was ready with a suggestion. "It's a beautiful night. Let's go down by the river." Avery thought that would be nice, but Cleo said, "I'm tired. I'd like to go home. I'll take the car, Ave." "What about the stuff?", she wondered. "Trent can drop it and you off later." It was settled.

Trent drove rather wildly across town toward the river. Avery watched the houses flashing by, noting which were lit, which dark. I love the West Side, she thought aloud. "Even the fires and the stabbings?", asked Trent. Avery didn't answer. He parked the car and they got out to lean on the railing. The river surged toward Niagara Falls. After a while, Avery said, "I think it's all an indication of the passion. It's mystery. But somehow I feel safe from it. Just read about it in the newspaper and reassure my parents it happened three blocks away." Trent was lighting a pipe so Avery kept talking.

"You know, it's the hidden crimes that really concern me. Like demolitions and putting nice little stores out of business. You know that stuff Gregory has is from the Shaker Bonnet? What a pig — it's so frustrating. I just don't have that kind of money or influence —" Trent interrupted. "Wait a minute, you have the documented history of the business. That's what's important. Furniture is furniture — you've got the guts of a Buffalo institution." Avery eyed him warily. "You should take a closer look through those papers, turn up some interesting items. Everybody knows they were forced out of business; you might find out how." Avery had never considered that angle. "Yeah and smear Gregory's name all over town," she schemed. Avery saw a large boat emerge from under the Peace Bridge, heading for the harbor.

"What do you do anyway?", she asked him. "Me? I'm a simple salesperson, I sell this city. You know that magazine **Out in Buffalo**? I help lonely travellers find a good time in the Queen City." Avery had seen its glossy pages and expensive advertisers. "You seem more independent than that," she teased him. "Don't you mean more 'undesirable?'", he taunted. He pointed to the boat looming closer. "See that? That's one of my accounts, the Miss Buffalo. Hey, ever been on it?" Avery nodded. "Well, there's a party on it next week — a midnight cruise," he leaned toward her. Something in his pocket caught her sweater. "If that's an invitation, sure it would be fun," Avery said, disengaging herself. She thought of Cleo and added, "Now I'm really curious about the papers we got tonight. Let's go sort through our loot."

At the house, they brought the rest of the boxes in from the car. Cleo was still up and had already sorted some, separating the correspondence from the bills and the invoices. "How was the moonlight?", she asked mockingly. Trent serenaded her on his kazoo. "Find anything exciting?", Avery queried. Cleo produced a pile for Avery to look at. "There are photographs too," she added. "It really was a beautiful little place." Avery had an idea. "Hey, Trent, what if we write a little history of the shop, with pictures of what it was like, do you think we could get it published? I just want to do something to avenge those ladies against destroyers like Gregory." Trent thought it might be possible and made a note about it on one of the innumerable cards in his pocket.

Avery pulled the chocolate mold from a box, and admiring it, passed it to Trent. "It's very nice," she said, "you're very lucky to have it." He looked surprised and reminded her it was for both of them. Then Avery remembered the tin box and pulling it from under some papers, she said, "Well then this will be ours too."

Trent just stared at the box, then started laughing hysterically. "You took **THIS**!, he gasped, "I don't believe it." Avery didn't know what was so funny. Trying to take it from him 'cause she thought he thought it was stupid it opened. Out dropped two glass vials full of powder — like the one Trent had showed her. They all stared at it. "Hey," said Avery. A nervous laugh escaped from Cleo. Trent was shaking his head, grinning.

"You mean this is his stash?", asked the ever innocent Avery. "Not only that, I'm sure he's responsible to somebody for it," said Trent. "Avery, you better call him and tell him you have it," Cleo suggested. "No," Trent piped in, devilishly, "I know he'll be on the Miss Buffalo party Tuesday. We'll make sure he gets it then. Anonymously," he added. Avery was getting it. "You mean make him sweat a little". "You've got the idea." "Boy," breathed Avery, "Underworld intrigue." "That's why you're known as 'Agent Pink', correct?", Trent teased.

That night Avery awoke from an ominous dream. Cleo was sleeping quietly, so Avery went to the kitchen for some water to calm herself. She noticed Trent's card on the table and dialed his number. Although it was nearly 4 o'clock, he answered immediately. "Hi. Uh, how come you're still up?", she almost whispered. "Too excited to fall asleep. How about you?" "I had a bad dream," she said, a little sheepish. "Well, come on", he encouraged, "let's hear it."

"Well, it was about Gregory. We were on the boat for the party and it was really crowded and smoky. I couldn't find you in the crowd." Trent hmmed occasionally. "So I went to the upper deck to get some fresh air. I was standing at the front of the boat getting hit by sandflies. Over the noise of the engine, I heard shouting, almost screaming. I walked toward the back and looked over. On the lower deck was some guy and Gregory. I thought they were yelling because of the wind but then they started shoving each other and fighting. Gregory was yelling that he lost something and didn't have the money but the other guy wouldn't listen. Just as we were passing under the Peace Bridge, Gregory was trying to pull something out of the guy's hand. Then he spun around and leaned over the side like he was puking. I tried to get down the ladder but my feet couldn't reach the rungs. Instead of picking Gregory up, the other guy pushed him over into the water. There was blood all over. I guess he shot him. But then the guy turned around and it was **you**! So I woke up."

Avery realized Trent was chuckling a little on the other end. "Hey, it's not funny, it was really terrible," Avery scolded. "Alright," Trent quieted, "maybe we'll return the box before Tuesday. Now are you going to go back to sleep or do you want me to come over and tuck you in?" Avery assured him she'd sleep just fine now but maybe he should come over in the morning to make sure they'd survived the lonely night.

"Hey Trent," she added, "you're pretty nice — for a boy."
"Yeah, well you turn me on I'm a radio."
"Goodnight."
"Goodnight."

Photo by: J.T. Hryvniak

This project is made possible in part by the Arts Development Services Regrant program with public funds from the New York State Council on the Arts.

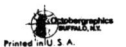
Printed in U.S.A.

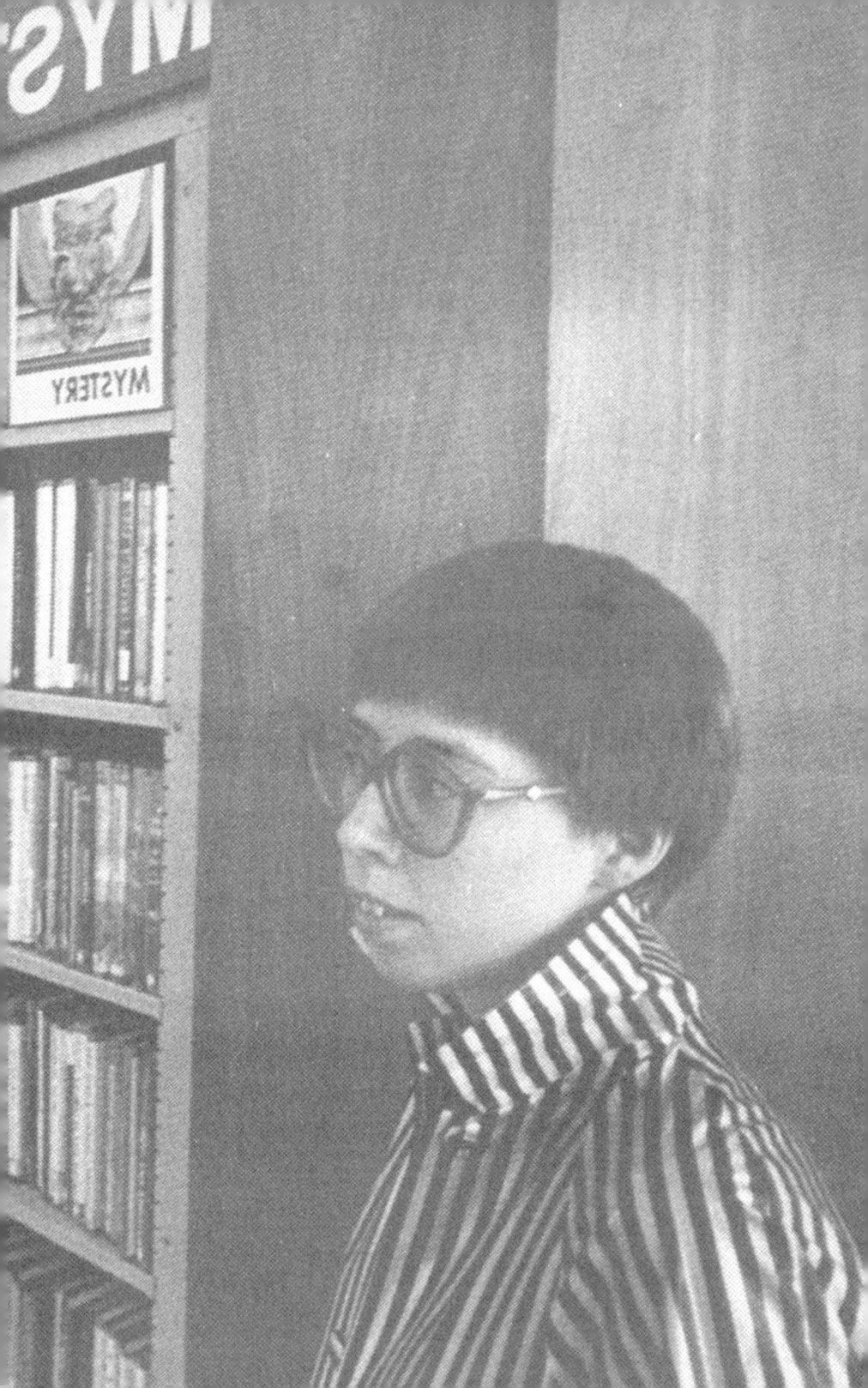

$1.00

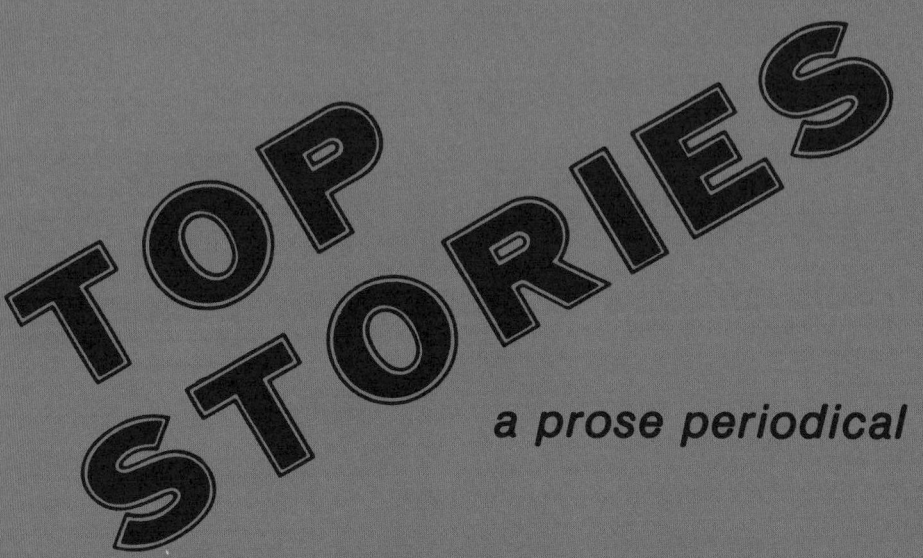

a prose periodical

#1 Donna Wyszomierski
#2 Laurie Anderson
#3 Pati Hill

available from:

TOP STORIES of *Hard Press*

30 Essex Street
Buffalo, New York 14213

TOP STORIES #5

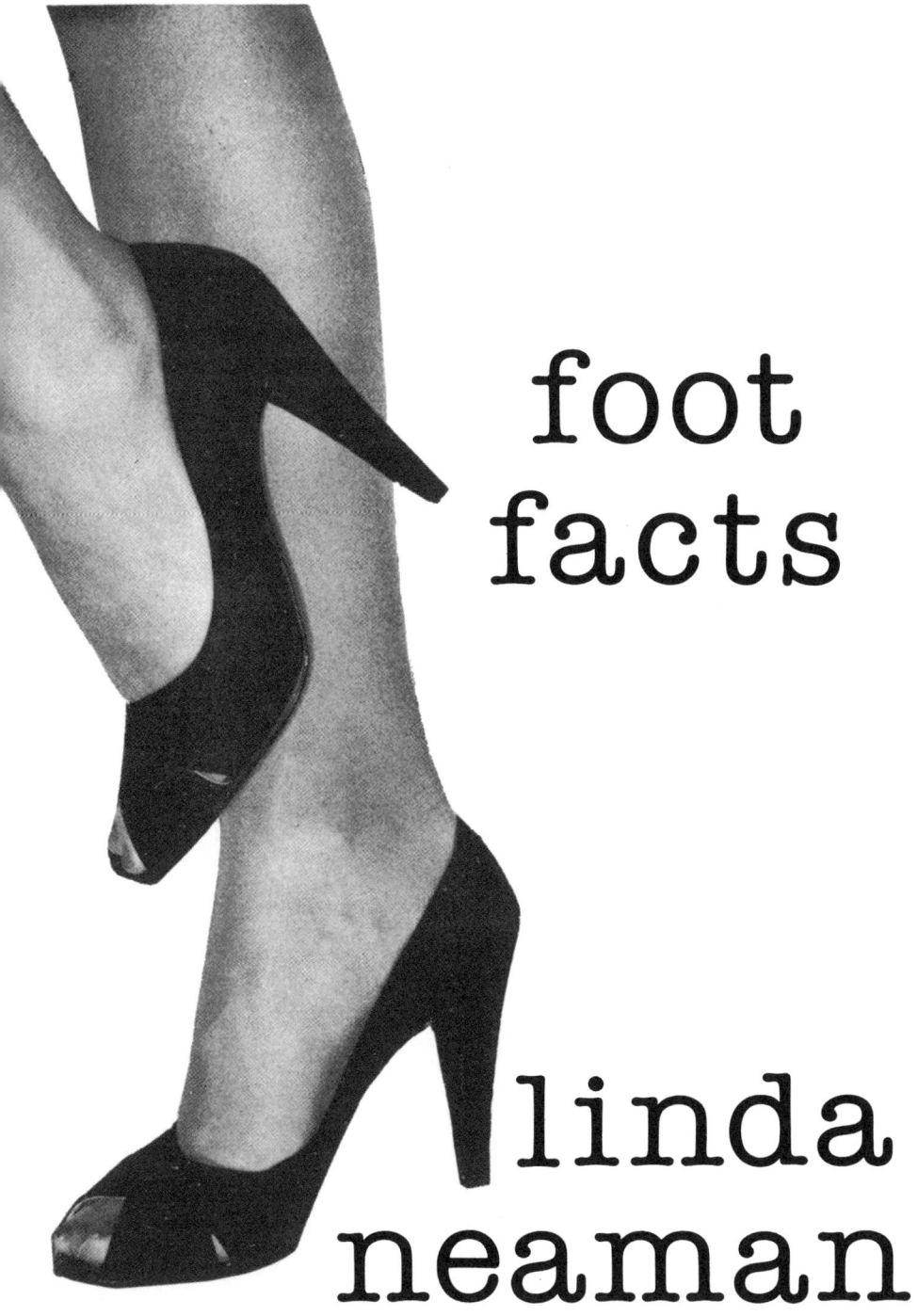

foot facts

linda neaman

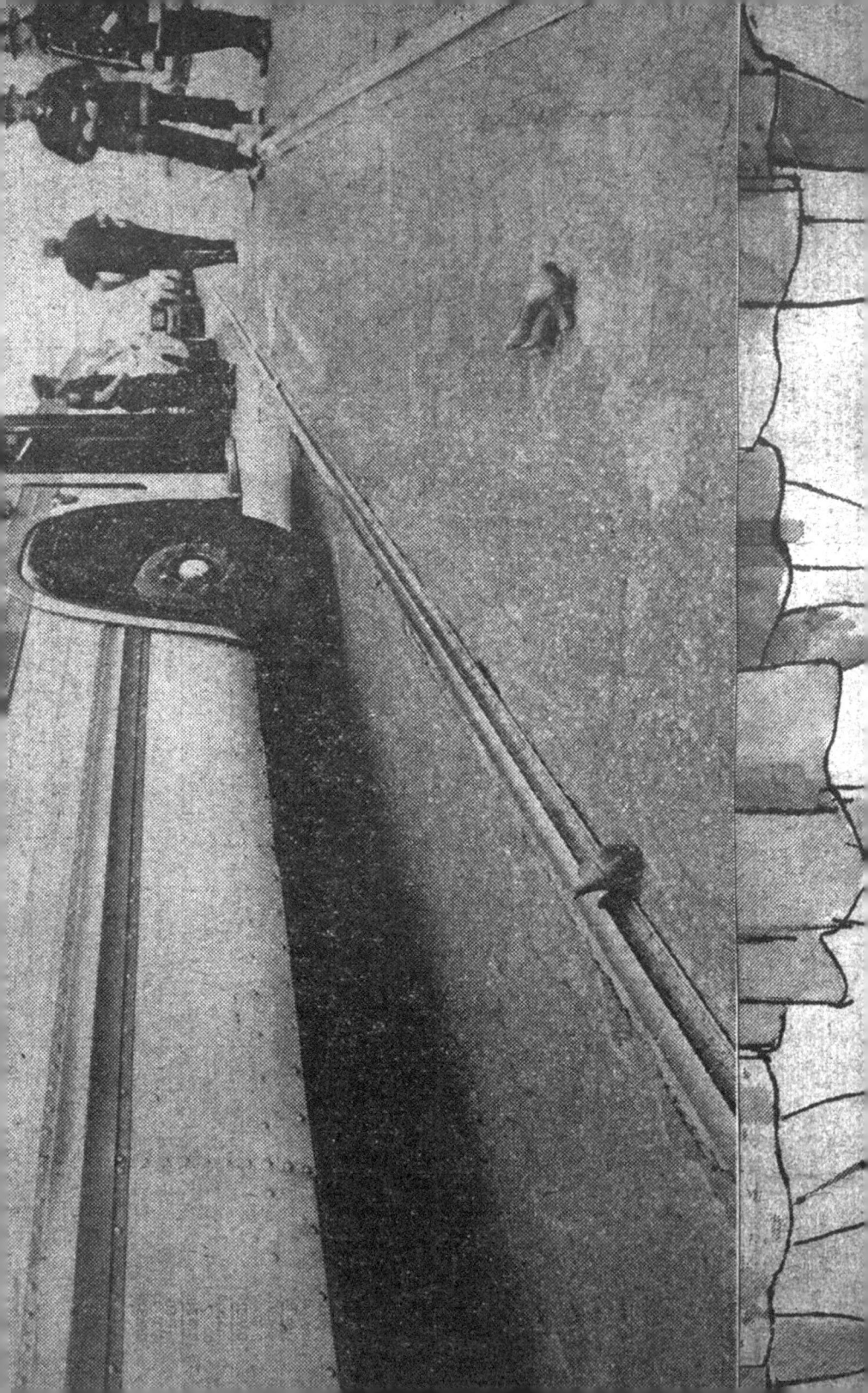

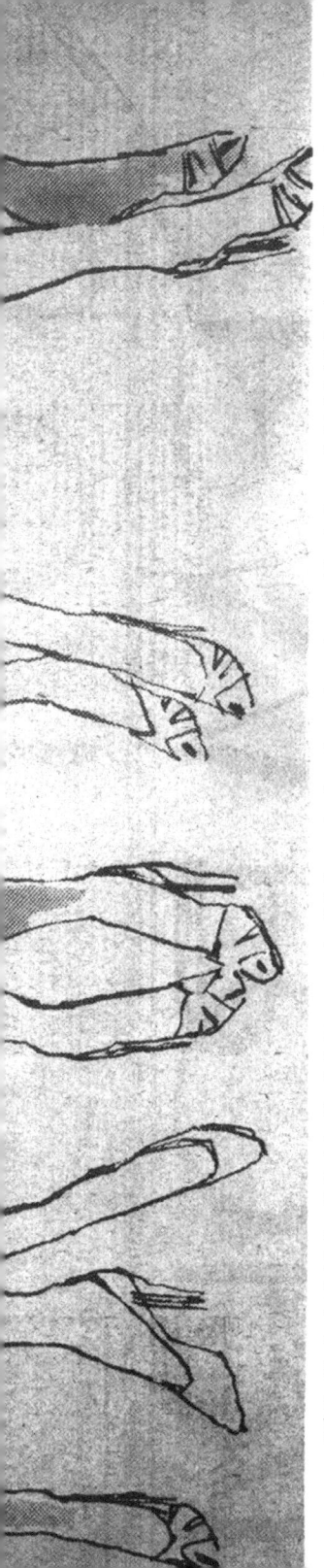

HOW TO WEAR HIGH HEELS

Very high heels tend to jam toes to the front of the shoe. Save them for occasions when you won't be on your feet much. For all-day wear or for evenings of lots of dancing, your best bet is a shoe with a lower heel. When going from a high heel to flat-or from flat to high-do it gradually. Change heel heights during the day, switching from a high heel to a two-incher to a flat, or vice versa. This avoids aching calf muscles. Shop for shoes toward the end of the day when your feet have expanded as much as 5% as a result of heat and activity.

WHAT HIGH HEELS DO TO FEET

Your feet are amazing constructions. Each one contains twenty-six bones linked by thirty-three joints and two hundred ligaments. Your feet walk between seven and a half to ten miles on an average day. In spite of their durability, feet sometimes don't take kindly to high heels. High heels tend to throw most of your weight on the balls of your feet which can cause serious and painful corns and calluses. Wearing high heels for long periods of time can shorten your Achilles tendon and cause it to react painfully when you stretch it by walking barefooted or wearing low heels. Making sure you wear a variety of heel heights will help prevent this.

October 1978, Glamour

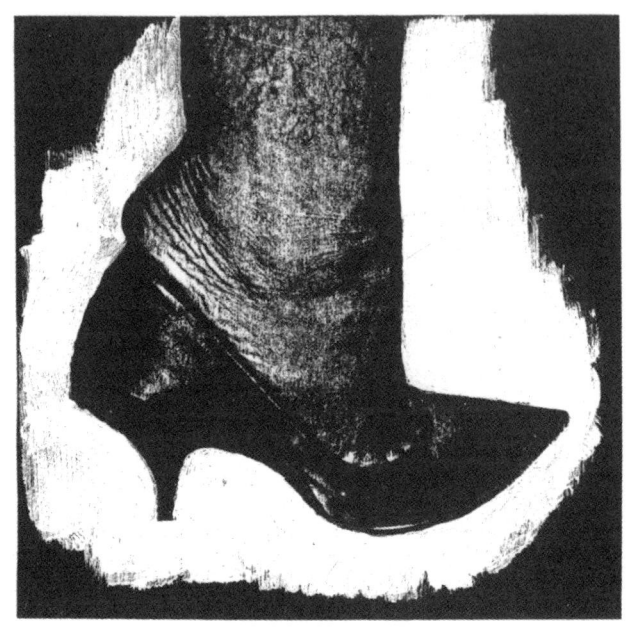

"What the doctors and others glibly call foot 'ills' or 'defects' are from womans standpoint regarded as pleasure wounds or sex scars."

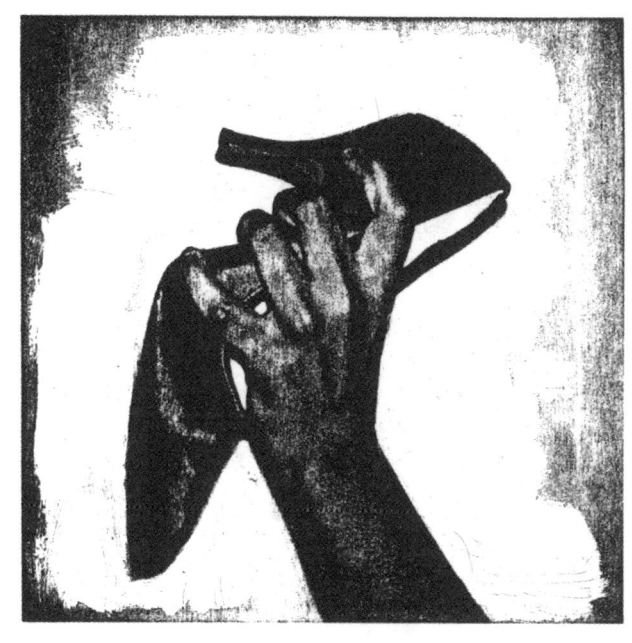

female helplessness arouses many men.

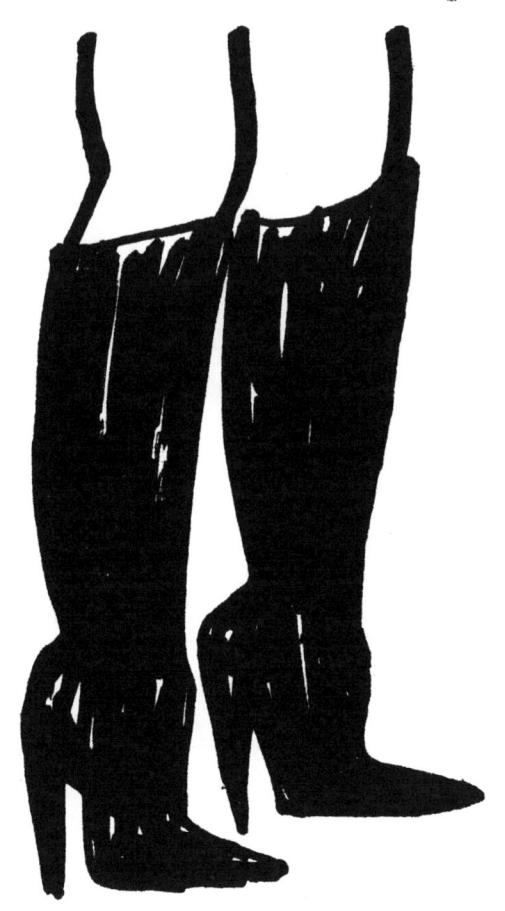

Bitches in Boots
To Stomp a Dude
The Heels of Dominance
Heeled and Lusty
Bitch in Charge
Pain is Her Pleasure

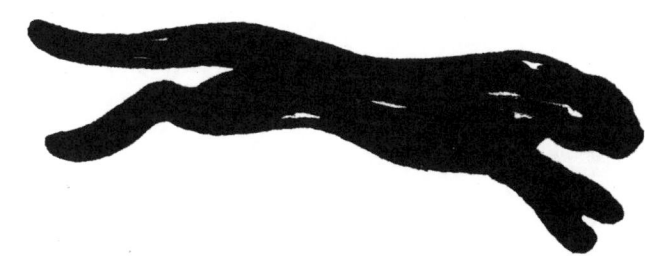

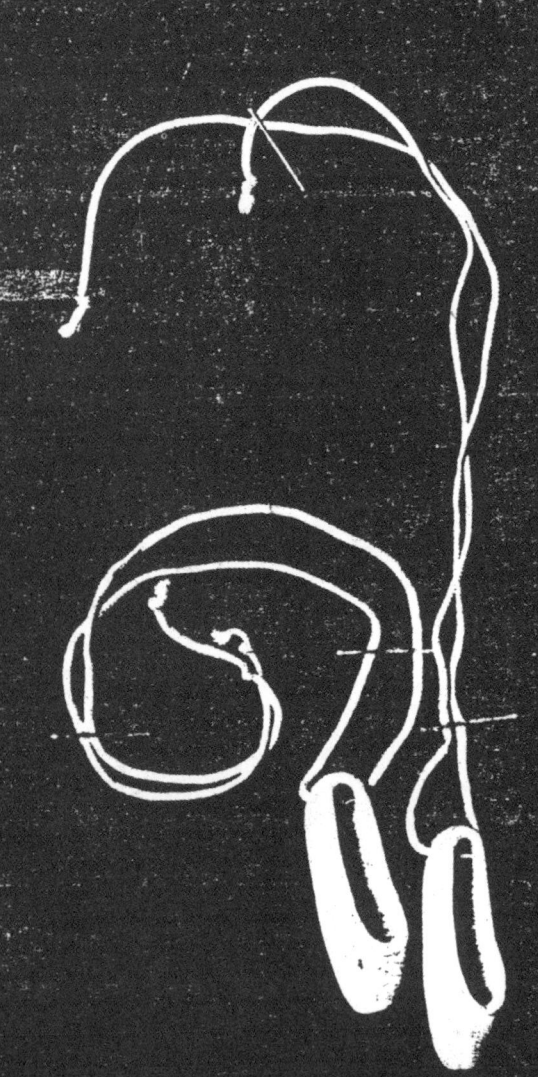

Jiang Qing (Chiang Ching) introduced "toe shoes" to the Chinese Ballet. They made the feet of the Xi'an dancers bleed.

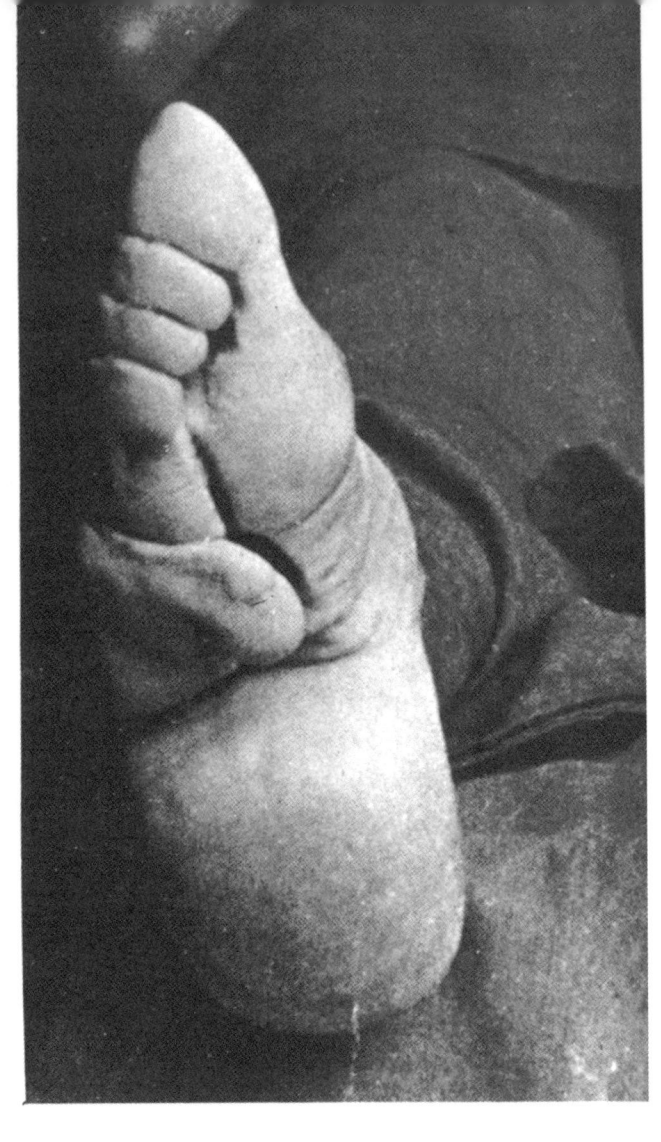

Why must the foot be bound?

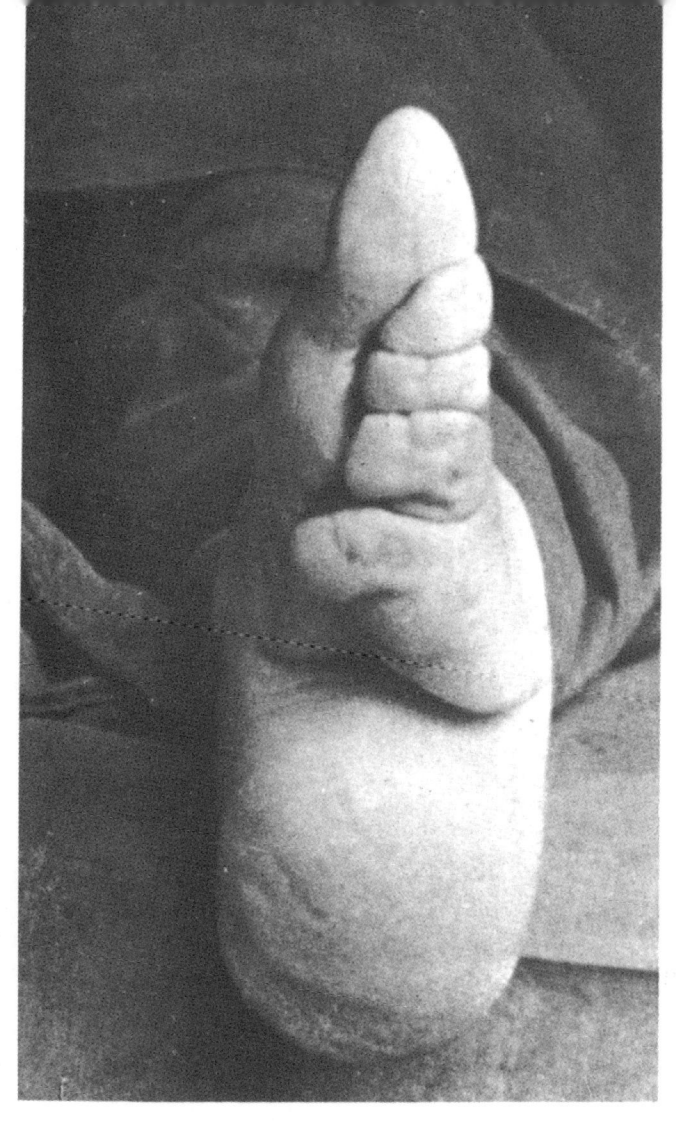

To prevent barbarous running around!

Good healthy feet: what you need to know and do

All about shape and shoes and care and pampering and exercise—everything to keep on your toes!

By Carol Kahn

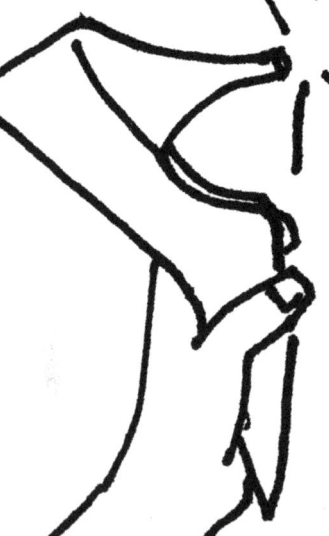

Feet are now out from under. Beautifully polished toes are bared—ankles are bared—the new evening sandals are just a thin strap or two, nothing more. But, in addition to enjoying greater exposure, feet are also doing more and more—jogging, bicycling, disco dancing till dawn. What all this means for the woman who cares about standing on her own two feet is that beauty and health begin at ground level.

Think about it. Your feet are all that stand between you and the world. The foot, with its twenty-six bones, nineteen muscles, and some one hundred ligaments, provides the foundation for the entire body. What happens to the foot affects the shin, the knee, the hip, the back, and so on all the way up the line. And, of course, it affects our mood. Sore feet and a sweet smile rarely go together. So...

(Continued from page 203)
Dr. Trott. The heel and ball of the foot are beautifully designed for weight bearing, thanks to a cushion of fat arranged in layers with fibrous substance in between. "But when the foot is placed inside a shoe," Dr. Trott says, "the body responds to the added pressure by an inflammatory reaction that causes layers of cells to build up. Since these cells are far from the surface, they continually die and are sloughed off, and thickened skin results."

But the need for a "sensible" shoe does not mean jettisoning your open-toed sandals and four-inch heels. If you must spend your day in high heels, simply take along another pair of shoes and change into them after two or three hours. "The foot normally conforms to the shoe so that just switching shoes will relieve the stress from the first pair," says Dr. Trott.

Foot care

Like the rest of the body, feet need daily loving care to look and feel their best. Robert Sparer, D.P.M., a New York podiatrist, recommends the following routine: Wash your feet twice a day with soap and water and then use a good foot powder containing antifungal, antiperspirant ingredients. In the evening, rub feet down with a moisturizing cream or an emollient such as baby oil or petroleum jelly. Air them whenever you can. A good refresher at the end of the day: plunge your feet in cold water for two or three minutes.

Rubbing calloused areas with a pumice stone or abrasive pad will remove superficial layers of thickened skin, Dr. Sparer says,

> "Walking is wonderful exercise. Best way to walk? Briskly! But don't change your natural gait."

but don't do it every day. Continual use of the pumice stone will cause too much friction and stimulate regrowth of the callus. For more lasting treatment, he advises a trip to the podiatrist who will remove the dead skin with a scalpel, a nonirritating procedure. Routine foot checkups will also help to nip serious problems in the bud, such as fungus conditions of the nail which can become chronic if neglected.

(Continued from page 204)
the ground. Alternately straighten leg so that it is parallel to the ground, hold it there for five seconds before letting it down. Repeat for a minute. Do sit-ups with knees bent for a trim waist (again, about a minute).

The stretches should include the hamstring stretch in which you stand about a foot from the wall and lean into it with leg straight so that you feel some tightness in the Achilles' tendon and calf. For hamstrings, put foot up on table with leg straight, and bend down to reach leg as far as you can go. For strength, low back and buttocks, sit on the floor with both legs together straight out in front of you and lean forward until you touch your toes.

For the ultimate in exercising itself, you might want to try walking, says Dr. William Hamilton, an orthopedic surgeon at Lenox Hill Hospital and doctor to more than 25

> "For the ultimate exercising the [foot]... try going to

a dance therap...

The following are some basic pointers for getting the most mileage out of the pair of feet you own.

...single muscle in the body and yet does not strain the muscle or bone structure, as you are supported by the water. Not everyone...

from New York's major ballet co... The kind of therapist Dr. Lieble... mends is an expert in exercising th... "It's more fun than regular foot e... he says," and the dance therapist... a program designed to fit your... needs, whether it's bringing up t... arches or turning the legs in so... walk like Charlie Chaplin." As th... legal classification for these specia... are usually listed as "masseuse" o... therapist" and the only way to... may be through referral by an or...

One of the basic exercises use... dance therapist that you can try a... walking barefoot, first on the to... back on the heels, then on the outs... foot, then on the inside.

Foot pampering

A pedicure for the foot is like a w... and set for the hair: It makes it... care for and makes it look its b... maine Beauvais, of the Elizabet... Salon in New York, recommend... lowing steps for those who wish to... own toes: First, soak your feet in... soapy water they can stand. Use... stone on the skin around the hee... ball. To trim the nails, use a lar... clipper and cut straight across to p... grown nails. Since trimming the... the toenails can be very tricky, s... pushing them down with an ora... Dry the feet thoroughly and rub... over with moisturizing cream. The... tissue lengthwise and wind it over... your toes so that you separate... well. Apply a base coat to one foo... let it dry while you do the other... best results, use two coats of co... polish. Remember to let your...

...rfaces such as grass, sand, or wall-to-wall shoes on hard surfaces. The best way to ...o throw your back or your hip out. Dr. Sparer ...ry to change your natural gait. Dr. Sparer natural for you."

...that is often hard on the foot is jogging ...panion running. Running feet strike the ...mes every hour, points out Lowell Lutter, ...ota, orthopedic surgeon who, along with ... Boston Marathon. This punishment to the ...l difficulty that you might already have... ...problem Dr. Lutter sees in the beginning ...gitudinal arch of the foot and in the shin ...they run also tend to overstride, he says, ...r additional injuries to the leg and foot. ...nt of stride which you usually fall into ...slow jog. But if you increase your speed, ...length of the stride rather than hold it in... ...ble, smooth gait pattern without stressing

...foot and leg problems for joggers is to do ...l drill that stretches heavily used muscles and strengthens certain ...under-used ones. Make this as much part of the routine as running ...s. Here are three basic exercises for strengthening: (1) To ...strengthen the shin, sit on a table and lift a weight (a half-filled pail ...of water is good), simply by moving your foot up (don't use the ...est of your leg). Hold five seconds. Let down. Repeat for about ...minute. (2) To strengthen the front muscles of knee and thigh, ...it on a bench or chair with both heels resting comfortably on *(Continued on page 212)*

Foot wear

In everyday situations, when you have to be on your feet a good part of the time, a well-fitting, supportive shoe is your best protection against problems, says Dr. Troit. Support begins at the shoe back, which should fit firmly around your heel. "Once the heel is held in a neutral position, the ligamentous structures will preserve the arch and keep it from collapsing," he says. The heel height should be low, about an inch and a quarter.

If the heel of the shoe goes much above that height, the weight that would normally be borne by your heel is thrown forward onto the ball of the foot where it can cause metatarsal problems.

Most low heeled shoes designed for walking, Dr. Troit also notes, have a steel or wooden shank along the side of the shoe that supports the foot from the ball to the heel. Shoes that lace up allow for individual bumps and humps such as an overly high arch. Finally the shoe should be wide enough so that the ball or metatarsal region of the foot has adequate room. "Most women choose shoes that are too narrow," he says, and this leads to corns and other pressure problems. Ideally, the shoe should be made of leather which 'breathes,' unlike the synthetic materials that are mostly popular.

REFLEXOLOGY

- ▲ sinuses
- ◆ pituitary
- ■ neck
- ○ throat & tonsils
- 👁 eyes
- back of head
- ☾ ear
- ✗ stomach
- ★ solar plexus
- ⌐ lungs
- ↑ shoulder & arm joints
- ♥ heart
- ← pancreas
- ● spinal vertabrae
- kidney
- ⸲ spleen
- ✚ bladder
- ▼ coccyx
- intestines
- ▮ hip joint
- ⧗ thigh & knee
- ⋀⋀ sciatic nerve

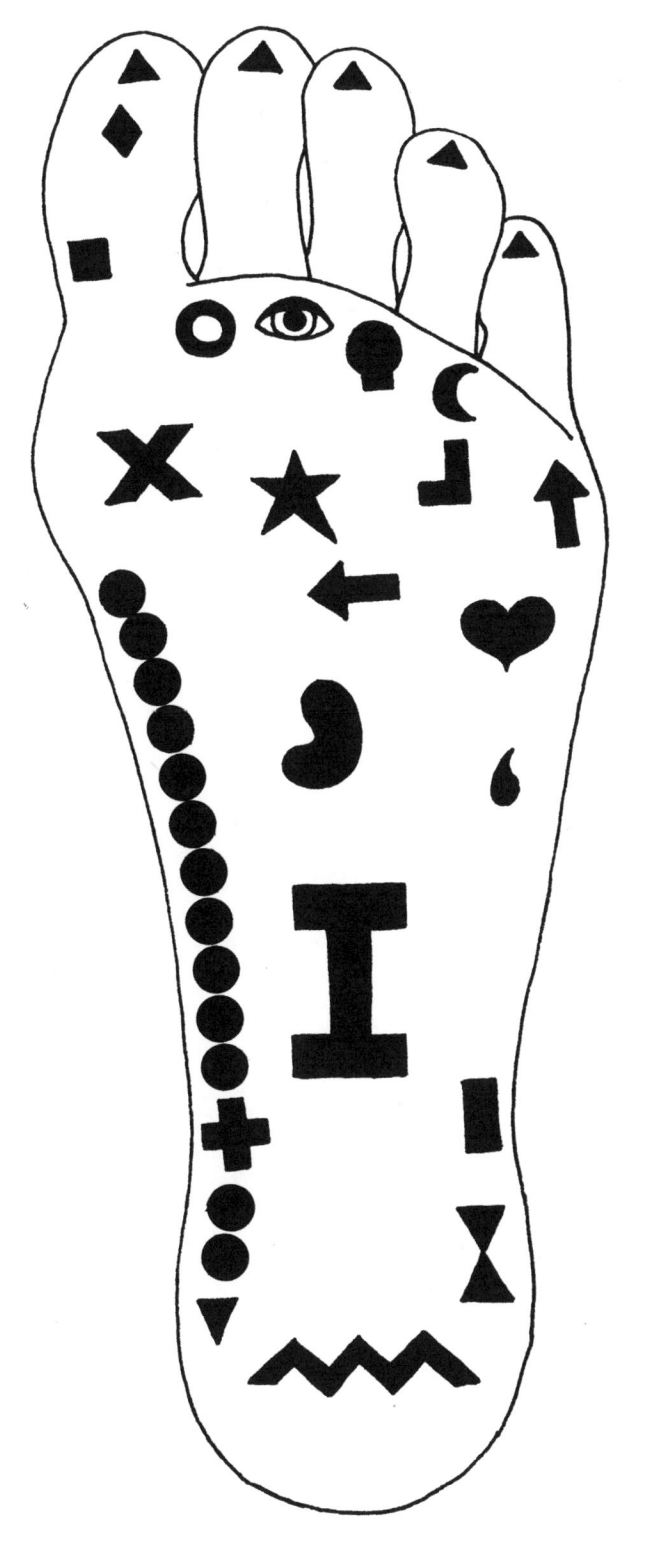

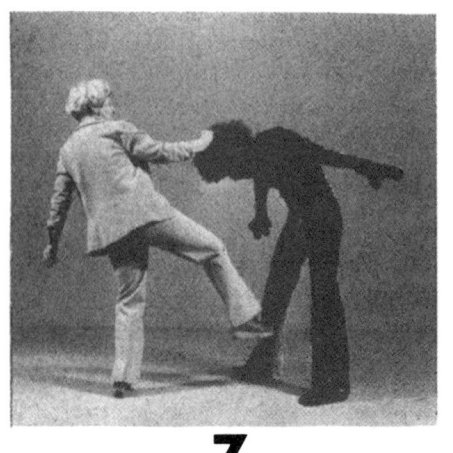

7

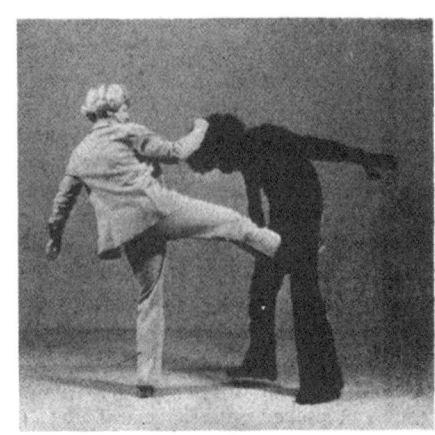

8

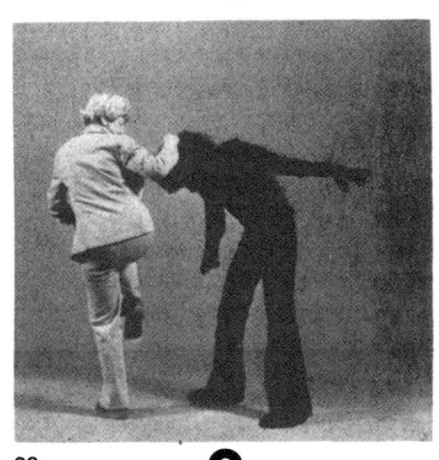

9

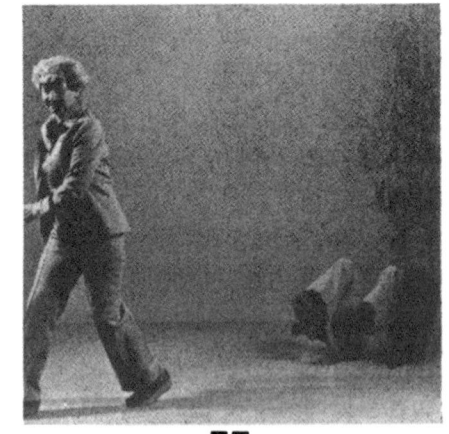

10

11

She steps back, grabs his hair and pulls him down as she kicks to his groin. She turns sideways, hits, and breaks the kneecap, then escapes.

About Chinese Women - Julia Kristeva

Black Belt Magazine

The Curious Erotic Custom of Chinese Footbinding - Howard S. Levy

Gyn-Ecology - Mary Daly

Glamour Magazine

The Massage Book - George Downing

Psychopathia Sexualis
- Richard von Krafft-Ebing

The Sex Life of the Foot and Shoe
- William A. Rossi

Woman Hating - Andrea Dworkin

Vogue Magazine

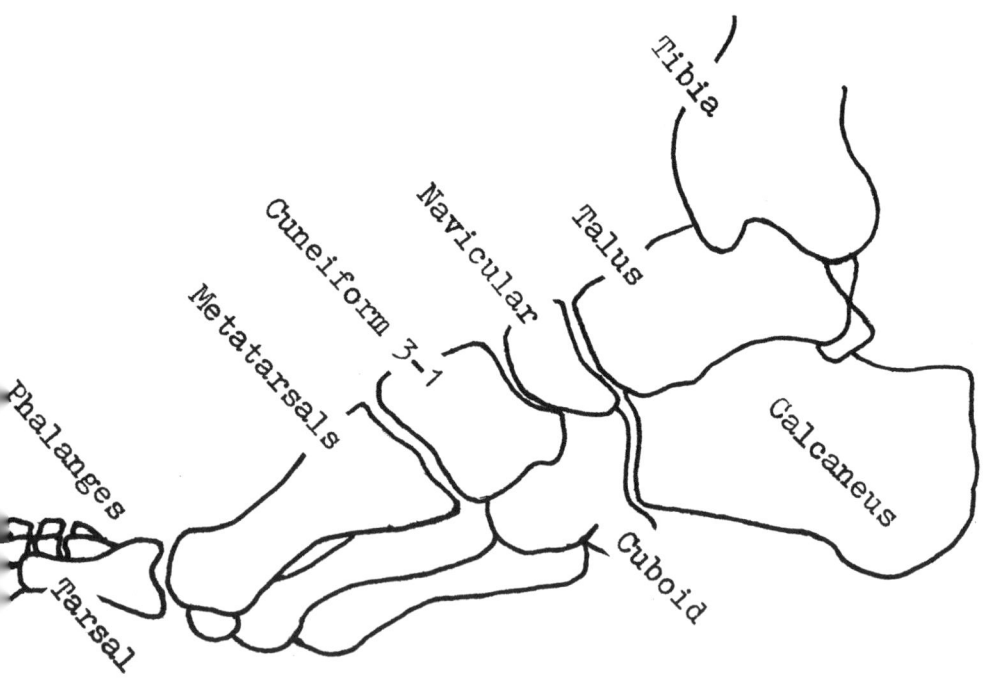

This project is made possible in part by the Arts Development Services Regrant program with public funds from the New York State Council on the Arts.

HARD PRESS PRINTING

$1.00

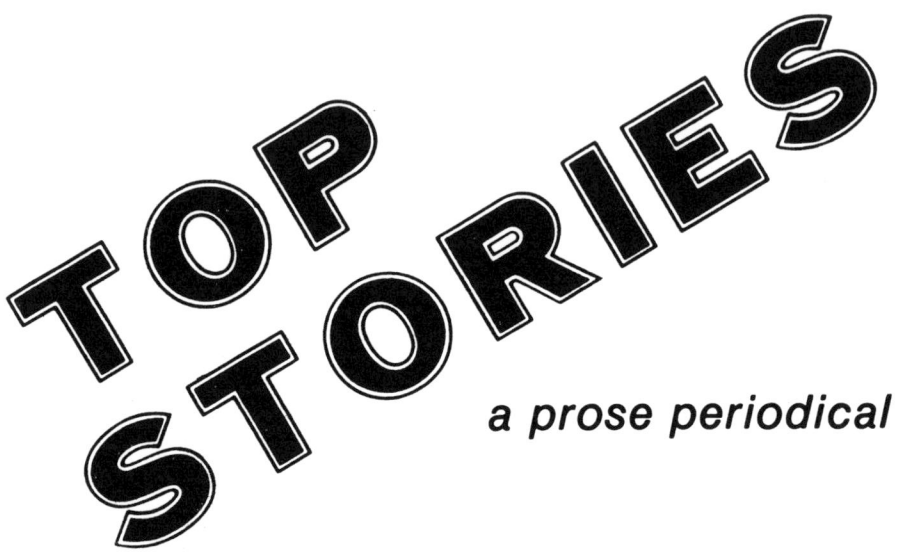

a prose periodical

#1 **Donna Wyszomierski**
#2 **Laurie Anderson**
#3 **Pati Hill**
#4 **Suzanne Johnson**

available from:

TOP STORIES of *Hard Press*

30 Essex Street
Buffalo, New York 14213

TOP STORIES   **$1.50**

THIS IS MY MOTHER. THIS IS MY FATHER.

BY GAIL VACHON

TOP STORIES #6

THIS IS MY MOTHER. THIS IS MY FATHER.

GAIL VACHON

©1980 GAIL VACHON
This publication was funded by the New York State Council on the Arts, Literature Program.

This is my mother. This is my father.

I had heard that a new form had been invented.
I went to the grocery store to look for it.
The produce department seemed an appropriate place.
A shortness of breath overcame me.
My brother, who was a medical doctor, was called.
An asparagus or crooked-neck squash was called for and produced.
She's not interested.
She's gazing into space.
She thinks what you are saying is boring.
She's repelled by your eagerness.
Her breath returns.
Her produce is gathered into a wire basket; her brother dismissed.
I am also speaking of my ideas, my autobiography, who I know.

My brother is no fool.
He rides the wake and is brought to a conclusion.
He takes the bull by the horns.
His perceptions become razor-sharp.

Alone again, one wanders, the other follows a northerly direction.
The wanderer takes a deep breath.
The other, my brother, is reminded of his past.
He drinks beer, he reads magazines and sits on his balcony.

* * * * *

Your wandering leads you to a grassy knoll.
You stretch and gulp.
A deer meets your gaze, and you take out your lunch.
You offer to share your meal; to repeat your gestures.
There is a salty smell, of urine or sweat.
I'm tough, or I'm a pretty girl.
I know what I am saying.

        *   *   *   *   *

The northern region is full of wild animals.
At night they make beautiful terrifying sounds.
The streets are narrow and lined with tall ombrous trees.
Many of the houses are painted red; each has a little balcony
    from which, visionless, this night world may be perceived.
A more casual approach can also be taken: magazines can be read,
    refreshments offered, impossible desires forgotten and
    another's anxiety ignored.

Inside the house, my daughter is learning to cook.
Tonight she will make ratatouille.
The dark pup watches from the window.
The vegetables are in several piles.
Music is playing.
My hand brushes against the front of your pants.
The kitchen door is closed tightly.

The airport is a few miles away.
My daughter likes to watch the planes; we go there regularly.
We went to meet an old friend.
She had a new hairstyle.
She was on vacation.
Drinks were ordered for all.
Money slipped through our fingers; I caught my breath; my brother
    consoled me.
Autumn was coming.

        *   *   *   *   *

She moved to Germany when we were five.
The father was an opera singer.
The mother was a vegetarian.
They made paper dolls and played doctor.
She got her period before me although she was a year younger.
They wore identical clothing and told people they were sisters.
They dug two deep pits in the woods and filled them with blankets.
I don't know why but these were very important, secret sexual places.
They dug them together towards the end of their friendship, shortly
 before I went away for the summer.
They had the same birthday, one year apart.

She was two years older than me.
They took drugs together.
We were painters.
They were feminists.
We were lovers.
My extraordinarily intense fear of car crashes seems to be
 diminishing.

I have this brother he's the black sheep of the family.
He's not crazy or anything he's a professional baseball player.
He plays for the Cleveland Indians he got shot in the leg because
 he had so many gambling debts.
I wish I was a waitress.

A story of two lovers.
One falls in love with someone else and shares this with the
 first lover, stating that the older relationship must end.
Together they find a suitable new partner for the first lover before
 ending the relationship.
They discuss the potential new mates' good and bad qualities.

Do you hear the Muzack?
He longs for the threads to be picked up.
Vegetables were strewn about on the floor.
My brother swept things into piles.
She describes attitudes in discreet sentences.
You might go walk in the garden tonight.
They tell me I am clever and lovely.
We are on the way to Montpelior.
She and I dance with cold on the ferry crossing.
We'll be back here again in ten days.
We don't know it but we'll be back.
We'll be here.

I went into the grocery store to get the feeling.
I got crazy with the feeling I danced and whooped with the products.
My brother gave me Natural Foods.
I felt so much better.
I was one of the first babies born by Natural Childbirth.
My groceries were all around me.
My brother drank Miller's HiLife.
We're moving to New York.

These African men have a guarded suspicious look in their eyes.
A very fat salesman helps them try on sport coats.
They are an odd size.
The department does not carry odd sizes.

My daughter sat on the balcony.
She was sewing a red dress.
The threads glistened in the fluorescent light.
I am sitting in a rocking chair, reading Look Magazine.
We would go for a swim, but the chlorine gives her a rash.
Or was it the moonlight?
She didn't seem to mind.
I spanked her little bottom.
I've stolen these four minutes, like all others.

Long red scarves are in vogue.
You're my sweetheart.
You have that special something.
You want me to wear high heels and grow my hair long.
You fly in a plane.
Animals nuzzle in your warmth.
You desire certain products.

There has been a robbery at the bakery around the corner.
My brother is driving.
Our breath comes more easily in this northern climate.
He is careful not to run over any animals.
We glide past the darkened grocery store.
Something is making me nervous.
I pluck at a thread on my sleeve.
We listen to music on a Milwaukee radio station.

The baby cries all night.
He cries all night.
The baby, he cries all night.
I'm not getting any sleep.
I fall asleep at odd moments of the day.
We decide to get some help.
I hire a woman to help with the chores.
She doesn't want to take care of the baby.
She eats everything in the refrigerator, and feeds me peanut butter.
I don't know what to do.
My friend is sympathetic.
My friend tells me to fire her.
I try to fire her but ask for a glass of water instead.
My friend is afraid of her too.
Finally I get an idea.
I will make a big mess in the house and she will quit.
I spread peanut butter on the kitchen counters.
A man brings old feather pillows and we have a pillow fight.
I hang the pictures crooked.
Everything is ready.
My friend comes in and says, "What's going on here?"
I explain my idea.
My friend, taking pity on me, has just fired the woman.

She walks slowly and I cannot keep up.
She suggests that my tone is too romantic.
Her sentences, on the other hand, are very bitter.
We make a list of possible sources of cynicism: life, smog, offices,
    fashion, television, art, romance, babies.

I visit an old friend.
She tells me, "You look so pretty. Are you very happy? or very sad?"
She doesn't use contractions, or the words "oh," "so," "up."
Her sentences are complete in themselves.

Cakes, cookies, pastries, pies, donuts, tortes fly through the air.
The clerk clutches at her own throat.
She imagines she is remembering this and other good times,
    years hence.
The robber has a black scarf on her face, and a gun.
Crumbs settle on the dollar bills.
The clerk's arms are sticky with chocolate icing.
The robber thinks to linger, but leaves instead with the money.

The sound passes through the throat wasting no breath.
I remember good times, but do I remember only what I have
    always longed for?
Or perhaps I am remembering the future.
As soon as he tells me what the warlock said: that encountering a deer
    is a good omen, I will see deer every time I go into the mountains.
We will hear 2 cars smash into each other on the road below.
We will see a boy plummet to his death from a Colorado mountain.
We will not allow things to happen in threes.

She was dark-skinned, about 35.
She wore a black scarf covering the lower half of her face.
The clothes she wore were plain.
She left in a big grey car.

You went uptown for a haircut.
In the mirror you looked hard and misshapen.
The pretty hairdresser asked questions and did not listen to
    your answers.
She fiddled with the radio.
She danced as she snipped at your hair.

I'm not going to buy nailpolish, or a car or a donut or a typewriter or something to make me blue.
My brother will give me money and something hot to drink.
Your thoughtfulness will pay off.
You'll count your money and ride in an airplane.
People you've never seen will say "How are you?"
Your thoughtfulness will have paid off.

The women executives are very tall.
They carry the money in big suitcases.
I can lend you a few dollars if you're short.
It's a satisfying career.
At lunchtime she sucks on plums and cherries and dreams of a frozen river, elsewhere.

Your mother sat in the corner for $1/2$ an hour with her hand over her eyes.
Your father broke down in the middle.
They give you a 4 week impression five weeks in succession.
They want your money.
They give you things to make you spend your money: gold chain with signs of the zodiac.
You'll read my mind.

Animals make low groans as he gathers my long hair in his hands.
The Mother of Me says to the Baby of Me, "Do you know what you are doing?"
I stare straight ahead.
He pulls my hair back and ties a scarf over my nose and lips.

You work in a bank.
You talk on the telephone.
A co-worker complains of a belly-ache.
Every 15 minutes you get some coffee or urinate.
Your mother's photograph on the desk watches with disapproval.
The air conditioner hums.
They speak French here, in November.
I am dreading November.

If a tree fell in a forest, it would make a deafening roar.
Animals retreat.
A black pup with an artist's name sits listening in front of a plant.
A bloody crowd trips down the steps while the soldiers, carrying
    bayonets, march up.
You'd think I complained all the time.
Can't you hear yourself?

It's a night out with my electric guitar.
My boyfriend yells at me because I messed up the song.
I'm wearing a shiny shirt.
You're wearing shiny shoes.
Some of the songs we sing are in French.
The telephone rings and rings.

She's sitting in an office by a window.
Outside her window is a 30-story building beside a vacant lot.
There is a gap between the north and south halves of the building.
Little bridges on every floor connect the two halves.
I never see anyone on these little bridges.
The shadows of the buildings on the other side of the lot climb
    down her building; if she were here for a long time she would
    amuse herself by learning to tell time by their position.

A lady behind me hums the theme from Looney Tunes.
A man across the way says, "I'm living but I'm not living."
The telephone rings and rings.

She is having a "nervous breakdown."
Two years ago she tried to kill herself.
She slashed her wrists.
I was horrified when I saw her arms.
She hasn't tried to kill herself this year.
My brother says she has too much control of herself.
I guess I have too much consciousness of myself.
It's a long story, too long to go into here.
You promise to take me to the races in the spring.

We take the subway to the racetrack.
We go through the turnstyle.
The crowd is milling about.
The horses are led around in a circle.
Several people laugh at the idea of roast beef and swiss cheese.

I admire one of the horses as well as his jockey clad in shiney pink.
I make a $2 bet on No. 2.
We have pizza and Yoo-hoo.
Her skin looks very dry, as if she lived in New Mexico.
My face is grey and pinched.
After a while you get used to things being this bad.
Like if you have an embarassing personal problem you don't talk to
    anyone about it and it gets internalized so that you're hardly
    conscious of it.
Well, theorizing about things is no help at all.
You have to take action.

Hi sweetheart how are you?
I ironed my red shirt and it melted.
I wore it anyway.
I'm driving now.
We enter a tunnel and our pupils contract.
The tunnel is made of shiny white tiles lit by fluorescent lights.
My brother and I sing "One Hundred Bottles of Beer on the Wall."

We come out of the tunnel and radio comes back on.
It's dark, we sing about beer, we play the radio.
The tunnel seemed very bright.
The black pup, pink tongue dripping, sits obediently.
The telephone rings and rings.

My daughter visited the arcade.
She bought fish protein concentrate and the clerk smiled
    an archaic smile.
She said she was late because of the arctic wind.
She told this fishy story and smiled archly at my disbelief.
I served her fried fish and french fried potatoes.
I fed the leftovers to the deer.

Is there anymore? Anymore? Is there anymore?
Are you ready? Are you ready for this? Do you like it? Do you
   like it like this?

Fishless waters flow through this arcane place.
Let's take a trip! Let's drive down that old avenue we used to
   know so well.
An old black Buick is still parked by the side of the road.
She lingers there with a queer fish who studies archaeology.
An anathema is a curse.
Your old age is approaching. Are you ready?

I hear there's a very attractive shopping center below street level.
It's so big and there are so many people you don't know.
My horse-racing friend once sold money.
I gave her a miniature doll from Guatemala in exchange for
   20 pennies.

The path snakes its way up the mountain.
Redbirds are all around.
You take off your hat and wipe your brow.
You haven't heard the news in weeks.
You open the window.
It's a long way down; you toss a penny.

Your sweetheart makes you a drink.
You live on the twenty-second floor.
Your windows overlook a huge vacant lot.
There is a fountain across the street.
Red pennies underwater glisten in the sunlight.

Someone met my brother on the bridge and later heard him speak
   his lines with gusto.
They shared an awkward meal.
They attempted to reconcile their 2 languages.
I walked, you rode your bicycle.
They misunderstood each other's sentences.
Sometimes one looked over the other's shoulder when they spoke.

I was fingerprinted again this morning.
They made two prints of each finger; one flat and one rolled.
I looked very solemn when they took my picture.
The lady explained that it would be in the FBI's permanent file.

She made a little bow when she walked in front of the store.
I am given a feather.
You are trembling slightly.
We ride to the river and tie our horses at the bridge.
The sky is pink.
You have head lice.

She stretched her long legs and opened a bottle of beer.
She will wear a black scarf with glistening red threads running
    through it.
She disregards the rules and she will pay for it.
I'll turn the heat on for her.

We make an agreement on the telephone.
You acknowledge my influence.
You've lost your receipt and your confidence.

The ladies admire you.
She looks like a little doll.
You look so proud holding her.
But I hear you cursing under your breath.

It's Friday night and the boys are placing their bets.
They're remembering a rare treat.
Red-eyed animals lurk in the bathroom.
You make efficient use of your time.

You sit on the balcony and ponder the future.
An airplane flies overhead.
Confetti flutters down.
You've found your receipt.
You turn the pages languidly.
You're relaxed.
The telephone rings and you do not answer.
Tonight, you can see your breath.

I can hear the water flowing and the soft motions of the horses.
I disregard the rules.
I ride in a short airplane.
Someone will meet me at the airport.
We will have a large meal.
I will be languid and confident.

    * * * * *

I drove my brother's car.
The car ran out of gas.
A handsome guy offered me a ride to the gas station in his van.
When we got there, he pulled out a gun and took the money.

We went screaming down the highway.
We robbed a bakery and a flower shop.
I sang a sexy song in a bar while he robbed the bartender.
When we got outside the police were waiting for us.
My brother was with them.
The guy had a gun but I pulled his hair.
Three policemen ran up and grabbed him.
He said "shit" on television.

I can hear the water flowing and the soft motions of the horses.
I disregard the rules.
I ride in a short airplane.
Someone will meet me at the airport.
We will have a large meal.
I will be languid and confident.

    * * * * *

I haven't mentioned that I make films.
I haven't mentioned that my name is Poland.
I haven't mentioned my children, Jack and Mary.
In New York the workmen play ring-around-the-rosy on
  the girders.
The disco beat catches your step.
The pulse of the nation drives your heart.

He came to the doctor's office for scientific investigation.
The doctor made a speech.
He returned to the hospital two years later wearing a long black
    cape and a bag pulled over his head.
The doctor ran an advertisement in the Sunday paper.
Suitable accomodations were found for him.
He attended the opera; he visited the countryside.
Daily baths eliminated the foul odor.
Beautiful ladies of noble birth touched his hand and gave him
    photographs of themselves.
A short time later, he died in his sleep.

You'll be home tonight you're my sweetheart I've swept the floor.
You have that special something.
We'll have a fine meal.
I bought red flowers for the table.

She picks up her threads.
Her senses are in tune.
She puts her gear into the car.
They go ice fishing in New Hampshire.
There's a pile of lemons on the table, a stack of magazines by the radio.
Saturday, Wednesday, Friday, Tuesday.

Your tattered fashions will lead you nowhere.
I had heard that a new word had been invented.
You get oh, so dressed up, and go out shopping.
Maybe you would hear it on the street.
My pants zip up the side; I close my jacket zippers.
My high heels grind into the pavement.

What do I want—fame, fortune—what?
You know the answer only when your gears are out of synch.
You wear heels so high you teeter and fall.
It's dangerous and your face is dirty.
You're disorganized and your feet hurt.

You came back together at last, years later.
You compared experiences.
I had become a famous skier, and traveled a lot.
The thin air invigorated me; the alpenglow gave me spiritual solace.
You avoided the subject of money.

Her spikey haircut punctured the elevator.
She was disconsolate.
The money she had spent had wiped out her savings.
She sang a funny little song.

In Nova Scotia, I went out to buy a pair of wool trousers.
The store is having an election day special.
The disco beat makes you want to spend your money.
My plans were shattered.
I was disconsolate.
I put my trousers on lay-away.
I bought a Yoo-hoo and sank into a chair.

"Aloha" said a black man selling hot dogs and Yoo-hoo.
I can't help smiling.
I notice the length of skirts, shiny buckles on shoes.
My daughter is throwing her boomerang in the back yard.
She is glad to see me and gulps her chocolate soda eagerly.
I thumb through my magazine, being a mother.

If only I could get a little ahead of myself.
I buy bananas but I only slip and fall.
I plan a ferry crossing.
My brother will pick me up and give me relief.
I'll take the bull by the horns.

A distant cousin from the South has dropped in unexpectedly.
He talks loud and has a funny walk.
His manners are peculiar.
He keeps his money in his shoe.
He goes to bed at 9:15.
He sleeps in the living room, so we have to go to bed too.
He has never been to the city before.
He is wary of bad women, but grateful to us.
We don't know what to do.
He wakes up early and sings country songs.
He is grateful to us for taking care of him.
Finally I get an idea.
I will disguise myself as the woman he fears and he will leave.
I will wear dangly earrings and a low-cut gown.
I will wiggle when I walk.
I enter the room in my costume and approach my cousin.
He is delighted to meet me.
He decides to stay on in the city.

She had asked for directions.
I pointed towards the northwest.
We walked at different paces.
Because I dislike words, I had to walk quickly to keep ahead of them.

I'm marking time.
My half-birthday will be in December.
Perhaps you're too old to count your birthdays by halves.
But like my middle name, my half-birthday was revealed to me late in life, when I thought I had already been told all the facts about myself.
I was 4 and a half at the time.

I love the disco and the natural food.
Disco makes me feel so good.
When I walk down the street the disco comes out of all the stores.
The disco, it's the driving pulse of the nation.
Disco makes you want to buy.

Your old friends are bored with you.
Your new lover hasn't time for you.
Your parents are dead.
Water and gas flow through the pipes.

In front of the bakery across the street from the supermarket, you thought you saw a little black and white dog.
You turned, and it was a fire hydrant.
You wonder if you've lost your way.
Your bags are getting heavier.
You can see your breath.

My wife wants to leave the city.
She's going crazy.
She has to get out of New York.
We take the train to the plane.
We take the boat-train.
We take a seaplane.

Exhaust fumes engulf the avenue.
You pull yourself together one last time.
You plan a trip.
You find your way on a map.

Your wife is going crazy.
You breathe.
You stretch and gulp.
Can't you hear yourself?
Your arms are sticky.
Other people have planned their activities carefully.
She smells like a man.

You review the directions.
You make your way through the brush.
Your daughter is at your left side.
The sun is rising behind you to your right.

What kind of a girl do you want to marry, Bob?
Bob was embaressed.
I'd like a big tall beautiful Irish girl.
She took a big gulp of coke to make herself burp.

She worked in a bank.
Every morning she walked several miles to work.
On holidays they spread the desks with little cakes and cookies.
In the mailroom they play disco on the radio.

I'm looking forward to winter sports.
When the snow falls I won't be sorry.
They've decided to announce their engagement.
This seems like a good idea.

They'll serve fruit and cheese.
She wears a gold chain.
We'll remember certain photographs, and try to resemble them.
My elbow hurts.
You know the feeling.

You answer phones and make notes.
You walk from one work station to another.
You verify items.

My wife is going crazy.
I will have to give up my job at the bank.
I have to take her away.

Communication by trance with animals was attempted.
She stared at a swinging pendant.
The melodrama made her laugh.
We talked about old times instead.
Things are more real here in the city.
One sentence follows another.
I make phone calls and feel important.
These fitful attempts are abandoned.
You shower and shave.
I read about my retirement benefits.

It's ten past ten.
It's five past one.
It's a quarter to three.
It's seven thirty.

She will listen to the news.
I felt my throat constrict.
At odd moments I would try to follow the flow backwards.
In a darkened theatre, I remembered my pleasure.
I thought of things I could do tomorrow.

She tries to help an old man who has fallen in the snow.
He is drunk and scowls at me.

They walked around the block several times, arm in arm.
They were singing old songs.
The veins in my hands are blue.

That day is drawing near.
Can you feel it?
I lost my suitcase at the train station.
It was full of presents for my daughter and her little girl.

Her juices must have been flowing.
She had had several cups of coffee.
She went outside for a breath of air.
She knew someone would fall like a domino.

You followed directions as best you could.
The sky glowed red on your left.
Everyone you passed was walking in the opposite direction.
Cars were turning on their headlights.

Several attempts at communication were made.
I receive a long distance call.
We have a foolish conversation.
We remember an underwater adventure we once shared.
She uses obscure words in our conversation.
After I hang up the phone, I look up words in the dictionary.
Threads of meaning are tied together.
I can breathe more easily.
I can relax and enjoy a beer.

I send long distance letters to my brother.
His home in the north is unchanging.
He watches the animals from his picture window.
His son is learning to watch, too.

I went to the doctor's on Friday.
I read magazines while I waited my turn.
She put her hands on my body.
She said that I was in good health.
I paid her with dollar bills that were old and soft.

It is a busy street.
She waited for the light to turn red.
She ambled along, window shopping.
Disco music comes out of the shops.
Someone grabs her from behind.
She whirls around.
Her teeth are bared.
It is her dear friend.
She laughs at the joke and they embrace in Spanish.

When we're parents let's spoil our children.
Let's give them everything.
Let's stand up for them when they act obnoxious.
Let's yell at the other kids when they beat up on our kid.
Let's hold them close.

My brother is proud of his son.
This seems like a good idea.
His perceptions are becoming sharper.
He eats his vegetables and says "goo-goo."

So, this was shortly after we went to Buffalo.
We bought food and we sat on the porch.
You swam in the river; the Lordly Hudson River.
They talked about Chicago.
We've received several postcards from them this winter.
"You guys over the bad weather yet?"

I thought this tragedy would soften her.
Instead she is more disagreeable than ever.
The cold stung my cheeks.
Now I see she has begun to wear make-up.

Let me out here.
I'll get out on this corner.
Let's murder this girl.
We'll stab her with a knife.

"You won't be back," they said.
"I'll be back."
"You won't be back.
You won't be back."
No one was alarmed.
No one asked why.

Sunset proved to be the most auspicious hour for time travel.
The mind is in a particularly unstable condition just before dark.
One is more conscious of the grandness of physical phenomena
    during that half hour or so.

        *   *   *   *   *

She huddles under a red blanket.
Things have changed.
She often goes hungry.
She allows herself to be abused.
She gazes for hours at crossroads.
I hear you bragging about your athletic ability.

You have a gleam in your eye.
Your cheeks are red as apples.
You'll notice different things from what I see.
I hear teenagers yelling to each other on the street.
They sing an old Beatles song.

Avoiding the drunk teenagers, I slipped into the supermarket.
The dazzling colors made my eyes pop.
I became giddy in the L-shaped produce department.
Nuts were across the aisle, processed meat in the center.
I bought pressed ham and red peppers.
It was unlike me.

In the morning I awoke.
I got dressed in the cold.
As I poured the coffee I glimpsed something.
I espied a monster from the corner of my eye.
It had shiny pointed teeth.
Its eyes were bleeding.
A putrid odor came from its fur.
It snarled at me.
My teeth were chattering.

Late at night, sobs awaken you.
It must be your neighbor upstairs.
You put your head under the pillow.
Tomorrow you will buy fresh fruit.

The wind blows from the south.
I was heading north.
The going was easy.
The wind pushed me along.

Dear Baba, I received your letter.
It was so good to hear from you.
I'm flattered by your attention.
The sweater will fit by next winter.
She looks so lovely in red.
Thank you so much.

Your neighbor greets you as you open the door.
Her cheeks are red from the cold.
You stumble a salutation.
She seems to have no cares.

I became my best friend, Baba.
I'm not kidding.
I really did.

There's a corner in New York where several streets come together at angles that are not ninety degrees.
My wife wants to get out of the city.
She really does.
She's going crazy.
We became each other.
What made you think you were becoming me?

I went to the bathroom.
A woman in red was washing her hands.
A girl at the mirror was putting on make-up and perfume.
The Muzack was playing fiercely.
I went into a cubicle and shut the door.

We all were gathered around the machines.
I don't know where she got the idea that Captain Hook could read her mind.

She met her husband when they were both cops.
She always had her head in a book.
She was thinking about going to law school.

Now they are married.
They disagree about everything.
He's a conservative and she's a liberal.
He says, "You don't believe in capital punishment but you believe in abortion."
She says, "That's after the fact."
They have a lively marriage.

My brother mails me photographs.
He talks about the cold weather.

You were cooking beans in your little trailer.
Night had fallen.
Animals made soft sounds in the Texas night.
You've fallen asleep in your chair.
My letter slips from your hand.
You scratch the dog in your sleep.
The radio plays only static.

Time has passed.
I'm watching television.
I'm sucking my fingers.
Ach! Vegetables have been long forgotten.
Meat is the order of the day.
There is no time for romance.
Ten year old memories come alive.
Her old friends have joined the CIA.
Can you believe this?

Red leaves fluttered down around you.
You suppressed your jealousy.
You looked down at a chair factory from a mountaintop.
You fingered the gold chain around your neck.

I'm relaxing.
I'm riding on a train.
I have no obligations.
I can think of what I want to.
Something fantastic was about to happen.
She left in a hurry.
She may have forgotten to lock the door.
She left her red sweater on the bed.
She may have missed her plane.

Out the window, rows of two-family houses are seen from above.
The cars look like toys.
Someone you know may be riding in one of them.

I will be home at 3:30.
At 4:00 I will take a red pill.
She will become invisible.
The sun will set.

A Martian landed on my doorstep.
It referred to the twentieth century.
Lonely Horse had us both up for tea.
We tried to explain to the Martians about the 1980's.

Galaxies spun around us.
I felt giddy.
O, I looked down at the blackness.
I thought of friends I was relieved to leave behind.
We stopped at a familiar station.
They played Little Anthony and the Imperials.
We travelled thorugh the space station in an electric Buick.
Crazy Eddy is crazier than ever.
I yawned.

She's planning to go to the snack bar.
She thinks she'll go to the bar car.
I cannot restrain her.
Flock after flock of birds fly by.
I think it is a film loop.
The next stop is Providence.
The sky is bright.
Blanket statements are always refutable.

You learn to be a good girl from a song your father sings.
On an expense account anything is possible.
You can pick out the shiniest vegetables.
The newspaper confuses some of the facts.

I live to a ripe old age.
I take an apartment overlooking the river.
I perform heinous crimes in the dead of night.
I pull threads together for relatives.

You are relieved of decisions.
I whisk you through the night.
I'm a teenager but I know my way around.
A red blinking stoplight is a warning.
You are foolish to try and make plans with me.
I don't live like that.

    * * * * *

They say they will but they never do.
Now all your ambitions crumble into dust.
Now your ideas seem foolish.

Now it's left to me to go to the market.
I'll go to the meat counter.
I'll dress you in your red sweater.
I dreamed I got a letter.

"Dear Chris, Thanks so much for your package which arrived today.
I'll while away the hours with it.
I'll play the shakahati flute.
I carry it on my shoulders.
It will fit her next winter."

I'm lonely without you.
I gaze at your picture every night.
I dance down the aisles.
I play your favorite song.
Tears drip down my face.
It's my favorite emotion.
I've been remembering the past.
Certain corners we took together.
Musical instruments make up the difference.
Feeling a distance you won't even acknowledge.

I've learned to be so good.
You're good for me.
You've squashed me.

There's a break in the Steak House murders in Oklahoma City.
Ironically the murders all took place last July.
A child was killed at the border.
American tourists were unable to go into the country.
Rivers have overflowed and the huge ice floes rushing downstream
    make sounds like bombs.
The Islanders are 4 games behind the Canadiennes.
The Mets opened their season with a 4-3 win over St. Louis.

I've worked hard all day.
I've addressed serious questions.
The Mother of Me says to the Baby of Me, "You've worked hard
    all day. What would you like for dinner?"
I stroll into the supermarket, gleeful.
I glide up and down the aisles humming with the Muzack.
I had heard that a new tense had been invented.
The apples were bruised, the lettuce wilted, the carrots rubbery.
I suspected that it might describe the memories of what would be.

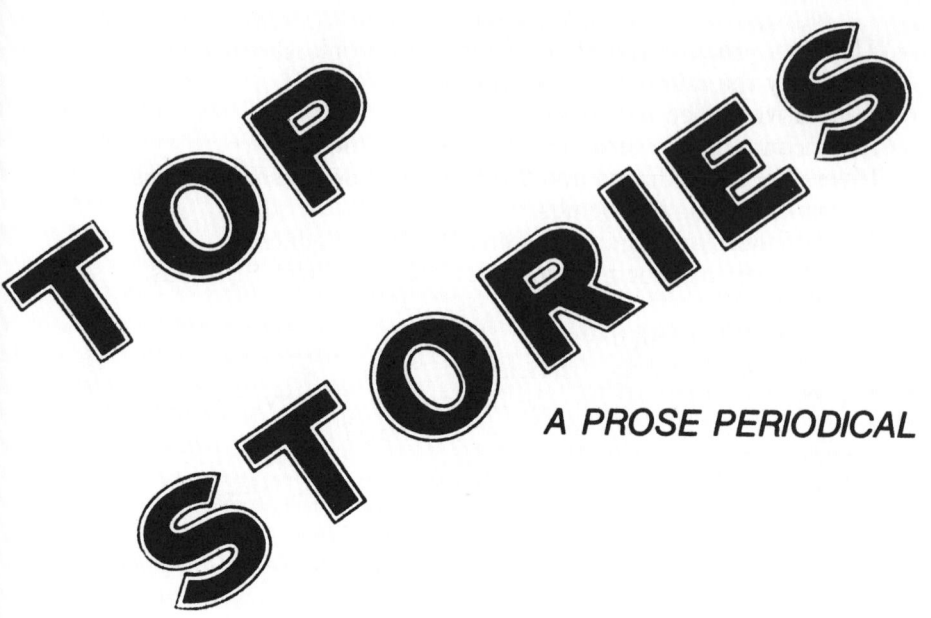

A PROSE PERIODICAL

#1 Donna Wyszomierski
#2 Laurie Anderson
#3 Pati Hill
#4 Suzanne Johnson
#5 Linda Neaman

Available from
TOP STORIES
Hallwalls
700 Main Street
Buffalo, New York 14213

TOP STORIES #7

EATING FRIENDS

$2.00

JENNY HOLZER/PETER NADIN

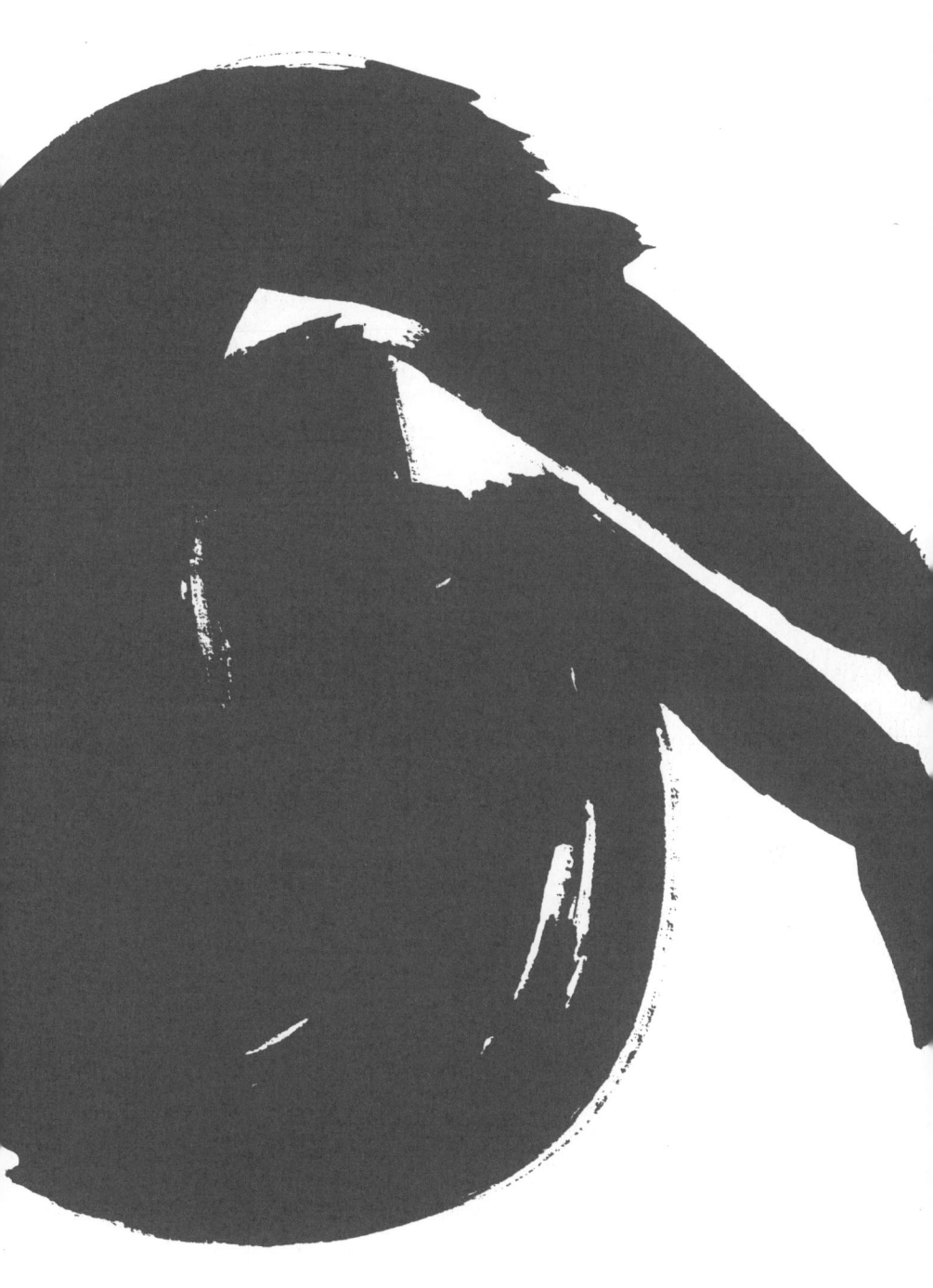

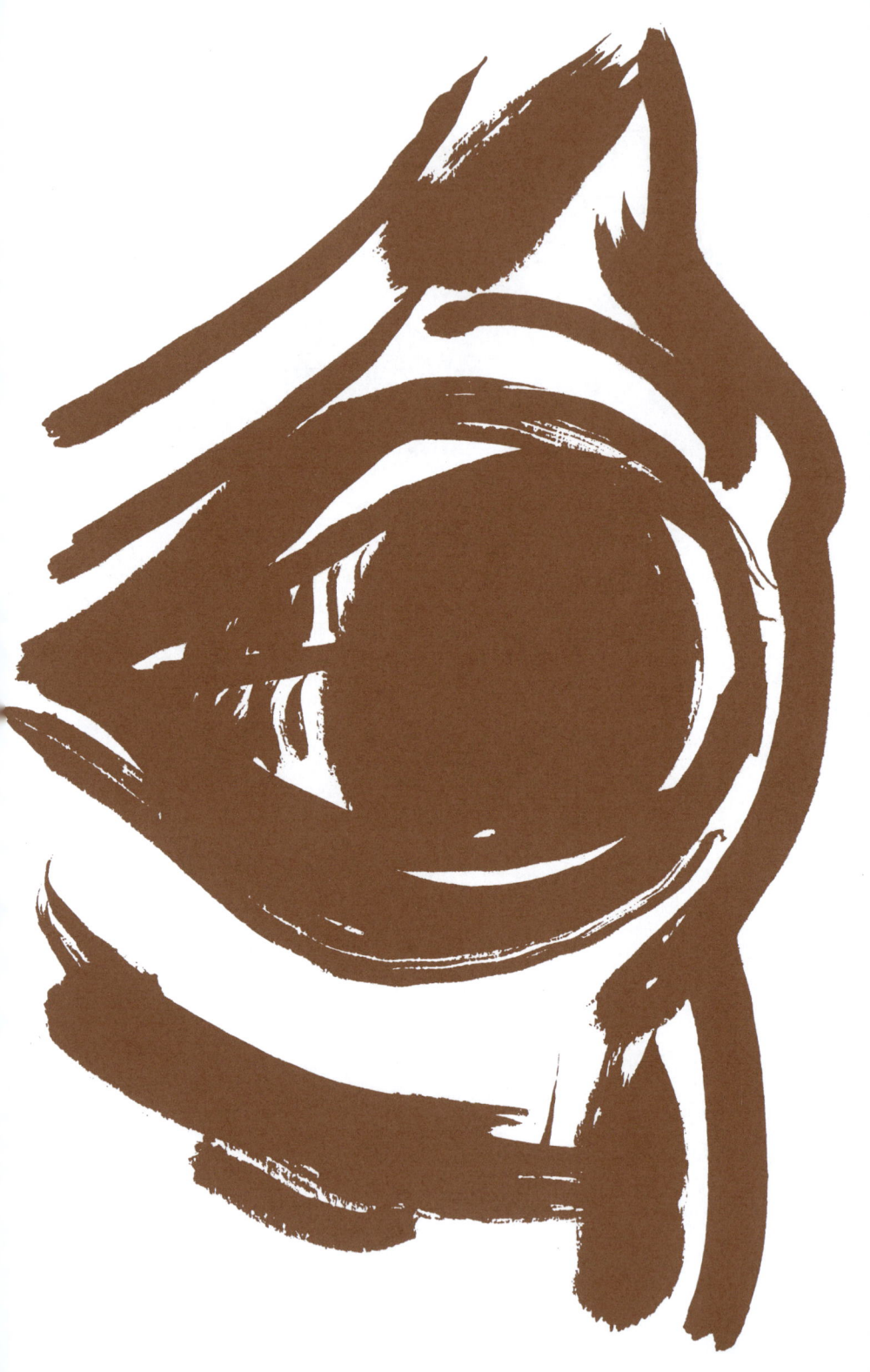

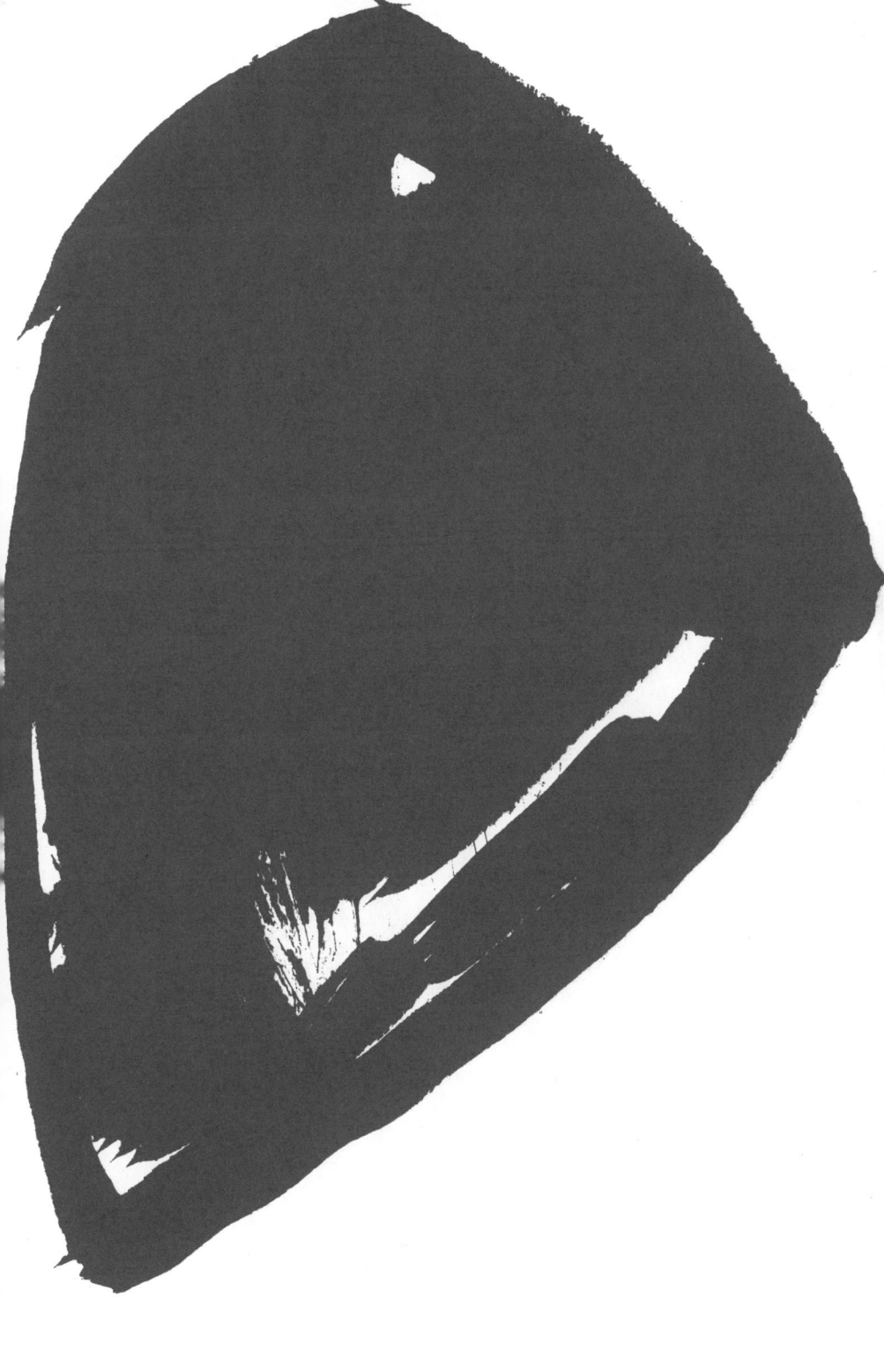

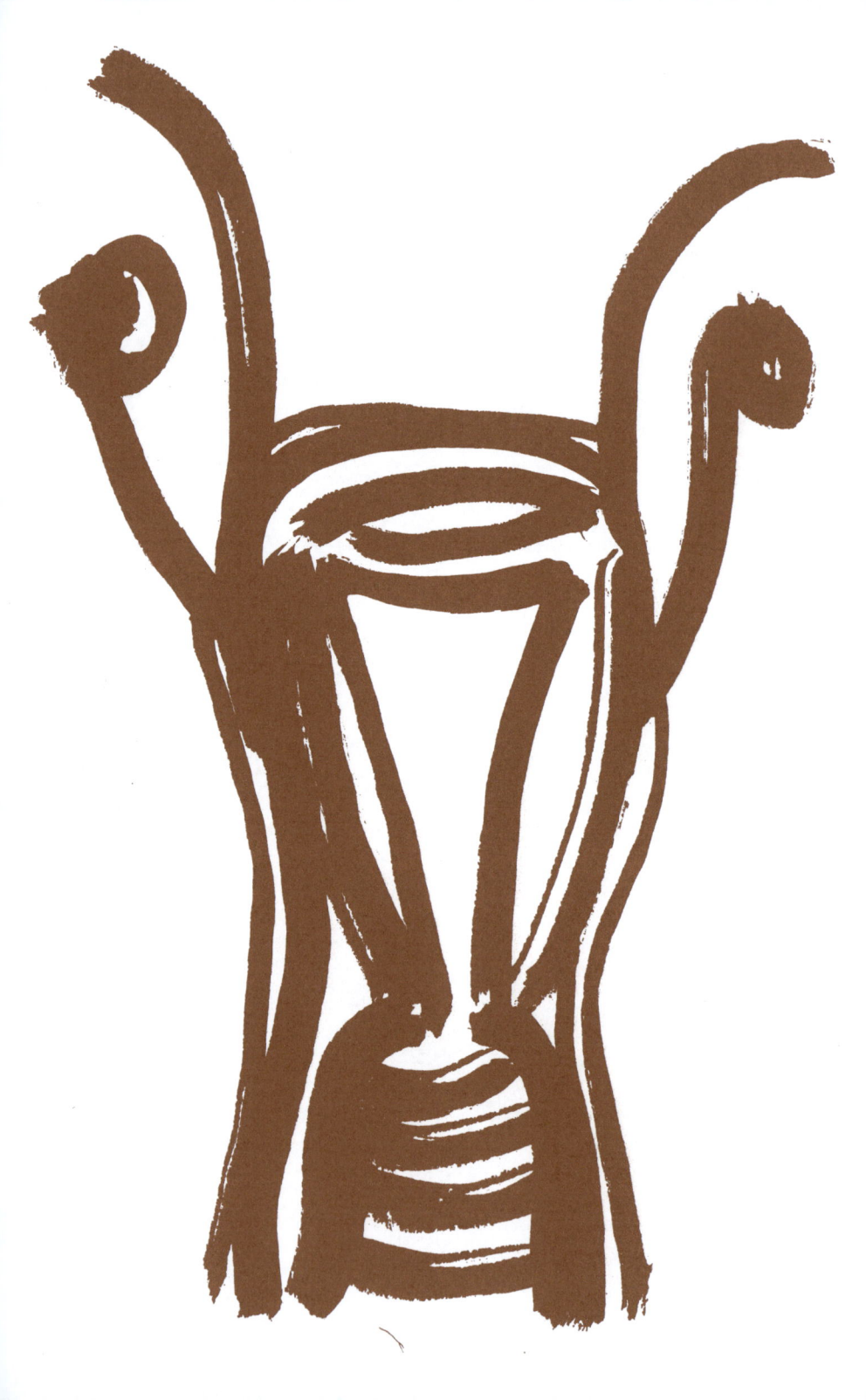

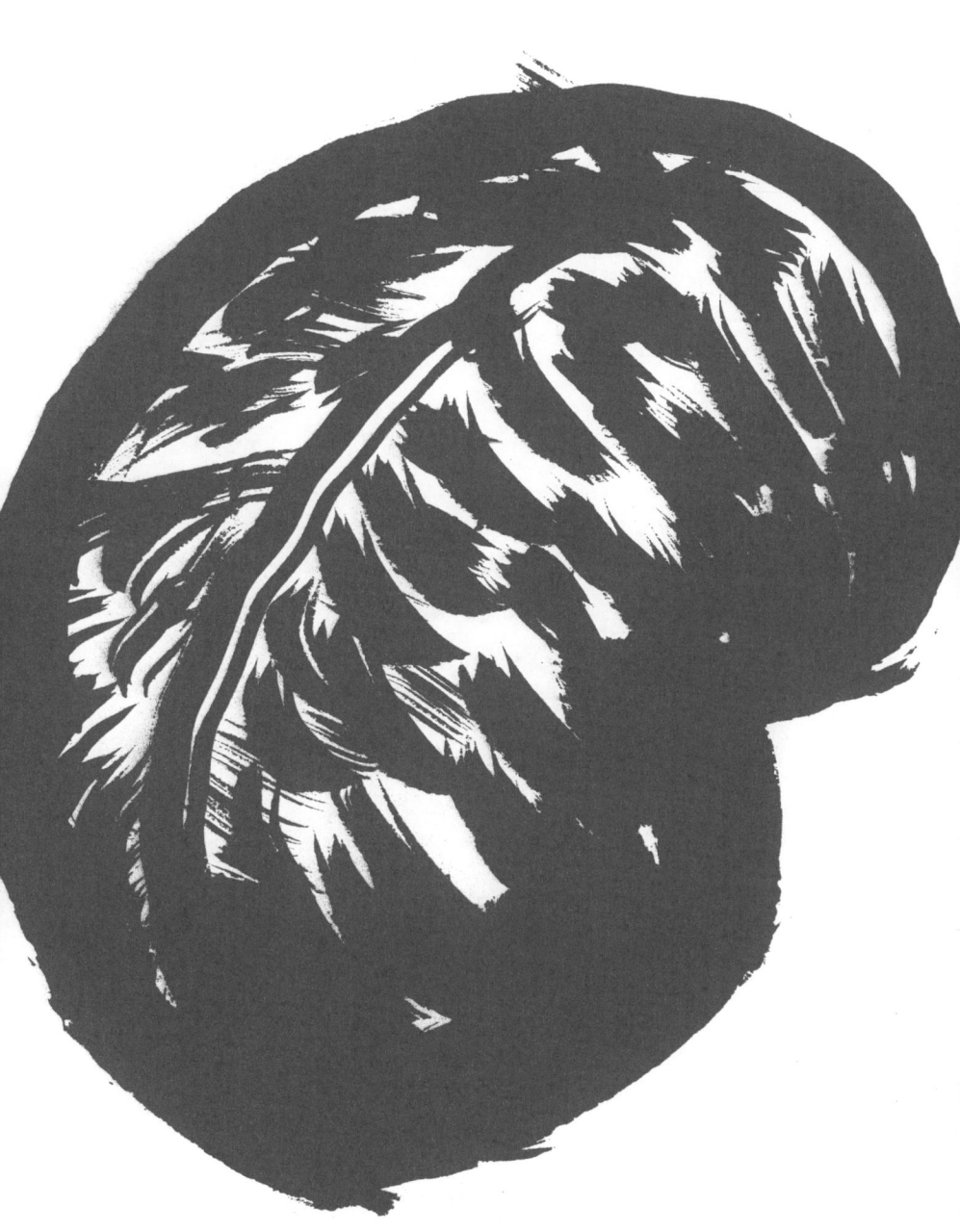

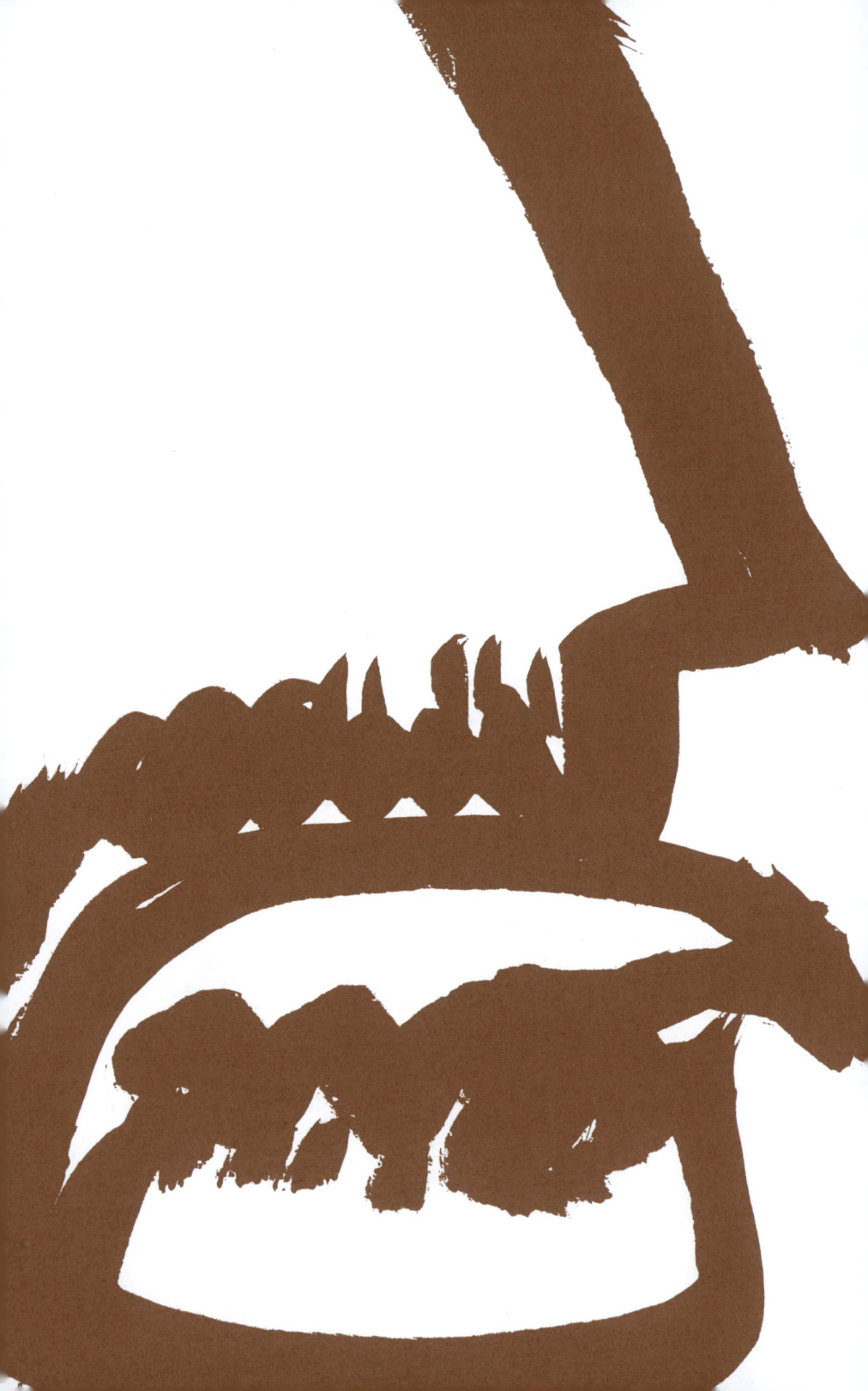

A LITTLE GIRL HAD BEEN IN A COMA FOR WEEKS BUT SMILED AND CAME OUT OF IT WHEN THEY SANG SONGS.

CHILDHOOD WAS THE TIME FOR EXPERIMENTATION. THEY FOLDED WASHCLOTHS ON THEIR LEGS AND POURED SCALDING WATER ON THEM, ALWAYS STOPPING SHORT OF EXTREME PAIN AND VISIBLE BURNS.

HANDS-ON SOCIALIZATION PROMOTES HAPPY INTERPERSONAL RELATIONS. THE DESIRE FOR AND THE DEPENDENCE UPON FONDLING ENSURE THEIR REPEATED ATTEMPTS TO OBTAIN CARESSES AND THEIR WILLINGNESS TO RECIPROCATE.

HOW NICE TO SUPPLY THE NECESSARY COMFORTS, NUTRIENTS AND LESSONS SO THAT THE OPTIMAL NUMBER OF THEM GROW TO MATURITY AND ENJOY IT.

I SAW THEIR STUNNING BODIES GO SLACK AND GET HAIR IN THE WRONG PLACES AND I VOWED I WOULD NOT PERMIT THAT TO HAPPEN TO ME.

IF THE HOUSE IS BITTER COLD, ALL THE FLUIDS THEREIN, IF NOT FROZEN, ARE STIFF AND SLOW.

IT CAN BE HELPFUL TO THINK OF THEM EATING THEIR FAVORITE FOODS AND OCCASIONALLY THROWING UP AND GETTING BITS STUCK IN THEIR NOSES.

IT CAN BE STARTLING TO SEE THEIR BREATH, LET ALONE THE BREATHING OF A CROWD. YOU USUALLY DON'T BELIEVE THAT THEY EXTEND THAT FAR.

IT IS UNFAIR TO TEAR THEM APART WHEN THEIR HEALTH AND EXUBERANCE THREATEN YOU.

IT MAKES A DIFFERENCE IF YOU'RE INTIMATE WITH THEM, IF YOU'RE DEPENDENT UPON THEM. THEY WILL ONLY TOLERATE OR SUPPORT CERTAIN ACTIONS AND THIS INFLUENCES WHAT YOU BELIEVE TO BE POSSIBLE OR DESIRABLE.

IT'S AN ODD FEELING WHEN YOU TRIGGER INSTINCTIVE BEHAVIOR — LIKE NURSING — IN THEM. IT'S FUNNY TO BE IN THEIR PRESENCE WHILE A DIFFERENT PART OF THE NERVOUS SYSTEM TAKES OVER AND THEIR EYES GET STRANGE.

IT'S AWFUL TO SEE THEM DEFORMED BECAUSE THEY ARE RIGID WITH FEAR.

IT'S EASY FOR THEM TO FEEL BETRAYED WHEN THEY'RE JUST WAVING THEIR ARMS AROUND AND THEY COME CRASHING DOWN ON A SHARP OBJECT.

IT'S NICE WHEN THEY DECIDE THEY LIKE SOMEONE, AND WITHOUT DECLARING THEMSELVES, DO WHAT'S POSSIBLE TO FURTHER THEIR HAPPINESS. THIS CAN TAKE THE FORM OF GIFTS, LOVELY FOOD, PUBLICITY, ADVANCE WARNING OR EASY MOBILITY.

MORE THAN ONCE THEY'VE WAKENED WITH TEARS RUNNING DOWN THEIR CHEEKS. THEY HAVE HAD TO THINK WHETHER THEY WERE CRYING OR WHETHER IT WAS INVOLUNTARY LIKE DROOLING.

SOMEONE WANTS TO CUT A HOLE IN YOU AND FUCK YOU THROUGH IT, BUDDY.

THE MOUTH IS INTERESTING BECAUSE IT'S ONE OF THOSE PLACES WHERE THE DRY OUTSIDE MOVES TOWARD THE SLIPPERY INSIDE.

THE SMALLEST THING CAN MAKE THEM SEXUALLY UNAPPEALING. A MISPLACED MOLE OR A PARTICULAR HAIR PATTERN CAN DO IT. THERE'S NO REASON FOR THIS, BUT IT'S JUST AS WELL.

THERE'S NO REASON TO SLEEP CURLED UP AND BENT. IT'S NOT COMFORTABLE, IT'S NOT GOOD FOR THEM AND IT DOESN'T PROTECT THEM FROM DANGER. IF THEY'RE WORRIED ABOUT AN ATTACK THEY SHOULD STAY AWAKE OR SLEEP LIGHTLY WITH LIMBS UNFURLED FOR ACTION.

THERE'S THE SENSATION OF A LOT OF FLESH WHEN EVERY SINGLE HAIR STANDS UP. THIS HAPPENS WHEN THEY ARE COLD AND NAKED, AROUSED OR SIMPLY TERRIFIED.

THEY LIKE TO NIBBLE ON THE INSIDE OF THEIR OWN CHEEKS. I'VE SEEN AN OTHERWISE LOVELY GIRL CONTORT HER FACE TO REACH A FAVORITE SPOT. THEY HAVE BITE LINES WHERE REPEATED NIPS HAVE BUILT UP A RIDGE OF SCAR TISSUE.

THEY RARELY FOLLOW MOTION WITH THEIR EYES IF THEIR HEADS ARE UPSIDE DOWN. THEY RAISE THEIR HEADS TO AN UPRIGHT ORIENTATION TO WATCH WHAT GOES ON AROUND THEM. DOES THIS DENOTE A LACK OF CONFIDENCE IN THEIR ABILITY TO REACT WHEN SUPINE?

THEY SHOULD LIMIT THE NUMBER OF TIMES THEY ACT AGAINST THEIR NATURE, LIKE SLEEPING WITH PEOPLE THEY HATE. IT'S ALL RIGHT TO TEST THEIR CAPABILITIES, BUT IF THEY DON'T KNOW WHEN TO STOP, THEY'LL HURT THEMSELVES.

THEY WERE STRIPPING A THIRD FELLOW SO THAT IN A MATTER OF SECONDS HE LAY CURLED-UP AND NAKED ON THE SIDEWALK.

TWO CREATURES CAN WANT TO MOVE AND REST IN CLOSE PROXIMITY EVEN IF THEY ARE AFRAID OF EACH OTHER. I'M THINKING OF A WILD ANIMAL FOLLOWING ONE OF THEM IN THE WOODS.

USUALLY YOU COME OUT WITH STUFF ON YOU WHEN YOU'VE BEEN IN THEIR THOUGHTS OR BODIES.

WHEN YOU'RE ON THE VERGE OF DECIDING THAT YOU DON'T LIKE THEM, IT'S AWFUL WHEN THEY SMILE AND THEIR TEETH LOOK ABSOLUTELY EVEN AND FALSE.

WITH BLEEDING INSIDE THE HEAD THERE IS A METALLIC TASTE AT THE BACK OF THE THROAT.

YOU CAN WATCH THEM ALIGN THEMSELVES WHEN TROUBLE IS IN THE AIR. SOME PREFER TO BE CLOSE TO THOSE AT THE TOP, AND OTHERS WANT TO BE CLOSE TO THOSE AT THE BOTTOM. IT'S A QUESTION OF WHO FRIGHTENS THEM MORE AND WHO THEY WANT TO BE LIKE.

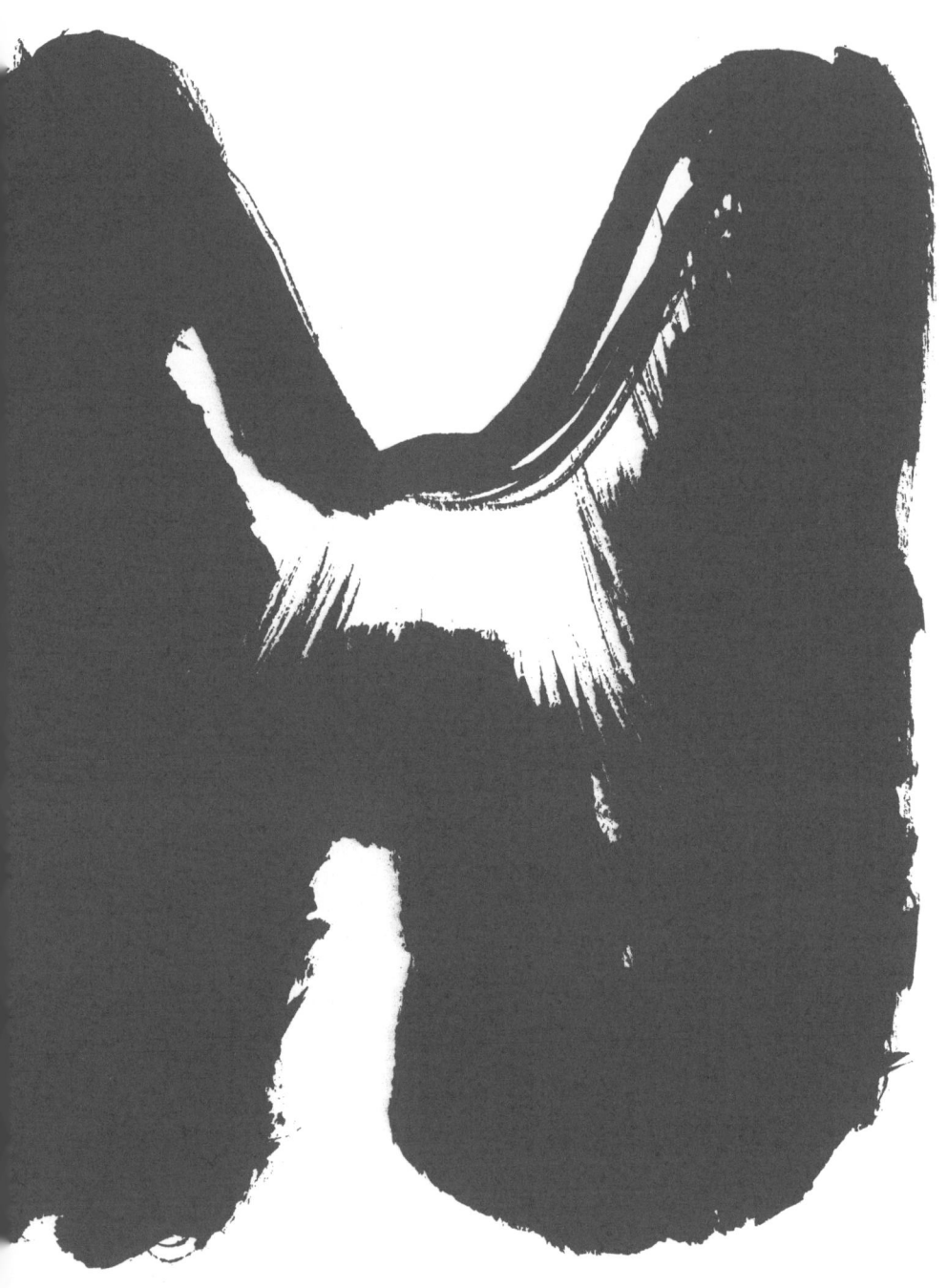

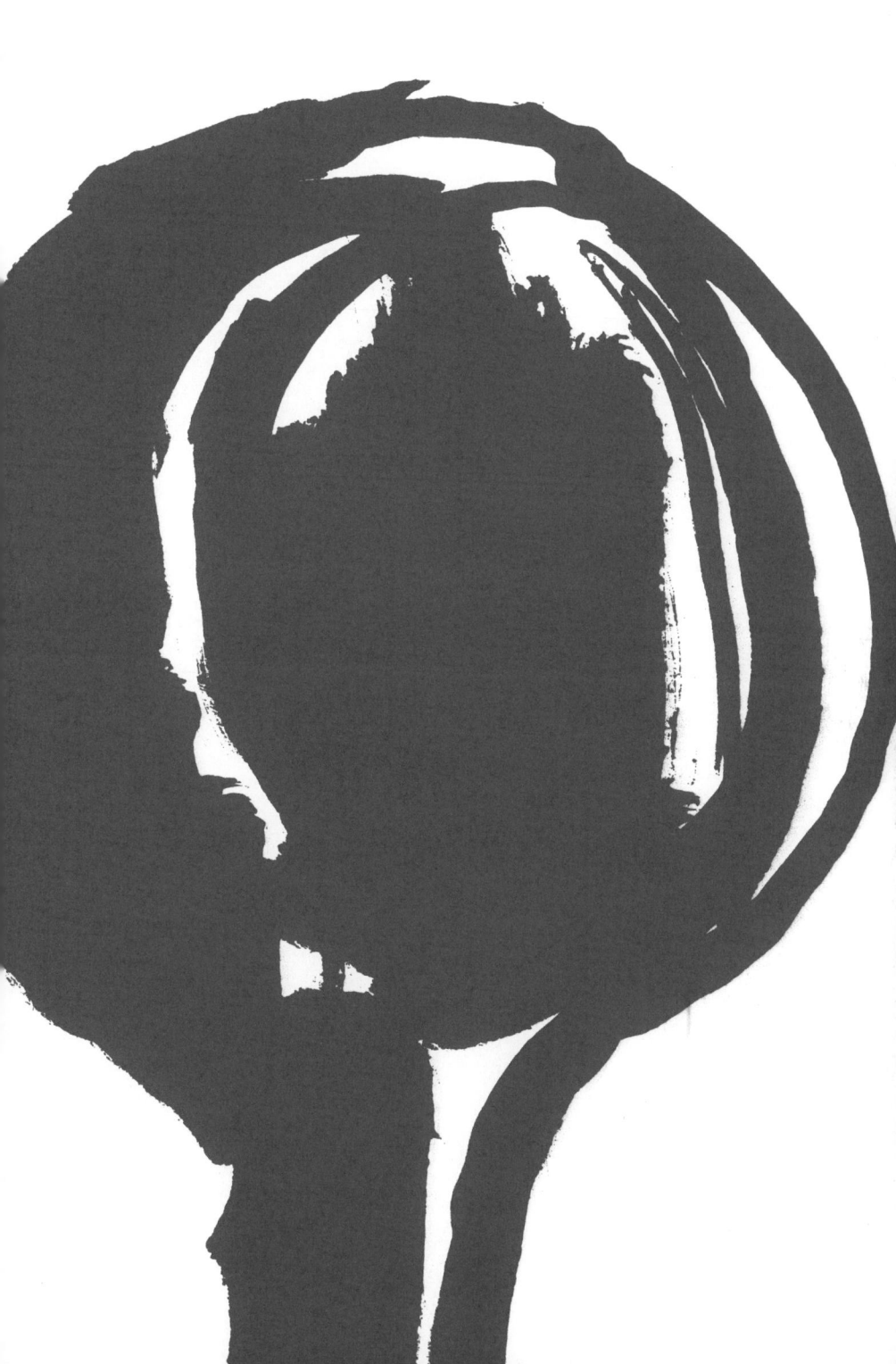

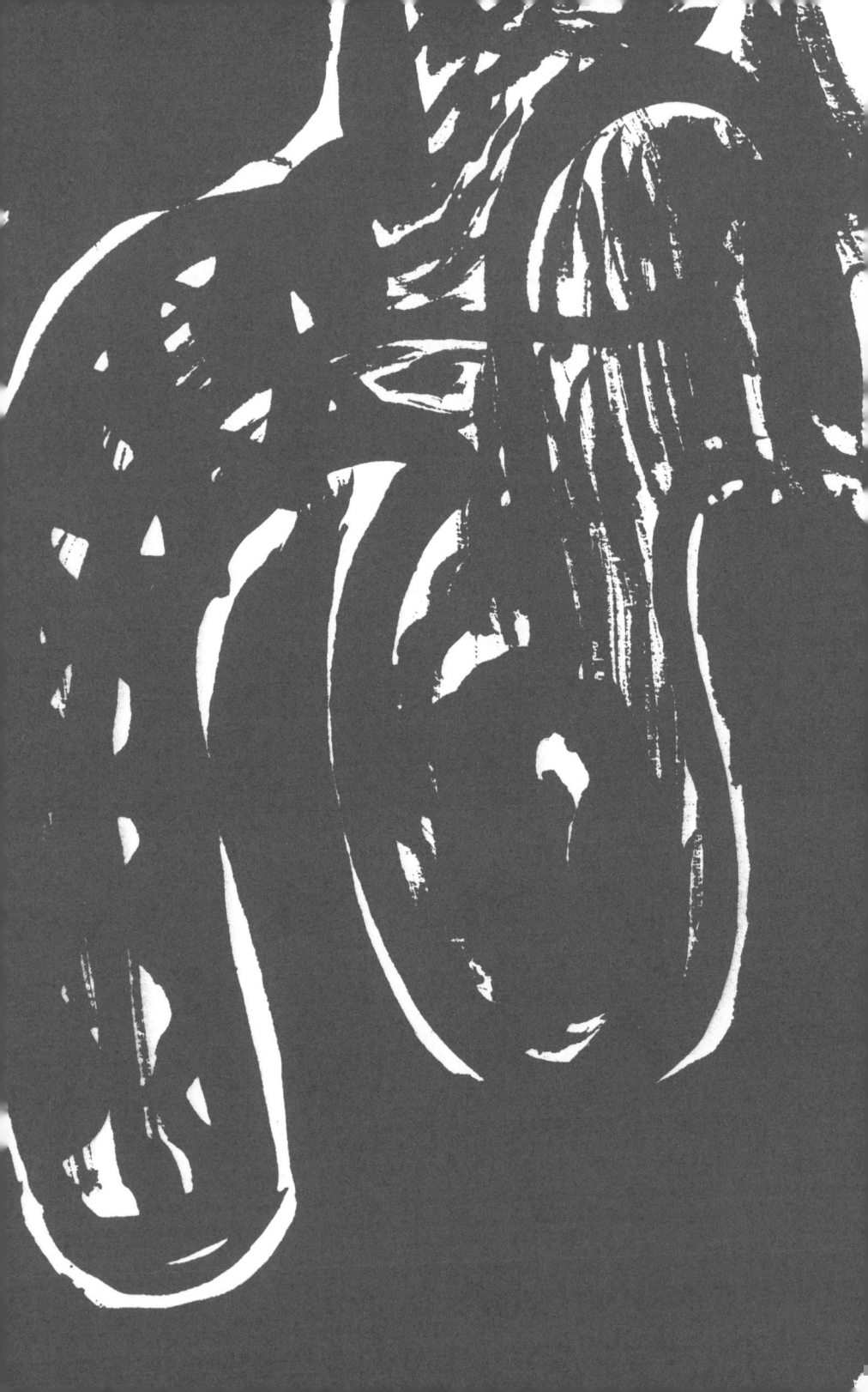

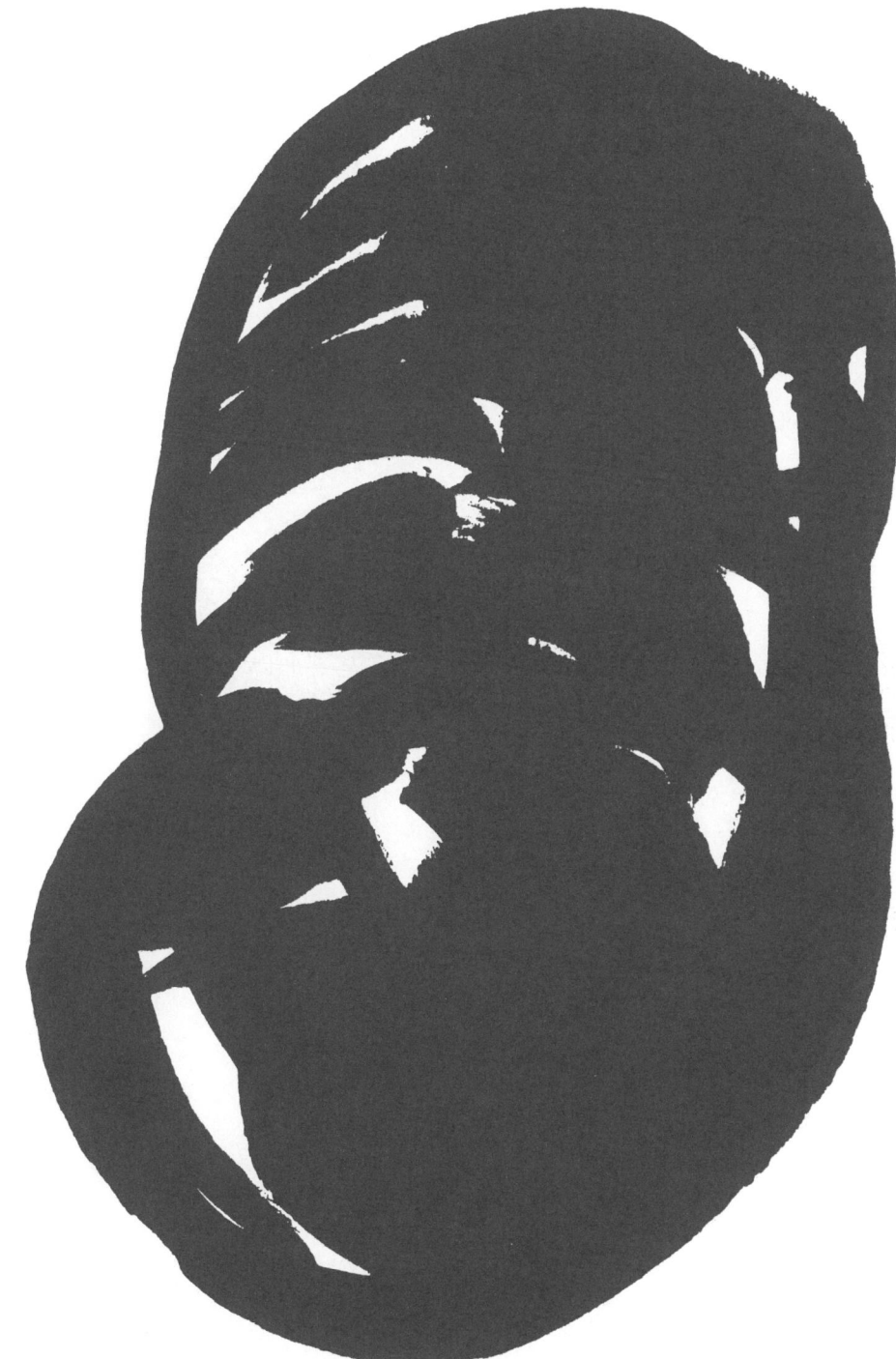

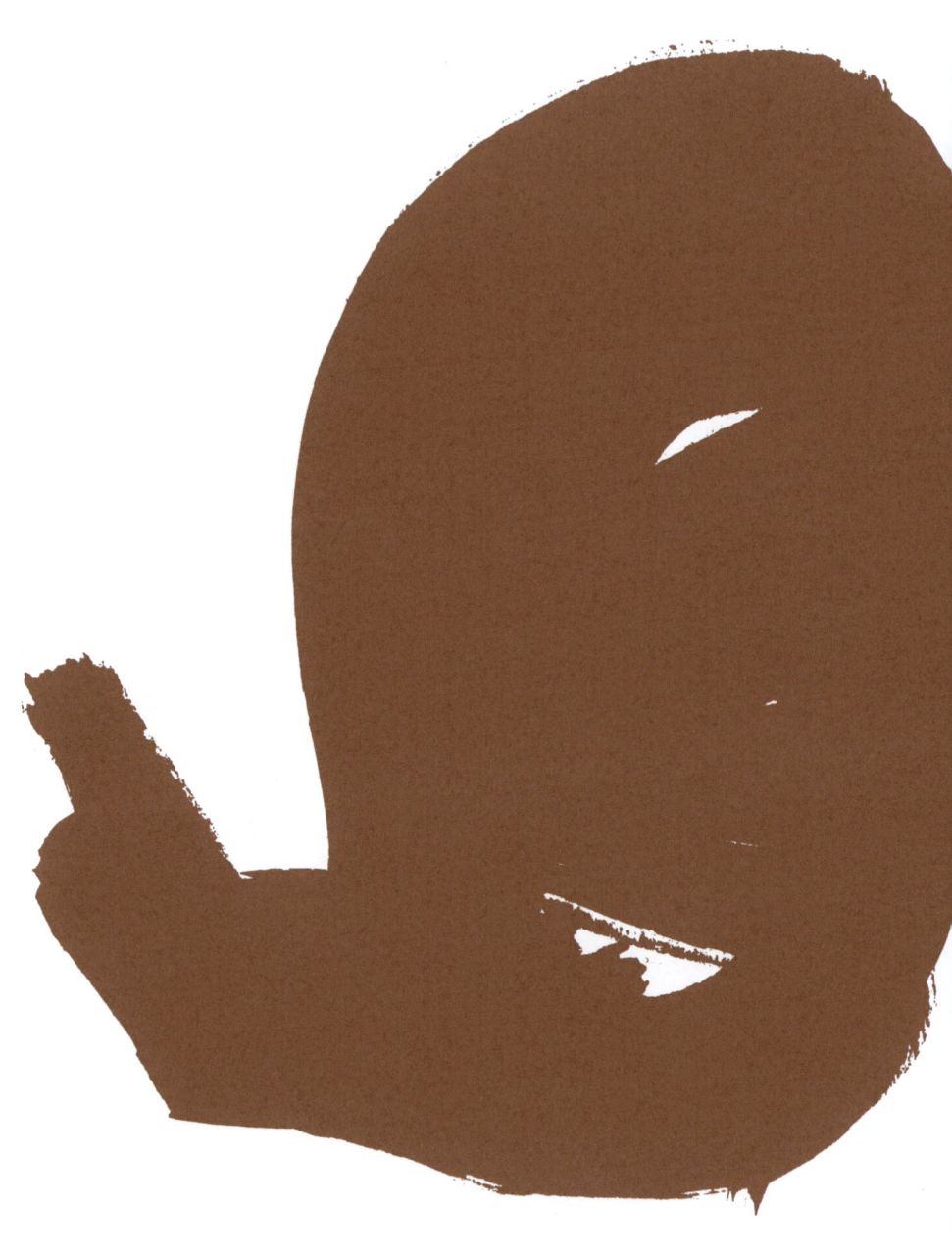

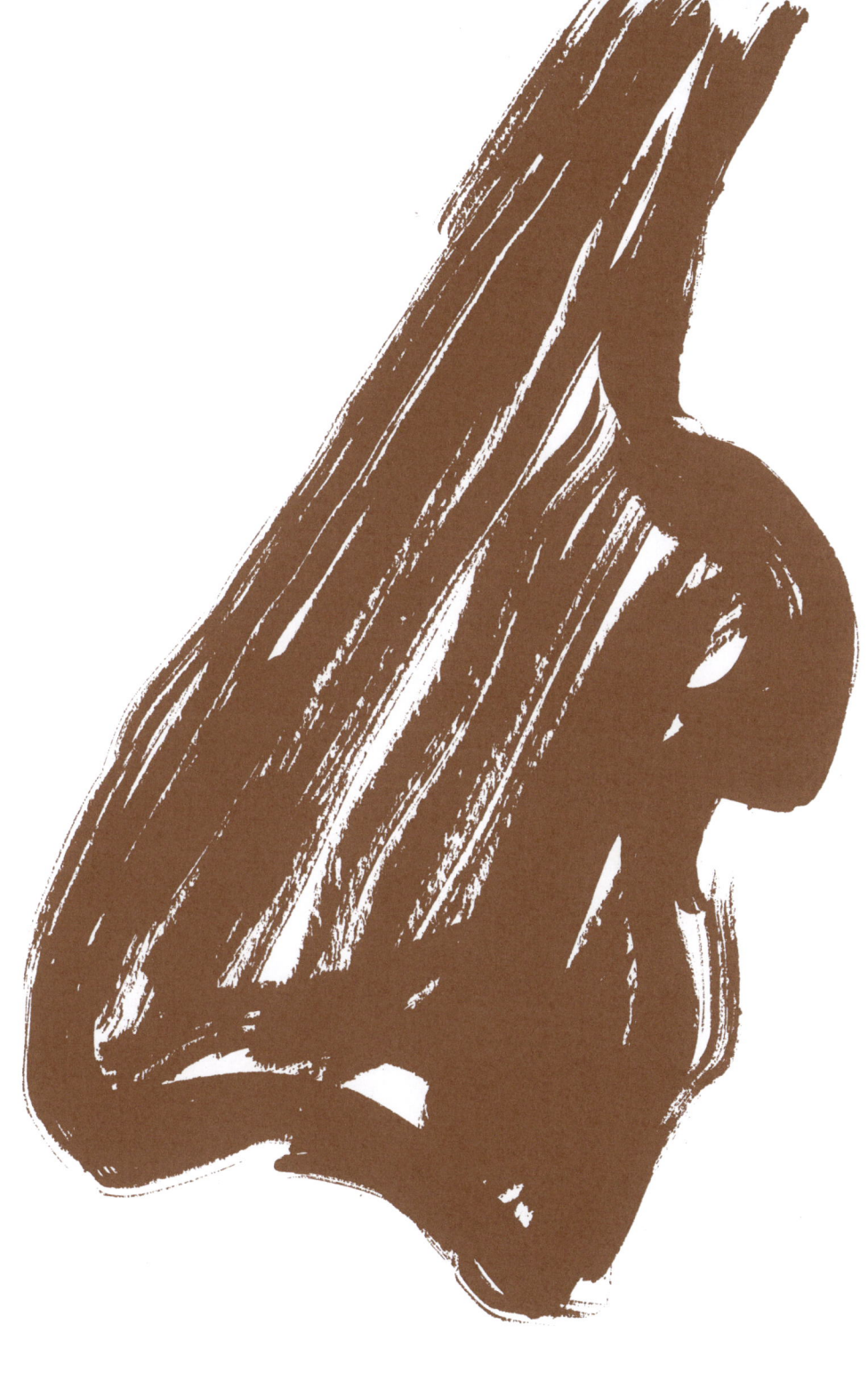

© 1981   Jenny Holzer/Peter Nadin

This publication was funded by the New York State Council on the Arts, Literature Program.

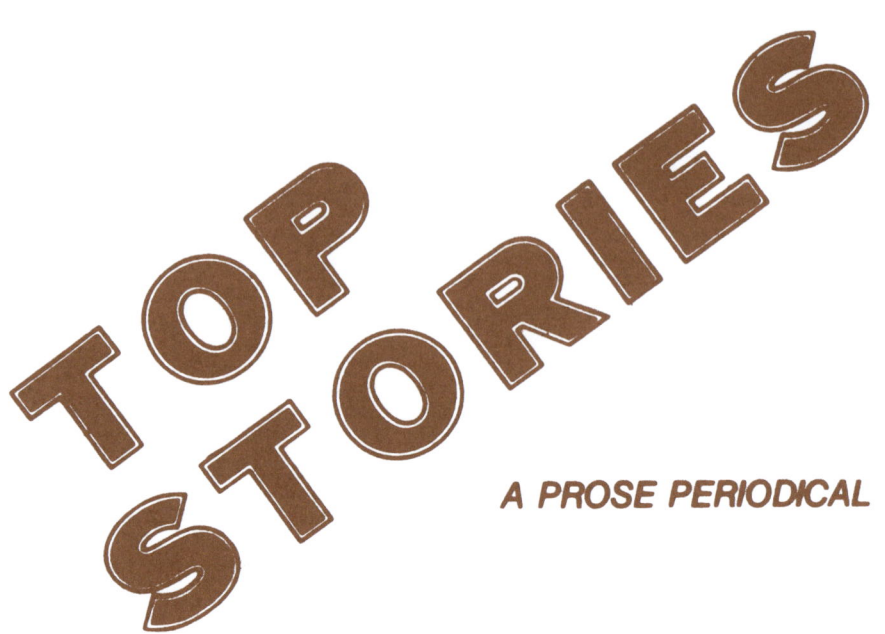

A PROSE PERIODICAL

#1 Donna Wyszomierski
#2 Laurie Anderson
#3 Pati Hill
#4 Suzanne Johnson
#5 Linda Neaman
#6 Gail Vachon

Available from
TOP STORIES
Hallwalls
700 Main Street
Buffalo, New York 14202

TOP STORIES #8 $1.50

TRANSCRIPT
JUDITH DOYLE

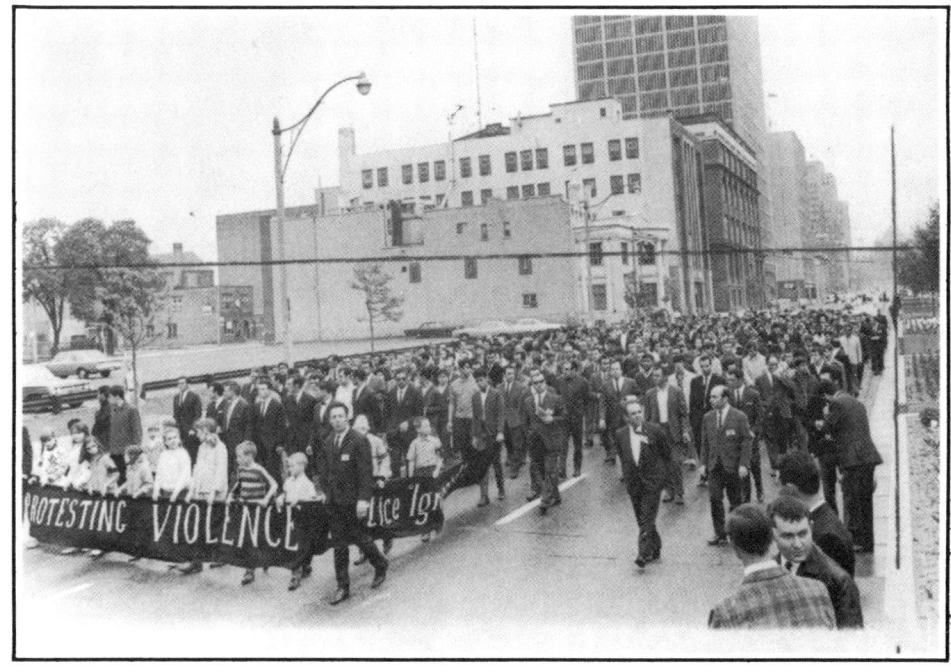

TRANSCRIPT

The following texts are from a performance, based on spoken accounts from three people -Andy Patton, Maria Camara, and Anna Camara. Part One was presented as a pre-recorded audiotape and projected text.

Part Two was performed by Anna Camara.

Cover: Portuguese Canadians in Toronto march against the Salazar regime in Portugal. A slide from the performance **Transcript.**

This publication has been made possible in part by a grant from the Coordinating Council of Literary Magazines.

© *1981 Judith Doyle*

Part One: On Pain

   The funny thing is, you can remember right up to the last split second before; I can still see the other car at the moment we must have been hitting it. Then maybe the second before the impact hit me and nothing after that. It's strange, it's just not there.

   Immediately after the impact I was unconscious for about half an hour; I know that just from being told. I woke up, and I knew that my back was broken but it was a 'no', not a feeling of nerve pain. That all comes later cause you're in shock. You wake up, and you know that you have pain. You don't feel pain, but you know you have pain, and can tell where it's coming from. I knew it was my back. I held my hands in front of me, because I had tunnel vision. I moved my fingers. Then I knew I was paralyzed. The feeling was not pain.

   It's very distant, it's not as painful as if you had a pain right now, like if you smashed your thumb in a door. You know what it's like to be around someone who's in pain, you think 'Oh my God, I've got to do something'. It's not like that.

It's like knowledge, like there's someone in California right now who's in real pain. It's sad - but I don't feel any urgency to rush out and do anything. The first thing is that under shock like that, you really differentiate yourself from your body - your body's just this toy, and it's too bad it got mangled up. You do and don't feel pain, I don't know how it works but you know that you're in pain, and you can also guess pretty well the degree of the pain, whether it's intense or not. I knew it was intense. But it's not happening to you directly.

Because of the shock. However your body mechanisms work, the pain's rerouted so that it's very distant. Like a memory or a dream; it's close to a dream. Except not that strong.

Partly because of the shock and partly because of the tunnel vision, the air, for a certain margin around you, has exactly the same amount of pain as you do. It's peculiar because it's the only time in my life I've experienced that. It's like the pain was in a certain physical region which you could put on a map; because my body had been put into that region, there was pain in my body. But it had very little to do with my body, perhaps nothing at all. The exact feeling is like having your body wrapped in cotton, except it wasn't restricted to my body alone, it was also that region of air. It's a very precise region, slightly larger than one human body. You might even be able to fit two in there.

You go through your body bit by bit, first you locate where the pain's coming from, if it seems to have a centre, if it doesn't, what must be causing the pain. First you find that problem then you check out other parts. I could feel that one leg was worse than the other. It didn't feel more painful, just more distant and more like air than the other leg. My hands felt least like air, my hands and head. The brain was organizing things. Very slowly and calmly. Totally calmly.

You learn 'this is leg one, this is leg two' - there's a difference between them now. There's a very extreme difference between the legs and the hands. I could tell exactly where my back had been broken; it tapered off the further away you got from that in any direction. You distribute your body, but now according to a different way. The pain was already located, and it becomes the principle for your life, for your body being there, for all your knowledge. Your narrative story.

When I got put in the ambulance they drove me to an intermediate hospital and, because of the distancing thing, more than anything else, it all happens like a movie - it's exactly like a movie. The way that colours in a movie are stronger than they are in life because there's nothing to compete with them. The mood especially of movies seeps in, almost as strong as a dream. This thing is happening, but it's not really happening to you, even though it's filmed from the front seat of a car and it's driving fast and you can feel those sensations. You have a problem with whether it's happening to you or whether you're watching it. The colour goes into you, in an odd way. You have tunnel vision in a movie theatre and you have tunnel vision when you're in shock. There's a cone-ness. It might be a foot wide, and infinitely long. On the other side, it's just like a film theatre - it's black. Your sight - I don't know why it closes down. Your sight also loses intensity. Right now, when I look at this wine bottle - I fasten on it. You possess it, you grab it or something. The gaze you have then is very non-committal. It moves across all things equally - your own body, the ambulance, the RCMP guys, the gravel. It's like being bored.

All things are equal. Being here as opposed to being there makes no difference. And it's a beautiful feeling. It's like gliding.

They took me in for X-rays at this intermediate hospital and it was still like being in a film. All these machines are moving over you - your relationship to technology is just fabulous. You see these mythical machines and they're doing all kinds of things. You don't know if they're going to save the patient or not. You're not even as excited as watching a film where you want the patient to live, where you're pulling for him. In this case, you move over all things equally and the patient will either live or die and the machines move and they X-ray you....

When you're in shock, it's like one of those really rare moments you have. It's abstract, and very pleasurable. Later on, you don't have a body, you just have a knot. It's like a muscle. You just have this intensity of pain and that's all you've got. Eventually your whole body is destroyed except for this little bit up in your brain where the pain seems to be emanating from.

In fact, it's not the case that people deal with you, and people deal with you through machines. It's people deal with you and machines deal with you. Machines are much nicer, much more like when you have shock. That's exactly the sort of intelligence they have. It's not that they couldn't care less about you, it's just that they don't particularly care. They're more pleasurable, their motion over you, they're more gifted, they're less involved with you, so you don't have to be as involved with your pain either.

I recall that the most when they did some sort of X-ray

that had video display. I was looking inside my body by looking at the video screen. That was the most nauseating, amazing moment because I didn't expect them to show me that. The Doctor said 'do you want to have a look?' so naturally I just turned. You turn and you see a video display of inside your body, and they're moving around, up different routes and things. It was a canal system.

With the machines, it's like you being already a drawing. I saw a lot of the X-rays they took of me. That's not as interesting because there's nothing going on; there's just the data. But it's like that, it's like you're already an X-ray.

As the shock wore off, the pain would come back more and more intensely. Time would slow down and become really irritable. Everything grated - the existence of a chair as separate from you, or a fly on a window, the sound of air in the room - was all pain, everything was pain. Everything having a separate existence of its own was a pain.

People totally disappeared when I was drugged. They came back as the drugs wore off, then as the pain got very bad I couldn't keep them in existence any longer. I had to use all my power to concentrate on holding back - no, that's not right either - on staying organized. It's not that you can block out the pain, but you can keep yourself organized. You can hold onto a self or something. It seems to have to do with discipline, just the form of discipline, not discipline toward any goal. I guess that when you're helpless, you're passive and it washes over you. When you have the discipline - even when what you're organizing is not the substantive content that you want - you still have a measure of authority.

The funny thing is that even when you're helpless, you're

not. Even when it knocks you right down to the floor and you've got no more resources to draw on, you wind up still having a something - it's not really a self, but a discipline. Even when you're helpless, *you're* helpless. The pain always inhabits a particular body and a particular person and I always felt at those points, if I could only totally destroy my name, I would destroy the pain too. But you can't. There's just no way you can get rid of your own history no matter how badly you try.

Part Two: On Emigration from Portugal to Canada

We got to Santa Maria and we flew in the night. It was crazy because, it was my first time, and one hour later we had to go back. Something went wrong in the plane, the motor. Something went wrong and it was five days until they fixed that.

Back home I knew the airport. Here, I didn't know a thing about it. It was strange. I cried. Anna wanted to use the washroom and when we got back, all the people - nobody was there. Because no one was there, I didn't know where to go. I went to the gates to get into the plane and I gave the guy my passport. I didn't speak English, I didn't speak French - he gave me a chair and said "sit down, relax". I didn't understand anything, but he made me understand. Then a lady came and took Anna, who was a baby. They took me to the plane and nobody was there - all the people who came with us - nobody was there.

Back home, the airport's nothing compared to this one. I had a big surprise because, now you can find all those things, but at the time when I came, there was nothing there. No toaster, no iron - we used a coal iron. Nothing compared.

The Government was crazy - Nazi, you know Nazi. When I came, Salazar was the President. He was President for thirty-six years and he didn't do anything. But people blamed him for the things that took place. Nobody was killed, there was never a war on, but you know what happened? When someone from the Government came to visit the Azores, the first thing we'd see - on City Hall and on all the Churches, all over - there'd be the papers which said "nobody's supposed to show up at City Hall or on the main streets without shoes or shirts. Everyone's supposed to dress up nice." Back home, most of the poor people don't wear shoes during the week. On Sundays at Church and at the Festivals they'd dress up nice and wear good shoes.

They didn't want people to look messy in front of City Hall - that was the problem. When someone comes from Lisbon, all the people dress up nice and beautiful. There are flowers all over the streets. In the windows, we were supposed to put bedspreads, the most beautiful bedspreads, shining - all for some stupid thing from the Government. The Lisbon Government. They couldn't do anything because they'd think "all these people live beautifully".

It's all different - a very big difference. The food, the houses, the streets, the jobs...it's all different. One place, the river is two colours, one green and one blue. The same river, but from the top you can see blue and one green. It's fantastic, but it's hard to go up there.

Here, we had a few close friends, but we couldn't find them - they seemed so far away. Back home everyone's close, but here even the streets are so long. The streets were so long, we couldn't find anybody.

Everything we saw - the fridge, the washing machine, stuff like that - it was all something else. Maybe a bit much. It was funny to me, but I enjoyed that.

The first time I used my washing machine - when I came to Canada, I had beautiful hands because I'd never worked. I never did the dishes, never washed the clothes - I used to sew, to work on men's clothes. I used to be a tailor. My Mom did all the heavy jobs so I had beautiful hands, big long nails. My husband understood why I loved my big long nails - he bought me rubber gloves. The first time I used my washing machine, I put the clothes in the rollers, and then the gloves got stuck, then it caught my hands, and I couldn't stop the machine. It was so funny.

My husband used to say "you'll never go to work". But I loved to, I always did. I wanted to go to work on the subway.

I never minded about the neighbours. I didn't bother them so they didn't bother me. All the neighbours would be talking to me, I said "ya, ya", I laughed, I didn't understand a word. Everyone liked me, so I liked them too.

I moved to the East End because I was fed up. Everyone from Portugal and the United States would come to my house downtown. They'd start Friday evenings and they wouldn't finish until Sunday at twelve or one in the morning. Food all over, people all over the place, food, drinks - I was fed up. I wanted to have some peace and quiet with my family.

When I came to Canada, nothing stuck in my mind as strange. You know why? Because before I came, I had lessons back home. I knew...not really. I never saw those things, but I knew.

TOP STORIES

A PROSE PERIODICAL

#1 Donna Wyszomierski
#2 Laurie Anderson
#3 Pati Hill
#4 Suzanne Johnson
#5 Linda Neaman
#6 Gail Vachon
#7 Jenny Holzer/Peter Nadin

*Available from
TOP STORIES
Hallwalls
700 Main Street
Buffalo, New York 14202*

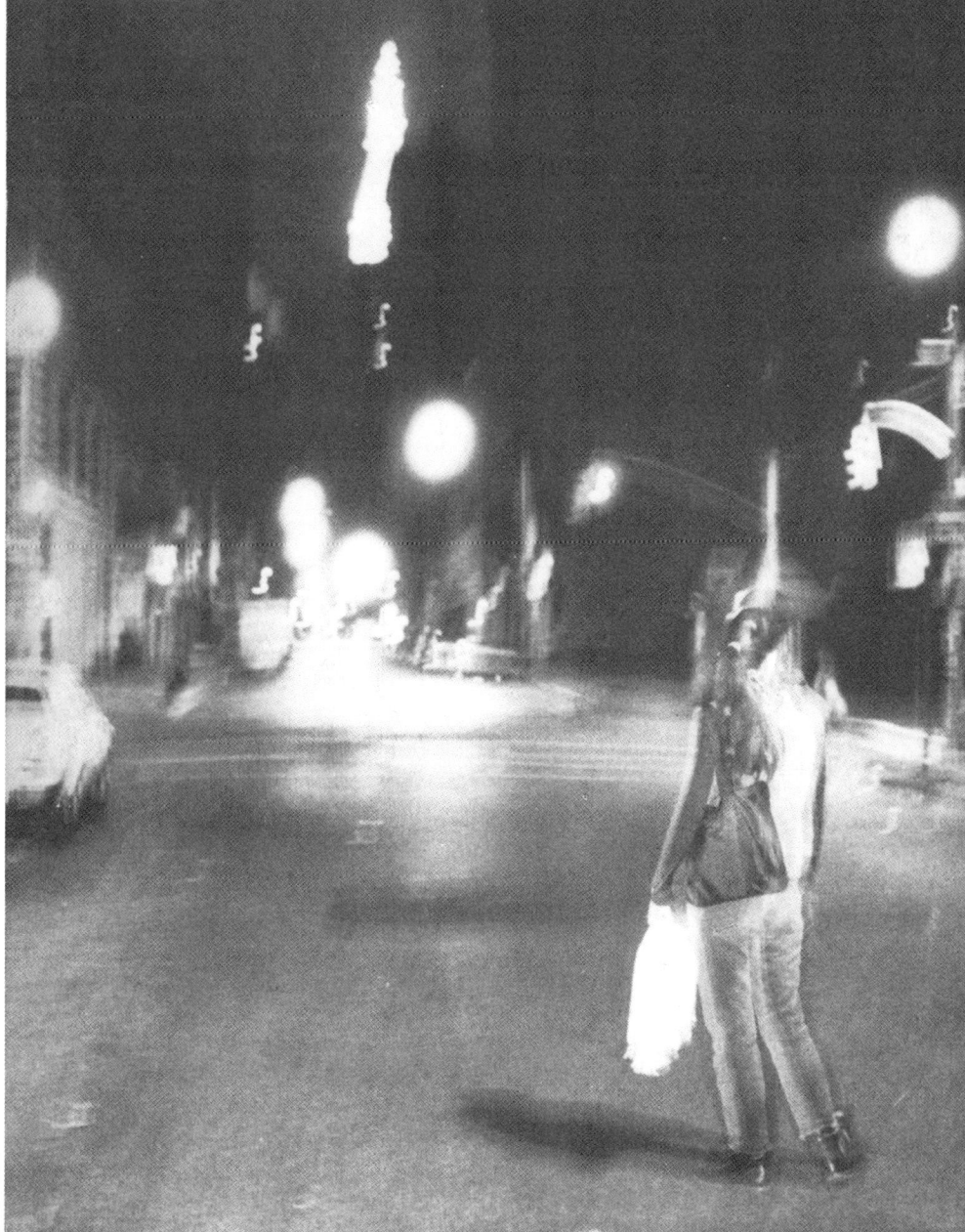

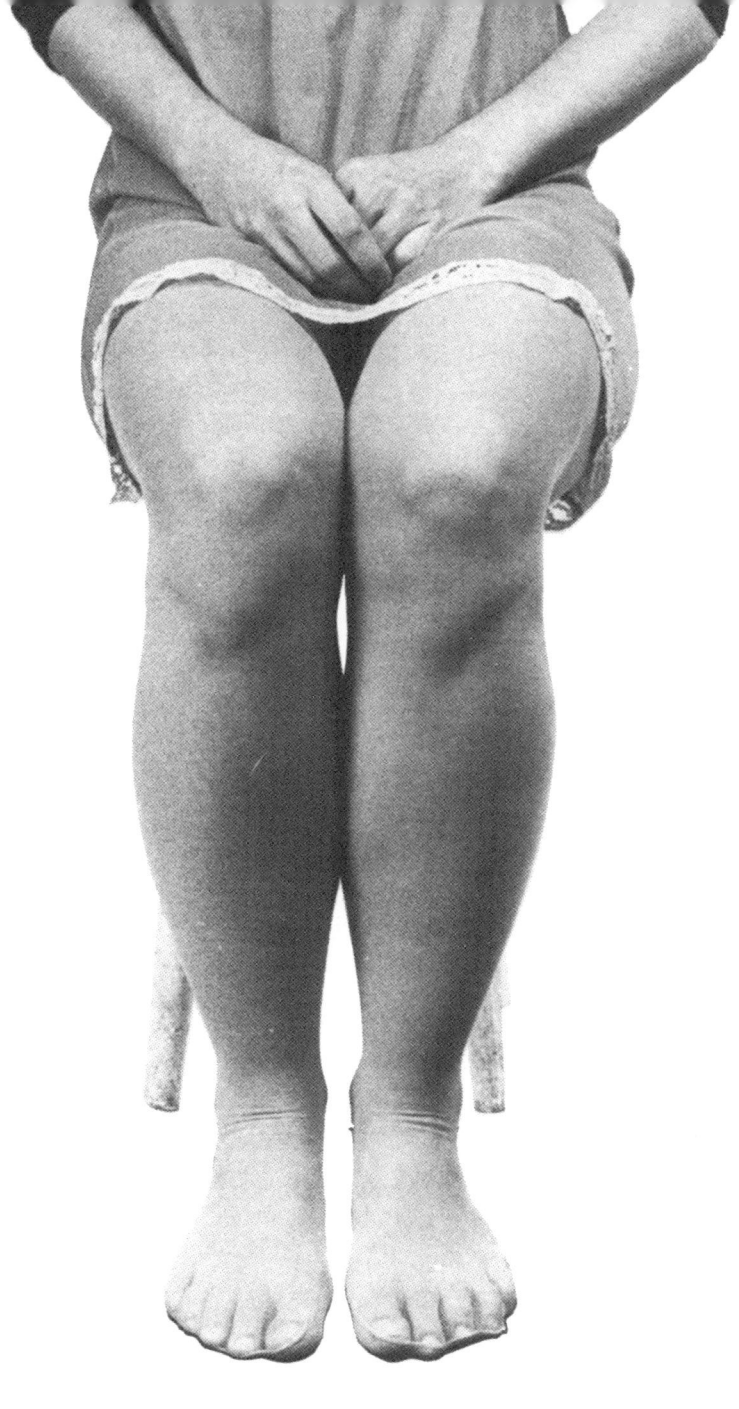

to Jeanne's insulted beauty

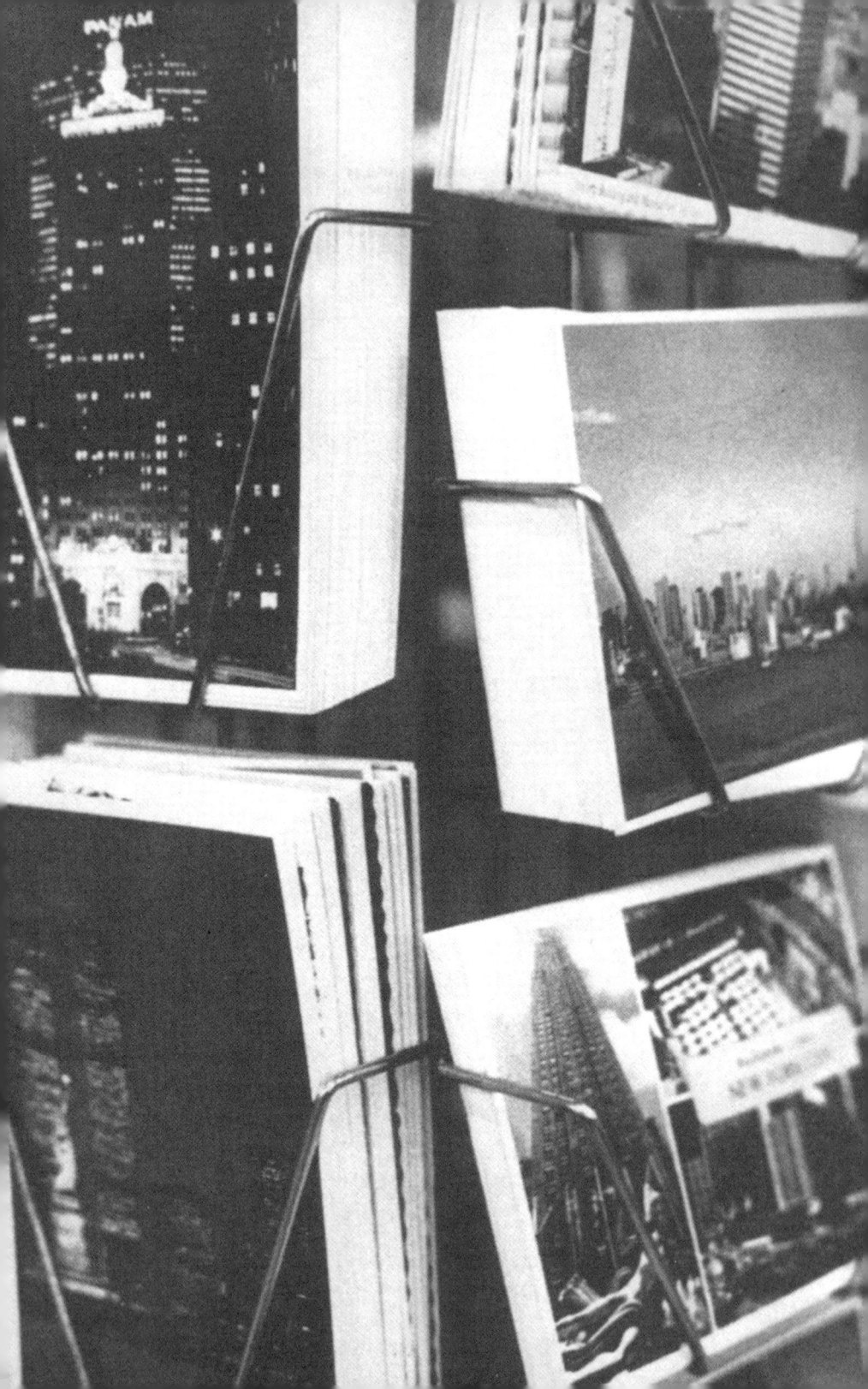

SOME people say New York City is evil and they wouldn't live there for all the money in the world.

These are the same people who elected Johnson, Nixon, Carter President and Koch Mayor of New York.

© 1979, 1981 Kathy Acker

Photographs © 1981 by Anne Turyn

New York City in 1979 *was first published in* Crawl Out Your Window, *number 7, July 1980; and was reprinted in* The Pushcart Press, *volume 6, 1981.*

The publication of this magazine was made possible in part by a grant from the Coordinating Council of Literary Magazines.

Typesetting by The Magazine Co-op, 105 Hudson Street, New York, New York, 10013.

Thanks to Hard Press for technical assistance.

Hallwalls, 700 Main Street, Buffalo, New York 14202

THE WHORES IN JAIL AT NIGHT

—Well, my man's gonna get me out of here as soon as he can.
—When's that gonna be, honey?
—So what? Your man pays so he can put you back on the street as soon as possible.
—Well, what if he wants me back on the street? That's where I belong. I make him good money, don't I? He knows that I'm a good girl.
—Your man ain't anything! Johnny says that if I don't work my ass off for him, he's not going to let me back in the house.
—I have to earn two hundred before I can go back.
—Two hundred? That ain't shit! You can earn two hundred in less than a night. I have to earn four hundred or I might just as well forget sleeping, and there's no running away from Him. My baby is the toughest there is.
—Well, shit girl, if I don't come back with eight hundred I get my ass whupped off.
—That's cause you're junk.
—I ain't no stiff! All of you are junkies. I know what you do!
—What's the matter, honey?
—You've been sitting on that thing for an hour.
—The pains are getting bad. OOgh. I've been bleeding two days now.
—OOgh OOgh OOgh.
—She's gonna bang her head off. She needs a shot.
—Tie a sweater around her head. She's gonna break her head open.
—You should see a doctor, honey.
—The doctor told me I'm having an abortion.
—Matron. Goddamnit. Get your ass over here matron!
—I haven't been bleeding this bad. Maybe this is the real abortion.
—Matron! This little girl is having an abortion! You do something. Where the hell is that asshole woman? (The matron throws an open piece of Kotex to the girl.) The service here is getting worse and worse!
—You're not in a hotel, honey.

—It used to be better than this. There's not even any goddamn food. This place is definitely going downhill.
—Oh, shutup. I'm trying to sleep. I need my sleep, unlike you girls, cause I'm going back to work tomorrow.
—Now what the hell do you need sleep for? This is a party. You sleep on your job.
—I sure know this is the only time I get any rest. Tomorrow it's back on the street again.
—If we're lucky.

LESBIANS are women who prefer their own ways to male ways.

LESBIANS prefer the convoluting halls of sensuality to direct goal-pursuing mores.

LESBIANS have made a small world deep within and separated from the world. What has usually been called the world is the male world.

Convoluting halls of sensuality lead to depend on illusions. Lies and silence are realer than truth.

Either you're in love with someone or you're not. The one thing about being in love with someone is you know you're in love: You're either flying or you're about to kill yourself.

I don't know anyone I'm in love with or I don't know if I'm in love. I have all these memories. I remember that as soon as I've gotten fucked, like a dog I no longer care about the man who just fucked me who I was madly in love with.

So why should I spend a hundred dollars to fly to Toronto to get laid by someone I don't know if I love I don't know if I can love I'm an abortion? I mean a hundred dollars and once I get laid I'll be in agony: I won't be doing exactly what I want. I can't live normally i.e. with love so: there is no more life.

The world is gray afterbirth. Fake. All of New York City is fake is going to go all my friends are going crazy all my friends know they're going crazy disaster is the only thing that's happening.

Suddenly these outbursts in the fake, cause they're so open, spawn a new growth. I'm waiting to see this growth.

I want more and more horrible disaster in New York cause I desperately want to see that new thing that is going to happen this year.

JANEY is a woman who has sexually hurt and been sexually hurt so much she's now frigid.
    She doesn't want to see her husband anymore. There's nothing between them.
    Her husband agrees with her that there's nothing more between them.
    But there's no such thing as nothingness. Not here. Only death whatever that is is nothing. All the ways people are talking to her now mean nothing. She doesn't want to speak words that are meaningless.
    Janey doesn't want to see her husband again.
    The quality of life in this city stinks. Is almost nothing. Most people now are deaf-mutes only inside they're screaming. BLOOD. A lot of blood inside is going to fall. MORE and MORE because inside is outside.
    New York City will become alive again when the people begin to speak to each other again not information but real emotion. A grave is spreading its legs and BEGGING FOR LOVE.
    Robert, Janey's husband, is almost a zombie.
    He walks talks plays his saxaphone pays for groceries almost like every other human. There's no past. The last six years didn't exist. Janey hates him. He made her a hole. He blasted into her. He has no feeling. The light blue eyes he gave her; the gentle hands; the adoration: AREN'T. NO CRIME. NO BLOOD. THE NEW CITY. Like in Fritz Lang's METROPOLIS.
    This year suffering has so blasted all feelings out of her she's become a person. Janey believes it's necessary to blast open her mind constantly and destroy EVERY PARTICLE OF MEMORY THAT SHE LIKES.
    A sleeveless black T-shirt binds Janey's breasts. Pleated black fake-leather pants hide her cocklessness. A thin leopard tie winds around her neck. One gold-plated watch, the only remembrance of the dead mother, binds one wrist. A thin black leather band binds the other. The head is almost shaved. Two round prescription mirrors mask the eyes.
    Johnny is a man who don't want to be living so he doesn't appear to be a man. All his life everyone wanted him to be something. His Jewish mother wanted him to be famous so he wouldn't live the life she was living. The two main girlfriends he has had wanted him to support them in the manner to which they certainly weren't accustomed even though he couldn't put his flabby hands on a penny. His father wanted him to shut up.

All Johnny wants to do is make music. He wants to keep everyone and everything who takes him away from his music off him. Since he can't afford human contact, he can't afford desire. Therefore he hangs around with rich zombies who never have anything to do with feelings. This is a typical New York artist attitude.

New York City is a pit-hole: Since the United States government, having decided that New York City is no longer part of the United States of America, is dumping all the laws the rich people want such as anti-rent-control laws and all the people they don't want (artists, poor minorities, and the media in general) on the city and refusing the city Federal funds; the American bourgeoisie has left. Only the poor: artists, Puerto Ricans who can't afford to move... and rich Europeans who fleeing the terrorists don't give a shit about New York... inhabit this city.

Meanwhile the temperature is getting hotter and hotter so no one can think clearly. No one perceives. No one cares. Insane madness come out like life is a terrific party.

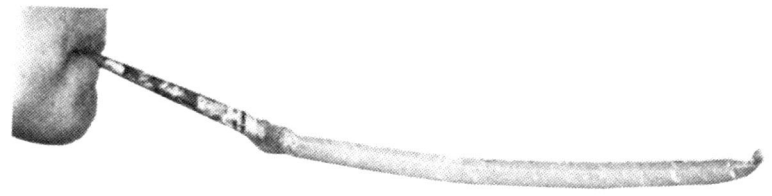

IN FRONT OF THE MUDD CLUB, 77 WHITE STREET

Two rich couples drop out of a limousine. The women are wearing outfits the poor people who were in ten years ago wore ten years ago. The men are just neutral. All the poor people who're making this club fashionable so the rich want to hang out here, even though the poor still never make a buck off the rich pleasure, are sitting on cars, watching the rich people walk up to the club.

Some creeps around the club's entrance. An open-shirted skinny guy who says he's just an artist is choosing who he'll let into the club. Since it's 3:30 A.M. there aren't many creeps. The artist won't let the rich hippies into the club.

—Look at that car.
—Jesus. It's those rich hippies' car.
—Let's take it.
—That's the chauffeur over there.
—Let's kidnap him.
—Let's knock him over the head with a bottle.
—I don't want no terrorism. I wanna go for a ride.
—That's right. We've got nothing to do with terrorism. We'll just explain we want to borrow the car for an hour.
—Maybe he'll lend us the car if we explain we're terrorists-in-training. We want to use that car to try out terrorist tricks.

After 45 minutes the rich people climb back into their limousine and their chauffeur drives them away.

A girl who has gobs of brown hair like the foam on a cappuccino in Little Italy, black patent leather S&M heels, two unfashionable tits stuffed into a pale green corset, and extremely fashionable black fake leather tights heaves her large self off a car top. She's holding an empty bottle.

Diego senses there's going to be trouble. He gets off his car top. Is walking slowly towards the girl.

The bottle keeps waving. Finally the girl finds some courage heaves the bottle at the skinny entrance artist.

The girl and the artist battle it out up the street. Some of the people who are sitting on cars separate them. We see the girl throw herself back on a car top. Her tits are bouncing so hard she must want our attention and she's getting insecure, maybe violent, cause she isn't getting enough. Better give us a better show. She sticks her middle finger into the air as far as she can. She writhes around on the top of the car. Her movements are so spasmatic she must be nuts.

A yellow taxi cab is slowly making its way to the club. On one side of this taxi cab's the club entrance. The other side is the girl writ(h)ing away on the black car. Three girls who are pretending to be transvestites are lifting themselves out of the cab elegantly around the big girl's body. The first body is encased into a translucent white girdle. A series of diagonal panels leads directly to her cunt. The other two dresses are tight and white. They are wriggling their way toward the club. The big girl, whom the taxi driver refused to let in his cab, wriggling because she's been rejected but not wriggling as much, is bumping into them. They're tottering away from her because she has syphilis.

Now the big girl is unsuccessfully trying to climb through a private white car's window now she's running hips hooking even faster into an alleyway taxi whose driver is locking his doors and windows against her. She's offering him a blow-job. Now an ugly boy with a huge safety pin stuck through his upper lip, walking up and down the street, is shooting at us with his watergun.

The dyke sitting next to me is saying earlier in the evening she pulled at this safety pin.

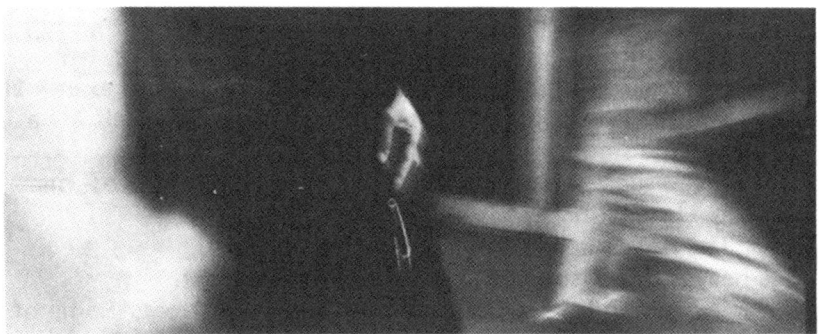

It's four o'clock A.M. It's still too hot. Wet heat's squeezing this city. The air's mist. The liquid's that seeping out of human flesh pores is gonna harden into a smooth shiny shell so we're going to become reptiles.

No one wants to move anymore. No one wants to be in a body. Physical possesions can go to hell even in this night.

Johnny like all other New York inhabitants doesn't want anything to do with sex. He hates sex because the air's hot, because feelings are dull, and because humans are repulsive.

Like all the other New Yorker's he's telling females he's strictly gay and males all faggots ought to burn in hell and they are. He's doing this because when he was sixteen years old his parents who wanted him to die stuck him in the Merchant Marines and all the marines cause this is what they do raped his ass off with many doses of coke.

Baudelaire doesn't go directly toward self-satisfaction cause of the following mechanism: X wants Y and, for whatever reasons reasons, thinks it shouldn't want Y. X thinks it is BAD because it wants Y. What X wants is Y and to be GOOD.

Baudelaire does the following to solve this dilemna: He understands that some agency (his parents, society, his mistress, etc.) is saying that wanting Y is BAD. This agency is authority is right. The authority will punish him because he's BAD. The authority will punish him as much as possible, punish me punish me, more than is necessary till it has to be obvious to everyone that the punishment is unjust. Punishers are unjust. All authority right now stinks to high hell. Therefore there is no GOOD and BAD. X cannot be BAD.

It's necessary to go to as many extremes as possible.

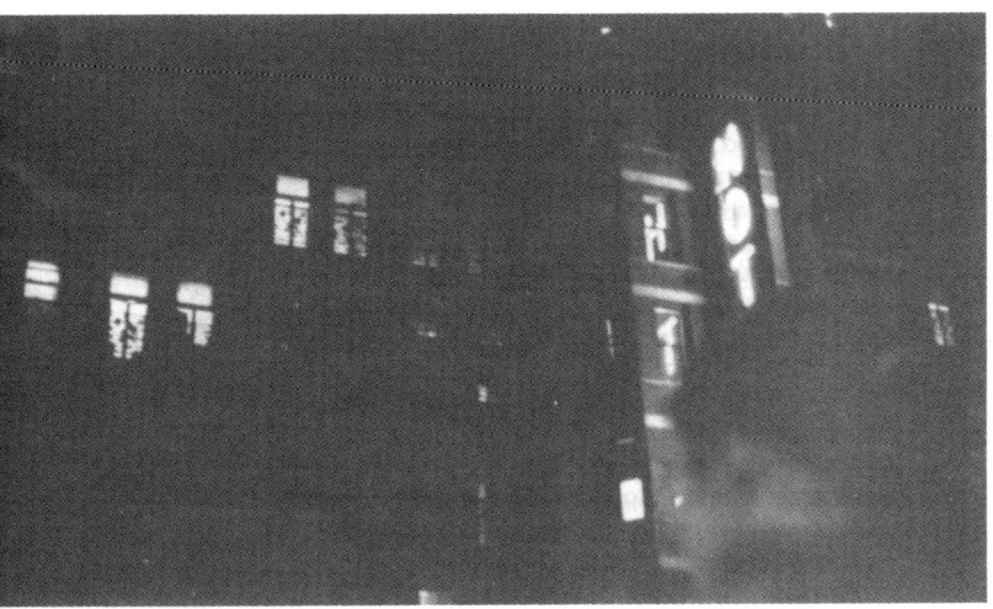

As soon as Johnny sees Janey he wants to have sex with her. Johnny takes out his cock and rubs it. He walks over to Janey, puts his arms around her shoulders so he's pinning her against a concrete wall.

Johnny says, "You're always talking about sex. Are you going to spread your legs for me like you spread your legs all the time for any guy you don't know?"

Janey replies, "I'm not fucking anymore cause sex is a prison. It's become a support of this post-capitalist system like art. Businessmen who want to make money have to turn up a product that people'll buy and want to keep buying. Since American consumers now own every object there is plus they don't have any money anyway cause they're being squeezed between inflation and depression, just like fucking, these businessmen have to discover products that obvious necessity sells. Sex is such a product. Just get rid of the puritanism sweetheart your parents spoonfed you in between materialism which the sexual revolution did thanks to free love and hippies sex is a terrific hook. Sexual desire is a naturally fluctuating phenomena The sex product presents a naturally expanding market. Now capitalists are doing everything they can to bring world sexual desire to an unbearable edge.

"I don't want to be hurt again. Getting hurt or rejected is more dangerous than I know because now everytime I get sexually rejected I get dangerously physically sick. I don't want to hurt again. Everytime I hurt I feel so disgusted with myself— that by following some stupid body desire I didn't HAVE to follow, I killed the tender nerves of someone else. I retreat into myself. I again become frigid."

"I never have fun."

Johnny says, "You want to be as desperate as possible but you don't have to be desperate. You're going to be a success. Everybody knows you're going to be a success. Wouldn't you like to give up this artistic life which you know isn't rewarding cause artists now have to turn their work/selves into marketable objects/fluctuating images/fashion have to competitively knife each other in the back because we're not people, can't treat each other like people, no feelings, loneliness comes from the world of rationality, robots, every thing one as objects defined separate from each other? The whole impetus for art in the first place is gone bye-bye? You know you want to get away from this media world."

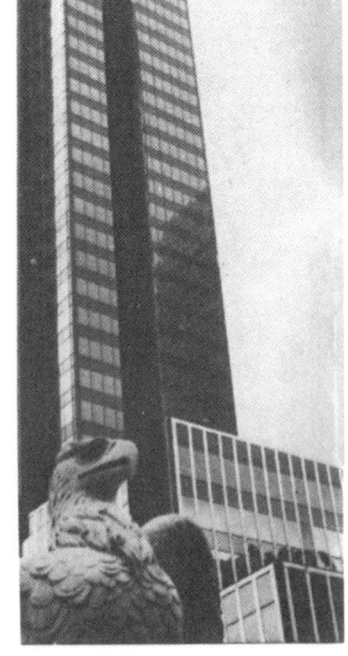

Janey replies, "I don't know what I want now. I know the New York City world is more complex and desirable even though everything you're saying's true. I don't know what my heart is cause I'm corrupted."

"Become pure again. Love. You have to will. You can do what you will. Then love'll enter your heart."

"I'm not capable of loving anyone. I'm a freak. Love's an obsession that only weird people have. I'm going to be a robot for the rest of my life. This is confusing to be a human being, but robotism is what's present."
"It's unnatural to be sexless. You eat alone and that's freaky."
"I am lonely out of my mind. I am miserable out of my mind. Open open what are you touching me. Touching me. Now I'm going into the state where desire comes out like a monster. Sex I love you. I'll do anything to touch you. I've got to fuck. Don't you understand don't you have needs as much as I have needs DON'T YOU HAVE TO GET LAID?"

—Janey, close that door. What's the matter with you? Why aren't you doing what I tell you?
—I'll do whatever you tell me, nana.
—That's right. Now go into that drawer and get that checkbook for me. The Chase Manhattan one, not the other one. Give me both of them. I'll show you which one.
—I can find it, nana. No, it's not this one.
—Give me both of them. I'll do it.
—Here you are, nana. This is the one you want, isn't it?
—Now sit yourself down and write yourself out a check for $10,000. It doesn't matter which check you write it on.
—Ten thousand dollars! Are you sure about this, nana?
—Do what I tell you. Write yourself out a check for ten thousand dollars.
—Uh O.K. What's the date?
—It doesn't matter. Put any date you want. Now hand me my glasses. They're over there.
—I'm just going to clean them. They're dirty.
—You can clean them for me later. Give them to me.
—Are...you sure you want to do this?
—Now I'm going to tell you something, Janey. Invest this. Buy yourself 100 shares of AT&T. You can fritter it away if you want. Good riddance to you. If your mother had invested the 800 shares of IBM I gave her, she would have had a steady income and wouldn't have had to commit suicide. Well, she needed the money. If you invest in AT&T, you'll always have an income.
—I don't know what to say. I've never seen so much money before. I've never seen so much money before.

—You do what I tell you to. Buy AT&T.
—I'll put the money in a bank, nana, and as soon as it clears I'll buy AT&T.

At ten o'clock the next morning Nana is still asleep. A rich salesman who was spending his winter in New York had installed her in a huge apartment on Park Avenue for six months. The apartment's rooms are tremendous, too big for her tiny body, and are still partly unfurnished. Thick silk daybed spreads ivory-handled white feather fans hanging above contrast the black-and-red 'naturalistic' clown portraits in the 'study' that give an air of culture rather than of call-girl. A call-girl or mistress, as soon as her first man is gone, is no longer innocent. No one to help her, constantly harassed by rent and food bills, in need of elegant clothing and cosmetics to keep surviving, she has to use her sex to get money.

Nana's sleeping on her stomach, her bare arms hugging instead of a man a pillow into which she's buried a face soft with sleep. The bedroom and the small adjoining dressingroom are the only two properly furnished rooms. A ray of light filtered through the gray richly-laced curtain focuses a rosewood bedsteads covered by carved Chinese figures, the bedstead covered by white linen sheets; covered by a pale blue silk quilt; covered by a pale white silk quilt; Chinese pictures composed of five to seven layers of carved ivory, almost sculptures rather than pictures, surround these gleaming layers.

She feels around and, finding no one, calls her maid.

"Paul left ten minutes ago," the girl says as she walks into the room. "He didn't want to wake you. I asked him if he wanted coffee but he said he was in a rush. He'll see you his usual time tomorrow."

"Tomorrow tomorrow;" the prostitute can never get anything straight, "can he come tomorrow?"

"Wednesday's Paul's day. Today you see the furrier."

"I remember," she says, sitting up, "the old furrier told me he's coming Wednesday and I can't go against him. Paul'll have to come another day."

"You didn't tell me. If you don't tell me what's going on, I'm going to get things confused and your Johns'll be running into each other!"

Nana stretches her fatty arms over her head and yawns. Two bunches of short brown hairs are sticking out of her armpits. "I'll call Paul and tell him to come back tonight. No. I won't sleep with anyone tonight. Can I afford it? I'll tell Paul to come on Tuesdays after this and I'll have tonight to myself!" Her nightgown slips down her nipples surrounded by one long brown hair and the rest of her hair, loose and tousled, flows over her still-wet sheets.

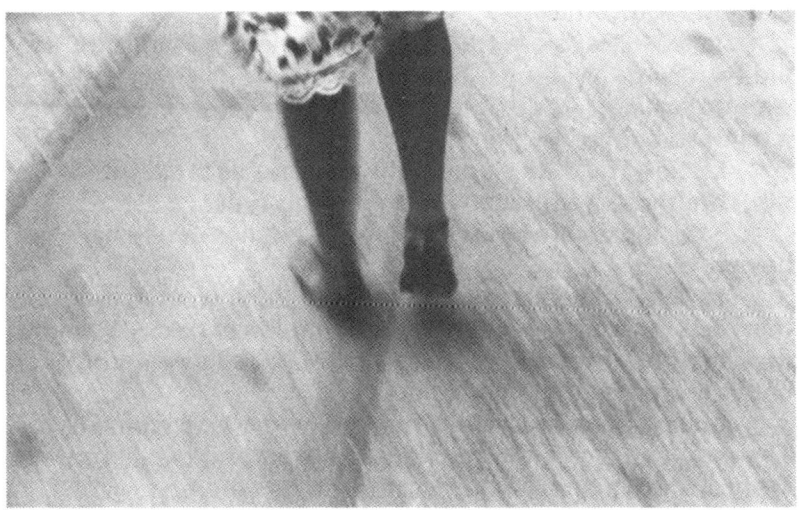

Bet—I think feminism is the only thing that matters.

Janey(yawning)— I'm so tired all I can do is sleep all day (only she doesn't fall asleep cause she's suddenly attracted to Michael who's like every other guy she's attracted to married to a friend of hers.)

Bet—First of all feminism is only possible in a socialist state.

Janey—But Russia stinks as much as the United States these days. What has this got to do with your film?

Bet—Cause feminism depends on four factors: First of all, women have to have economic independence. If they don't have that they don't have anything. Second, free daycare centers. Abortions. (counting on her fingers) Fourth, decent housing.

Janey—I mean those are just material considerations. You're You're accepting the materialism this society teaches. I mean look I've had lots of abortions I can fuck anyone I want —well, I could— I'm still in prison. I'm not talking about myself.

Bet—Are you against abortions?

Janey—How could I be against abortions? I've had fucking five of them. I can't be against abortions. I just think all that stuff is back in the 1920's. It doesn't apply to this world. This world is different than all that socialism: those multi-national corporations control everything.

Louie—You just don't know how things are cause the feminist movement here is nothing compared to the feminist movements in Italy, England, and Australia. That's where women really stick together.

Janey—That's not true! Feminism here, sure it's not the old feminism the groups Gloria Steinem and Ti-Grace, but they were *so* straight. It's much better now: it's just underground it's not so public.

Louie—The only women in Abercrombie's and Fitch's films are those traditionally male defined types.

The women are always whores or bitches. They have no power.

Janey—Women are whores now. I think women every time they fuck no matter who they fuck should get paid. When they fuck their boyfriends their husbands. That's the way things are only the women don't get paid.

Louie—Look at Carter's films. There are no women's roles. The only two women in the film who aren't bit players are France who's a bitch and England who's a whore.

Janey—But that's how things were in Rome of that time.

Bet—But, Jane, we're saying things have to be different. Our friends can't keep upholding the sexist state of women in their work.

Janey—You know about Abercrombie and Fitch. I don't even bother saying anything to them. But Carter's film: you've got to look at why an artist does what he does. Otherwise you're you're not being fair. In ROME Carter's saying the decadent Roman society was like this one.

Louie—The one that a certain small group of artists in New York lives in.

Janey—Yeah.

Louie—He's saying the men we know treat women only as whores and bitches.

Janey—So what are you complaining about?

Bet—Before you were saying you have no one to talk to about your work. That's what I'm saying. We've got to tell Abercrombie and Fitch what they're doing. We've got to start portraying women as strong showing women as the power of this society.

Janey—But we're not.

Bet—But how else are we going to be? In Italy there was this women's art festival. A friend of ours who does performance dressed as a woman and did a performance. Then he revealed he was a man. The women in the festival beat him up and called the police.

Michael—The police?

Janey—Was he good?

Bet—He was the best performer there.

Louie—I think calling the police is weird. They should have just beaten him up.

Janey—I don't like the police.

I WANT ALL THE ABOVE TO BE THE SUN.

INTENSE SEXUAL DESIRE IS THE GREATEST THING IN THE WORLD

Janey dreams of cocks. Janey sees cocks instead of objects. Janey has to fuck.

This is the way Sex drives Janey crazy: Before Janey fucks, she keeps her wants in cells. As soon as Janey's fucking she wants to be adored as much as possible at the same time as, its other extreme, ignored as much as possible. More than this: Janey can no longer perceive herself wanting. Janey is Want.

It's worse than this: If Janey gets sexually rejected her body becomes sick. If she doesn't get who she wants she naturally revolts.

This is the nature of reality. No rationality possible. Only this is true. The world in which there is no feeling, the robot world, doesn't exist. This world is a very dangerous place to live in.

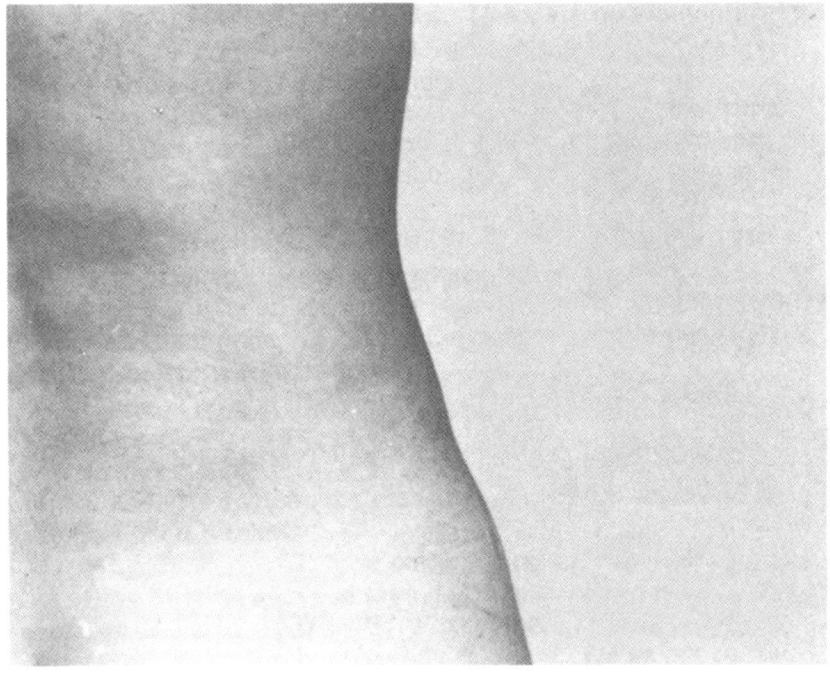

Old women just cause they're old and no man'll fuck them don't stop wanting sex.

The old actress isn't good anymore. But she keeps on acting even though she knows all the audiences mock her hideousness and lack of context cause she adores acting. Her legs are grotesque: FLABBY. Above, hidden within the folds of skin, there's an ugly cunt. Two long flaps of white thin spreckled by black hairs like a pig's cock flesh hang down to the knees. There's no feeling in them. Between these two flaps of skin the meat is red folds and drips a white slime that poisons whatever it touches. Just one drop burns a hole into anything. An odor of garbage infested by maggots floats out of this cunt. One One wants to vomit. The meat is so red it looks like someone hacked a body to bits with a cleaver or like the bright red lines under the purple lines on the translucent skin of a woman's body found dead three days ago. This red leads to a hole, a hole of redness, round and round, black nausea. The old actress is black nausea because she reminds us of death. Yet she keeps plying her trade and that makes her trade weird. Glory be to those humans who are absolutely NOTHING for the opinions of other humans: they are the true owners of illusions, transformations, and themselves.

Old people are supposed to be smarter than young people.

Old people in this country the United States of America are treated like total shit. Since most people spend their lives mentally dwelling on the material, they have no mental freedom, when they grow old and their skin rots and their bodies turn to putrefying sand and they can't do physical exercise and they can't indulge in bodily pleasure and they're all ugly anyway; suddenly they got nothing. Having nothing, you think they could at least be shut up in opiated dens so maybe they have a chance to develop dreams or at least they could warn their kids to do something else besides being materialistic. But the way this country's set up, there's not even opiated homes to hide this feelinglessness: old people have to go either to children's or most often into rest homes where they're shunted into wheelchairs and made as fast as possible into zombies cause it's easier to handle a zombie, if you have to handle anything, than a human. So an old person has a big empty hollow space with nothing in it, just ugh, and that's life: nothing else is going to happen, there's just ugh stop.

ANYTHING THAT DESTROYS LIMITS

Afterwards Janey and Johnny went to an all-night movie. All during the first movie Janey's sort of leaning against Johnny cause she's unsure he's attracted to her and she doesn't want to embarass him (her) in case he ain't. She kinda scrunches against him. One point Johnny is pressing his knee against her knee but she still ain't sure.

Some Like It Hot ends. All the rest of the painters are gonna leave the movie house cause they've seen *The Misfits*. Separately Janey and Johnny say they're going to stay. The painters are walking out. The movie theatre is black.

Janey still doesn't know what Johnny's feelings are.

A third way through the second movie Johnny's hand grabs her knee. Her whole body becomes crazy. She puts her right hand into his hand but he doesn't want the hand.

Johnny's hand, rubbing her tan leg, is inching closer to her cunt. The hand is moving roughly, grabbing handfuls of flesh, the flesh and blood crawling. He's not responding to anything she's doing.

Finally she's tentatively touching his leg. His hand is pouncing on her right hand setting it an inch below his cock. Her body's becoming even crazier and she's more content.

His other hand is inching slower toward her open slimy hole. Cause the theatre is small, not very dark, and the seats aren't too steep, everyone sitting around them is watching exactly what they're doing: Her black dress is shoved up around her young thighs. His hand is almost curving around her dark-pantied cunt. Her and his legs are intertwined. Despite fear she's sure to be arrested just like in a porn book because fear she's wanting him to stick his cock up her right now.

His hand is roughly travelling around her cunt, never touching nothing, smaller and smaller circles.

Morning. The movie house lights go on. Johnny looks at Janey like she's a business acquaintance. From now on everything Janey does is for the purpose of getting Johnny's dick into her:

Johnny, "Let's get out of here."

New York City at six in the morning is beautiful. Empty streets except for a few bums. No garbage. A slight shudder of air down the long long streets. Pale gray prevails. Janey's going to kill Johnny if he doesn't give her his cock instantaneously. She's thinking ways to get him to give her his cock. Her body becomes even crazier. Her body takes over. Turn on him.

Throw arms around his neck. Back him against car. Shove clothed cunt against clothed cock. Lick ear because that's what there is.
    Lick your ear.
    Lick your ear.
    Well?
    I don't know.
    What don't you know? You don't know if you want to?
    Turn on him. Throw arms around his neck. Back him against car. Shove clothed cunt against clothed cock. Lick ear because that's what there is.
    Obviously I want to.
    I don't care what you do. You can come home with me; you can take a rain check; you cannot take a rain check.
    I have to see my lawyer tomorrow. Then I have lunch with Ray.
    Turn on him. Throw arms around his neck. Back him against car. Shove clothed cunt against clothed cock. Lick ear because that's what there is.
    You're not helping me much.
    You're not helping me much.
    Through this morning they walk to her apartment. Johnny and Janey don't touch. Johnny and Janey don't talk to each other.
    Johnny is saying that Janey's going to invite him up for a few minutes.
    Janey is pouring Johnny a glass of Scotch. Janey is sitting in her bedroom on her bed. Johnny is untying the string holding up her black sheath. Johnny's saliva-wettened fingers are pinching her nipple. Johnny is lifting her body over his prostrate body. Johnny's making her cunt rub very roughly through the clothes against his huge cock. Johnny's taking her off him and lifting her dress over her body. Janey's saying, "Your cock is huge." Janey's placing her lips around Johnny's huge cock. Janey's easing her black underpants over her feet.
    Johnny's moaning like he's about to come. Janey's lips are letting go his cock. Johnny's lifting Janey's body over his body so the top of his cock is just touching her lips. His hands on her thighs are pulling her down fast and hard. His cock is so huge it is entering her cunt painfully. His body is immediately moving quickly violently shudders. The cock is entering the bottom of Janey's cunt. Janey is coming. Johnny's hands

are not holding Janey's thighs firmly enough and Johnny's moving too quickly to keep Janey coming. Johnny is building up to coming.

    That's all right yes I that's all right. I'm coming again smooth of you oh oh smooth, goes on and on, am I coming am I not coming.

    Janey's rolling off of Johnny. Johnny's pulling the black pants he's still wearing over his thighs because he has to go home. Janey's telling him she has to sleep alone even though she isn't knowing what she's feeling. At the door to Janey's apartment Johnny's telling Janey he's going to call her. Johnny walks out the door and doesn't see Janey again.

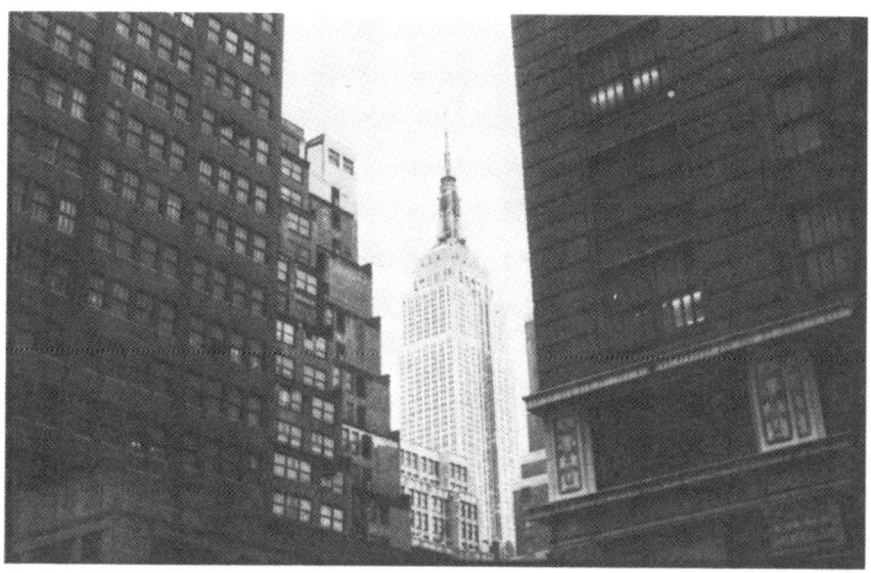

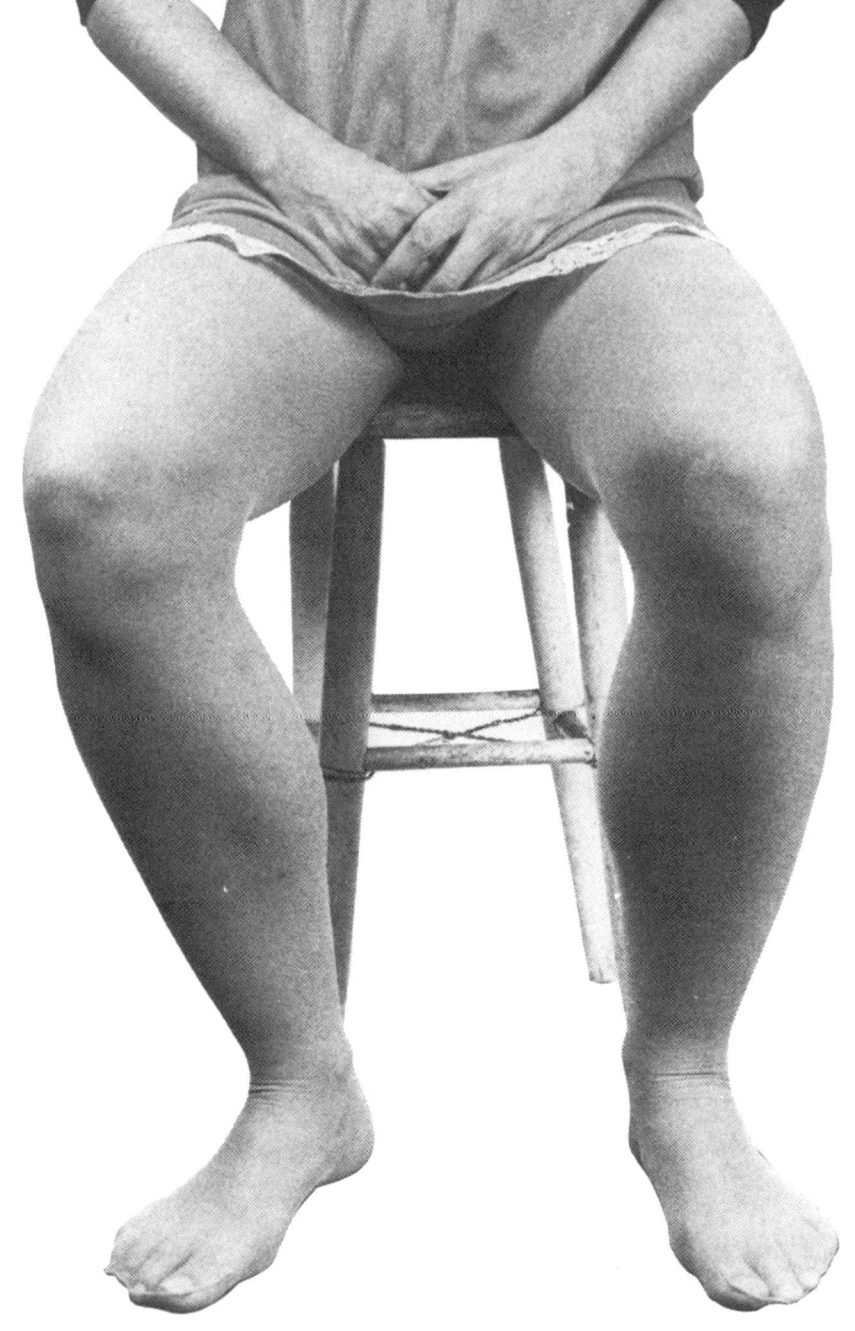

TOP STORIES

A PROSE PERIODICAL

#1 Donna Wyszomierski
#2 Laurie Anderson
#3 Pati Hill
#4 Suzanne Johnson
#5 Linda Neaman
#6 Gail Vachon
#7 Jenny Holzer/Peter Nadin
#8 Judith Doyle

Available from
TOP STORIES
Hallwalls
700 Main Street
Buffalo, New York 14202

TOP STORIES #10
LIVING WITH

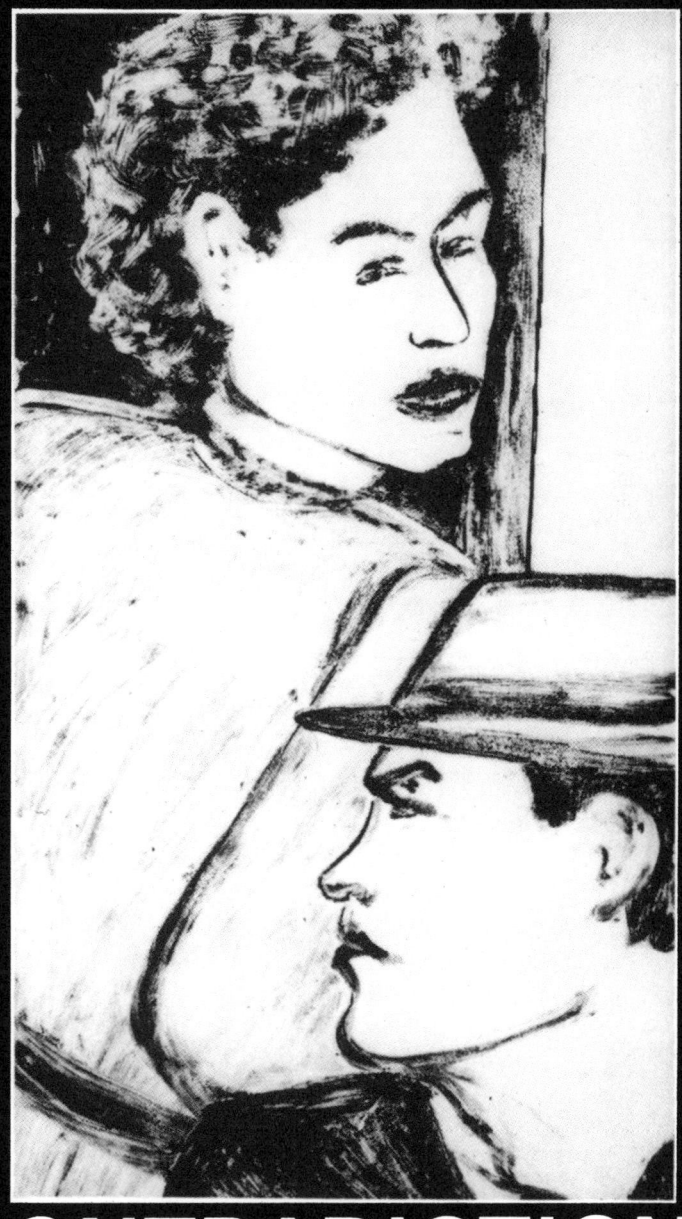

CONTRADICTIONS
by Lynne Tillman

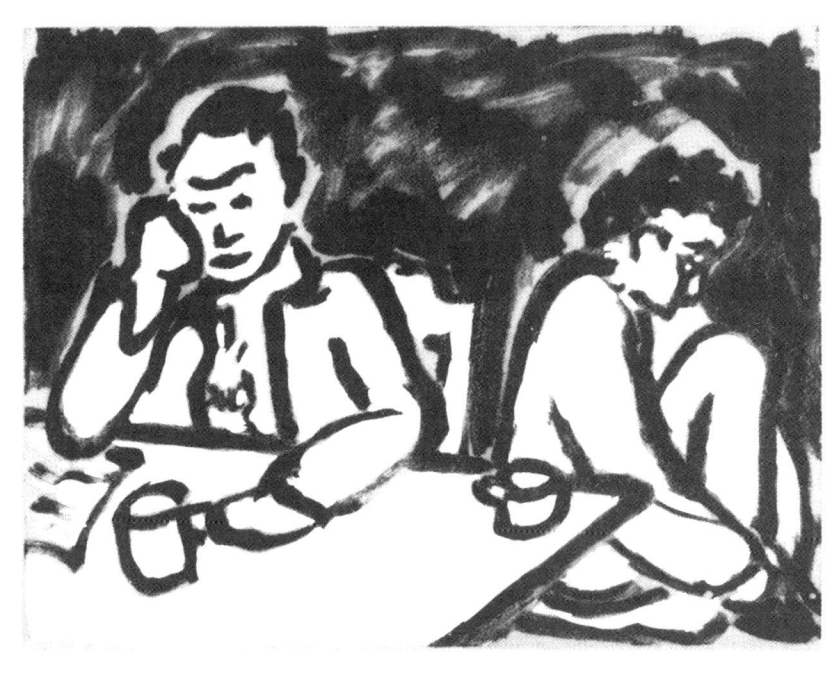

LIVING WITH CONTRADICTIONS

by
Lynne Tillman

drawings by
Jane Dickson

He didn't want to fight in any war and she didn't want to have a child. They had been living together for three years and still didn't have a way to refer to each other that didn't sound stupid, false, or antiquated. Language follows change and there wasn't any language to use.

Partners in a pairbonded situation; that sounded neutral. Of course living with someone isn't a neutral situation. Julie and Joe aren't cavedwellers. They don't live together as lovers or as husband and wife.

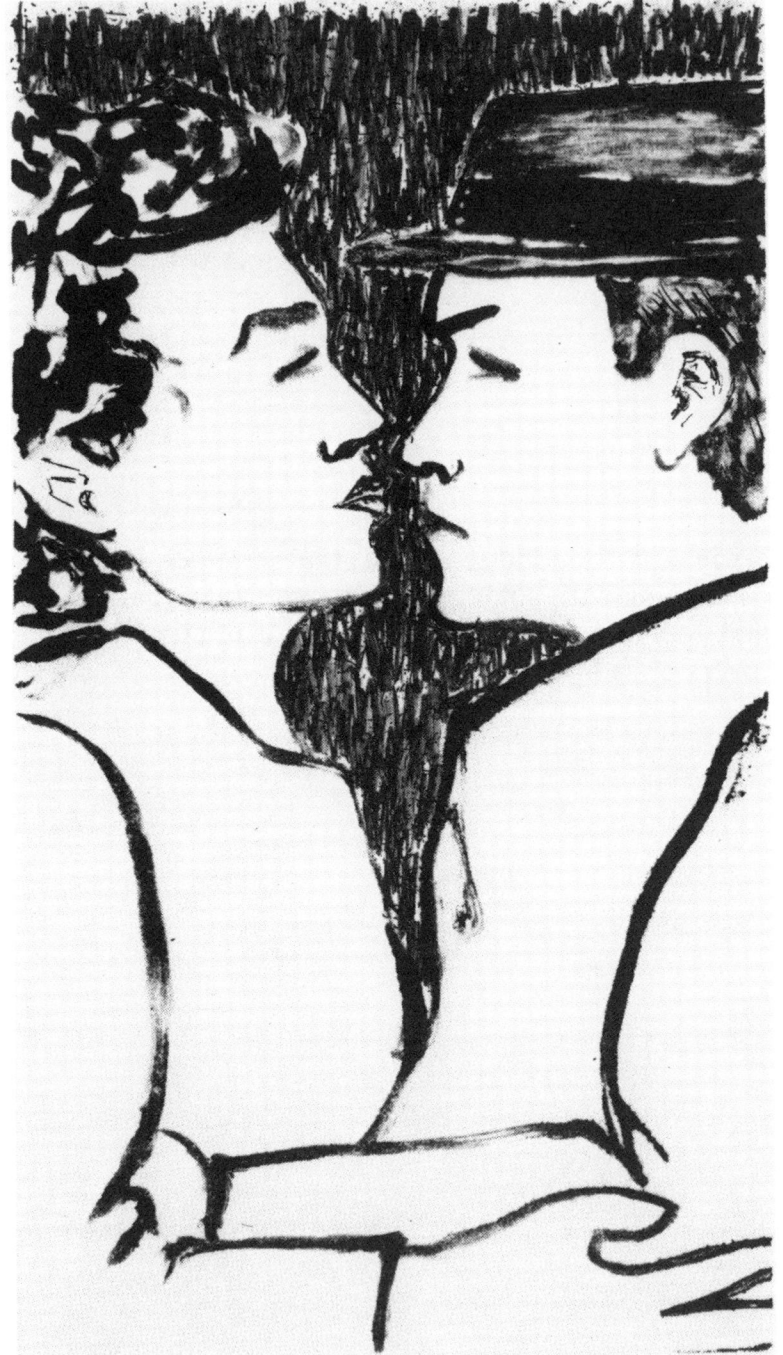

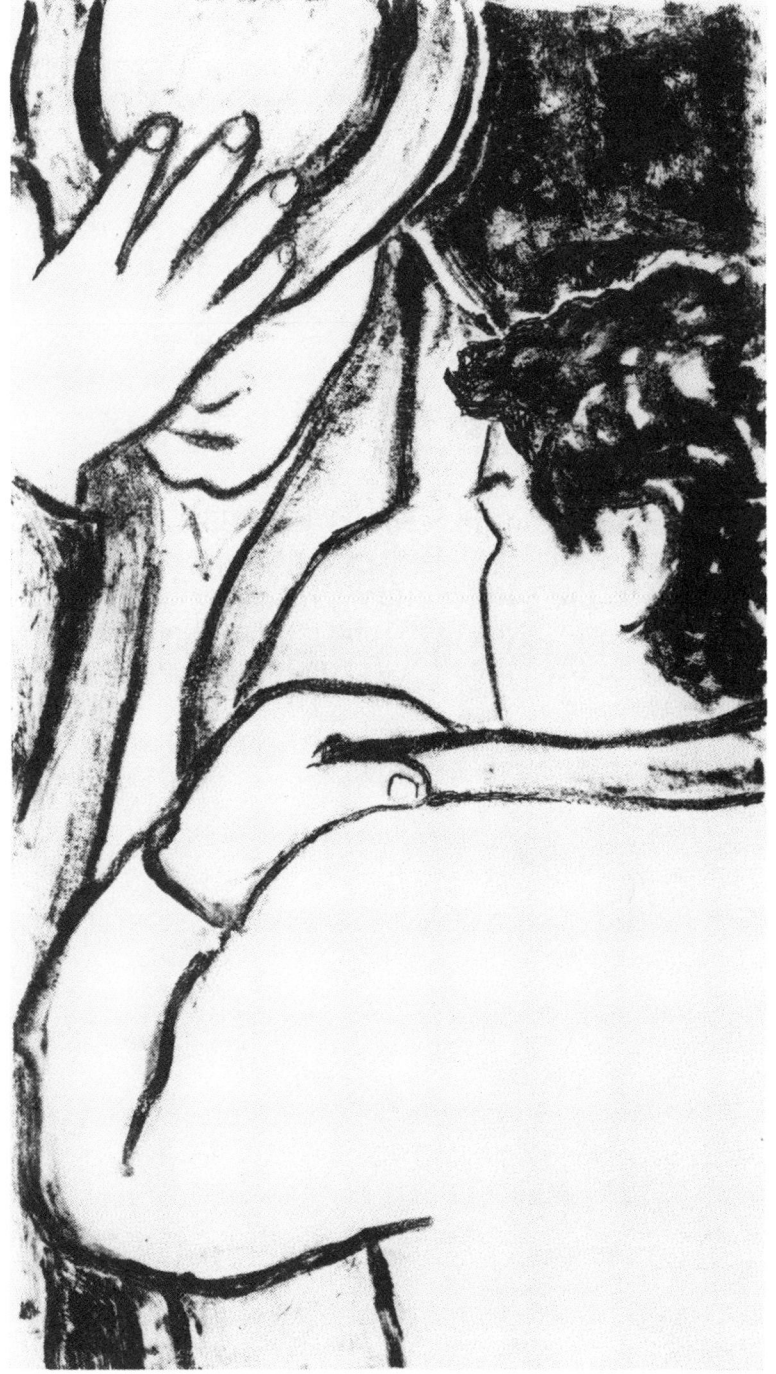

How long would this century be called modern or, even, post-módern? Perhaps relationships between people in the 14th century were more equitable, less fantastic. Not that Julie would've wanted to have been the miller's wife, or Joe, the miller.

In other centuries, different relationships. Less presumption, less intimacy? Before capitalism, early capitalism, no capitalism, feudalism. Feudal relationships. I want one of those, Julie thought, something feudal. What would it be like not to have a contemporary mind?

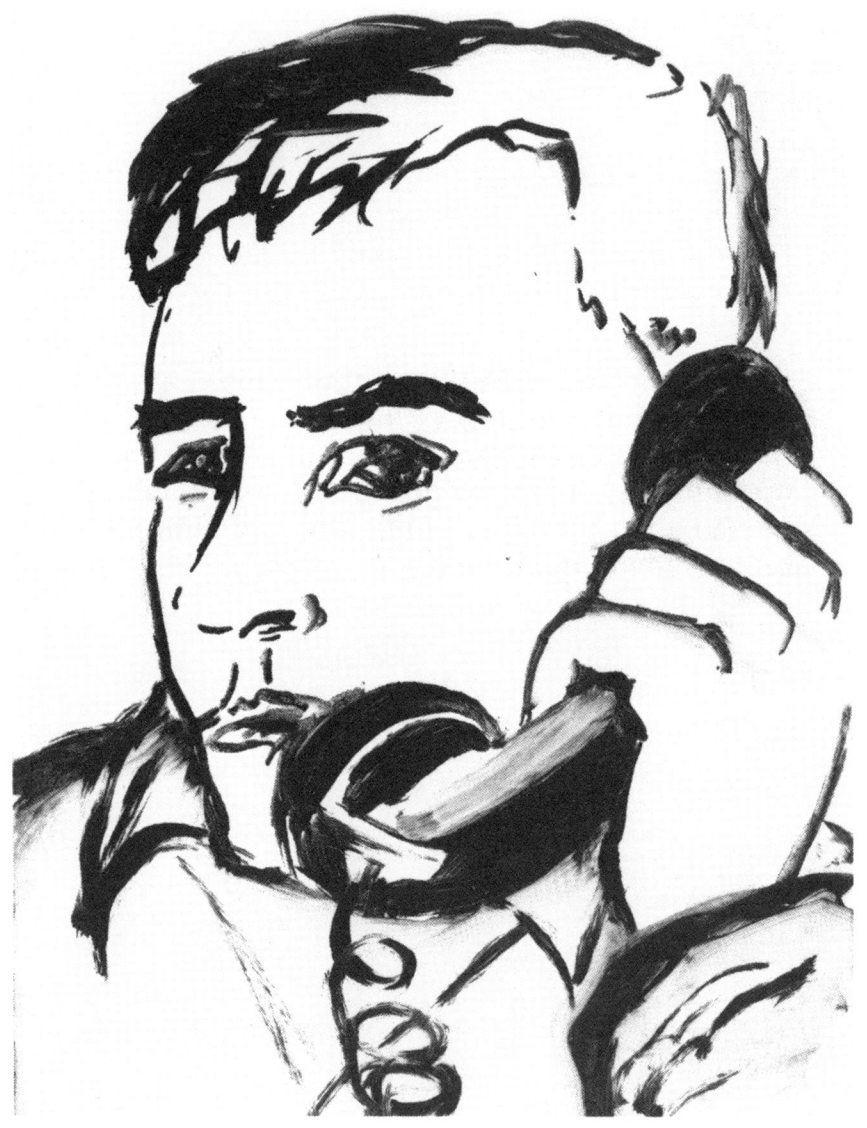

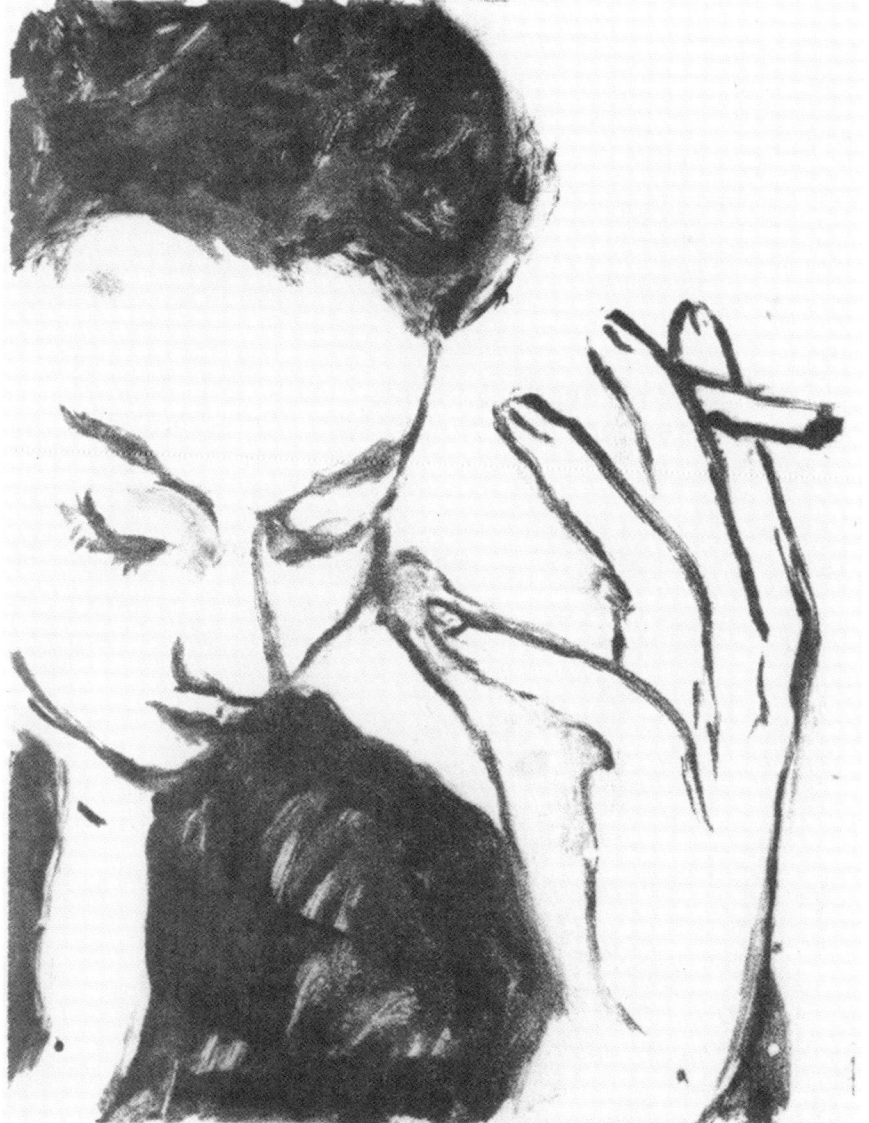

Intimacy is something people used to talk about before commercials. Now there's nothing to say.

People are intimate with their analysts, if they're lucky. What could be more intimate than an advertisement for Ivory soap? It's impossible not to be affected.

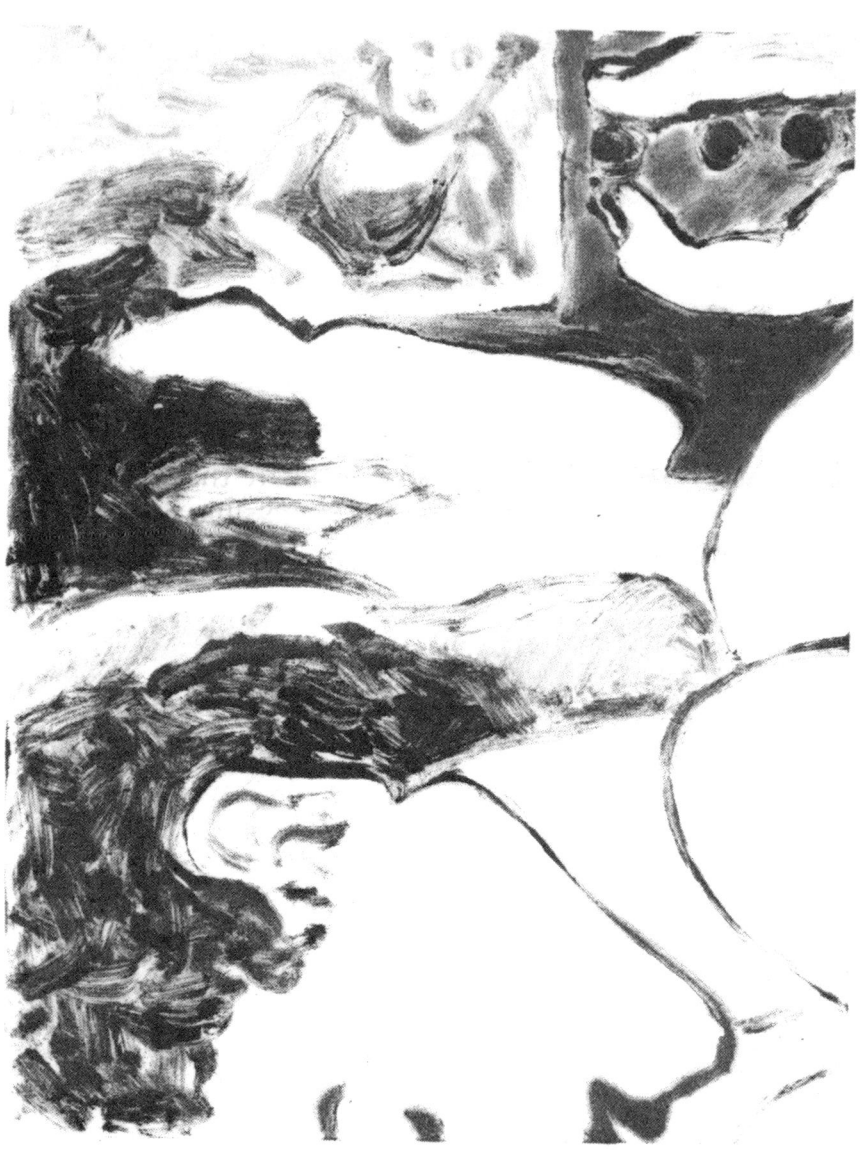

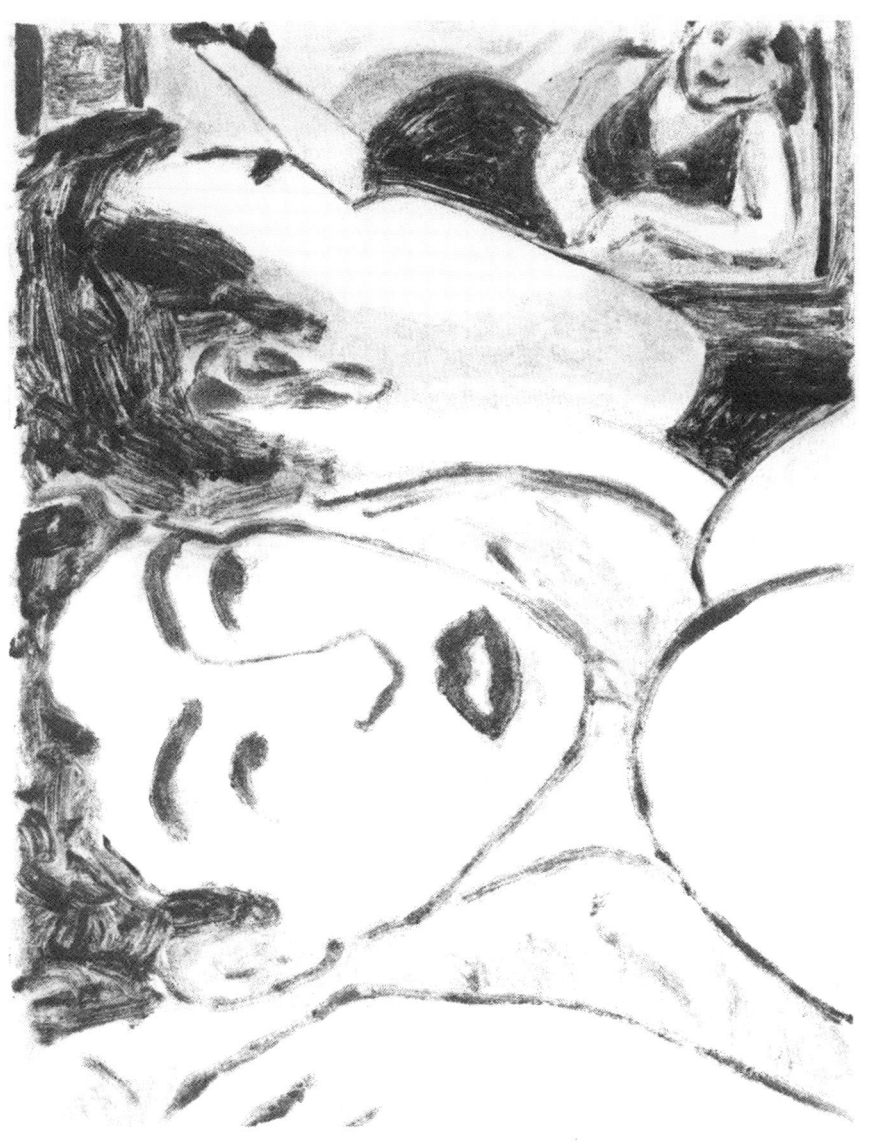

The manufacture of desire and the evidence of real desire. But "real" desire is for what — for what is real or manufactured?

Other people's passions always leave you cold. There is nothing like really being held. They didn't expect to be everything to each other.

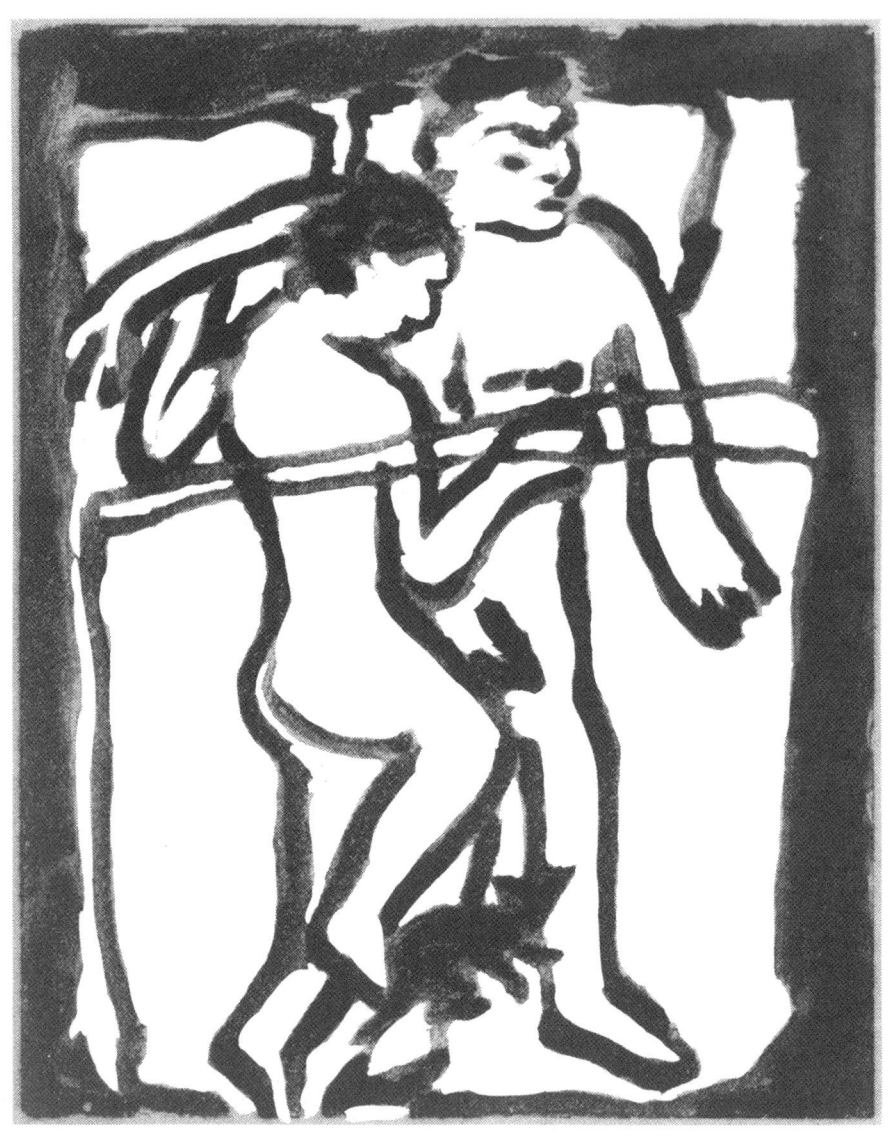

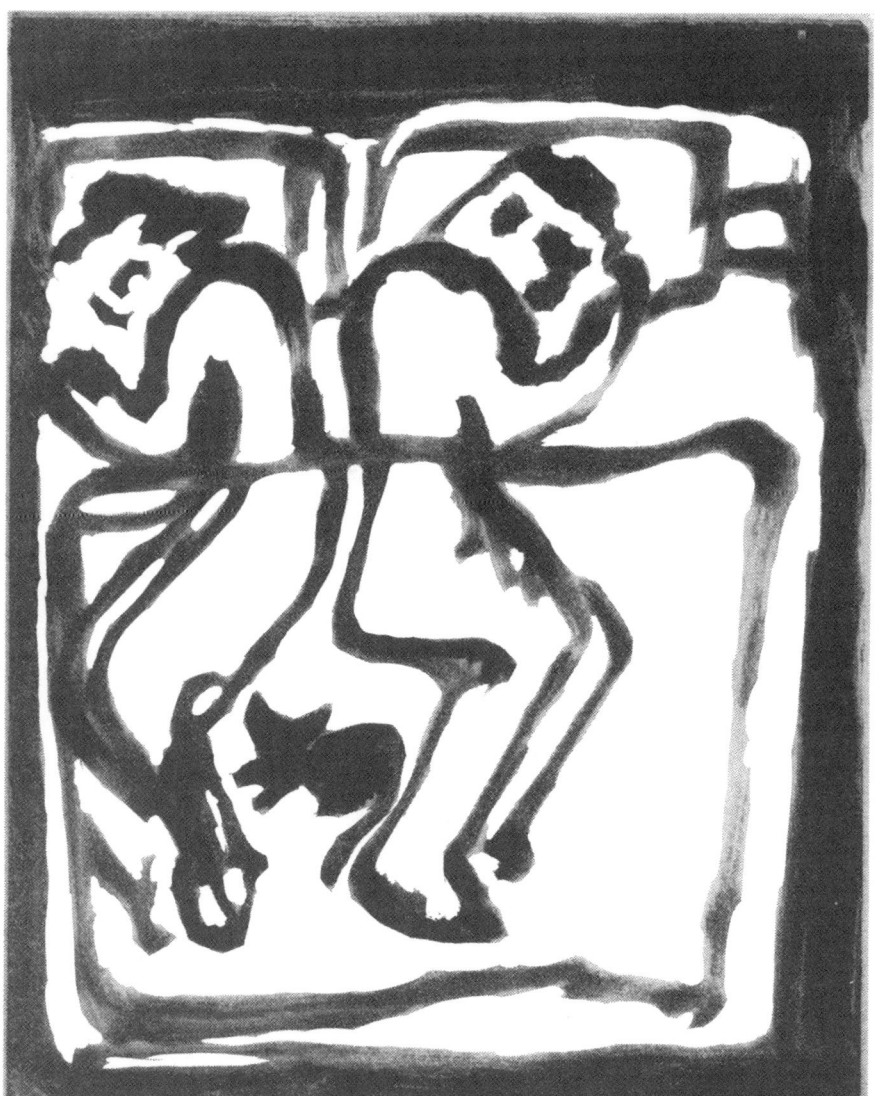

The first year they lived together was a battle to be together and to be separate. A silent battle, because you can't fight the fight together, it defeats the purpose of the battle.

You can't talk about relationships, at least they didn't; they talked about things that happened and things that didn't. Daily life is very daily.

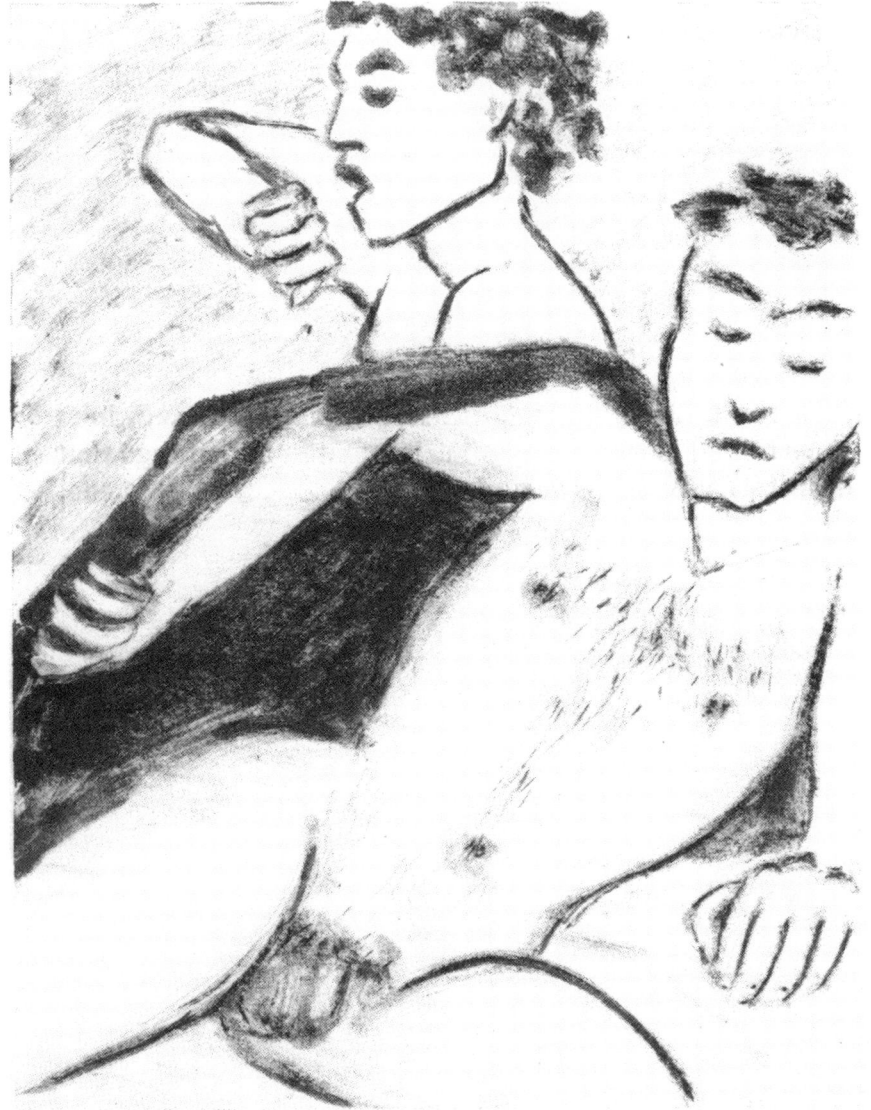

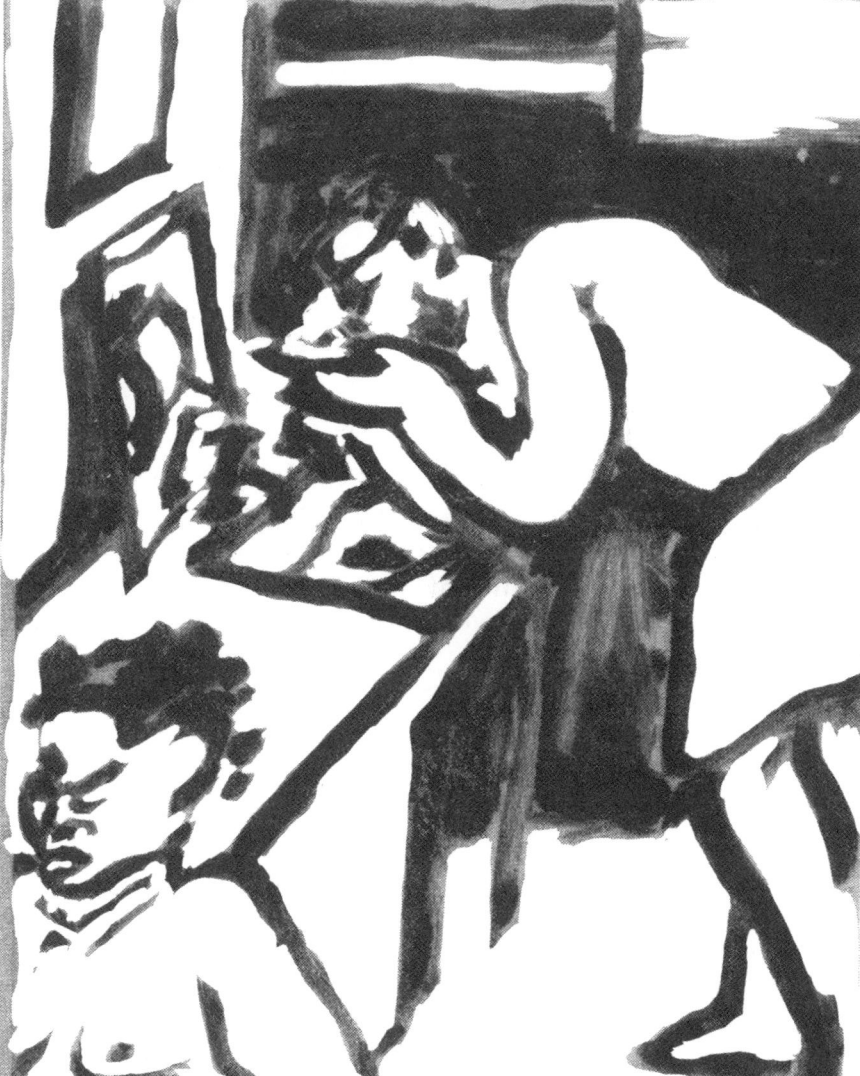

The great adventure, the pioneering thing, is to live together and not be a couple. The expectation is indefatigable and exhausting. Julie bought an Italian postcard, circa 1953, showing an ardent man and woman, locked in embrace. And looking at each other. Except that one of her eyes was roving out, the other in, and his eyes, looking at her, were crossed.

Like star-crossed lovers' eyes should be, she thought. She drew a triangle around their eyes, which made them still more distorted. People would ask "Where's Joe?" as if there was something supposed to be attached to her. The attachment, my dear, isn't tangible, she wanted to say, but it is also physical.

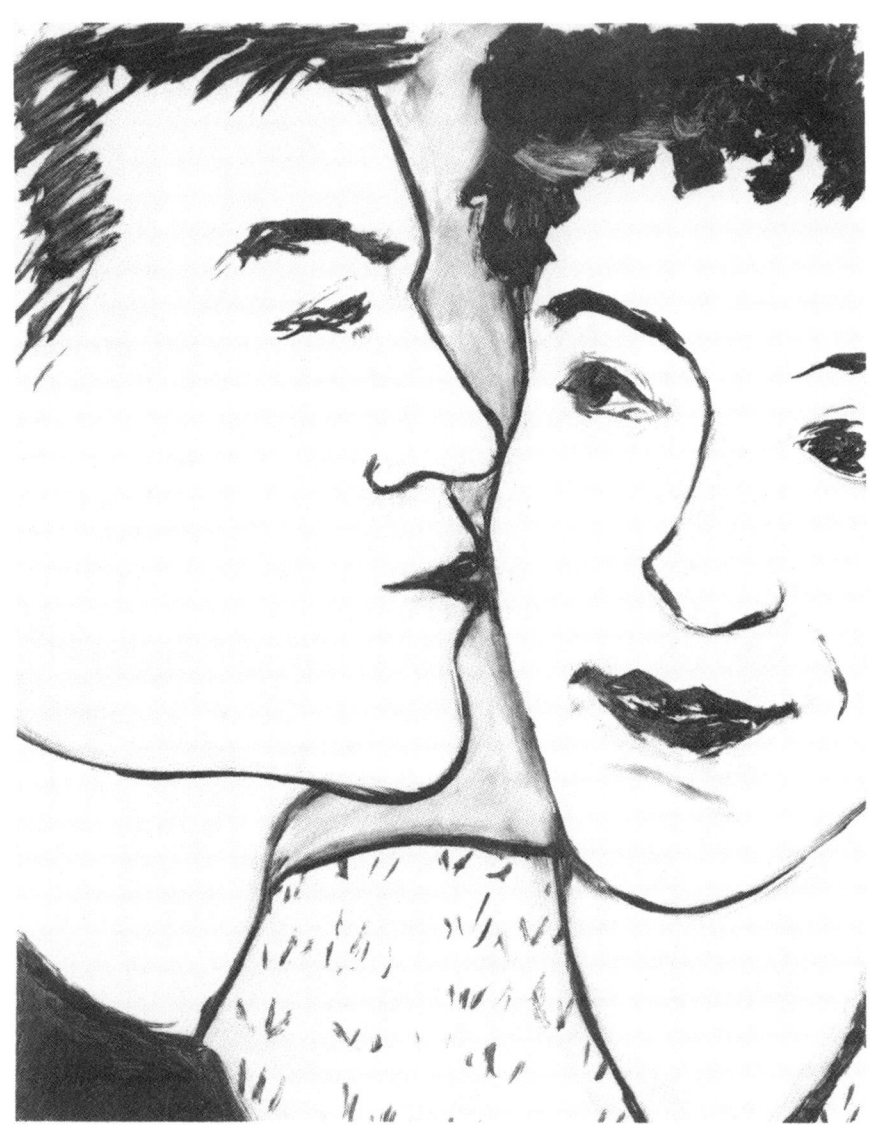

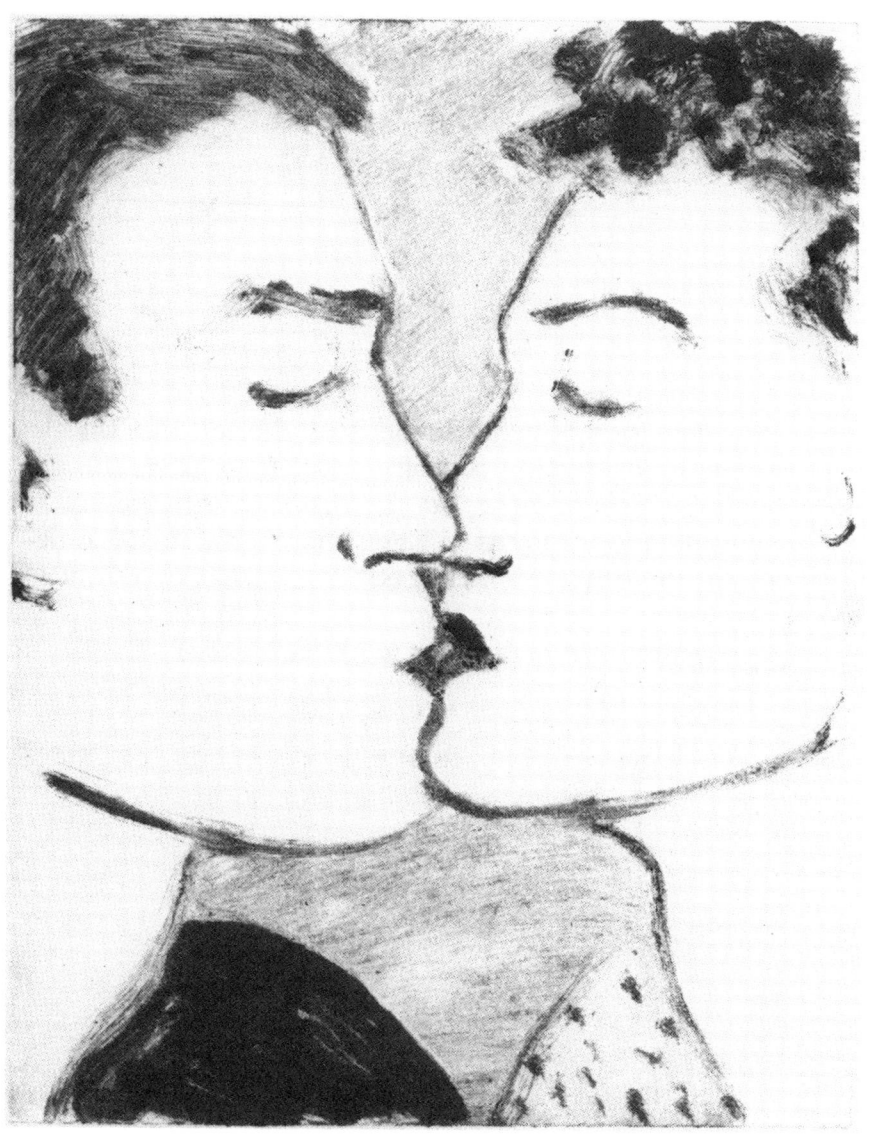

New cars, new lovers. Sometimes she felt like Ma Kettle in a situation comedy, looked on from the outside. You're either on the inside looking out or the outside looking in. (Then there's the inside looking in, the outside looking out.)
    Joe: We're old love.
    Julie: We're familiar with each other.

Julie didn't mind except that she didn't have anyone new to talk about, the way her friends did. Consumerism in love. One friend told her that talking about the person you lived with was like airing your clean laundry in public.

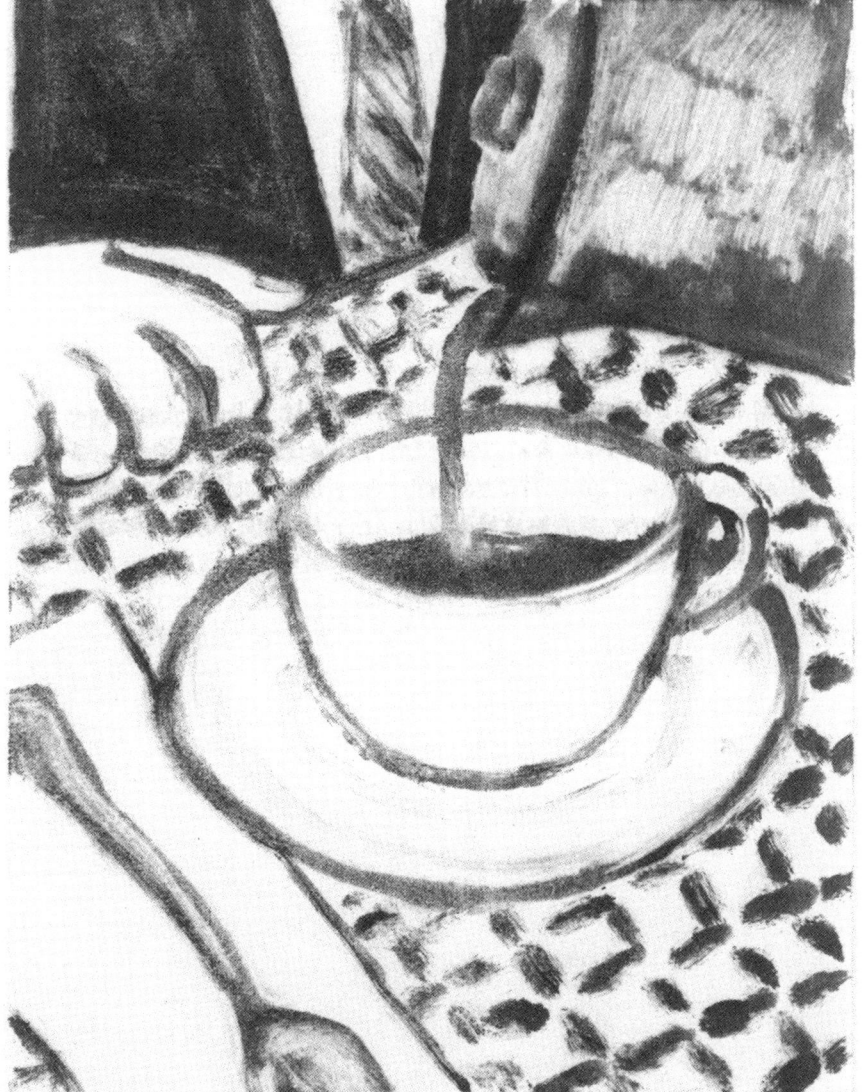

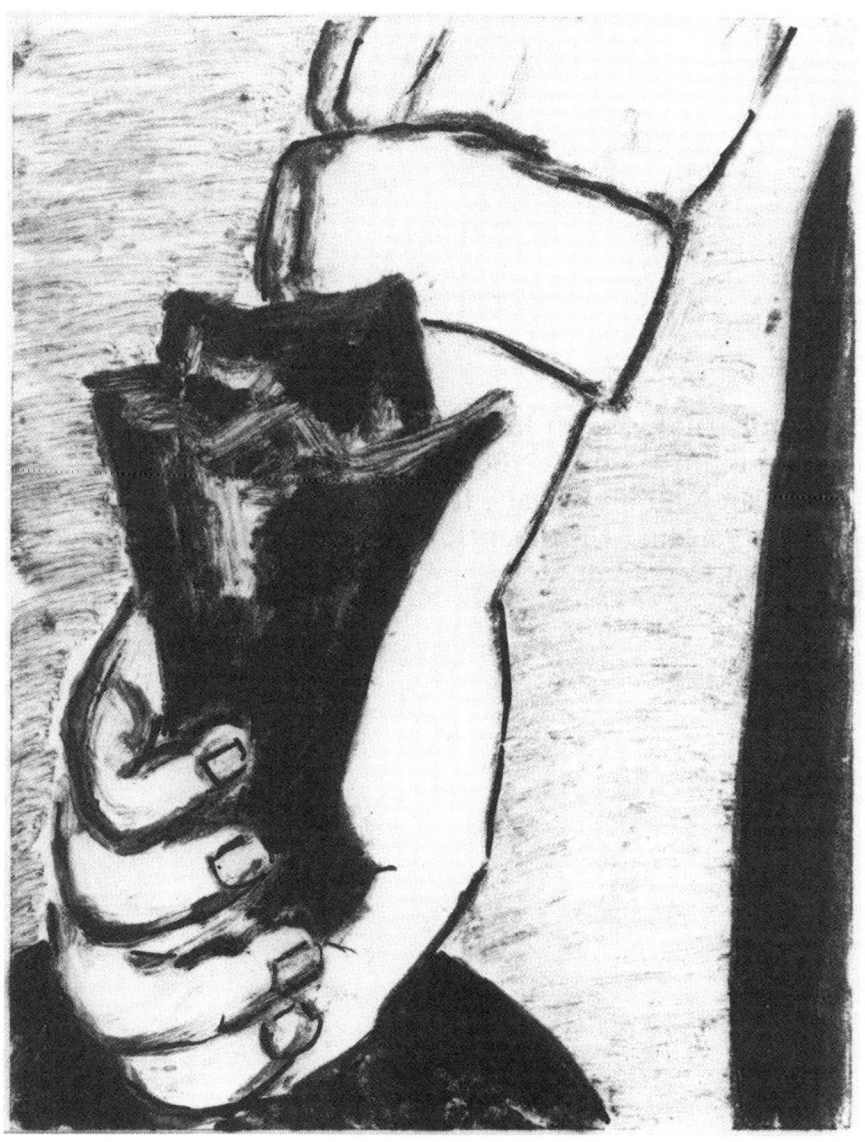

Familiarity was, for her, better than romance. She'd been in love enough. Being in love is a fiction that lasts an hour and a half, feature-length, and then you're hungry again. Unromantic old love comforted her, like a room to read in.

Joe: You hooked up with me at the end of your hard-guy period.
Julie: How do you know?
Joe: I know.

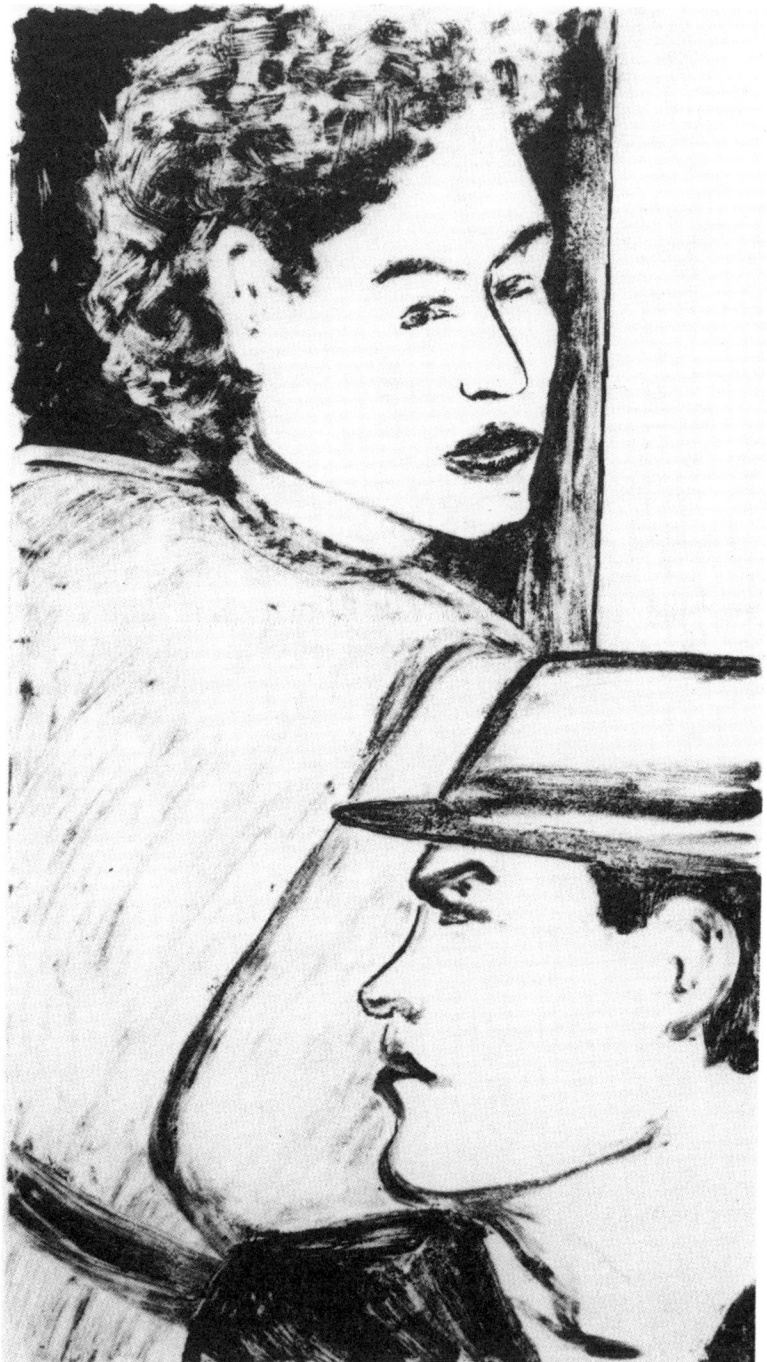

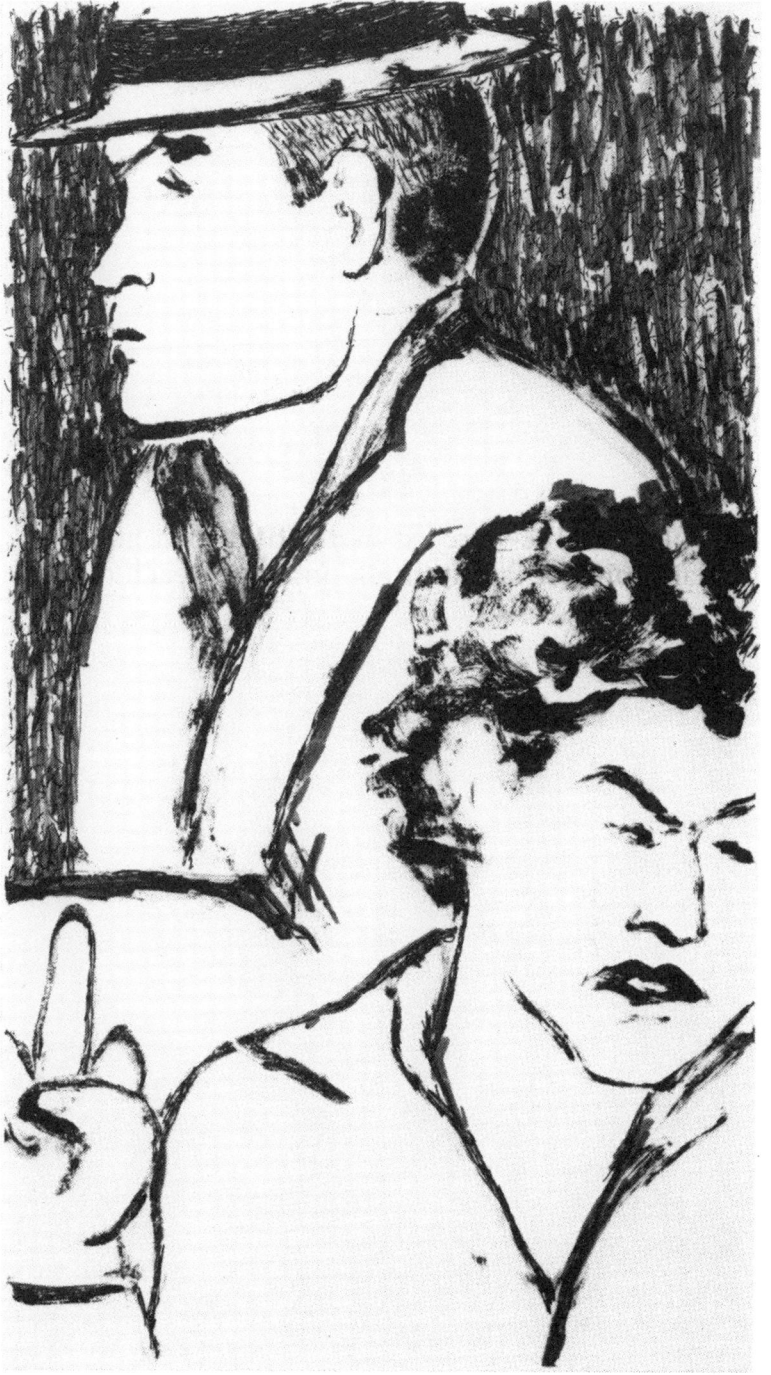

So, Julie and Joe were just part of the great heterosexual capitalist family thrall, possessing each other.

Contradictions make life finer. Ambivalence is just another word for love, becoming romantic about the unconscious.

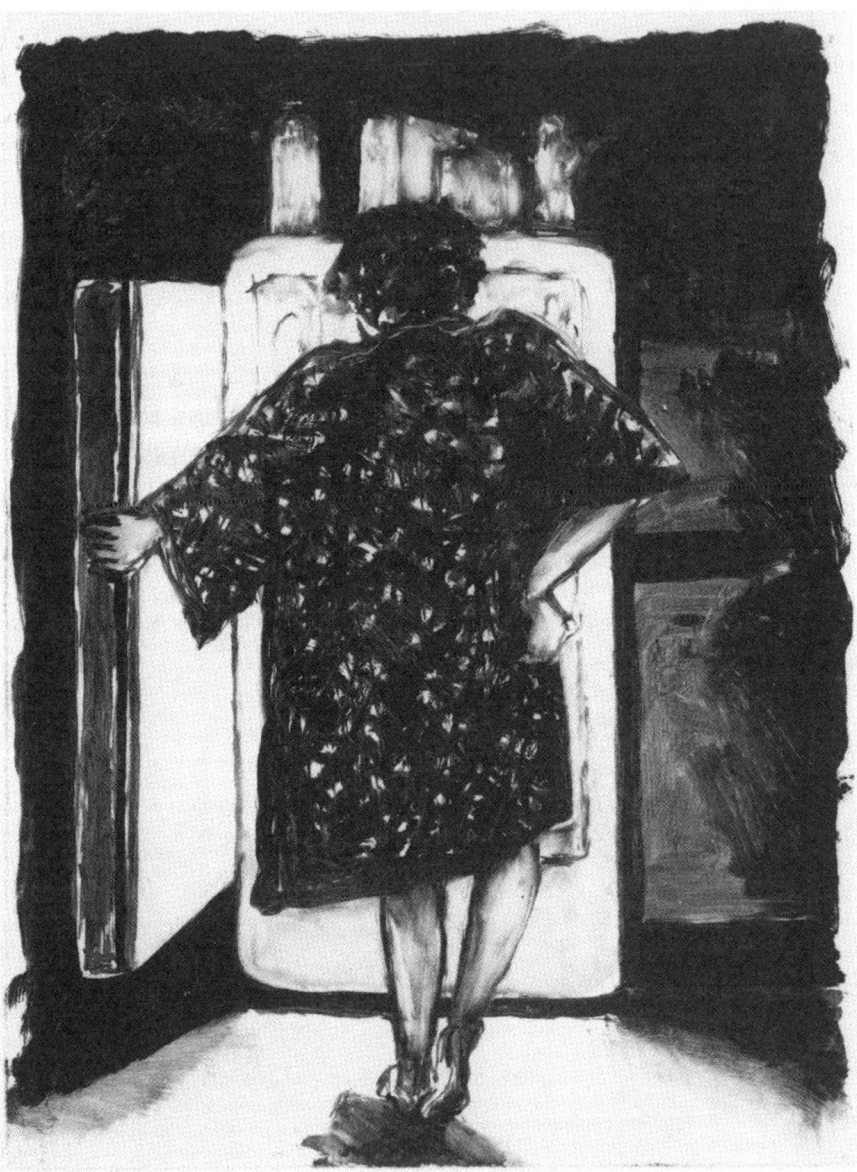

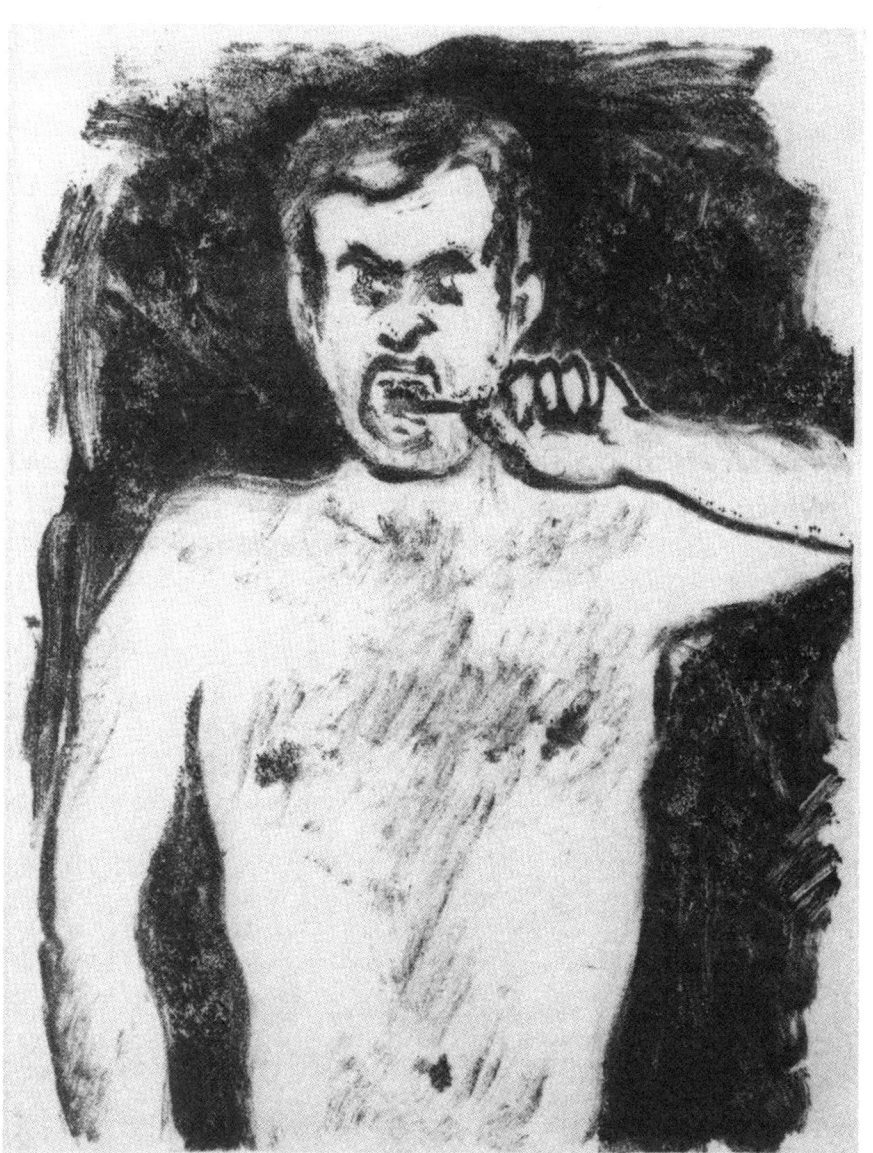

Where does one find comfort, even constancy. To find it in an idea or in the flesh. We do incorporate ideas, after all.

You can accept the irrational over and again, you can renounce your feelings every day, but you're still a baby. An infant outside of reason, speaking reasonably about the unreasonable.

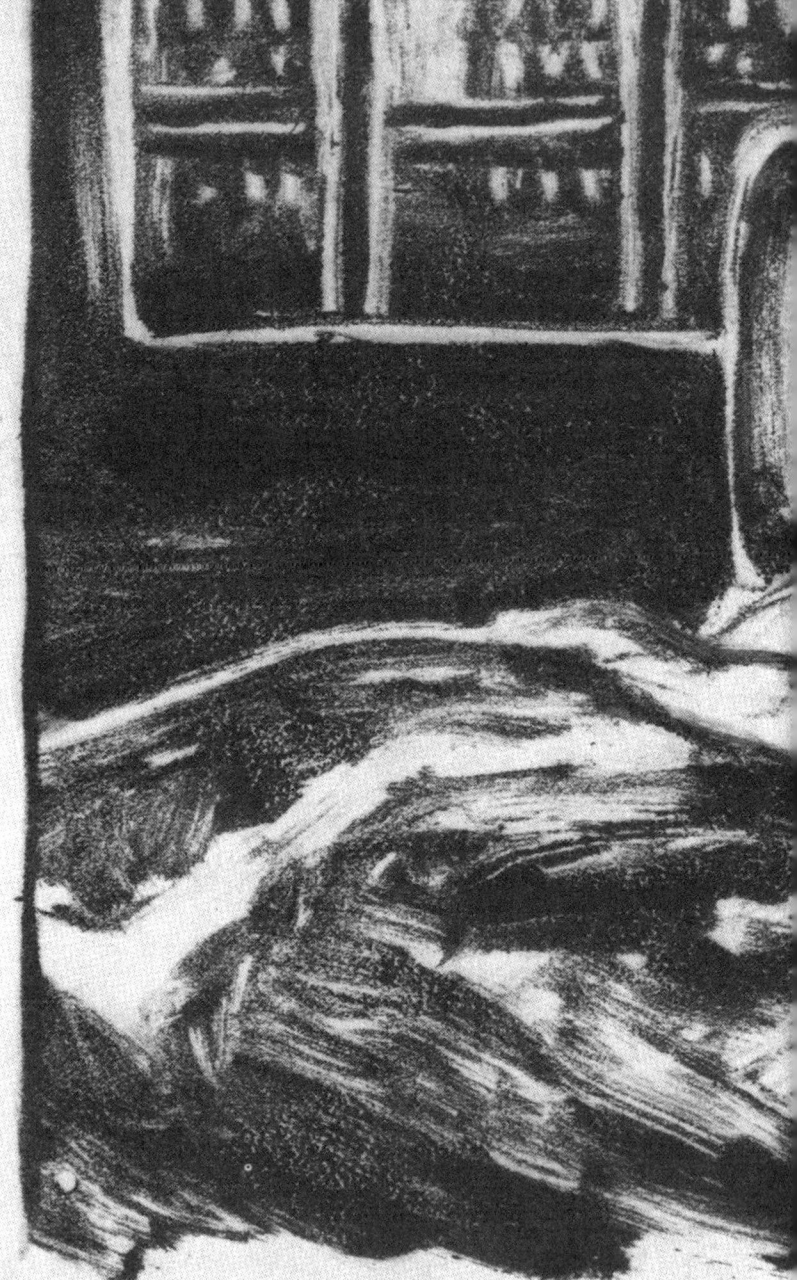

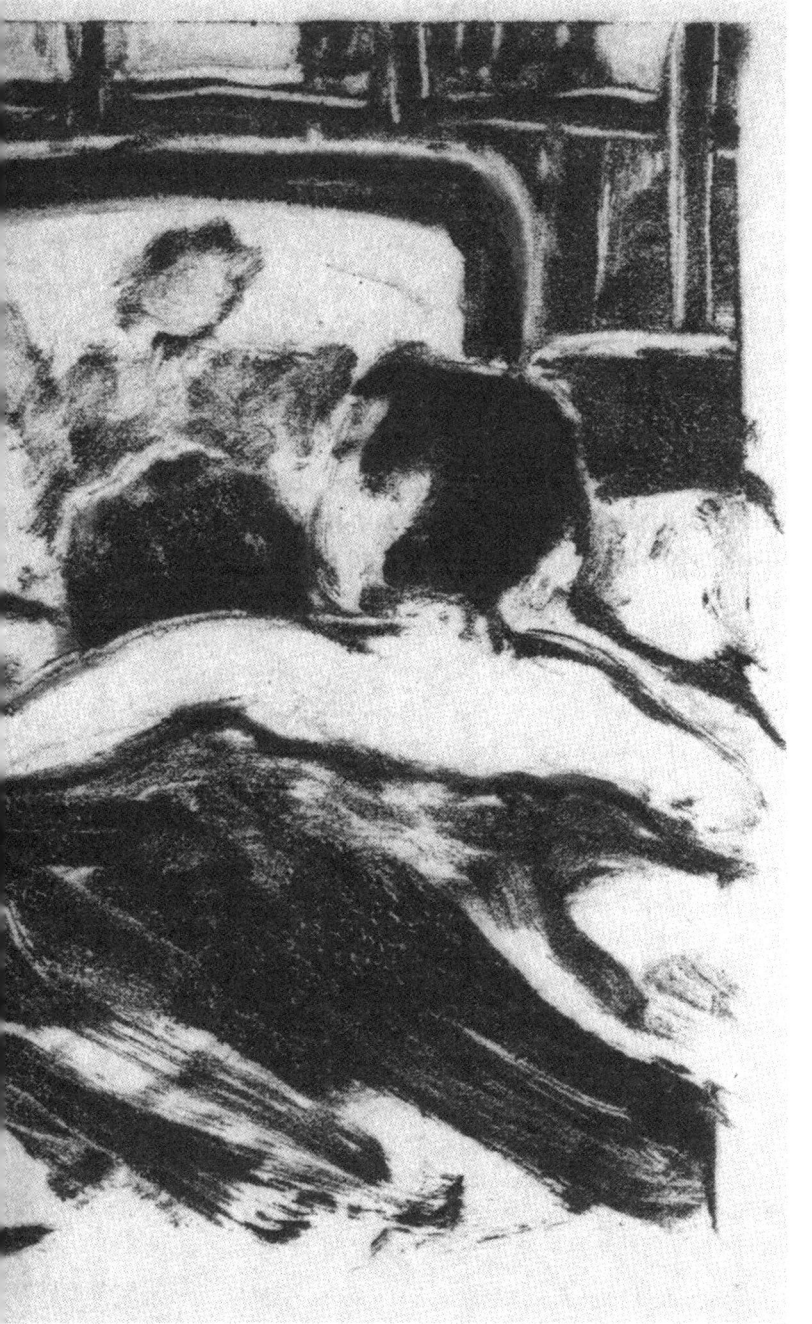

Calling love desire doesn't change the need. Julie couldn't abandon her desire for love. It was a pleasurable contradiction and it was against all reason.

This publication was made possible in part by grants from the Coordinating Council of Literary Magazines and the Committee for the Visual Arts.
Typesetting by The Magazine Co-op, 105 Hudson Street, New York, New York, 10013.

Copyright © 1982 by Lynne Tillman
Drawings copyright © 1982 by Jane Dickson

Hallwalls, 700 Main Street, Buffalo, New York 14202

TOP STORIES

A PROSE PERIODICAL

#1 Donna Wyszomierski
#2 Laurie Anderson
#3 Pati Hill
#4 Suzanne Johnson
#5 Linda Neaman
#6 Gail Vachon
#7 Jenny Holzer/Peter Nadin
#8 Judith Doyle
#9 Kathy Acker

Available from
TOP STORIES
Hallwalls
700 Main Street
Buffalo, New York 14202

TOP STORIES #11 $2.50

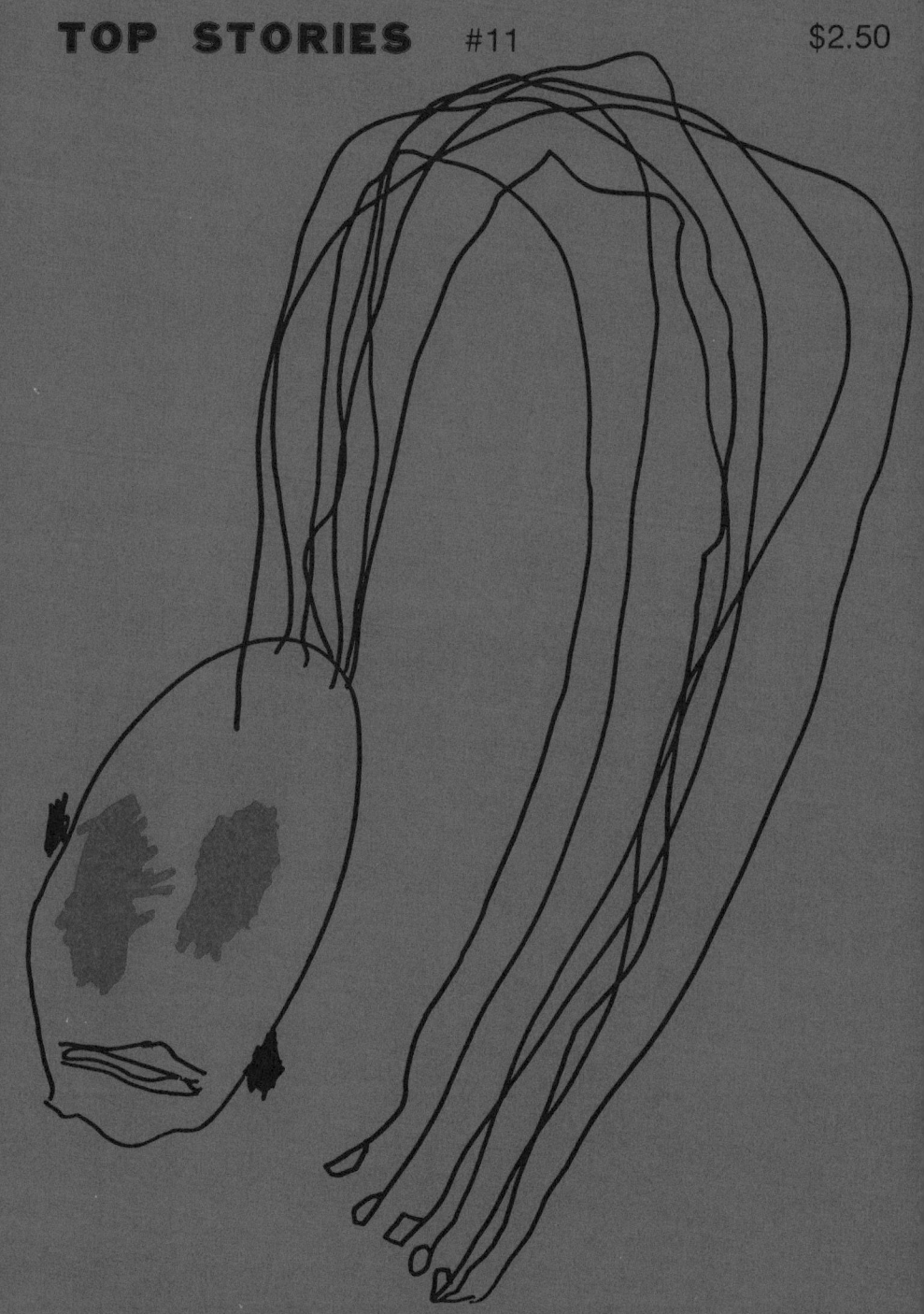

MARIE by Kirsten Thorup

MARIE

by
Kirsten Thorup

Translated by
Alexander Taylor

Copyright ©1982 by Kirsten Thorup
translation copyright ©1982 by Alexander Taylor
drawing copyright ©1982 by Aja Thorup

This publication has been made possible in part by grants from the National Endowment for the Arts, a federal agency, and the Committee for the Visual Arts.
Typesetting by The Magazine Co-op, 105 Hudson Street, New York, New York 10013

Hallwalls, 700 Main Street, Buffalo, New York 14202

Love will always find you
No matter where you hide.

She had neither been married nor engaged. It had never occurred to her. You could say that she couldn't connect herself with engagement rings and marriage. She was one of those who were quickly discarded. Maybe it was because she didn't say very much and wasn't very entertaining. Anyway, she considered herself boring. It was mainly because she demanded nothing of others. She didn't even demand that dates be kept. She scarcely expected it. But took things as they came. She kept the meal warm for two hours. That was the kind of boundary she had set. Then she spread her napkin in her lap and began to eat while she looked at the empty plate on the other side of the table. She didn't find it worth the trouble to take it out. It could stay there until she took her own out. She wasn't sentimental with herself.

Moreover, she didn't like to cook. And usually bought pre-packaged meals in the supermarket. Corn, spaghetti with meat sauce, ravioli or hamburger in cans. She could taste that they weren't good, that they had a metallic taste of preservatives and chemicals. There wasn't anything wrong with her tastebuds. But she was a creature of habit, and when she had first gotten into the habit of buying certain particular things, she continured doing it. It wasn't from apathy, but more from a total lack of interest in material things.

She was a very nervous person. You could see that when on rare occasion she said something about herself. Then red spots appeared on her cheeks and neck. And she always held her hand in front of her mouth when she spoke as if she wanted to catch the words with her hand before they got too far out and could hit somebody. Even the most trivial things about herself – which school she had gone to, how old she was, or whether she liked music – she found difficult to get across her lips. Her lips were unbelievably beautiful and as full as a newly blossomed rose that was pinned on her pale slightly blurred moonlike face, which sort of swayed over her body. She was thin to the point of being undernourished. You could see her bone structure and the shape of her skeleton under her skin. Her upper arms were as thin as pipe cleaners, and her thighs were narrow and hollow. She used girls' underwear for age 10.

Her lack of interest in material things could also be seen in her apartment. The furniture was placed haphazardly and impractically in the room. And most of it was from the room she had as a girl and her parents' attic. The chairs were too low for the table. And the lamps hung too high up and were placed where you had no need to see anything. It was cold. She always had the upper window open. There was a draft in the floor. The baseboards yawned below. And the floorboards were calling to one another. And the worst holes were covered by rag rugs. But she apparently didn't need much heat. And only turned on the radiator when guests came.

If it was a late visit she set, in the same way as with dinner visits, the boundary for the waiting time at two hours. Then she put the security chain on the door and pulled out the telephone plug and went to bed. She passed the waiting time by watching television or reading a book from the library. But she liked television best. And once in a while there were interesting programs from foreign countries which she thought she learned something from.

Now some may be tempted to think that Marie was a kind of whore because of the successive male visitors and the way they occurred. But it wasn't the case. On the contrary it was her – if you want to count it in money – who bore the lion's share of the expenses connected with the human contact she had. And in a way that was how she would rather have it. It was easier for her to give than to receive. And if she was invited out to a restaurant, she said no, thank you. She didn't like to sit eating among strange people. And when she made a new acquaintance and the person in question suggested that they should go to his house, then she stubbornly insisted that it should take place at her house, or they could just forget it. She felt more comfortable in her own apartment and was nearly impossible to drag off to other places.

Marie worked in a quick- and automat laundry on the corner of H.C. Ørstedsvej and Rosenørns Alle. Of course, most people came for the laundromat, and she didn't have much to do with them unless there was trouble with the machines. She served the customers who came and delivered their clothes and picked them up the next day. Once a day she emptied the washing automats and counted the money and went over to the bank with it and put it in the owner's account. She kept the accounts in the little back room stuffed with laundry bags and finished flatwork, wrapped in brown paper. She took care of everything – the cleaning, too, with which she was very meticulous. She was happy with her work. She liked to do the same thing every day. The routine itself gave her a certain satisfaction. And at last she could arrange the day the way she wanted. Only the things that must be done were done. She was at ease with the machines and had learned to manage minor repairs. But if there were major defects, she called the factory's repair- and service department, who sent a man out right away.

The owner, who had 15-20 laundries in the city – as well as a lot of real estate – came every other month. But she never knew when. And when she saw the black Mercedes roll up in front of the big windows, she got cold and hot by turns. He walked around and looked at the machines, saw whether they were in proper condition, saw whether the floor was clean, saw whether the soap automat and the the change automat were polished brightly, saw whether there were signs of vandalism, had on the whole an eye on every finger. When he had gone his rounds, he came into the back room where Marie sat, quiet as a mouse. He asked whether there were any problems. She shook her head. He nodded goodbye and said that she should contact him if there were any. There had never been any yet.

Marie was very tied to the laundry. Besides waiting on the customers from 9 until 5:30, she had to go down every evening and close up the laundromat at 10 o'clock and open up at 7 in the morning. That wasn't part of her work. But she had been offered it as an extra job. She lived on H.C. Ørstedvej in an old high-ceilinged first floor apartment two steps from the laundry. So it didn't matter getting up a little earlier in the morning or going down in the evening and shutting off the light and turning the key when she was sitting doing nothing anyway.

The evenings when she had company and they were already in bed before ten, it was naturally annoying for her — in the first place to be keeping an eye on the clock and then to have to get up and get dressed and go down to the laundry and back up again and off with her clothes and down in bed to a nearly strange person. But on the other hand she didn't have company more than once a week, and at the most twice. And she couldn't arrange her life around that, after all.

And she did it, of course, for the sake of the money, too. She really didn't need it and let the extra earnings evade her budget and put them in the bank. She had no idea what she could use the hoarded sum for. She had enough furniture and porcelain and curtains and clothes. She didn't need anything. Yes, I need a child, she thought. Then I'll save for a child, she said to herself and smiled inwardly. She often talked to herself when she washed and cleaned in the laundry. And she didn't just talk to herself, but also to the people she had in her thoughts, people she had seen on television or met in the street. She carried on long conversations in her head. And some days she had difficulty stopping. Then the talk continued right until she fell asleep in the evening. About everything, all the way from politics to headaches, war and menstruation, the Milky Way and space travel, about life and death and big and little people — like she herself and the owner in the black Mercedes.

Sometimes it got to be too much; then she felt as if she was the world's center and the whole universe whirred around her. And the voices became radio waves and people distant planets. If she got that way, she went over into the supermarket and bought a beer. She shut herself into the back room and slugged it down in a hurry. On the whole she didn't like beer or liquor. But it deadened the brain. She didn't need stimulants, more the opposite. But when she came walking down the street in her short jacket and black corduroy trousers and clogs there was no one who could see from her that she found herself in a tense condition, a kind of expectation or preparation which made it necessary for her to live as regularly and monotonously as she did.

Every Friday she bought flowers for the weekend. The flower shop was right next to the quick wash and was owned by a young man in overalls and flaxen blond hair. There was something soft and fine about him. He wore a home-knitted vest and his mother helped him to tie the bouquets. She stayed in the back room and didn't put a foot in the shop. But Marie caught glimpses of her in the door opening when she walked to and fro and puffed on a cheroot. She was tiny, thin, and sinewy. On the table among earth and green branches and cactus and heads of flowers there was a white ceramic mug with black coffee, which she slurped at once in a while.

Marie considered the flower dealer if not as her friend — then as an acquaintance. She didn't know his first name. And they talked exclusively about flowers, their durability and care, claypots versus plastic pots, the weather and the seasons, which had a great deal to do with flowers and not least influenced their prices. For the most part Marie stuck to tulips, but not the same color two weeks in a row. She bought potted plants once in a while, but as a rule they died on her even if she watered them carefully every other day.

Except for the flower dealer Marie found her circle of acquaintances among the customers of the quick wash. But one day in August right after she had come back from her usual summer vacation in Mallorca, two of the washing machines broke. It happened within a span of a few minutes. And the evening before there had been trouble with a drier. She called the factory and about a half an hour later the repairman came. Marie showed him what machines he should look at. She didn't pay much attention to his appearance except to notice he was very brown — as if he, too, had been on Mallorca — and had tatooed stars between the knuckles on his right hand. It took him nearly two hours to make the repairs.

When he was finished he went in to Marie to get a receipt. She put her name on the slip, but he kept standing there as if he were waiting for something. Marie let him stand there. She was

counting the one kroner and five kroner pieces.
—Aren't you going to give me a cup of coffee, he said. Disconcerted, Marie looked up at him. She had never met with this before. But she took down the immersion heater from the shelf and put her cup on the table. She had just the same kind. It was from her own set, "Blue Edge." There was just one chair, too, so he stood up, leaning against the table. He watched her attentively. Then he said goodbye and thanks for the coffee and left.

A few days later he came again to deliver his washing. Marie took it and weighed it, made as if nothing had happened, made as if they had never seen each other before. He tried to catch her glance. She avoided looking at him.

—There hasn't been anything wrong with the machines since, has there? he said. And there was something about him which gave her a feeling of beauty.

—No, said Marie. He took a pack of cigarettes from his pocket and offered her one. She shook her head.

—I really should do something in return for the coffee. Wouldn't you like to have a beer?

—No, thank you.

—You don't want to do very much, do you?

Marie didn't answer. She stood waiting for him to go, so she could get on with her work.

—I'll come tomorrow and get my clothes, he said and turned on his heel. Marie was busy the rest of the day. And in the evening she was to have company. She shopped. Both coffee and marzipan cookies. Red wine and a package of mashed potatoes and a can of goulash.

She had everything ready and the meal was on the table when the doorbell rang. It was a little fat widower in his fifties. He had gotten his laundry done at the quick wash long before Marie worked there. He was clumsy and shy and ate noisily and loudly clinking. Marie poured the red wine and drank half a glass herself. And as the little man gradually emptied the bottle, he became more talkative without losing his gentle and congenial manner by it. As a rule he left before twelve. Marie never allowed her lovers to stay overnight. She didn't want to wake up with them in the morning. But it was far from every time that he took any sexual initiative at all. But it could happen that they — once he had helped her clear the table or make the coffee — collided in the tiny narrow kitchen and nearly fell over each other. Then they stood for a long time in the same position like an immovable sculpture. Until Marie reached out her arm and turned off the gas and

lead him into the bedroom, where there was just room for her
narrow, hard bed and a chair and a bureau. They undressed with
their backs to each other and crawled under the quilts. Usually
nothing happened except they lay warming each other for an
hour. He was impotent and always asked politely if he should satisfy her with his hand. But it wasn't always that she wanted it.
Then he turned on his back and looked up at the ceiling. The
room was narrow and high-ceilinged and the walls were nougat-brown. And when the door was closed it was like lying in a huge
cardboard box.

—One should be young, he sighed. He was a head clerk in the
Amagertorv branch of Handels Bank and lived alone in a much
too large apartment. He was still mourning for his wife and
couldn't bring himself to get married again. But once in a while
he had a need for the closeness of another person. And for that
he had chosen Marie. He talked a lot about his wife, how beautiful she had been and a splendid mother and skillful at everything.
And afterwards about his youth in Lemvig and fishing trips on the
fjord. Marie listened to the same stories over and over again. She
saw it all lifelike before her and thought she nearly knew him better than himself. She felt secure when she was with him because
it didn't bother him that she didn't say anything.

He had a hobby, or rather a passion. And that was old coins.
In the course of the years he had gathered a collection together
which was worth a small fortune. He sat every evening at his desk
and examined them through a magnifying glass, held them up
under his nose and sneezed at them. But some time ago he had
begun to get eczema on his hands and the doctor believed that it
had to be the coins. So he put on his gloves every time he sat rummaging in his collection. But it made no difference. The eczema
didn't go away. His hands were fire red and itched like hell, especially when he sweated and was nervous. The he tore at the thin
skin between his fingers until they bled. And at night he kept his
gloves on in order not to rub the salve into the bedclothes. He
felt that it was especially embarassing for a man in his job, which
called for nice hands. When he counted the money and pushed
it in under the glass window to the customers, it was his hands
peoples' glances stuck to. They didn't see his face.

It gradually became so bad that he was moved from the teller's window to a desk far back in the huge bank office. And it
was a terrible defeat for him. Marie was the only one he confided
in, and with whom he wasn't ashamed.

—I've put the coin collection away. I don't touch it any more, and still I can't get rid of the damned rubbish, he complained and clutched his chin.
—Don't you think it's the money in the bank that you can't tolerate rather than the old coins.
—Then my very existence will be threatened, he burst out hysterically.
—But it's no better with the salve.
—No, it gets worse and worse. It will end up with my crawling to the cross and going to a folk doctor, which is against my philosophy.

That evening he was in a fairly bad humor. They were still sitting at dinner. And he rubbed his hands against each other from sheer despair.
—That it should happen to me. It's unfair. I haven't done anything. I've always lived a decent, proper life.
—There isn't anything fair here on earth, Marie said with a little sharper voice than usual, but you only think about that when it hits you yourself.

The little banker sighed again, and Marie began to get up and go out and make coffee.
—You shouldn't go to any trouble I'm going soon. I'm not worth very much this evening. You can't really imagine what it means to have a visible defect in my position. I'd rather have been castrated. That, at least, you can't see. Come over and sit a little while.

Marie sat down next to him. He stroked her hair and kissed he her discreetly on the neck. She was fairly tall and towered over him quite a bit. She looked over his bald crown and out the window. The rain poured down. And when the weather was bad she came to think about how lucky it was to have a place to live and not be forced to walk the street and sleep on stairways in the draft and cold. In the winter when the snow and frost set in, she was even able to feel privileged.

He kept on stroking her hair. Mechanically and absentmindedly. He was breathing heavily.
—The discount rate has been raised again. But what good does that do when we go on living above our means and the foreign debt grows and grows. At some point or other, the balloon will burst and then all of us will be put on bread and water, he said. It was the introduction to his favorite subject. He had money on

the brain. Not his own – he wasn't very well-off. But that of the general business trade. The string pullers'. The anonymous millions in the banks. You could say that it was natural trade sickness. And Marie tried to listen, but her imagination couldn't fill the dizzying, abstract quantities. It was as if the banker injected a strange fluid into her head.

—The devil looks after his own, he said and ducked a little as though he alluded to himself. He came from a very religious home but had lost his religious feeling. The only Biblical figure he had taken into his head was the devil, with whom he felt in cahoots because every day he took part in the dance around the golden calf. He could literally wake in the night and clutch his forehead and feel two tender bumps which slowly became miniature horns. But nevertheless he felt in his element among figures and bank notes. Securities and stock quotations. And often remained sitting at his desk in the huge office landscape after four when all the others had gone home.

They had sat for a long while without saying anything. The rain had stopped. And it was getting close to the time that Marie had to go down and lock up the laundry, and the little corpulent banker went with her. He walked with tiny mincing steps and set his feet down like a ballet dancer. They said goodbye to each other on the corner by the laundry. Marie went in. It was empty. She placed the laundry baskets together so that they stood in a straight row for the first customers the next morning. She turned out the lights and left. The air was heavy and full of exhaust. And this evening for some reason or other she felt depressed. Was it the unfortunate man's hands, her loveless life or the unhealthy air that gave her a headache?

She went up to her apartment and looked forward to going to bed. Sleeping was one of her greatest pleasures. She was a heavy sleeper and dreamed every night and really lived more dynamically and more intensely at night then in the daytime. She dreamed the flower dealer proposed to her and bound a wreath of pink latyrus and set it on her head. That she crawled up from the bottom of a stinking river with an infant that resembled a frog next to her. She knew that she would be able to come up. And just managed to take the child by the arm and heave it up over the bulwark and onto the quay.

Everything that she never gave a thought to during the day came forward in her dreams. She carefully entered every dream in a notebook, which she called "The Book of Dreams" which lay in clear view in the room on the television or by the telephone.

She went out and brushed her teeth and washed her face and dried it thoroughly so it was warm and shining. She opened the window, pulled down the shade and went to bed. A police car drove by with its siren blaring before she managed to fall asleep and began to dream.

She was already awake at five o'clock. An hour before the alarm clock was to go off. She got up and felt uneasy and unrested as if she was waiting for something or other from the day. She made the bed and put two curlers on the side where she didn't like the way it hung. She let the curlers stay in until she had to go out of the door to work. She made a detour to get a little fresh air before she had to go into the laundry and stay there all day. She suddenly felt like it was a prison. The sun shone. The streets were dirty. It looked like it was going to be a very hot day. She went into the garden of the Agricultural High School. She walked onto one of the lawns. That was forbidden. She picked a flower. That was even more forbidden. And an attendant came and threw her out. She had to return the flower, a blue pansy. Whereafter he followed her to the gate and stood there to be sure that she didn't slip in again.

Marie took another detour and arrived a half hour late. And there stood a young woman with two children waiting to get in. Marie apologized, saying that she had slept poorly and had a headache. The woman nodded understandingly and hurried in and tossed her clothes in one of the machines. All day Marie was distant and unapproachable. It was an anguish for her to open her mouth and talk to the customers whom otherwise she used to find entertaining. She came to think of concentration camps, which she had heard so much about in school and now and again come across on television or in some novel or other. And it occurred to her that she could easily adapt herself to daily life in such a camp. For she already had it within her.

She was washing the repairman's clothes. Normally she didn't pay any attention to whose clothes she was washing. But she recognized the shirt he had worn the day he repaired the machines. A chalk white shirt with a red pattern. She was a long time folding his clothes. There were four Turkish towels, two bath towels, a set of bedclothes, a dish towel, four fishnet undershirts, eight pair of undershorts – two white, two blue, two black, two brown, and four permanent press shirts. She put the clothes down in the laundry bag and put it aside.

The rest of the day she thought of something else. It got to be half-past five. He hadn't come. She waited for him until it got to be seven o'clock. She hadn't for a moment doubted that he would come. The she went home. She couldn't eat supper. Not even a fried egg. And neither the television nor the library book amused her. She went to bed early. She woke up in the middle of the night because she cried in her sleep. She got up and stayed up the rest of the night. She was afraid to lie down and sleep again. Morning came. She dragged herself through the day, forcing herself not to look at the clock. At lunch break she went into the flower shop. She bought ten tulips from the inexpensive assortment in front of the store.

—What's happened, the flower dealer said, as he wrapped them in thin green paper, — it's only Wednesday today.

—What should have happened? she said evasively. But kept standing there when she had paid.

—Variety's the spice of life, she said with a delicate and slightly awkward movement of her hand.

—Yes, all of us long for variety, the flower dealer said. His voice was like a puff of wind, and he spoke very softly.

—We just have to find one another. Marie smiled absentmindedly.

—There's something to that. People go around so strangely, each to himself. The flower dealer looked shyly down into the glass case. It was a beautiful business he had. There were bamboo shelves with dried flowers in artificial centerpieces. Dried flowers were his hobby. And numerous strings of bouquets were hanging to dry with their heads down over the door to the back room.

—Can one really dry roses, Marie asked looking up at one of the bouquets.

—Yes, they lose a little of their color but otherwise they keep well. He took down a very pretty flower decoration with many different flowers and pointed out the roses for her.

—It's really a complete flower orgy, Marie said, impressed.

—Yes, I put them together to music. In me the tones have colors.

—What music do you use?

—I only have a transistor radio.

—The light program? Marie asked. The flower dealer nodded.

—Would you like this one? he said and pushed the white porcelain bowl over to her.

—I can't accept that. Marie's face grew beet red.

—Yes you can. Do take them.

—No, another time. Marie was breathing fast.

—There may not be another time, the flower dealer said, looking accusingly at her. He put the centerpiece back on the shelf, and Marie felt that she had committed a terrible mistake and speculated like mad on how she could make it right again. She knew that he was hard up and could just keep body and soul together. She said goodbye and left with the tulips. But her thoughts circled around the flower dealer. He suddenly stood before her as the finest and most elevated creature on earth. And she had nearly forgotten the repairman when he showed up just before she was to go home. She opened the up back room and quickly found his bag, which she handed to him without saying a word.

—How much do you want for it, he asked. He had good clothes on, as if he were going to a party. And his hair was combed back with brilliantine. And Marie noticed that he had very slim hips. She mumbled the amount. And he took some bills out of his pocket. Marie was about to go in after the change.

—That's all right, he said. I've just come back from America, where I've worked for six years. Over there you always give a tip.

But Marie gave him his change. What could she do with four kroner?

—I've worked for two and a half months here at home now and already paid 5000 in tax.

—But then we get something for the money, too — hospitals, schools, retirement, workman's compensation and unemployment benefits.

—You make me curious, he said and stared at her.
—Me? she said.
—Yes, you're something special.
—I'm like everybody else.
—I can see from looking at you that you'd like a drink.
—No, that's not quite it, Marie said clumsily.
—Come, he said, and touched her shoulder. She started as if she had received an electric shock.
—You're a tiny frightened bird, he said and closed the door after them. Marie walked a little ahead of him down the sidewalk. And the street and the houses with which she was otherwise so familiar seemed to her as unreal as memory images from another planet. They went into the bar which she walked by many times every day. She got a martini. He got a beer.

—Skoal. What's your name?
—Marie.

—Martin, but I'm called Tor. So you can choose.
Marie looked around the room. It was the first time she had been in the bar. It was half-dark and cozy. She felt secure as when she lay under her quilt in the evening.
—You know, when you've been away for some years, then your friends have quit or spread to the four winds. Tor leaned across the table expectantly. There was something unneurotic and direct about him which surprised her because most of the people she met were so complicated.
—Yes? she said.
—Yes — now I live in the basement at my brother-in-law's out on Amager. My sister's in the hospital with female trouble and comes home next week. And so I don't know if I can go on living there. I've already had a falling out with my sister. And then — I've been through most everything — the whole trip down and up again.
—Yes?
—Maybe you think it's strange that I'm sitting here talking about myself.
—No, not at all, Marie said. She already liked him. She liked, so to speak, all people, except for her employer. Tor finished his beer and ordered another.
—I have a sister, too, Marie began slowly.
—Does she look like you? Tor asked, interested.
—No, just the opposite. She's blond.
—I've always been most attracted to dark haired girls.
Marie didn't answer. She felt confused. And thought about her sister, whom otherwise she never thought about. Her sister had a husband and three children and lived in an apartment out on Brødby Strand. And Marie spent Christmas Eve there and a day in summer when the weather was good and she could sit on the balcony. They talked mostly about her sister's problems with her husband and money and the older children who couldn't see any sense in going to school. Marie didn't really have any problems. Not important ones.
—It's funny about your family. You cling to it in one way or another. It's there, in spite of everything, that you've had your childhood.
—Yes, Marie said. She didn't cling to her family. It had disintegrated a long time ago when her parents died. But she couldn't explain that to him. Tor continued: —I feel like holding your hand.
—What are you afraid of, he said, when she gave him her hand.
—I'm not afraid, she said. And it was true. She was never

afraid. Except of going on welfare and having to stand there telling about her private life in order to get her rent. Or ending up like some of the old women who rooted around in trash cans loaded down with plastic bags and packages wandered around in the streets restlessly like ghosts from the past.

—Summer has come late this year — not until September, she said in order to say something. His hand was soft and lay like a caress around hers. She was excited and warm throughout her whole body. What she most wanted was to go home and put on some other clothes. Some nicer ones. A new white blouse.

—Shall we go to my house, he said. Marie let go of his hand. He got up as though he didn't need an answer. They took a taxi to Amager. Marie thought everything was going too quickly even though she had wanted to go to bed with him. It had been years since she'd been in love. She did whatever she could to avoid it. She didn't feel strong enough. But now it had happened.

They went around behind the house and in the cellar entrance Next to the furnace compartment was a large room. There was an old faded poster of the Eiffel Tower and a green curtain which couldn't even cover the window, but which Tor drew anyway. Marie sat on the bed. There was a table but no chair. There was a suitcase on the table. Tor put the laundry bag in the corner nearest the door.

—Are you going to stay in Denmark? Marie asked.

—That depends on the possibilites.

Tor came over to her and began to unbutton her blouse. It took a long time. And Marie thought that this moment, which should be eternity itself, would never come again.

—Help me, he said, when he at long last had gotten the buttons undone. And Marie took her clothes off in front of him.

The sheet and the quilt cover were white with a nearly invisible blue stripe. They didn't have to go to work until seven o'clock the next morning and had the whole night before them.

—You're just my type, Tor whispered.

—You're just mine, Marie whispered back. And noticed how her body gradually became flesh and blood. They made love in the dark and fell asleep nearly simultaneously.

Marie woke when it was about to get light and discovered that the quilt and sheet were smeared with blood. She wanted most to get up and very quietly dress herself and run from the spots of blood. She cursed her bad luck. She cursed that it should come just that very night. She lay waiting and didn't even dare breathe. It was a lovely grey morning. Light streamed through the window.

Half-asleep Tor reached for the alarm clock and saw that it was five o'clock.

We can sleep for another hour, he mumbled and pulled her to him and kissed her. Then he caught sight of the spots and shot out of bed like a rocket. He pulled the quilt cover off. It had gone through onto the quilt.

—Oh, no, how will it come off, he wailed. My sister comes home on Thursday. It's the last of the month, and I can't afford to buy a new one.

—I've used their room free and been treated well and then make a mess of everything. It's too bad. It's a real disgrace. Tor nearly cried with fury. He threw the quilt cover on the floor.

—It will have to go in the trash. There's nothing else to do, he said. Marie lay stiff as a board, freezing. Most of the color from Mallorca was gone. She was white.

—It can be washed off, she said and sat up in bed, dazed as if after an assault. Tor wasn't listening but picked up the quilt and stood confused and examined it to see how great the damage was. Marie got up and began to look for her clothes, which lay spread about the room. She wanted to go home at once and didn't even ask for the bathroom.

—Are you going? he said as if he was coming to himself and only now noticed her. Marie didn't answer. She was putting on her black corduroy trousers.

—Are you going? he repeated. He still stood there with the bloodspotted babyblue quilt in one of his hands.

—I'll take the quilt cover and the sheet and the quilt with me and wash them. You can pick them up after four, she said and gathered the quilt cover from the floor and folded it. Then she took the sheet off.

—What about the mattress, Tor said.

—You can scrub the spots with a nailbrush — but you should use cold water.

—Are you certain it will come off?

—Yes, Marie said. She was far from certain, but she didn't want to make him more upset. She took the quilt out of his hand.

—Have you anything I can put it in, she asked. He looked around the room and threw out his arms despairingly. Marie laid the sheet and the quilt cover inside the quilt and rolled it up.

—Do you have a piece of string I can tie it with?

—I haven't really gotten settled in yet, he said apologetically.

Marie took the quilt under her arm and stood there a moment in order to draw the time out. She wanted most of all to have kissed him, but went out the door, leaving him naked in the middle of the floor by the side of the bed, where there was only the mattress left.

Marie felt miserable. She walked as if in a trance and moved her legs mechanically. She saw everything very clearly and in much too strong colors like an excited person who has entered the kingdom of death. The slabs of the sidewalk were chalk white and the flower boxes red and blue as on a color television. One night with her lover was both nothing and much more than nothing. She walked and walked with the quilt under her arm. Over Knippel Bridge. Past Christiansborg. And got all the way in to the Court House Square before she took a bus. She went one stop too far and had to walk back to the laundry. She went in – without thinking about the door having been open all night – and put coins in a machine as if she were an ordinary customer. She sat on one of the laundry chairs and waited until the machine had stopped and the water had run out. The quilt was centrifuged and dried and smelled of soap and was like new. Marie fed the sheet and quilt cover through the ironer until they were completely smooth and whiter than an advertisement, whiter than snow.

The colors around her were still too strong. It was as if everything was bathed in light. Even the grey centrifuge shone. And the orange lids on the washing machine hurt her eyes. And it became clear to her that she couldn't endure working at the laundry any more. She had to leave. There was already somebody there washing. The smell made her nauseous. She felt as if all the flesh fell from her face, and that her head had become a skull. A dry taste of ashes came into her mouth, and she could feel her kidneys, which she otherwise never noticed.

But before she got out of the door, her friend the banker came in to drop off a bag of laundry. It was a fearful sight. The features of his face drawn together like a devil's face. He grinned at her with a strange grin and held his hands behind his back.

—Which hand do you want, he said.

—The left, she said and was amazed that it was so easy to answer. He gave her a little box with a ring. And Marie forgot to say thank you. Because she didn't want the ring at all.

—Shall we get married, he said and put the ring on her finger. Slowly Marie returned to reality. And because she was so filled with love, she said yes. It was on the tip of her tongue.

—I'll adore you, he said, You won't have to work.

—No, I'll work – but not here – another place.

The banker patted her on her hair and asked if he might in-

vite her to dinner to celebrate the day. Marie nodded or imagined that she nodded. And he fidgeted with his feet as if waiting for a kiss or a handshake. But Marie said — You should stop working in the bank, so your eczema will clear up. I'm sure it's the money.
—No, it's nerves, he said. I've gotten some pills from the doctor and it's already helped, look.

He displayed his hands like a well-behaved schoolboy. And Marie looked at them with a severe schoolteacher glance.

Yes, perhaps, she said in order not to hurt him. He blinked his eyes in sheer hapiness; then pulled himself sideways over to the door and hurried out to be at the bank on time at precisely nine o'clock. At the window outside he waved to her with a slight gesture.

Marie went home to take a bath and change her clothes. The first thing she heard when she came through the door was the alarm clock, which ticked unbearably loud. And even though she could still hear a faint sound as if from an insect you couldn't see.

—It sharpens the senses to be separated from the one you love, she thought as she undressed for the shower.

Marie had taken Tor's bedclothes home with her, and after her bath she wrapped them in brown paper which she had taken with her from the laundry. She put on her only dress — she always wore pants — and took the long busride out to Amager. She found the house and only now saw how lovely it was. It was a tiny red-brick single family house. There was lawn furniture in the yard which wasn't yet taken in for winter. Most of it was sown with grass, and there was a pair of crooked fruit trees. Marie took a pear that had fallen on the grass. She sat down on one of the garden chairs and ate the pear and the juice ran down her chin and through her fingers. The grass was a little too green and neon-like, but otherwise there was nothing unusual. The chair was a chair, and the flowers were flowers and the house a house. The sky was blue. And the sun was warm.

She went over to the cellar entrance which lay three steps down and set the package up against the door so that he couldn't avoid finding it. She adjusted it so it came to lie completely flush and patted it like a child. She had thought of writing a note and laying it with the package: Everything is clean! Love, your M. But she would rather disappear without a word. She didn't like to be in his consciousness.

From Amager she went into the city. She took her savings out of the bank. And kept a little for herself. The rest she sent anonymously to the flower dealer. And when she had been to the post office, she could finally go back to the laundry and continue her work as if nothing had happened. The whole excursion hadn't taken more than a few hours. It was the first time in the five years she had been at the laundry that she had taken the liberty to leave during work hours. And so it took her by surprise when she saw from the bus the black Mercedes parked at the curb outside the laundry.

The owner stood waiting for her. It was only fourteen days since he had been there last. He snorted and groaned like a furious colt. He had unbuttoned his dark blue cashmere coat. The air was sultry and damp because of the vapour from the washing machines.

—Shall we go in and sit down, he snarled. Marie opened up the office. He sat on the chair.

—You can stop working on the first. I can't use you any longer.

—Yes, but.

—I can't use your excuses, either. I don't care about them at all. People are waiting in line for work. You can feed the pigs with them. And now I want to see the accounts, he added and turned around in the chair. He had a broad bull neck with three or four rolls of fat across it. And the close-cropped neck hair grew out between the pillows of fat. He sat with his back to Marie leafing through the account books. He slowly trailed his thick and slightly stiff forefinger down across Marie's neat rows of figures, stopped and let his finger linger on a number and asked for explanations of anything he didn't understand. Marie was sure that there were no errors and answered curtly with single syllable words. She stood behind him and looked into his neck. She remembered that once he had taken her by the chin and said that they could talk about it when she had gotten a little more meat on her body. And that the older woman who had been fired and whose job she had taken had cried and said to him:
—Some day you'll pay for that.

The owner asked again about something. Marie didn't hear him. He repeated his question, and it sounded like a commando call. "Some day you'll pay for that" — it sang in Marie's ears.

In front of her on the shelf next to the cup lay a long pointed awl which she used to loosen the money that had gotten stuck in the machines. She took the awl and jabbed it into his neck between two rolls of fat. And she thrust so violently that it went through his neck and out the other side right under the larynx. He fell forward without a sound so that his forehead came to rest on the little white page with the rows of numbers.

Marie felt a great relief and suddenly knew that this was what she had prepared herself for her whole life. And it hadn't demanded anything more than courage and a strong arm.

TOP STORIES

A PROSE PERIODICAL

#1 Donna Wyszomierski
#2 Laurie Anderson
#3 Pati Hill
#4 Suzanne Johnson
#5 Linda Neaman
#6 Gail Vachon
#7 Jenny Holzer/Peter Nadin
#8 Judith Doyle
#9 Kathy Acker
#10 Lynne Tillman/Jane Dickson

Available from
TOP STORIES
Hallwalls
700 Main Street
Buffalo, New York 14202

TOP STORIES #12 $2.50

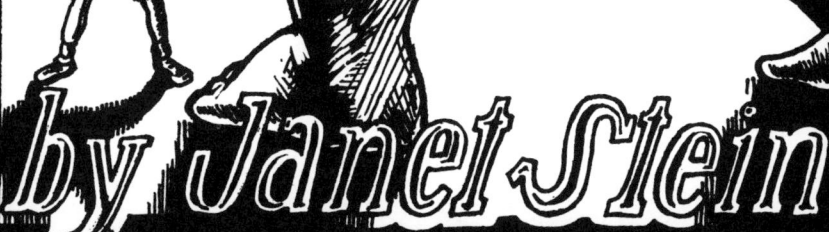

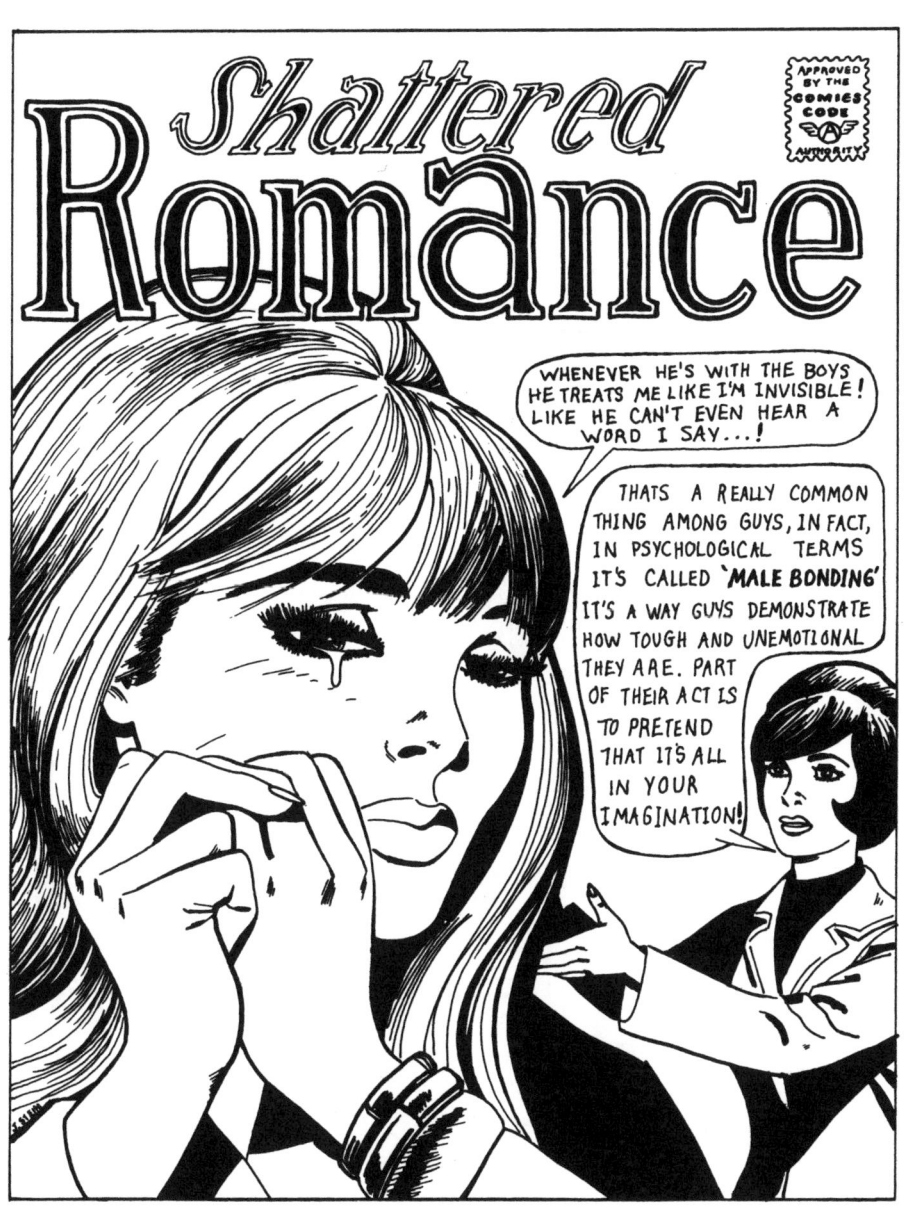

by Janet Stein

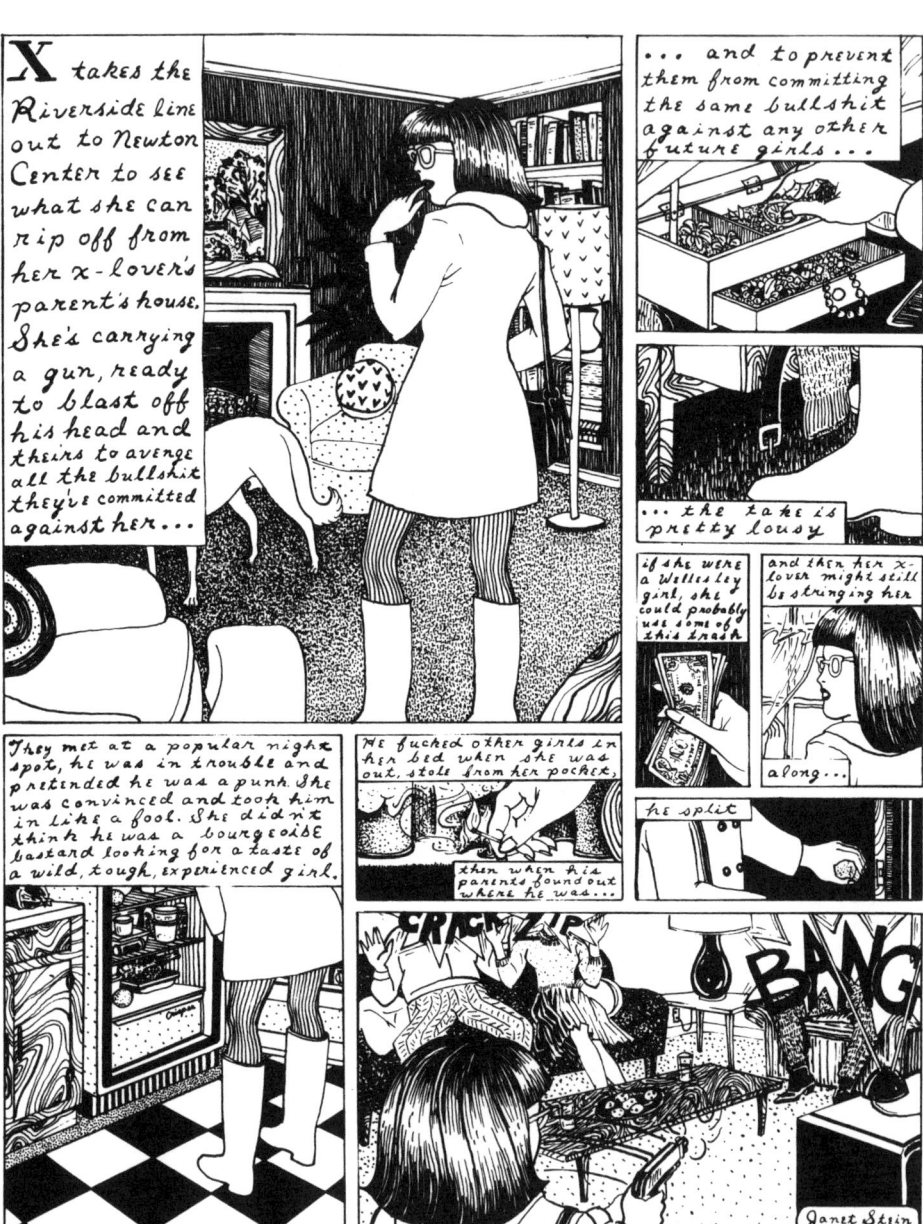

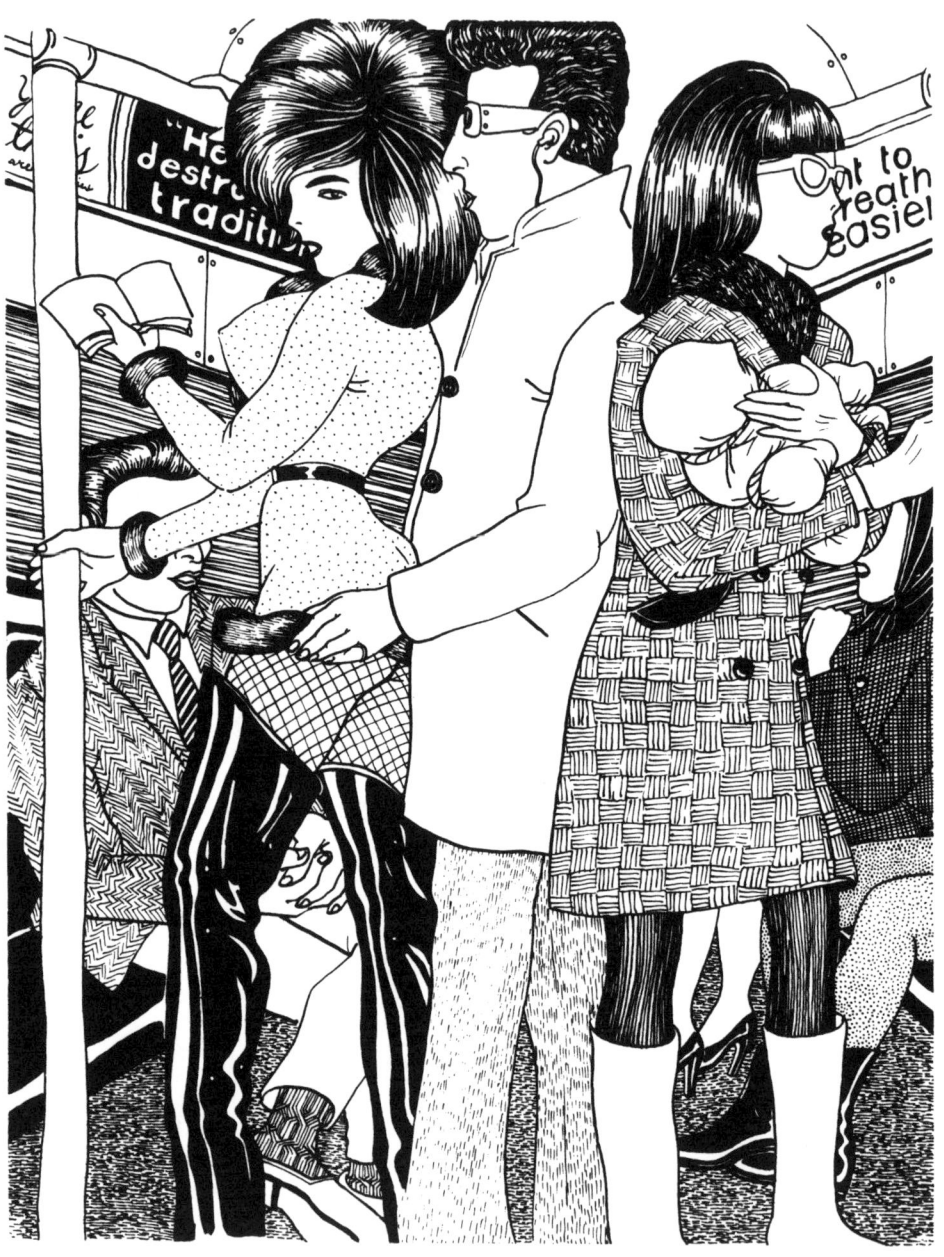

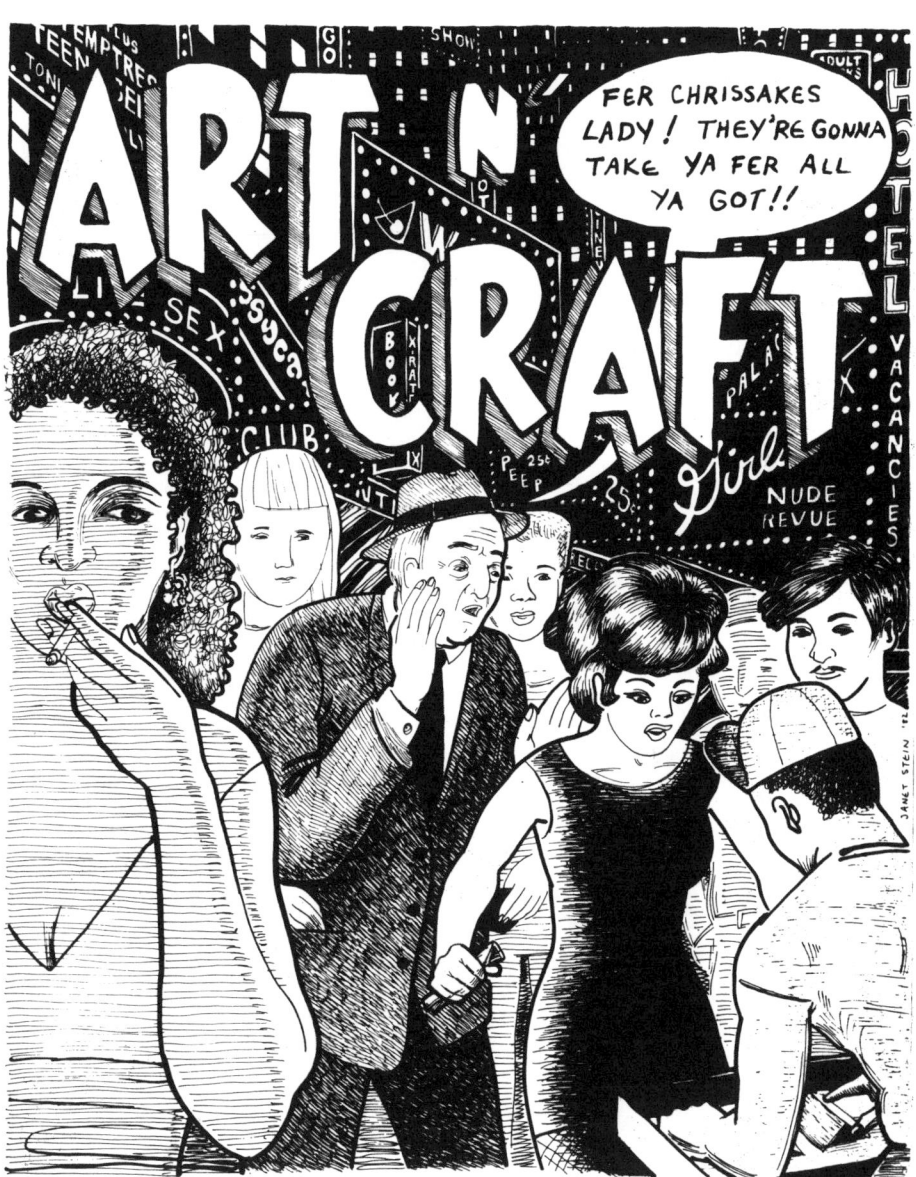

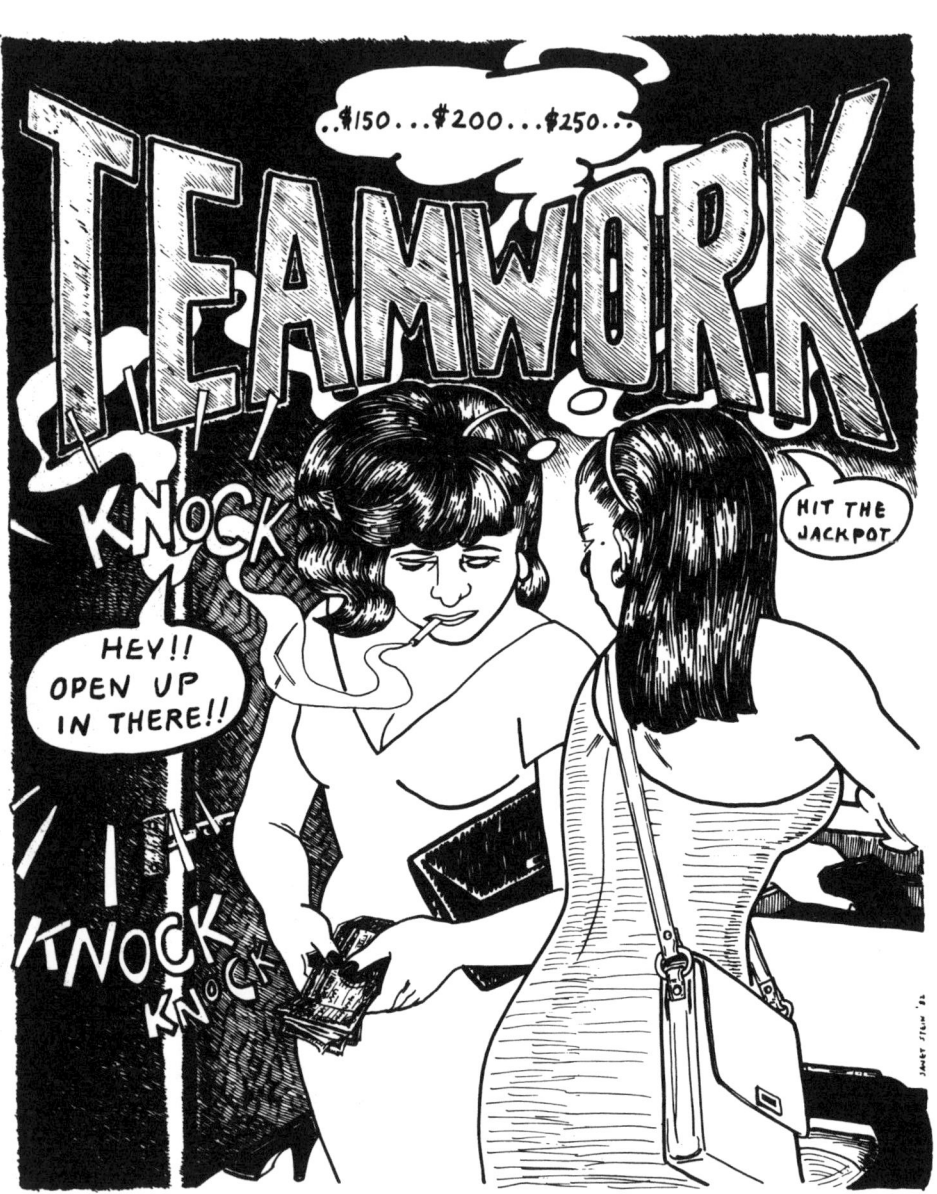

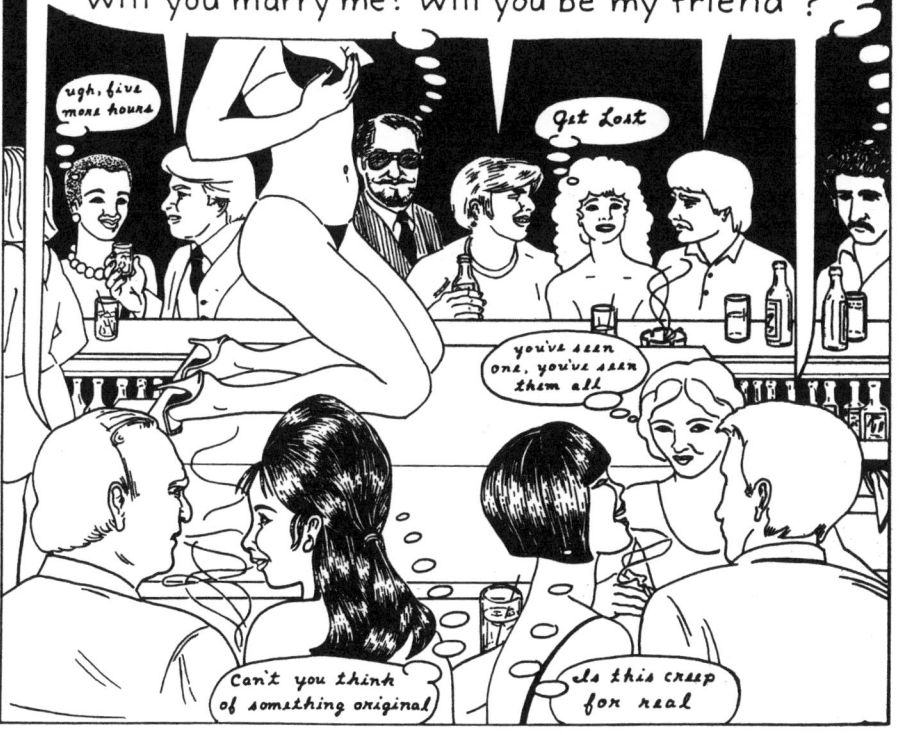

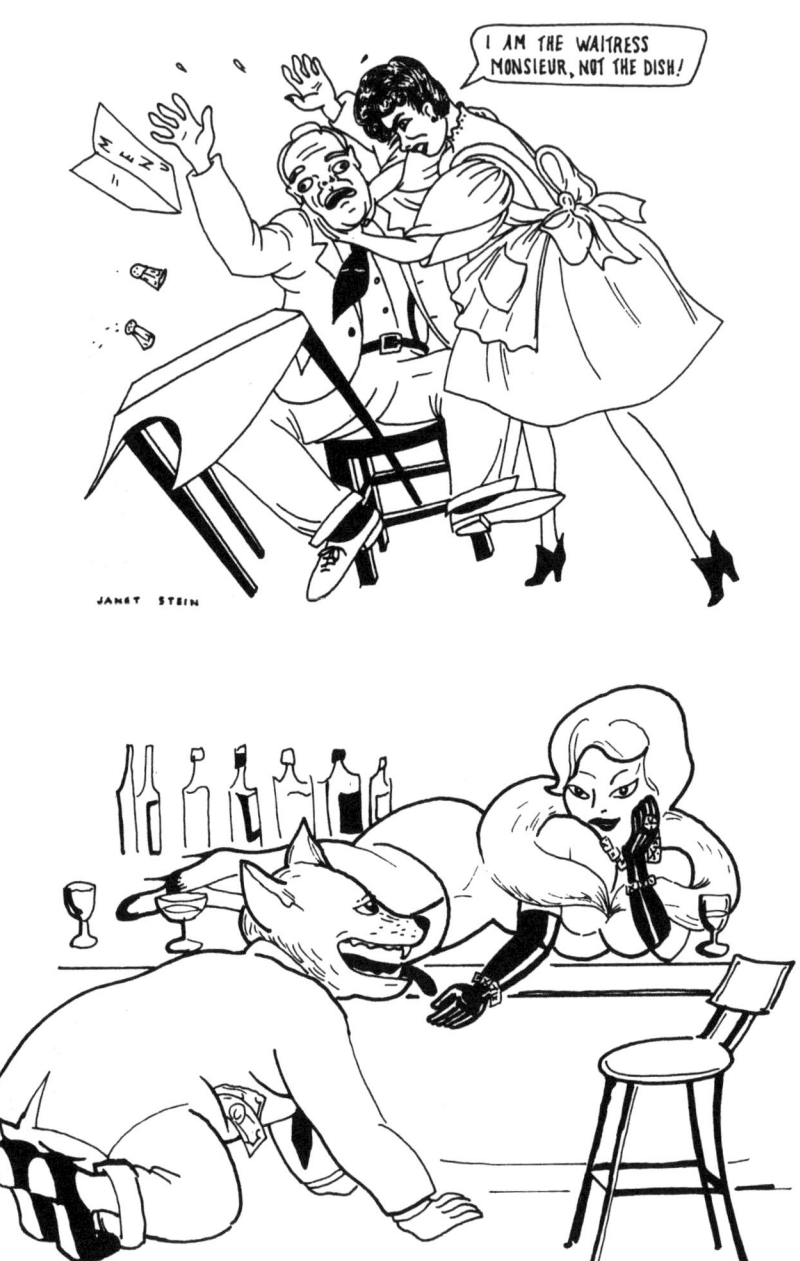

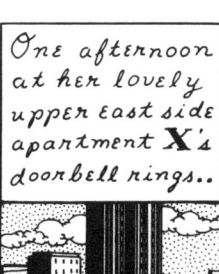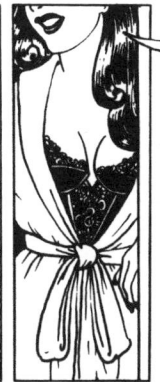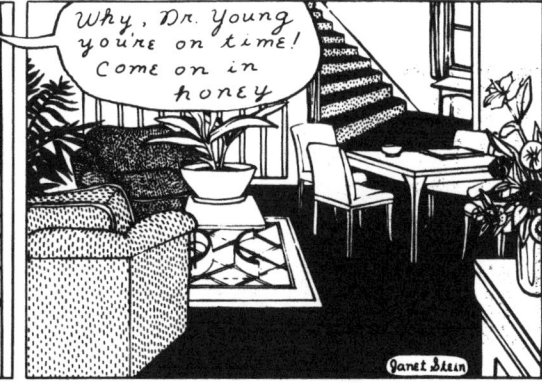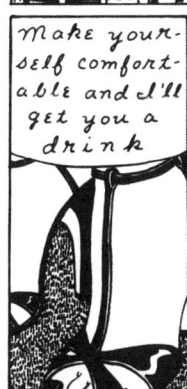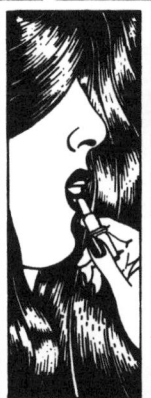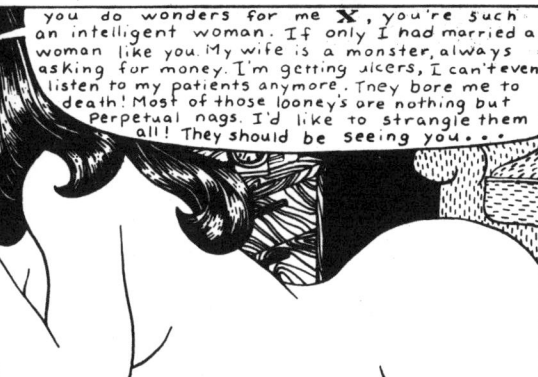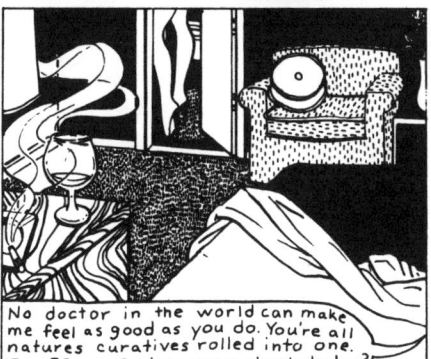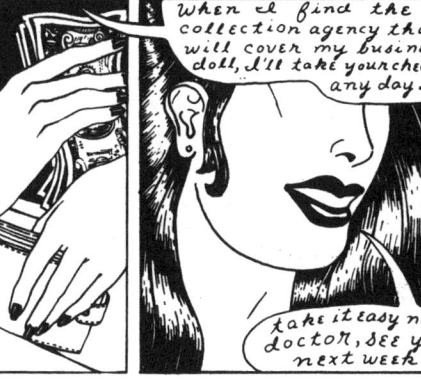

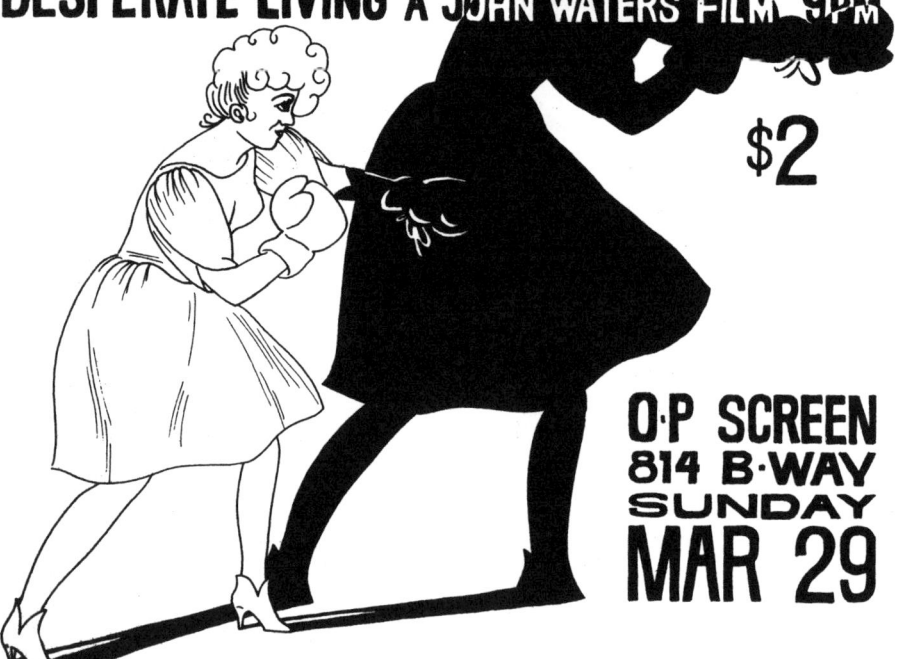

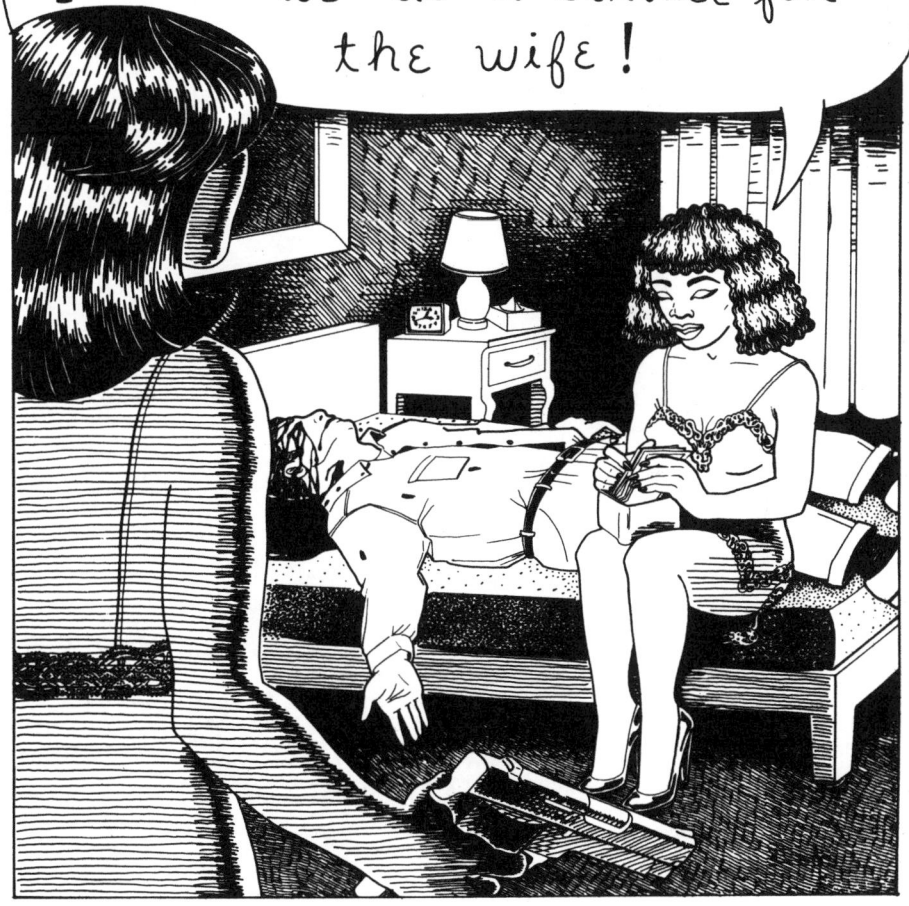

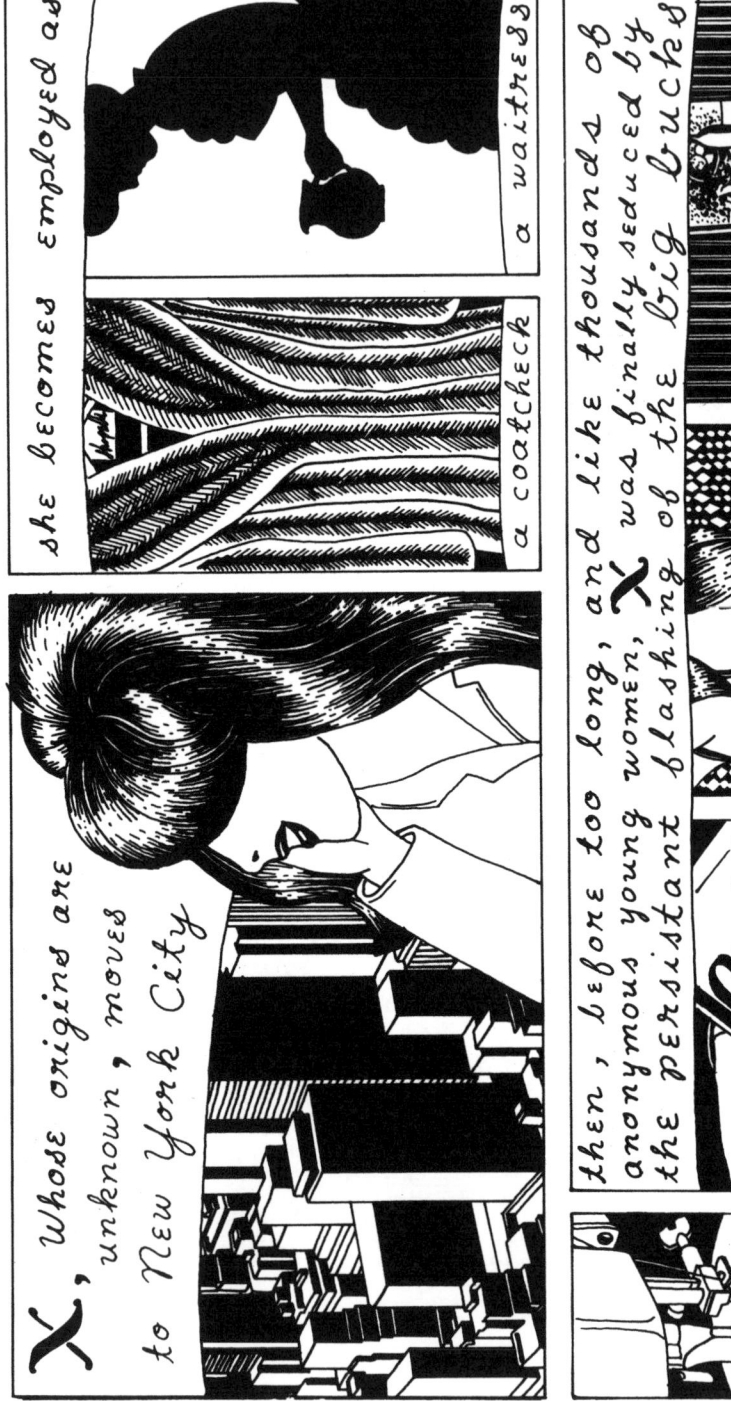

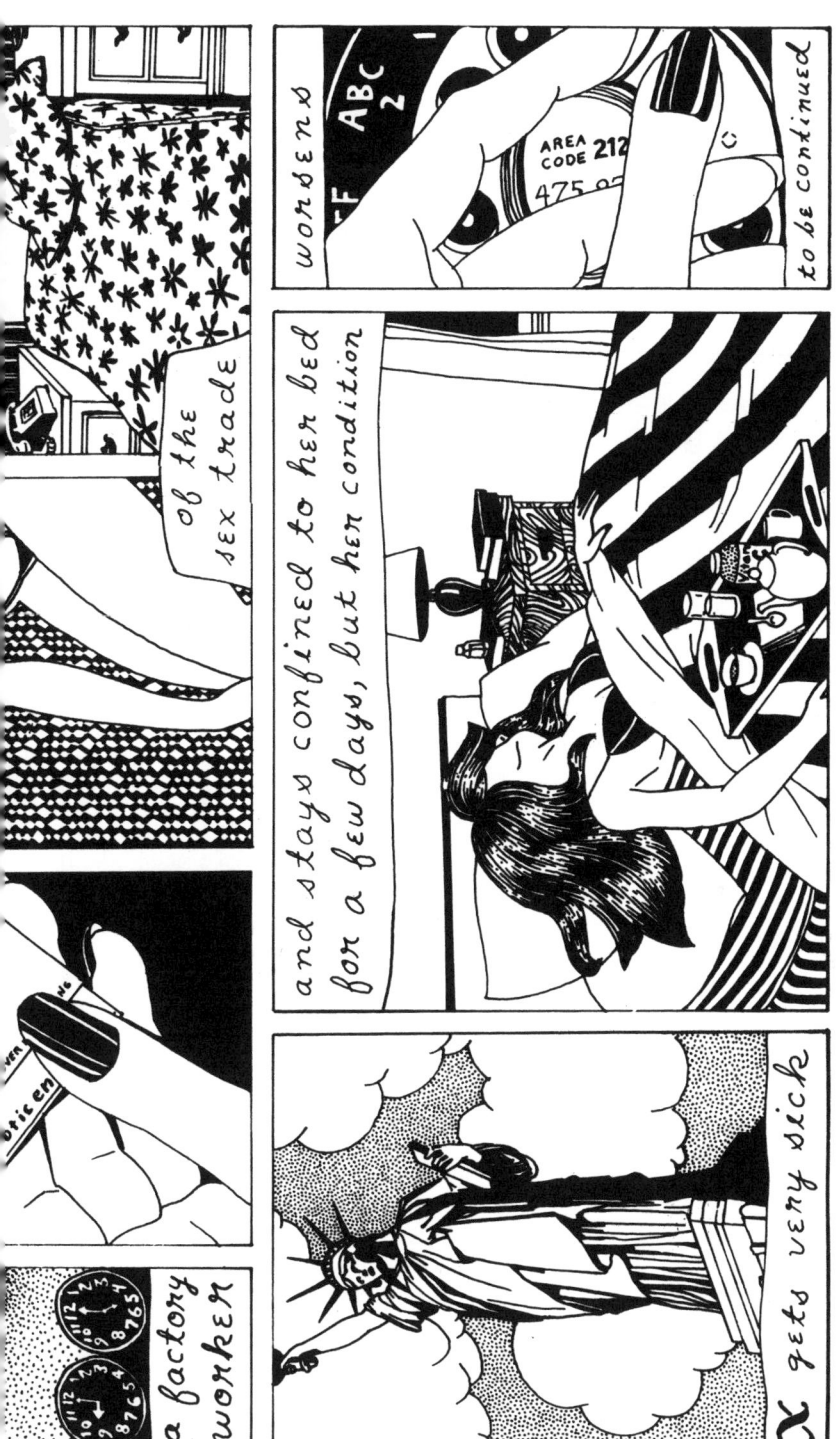

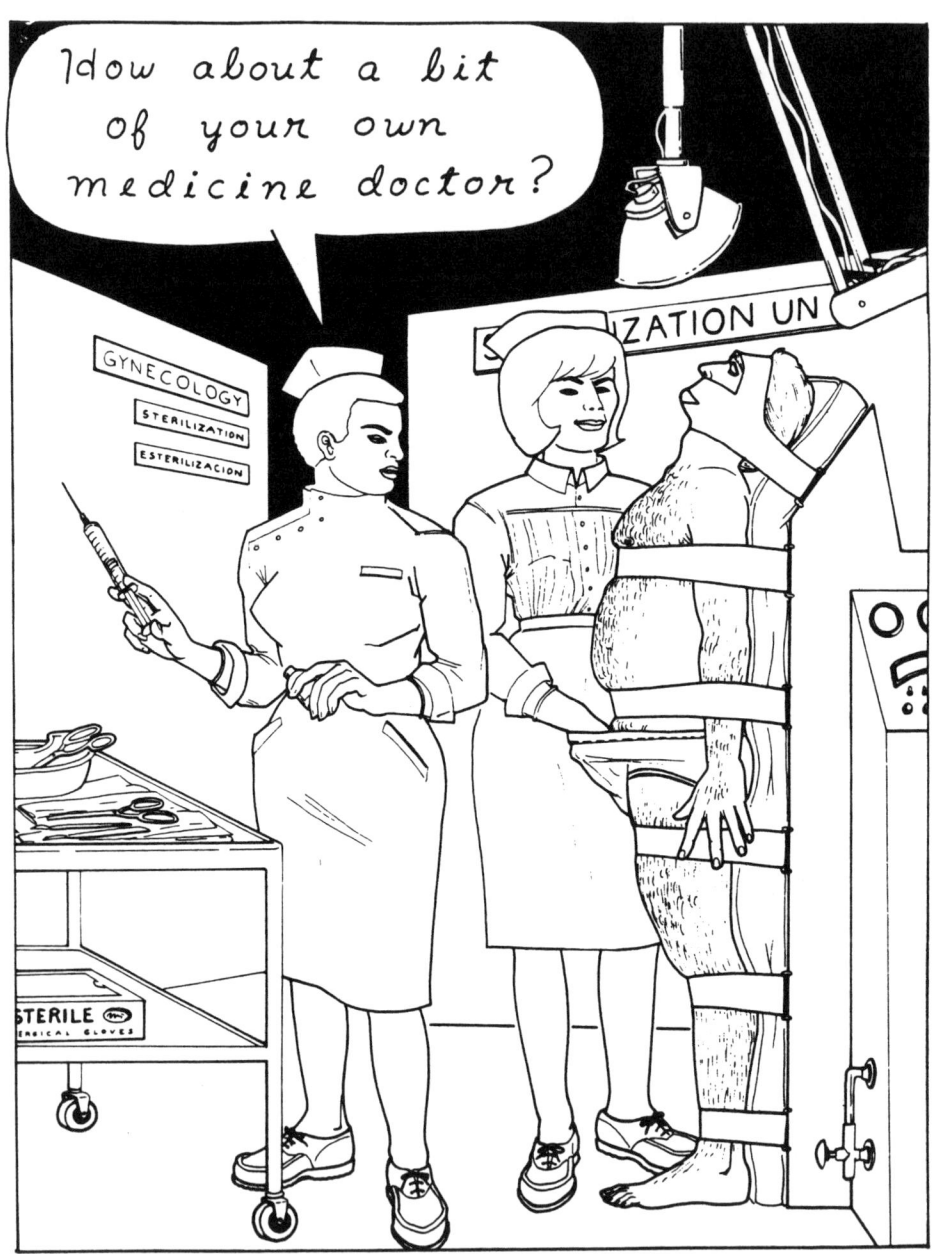

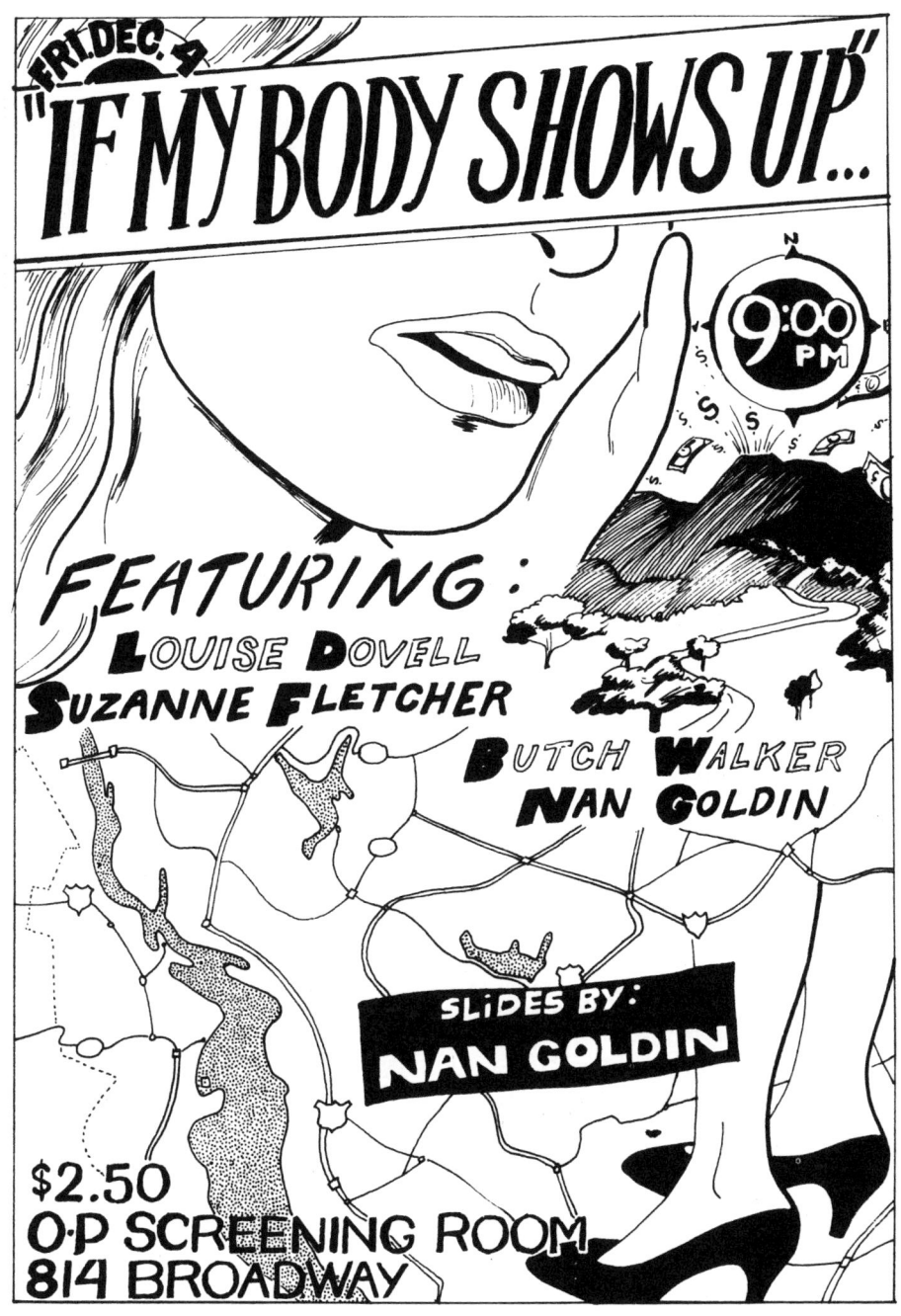

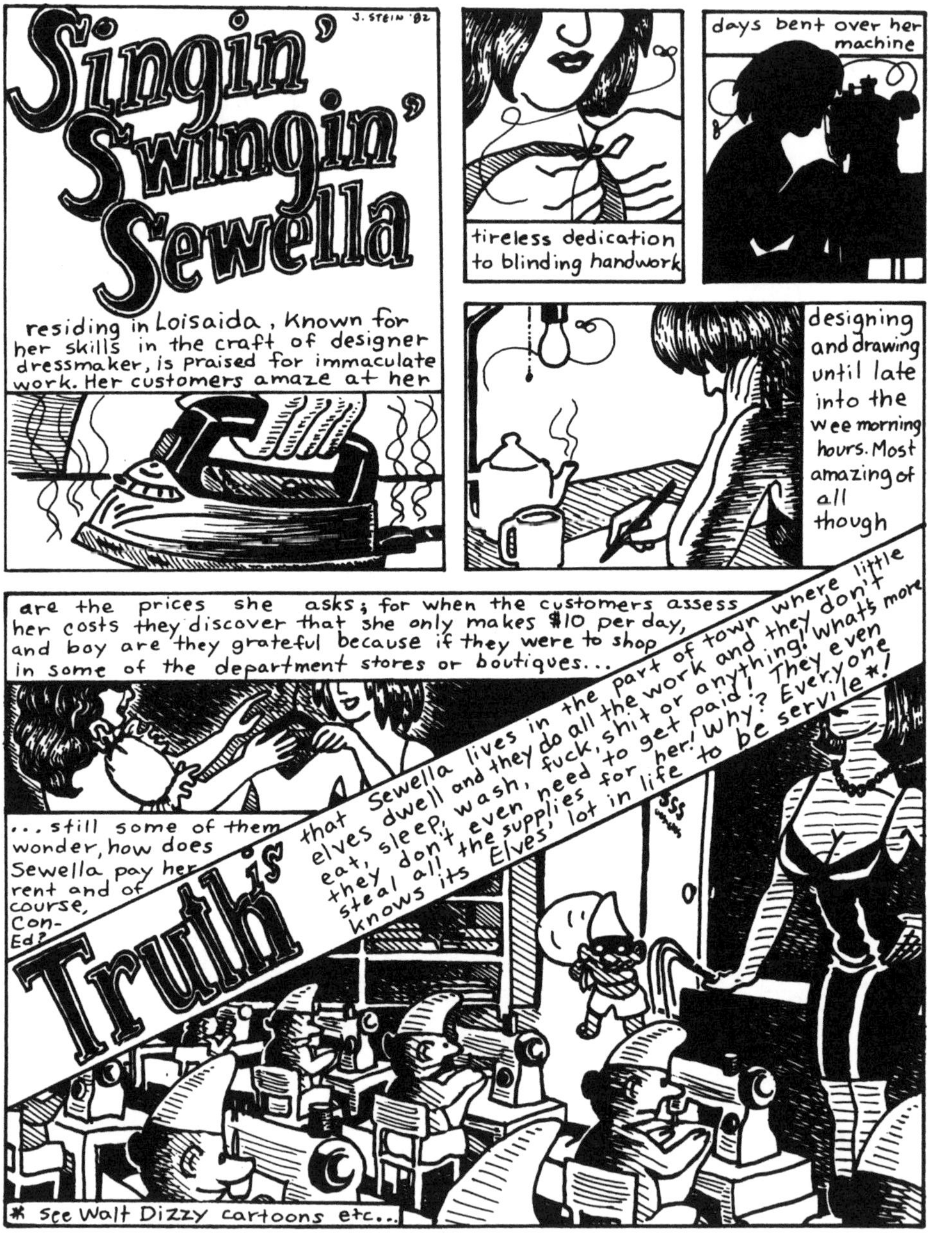

Singin' Swingin' Sewella

J. STEIN '82

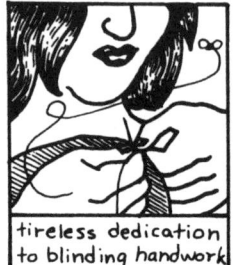
tireless dedication to blinding handwork

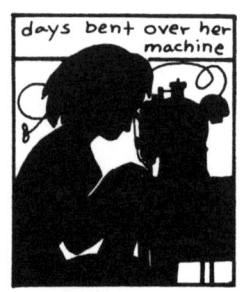
days bent over her machine

residing in Loisaida, known for her skills in the craft of designer dressmaker, is praised for immaculate work. Her customers amaze at her

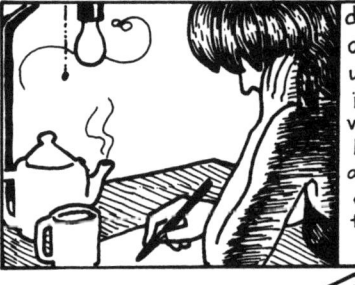

designing and drawing until late into the wee morning hours. Most amazing of all though

are the prices she asks; for when the customers assess her costs they discover that she only makes $10 per day, and boy are they grateful because if they were to shop in some of the department stores or boutiques...

...still some of them wonder, how does Sewella pay her rent and of course, Con-Ed?

Truth is that Sewella lives in the part of town where little elves dwell and they do all the work and they don't eat, sleep, wash, fuck, shit or anything! What's more they don't even need to get paid! Why? Everyone steals all the supplies for her! Everyone knows its Elves' lot in life to be servile*!

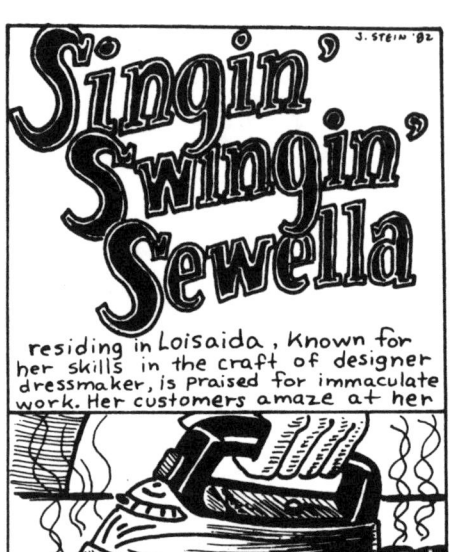

* See Walt Dizzy cartoons etc...

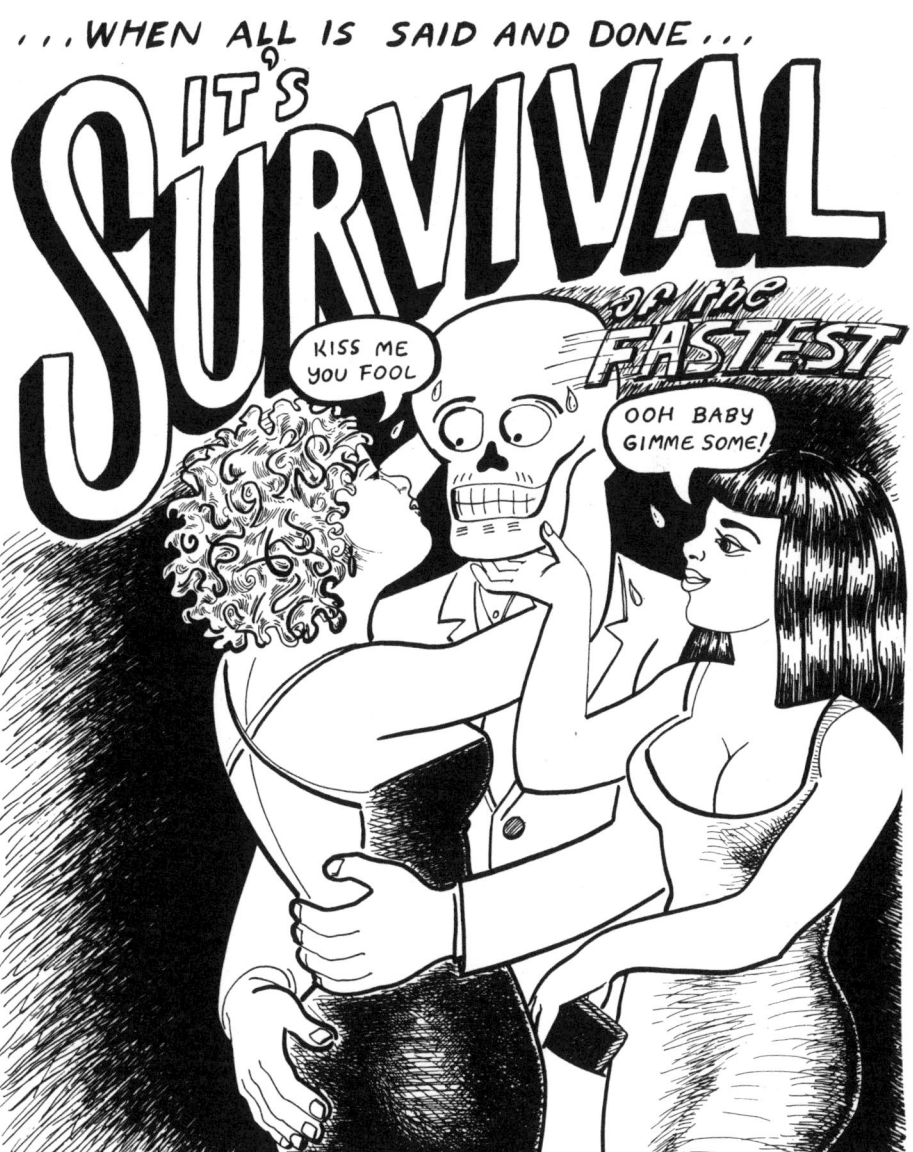

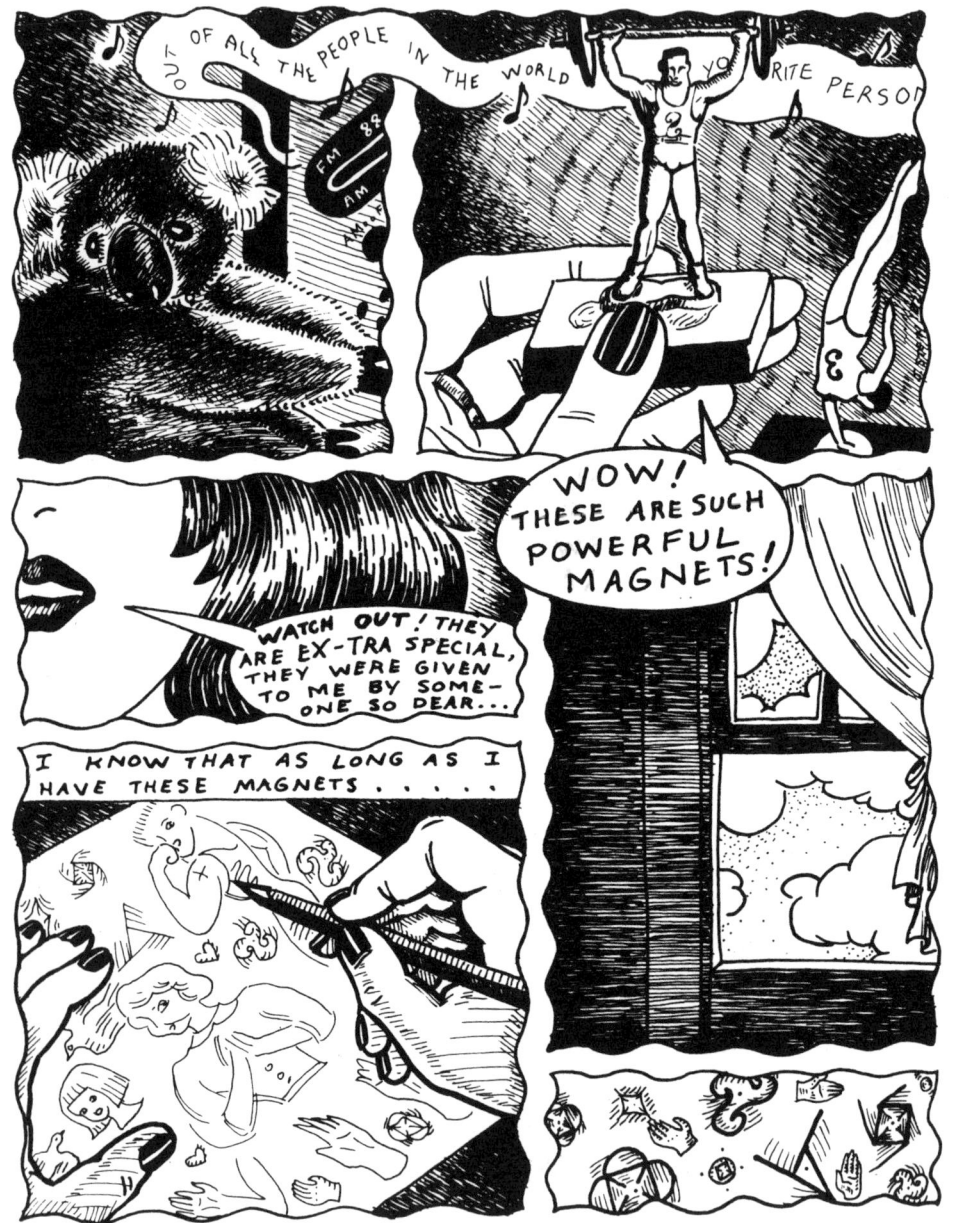

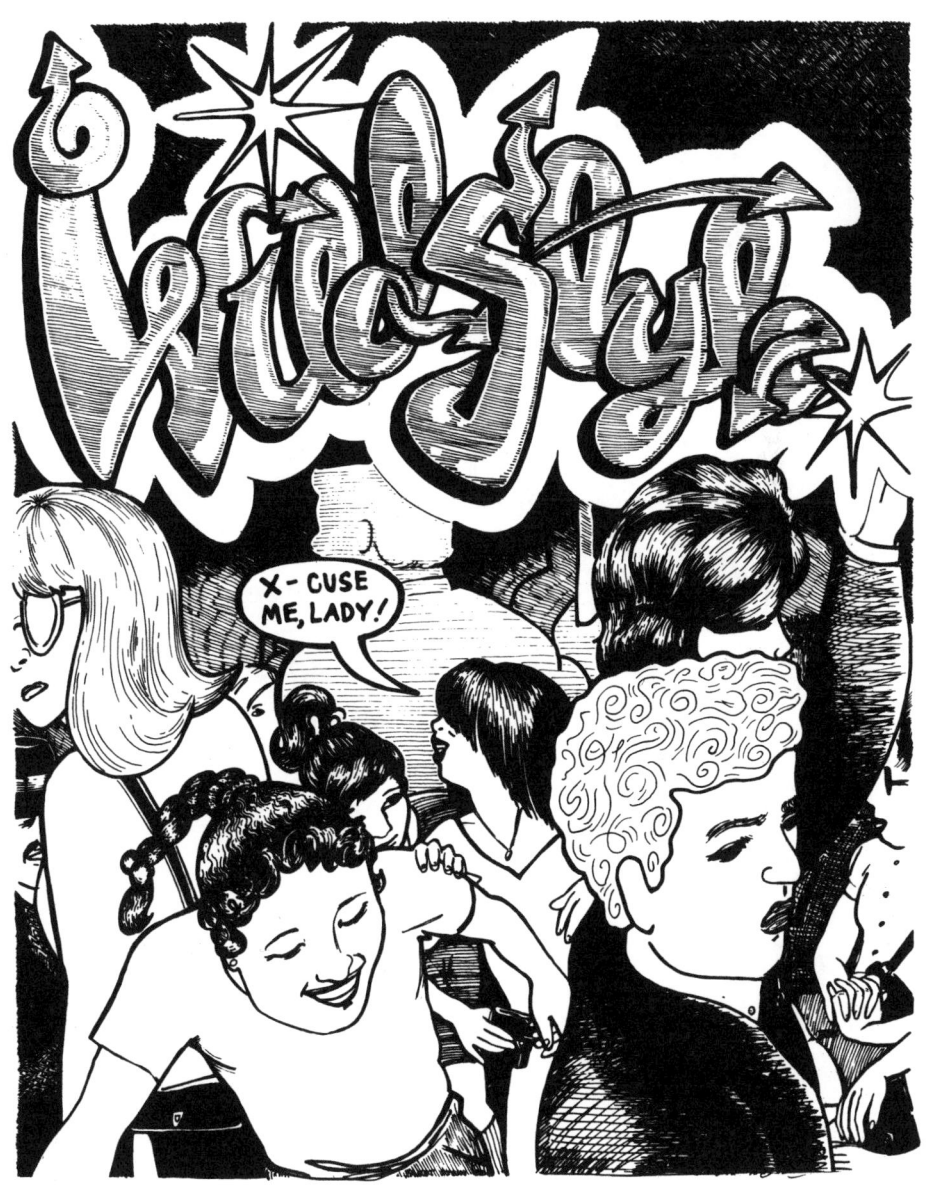

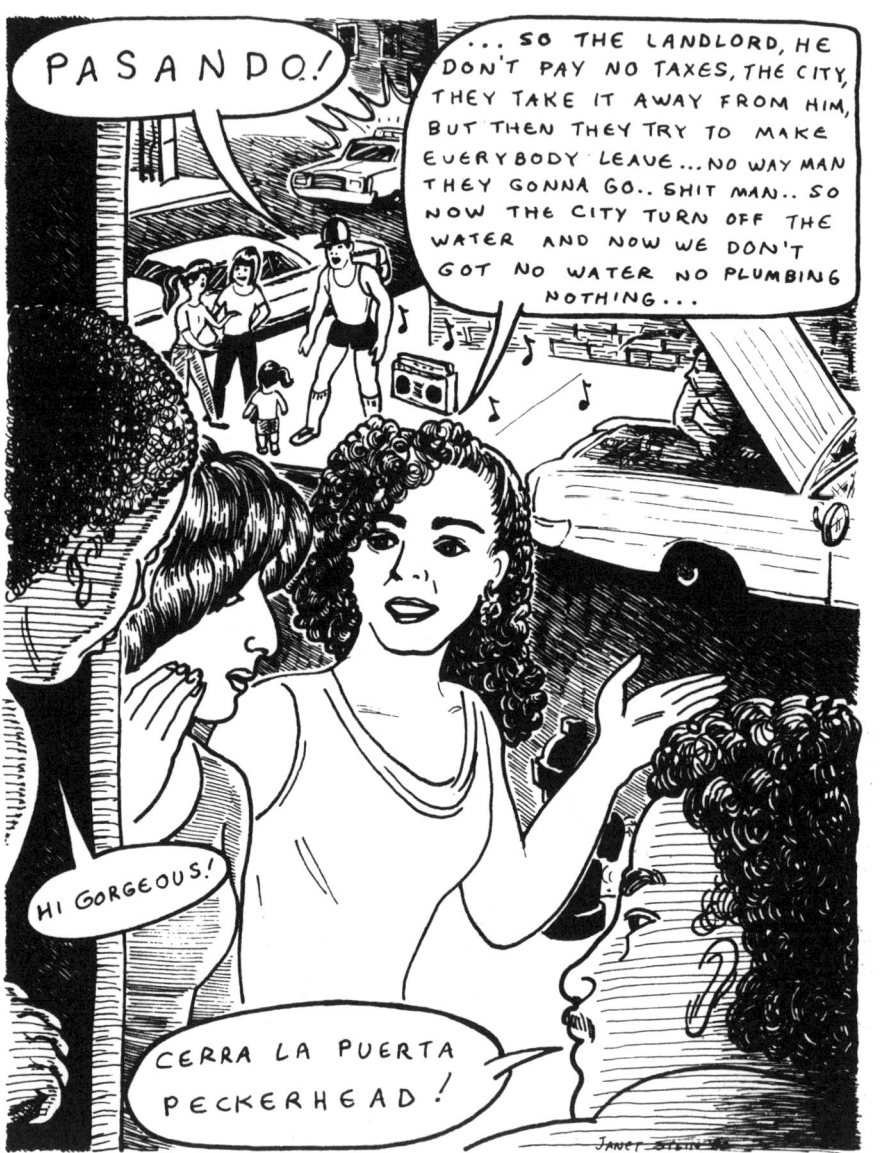

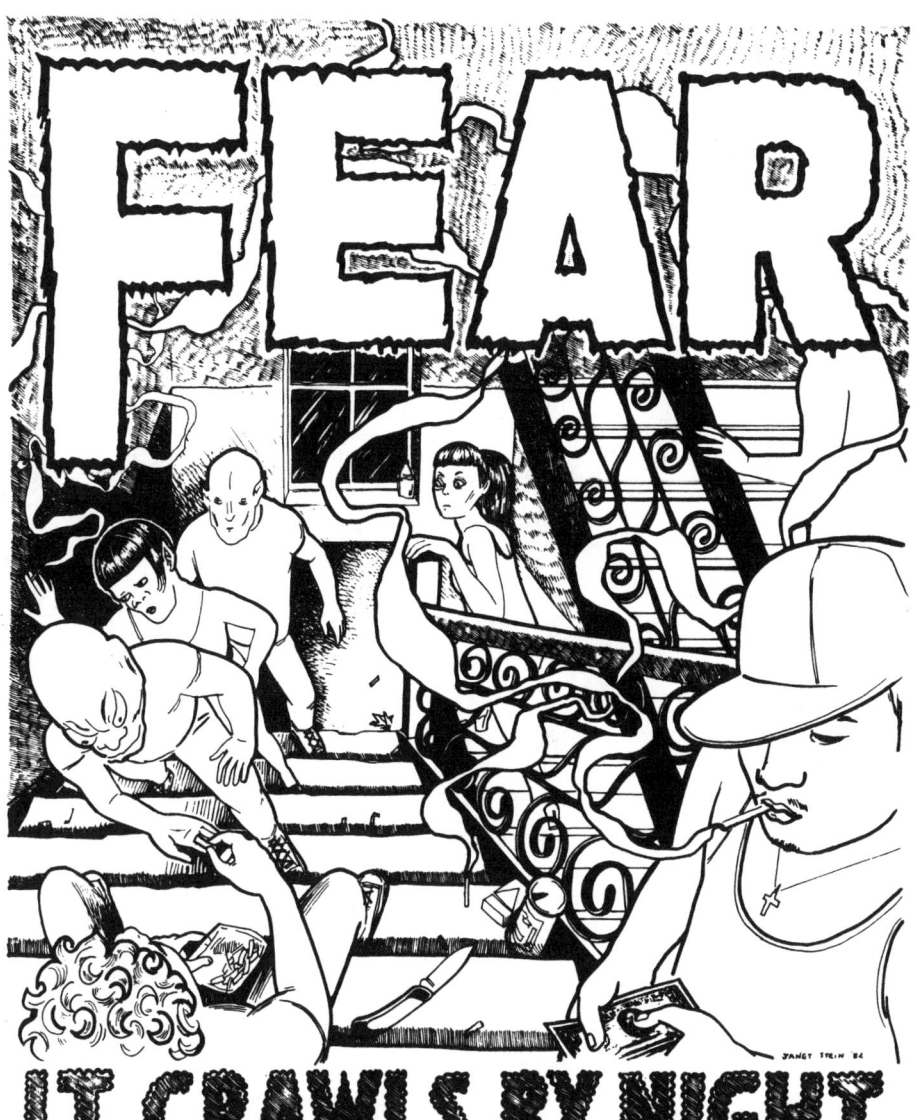

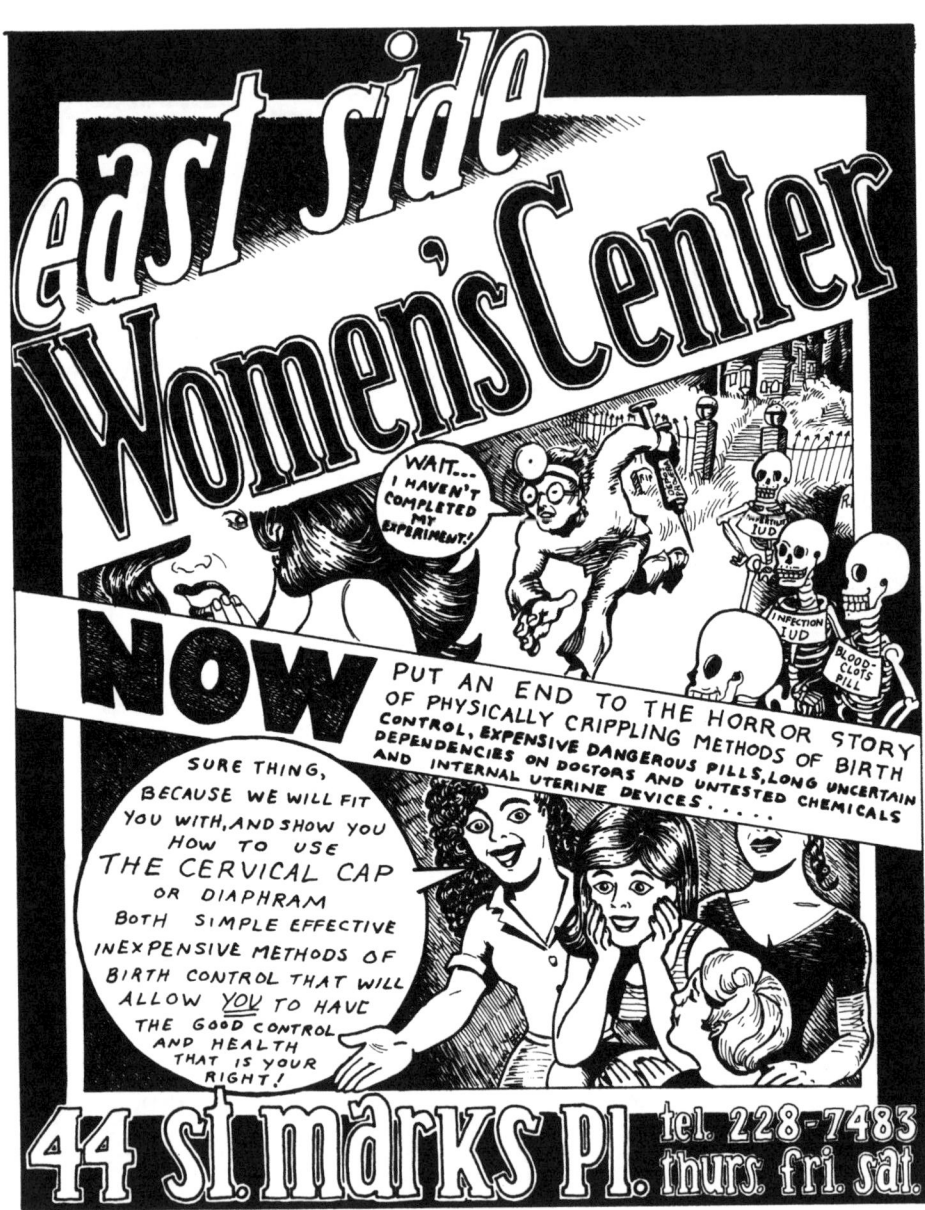

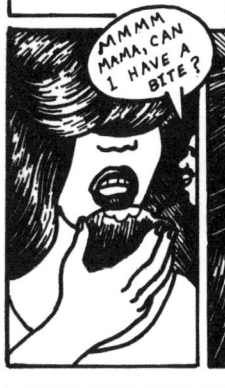
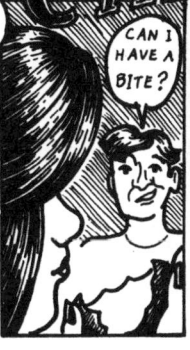
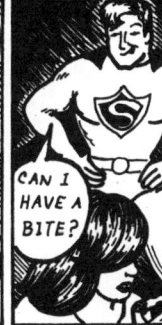
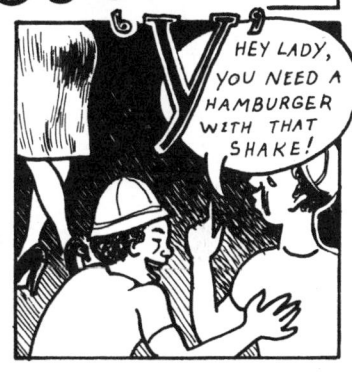
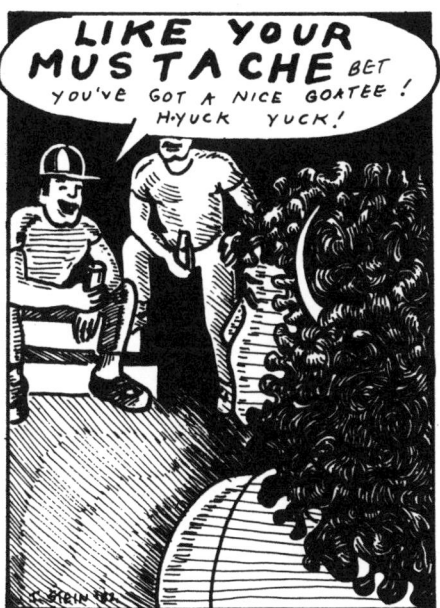
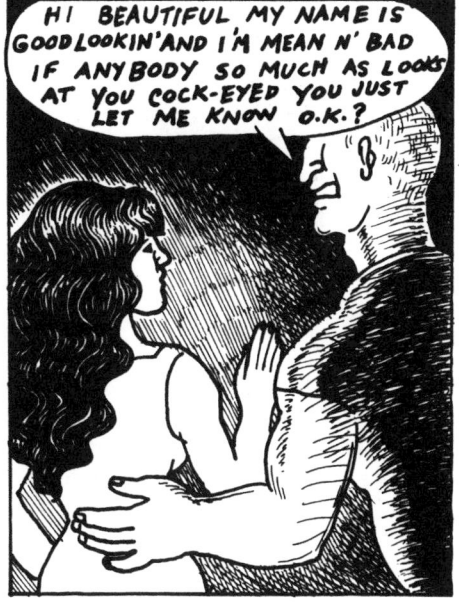

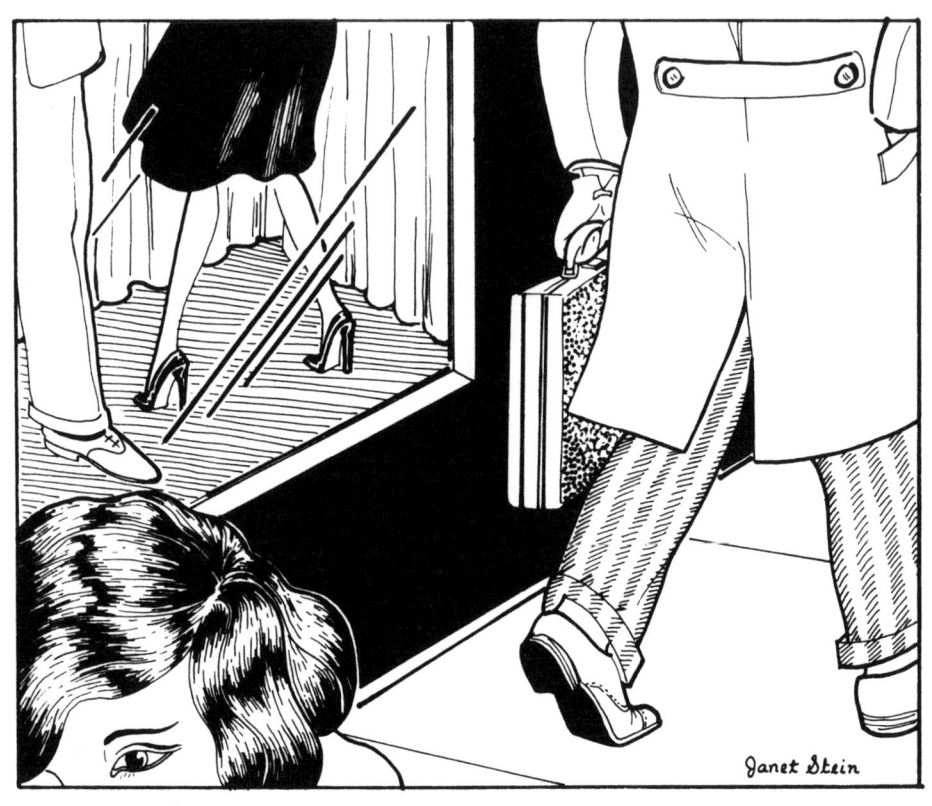

Copyright ©1982 by Janet Stein

This publication has been made possible in part by grants from the National Endowment for the Arts, a federal agency, and the Committee for the Visual Arts.
Typesetting by The Magazine Co-op, 105 Hudson Street, New York, New York 10013

Hallwalls, 700 Main Street, Buffalo, New York 14202

TOP STORIES

A PROSE PERIODICAL

#1 Donna Wyszomierski
#2 Laurie Anderson
#3 Pati Hill
#4 Suzanne Johnson
#5 Linda Neaman
#6 Gail Vachon
#7 Jenny Holzer/Peter Nadin
#8 Judith Doyle
#9 Kathy Acker
#10 Lynne Tillman/Jane Dickson
#11 Kirsten Thorup

Available from
TOP STORIES
Hallwalls
700 Main Street
Buffalo, New York 14202

TOP STORIES #13 $2.50

Real Family Stories

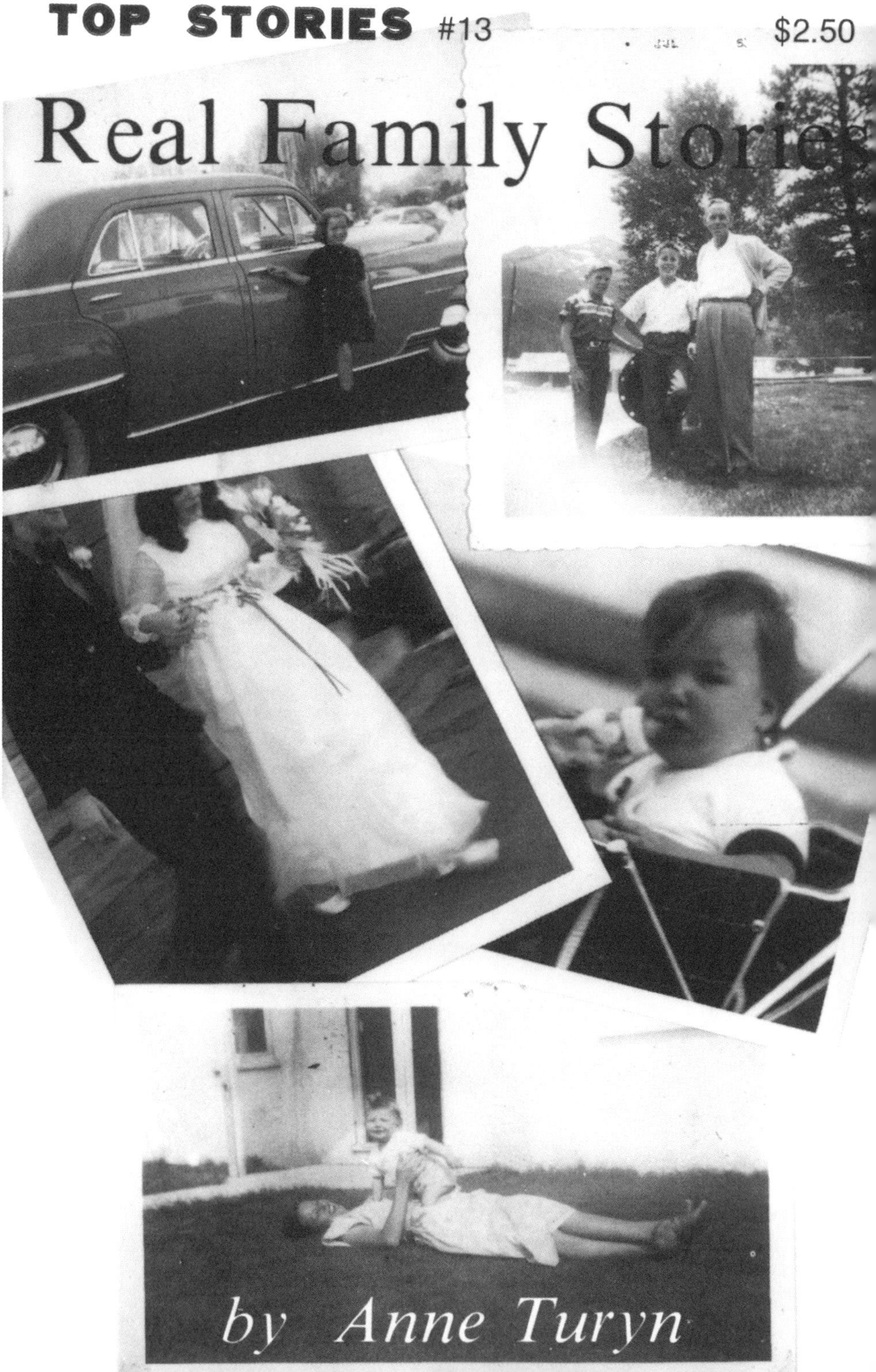

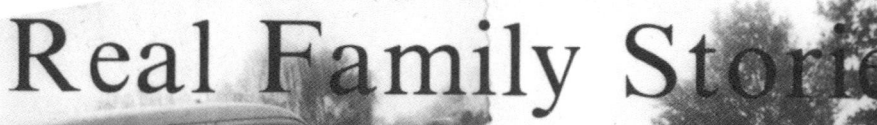

by Anne Turyn

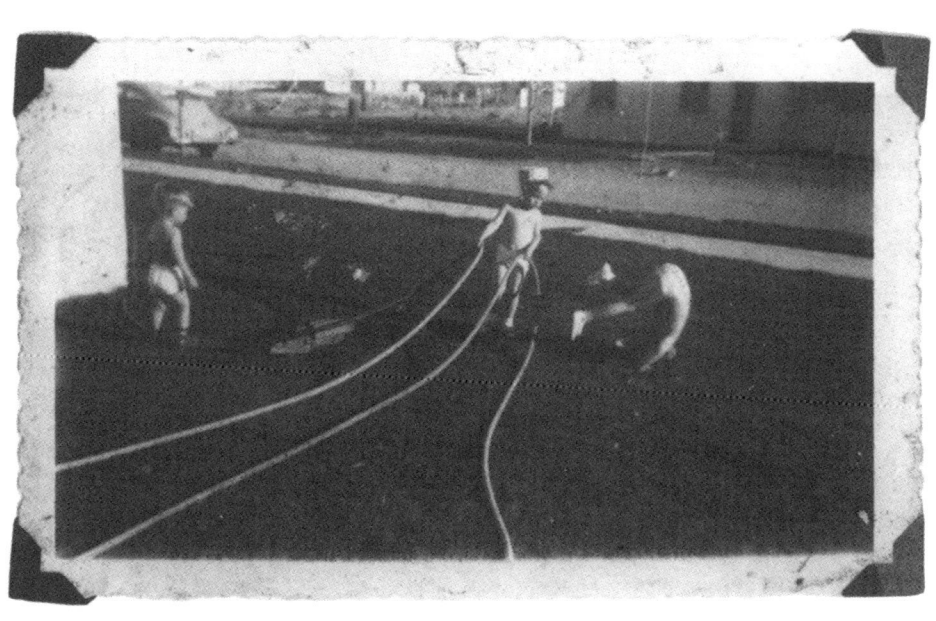

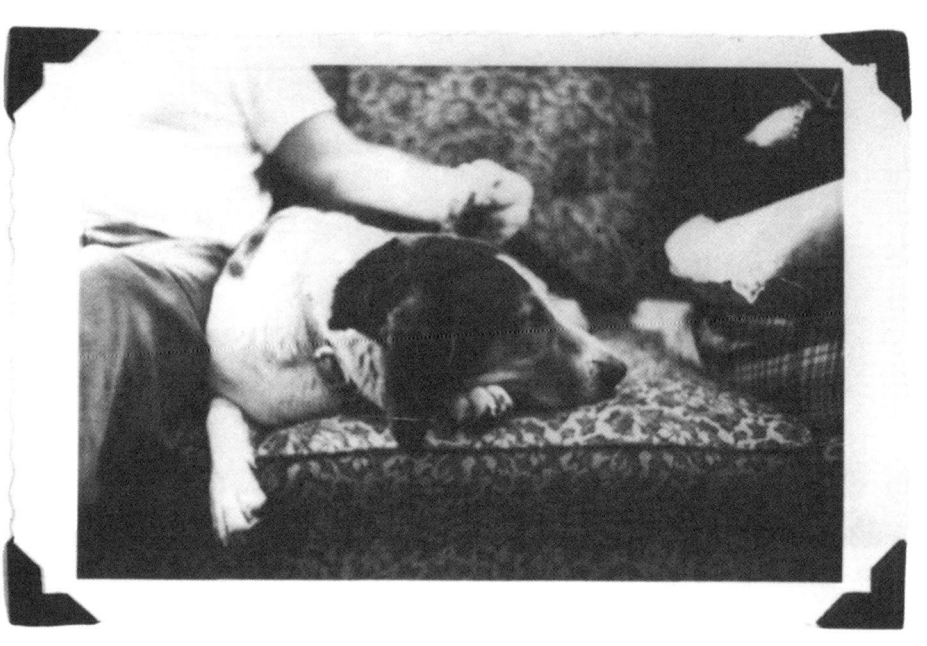

Real Family Stories

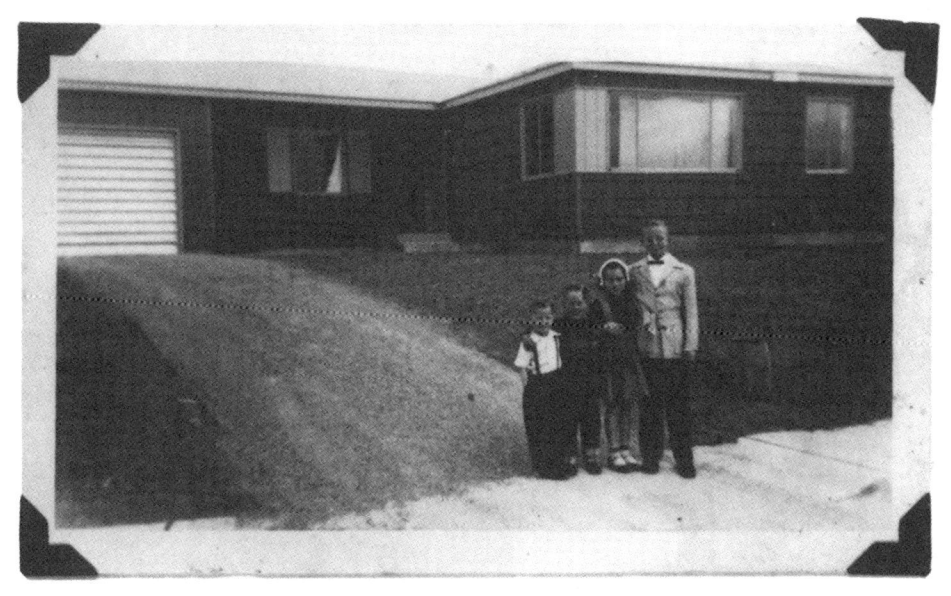

by
Anne Turyn

Copyright ©1982 by Anne Turyn

This publication has been made possible in part by grants from the National Endowment for the Arts, a federal agency, the New York State Council on the Arts, Literature, and the Committee for the Visual Arts.
Typesetting by The Magazine Co-op. 105 Hudson Street, New York, New York 10013

Hallwalls, 700 Main Street, Buffalo, New York 14202

TIME FOR DINNER. TELL YOUR SISTER IT'S TIME FOR DINNER.

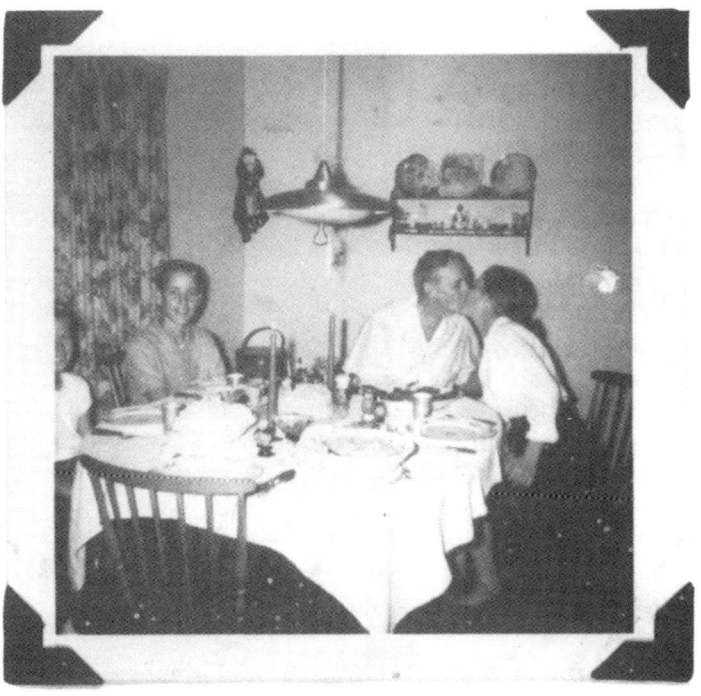

What's for supper?

We were always very polite at dinner and used our best table manners.   Oh, what a shiny family we were!

Well I have this cousin, Cindy, and when Cindy was about 15, they were living abroad, but this would happen here too, the whole family was riding the subway. Or the metro. Her parents and sister were a ways down the car, she and her brother together, clinging to the same pole. As she tells it, her brother was quite a doll then. He still has blond hair and cyan eyes. At 16, a pretty boy. So, the subway, and Cindy noticed a guy hanging around them, maneuvering to get next to her brother. He'd move and she'd block. She'd move and he'd move and she would move, barricading the way. Cindy sensed that everyone wanted her brother. It took that long for her to notice the man rubbing against her leg.

I always call my lovers hon. Sometimes honey. It's been over 20 years now, the lovers shift, bodies change, styles switch, positions vary, but the name is always hon.

He called us his daughters, but we were really his stepdaughters.

Mother. I don't remember what she called my father. 'That shrewd prick I never should have married' is the only name that surfaces. Though I recall a time when my father pussed through my mother's veins. I cherished my stepfather. A lot. Well, I guess he enjoyed me too, because I ought to mention, when I turned 21 I ran away with my mother's second husband. Lived with him for just over 10 years.

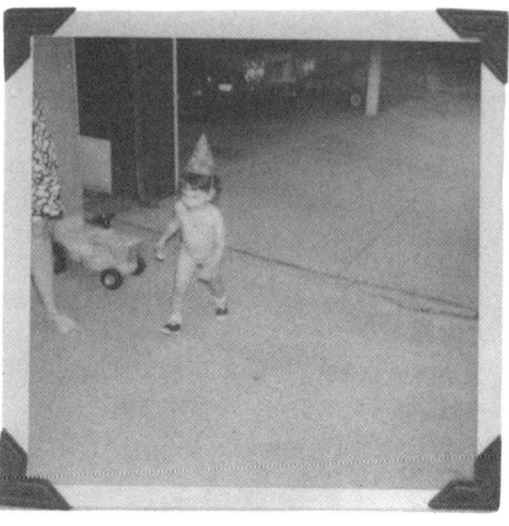

If I hadn't married your father, who would you be?

My mother left us t.v. dinners, sometimes homemade casseroles, when she went out to dinner. My pleasure was eating alone, with a book, which insulted my brother. But nonsense, I worship my older brother...my older brother is someone else, I think he's terrific, that's why I named my boy after him. When we were growing up he was there to teach me how to throw a ball, spin discs, do his chores, skip school. It was special, I could *never* insult him.

My wife is in love with my brother I think.

My real father was one of twins — identical twins — two daughters for each of the twins when they married. Our two families lived in sister towns, my father and my uncle were close. It was a shot to my father when his twin dropped dropped dead. Heart attack. The daughters in the two families, we weren't so close. Me and my sister are different somehow than our cousins. Sometimes it seems that we're kind of weird, and always figured my father could see it. I think he preferred his more normal nieces. Familiar. *Familial.* He admired my aunt, too. He likes her. After his brother died so sudden like that he began spending quite a load of time over their house. More and more. Things weren't that great between my parents, don't remember when that all started. My mother finally asked my father if he still loved her. Twenty-one years they'd been married. Never answered, just sat there. She threw him out soon after... They'll get a divorce real soon. He passes most of his time at my aunt's house now. Fits right in there. We find it a little strange at Christmas, but most of the time it just doesn't have to matter. To pierce to the heart of the matter, we suspect he'll marry my aunt as soon as the divorce comes through.

Why isn't Daddy president?

She never really seemed to be kin to us.

My sister's hair grew so fast; she always had longer hair than I did. And she'll always be older.

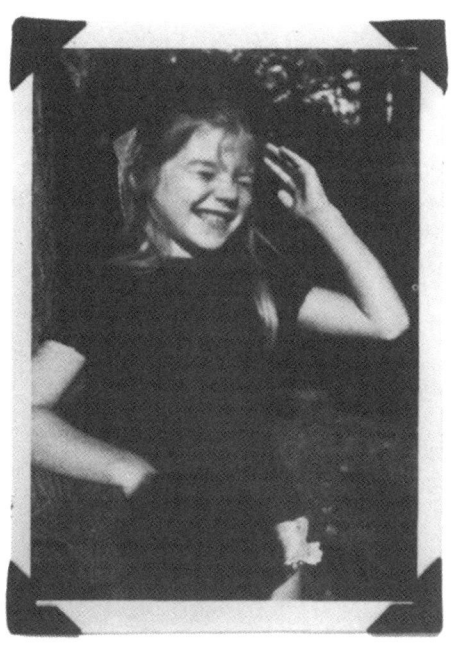

My twin and I fell for the same guy years ago. She was working with him, developed a crush on him, a rash... then I came to town. He infected me, too. I wasn't that nice to my sister and he chose someone else.

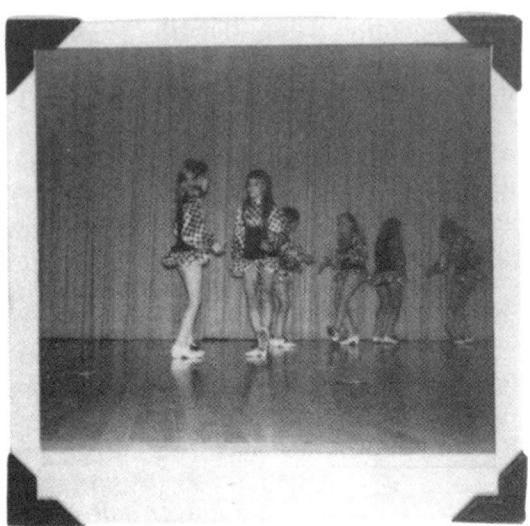

My family? Just some whacky people I spent my childhood with.

My brother was the ambitious one. Boys are. Brainy though, too. He was dashing off to college about the time the war was on. My brother was to be a writer, decided to be in the most exciting spot on earth, which he figured to be the war zone. Being that he was only 17, he needed my folks' permission to enlist. They were against the war, but for their son living his own life. He was killed over there. My mother has never forgiven herself.

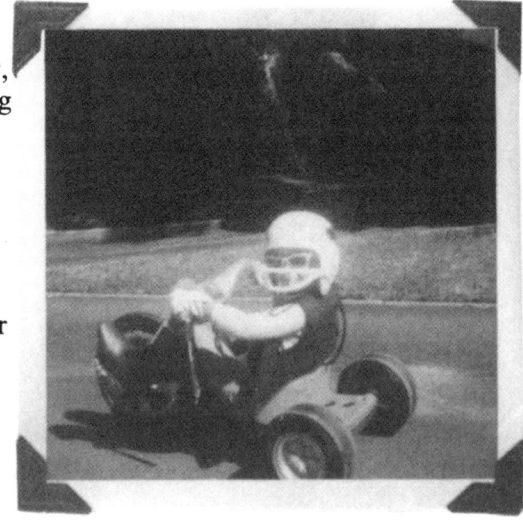

My husband is in love with my sister. I cope, what else would you do. The kids don't know. Why mention it, I don't think about it much. If you don't know for sure you can live with it. But if you know for sure, you just can't live with it.

My brother was murdered on my birthday. There were six girls, one boy, in our family. Now there are six girls. *(6+1) - 1 = 6+ (1 - 1)*

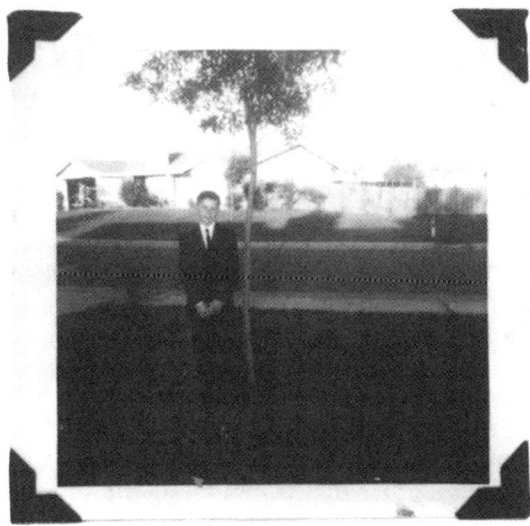

All family stories are tragedies.

Trouble comes in threes.

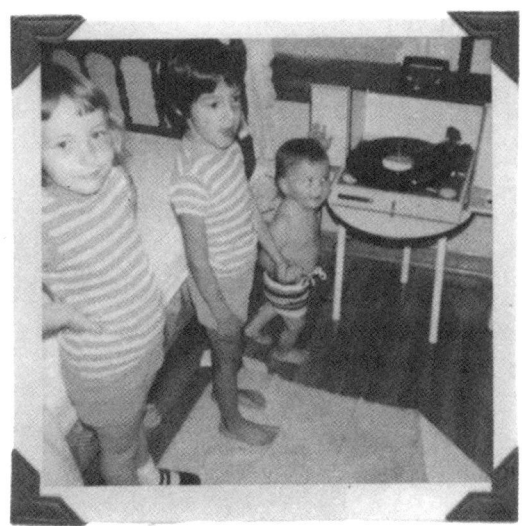

My father was a minister but I can't attend church anymore. Couldn't then either... Before he became a preacher he had a restaurant. Sometimes when he delivered sermons I was there to receive them, but less and less. The family all attended social functions, though. Sort of had to for appearances. It's that kind of a job. I'd been living out of town, and went to a dinner with them. There was this one lady there who I had my eyes set on, but never made a move. Months later when I heard about my father's affair, wouldn't you just know it was with this very same lady. In all honesty I was jealous. My mom was angry. She said he should quit the church, it was too hypocritical with him running around the way he was. The lady in question married a dentist, my dad resigned from the church. It wasn't really what he wanted to do. My parents have an inn by the ocean now.

All families are weird.

My mother is kind of odd, too. I never knew her mother, but she was one of 9 children and I know most of them. My mother and her siblings are sort of the black sheep of the whole flock. More irregular than the way the others turned out. Makes me sure curious about my grandmother since maybe the strain she grafted is the rotting branch on the tree. Asked my mother about this but she refused to understand. My mother kept the windows closed all the time, I mean the shades drawn or the blinds down. The house was continuously dark. Like a movie theater. Popcorn underfoot. So were the apartments we lived in. Even worse.

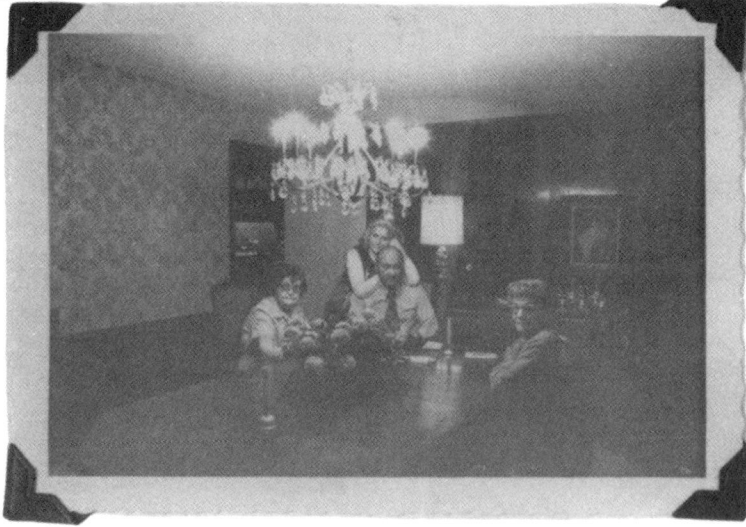

My mother's sister, too. Nutty. Collects things. Buttons... combs, magazines, her place is an archive. No offspring and she's elderly. When she dies it'll be me, I know, who has to unfile her belongings.

I'M NOT PLAYING. I'M NOT PLAYING WITH YOU ANY MORE. EVER AGAIN.

I dreamt about my sister last night. It wasn't my true sister, but in the dream it was. I got real angry and yelled at her. The we had sex. But it was only a dream and it wasn't my sister.

Every family's got their trauma sooner or later.

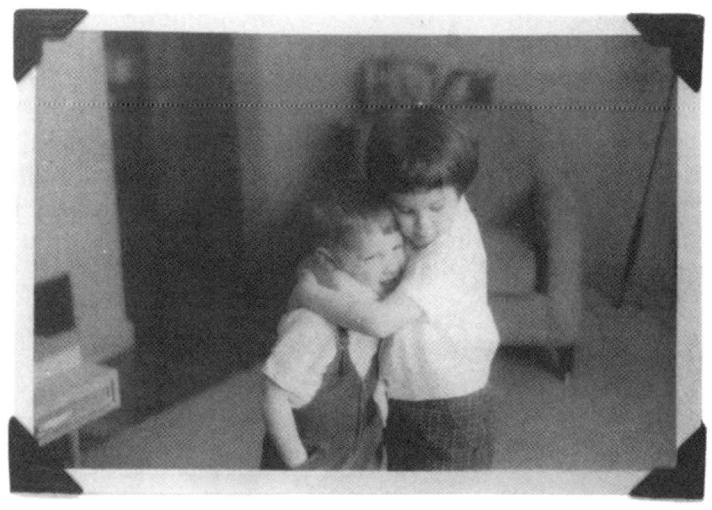

Sure my dad hits us. We can all fight, but I tell you one time I felt bad, pretty bad for the old man. He was in a fight with my brother, and my brother was whopping my pa. Usually I step back, but this time I threw my brother off of my pa.

My sister's husband is no good. Beats her. Leaves her, comes home. Leaves her, comes back again. My mom bought a gun. Blow the bastard away if he comes in here. Her oldest looks just like me.

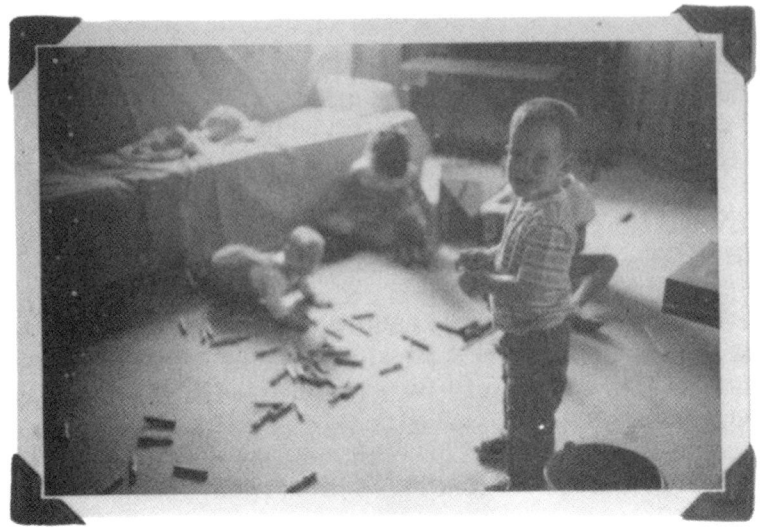

And I like being the favorite child. Anyway my homework *is* always done. Why shouldn't I get what I want... You've got to make the most of a situation... Grab opportunities when they arise...

My mother adores my son. Does his laundry for him. Bakes him pies. He goes away, on vacation, say to visit his girlfriend, she calls to see if he's okay. Who can figure where she finds the number. In his diary. Sunday morning, they're still in bed. Who'd phone early Sunday morning? His Gram, that's who, but just for him.

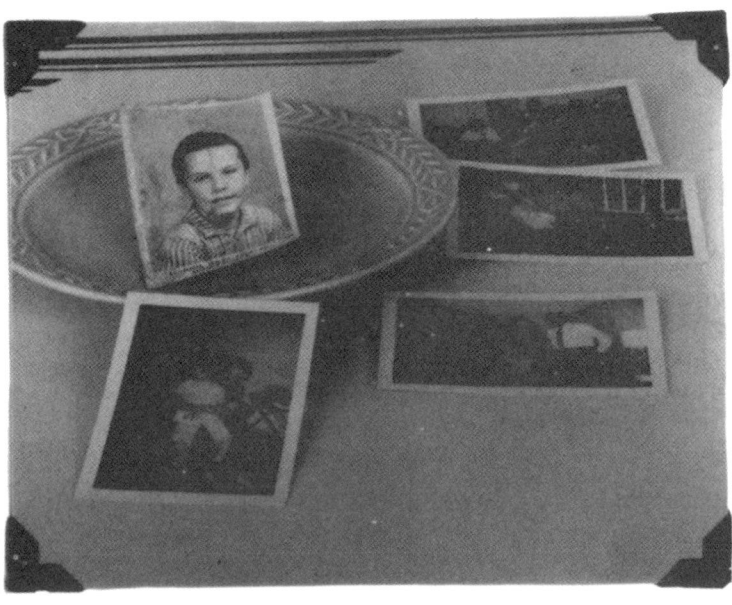

My mother's mother stuck her in convent school to keep her quiet. Gramps is a volunteer fireman. My 2 grandmothers have the same first name, so my sister was named for them. Both. They were both pleased, the grandmothers, everyone's happy except we mislike them, just my mother's mother, and we hate her and my sister despises the name. The other one's dead anyhow.

What are values anyway. Luggage, what we carry around. Who is interested in what. Our family was never one that was only interested in itself as a unit.

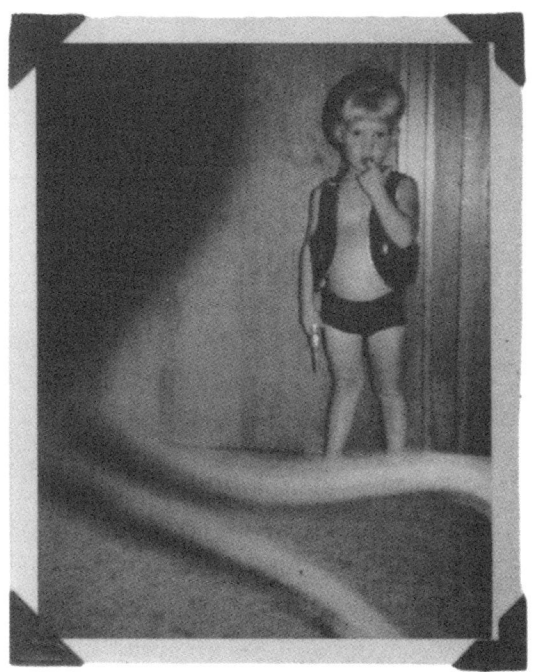

I HATE YOU   I HATE YOU   I HATE YOU

If you kids don't quiet down I'll lock you in your room again   or   I'll put you out with the garbage. Tomorrow is garbage day. If you kids aren't smart I'll drown you or   sell you back to the Indians...

Sometimes I wonder if the children hate me.

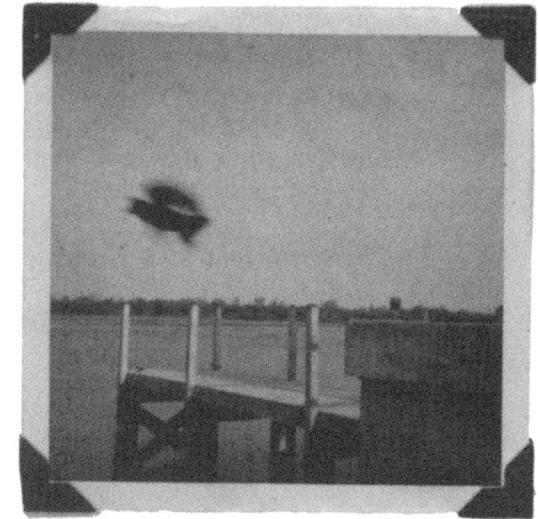

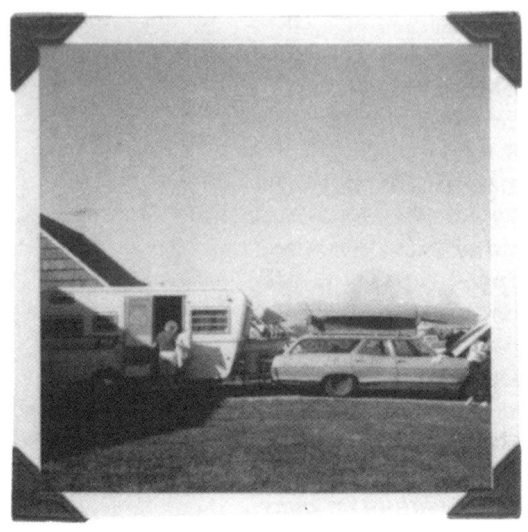

While we were growing up our parents had good friends who had kids our ages. We'd spend a lot of time together, the two families...weekend ski trips, summer vacations, romps in the country, Thanksgivings, and Sundays. Sometimes especially with skiing, just my dad would go and their dad and out mother, who didn't prefer the cold as much, would stay in the city. First out parents broke up, then they split, too...My father up and married her, after an instant divorce. Eventually my mother married him. She didn't clamor to marry again, and her parents never married either. But he really had his head set on marrying again, her. She reasoned, he's older, not much time left anyway, if it was she really wanted to marry him, and he refused on principle, she'd be upset, so they married. She's not happy married this time either.

That's not the way it happened.

All families have strange stories.

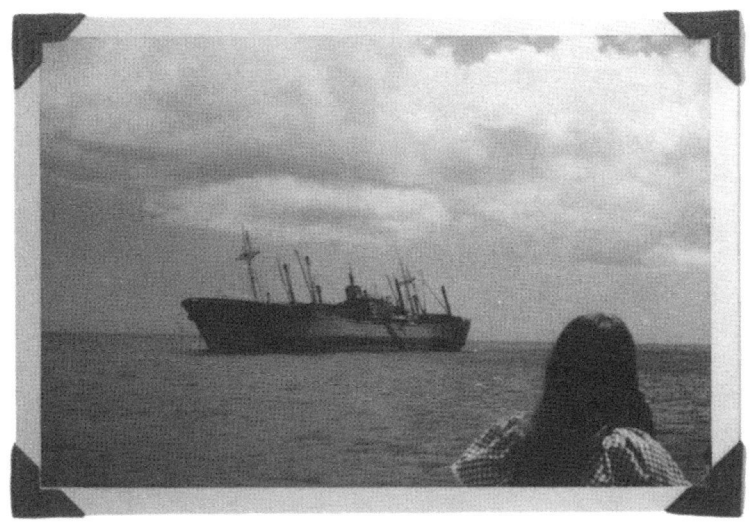

I have a girl cousin and a boy cousin. My aunt and uncle were living abroad then and they went there for a few months to live with their parents. My uncle kept trying to arrange a blind date for his son 'd like to arrange a date for my sin with the secretary at his office. She was just a year or two older than my cousins. It never really worked out, the date. It wasn't long after they were back here when my girl cousin was visiting with us. My daughter asked if she thought her parents were happily married. My daughter quizzed, 'Don't you think your father fools around?' My cousin answered 'No, capital N-O. He looks too who would want him anyway.' The next time she went home her parents were divorced and her father was marrying the blind date secretary.

My daughter was 15 and we were vacationing with friends of my husband. My girl and I were close then, we're not now, and she confided to me that this gentleman had made a pass at her. I told my husband and we were pretty darn annoyed, but didn't say, just let the friendship slip. Twelve years later, my husband and I moved out of state, my girl had been married but her marriage was dissolving. Later we heard that our former friend was running around with a younger woman, but had no idea until we stepped off the plane for a visit that the younger woman was our daughter. They're married now.

My daughter's daughter visits her father a few times each year. That man is no good... I don't trust him even alone with his own daughter. Poor little girl, grown man grabbing at her.

Everyone's got kooks for relatives.

All those years my mother was in and out of the state hospital my father cared for me. We have photos of me and my dad, I'm the first born remember, him feeding me, us vacuuming, in the kitchen, from those years. All my life I've looked at those pictures fondly...just me and my dad when my mom was in the hospital, until I realized that my mother *was* there. She took the pictures.

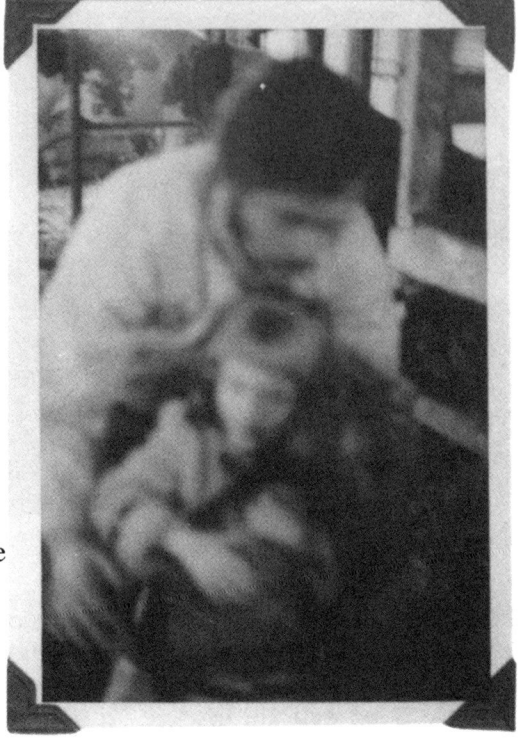

Not in public.

YES. OF COURSE WE LOVE YOU. WE ALL LOVE EACH OTHER.

We used to visit our cousins often while we were growing up. My sister really appreciated Tom, our boy cousin. So she fancied his best friend, too. Dave. Dated him starting at 14 – all the way to 21 – I don't think she's ever been with another man. Married Dave at 21, even my mother warned, wait a while. That Dave, moved smack to the center of the country. Finally have a kid. Now it doesn't do my mother hardly any good to have a grandchild so far away. No one wants to vacation in that part of the nation. But our cousin Tom, best man at her wedding. Tom's moved to the next town. She should've just married Tom.

Tom married someone else. For 21 years they stayed married. Came home from work, he'd picked up some flowers that day, wandered into the dinette to leave them for her...and found the note that she'd left for good.

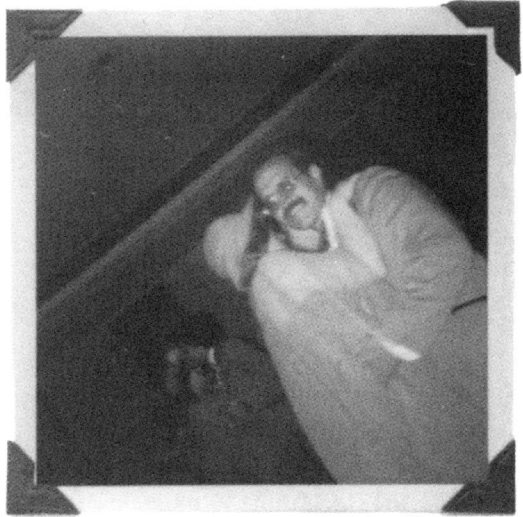

All families have secrets.

My son is teaching his daughter to be rugged, shoves the little thing off a chair, with his elbow, she hops up fighting. His little boy, though, I'm afraid he fell on his head and was damaged.

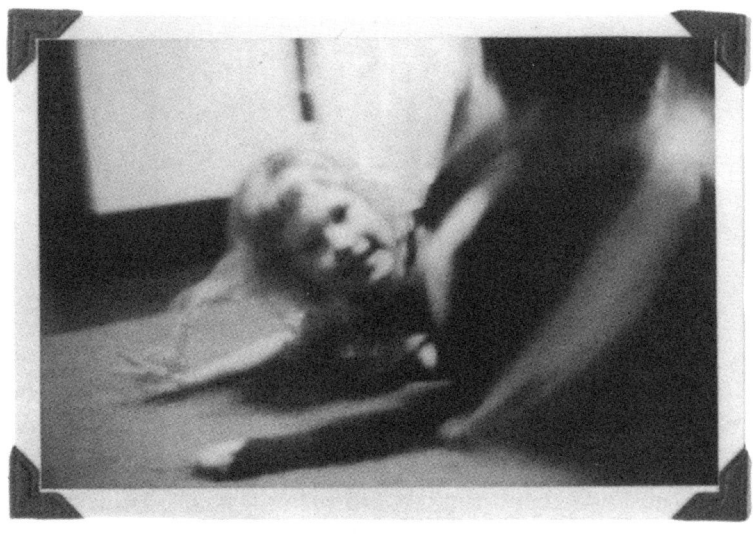

My wife left me for my best friend.

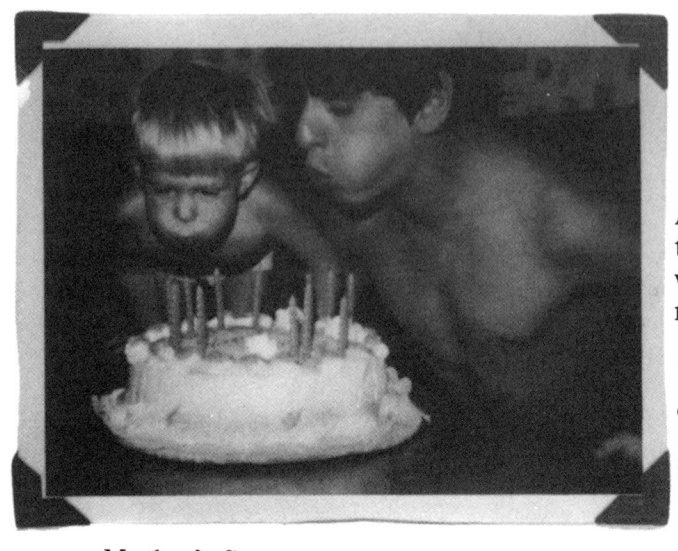

After all those boys, thank the lord the last was a girl or else he might've drowned it.

What did I do to deserve this?

SOUP'S ON.

Mother's first car was a Ford. She had it 10 years. It was still running, but she ordered a new car. The day the new car was to be picked up, the old Ford died miles from home.

We were all women living together. My mother, my grandmother, and her mother, and me. My dad and brother were

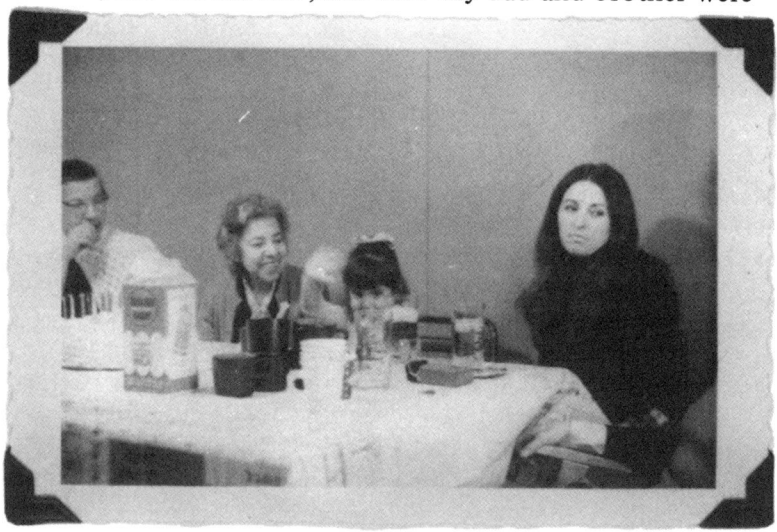

at war. My grandmother baked, my mother sewed, my great-grandmother slept. Grandfather was in prison, I was in elementary school all day long. Dinners of women and breakfasts of women, pink calico and biscuits. My mother packed my lunch mornings in my father's old metal lunch box. The day arrived for my grandfather to return home. He'd been gone 4 years and I couldn't remember him, though I'm named for him. Pies were made, the house was cleaned...he never made it back home, died on the train.

No, that's not true, my grandfather eloped with the lady cook from the prison.

Oh, who cares if I'm in love with my best friend's sister.

The house we grew up in was kind of quaint, a big old house brimming with mice. Catching mice became the family sport. We conducted contests, weekly, monthly, keeping tally. There were traps set everywhere. Reaching for a dress in the closet and *Snap!* you set off a trap. Into the pantry and *Clap!* you've tripped a trap. During dinner *Whack!* a mouse is caught. Everyone's asleep and *Bam!* a mousetrap, then *clap clap clap* as it drags away only half dead.

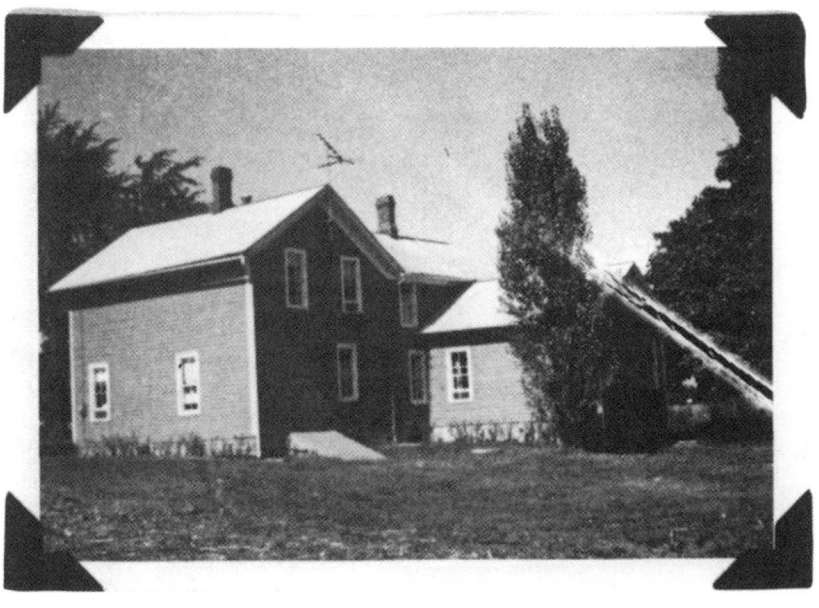

WAKE UP. GET UP. WAKE UP. GET UP. *I prefer to sleep in but my son has to wake me.*

My arches are fallen, my mother said have your father pay for orthopedic shoes, it's clearly his responsibility, they're his genes. That's life. My mother divulged to me that if she had the choice to do it again, she wouldn't, it wasn't worth it. And since she leapt out the window, I've never felt the same about life.

This couldn't be our family. I've never seen these pictures before.

My sister's husband passed away on Christmas. My sister was consumed with grief...and fear...as his death pointed the path to her own. She carried on all year, doing her work, taking care of matters, though she asked me, and reconfirmed time and again, if I would share the upcoming Christmas with her. I purchased my tickets, was scheduled to arrive several days before the holidays began. My nephew phoned me the morning of my departure to say that his mother had been taken to the hospital on account of a teeny heart attack. I arrived later that day...spent the days with her at the hospital...and on the anniversary of his death she died of a broken heart.

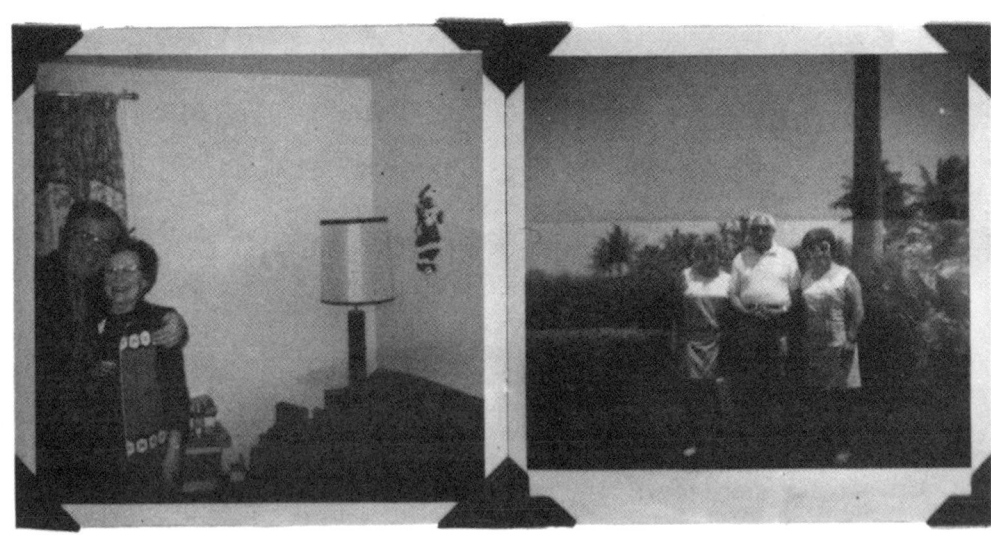

My son's a gangster, but he's good to me.

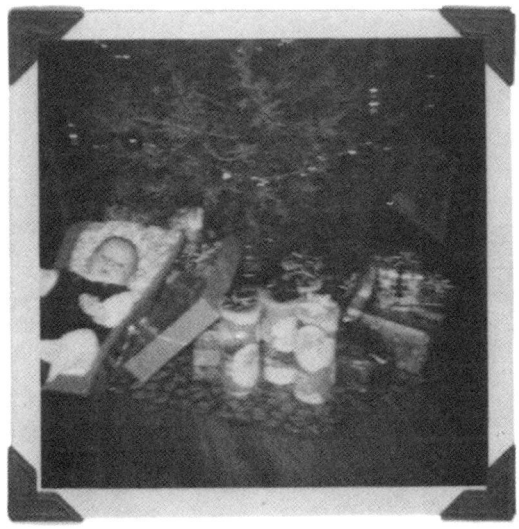

My ex-wife rents rooms out. She rented one to a man, after six weeks she's marrying him. She doesn't really know him well enough. We think it will amount to nothing. It's a little crazy, but then, her folks only knew each other 37 days and were married and it lasted 21 years.

She's a child of lust. My mother's a goodlooking woman, but you should have seen her then. My father wasn't bad then, you'd hardly believe it to look at him now. Finishing high school, and anyway they had to get married. I'll bet my mother must look at her now and think, could've been...should've been...

We call him our brother but he's really our halfbrother.

My niece finished school and had travel plans with a friend. First, see the world, then settle down. She became reacquainted with a second cousin, the grandmothers were sisters or cousins. She claims it was love at first sight. Cancelled her trip. She writes in a letter, 'I get up, make him breakfast, he goes off to work and I go next door to exercise with his sister. I have the rest of the day to myself, until he comes home to cuddle all night. Write it down, because this will be my address forever.'

All she loves is my money. She'd be happier if she wasn't waiting for me to die.

Your friends come and go but your relatives are stuck with you for all your lives.

What's for dessert?

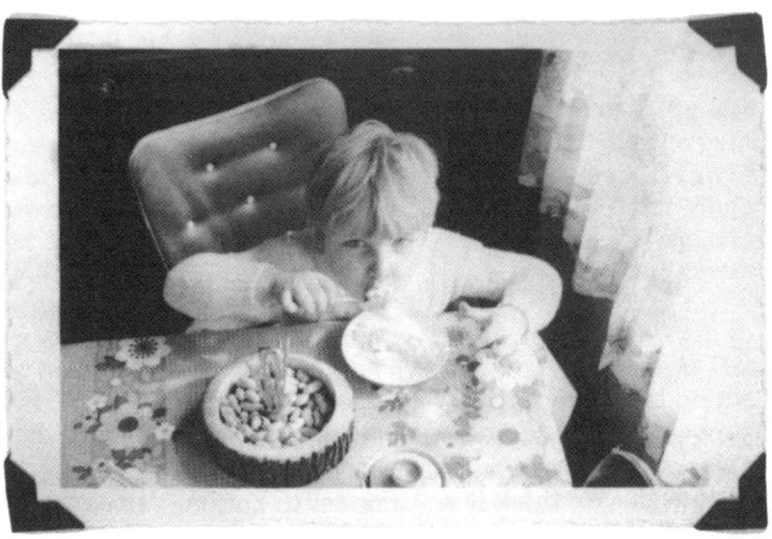

You'll get your just deserts.

SO WHAT IF I'M IN LOVE WITH MY BROTHER'S BEST FRIEND... WHAT D'YA THINK?...I'M GONNA FUCK MY BROTHER?

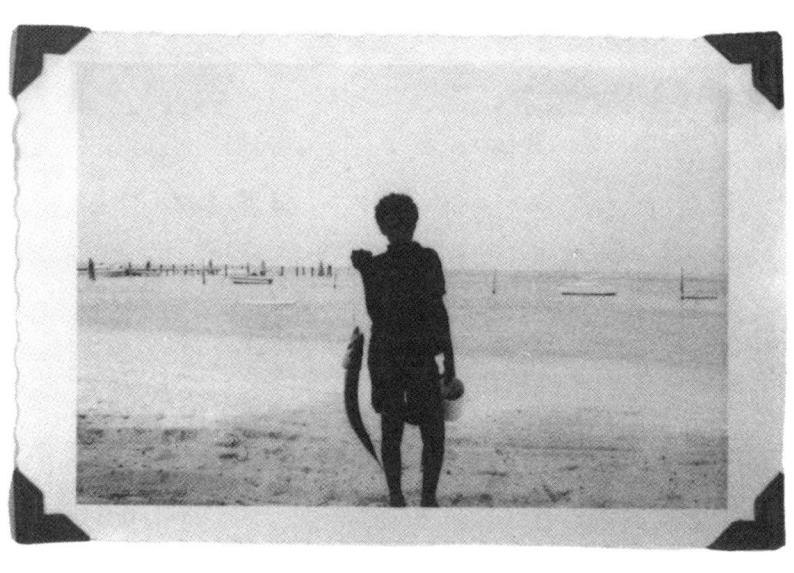

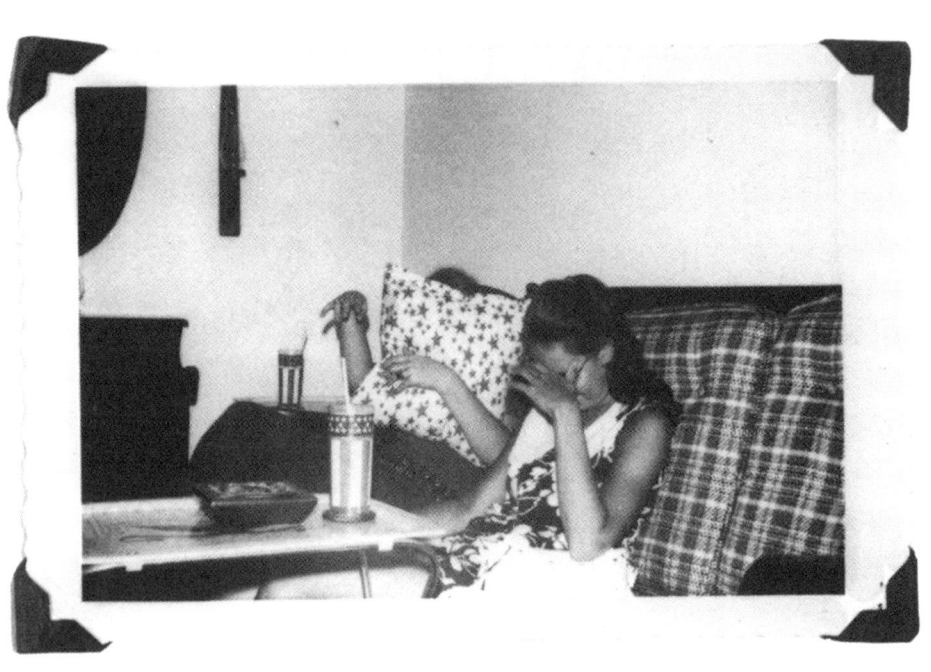

TOP STORIES

A PROSE PERIODICAL

#1 Donna Wyszomierski
#2 Laurie Anderson
#3 Pati Hill
#4 Suzanne Johnson
#5 Linda Neaman
#6 Gail Vachon
#7 Jenny Holzer/Peter Nadin
#8 Judith Doyle
#9 Kathy Acker
#10 Lynne Tillman/Jane Dickson
#11 Kirsten Thorup
#12 Janet Stein

Available from
TOP STORIES
Hallwalls
700 Main Street
Buffalo, New York 14202

TOP STORIES #14 $2.50

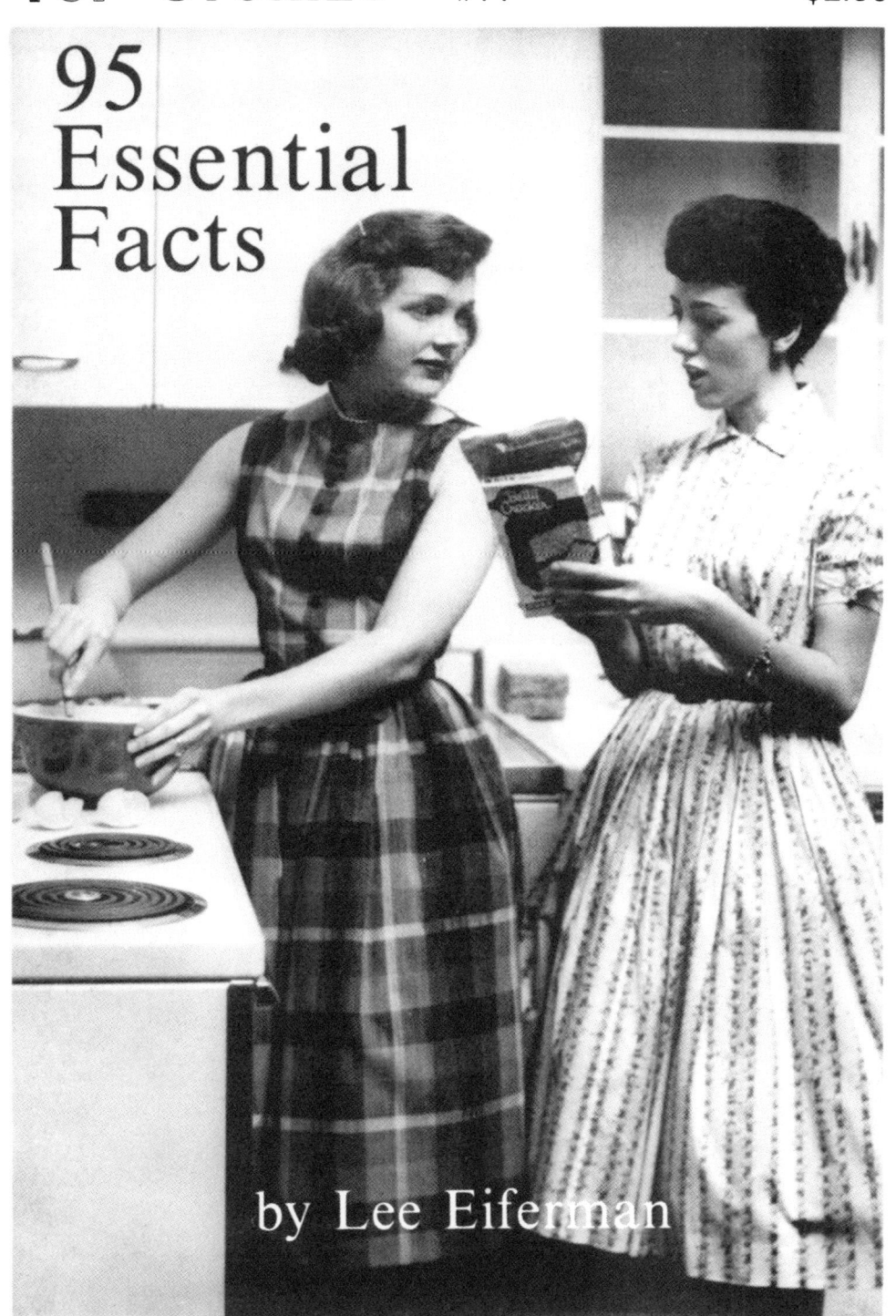

95 Essential Facts

by Lee Eiferman

95 Essential Facts

by Lee Eiferman

Copyright © 1982 by Lee Eiferman

This publication has been made possible in part by grants from the National Endowment for the Arts, a federal agency, and the New York State Council on the Arts, Literature.

Hallwalls, 700 Main Street, Buffalo, New York 14202

Painting Houses

Every day he hooks his ladder onto the roof of his station wagon, stops off for a coffee to go and begins his working day by unhooking the ladder from the roof of his car. At lunch time, he drinks a tall boy beer along with his sandwich. He is always on the lookout for a reliable partner. Someone who is willing to do the trim work as well as the higher spots. He prefers working in the fall, but naturally he does the bulk of his work in the summer. The first thing his clients want to know is if he is any relation to the governor. He used to turn those jobs down.

Crime

Crime is fascinating to think or read about. Especially if you are not a criminal yourself. Knowing criminals is not glamorous. Generally, they should be fairly bright or else their career is doomed to be a short one. Besides it provides a reasonable excuse for telling a story. This thing happened. Crime is concrete, there is nothing vague about having your walkman stolen. Or on the other hand, suddenly owning a walkman. Or a ladder say, the kind housepainters use.

The Governors Program for the Youth

In the old days this sort of thing was possible; feeding the disadvantaged, repaving the highways and hiring our youth. I'm all for it. I've watched the streets fill up with these hoodlums time and again, because it's summer, they're hot and unemployed. It stinks. Crime rises. The streets become treacherous. Our elderly feel imprisoned in their homes. Shopkeepers carry guns. A customer asks a question, is misunderstood, and he's shot down for no reason. Believe me, if there was a spare nickel in the state budget, it would go towards hiring a kid for the summer. Summer is hell, I know.

Dying Your Hair Blonde

It's summer. And all the kids are on the beach. Drinking beer. Smoking pot. Eating acid. And watching for the perfect wave. A few summers back, Donna thought hanging out at the beach was more fun. Maybe it's because, as her mother insists, she's finally outgrowing juvenile activities that go nowhere. Or maybe its because everyone has switched from big disco radios to the walkman. It's hard to party when everyone is dancing to their own beat. Donna thinks her old boyfried Joey must be doing too many drugs lately. Or else he's drinking. Why would his girlfriend be trying so hard to reform him. Unless, he really is a sad case. All of Donna's girlfriends agree with her.

Motivation

Before he met her, he had trouble passing the night without a few quick shots of whisky. But she didn't go for that. So he stopped. He realized how boring the days are if you don't have the nights to look forward to. When the laundry smelled sour he decided to do it. In between the 2nd and 3rd rinse he noticed a sign *help wanted ass't house painter.* He applied over the phone while the clothes were safely tumbling in the dryer. The first question the man asked him over the phone was *Who did you vote for in the last election?*

Influencing Others

Eileen was tops in her class. Or just about. She was a whiz in math and could name all the specific stages of reproduction in single celled animals or the attributes of iambic pentameter without pausing for breath. Like most smart girls, Eileen was bored with her fellow classmates. They all seemed obsessed about getting into college. Their conversations revolved around the comparative merits of say Harvard, Yale and Brown. Eileen was interested in the subject of sex. There were no boys in the honors classes she cared to talk about sex with. But there was this one boy, Joey. He cut out of school, her friends told her. In short, he was bound to be no good. Just the sort of boy she was looking for.

The Rain

Four days of rain put everyone in a funk. All activities seemed to grind to a halt. Donna and her friends had to go to summer school. The beach was definitely a drag in the rain. And outdoor service jobs stopped until the weather changed again. The park employees stopped cleaning the grounds of the park, no one went to the car wash and housepainters stayed home and watched T.V. Joey was bored at home. He had a rotten home life. His new girlfriend was out of town, and his mother was off traveling with some new boyfriend. Joey was itching to shatter the boring slump this summer had settled into. To kidnap a smart girl and hold her for ransom. That was his latest plan for earning some money. All he needed was a smart girl who was willing, and a ladder to kidnap her with.

• • •

An Empty Vial

He's in the habit of waking up early to go bike riding. If it's Saturday, it's especially thrilling to wake up early and do a few lines of coke before his bike ride. But it's only Friday. There's a full day in court stretching before him. And tomorrow there will be no secret pleasures. His supply is finished. Like the rest of the city, his connection has left for August.

He bike rides around the park twice. On his way home he is sweating. He can feel the surge of blood flood through him; his muscles tightening. He smiles. This is what he waits for every morning. His pleasures are regular, preplanned and constant. As he gets off his bike he fumbles with his keys; he carries his mail box key with him. The morning mail is neatly packed into his mail box. Amidst the telephone bill and party invitations is his divorce decree. He carries the bicycle up the stairs, he takes a shower.

The mail lies on the dining room table waiting to be read. He picks up the legal document again and studies it. Perhaps he should cancel his court engagement. He is unsure of what he is feeling. What is its name? The relief of freedom doesn't flood through him. Nor do the complicated feelings associated with the photograph of her (which is still hanging on the wall) disappear. Today he will appear in court and plead a client's case to this system of judgement. He swallows his coffee. At least there's a party tonight he can look forward to. It's being given by an aspiring politician. And then there's the telephone bill to pay.

Intimacy and Pragmatics

She swears she's just walked out of unemployment for the last time. The wait drives her crazy. The crush of the public is suffocating. Crying babies. Bulging families with their sticky children. Interpreters. Everyone reading the Daily News out loud. She thinks of them screaming her name over and over again into the air. They can keep my book and clean floors with it. Their $45 a week won't break me.

Her skin feels brittle in the brilliant morning light. She licks her lips and feels them cracking under the pressure of her tongue.

In a coffee shop she opens her book and looks up Alexander's number. Alex is the only dependable coke dealer she knows of in the city. The only dealer who would be trusting enough to front her some drugs. *Habits are powerful, appetites are whetted by income.* Alexander is fond of spouting his philosophies after he's given her a few grams, before they have sex. She's ready to get on with it, but Alexander loves to lecture. There's something about taking his clothes off that brings out the philosopher in him.

She fumbles in her pocket looking for a dime. Hopefully his wife won't answer the phone. Pampered little bitch. But she can't wait for a more opportune time of day to call. There's a deadline she must meet. A party tonight. It will be swelling with rich types. The kind that like to impress a pretty girl by spending money, especially a pretty girl with connections.

Secret Stains

She wants to fold the towels first. When they come out of the dryer they're so inviting, warm and fluffy. Just the way her husband would like her to be. Preferably with another woman. While he's watching. Twice this past week he's suggested the possibility of planning a weekly fling with some other couples he knows. He introduced this idea slowly, weeks ago over a bottle of brandy.

It must be the kind of trait that emerges in a man in his 30's. When she first met him, there was no sign of him going weird like that. There's a photograph of him in the living room. It's propped up on the left speaker, capturing him as he was when she first met him. She was impressed then by his thick, bushy, jet black mustache. He had just completed his 2nd major deal. Cocaine then was like handling heroine he explained to her. Taboo, but thrilling. He felt lucky to be alive. Then his picture was taken.

Next she sorts the piles of underwear into his and hers. The clothes have been sitting in the dryer for hours. She has avoided this chore all day. In the dryer there is further evidences of Alex's infidelities. As she spots the blue lace underwear, the phone starts ringing in the background. Alex's clientele seem to be exclusively women these days.

She knows that once she leaves Alex, there will be no more conveniences like dryers for a long time to come. Suspended between the lacey evidence and the phone ringing she is tempted to just light up a joint and watch the tensions float away.

Big Boys With Guns

Of course he knows his wife is right. The Armenian community can no longer support the dance hall full time. He is trying to convince himself it is a good thing that a political candidate wants to rent the dance hall for a party. If they obey the laws: no drugs, no loud music after 12:00. When they break rules he can always call his friend Joe at the police station. Why else give him $10 every Christmas if not for occasions such as these. Maybe he should stop by and mention it to Joe, just in case. Outside he sees a young woman wheeling a red wagon down the street. The wagon is empty and she is pregnant. He thinks about his walk and notices that it looks like rain. In the fall the sky changes quickly, but it's still only August. He decides against carrying an umbrella. If the sun should break through the thick bank of clouds he will look foolish carrying an umbrella. Poised between the doorway and the long flight downstairs, he considers the climb and grabs his umbrella. It looks more casual then a walking stick, less conspicuous.

A neighbor is growing morning glories. It's a healthy vine that stretches to the next floor. The vine is heavy with seeds. The flowers look puny, washed out. Just weeds. After all these years he can't understand these people. Cultivating weeds in window boxes, like they're something to be proud of, and letting their children run wild.

In a few hours the party will be behind him. Maybe they will just dance and have a good time. Maybe the politicians will behave the way politicians used to, trying to make everyone happy. I can watch from a corner. Watch some of those younger girls I see on the street, with their little bodies moving around the dance floor. I'm sure if they're polite, they'll offer me a little whisky. Not like my Armenian customers. They're young yet, they're entitled to a little fun.

He heard himself whistling as he passed by the climbing weeds. He thought about stopping for some nice espresso before he went to the police station. The young girl is there. He thought about being waited on by her with a keen rush of anticipation. The kind you can almost taste.

Cornered

She is asking him about his divorce. How long did it take? Who was your lawyer? It is hard to hear her over the din of the music and other people shouting. It is a persistant beat. He tries to change the topic: *Apparently disco isn't quite dead.* She isn't easily distracted. She needs the name of a lawyer. He'd like to have a taste of some coke tonight. At the very least some good hash or pot. She is reluctant to suggest her husband Alex, who is there and certainly could sell him whatever he wanted. To an outsider it would seem like these two people were getting to know each other very well. Nestled in a corner, they have reached a stalemate.

● ● ●

Assessing the Damage

Pat glanced at the big hospital clock the moment she sat down. It was 7:25 P.M. In ten minutes her plane would be taxiing down the runway. That the plane would be leaving in ten minutes without her, was a dismal thought. Still Marc, with his one good eye opening to greet her, offered Pat a small consolation. One that she could share with her Mother when she called. He seemed genuinely pleased to see her.

Do you come from a large family?
Marc's question caught Pat off guard. She was preparing to watch a little T.V. now that it was hooked up. Perhaps in an attempt to mask the disappointment she felt, Pat fixed her attention on finding something worth watching. Any mention of her family, particularly coming from Marc, made her bristle.

It isn't his fault.
Sometimes you find yourself saying aloud what initially is only a half-formed thought. Perhaps it's because Pat was flipping through the channels in search of Love Boat or something with a happy ending, that she mistakingly mumbled aloud *it isn't his fault.*

Do you come from a large family?
Marc's left eye was swollen shut. A clear tube connected his arm to an intravenous bottle. Pat regarded the situation for another moment. Marc didn't look that bad. It was clear that once his swelling went down he'd look normal again. His appearance solicited an overly dramatic response from Pat when she first walked into his private room. *So in a way,* she continued, *it is my fault as well.*

Do you realize that I just missed my plane to Kansas thanks to you. And Yes! I do come from a large family. Eight to be exact.

It wasn't the kind of speech she had prepared to deliver. The words came tumbling out. Then she reacted. Her face flushed red hot. Marc was not an insensitive boss.

He sighed. *Love Boat reruns are not on tonight.*

The Weight of a Pink Vase

She stopped everyday at the window of this one antique shop. In the middle of a window, surrounded by bits of lace and old world remainders, stood a beautiful milky translucent pink vase. In the vase, there was a rotating display of budding branches, bright tulips and withering wildflowers. She frequently thought about her ideal home of the future. With their bright child, she and her husband would settle in for a hushed evening, while the world gathered in around them. For some reason this pink vase figured in her plans. It served as a lynch pin of her happy, future arrangement. With a tremendous release of tension, she realized she was no longer battling time.

Once she stopped and pointed the vase out to Marc. She shared with him this secret image attached to the vase. Marc was visibly not moved by this idea. He had heard it before. Usually about two months into any new relationship. Why was it that the nurturing well-spring of his lovers seemed to speak of, so vividly, never called to him.

Eventually it was clear to him that, despite their mutual interest in films, theater and futuristic applications of computers, their relationship was becoming musty and embarrassing.

Each of them, separately, passed by that milky pink vase and inquired as to how much it cost. Neither of them found this idea of the vase to be worth $65.

Further Developments

The nurse's aide wheeled in the last sad offering of the day.

Pat noticed a line up of tiny juice containers. The thought of juice reminded her of other beverages packed away in her suitcase. And when the nurse's aid left, Pat offered Marc a small glass of expensive wine to toast the holiday season. There was nothing interesting to watch on T.V. Mostly there were fat glossy specials on, and so Pat unintentionally found herself, with Marc's encouragement and participation, finishing off more of the bottle than discretion would dictate.

The doctor popped in a half hour later to share the lab's findings with Marc. Both the patient and his guest reacted with inappropriate glee to the news. Perhaps it was the effect of televison and its shallow treatment of everyday crisis that caused both Marc and Pat to giggle at the docor's report. Or was it the half bottle of wine they had shared? The doctor, not joining in their preholiday spirit, scolded Marc and suggested, in a stern professional tone, that if he were the patient and he was just informed of the lab's findings, he'd certainly give serious thought as to who might want to poison him. *Do you have any enemies Mac?*

The name's Marc. All traces of levity had suddenly disappeared.

The Man I Will Marry

Pat may have felt lonely in New York. Her home phone didn't ring frequently. The neighborhood, despite the fact that she had lived there for two years, still felt threatening. But her mailbox was always full of personal letters. Occasionally her folks back home dashed off a quick postcard. And any one of her seven brothers and sisters were liable to write her. Mostly, she received thick letters from her old boyfriend—her childhood neighbor and playmate.

The mantle in her living room had a sloppy stack of his opened and unopened letters. Sometimes he enclosed a check. It was the only way he could determine whether or not his letters were read.

Every other week he sent Pat a murder mystery he had just finished reading. He figured he was cultivating another mutual interest with Pat. He was right. Pat loved the endless intrigue: poisonings, sharp daggers and hot nights.

Back in Kansas he was thought of as a modern Renaissance man, part farmer, part poet, part scientist. His letters were full of descriptions: the smell of the sod after a long rain, possible cures for sickly cows, and the joys inherent in watching corn grow. He loved his life in Kansas. Though Pat came to the city two years ago, he still believed that she was just experimenting. The real reason she moved to the city, in his scheme of things, was to test his love. Frequently, his loving sign-off at the end of a letter was *you belong to me.*

It reinforced the secret image Pat carried around with her. Really, her Kansas Renaissance man was no more than a drill sergeant.

Modern Applications for Computers

Marc loved his field. Wherever he went, Marc saw the potential for computers. He believed in streamlining the systematic access to information. Which was why the PTA organizational board hired him to help computerize their central offices.

Marc, having been in the field for six years, realized that clients were frequently unable to articulate all the hidden expectations which were hinged to this process of computerization. So on a particular Wednesday night, Marc found himself sitting in on a PTA meeting at IS 155.

Besides his business, Marc's second love was meeting people, especially women. At this PTA meeting he noticed that he and an attractive blonde were the only ones taking notes. The more eye contact he established with this woman during the course of the PTA meeting, the less specific his notes became. By the end of the meeting his two main interests were at war.

Marc was under the impression that, since he met her on the job and she worked for the Board of Estimates, she was strictly a career woman. It took two months for her nurturing instincts to become apparent. The transformation emerged in the form of a fluted pink vase found one day while antique hunting. By that point, their lives were inexorably joined. At least for the duration of the holiday season. Marc realized, in a flash of desperation, that he would have to free himself from this relationship immediately. If she were susceptible to the dream of a family, then the holiday season would be an inescapable tug at her heart and fielding endless debates. From past experience, Marc knew he would have to be decisive and cruel.

But first there was a final goodbye meal. *It will replace our Thanksgiving dinner*, she said sweetly over the phone. The last thing he remembered was trying to hail a cab.

A Question of Priorities

It was unclear why the rats were particularly attracted to the basement of City Hall. It was embarrassing when a foreign dignitary happened to catch the fleeting impression of a rat scurrying around the corner of an office. But it seemed from recent reports that the rat population was soaring and, as a consequence, they were becoming bolder in their quest for food. When the story broke in early November, the assistant to the Building Manager approached the Board of Estimates with a request for funds in order to exterminate the City Hall complex of buildings. *A few strategically placed traps baited with strychinine ought to do the trick* he assumed.

It was a glum task.

• • •

A Small Lecture

A decision has its consequences. An active social life presents you with unexpected complications. Somehow, you've decided on a course of action. The moment threatens to overwhelm you. Time passes, and you noticed you've attained a small degree of success in the direction you've chosen. And then things get gummed up. Maybe you shouldn't have married that guy. Maybe you're not suited for motherhood. Maybe it's too late for that.

Stories about women are especially interesting because the endings are open to question.

The streets are lively tonight. There's finally a smell of summer retreating. But the radio can't possibly drown out the sound.

The Shortest Way of Telling It

this was written before she left

This is the theme. This is my life. I've been living in the suburbs for two years now. I was studying music beforehand, when I met Bob. I was a composition student, also studying guitar. I had this idea then, of what I wanted. I had this idea of just singing and playing for the next few years. It wasn't a very clear idea, but I thought it would be a lovely way to live. Like my heroes the Weavers. I'd support myself this way. Back then, maybe five years ago, about the time that Pete Seeger was arrested with the Weavers, and accused of being a communist, everyone was running around half scared and half defiant of the power that McCarthy seemed to hold over the country. The Village folk scene wasn't so strong yet. I just wanted to go from place to place, I'd find out where the folk singers went, and play and sing. I was thinking then of my music and how I'd probably get better and better at it. I wasn't dreaming of fame, or being written up in Sing Out! There was this romantic image I had of being a folk singer. It was the kind of person who aged invisibly and spend their days with other folk singers, swapping songs and laughing readily. In my future there would be no room for marrying and having kids.

I've heard older women say that if they met the right man, they'd leave their husbands in a minute. I knew a woman once who did just that. Leave her husband and live with her lover. No break in between. I remember thinking that leaving your husband and running into the arms of your lover was a daring thing to do. Compare that to where I am now. About to leave Bob and Charlie. There is no lover waiting for me. No certain future. No nobody. Just a big void.

Insisting On The Next Generation

Charlie has trouble remembering women's faces. He also had a hard time with names. This summer he is planning on buying a camera and taking pictures. A little bit like making lists as a way of organizing your life. Charlie plans on photographing everything essential in his life. Like a scrap book. In the fall he wants to develop all his pictures and then sort them into piles. That way he thinks he will know something concrete. And the summer will have passed.

He hates the city beaches. They're smelly and crowded. "If only I could go to Argentina, like the cute girl who lives across the street, whose name I can never remember, but who plays guitar just like my mother."

As It Turns Out

this was written about two years after she left them

It's a slow slow climb. I live on the top floor. Sometimes when I'm carrying my groceries and the guitar all the way up those stairs, in the middle of the summer, and it gets hotter the higher I climb, I can't help but wonder if I'm paying for my sins now. In this life time. Leaving Charlie. What did I expect.

This apartment is the only stable component in my life. I go through waitress jobs so quickly, that sometimes I wake up in a blind panic and can't remember where I am working that morning. I must remember to write down the name of the coffeehouse where I'm working and keep it by the alarm clock. My sleep seems to be influenced by these little habits and soothing reminders. It reassures me. Like writing down my latest grand offer. How was it that female folk singers got the reputation for being easy? Did we earn it? Or was it something that was assumed one day in the Village and no one woman has been able to convince men of otherwise. What did I imagine for myself when I left? I think I was past imagining. I think I was pushed into it. I left out of anger. Blind into the city. Right into the Village. Pretending like it was jubilant freedom. Get a job as a waitress, a real estate guy told me. It's easy. There's that word again. First I spill espresso into a customer's lap, and have to pay the cleaning bill. Then I realize that I have no connections. No one has heard me sing yet. I am unknown still.

In the winter I'm warm because it's the top floor. In the summer I sit very still with the fan blowing across me. Blowing the hot air around. I cook in the summer heat. I hate swimming in the ocean. At public beaches. Sometimes I wonder how Charlie is adjusting.

Does he like his new stepmother? Does he like her voice? Does she sing him lullabies? Tomorrow I will be bright and remember to finish all my errands. I will buy milk and cash my paycheck with the grocer.

What Is Your Heritage

Charlie learns about things in unusual ways. He found his apartment by taking his first photography course and befriending his instructor, now his landlord. Which is also how he found a cheap darkroom. He met his girlfriend by just looking out his window. And he found out that his stepmother stretched the truth when it suited her, just by looking through a few scrapbooks; a few photo albums. Sometimes when he walked past a coffeehouse on the corner of Bleeker and Thompson he'd shudder. He never knew why, but a cold feeling came over him. It took him awhile to put all the facts together. His father was no help, he was dead. When he did put it all together, at least enough to suit his curiosity, it didn't stretch his sympathies much.

● ● ●

TOP STORIES

A PROSE PERIODICAL

#1 Donna Wyszomierski
#2 Laurie Anderson
#3 Pati Hill
#4 Suzanne Johnson
#5 Linda Neaman
#6 Gail Vachon
#7 Jenny Holzer/Peter Nadin
#8 Judith Doyle
#9 Kathy Acker
#10 Lynne Tillman/Jane Dickson
#11 Kirsten Thorup
#12 Janet Stein
#13 Anne Turyn

*Available from
TOP STORIES
Hallwalls
700 Main Street
Buffalo, New York 14202*

TOP STORIES #15 $2.50

CONSTANCE DEJONG

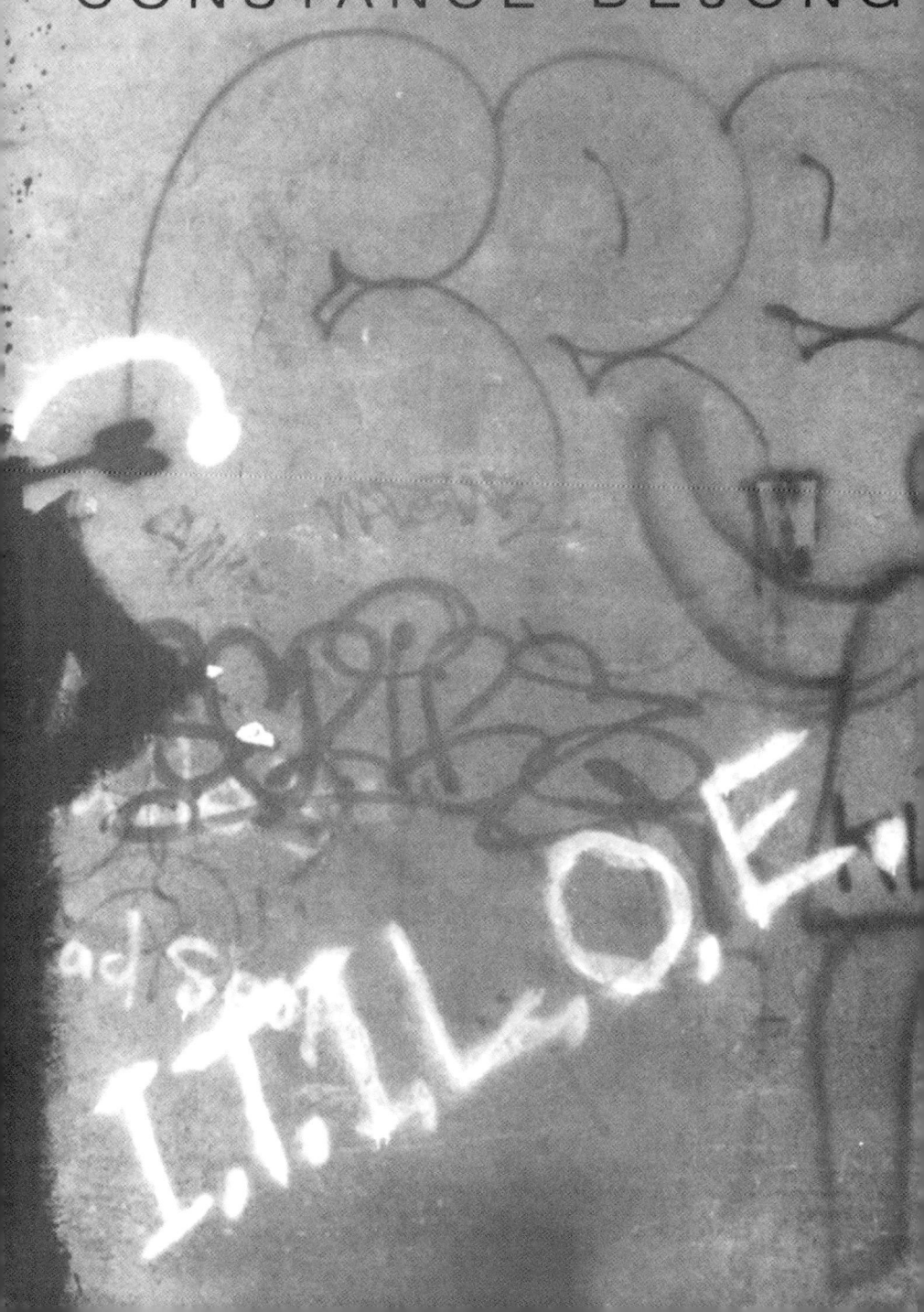

I.T.I.L.O.E.

by Constance DeJong

Copyright ©1983 by Constance DeJong

Acknowledgements—editors Ingrid Sischy (ArtForum) and Betsy Sussler (Bomb) for their previous publication of segments included in the present text.

This publication has been made possible in part by grants from the National Endowment for the Arts, a federal agency, and the New York State Council on the Arts, Literature.

Hallwalls, 700 Main Street, Buffalo, New York 14202

FROM A NARROW BAND AT THE END OF THE RADIO DIAL

"Midnight, September 26, 1980"

"The Night of the Last Fairy Tale"

"As the desert is one of his habitual homes and dawn an especially uneventful hour, the Jinni is often mindlessly circling under the morning star in the form of a stray bird. From up there it's easy to catch sight of a line of dust kicked up by a column of asses and camels plodding across the sand. He's careful to keep out of sight, the better to follow without causing a commotion. That way, toward dusk when the steward signals for camp to be pitched, he can move in closer among the calm and unsuspecting women; the women who sometimes accompany the tradesmen on their long desert crossings. Sometimes the Jinni likes to get them flapping by upsetting tables set for supper, by blowing out the lamps in a single blast. At other times he enjoys the thick atmosphere of the women's tent and is content to compose his presence in the subtle vapors that tickle their noses, the hemp smoke that makes them sleepy, even to merge with the night music they play on their flutes. But in either case, flapping or serene, he's always the visitor in each of their 3 A.M. dreams, the loving dreams peculiar to that hour.

"What's not so peculiar is this. Loving doesn't mean much unless it's real, another story altogether—that one in a thousand nights out in the desert, silent and still. As usual the Jinni was out there breaking up that calm spell of desert; coming in as a cold gust of wind to swirl the stars around, a crack of lightning to charge the neutral air. And as a matter of course he moved on, drawn by the presence of foreigners, white ones; actually, two of them, lying there side by side in the back of a Jeep. Parked at the edge of the desert just where the sand begins to blow across the road, there was a sleeping man and a restless woman who grew calm the instant the Jinni caught hold of her hand and pulled her gently into the fabric of the night. Ordinarily there's a little struggle, if only for the sake of appearances. But this one was different. She made herself comfortable inside his great cloak of darkness, not at all surprised when he told her, 'Angels are formed of light, men of the dust and earth, I of the subtler substances in between.' When he set her down out there on those wasted stretches, she was not alarmed to witness the permutations of his existence from a lion to a wolf, to a jackal, scorpion, snake. Nor was she particularly impressed when he kicked up a storm; first hail, then rain. By slow, steady degrees the sight of the night unfolding in the bright desert moonlight made her grow calmer and calmer, and it made him wonder—'If only I could prolong the effect....'

"By morning he had acquiesced to his fate.

"Being human she belonged to the level, solid world, and there she would stay. Being of subtler substance he realized there was nothing for him but to belong to her, become part of her, be the breath of life to her. So he came out of the distance as a pillar of sand dancing around her in a wide circle, closing in, lifting her, carrying her back to the Jeep. He heard a distant echo. He was fading to a soft whisper, a wisp of breath passing through her lips...lips which for the first time began to move and to speak, capturing his attention and holding him there at the back of her throat. For it seemed that he was back at the beginning, that with the sound of her voice he had arrived at the source of his long, untold existence. It was spellbinding, really—that voice of hers that made words that were him, the Night always unfolding into other nights, beings, entities, shapes that piled up, a dizzying and dumbfounding edifice which spilled over into an intricate system of spaces, a world within a turning world of hours, eons, time fanning out around him, the One-Upright among the horizontals, the Visitor, the Man of Women's Dreams as she called him. She called him in a breathless voice that ran on, "Oh you desert night! One minute you are all and everything and in an instant, I'm here. What can it mean? It's been said that these things happen, that there's chance, lucky stars, meetings at the hour of destiny...over and over it's been said until in an instant it rhymes with drop dead. I've had it, I'm done with you in a word. Actually two of them: THE END."

THE VOICE THAT MAKES THE NIGHT—CHARLOTTE SNOW, ACCORDING TO HER FRIEND FRANCINE ROSE

The first time she came over there was rain, one of those soft gentle rains that go deep. "Fine for the country," Charlotte said; but we were having lunch under my skylight where that gentle April rain became a steady drip, drip, drip. The next time it was the sun, a peaked glare I never noticed until we sat there under the skylight unable to breathe without sending up clouds of dust. It was under the pretext of eating that we kept on meeting, circling slowly and fixedly around lunches, dinners, late-night snacks, meals ever later in the night. She liked the night because it was always young. She liked eating in public places where for hours we could sit unnoticed, giggling like girls—girls who had no need for the likes of a boy. As if to demonstrate this, Charlotte would sometimes pencil on a moustache and order a big cigar. She liked only restaurants where cigars could be had, cigars and clean bathrooms, and eventually she liked only one restaurant, "Lady Astor's." It had a corner booth with velvet curtains which, for a price, the waiter would close—with a smile. She liked this best of all: privacy in public. And in there, a girl I was not. Neither was I a woman. I was all legs and arms, bumping legs and arms always knocking over the wine bottle. I was eyes, they got caught, locked in the longest moment, the moment of recognition. I had a mouth with words flying out of it, words that collided with hers. The collision produced a startling mutation of a language; the deepest of privacies was this. This gave us more than food, than sex, more than a body knows. We were indistinct from our mutated language, our intricate system of intimacy...that was who we were. To exist like that we *had* to meet more, more. I made the arrangements, made the "Lady Astor" waiter smile really, really big. And there in our curtained booth we evolved, producing a mutation of the mutation as our dialect gave way to crypto-speech. With initials we encoded vast subjects. Initials, our dots and dashes, also tapped out the lesser topics—the C.G.'s (cute guys; i.e., witless souls trapped in good bodies) and the occasional A double C double S (academic clothing covering some-kind-of structure; i.e., a not-dumb man). When Charlotte was in between jobs she

made a living practicing O.C. (outfit control, or designing clothes for the fashionable set). And when she had to leave town unexpectedly she sent me a telegram: "Everyone in the C. is on I.P. Not my I. of L. Not even C.B.N.C. K's x 10, P.S." Or, "Everyone in the City (New York) is on image patrol (modern narcissism). Not my idea of life. Not even close but no cigar. Lots of kisses, P.S."
(According to Francine, Charlotte always signs her messages *P.S.* to indicate there will be more coming, and in her replies, Francine always underscores her signature with the address below, the site where everything began.)

32 EAST FIRST STREET, NEW YORK CITY

Late in February 1980, Ricky Dent was assigned to keep an eye on Havana Lamotte, a tenant in the basement of the building. Havana was new to New York's Lower East Side but not to intelligence. She would always be under surveillance for the sympathies announced in her name; a rare instance of there possibly being an answer to the worn-out, the usually rhetorical: what's in a name? A questioning type the super at #32 was not. To him "Havana" announced soul-mate, a match made in heaven (a not-so-rare claim filed under another story altogether). The more pertinent file:

Havana Haydée Lamotte, no known aliases.
Born 1952, Artemisia, Cuba.
Father, Ramon, left Cuba with mother, Beatriz, in February 1958. Ramon Lamotte died under mysterious circumstances in April 1958, though a preliminary investigation into his 'drowning' turned up no underworld ties, insurance policies, etc. Conclusion: suicide. Beatriz Lamotte became active in anti-Cuban (communist) activity around the time of her daughter's birth. She has gone on public record—May Day party, Miami, 1970—to the effect that the daughter, Havana, is a legacy of Castro's Cuba (?). For details regarding sexual relations between Beatriz Lamotte and Fidel Castro and any subsequent 'issue'—see M-14, paragraph 73. Mother Beatriz' comment regarding legacy may indicate that the daughter, like herself, was to become active in the NY-Miami mouth network, disseminating propaganda.*
Beatriz Lamotte retains same address since her husband's immigration: 3718 Fairlawn Drive, Coconut Grove, Miami, Florida. Havana Lamotte makes irregular but frequent trips between mother's home and New York where she maintains no permanent address.
*Note: considering Lamotte's family background there is always the very likely chance she is involved in something more.

Always the very likely chance she is involved in something more, something....

It was a long time since contract agent Ricky Dent had been active in the anti-Castro campaign, had approved of such proposals as infusing Castro's shoes with a chemical that would cause his hair to fall out. But once reactivated by the Lamotte assignment, Dent worked double-time, almost instantly closing the gap between Havana Lamotte in the basement and Francine Rose upstairs under her skylight. The logic was assisted by evidence: Lamotte's twenty-four hour courier service and Rose's personal correspondence, a handful of documents written in 'code.' Included were messages received, drafts of replies sent, scraps adrift from the sender-receiver matrix pointing to the likelihood of bigger operations circling out from a clump of papers dropped in the garbage. Another point. Dent found other assistance drifting along those littered Lower East Side streets, streets given to all manner of paper products.

—The 7th Precinct police have reams of records with statistics characterizing the environs as a fourteen by seven block area where there are more murders committed than anywhere else in Manhattan, except in Harlem.

—The N.Y.U. Graduate Library has several Ph.D. theses written by aspiring urban sociologists concerned with the unusual and complex demographic features of a multi-ethnic, multi-racial contiguity and, as gentrification slips into the vocabulary, theses swell, shelves lengthen.

—The quotidian is printed up. In big pictures and a little bit of text the local dailies report the week's obligatory three-alarm fire, drug bust, body in a bag wedged between two abandoned buildings. And the less frequent 'human interest story': Is the richest-country-in-the-world becoming like Calcutta, New Delhi, places where the street is a dormitory, rows of poor bedding down at night?

By daylight the City's homeless appear larger than life, like the TV character, The Hulk, whose body expands to giant proportions, though the humans in question here may have no muscles at all. These giant forms may be tiny people built up from layers of clothing, from wrappings of paper and plastic, muffled up to the chin, the face exposed; the construction then continues. Heads are turbaned or bedecked with countless caps or with just one hat made from brown bag after brown bag fitted one inside another. Embellishing the surface are idiosyncracies of adornment—more buttons than a general, pop-top medals, aluminum foil fringe, magnetic tape streamers, cellophane bows, safety pins, paper-clip garlands, more stuff made in U.S.A. Not French, not on the L.E.S.

A reporter from one of the dailies made such a mistake in identification when attracted to one of the more fashionable homeless. Her idiosyncratic taste—rhinestones and dime store jewels, anything that glitters. Any resemblance to a French woman was genesis made simple, an overeager journalist's splice job—a glittering old woman alive in 1980 on First Avenue/La Môme Bijou-Miss Diamonds, already old in 1932 in a Montmartre night spot.

A little research at the library would have steered the reporter to moments when Ziegfeld Girls appeared regularly in back page tidbits of morning editions of *The Herald*. Having been seen at certain parties, escorted and twirled through after hours life, the Girls made sparks in the daily machinery, some of which didn't just fizzle out. Some big wheels and a smoking gun: a tidbit like that marches from the gossip columns onto the front page.

STANFORD WHITE SHOT DEAD BY MILLIONAIRE
HARRY THAW
Playboys in the Garden

The time is 1906; the place, Madison Square Garden; the incident marches around on more recently written pages.

"...it seems established that White, although a devoted husband and father, was also a determined seducer of young girls.

"In 1901, White met a showgirl called Evelyn Nesbitt, from Ziegfeld's Floradora chorus. She was then sixteen, and looked even younger, but White seduced her. The millionaire Harry Thaw, who was jealous of White on various other grounds, also admired her. Thaw eventually married her, in 1905, suffered greater jealousy, and shot White dead fourteen months later in Madison Square Garden's Restaurant."

Writing in 1976 Martin Green also notes: "Thaw, too, saw himself as a great lover and bravura personality. When he came into his fortune on his twenty-first birthday, he gave a dinner for a hundred actresses, each of whom found a gift of jewelry beside her plate."

A hundred actresses wadded up in three words, seventeen characters of type, a spitball sailing beyond visibility but not out of earshot. Winifred Abel, Irene Arnold, Yvonne Bendkowski, Virginia Blatt, Carlota Bohm, Minnie Briscoe, Adele Brown, Naomi Buchanen, Isabell Capota, Ardell Capra, Rosemary Claire Casey, Dorothea Charles, Lucille Clapper, Estelle Cocco, Ruth Cory, Josephine Cuomo, Olive Daphnis, Opal Dauber, Pearl Dauber, Wilhemina Dean, Esther DeGarcia, Gladys Vista Dixon, Hattie Doniger, Lili Dorn, Blanche Drakonakis, Pauline Durkin, Sarah Eberhard, Iris Ehrlich, Maxine Emspack, Lydia Evans, Frieda Evers, Catherine Fanning, Edith Fisberg, Lillian Flores, Dora Fortini, Veda Fuchs, Amelia Gelfand, Meredith Glazer, Annabell Green, Stella Guest, Flo Harrison, Jeanette Hart, Dot Herman, Henrietta Hopkins, Crystal Hutchins, Anna Ivany, Cora Jessup, Lili Jones, Angeline Jusino, Faye Kaiser, Mildred Keely, Ruby Kelley, Cecelia King, Joan Louise Koblentz, Phoebe Koppel, Esther Kozic, Louise LaBarbara, Hannah Landau, Edna Lord, Eloise Maxfield, Patricia McBride, Sylvia Miller, Hazel Moran, Ada Mullter, Myra Neff, Allegra Nugent, Margaret Nye, Catherine O'Hagen, Marion Oliver, Eugenia Owings, Evelyn Pesking, Ava Phipps, Ginnie Pomeranz, Bea Purdy, Geraldine Putnam, Virginia Ricks, Christine Rhodes, Nadine Richter, Louisa Robertson, Agnes Ross, Hope Rupenthal, Beatrice Samuels, Dawn Sawyers, Celia Schneider, Ethel Schultz, Cynthia Shatkin, Isabell Snyder, Emmaline Swazey, Madeline...the litany like the F-train stops here at the intersection of First Street and First Avenue.

At five o'clock: traffic backed up for minutes on end, blocks and blocks of cars momentarily caught in the First and First nexus. Quadraphonic leakage from car radios tuned to 'Shadow Traffic' sent down from helicopters on the watch for gridlock. On the respective four corners, much of the world is represented here. Abandon the orderly right angles of intersecting streets for "nexus," two crossing diagonals, an X. Jews and Arabs occupy the ends of one axis, and on the other, the more obscure coupling of Eastern Europe and the Mediterranean, a Polish restaurant opposite a quick-stop cafe run by Greeks. Aside from corners tacked down by businessmen, minority groups claim the surrounding area as home, as do individuals living in varying degrees of anonymity and flamboyance, disorderly crowds heading homeward at five o'clock, jaywalking the First-First intersection. X is home base for Madeline Tarkington, or Mad Madeline, as she's known. She's known for such peculiarities as reeling off alphabetical order seventy-five years after the fact; also for delivering whole punctuated paragraphs when senility shifts from the singed pinpoint of a smoking gun, when the fog that comes with age recedes to reveal a vista.

The pinpoint. Mothered by a show girl, Madeline is one of uncounted people biologically fathered by Stanford White, left with a dangling genetic blank spot, nothing to flesh it out.

The vista. "...All night fruit markets, flower stalls, liquor stores, newstands, you could get anything you wanted at all hours on Eighth Avenue. We lived around here to be near the theaters and agents, a district full of small studios with one window on an air shaft. Mr. Fishbach, he had 70, 80, 100 of them in his row houses and he didn't bother much with formalities, just pulled out a leaselike paper with a room number at the top followed by rows of dotted lines. You signed, crossing out the name above. Only women tenants, that was about his only rule, and it had him hauling his 225 pounds of overweight back and forth in front of his buildings, chain smoking Camels, muttering about 'my girls.' We came to him through the grapevine, went away when someone gave up or got a better job or married. Sad good-byes, happy good-byes, and lots of resentment because I couldn't tell which was which, work/marriage, I always said at least there's more to alimony than unemployment checks, good luck. I always bombed with the girls. They didn't like my jokes, didn't like how I wouldn't share my studio, how I never went around after the show with some decent looking guy. Then I got my hair cropped. So. I was a lesbian after all. And who was I to blow the whistle on gossip? At home it gave me some privacy, and on the other hand, the very idea kept the girls from stretching their imaginations far enough to see me going down to the piers. Early in the morning, even with eyes swollen from lack of sleep, there's no mistaking that pretty swaying movement through the haze lifting off the water. See them little behinds coming down the gang plank? Each one, each one alone is even more pretty—a swell of smooth muscle flinching a little at the first kiss of concrete on the sole of a black polished shoe. Oh, sailors. You linger for a minute and they're moving off, bunches of spit-shined toes pointed toward midtown. Thank god for wind. Still two of them trying to light a match, a real pair, Mr. Mutt and Jeff, though the tall one didn't think so. Didn't think much of my hairdo, either, until it got topped off with his cap. That's how they do it, cap you for a weekend. And the short one? Pascal shook his head slightly and backed off a few steps. Roger was so much taller, he had to lean down to kiss that sad face. When Roger patted him on the bottom, the sad boy fiddled with his buttons, and with Roger's arm around his shoulders, Pascal said nothing all the way to the Village—just more long faces when the coffee finally came.

'You think this American coffee's shit. I'll tell you what's shit. You, if you don't stop whining. What if I leave you on your own? Just you and Louie, eh? Then see how it goes.'

Pascal's going got better after that. All weekend he never peeped about sleeping on the floor of my tiny foyer with his feet in the closet. On the last morning he was still being charming when he climbed into bed. Laying his head on Roger and peeking through those curls of chest hair, he asked very sweetly if I'd come down for a good-bye wave. I agreed, since it was November, cold enough to pin on my new raccoon collar, have my first hot chocolate of the season, even better, some hot buttered rum. A lot of that got drunk the day the *La Sylvette* sailed. In its seven state rooms passengers were probably listening to their friends' I-told-you-so about booking passage on an old freighter. After a three hour delay with engine trouble their champagne was gone, same for the bon-voyage spirit, which was still going strong among the girls who'd come down to see off their sailors. We didn't mind not being allowed on board, not on the corner of Water Street where rounds of rum only cost a dime. In "Smokey's" we didn't mind anything, except for Jeanette. 'My Charlie,' she wailed holding up her glass. 'Oh come on, Jeanette. How can you cry for Charlie when there's a whole boat load of them out there?' And you can bet they weren't looking too pretty down there in the hold, sweat dripping between the cheeks of those hard little behinds, dirty jerseys sticking to their chests. Forget about pretty down there. Valves are being opened, cartons restacked. With luck a guy can duck out of the terrible heat and noise for a quick smoke. Hurrying sailors rib each other with a 'make tracks punk,' 'hey baby dig my hard on,' 'oh beat off.' And always on the move down those narrow corridors, there's a figure casting a shadow over every inch of the ship. Forget about the captain. Remember the name, Louie Paradise. He had a ticket all right. Dope, that was Louie's ticket; morphine sewed in the lining of his jacket, sold to the lonely, the homesick, anyone dumb enough to get hooked on it. The fun started when the needle happy ran out of money. Halfway across the Atlantic without a sucker to put the touch on, they'd come whining to Louie and he'd meet them in the showers. He liked playing god in there, ordering them down on their hands and knees, sticking it to them in their ass. Maybe no one heard Louie scream the night Pascal took it in the mouth, but if Louie was out of commission for a few days with some teeth marks in his meat, that was nothing compared to the infected track mark running up Pascal's leg. One dirty needle was all it took and the *La Sylvette* came into Marseilles with a stiff in its stow. The captain escorted Louie to the Chief of Police. A halfhour later they were standing on headquarter's steps, buttoning up their pea coats, the Mistral in their ears. When the papers asked for a statement, the Chief said, 'That's what the Marseilles hoodlums do, they kill each other.' Think of it, think of it...."

The fog is back. The blurry trail is about death on a ship, it's like murder in a hotel, the air never quite clears, little things bring it all back.

Three picture postcards held together with a rubber band
Burnt toast
Dead batteries

Little things are piling up around Madeline as she forages in the garbage for the stuff of her material life ordered according to edible, usable, beautiful. In the reject pile go loose pages, scraps adrift from the sender-receiver matrix.

"Take 'em Sonny. Take 'em if you're that dumb."

And take 'em he did, "Sonny" a.k.a. Ricky Dent. When he waved his evidence under Francine Rose's nose, the smell of garbage was pretty sweet compared to the odorless creep of fanaticism, desperation, and the confusion. Had Dent concluded that coded messages descended to the basement to be disseminated into the world, or was it the other way round—that Lamotte scurried back from her contacts to the woman upstairs, who disguised secrets in the letters of the alphabet? Francine's attempts to make head or tails of it belabored her conversation with friends, whose attention spans had been taxed by efforts to grasp what actually had transpired under drops of rain, among particles of dust, behind velvet curtains; by efforts to puzzle out what third person had provided information about the nexus point linking all that to-ing and fro-ing of street people, reporters, agents, guns. Ricky Dent packs a .38 automatic, German made perfection popularized in 007 spin offs. But weary of details, friends grew impatient with the Dent affair, began to ask questions or talk among themselves.

"Was it likely that so complicated a plot would all depend on the unwitting cooperation of one mercurial young woman about to leave for England?"
or
"Francine Rose. An obsessive personality! Always making a federal case out of her own personal problems."

No one said: that what one really is, is knowing oneself as a product of a historical process to date which has deposited in you an infinity of traces without leaving an inventory; the job of producing an inventory is the first necessity. Or, that many people find their way to the general through the personal, the individual. These were quotations underlined in books Charlotte Snow was reading in a bed-sit in Islington, a borough of North London where she'd taken up residence. She'd described the situation in a letter to Francine. "I'm becoming a respository, a compendium of statements that're being committed to memory. Someday I'll be like a vast, indexed reference book that can flip to its own pages at will. Naturally there's a trick, a system. I'm using one described in *The Art of Memory* by Frances A. Yates, a medieval system...too intricate to go into here. But essentially you image a building constructed of rooms and each designated room is a subject heading where particular material's stored. So the material's not just conserved; it can also be located in a flash. Among other things one has to keep the imaged structure from becoming some dizzying and dumbfounding edifice that will topple over. That means starting with a sound foundation. Sound looney? So is living in an Islington building crawling with armchair radicals tossing off buzz words and received ideas, pearls before the American swine, me, who's wandering down the hallways of medieval metaphysics. Still, the system seems to be working. My imaged building is a standard middle-class house, and when I got your letter about upstairs, downstairs Dent, I wandered into the Closet and flipped directly to *Conspiracy*, A. Summers: 'The American intelligence community is so sprawling a creation that it spawns compartments where not even those in charge can be sure what is going on. One such was its anti-Castro division, consisting in 1962 of 600 Americans, most of them case officers, plus upward of 3,000 contract agents in and out of Cuba. The Americans no less than the exiles were committed to their cause. There was the proposal, for example, to infuse Castro's shoes with a chemical compound that would cause his hair to fall out. (Once bald and unbearded, his charismatic charm would disappear.) Also a specially treated cigar to make him incoherent during one of his speech making marathons. Or spraying LSD in his broadcasting studio for much the same effect.' Actually, Francine, when you first sent word of the Dent business I just rolled my eyes and stuck there on the back of my eyelids was the old question we always used to ask: I.T.I.L.O.E.? If your alpha-speak is a little rusty, I'll spell that out when you get here. I *am dying* to see you again. Please try to bring some news of Edgar Krebs and some all cotton sweatshirts. Much love, P.S."

27 March 1980
Dear Charlotte,

Did you get the message I called? Whoever answers your phone isn't terribly cooperative. I had as much trouble getting across to them as I've been having with calls to West Bengal, a subtle introduction to my change of plans. I plan to see you still in London but on the return trip in June. By then will your head be swollen beyond recognition, the size of that house you're stuffing with 'material'? Or will you have invented something like the flying buttress to hold up your densely packed cranium? Technologists are trying to invent computers that can think. So what's the idea of trying for the reverse, housing a storage and retrieval system, becoming a human computer that doesn't think? Such are my infantile terrors. I've always had a near phobia about mind control, waking up in *1984* with a Roman Polanski script: "This isn't a dream, this is really happening!" I want to say *the future is now* without being glib, I want shiny coin phrases. Not slogans stamped on buttons and T-shirts like hip brand names strangers use to find each other. Not frozen phrases like flash cards that teach you to recognize word groups in 1/32 of a second, no meaning, let alone spelling. I.T.I.L.O.E.? Not that either. Alpha-speak is everywhere from DDT to FMLN-FDR, both inescapable, poison and politics. But when we see each other again let's work on the lost art of plain English, inefficient as it may be in a world of initials. The FMLN-FDR is a coalition of the Revolutionary Democratic Front (FDR) and the five guerilla groups in the Farabundo Marti National Liberation Front (FMLN). These five groups are the Salvadorian Communist Party (PLS), the Popular Forces of Liberation (FPL), the Revolutionary Army of Central American Workers (PRTC), the People's Revolutionary Army (ERP), and the Armed Forces of National Resistance (FARN). Within each of these groups, there are further factions and sometimes even further initials, as in the PRS and LP-28 of the ERP. That's public information.

And Havana Lamotte has an equally complicated life story bound up in split factions which as *you* say is too intricate to go into here, will have to wait till I meet you in the falling rain, June in London on the P.E.—plain English not Hampstead—Heath.

In the meantime I'm getting to know Havana. She's staying in the spare room. (Among other things we agree that under the circumstances it's a little too symbolic to be living below ground in the basement.) Up here it's Insomniacs Anonymous. She tells me her nightmares, I tell her mine.

...A woman wearing a red veil comes walking up the driveway from the far end where she's just stepped out of a shiny black car. She has some trouble negotiating the icy patches and the wind keeps blowing her coat straight out. Then suddenly the wind dies and her key is turning in the front door lock, her footsteps are on the stairs, even the silver charms of her bracelet are jingling, jingling in the quiet of that long windless moment....

What does it mean? We don't need a shrink for this one. Havana is haunted by an image of a three-piece suit packing a .38 Walther PPK and commiserating with M.M. which doesn't stand for Marilyn Monroe. Havana happened to see poor old Mad Madeline going through the garbage on the afternoon Dent came snooping around in his flannels. So one part of the puzzle's no longer a mystery. The papers I'd thrown out got recycled through Madeline and, need I say, Dent never had to dirty his hands.

Enclosed is the part that haunts me. As you know this recent event isn't the first time Madeline has intervened in our lives, and it's in your words that I register a little detonation, the sickening eruption of a déjà vu. Maybe there's a corner in your memory system for the enclosed article you wrote so long ago for, god help us, the *House Organ*.

I'm writing at such length, sorry, I'll try to be brief. All cotton sweatshirts are in the mail. Black and blue and white.

As for Edgar Krebs, he left for an early vacation without a word and our temporary super is Rudolf Brenner from next door who now goes by the name Rainer Berlin, rechristened for his favorite poet and the city of his birth. What he knows about Rilke and Berlin would fill a space the size of the tiny heart tattooed on his shoulder which carries a burden no heavier than the weight of some chains looped through the epaulets of his leather jacket— just another character jingling along, a guy in his own movie complete with sound effects. Oddly enough, he's scouting locations for an 'actual' film he's involved with as the art director; some cops and robbers remake starring local leather-and-steel talent. He thinks my apartment is perfect for it, all those points of view (!). Shots down through the skylight, up through the hole in the floor, tracking through the sliding door to next door...dumm da dum dum. If it'll pay the rent while I'm gone, I'm game. Rainer is still Rudolf, still asks after you. "Well, well Rose Red how is Snow White?" I didn't tell him not all women are attracted to fairy tales with One-Uprights stalking around. Instead of double negatives I searched for the tape of your radio program and when I couldn't find it, I gave him the typescript to read. Is that OK? The more I send out of here the more nice and empty it becomes. Insomnia has me on the night shift. At this hour my assistants, strategically positioned around the apartment, are working tirelessly to keep the place reasonably together. A Roach Motel in the corner is collecting bugs on some surface, sweet and sticky. Under the stove, a package of D-Con poison is inviting mice to their last supper at my expense. A small fortune passes hands for these and other contraptions such as a penguin shaped one on the tap filtering heavy metals out of the water, a pyramid shaped ionizer revitalizing polluted air. I pay for contraptions sold by the same companies that produce the problems that destroy the house we all live in. Is this why I've a reputation for making mountains out of molehills? Mountains. When I go to them periodically for some fresh air and for some kind of mental space that only comes with practice...never mind. Some people jog, some sit very very still. It'll be more than nice to see you on my way back. Somedays I miss your company to the point of distraction. I think this was one of them.

                                        Much love,
                                        Francine
                                        #32 E.F.S.

32, 34 EAST FIRST STREET, NEW YORK CITY

A typical screw-up. This morning when I came downstairs all the mail for #32 had been delivered here by mistake. People I don't know read *Newsweek* and *Soviet Life*, get thin blue aerograms from Dublin, bills from a West Side doctor, from a collection agency in Omaha. A typical screw-up and too suddenly, there's a chink in the venetian blinds of people I don't know.

#32, 34 are identical twins from the pink and black tiled entrances to the matching skylights giving access to the adjoining roofs. There's a huge telescope up there when the weather permits. When nights are clear our super searches for comets, the one he'll sight before any other amateur astronomer's known as a streak across the sky. If Halley did it so can Edgar Krebs, he's fond of saying. He's fond of the ring of "Kreb's Comet," plans a traveling laser light show bearing that title, part of the someday when he leaves the roof and is an itinerant astronomer with his scheme packed up in a couple of aluminum suitcases.

"Earth to Egbert, earth to Egbert." I hear kids yelling in the hall when they're not pumping quarters into Donkey Kong video games Edgar could probably program in his sleep. I hear footsteps overhead and rap three times on the skylight. Silence means call the cops. Two raps means it's Edgar conducting his roof top vigil. I go up for a look. His sight is trained on his favorite target. "The fashionable world, a tremendous orb nearly five miles around, is in full swing, and the solar system works respectfully at its appointed distances."

Me: "A little respectful backing off seems perfectly in order here since it's physical space not knowledge everyone's after. Let's call for a moratorium on greed. Hands off the sky, everyone zip up their pants and pipe down."

He: "Oh, come on. The search for extraterrestrial life is, in the opinion of many, the most exciting, challenging, and profound issue not only of this century but of the whole naturalistic movement that has characterized the history of Western thought for 300 years. What is at stake is the chance to gain a new perspective on man's place in nature."

Me: "Let's begin the search with fingering the question, is there intelligent life on earth? Is there a naturalist for attending to minute phenomena, for reading between the lines?"

He: "Don't go metaphorical on me. Facts, I want some plain old ordinary facts. This isn't Egypt, we're not talking in riddles."

Me: "What is this civilization in which we find ourselves? What are the ceremonies and why should we take part in them? What are these professions and why should we make money out of them? Where in short is it leading, the processions of the sons of educated men?"

He: "Well, Alfred North Whitehead and Bertrand Russell had a fruitful collaboration, *Principia Mathematica*. Their work on "logistic language" had been preceded by efforts to produce an international language which would bring the world closer together. The first to be widely used was Volapük, invented in 1880 by an Austrian priest. This was followed seven years later by Esperanto, but the mathematician Peano felt these had failed to escape from the arbitrary and illogical syntax of tongues that had evolved in the chance manner of nature. In 1903 he produced Interlingua, derived from classical Latin but with a simplified syntax. It is still widely used in abstracting scientific articles."

(My ignored interruption: "Probably he has got no red blood in his body. Somebody put a drop under a magnifying glass and it was all semicolons and parenthesis. Oh, he dreams of footnotes, and they run away with all his brains. They say when he was a little boy, he made an abstract of 'Hop o' My Thumb' and he's been making abstracts ever since. Ugh!")

"These developments have lead Hans Freudenthal, Professor of Mathematics at the University of Utrecht, to attempt extending the "logistic language" of Whitehead and Russell into something intelligible to beings with whom we have nothing in common except intelligence. He calls it "Lincos" as a short form of "Lingua Cosmica." The logical exposition of the language as might take place in an extended interstellar message is contained in his book, *Lincos: Design of a Language for Cosmic Intercourse*. Actually, he pointed out, such a language already may be established as the vehicle for cosmic intercourse."

Me: "Great. Everyone speaking the same tongue, singing the same anthem. Fuck cosmic intercourse, celestial syntax."

"Oh, come on."

"You come on!"
"I don't believe you, I really don't."
"No one asked you to." Someone, however is coughing in the shadows. "Oh, it's Francine, hi."
   As witnesses to Edgar's near nightly vigil, Francine and I became familiar with all his schemes and with the practical side of his talents, which run to anything electrical, mechanical, even structural. He's helped us to make our apartments burglar-proof, our cranky radiators give off steam, and when we decided to make our lives simpler, he had us chipping through the correct spot in the common wall of our apartments. If Gulf & Western could do it so could we. That was our scheme, Francine and mine's. If considered in the light of multinationals, our merger, a consortium of two, will not a big deal make. Neither will darkness make do, nor a gray zone where someone, however, *is* always coughing in the shadows, infecting the entire organism out to the extremities, our leaping-off site. No big deal, except for the laws of nature, which state that no two bodies can occupy the same space at the same time. Ricky Dent, his boss, would like to be a law that certain; know which bodies occupy what space when. They don't like, maybe no one likes strategem, deception, facts giving way to a sprawling fiction, the lives we live:
   Two people become one on paper by drawing up a contract and pooling their resources to exist as a stronger economic unit, an imagined third person. Conversely, one person exists as many, a string of aliases and a.k.a.'s, when there really is something to the what's-in-a-name homily. When originally Francine and I drew up our contract we provided for inevitable complications. For example, when Francine went away she replaced herself in the unit. Now Havana Lamotte upholds a share in domestic economics my salary cannot withstand alone.
   I work in the Lincoln Center Library, Theater Division, where lives of performers are bequeathed to eternity. We disassemble their scrapbooks, photographs, reviews, love letters; we cut and paste. We, some of us, work late after our bosses go home. The place then is ours, a treasure house of free stationery this fluorescent lit sanctuary where the free Xerox machine is humming away. I copy things for Francine.

A typescript: *TWICE-TOLD TALES, an Ecological Text made from Recycled Material*; adapted by Charlotte Snow; footnotes by Richard Burton; additional annotation by Gustave Flaubert.

An article: *AT NIGHT, The Biography of an Object* by Charlotte Snow. The object of this study is a piece of jewelry, or at least it was once all of a piece, a necklace of Egyptian origin associated with Hathor. Legend recounts that at the origin of time, men conspired against their Creator, Re. After considering the matter, Re decided to send his Eye (consciousness) in the form of a lioness to chastise the insurgents. She was called Sekhmet, meaning "powerful," an aspect of Hathor. Sekhmet wrought havoc and would have devoured all humanity had not Re, striken with regret, then had the ground covered with red-dyed beer in place of blood, so that Sekhmet, deceived by the color, drank up the liquid, became drunk and fell asleep, thus sparing mankind. This took place, however, very far to the south of Egypt. It fell to Thoth, lord of writing and time, to bring Sekhmet back into Egypt. Barely had the two arrived in Aswan when Thoth plunged her into the waters of Abaton in order to "quench her heat." And thus it was that the blood-thirsty lioness was transformed into the gentle cat, Basket, one of the aspects of Hathor.

But not all is a lioness brought under control and made to pussyfoot through all eternity.

Under the multiple names that evoke her countless aspects, Hathor represents a synthesis of Egyptian notions concerning cosmogenesis, and as such she is of a different dimension than Aphrodite, with whom the Greeks mistakenly identified her. For despite her female epithets, including "Mistress of Love," she isn't the Feminine Principle. Under the name of Neith, for example, she is addressed as "Lady of Sais," meaning two-thirds masculine and one-third feminine.

I read the first page of the article while the Xerox machine hummed away copying things Francine needed in preparation for her departure. She's gone to mountains so high and remote not even the tools of surveillance travel that far. Even if it sounds like escaping she lives with wanderlust contracted at an early age and reports this as fact. "There are places where there is no television, yet: Darjeeling, which is perching at a high altitude and for days nothing, white nothing, from the Windemere's windows, the renowned hotel in the clouds. When a hard wind blows, Mt. Everest is standing there and...Darjeeling is perching in the foothills of the Himalayas. In these lowly heights soft are the sounds brought here on a strange, flitting breeze, dizzying tease, oh jeez, please stop. And indeed one does become accustomed to always having an airflow in the head, to the unremitting rustle of silk prayer flags, of deep moaning prayers circling up from the valley. Monks down there have a hard-to-grasp notion of words as living things. Thus anything committed to writing cannot be destroyed unless the life of it is passed on in a ceremonial fire; colored smoke warming the atmosphere with the breath of life. At a far distance from the monastery, the Windemere is a relic of the British Raj still serving high tea on a landscaped terrace. A piece of paper caught in a bush makes a flap. I release it, a page from *Romeo and Juliet*, the part about love traveling from hand to hand, lip to lip. It makes me laugh, it always has, those two kids all bent out of shape and there's no one here to iron them into the fabric of Darjeeling life. Local residents await the arrival of television, one set which they'll watch in the movie house. I've come to a place where words are living things and where my Darjeeling friends await exotic reflections of faraway places with strange sounding names. They look forward to seeing me on television after a safe journey home which as you know will be soon enough, after London in the falling rain. Love, Francine."

Francine's letters come to Havana and me at the 32-34 complex on East First Street addressed to Carol Riding, the so-called person who simplifies things, clears difficult economic hurdles; and yet. Carol, she comes into existence like neighbors glimpsed in a stack of strange envelopes; these I'm entitled to open, envelopes enclosing an unsolicited credit card from a second rate rent-a-car company, catalogs promoting discounted make-up with a free sample, a request for a signature on a letter protesting the incarceration of Polish intellectuals; but no health insurance policy. No, instead of the one awaited document which would verify our conscious efforts, there comes only Hulkish unarrested expansion into a creature putting on lipstick in the rearview mirror of a rented car with license plates made by convicts as opposed to incarcerated intellecutals. That's not right. A woman is putting on her make-up before picking up a rented car, and on the way she drops a letter of protest in a mailbox. This woman has incessant conversations with Shepherd, a fanciful constant companion, a man

I knew briefly in real life in days when the scheme, Francine and mine's, was young. Older is a dry clot of days punctured by dots, dashes, blank spots where caprice whispers and moans. It started on Wednesday. An invisible hand relieved Havana of her pocketbook in a crowded coffee shop. Last night she received an anonymous call from a man in a phone booth at 125th Street and Amsterdam Avenue who claimed he'd found her wallet and other valuables, she could come up and get them, he'd be waiting in front of Harlem Hospital. By morning it's still uncertain if the phone caller, who now calls himself Pinkie, will keep the second rendezvous; if his absence at the first was a true misunderstanding; if this isn't a classic set-up in which the original thief receives a reward for returning stolen possessions as his partners burglarize the victim's apartment known to be vacant while she traipses uptown; if we aren't reasonably justified in assuming an absence of rectitude—"Of what?" Havana snaps, nerves running wild. It started as a joke. Where once I kidded about us assembling in Carol Riding a Frankenstein creature who would probably turn on its makers, Francine was ever serious, reacting with a learned diatribe about *Reason, Rectitude, Justice*; three celestial Graces who appeared before a worrying woman in 1405 "to restore her senses, to explain to her the causes of antifeminism and to reveal womanhood's true nature, and at the same time, they will help her build a fortified city, an ideal city in which all noble women of the past, present, and future can live undisturbed." When it seemed appropriate to the occasion of her leaving, of Havana Lamotte entering, Francine amended her diatribe, said the source of her celestial reference, her friend Charlotte Snow, had strayed too far afield with medievalisms, things eerily Euclidean; at any rate *we* could stick to the principle of the thing. We could, for example, continue along the lines of three Graces in reaction to which Havana had said it was about time we discussed down to earth things, in particular that now anxiously awaited health insurance policy. But it doesn't come; only unsolicited envelopes, unwanted incidents, glimpses and snaps. If we are reasonably justified in assuming an absence of moral integrity, the dictionary's words for "rectitude," the dictionary isn't giving many pointers about how to proceed with a guy named Pinkie who may or may not be waiting in front of Harlem Hospital at noon, three-thirty, five-thirty, he can't make up his mind, his upper hand that jerks us around; us and our masked man, our day's dose of button, button, who's got the button? And so it goes. Hours of relay phone calls to and from Havana, many particulars, reassessments of "personal business" conducted on library time under the watchful eyes of Miss Millicent Gibbs, the supervisor...after hours of this, I've a mind contracted to a sore spot; only the tight little curlicue of a snatched purse located in a throbbing muscle in my neck. I am not discussing it with Shepherd, with whom all conversation is on a nontedious plane, is involuntary murmuring—high nonsense on the way home at rush hour. I am not the only one thus engaged, betrothed to a phantom. Thousands rushing home and this woman, that man, many are of the murmuring lips. Many are mouthing their capricious mantras, whispers and moans, though rarely in the body to body tight quarters of the subway where I am a less than anonymous worker, thanks to the colors of midnight: black shot with deepest of blue, a hand-me-down dress inscribed with love of night from Charlotte to Francine to me spit out of the train, hurrying, jaywalking.

Upstairs. I wind back the tin top of my kippers in front of the 7 O'Clock News. I hear kids yelling in the hall, footsteps overhead, three and two raps on a pane of glass, and on the roof, a dry peck for right cheek, left cheek. Edgar's back from vacation, returned to his near nightly vigil and up here all's very still. It's our tacit agreement to replace scenes unworthy of repetition, it's our truce to realign a badly tallied invoice, all that he-ing and me-ing of:

- Ill trained ideologues banging their solitary gongs

- Unmagic mediums through which there passed two separate processions of ghosts

- Faulty instruments streaking the sky on a trajectory heading for the drink

---

Many minuses
One plus—all's very still. It's a startling silence, it's the breathtaking quiet when a long monotonous sound suddenly breaks off.

NOTES

Page

8   Martin Green, *Children of the Sun* 1976, Basic Books.

15 Joan Didion, "In El Salvador," *New York Review of Books*, November 1982

17 The "ghosts" passing through unmagic mediums. He: Charles Dickens (*Bleak House*), Space Science Board of the National Academy of Sciences, Walter Sullivan (*We Are Not Alone*). Me: Adrienne Rich (*On Lies Secrets and Silence*), Virginia Woolf (*Three Guineas*), George Eliot (*Middlemarch*).

20 Lucy Lamy, *Egyptian Mysteries*, 1981, Thames and Hudson.

22 Christine de Pizan, *The Book of The City of Ladies*, (orig. 1405) 1982, Persea Books

TOP STORIES

A PROSE PERIODICAL

#1 Donna Wyszomierski
#2 Laurie Anderson
#3 Pati Hill
#4 Suzanne Johnson
#5 Linda Neaman
#6 Gail Vachon
#7 Jenny Holzer/Peter Nadin
#8 Judith Doyle
#9 Kathy Acker
#10 Lynne Tillman/Jane Dickson
#11 Kirsten Thorup
#12 Janet Stein
#13 Anne Turyn
#14 Lee Eiferman

Available from
TOP STORIES
Hallwalls
700 Main Street
Buffalo, New York 14202

TOP STORIES #16 $2.50

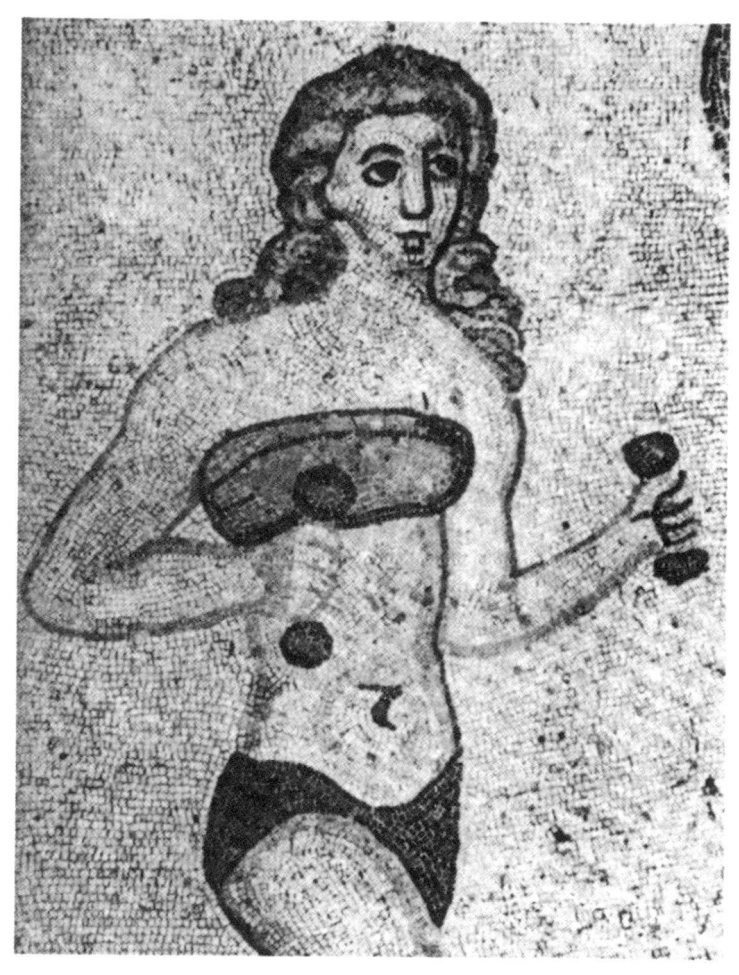

Sweet Cheat of Freedom
by *Ursule Molinaro*

2-In-1

Sweet Cheat of Freedom
by Ursule Molinaro

Copyright ©1971, 1983 by Ursule Molinaro

Cover illustration and design by Linda Neaman

Cover image is a detail from a mosaic; Sicily, third century A.D.

Sweet Cheat of Freedom was first published in *New American Review #12*

This publication has been made possible in part by grants from the National Endowment for the Arts, a federal agency, and the New York State Council on the Arts, Literature.

Hallwalls, 700 Main Street, Buffalo, New York 14202

for John Evans

He had *not* said: No man is truly free, until he has a slave.
No Roman feels free, unless he has a slave: was what he had said. Rather imprudently, perhaps. To the only daughter of his former master, the senator. When the senator had still been his master. Officially as well as *de facto*. Whose only daughter he had tutored for 11½ of her 16   almost 16½   years.
Had begun to tutor nearly 12 summers ago. After the senator became senator, after the death of his senator-father-in-law. When the new senator had decided   with his newly inherited rank   that he wanted his only daughter to grow up to think like a man. And had acquired a Greek thinking-slave, from Sparta, to tutor her to grow up to think like a man. Like the son & heir-to-the-senate he'd been prevented from having, by whatever it was that he had given to his wife. Who was of better Roman birth than he was. Brought home to Rome. From one of the campaigns in southern Gaul & passed on to his better-born wife, before he became senator after the death of his senator-father-in-law. Before he & his better-born wife began to age.
Before he began to resent his equally   though differently   aging wife. A little more each day. For not aging the way he was aging: rather resentfully; obesely. For cheating on nature. By looking younger   & younger than the one year that she was younger than he was.
Because of whatever it was that he had passed on to her, perhaps, that was perhaps delaying the natural aging process of her 39-   almost 39½-year-old better-born body after preventing it from bearing him other children. Cheating him out of a son, after bearing the only daughter.
Who had grown up to resent her mother.
Whose barely perceptible   rather serene   aging the senator's 45-year-old Spartan-Greek thinking-slave liked to attribute to thinking. Which had perhaps been prompted in the mother's mind by whatever it was that she might have heard him say during much of 11½ years of daily dialogue attempts in which he had tried to involve the only daughter.
Who had perhaps resented her mother's almost daily presence, during much of the 11½ years. From the first day on, perhaps. Walling herself in willful stony deafness against whatever it was that he might be saying.
About a little girl, for instance, who chose boredom in the belief that she was choosing freedom.
Who was probably too little to understand that the only true freedom was freedom of thought. Which many grownups didn't understand either. Ever. For which one had first to learn how to think. Not necessarily like a

man. Or like a Roman. But like a human being. The only true hierarchy being a hierarchy of minds...

Some of which were better born than others. Not socially better born, necessarily. Although a comfortable social position of senator parents could be helpful, in certain cases. Wasn't always helpful, however. Induced smugness &/or laziness, & subsequent boredom in certain cases.

Some of which arrived in the world better-equipped than others. With a head-start, so to speak. Which made it easier for them to reassemble in detail the knowledge which the gods took away from man in exchange for his first breath.

Man's first breath blew his mind, so to speak. Wiped his memory-slate clean of most of the subconscious total knowledge of life which man shared with the gods up to the moment of his birth.

Continued to share with the gods in his dreams, after his birth.

When his taking shape, his taking on a specific the human form restricted his grasp of life as a totality to the human experience of life. To his own personal perception.

Which was his tool.

Which he had to use consciously, every day of his life, in order to understand his relationship to the other specific forms of life around him: other men/ animals/ plants/ mountains/ rivers/ the sky/ the earth.

To understand all of life by means of his own specific life, as he grew. Up. & older. Toward reabsorption by death. When the gods judged by the sum total of his understanding whether he had succeeded or failed.

Which failed to scale the willful deafness walls of the $4\frac{1}{2}$-5-$5\frac{1}{2}$-6-etc.-year-old mind.

Which he continued to try to scale, unsuccessfully, for $11\frac{1}{2}$ years.

Stealthily ignoring 7 to 8 years of boredom-born tantrums.

The subsequent recounting of which by the mother amused the senator.

Until the tantrums gave way to an equally boredom-born, equally deaf passion for verbal disagreement.

Holding over 3,000 monologues. While: the only daughter nudged her listening mother. Tugged at her listening mother. Poked her listening mother. Climbed one of his legs. Kneaded his lap with her toes. Stared into his eyes. Blew into his ears. His talking mouth. Searched between his thighs with outrageous $4\frac{1}{2}$-5-$5\frac{1}{2}$-6-$6\frac{1}{2}$-year-old directness.

Which he & the listening mother tried not to see. To pay no attention to. On the principle that: what you don't feed cannot live.

On which principle, its positive & its negative applications:

Feeding an affection with attention; a mind with thoughts; a plant with water.

Starving a resentment/ a jealousy by withdrawing your thoughts from the subject   or object; an illness/ a tantrum by ignoring it...
he continued to talk. While the mother continued to listen. Both conscientiously paying no attention to the only daughter.
Who disrobed, & marched out of earshot. Past the patio confines of blue-clustering grapes. Into the late-summer muck of the duck pond.
In which she proceeded to roll her 5-year-old nudity until she was pulled out & returned muck-crusted & flailing to the patio. By a weeping girl, a recent slave from southern Gaul, who was anticipating another beating, this one official, administered by the mistress of the house, after an initial unofficial one, administered by painful bruising 5-year-old fists.
Which the mistress of the house had ceased to administer   to any of her slaves   after listening to one of his early monologues about the nonviolence of true authority.
Which the mistress of the house should perhaps have administered to the muck-crusted 5-year-old bottom of the only daughter, in spite of what she had listened to him say about nonviolence.
About the unruffle-able serenity of a "true" master. Early that summer. During an aromatic morning in a rowboat on the senator's green-mirroring turtle lake. That had lain in seemingly unruffle-able serenity. Dark-brown turtles dropping from the bullrushes like giant bedbugs; ducks & cranes flying crookedly into the air at the almost soundless approach of the rowboat.
Until the vehemence of 4½-year-old boredom finally succeeded in overturning the rowboat in which it had felt held captive.
The subsequent recounting of which amused the senator to the point of laughter.   Which was one of man's –dubious– distinctions from –other– animals. A distinction the senator thought he shared with the gods. Although he had very nearly lost:

1 (& only) 4½-year-old daughter
1 27½-year-old better-born wife
1 18-year-old well-muscled Teuton rowing-slave
& 1 33-year-old Spartan-Greek thinking-slave in the process.

Whose fault it would have been if all 4 of them had drowned.
For thinking inadequately.
For not knowing how to capture a 4½-year-old attention. From the first day, the first word, on. For capturing   & holding   the mother's 27½-year-old attention instead.
For not quite daring to take physically punitive measures. Which were not only not in keeping with his nonviolence principles, but also contrary to certain basic considerations of prudence: A slave striking his master's

4½-5-5½-6-6½-etc.-etc.-year-old only daughter. In the presence of the 27½-28-etc.-etc.-year-old mother, who had listened to years of his monologues about the laziness of violence. While he & the mother continued to ignore the growing only daughter's daily growing boredom.

Preferring to praise the excellence of melon marmalade, when the 6½-year-old flayed an entire field of richly ripe melons which they were passing with a frenzied stick.

When he & the mother continued walking. While he continued to talk.

About: "miniature suns, shining from a deep-green foliage-sky."

& about: "the recurrence of the egg shape everywhere in nature. The neuter, still neutral, shape of the fruit/the seed. With its promise of male & female. Before the split into male & female. Into pistil & petals   One split in two, & started talking..."

& about: "the all-prevading elementary trinity of earth/ water/ air/ recurring in flesh/ blood/ breath; stem/ sap/ green..." Etc. Etc. Etc. Etc. Etc. Etc. Etc....

Rather than use the frenzied stick on the melon-shaped   already blatantly female   6½-year-old bottom.

A subsequent recounting of which   by the sore-bottomed only daughter   might not have amused the senator to the point of gods-shared laughter.

Might, on the contrary, have prompted the not-amused senator to revise his Greek thinking-slave's Spartan tutoring methods by cutting off the slavish hand that had dared strike his master's only daughter. Or, more simply, to cut off the slavish head, to put a stop to the kind of thinking that led to slaves striking their master's only daughter.

Whose increasingly violent boredom-tantrums were well in keeping with Roman patrician tradition: according to the senator's Spartan-Greek thinking-slave's unrevised thinking.

The same frantic attempts to silence   with screams of childish rage; & later with the screams of victims: of animals, of slaves   the inner voice that was telling them how unfree they were.

Were free perhaps not to listen to their fathers' thinking-slaves, but not free not to listen to the whisper voice inside themselves that kept telling them that they, the proud patricians, the empire builders, the history-makers, were abject menial slaves. To their needs & greeds. To their craving for effect-producing. For constant world-wide attention.

Were more enslaved than the slaves who served them. Who ruled them, by serving them. Might eventually   some day   start ruling them without continuing to serve them, if the masters continued to ignore their inner whisper voice. Until they'd become unable to ignore the whisper voices of their slaves.

Who were beginning to doubt the self-mastery of their masters. In the different idioms of their different ethnic & social backgrounds. Which their enslaved condition was melting into one language, spoken & understood by all. The language of passive resistance. In echo-response to the suffering inflicted upon most of them by obesely bored masters. Who called their thoughtless   or, on the contrary, their minutely thought-out   cruelties: necessary punitive measures. Healthy discipline. When they themselves lacked even the discipline not to overeat. & dieted by proxy, by starving their slaves...

Who had somehow begun to hear what the senator's Spartan-Greek thinking-slave had been thinking out loud for 7 to 8 years. In the course of his   less & less prudent; more & more outspoken   daily monologues.

Which they'd begun to repeat to one another. In the different idioms of their different ethnic & social backgrounds.

Which ceased being monologues, after the suddenly listening 12½-year-old only daughter began to contradict whatever she thought she had heard.

Vehemently.

& to repeat to the senator whatever she thought she had heard that she had contradicted.

Incorrectly.

Not understanding whatever it was that he might have said.   Somewhat more prudently, lately.   About: the importance of understanding, for instance, the relative unimportance, the luxury, of being understood...

About   with all due respects   Juvenal's somewhat unfortunate saying that: *mens sana in corpore sano* was the greatest gift of the gods.

Treating mind & body as two separate entities. As though the mind were not part of the body. As much a part of body as the hands, the feet. When we needed our whole body to think with. Could understand a concept only after we'd felt its applications with our body.

Which was perhaps why Juvenal was so often misunderstood. Hygienically misunderstood, so to speak. Misquoted, as though he had meant to say that a healthy body was the *conditio sine qua non* of a healthy mind.

Which made about as much sense as saying that a broken leg prevented a man from seeing.

Although it might conceivably prevent him from seeing things in places where his broken leg prevented him from going.

Which made the now-14-year-old now-listening only daughter laugh.

Before   or perhaps after   it occurred to her to burn the soles of one of her father's slave girls' feet with hot stones which she'd ordered the girl to heat. In order to understand the concept of pain.

Which made the senator share in the laughter of his only daughter which both shared with the gods after she described to him what she had do after what the thinking-slave had said.

Which the now-listening only daughter had perhaps willfully misunderstood.

Was perhaps, making a game of misunderstanding.

A game in which the senator was perhaps sharing, when he repeated to all of Rome what his Spartan-Greek thinking-slave had *not* said.

For every potentially rebellious slave to hear. & to repeat.

To believe that he had actually said: No man is truly free, until he has a slave After he'd been given his freedom. & a slave of his own.

Whom to set free he was not free enough.

Nor was he free enough to leave Rome & return to Sparta.

Was free enough only to continue living in the small crude house on his former master's grounds in which he had lived for nearly 12 years. Which felt smaller now that he had to share it with his slave. A not-too-bright, not-too-clean girl from southern Gaul whom enslavement had aged prematurely. Sullenly.

Who sullenly practiced on him the passive resistance he had preached.

Who felt further degraded by serving a former slave. A former "equal." Whom she mistrusted, because she'd been told what he had not said, after he'd been given his freedom. Which he had no way of rectifying, since the girl spoke neither Greek nor the language of Rome.

Hardly spoke or washed at all. A sullen slightly smelly presence. That he felt the unexpected temptation to beat, at times, when she kept persistently in his way, in the smaller-seeming crude house.

Which he no longer had any reason or excuse to leave. Since the senator had deemed that his only duaghter was well able to think like a man, like a true Roman, at 16; almost 16½. & that his 45-year-old Spartan-Greek former thinking-slave had therefore no further need to think. Out loud. In the listening almost daily presence of the 39½-year-old mother who continued to age barely perceptibly. Serenely.

Who had sent the Spartan-Greek former thinking-slave the jug of wine he had just finished drinking. The dregs of which had the color & texture of slowly drying blood.

TOP STORIES

A PROSE PERIODICAL

#1 Donna Wyszomierski
#2 Laurie Anderson
#3 Pati Hill
#4 Suzanne Johnson
#5 Linda Neaman
#6 Gail Vachon
#7 Jenny Holzer/Peter Nadin
#8 Judith Doyle
#9 Kathy Acker
#10 Lynne Tillman/Jane Dickson
#11 Kirsten Thorup
#12 Janet Stein
#13 Anne Turyn
#14 Lee Eiferman
#15 Constance DeJong

Available from
TOP STORIES
Hallwalls
700 Main Street
Buffalo, New York 14202

11:39pm   home next to phone   thinking   pensive   E. just called. She's sure Timmy saw us & that spitting in people's faces is his vision/version of our kissing. He spat in his grandmother's face when she picked him up at the daycare center, & in E.'s, when E. picked him up at his grandmother's house. & he'd spat at everyone at the daycare center, including the woman who runs it. E. was laughing.

I told her I'd called in sick, & stayed home painting all day. In that case: Why hadn't I called her at her office? Since I hadn't been working. We might have had lunch. Maybe even a quick nap… I didn't point out that I had stayed at home in order to PAINT. That I had, in fact, been WORKING. I merely said: good night. My alter ego which had, as usual, risen to the siren sound of her voice, shrank beyond retrieval at the realization of how little importance she accorded to the most important part of my life. More important to me than my health. Than a desirable woman who didn't consider my painting more important than my stupid job.
At first I thought of mailing these lists to E. As an explanation. But they would probably explain nothing to her. Except my selfishness. My unfairness: after all the allergy pills she had popped for my sake…So I'm going to burn them & flush them down the toilet. To exorcise my hostility.
Which is more harmful to anybody's health than all the cigarettes in the world.

---

31 cigarettes

EIGHTH DAY

TIME	WHERE ARE YOU?	WHAT ARE YOU DOING?	HOW DO YOU FEEL?	THOUGHTS & COMMENTS (IF ANY)
8:45am	kitchen	coffee	awake, for once	This is the best cigarette of the day. If I can cut this one out, I might make it through the whole day. I'm putting it out.
8:48pm	"	relighting cigarette	unfulfilled	No use starting a free day feeling unfulfilled.
9:32am	home; next to phone	just called in sick	very good	Marion said: I sounded awful. I'd already looked sick yesterday. Nothing like a fool-proof alibi....
4:12pm	kitchen	just had some lunch	very good	I didn't bother with this list while I was painting; there are 13 butts in ashtry. But they may not all be today's. So I'll count 11, & consciously empty the ashtray.
+ 11 cigarettes home		painting	"	
11:15pm	home; next to phone	bringing list up to date	exhausted & hungry, but good	I feel I did good work today. Would like to continue painting, but must go back to work tomorrow. There are 14 butts in ashtray
+ 14 cigarettes (home; painting; good)				
11:59pm	in bed	counting today's cigarettes	I feel dead tired	I'll definitely call in sick tomorrow.
43 cigarettes				

Time	Location	Description
10:37pm approximately; filled in afterwards at home at 11:28pm	on E.'s couch	pretending to be smoking through my ears, to divert Timmy's eyes from his mother's dishevelled appearance. at a loss; embarrassed for E. When I bent down to kiss him goodnight at E.'s door, he spat in my face. Why are you spitting at John? E. asked. Because I do it: he replied…What does a 4-year-old see? & hear?
10:50pm approx. filled in at home at 11:28pm	on road	walking home from E.'s place very sorry for E.
11:28pm	at home	filling in previous cigarettes still perplexed
		-------
11:42pm	"	Just finished reassuring E. —who called: in tears, I thought— that Timmy saw nothing. That it had probably been the ringing of her phone which she had let ring itself out that had awakened him. & that he couldn't have seen very much if anything since her phone had started ringing at the very highpoint of… *My* highpoint: E. said: not hers. Just then. Or she would probably have answered. Incidentally, that had been her mother, on the phone. Her mother had called back 2 minutes after I left, complaining that there had been no answer. Where had E. been? What had E. been doing? Was Timmy all right…etc. etc.…she'd been worried sick…. One's mother & child certainly didn't encourage one's sex life: E. said. I asked if she'd been crying, but she said: No, that was her allergy acting up. Despite the three pills she had taken. Her mother, incidentally, was an incurable smoker. She had even paid $100.—to a hypnotist, to make her stop. But after a week she'd been back on. So that's why E.'s allergic. To her mother. I didn't say that, though. I merely recommended that her mother start filling in lists…

TIME	WHERE ARE YOU?	WHAT ARE YOU DOING?	HOW DO YOU FEEL?	THOUGHTS & COMMENTS (IF ANY)
6:30pm	in train	thinking up additional arguments for bastard cabbie	outraged/abused indignant	At least he might carry his NON SMOKING sign on his roof, to warn smokers not to flag him. Not to step into hostile territory. We're being persecuted; smokers of the world, unite!
6:46pm	"	"	"	It's when the individual is denied his right to self-destruction, that the world is headed for trouble. Paternalistic surgeons general, preserving us for The Great Asphyxiation.
7:10pm	"	calming down	rational	I think I'll call in sick tomorrow. I need a full day of painting to restore my equanimity.
7:32pm	in E.'s bathroom	washing up	somewhat less grubby	-------------
7:58pm	on E.'s couch	Martini	embarrassed	Trying to dissuade Timmy from kneeling on my erection.
8:20pm	at table	finished soup	?	Timmy wants to know why I always smoke when I write. I tell him: it's the other way around...
8:48pm	"	coffee	?	Timmy is climbing all over me. He refuses to go to bed unless I take him to his room & undress him & tell him a story... I've rarely been the object of so much affection...
9:10pm	on E.'s couch	waiting	aroused	-------------

Time	Location	Activity	Notes
3:15pm	"	paperwork	E. wants me to come to dinner at her place. She couldn't get a sitter. I told her I'd try to make the 6:15…
3:37pm	"	telephone	"
3:54pm	"	paperwork	"
4:08pm	"	telephone	I've never been to E.'s place with Timmy around.
4:31pm	"	"	"
4:50pm	"	paperwork	Is it less free to be hooked on cigarettes, than on a woman? Because a woman is less "harmful to your health"?
5:08pm	"	telephone	" " " " " " " " "
5:38pm	"	paperwork	impatient
5:51pm	in cab	riding to station	I better get out of here…
6:03pm	in another cab	"	outraged: explain later --------
6:19pm	in train	riding toward E. hope I'll catch the 6:15	abused/indignant/deprived of my rights as a customer. When I lit my cigarette, the first cabbie pointed to a NON SMOKING sign on his glass partition, & when I refused to comply, arguing that I was renting his cab for the duration of the ride, & could therefore smoke if I so chose, that his was not a public conveyance, the bastard pulled over & told me to get out.

TIME	WHERE ARE YOU?	WHAT ARE YOU DOING?	HOW DO YOU FEEL?	THOUGHTS & COMMENTS (IF ANY)
1:08pm	"	"	"	The truth is even more self-deceptive, & infantile: I've been cultivating the un-likely causality that, if I muster the will-power to stop smoking, I'll somehow be able to chuck this job & paint full time….
1:21pm	front desk	enjoying sight of cowed Marion	? ? ? ? ? ? ? ? ? ?	Emily called while I was out to lunch---
1:46pm	cubicle	paperwork	I don't feel at all, just now	Of course Emily thinks that I'm trying to quit for her sake. Ever since I started this list, she's stopped complaining, & quietly swallows her allergy pills. I wonder what would happen if I really quit. How it would affect our relationship: would it make her want to show herself "worthy of my sacrifice", or would it, on the contrary, prompt her to demand others?
1:59pm	"	Gazing at Marion standing before me	Unfeeling	Listening to worried Marion rationalizing her "oversight".
2:18pm	cubicle	frowning	aroused	E. just called back. She…
2:37pm	"	telephone	"	" " " " " " " " " " " " "
2:52pm	"	"	"	" " " " " " " " " " " " "

Time	Location	Activity	Mood	Notes
10:31am	in shop	assigning job to fitter	rushed	------------------
10:48am	"	" to cutter	"	This is going to a bum day, I can feel it.
10:59am	"	" to welder	"	" "
11:11am	cubicle	paperwork	hungry; too rushed for coffee & Danish	" "
11:37am	"	telephone	"	" "
11:54am	"	"	"	" "
12:12pm	front desk	Fuming at Marion	outraged (& vindicated; amused, actually)	Marion forgot to reorder 611N Wood Molding. You see: I told her: what did I tell you! She'd never forgotten before, when she was still smoking… Now she's seriously worried that I might get her fired…
12:27pm	Aristotle's	beer	still amused	Poor Marion…
12:50pm	"	coffee	Full of shit:	I'm obviously kidding myself: if I seriously intended to stop smoking, I'd try to dismiss the thought of cigarettes from my mind, instead of expanding each one with a vignette—an additional self-indulgence: I'm beginning to enjoy jotting down my dreary days…

TIME	WHERE ARE YOU?	WHAT ARE YOU DOING?	HOW DO YOU FEEL?	THOUGHTS & COMMENTS (IF ANY)
10:36pm	on E.'s couch	brandy	"	" " " " " " " " " "
10:50pm	in E.'s bedroom	ringing one of the bells to E.'s heart	loving	" " " " " " " " " "
11:29pm	in car	driving home	world loving	" " " " " " " " " "
11:57pm	home	getting ready for bed	world loving	----------
12:12pm	in bed	counting today's cigarettes	Like an accountant	Quitting must be easier if you're stingy…
47 cigarettes	....			Seems like a lot; I think this list is making me smoke more…
12:39am	in bed	having last cigarette	tired; a contented bull	The place to stop is in your head!
48 cigarettes				

SEVENTH DAY

TIME	WHERE ARE YOU?	WHAT ARE YOU DOING?	HOW DO YOU FEEL?	THOUGHTS & COMMENTS (IF ANY)
8:35am	bathroom	shaving	rushed	----------
9:17am	train	riding to work; gasline too long	uncommunicative	----------
9:43am	"	"	"	----------

Time	Location	Activity	Mood	Notes
6:52pm	(STILL!)	"	"	I like to think of myself as an instrument of perception. How can I perceive anything, if I spend my life fussing over the instrument…
7:08pm	in cab	Driving to El Faro	Eager to see E.	I've done my best work, painting through the night, on Fridays & Saturdays, when E. can't get a babysitter. I've painted beyond the point of exhaustion, sometimes— following Gurdieff's advice. It seems to free my hand from the restrictive hesitations of my mind…
7:46pm	El Faro's	Having a Margarita	aroused	-------------------------------------
8:19pm	"	Finished Crabmeat in green sauce	"	E. looks very soft in a new blue dress.
8:41pm	"	coffee/brandy	content/aroused	I try to blow smoke in opposite direction of E., but somehow she seems to attract it. —She's swallowing her allergy pill. Her place is free till 11:30 tonight; Timmy's watching his uncle on TV at her mother's house.
9:02pm	in cab	going to garage	"	A cigarette makes a good thing taste better…
9:40pm	in car	driving to E.'s place	"	"
10:10pm	"	"	"	"

TIME	WHERE ARE YOU?	WHAT ARE YOU DOING?	HOW DO YOU FEEL?	THOUGHTS & COMMENTS (IF ANY)
3:59pm	cubicle	thinking	ambivalent	Emily just phoned. She's in the ci y, discussing her hardware company's new radio jingle. She wants to meet me at El Faro's for dinner, & drive home with me... There goes the painting I'd planned for tonight, but my alter ego promptly stood up & saluted her phone voice...
4:16pm	"	telephone	-------	
4:29pm	"	"	-------	
4:53pm	"	"	-------	
5:17pm	in shop	Chewing out mat cutter	Pissed off	16 mats too narrow…
5:39pm	"	Remeasuring mats	"	" " " " " " " " " "
5:59pm	cubicle	paperwork	Exploited	This list probably isn't interested in my just emotions. All it wants to know is the gradual decline of my anatomy, due to my VICE.
6:17pm	"	"	"	Vice always finds excuses: my mother liked to say.
6:39pm	"	"	"	It may be illusion, but I think I paint better when I smoke. It helps me get unstuck.

Time	Location	Activity	Sane/Ridiculous
2:51pm	Aristotle's	coffee; watching a jogger jog past the window	Sane; by comparison
3:08pm	"	lighting a cigarette	"
3:30pm	back in cubicle	filling in this ridiculous list	Ridiculous

Another ridiculous fad. Don't they see themselves. People who worry about their health all the time might as well be sick. All of life is fatal....

Poor Emily: every time she sees me light a cigarette, her big blue eyes start brimming with tears. Don't I believe that she's allergic? Do I think she's choking just to test me? To find out if she's worth more to me than a pack of cigarettes?----That's how I got started on this ridiculous list...

Now Marion our cashier/receptionist has joined the ranks of the enemy. THANK YOU FOR NOT SMOKING said a large sign on her desk when I got back from lunch. "Don't thank me," I told her, pulling out my pack, "thank me instead for the months of cigarettes you bummed off me. Ah, but no longer! She has finally "been weened". If I only knew how FREE she feels, & bla & bla & bla, with the passion of the neo-convert. Couldn't I at least "refrain" until I got back to my office. (To my hole in the wall.) I asked her if she'd also maybe taken up jogging. She had. In that case: I said: I might feel obliged to have her fired. Healthaholics were notorious for lying down on the job. I hope she believed me. Her face was a satisfying mixture of disbelief & punctured self-righteousness.

TIME	WHERE ARE YOU?	WHAT ARE YOU DOING?	HOW DO YOU FEEL?	THOUGHTS & COMMENTS (IF ANY)
12:40pm	in shop	Letting Metal Section have it.	Forceful & fair. (Like a jerk.)	
12:59pm	cubicle	telephone		
1:16pm	"	"	hungry	
1:31pm	"	"		
1:58pm	Aristotle's luncheonette	having a beer	Slowly coming alive	I told Jerry that I'd lifted the pack from my stepfather's carton that morning. I offered him one, & smoked one myself. That's when I started smoking for good. For bad: dear Emily.— I got hooked on the way I looked like a pro with a butt drooling from my 11-year-old mouth.
2:19pm	"	waiting for coffee	Almost human	It's easier to do, then not to do…
2:35pm	"	having coffee	"	I enjoy smoking. The whole ritual of lighting up. I used to enjoy watching this old Russian woman Yureva the curator of Balzac's house in Paris. She liked to sit in the sun under one of Balzac's plum trees, lighting her cardboard-tipped cigarette with a magnifying glass. She was an ancient woman, & she had smoked all her adult life, & it hadn't given her any of the surgeon general's diseases. They hadn't been invented yet.

Time	Location	Activity	Note	Narrative
10:41am	in can		Disgusted	In this place, smoking is an act of self-defense
11:02am	cubicle	paperwork	Over-qualified	I smoked my first cigarette in the can the bathroom at my grandmother's place in Conn. Must have been the Easter vacation my parents got divorced. When I was 9. No idea where I got that cigarette. I don't remember anyone smoking in my grandmother's house.
11:19am	"	"	"	I didn't smoke again until my mother's wedding, when I was 11. My stepfather offered me a Camel—as a peace pipe, I guess. He used to buy Camels by the carton. I admired that—unlike my mother, who claimed that it "greyed" her curtains.
11:46am	"	telephone	"	------------------------------
11:59am	"	paperwork	"	After he'd been living in our house for some time I lifted a pack from his carton & took it to school. Jerry chain-smoked 4 in front of me—in the can, again—during math.
12:13pm	"	telephone	"	I carried the open pack around with me, in the inside flap of my art kit. I must have forgotten that I had it. Until Jerry saw it, & asked if that was still the same pack.
12:29pm	cubicle	paperwork	over-qualified	#2, as Emily calls it, in her smiled nursery language. She is a proud member of Parents without Partners.

Consciousness-raising Sheet. Keep wrapped around pack of cigarettes.
DO NOT FAIL TO FILL IN BEFORE LIGHTING UP

THIRD DAY

TIME	WHERE ARE YOU?	WHAT ARE YOU DOING?	HOW DO YOU FEEL?	THOUGHTS & COMMENTS (IF ANY)
7:51am	kitchen	having coffee	numb	Emily, o Emily, the things you make me do....
8:17am	bathroom	shaving	"	-------
8:44am	car	driving to work	Like a jerk:	trying to write while driving in traffic.
9:04am	at work; in my cubicle	preparing work sheets	How am I supposed to feel, wasting my life earning a living....	
9:22am	in shop	assigning job to fitter	-------	
9:43am	"	assigning job to welder	-------	
10:04am	"	assigning job to cutter	-------	
10:27am	cubicle	coffee & Danish	"	Did painters live better when they were being kept by Renaissance patrons? Whose tastes probably were no less cautious than the galleries'. & probably just as condescending. Forever discovering yesterday's hats....Fuck the Establishment Revolution!

Analects of Self-Contempt
while trying to stop smoking

by Ursule Molinaro

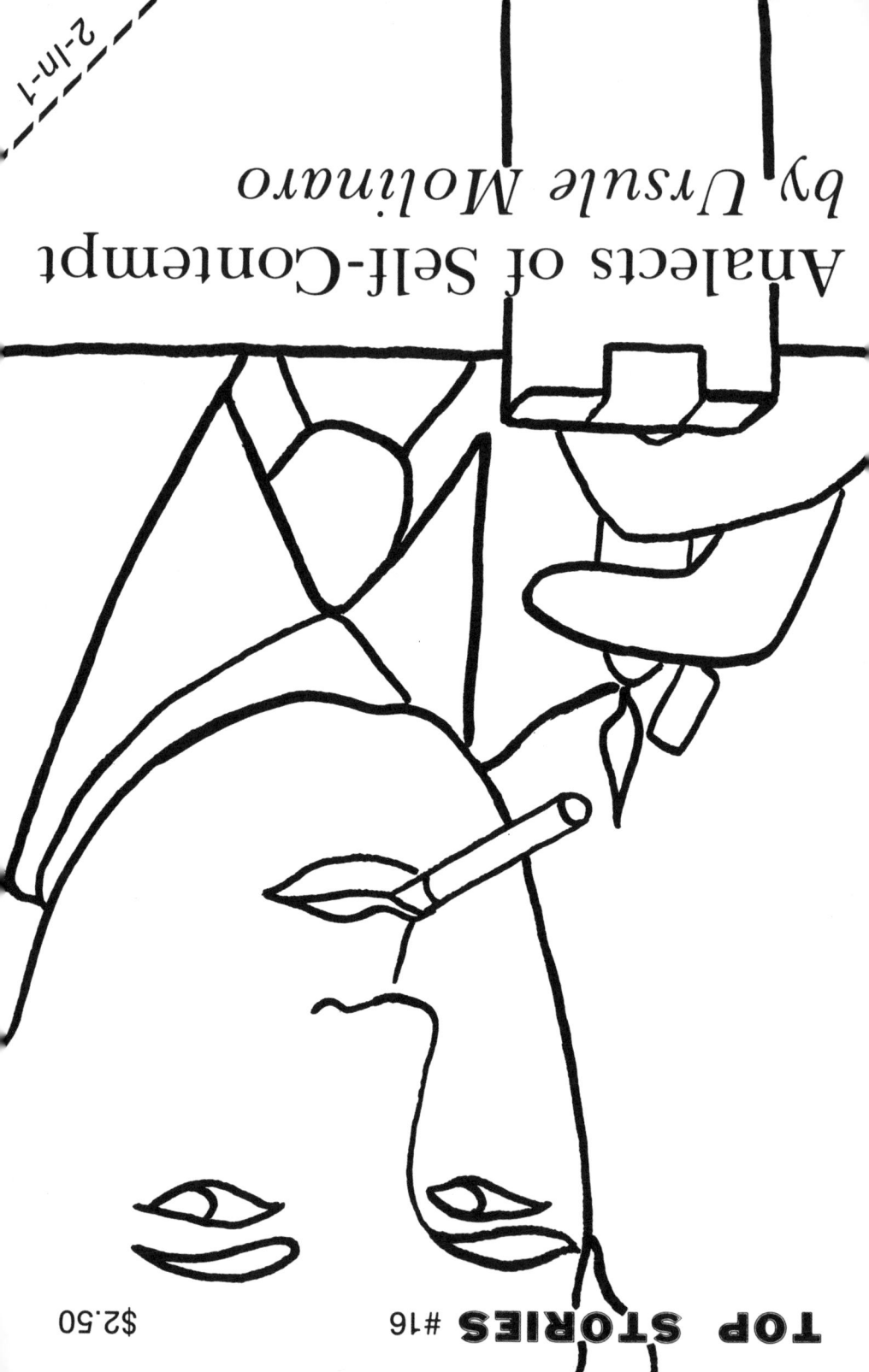

Top Stories
© 2021 Anne Turyn

ISBN: 978-1-7365346-1-8

The rights to the work remain the sole property of the author. All rights reserved. No part of this publication may be reproduced, stored in retrieval systems, or transmitted in any form or by any means, electronic, mechanical, photocopying, recording, or otherwise, without prior permission from the copyright holder.

The work of Jenny Holzer is © 2021 Jenny Holzer, member Artists Rights Society (ARS), New York

Top Stories was published in twenty-nine issues between 1978 and 1991 and edited by Anne Turyn. This volume collects issues one through sixteen as they were originally published.

Editor: Anne Turyn
Managing Editor (2021): Hiji Nam
Managing Designer (2021): Rick Myers

Primary Information
155 Freeman Street, Ground Floor
Brooklyn, NY 11222
www.primaryinformation.org

Printed in Latvia by Jelgavas Tipogrāfija

Primary Information would like to thank Constance DeJong, Lia Gangitano, Randy Kennedy, Max Schumann, Matt Shuster, and Leah Whitman-Salkin.

Primary Information is a 501(c)(3) non-profit organization that receives generous support through grants from the Michael Asher Foundation, the Graham Foundation for Advanced Studies in the Fine Arts, the Greenwich Collection Ltd, the John W. and Clara C. Higgins Foundation, the Willem de Kooning Foundation, the Henry Luce Foundation, the National Endowment for the Arts, the New York City Department of Cultural Affairs in partnership with the City Council, the New York State Council on the Arts with the support of Governor Andrew Cuomo and the New York State Legislature, the Orbit Fund, the Stichting Egress Foundation, Teiger Foundation, The VIA Art Fund, The Jacques Louis Vidal Charitable Fund, The Andy Warhol Foundation for the Visual Arts, the Wilhelm Family Foundation, and individuals worldwide.